Differences and Changes in Wage Structures

NBER Comparative Labor Markets Series
A National Bureau of Economic Research Series
Edited by Richard B. Freeman

Also in the series

David Card and Richard B. Freeman, editors
*Small Differences That Matter: Labor Markets and Income
    Maintenance in Canada and the United States*

Lisa M. Lynch, editor
*Training and the Private Sector: International
    Comparisons*

Rebecca M. Blank, editor
*Social Protection versus Economic Flexibility: Is There a
    Trade-off?*

Joel Rogers and Wolfgang Streeck, editors
*Works Councils: Consultation, Representation, and
    Cooperation in Industrial Relations*

Differences and Changes in Wage Structures

Edited by Richard B. Freeman and Lawrence F. Katz

The University of Chicago Press

Chicago and London

RICHARD B. FREEMAN holds the Herbert Ascherman Chair in Economics
at Harvard University. He is also director of the Labor Studies Program at
the National Bureau of Economic Research and executive programme director of comparative labour market institutions at the London School of
Economics' Centre for Economic Performance. LAWRENCE F. KATZ is professor of economics at Harvard University and a research associate of the
National Bureau of Economic Research.

The University of Chicago Press, Chicago 60637
The University of Chicago Press, Ltd., London
© 1995 by the National Bureau of Economic Research
All rights reserved. Published 1995
Printed in the United States of America
04 03 02 01 00 99 98 97 96 95   1 2 3 4 5
ISBN: 0-226-26160-3 (cloth)

Portions of the introduction have been reprinted by permission of the pub-
lisher from Richard B. Freeman and Lawrence F. Katz, "Rising Wage Inequality: The United States vs. Other Advanced Countries," in *Working
Under Different Rules,* edited by Richard B. Freeman (New York: Russell
Sage Foundation, 1994), pages 29–62.

Library of Congress Cataloging-in-Publication Data

Differences and changes in wage structures / edited by Richard B. Freeman and Lawrence F. Katz.
    p.   cm.—(NBER Comparative labor markets series)
  Includes bibliographical references and index. 1. Wages—Case
studies—Congresses. I. Freeman, Richard B. (Richard Barry). II.
Katz, Lawrence F. III. Series.
HD4906.D53 1995
331.2'1—dc20   95-11716
                                                     CIP

Contents

Preface

This volume contains twelve papers that explore and compare wage structure developments in the United States, Australia, Japan, Korea, and various Western European countries. The papers are the result of a broader research project on comparative labor markets and institutions funded by the Ford Foundation through a grant to the National Bureau of Economic Research (NBER).

The papers in this volume were presented at conferences held at the Center for Economic Performance (CEP) of the London School of Economics and at the NBER. We thank the many conference participants, particularly the discussants, for their many insightful comments. This volume would not have been possible without the valuable assistance of the staff at the NBER and the CEP. We are particularly grateful to Jennifer Amadeo-Holl of the NBER.

Introduction and Summary

Richard B. Freeman and Lawrence F. Katz

Earnings inequality increased substantially in the United States in the 1980s, and the real earnings of many groups of workers, primarily men, fell from the early 1970s through the early 1990s. In 1993, about 16 percent of the nation's year-round, full-time workers were labeled as low-wage workers by the U.S. Department of Commerce, earning less than the poverty level for a family of four ($13,483 per year in 1993 dollars)—an increase of approximately 33 percent over the 12 percent who had low earnings in 1979. Less educated young men suffered unprecedented losses in real earnings. Despite their costing employers less, however, these men were less likely to work at any point in time than in the past. In short, in the 1980s, if not earlier, the U.S. labor market experienced a massive twist against the less skilled and lower paid that reduced their living standards.

Was the twist in the job market against less educated workers unique to the United States, or was it part of a general pattern of decline in the well-being of the less skilled in advanced countries? Does it mark a new era in modern economic development—a reversal of the broad finding that income inequality tends to fall with modern economic growth? Have other countries avoided or ameliorated the rise in wage inequality that characterized the United States?

Motivated by these and related questions concerning the rise in inequality in the United States, the National Bureau of Economic Research (NBER) undertook the research project the results of which are presented in this volume. We asked U.S. and European economists to examine wage patterns and

Richard B. Freeman holds the Herbert Ascherman Chair in Economics at Harvard University. He is also director of the Labor Studies Program at the National Bureau of Economic Research and executive programme director for comparative labour market institutions at the London School of Economics' Centre for Economic Performance. Lawrence F. Katz is professor of economics at Harvard University and a research associate of the National Bureau of Economic Research.

changes in various countries for the purpose of enlightening the U.S. discussion about the increase in inequality in our country. Much of the research reports on the results obtained from computerized files on the earnings and employment of tens of thousands of workers in other countries. While the foreign surveys are not identical to the U.S. Current Population Survey (CPS), which most U.S. studies use to document changes in our wage structure and income distribution, the data from other countries are sufficiently similar to permit valid comparisons of changes in inequality across countries and, in most cases, of differences in wage patterns and inequality as well.

There are two basic ways to analyze economic patterns across countries. One approach is to examine developments in a single foreign country that the researcher implicitly or explicitly compares to his or her own. The other approach is to contrast the situation in a number of countries in a single study. Each approach has its advantages and disadvantages. By concentrating on a single country, the researcher can explore country-specific developments and data sets in depth but faces the danger that generalizations based on such analyses may not hold up in a broader setting. By examining a set of countries, the researcher gains a wider perspective on patterns of change, but at the cost of learning less about any single data set or mode of wage setting in any single country.

The NBER project sought to exploit the benefits of both methodologies by combining country-specific studies with broader cross-country studies. Some of the papers in this volume focus on the situation in specific countries, with the research undertaken by national experts with detailed knowledge of relevant data sets and of that country's institutional and market realities. One study, for instance, explores the pattern of wage inequality in Italy, a country that used a particular form of changing wages, the *scala mobile,* to reduce inequality greatly (Erickson and Ichino, chap. 8). Two studies focus on Sweden, one largely empirical (Edin and Holmlund, chap. 9), the other largely theoretical (Freeman and Gibbons, chap. 10). One of the big surprises to emerge from these studies was the similarity in patterns of wage change and in wage-setting institutions between these two countries, which are not normally classified as "kissing cousins" in terms of labor market practices. Another study (Abraham and Houseman, chap. 11) examines inequality in Germany, while yet another (Kreuger and Pischke, chap. 12) explores the effects of German unification on the wage structure in the former East Germany. Finally, one study examines wage patterns in the rapidly growing economy of South Korea (Kim and Topel, chap. 7).

Because the United States has shared a historical tradition with other English-speaking countries, our project paid particular attention to the experiences of Australia (Gregory and Vella, chap. 6) and the United Kingdom (Schmitt, chap. 5; Katz, Loveman, and Blanchflower, chap. 1). Australia has traditionally had a wage-setting system that is based on industrial tribunals and that differs substantially from that of the United States, while the United

Kingdom's labor market relies on a more decentralized approach to wage determination. While the evidence is a bit mixed for Australia, these studies found increases in inequality in both countries, with the rise in the United Kingdom during the 1980s being both quantitatively and qualitatively similar to that in the United States. We excluded Canada from this analysis because comparisons of the United States and Canada are contained in a separate volume (see Card and Freeman 1993).

Four of the papers examine patterns of inequality and pay differentials across several countries. Abowd and Bognanno (chap. 2) treat managerial compensation, an issue that continually raises controversy in the United States owing to newspaper stories claiming that U.S. executives are "overpaid" compared to their counterparts overseas. Blau and Kahn (chap. 3) examine the relative pay of women across countries in the context of the broader level of wage inequality within a country. Blanchflower and Oswald (chap. 4) explore the striking degree of similarity in the extent to which the level of pay negatively varies with regional (or industry) unemployment in each of ten nations, including the United States. Finally, Katz, Loveman, and Blanchflower (chap. 1) examine the evolution of earnings differentials in the United States, Britain, France, and Japan and assess potential explanations for the differences and commonalities in the patterns of changes in the wage and employment structures of these four nations.

With studies focused on individual countries as well as cross-country studies, we have greater confidence in the findings presented in the volume than we would have had were the analyses limited either to individual country studies or to cross-country comparisons that could not examine the patterns in a single country in depth.

Finally, the reader will notice that this research project pays considerable attention to labor market institutions as well as to the supply-and-demand forces that affect wages. The countries covered in this volume have similar advanced market economies (Korea and East Germany are the exceptions). They face much the same shifts in technology, demand, and, with some exceptions, supplies of labor. It is thus natural to look at differences in wage-setting and other institutions to account for some of the country differences in wage structures and changes in inequality.

The Main Findings

In capsule form, the research in this volume goes a long way toward answering the question of whether the substantial rise in earnings inequality in the United States since the late 1970s is universal among advanced capitalist economies or something more idiosyncratic. The findings also cast important light on the likely causes of the evolution of the wage structure and the growth of inequality in the United States.

With respect to the pattern of change in inequality across countries, the research shows that, during the 1980s, the United States and the United Kingdom—countries with decentralized labor markets and systems of wage setting—had exceptional increases in earnings inequality and in wage differentials by skill category. Only in the United States, however, was the rise in inequality associated with quite large declines in real wages for low-wage workers (even those in year-round, full-time employment). The huge decline in the real earnings of low-paid workers in the United States has been associated with sharp increases in family income inequality and growing rates of poverty among working families. Most other developed countries had moderate increases or in some cases effectively no rise in wage inequality, and real wages increased in Britain even for low-paid workers. Thus, the rise in inequality was especially harmful to low-paid workers in the United States. Nevertheless, most other advanced nations with less increase in wage inequality and faster increases in real wages than the United States suffered from much slower employment growth and sharper increases in unemployment/nonemployment among less educated and young workers (OECD 1994b).

The key forces behind the rise in inequality appear to be changes in the supply of and demand for skills: a secular shift in relative labor demand favoring more educated workers and workers with problem-solving skills compared to a slowdown in the rate of growth of the supply of highly educated workers relative to less educated workers. The shift in labor demand appears to be driven in part by skill-biased technological change partially associated with the "computer revolution" and by the growing internationalization of advanced industrial economies manifested in expanding trade with newly industrialized and less developed countries, large trade deficits in durable goods in some nations, and increased immigration pressure. Different analysts put different weights on the role of technology and trade forces as well as other factors (e.g., Borjas 1994; Borjas, Freeman, and Katz 1992; Bound and Johnson 1992; Lawrence and Slaughter 1993), but no one can gainsay that demand has been moving toward the more educated and more skilled. Shifts in demand are, however, fairly similar across countries, with the result that demand forces do little to explain country differences in the rise of inequality.

Hence, we also attribute a substantial role in the rise in inequality and the divergence between the United States and other countries to supply factors—in particular to the slowdown in the growth of the supply of highly educated workers between the 1970s and the 1980s in the United States. In the 1970s, rapid growth in the relative supply of highly educated workers (associated with the labor market entry of baby-boom cohorts and the rapid expansion of higher education systems) led to declining college or university wage premiums throughout the OECD, despite increased demand for these workers. In the 1980s, a more sluggish growth of the relative supply of highly educated workers (partly associated with the labor market entry of baby-bust cohorts and increases in immigration by less educated workers) permitted skill differentials to rise and accounts for some of the greater growth of inequality in the United

States. In striking contrast, the pattern of continued rapid educational upgrading in Korea was associated with a large drop in educational wage differentials (Kim and Topel, chap. 7).

The research also finds that labor market institutions contribute to the rise in inequality in two ways. First, differences in wage-setting institutions and in training and education systems explain some of the differential growth of inequality. Countries where labor market institutions—unions, employer federations, government agencies—play a greater role in wage setting and that provide better training or education for less skilled workers had smaller rises in inequality in response to demand/supply shifts similar to those affecting the United States (Abraham and Houseman, chap. 11; Erickson and Ichino, chap. 8; Edin and Holmlund, chap. 9; and Katz, Loveman, and Blanchflower, chap. 1). Second, changes in labor market institutions contributed to changing wage inequality. The decline of unionization contributed to rising wage inequality in the United States and the United Kingdom. Centralized wage-setting institutions weakened in some countries, including Sweden and Italy, lessening the forces that reduced inequality.

Generalizing from these findings, we offer a *supply-demand-institution* (SDI) explanation of relative wage determination to explain the rise of wage inequality in the United States compared to that in other countries. This explanation attributes differential changes in relative wages and employment among countries to long-term shifts in the supply of and demand for more and less skilled workers that work themselves out under different *and* changing labor market institutions.

There are three parts to this explanation. The first is that shifts in the supply of and demand for labor skills substantially alter wage and employment outcomes. This requires that shifts affect the wages and employment of different groups of workers in the manner predicted by the economists' supply-and-demand, market-clearing model. This in turn means that different demographic, education, and skill groups must be imperfect substitutes in production.[1] Further, we argue that shifts have their largest effect on young or less experienced workers on the active job market as opposed to experienced workers with substantial job tenure (Freeman 1976). The studies in this volume show in different ways that changes in relative supply and demand do in fact alter relative wages in the expected directions.

Since developed economies operate in the same world markets with similar technology, however, changes in demand move in broadly similar ways across countries. Supply changes will diverge more because different countries expanded their higher education systems at different times, but, even so, the proportion of the workforce that is highly educated has risen in all advanced countries. Differences in the pattern of change in supply and demand are thus

---

1. In technical jargon, the elasticities of complementarity (Hicks's term for the effect of changes in relative quantities on relative factor prices) must be noticeably greater than zero but less than infinite.

unlikely by themselves to explain cross-country variation in changes in wage inequality fully.

The second part of our explanation identifies country differences in wage-setting and other labor market institutions (described in detail in the various chapters in this volume and in other volumes in the NBER Comparative Labor Markets series) as an additional determinant of differing patterns of change in inequality. The more centralized a wage-setting system, and the stronger the role of institutions in wage determination, the smaller will be the effect of shifts in supply and demand on relative wages, and, as a consequence, the greater will be their effect on relative employment. In addition, education and training market institutions, which determine the level of workplace skills for the less educated and the degree to which more and less educated workers can be substituted for one another in production, will also mediate the effect of market forces on wages and employment (Lynch 1994). A more egalitarian distribution of skills should dampen the effects of market shifts on wages and employment. Finally, social insurance and income maintenance institutions also affect wage setting by influencing supply and demand behavior (Blank 1994). For instance, generous income maintenance or unemployment benefits programs that allow workers to remain jobless for a long period can reduce their willingness to take low wages to obtain work and thus reduce supply-side pressures that generate greater earnings differentials.

For the third part of our explanation, we turn to how institutional changes such as product market deregulation and changes in unionization alter the wage-setting calculus. In part, forces outside the labor market, such as political developments, will change labor institutions, but these institutions also respond to shifts in supply and demand. The important institutional changes in the 1980s were the decline in trade union power, which was exceptional in the United States, and the decentralization of collective bargaining that characterized diverse European countries. Both these developments are likely to produce greater earnings differentials.

We summarize next the dramatic changes in the American wage structure that motivated this study and then place these changes in the perspective of the developments in other advanced countries.

The Changes in the United States

As a starting point for examining what happened in other countries, we summarize the facts about changes in the U.S. wage and employment structure in the 1980s. Many researchers using several data sources—including household survey data from the CPS, other household surveys, and establishment surveys—have documented that wage inequality and skill differentials in earnings and employment increased sharply in the United States (Bound and Johnson 1992; Davis and Haltiwanger 1991; Gottschalk and Moffitt 1992; Katz and Murphy 1992; Levy and Murnane 1992; Murphy and Welch 1992). The finding that inequality increased is not sensitive to the choice of data set, sample, or wage measure. The following four "facts" summarize the changes in the American wage and employment structure that give us a benchmark for assessing the labor market performance of other countries:

Fact 1. From the late 1970s to the early 1990s, wage dispersion increased dramatically for both men and women, reaching levels of wage inequality for men that are probably greater than at any time since 1940. The hourly earnings of a full-time worker in the ninetieth percentile of the U.S. earnings distribution relative to a worker in the tenth percentile grew by approximately 20 percent for men and 25 percent for women from 1979 to 1989. The gap increased further in the early 1990s. This pattern of rising wage inequality was not offset by changes in fringe benefits favoring the less skilled[2] or by improvements in their chances of holding a job relative to those of more educated workers.[3] It marks a worsening in the economic well-being of lower-paid workers.

Fact 2. Pay differentials by education and age increased. The college/high school wage premium doubled for young workers as the weekly wages of young male college graduates increased by some 30 percent relative to those of young males with twelve or fewer years of schooling. In addition, among workers without college degrees, the average wages of older workers increased relative to those of younger workers. Only the gender differential declined. The earnings of women increased by 10 percent or more relative to men in all education and age groups in the 1980s.

Fact 3. Wage dispersion increased within demographic and skill groups. The wages of individuals of the same age, education, and sex, working in the same industry and occupation, were more unequal at the end of the 1980s than twenty years earlier. Much of this increase took the form of greater wage differentials for "similar" workers across establishments in the same industry.

Fact 4. Since these changes were coterminous with sluggish overall real wage growth, the real earnings of the less educated and lower paid fell compared to the earnings of analogous individuals a decade earlier. Most striking, the real

---

2. To the contrary, the same less skilled men who suffered losses in real earnings experienced losses in the likelihood that they would have an employer- or union-provided pension (Even and MacPherson 1994) and would be covered by an employer health insurance plan (Acs and Steuerle 1993).
   3. Despite the decline in the relative wages of less skilled men, the proportion employed fell relative to the proportion employed of more skilled men. This occurred by education and by deciles of the earnings distribution (Blackburn, Bloom, and Freeman 1990; Topel 1993). But note that, during the early 1990s, white-collar workers suffered more from unemployment than in the past. The unemployment rate of executives in January 1993 was 3.9 percent, the highest it had been since 1983 (4.4 percent). By contrast, the unemployment rate of operators, fabricators, and laborers was 11.9 percent in January 1993, compared to 20.6 percent in 1983.

hourly wages of young men with twelve or fewer years of schooling dropped by some 20 percent from 1979 to 1989 and continued declining in the early 1990s. In fact, the real hourly earnings of the median male worker appear to have declined since the end of the 1970s.[4]

Like most research on the widening distribution of earnings, this list of facts presents the evidence in terms of statistical measures of earnings distributions. But the same data can be organized in another way, one that some find more appealing: as changes in the share of jobs that provide "middle-class" earnings. For instance, rather than reporting the ratio of the wages for the ninetieth and tenth percentile workers, one can report the proportion of workers with incomes that fall in a fixed "middle-class" income band around the mean. Since the "jobs" measure of the change in the labor market is based on the same data as income distribution measures, it is likely to tell the same story.[5] When the distribution of earnings widens, there should be a decline in the share of middle-class jobs in the total; conversely, when there is a decline in the proportion of middle-class jobs, the earnings distribution should widen. Gregory and Vella's study (chap. 6) focuses largely on the jobs measure of inequality, which they find has worsened in Australia as in the United States, consistent with measures showing a widening earnings distribution.

Did the changes that took place in the 1980s break with the past or continue earlier trends? Figure 1 graphs the relative hourly wages for full-time workers from the March CPS from 1967 to 1989 to answer this question. The figure shows that the 1980s changes are largely a break with the past. The college wage premium plotted in panel A did not trend upward for decades. It increased modestly from 1967 to 1971, then fell through 1979, before jumping sharply in the 1980s, especially for the youngest workers.

Returns to experience graphed in panel B increased greatly for less educated men in the 1980s but not in previous years. The rise in the experience differential is, however, limited to the less educated; the earnings of male college graduates show no marked shift in favor of older or more experienced workers.

The reduction in the gender gap was also a 1980s development. Differentials in pay between women and men changed little in the 1960s and 1970s, then narrowed substantially from 1979 to 1990 (panel C).

The one change that began prior to the 1980s was the rise in within-group wage inequality for men. Panel D shows that, even after controlling for education and experience, the differential in earnings between men in the ninetieth

---

4. Information on U.S. wage trends through 1993 can be found in Mishel and Bernstein (1994).

5. Because earnings distributions can be altered in various ways, there is no one-to-one correspondence between all measures of change in the distribution and the change in the share of jobs in specified earnings categories. For instance, it is possible that the proportion of workers earning middle-class incomes remained unchanged while the very poor got poorer (reducing the earnings of the tenth percentile) and the very rich richer (raising the earnings of the ninetieth percentile). But observed changes in the distribution have not followed such a pattern.

percentile and those in the tenth percentile began to increase in the early 1970s. We note, however, that an analysis of usual hourly earnings in the CPS does not show this trend beginning until the 1980s (Card and Lemieux 1994; Mishel and Bernstein 1994).

Changes in Other Advanced OECD Countries

Did earnings differentials and overall wage inequality rise in other advanced countries as they did in the United States, or is rising inequality unique to the United States?

To answer this question, we summarize the analyses in this volume and elsewhere that gathered comparable data for many countries. The data come from diverse country sources, ranging from CPS-style household surveys, to establishment surveys, to surveys comparable to the U.S. Survey of Consumer Finances. While most of the analyses use micro-data files, in some cases these data were unavailable (Japan does not make public its basic data files), and the figures are limited to published data. Virtually all the data sets measure earnings before taxes.

There are, of course, numerous noncomparabilities among data sets for various countries (as there also often are for different data sets for the same country). Definitions of education and occupation groups differ depending on education and training systems and data-gathering procedures. Sample survey coverage and measures of earnings differ. The meaning of earnings also differs across countries. In the United States, living standards depend largely on personal earnings, whereas many European countries provide elements of compensation to all citizens or workers, such as health insurance, that Americans must buy with their take-home pay or through nonwage workplace compensation. Most other countries also have child allowances, among other benefits. If everyone in a foreign country has benefits that Americans buy through pay, measures of inequality based on wages will overstate inequality in that country compared to the United States. Differences in the progressivity of tax-transfer systems also vary across countries and affect the way in which differences in before-tax earnings translate into economic well-being and the use of nonearnings compensation. For instance, firms are more likely to give in-kind payments to workers, such as company cars, subsidies on transportation, lunch, and so on, in countries with high marginal rates. Abowd and Bognanno (chap. 2) explain part of the seemingly high compensation of executives in the United States as a result of relatively low marginal taxes, which favor direct compensation as opposed to unmeasured perquisites.

Differences in data and modes of pay make cross-country comparisons difficult. But they do not make such comparisons impossible or meaningless. In many cases, researchers know how reporting practices or definitions vary and can adjust results for these differences or, if that is not possible, specify the direction of bias in measures of inequality relative to the United States. More

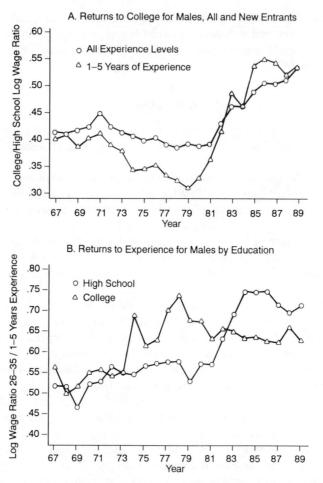

Fig. 1   Relative hourly wages for full-time workers, March CPS, 1967–89
Source: Katz, Loveman, and Blanchflower (chap. 1 in this volume).

important, in terms of changes over time, differences in definitions and reporting procedures that are constant over time are unlikely to distort trends in inequality.

Table 1 categorizes countries by the way their educational or occupational wage differentials changed in the 1970s and 1980s. From the late 1960s to the late 1970s, all the countries shared a common pattern of narrowing educational and occupational wage differentials. In addition, all saw the trend toward reduced educational wage differentials and a more compressed wage structure end by the early to mid-1980s.

In the 1980s, however, educational differentials moved differently among countries. In several countries, the differentials rose, but at more modest rates than in the United States (Katz, Loveman, and Blanchflower, chap. 1 in this

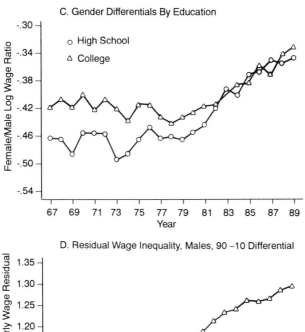

C. Gender Differentials By Education

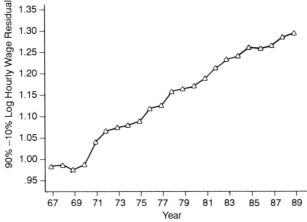

D. Residual Wage Inequality, Males, 90 –10 Differential

volume; Edin and Holmlund, chap. 9 in this volume; Freeman and Needels 1993; Abraham and Houseman, chap. 11 in this volume; Erickson and Ichino, chap. 8 in this volume; Gregory and Vella, chap. 6 in this volume; and OECD 1993). The one country with a pattern of widening wage differentials quantitatively similar to that of the United States is Great Britain. Canada, Australia, Japan, and Sweden had small increases in educational differentials beginning in the early 1980s, and the Canadian rise appears to have at least partially reversed itself in the late 1980s (Bar-Or et al. 1992; MacPhail 1993). Wage differentials continued to narrow in Italy and France through the mid-1980s, with some hint of expanding differentials in the late 1980s. There is no evidence of rising educational differentials during the 1980s in West Germany and the Netherlands and only slight evidence of an increase in Australia. The only country where educational/occupational differentials widened by an amount similar to that in the United States was Great Britain.

Table 1   Changes in Educational/Occupational Wage Differentials in
                           Selected Countries

Countries That Experienced:	1970s	1980s
Large fall in differentials	Australia Canada France Germany Italy Japan Netherlands Spain Sweden United Kingdom United States	South Korea
Modest changes in differentials: Modest fall in differentials		Netherlands
No noticeable change in differentials		France Germany Italy
Modest rise in differentials		Australia Canada Japan Spain Sweden
A large rise in differentials		United Kingdom United States

Table 2 measures changes in inequality in terms of the log of the ratio of the earnings of the top decile to those of the bottom decile from 1979 to 1990 (or the latest year available). The data show that the United States and the United Kingdom had by far the biggest increases in inequality. But there is a difference between the pattern of change in wages in the United Kingdom and that in the United States. In the United Kingdom, real earnings for all workers rose noticeably, with the result that, despite greater inequality, the real earnings for those at the bottom of the distribution grew (Katz, Loveman, and Blanchflower, chap. 1; Schmitt, chap. 5). By contrast, in the United States, real earnings at the bottom of the earnings distribution fell sharply. From 1979 to 1989, the real earnings of lower-decile American males *dropped* by 11–17 percent (depending on the survey used) compared to an *increase* in the real earnings of lower-decile British males of 12 percent.

That low-wage workers need not suffer losses in economic well-being even when inequality rises is also shown in the pattern of change in Japan. Inequality rose somewhat in Japan in the 1980s, but economic growth was so rapid that the living standards of the low-paid workers improved immensely. From 1979 to 1989, the real earnings of the tenth percentile Japanese male employee increased by more than 40 percent—an increase that exceeded that of the nine-

Table 2   **Wage Inequality for Full-Time Workers, Selected OECD Countries, 1979–90 (log of ratio of wage of ninetieth percentile earner to tenth percentile earner)[a]**

Country	1979[b]	1984[c]	1987[d]	1990[e]	Change from 1979 to Latest Year
Men:					
United Kingdom	.88	1.04	1.10	1.16	.28
United States	1.23	1.36	1.38	1.40	.17
Japan	.95	1.02	1.01	1.04	.09
France	1.19	1.18	1.22	1.23[f]	.04
Italy	.74	.69	.73	...	−.01
Netherlands	1.01	...	...	1.01	.00
Germany I	.78	.80	...	...	} −.06[g]
Germany II	...	.96	.91	.88	
Australia	.69	.76	.77	.80	.11
Austria	.97	...	1.00	1.01	.04
Canada	1.25	1.39	1.34	1.38	.13
Sweden	.77	.72	.72	.77	.00
Women:					
United Kingdom	.84	.98	1.02	1.11	.27
United States	.96	1.16	1.23	1.27	.31
Japan	.79	.79	.84	.85	.06
France	.96	.93	1.00	1.02[f]	.06
Italy	.87	.69	.69	...	−.18
Australia	.56	.64	.66	.67	.11
Austria	1.21	...	1.24	1.26	.05
Canada	1.32	1.46	...	1.38	.06
Sweden	.53	.57	.56	.60	.07
Men and women:					
Sweden, all	...	.66	...	.73	.06
Sweden, blue collar	.30	.30	.31	.35	.05
Denmark	.76	.77	.79	.77	.01
Norway	.72	...	.77	.68	−.04

Sources: The data for the United States, the United Kingdom, France, and Japan are from Blanchflower, Katz, and Loveman (chap. 1 in this volume); the data for Germany are from Abraham and Houseman (chap. 11 in this volume); the data for Sweden are from Edin and Holmlund (chap. 9 in this volume); the data for Italy are from Erickson and Ichino (chap. 8 in this volume); and the data for the Netherlands are from Hartog, Oosterbeek, and Teulings (1992). The data for the other countries are from OECD (1993, table 5.2, p. 159).

[a]The samples consist of full-time workers, with the exception of Japan. The wage inequality measures for Japan refer to regular workers. Wages are measured by hourly earnings for the United States, the United Kingdom, France, the Netherlands, Norway, and Sweden; weekly earnings for full-year, full-time workers covered by the social security system for Germany I; and gross average monthly earnings plus holiday allowances based on data from the German socioeconomic panel for Germany II. The data for Canada and Italy are for annual earnings of year-round, full-time workers. The data for Australia cover weekly earnings and for Austria monthly earnings.

[b]Category I is 1979, except in the following cases, where we recorded 1980 data for Austria (men; women), Denmark (men and women), and Norway (men and women) and 1981 data for Canada (men; women) and Sweden (men; women).

(*continued*)

Table 2   (continued)

^cCategory II is 1984, except in the following cases, where we recorded 1983 data for Germany I (men), 1985 data for Australia (men; women), Sweden (men; women), and Denmark (men and women), and 1986 data for Canada (men; women).

^dCategory III is 1987, except in the following cases, where we recorded 1988 data for Canada (men) and Sweden (men; women).

^eCategory IV is 1990, except in the following cases, where we recorded 1988 data for Germany (men), 1989 data for Austria (men; women), and 1991 data for Sweden (men; women) and Norway (men and women).

^fFrench data for 1990 are provisional updates from the OECD.

^gThis change is the sum of Germany I from the period 1979–83 and Germany II from the period 1984–88.

tieth percentile American male worker. Japan accomplished widely shared, rapid real wage growth while maintaining relatively low unemployment throughout the 1980s—although this pattern has been somewhat disturbed by the deep Japanese recession of the early 1990s.

We conclude that less educated and lower-paid American workers suffered the largest real wage decline among advanced OECD countries. The erosion in their economic well-being, in turn, produced the highest level of inequality of earnings among advanced countries and the seemingly anomalous situation in which low-paid Americans made less in purchasing power parity units than low-paid workers in other major countries, despite the United States having higher living standards on average (Freeman 1994).

What about workers at the top of the earnings distribution? Chief executive officers (CEOs) in America are paid more than CEOs in other countries, even after adjusting for differences in modes of pay, such as the use of various fringe benefits, according to Abowd and Bognanno (chap. 2). The advantage of CEOs over manufacturing operatives rose in the 1980s. But the American pay advantage appears limited to CEOs. Differences in pay between high-level managers and operatives do not differ noticeably between the United States and other major OECD countries.

Did the relative earnings of women improve in other countries as they did in the United States? Figure 2 shows that the gap between men's earnings and women's earnings declined in most countries in the period under investigation. Given the widening of the overall earnings distribution and the historical concentration of women in the bottom part of the distribution, the reduction in the male-female wage gap in the United States in particular was a significant achievement.

Why the United States and Other Countries Did Differently

Can international differences in changes in relative wages in the 1980s be explained by differences in supply, demand, and institutions? Why did inequal-

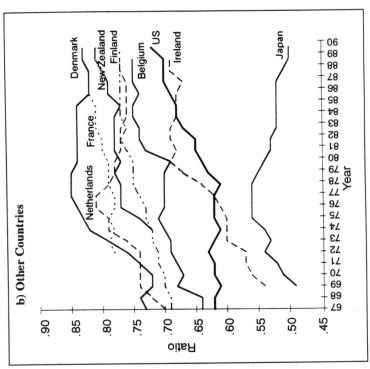

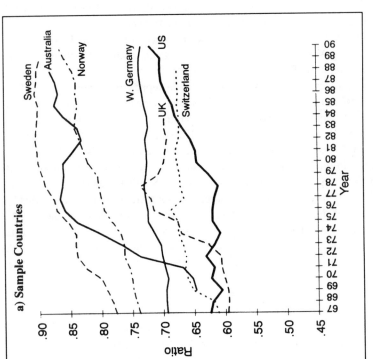

Fig. 2 Female-to-male hourly earnings ratios
Source: Blau and Kahn (chap. 3 in this volume).

ity increase more in the United States (and the United Kingdom) than in most other advanced countries?

Labor demand factors do not explain much of the differential growth of wage inequality or educational earnings differentials among countries in the 1980s. All advanced countries experienced large, steady shifts in the industrial and occupational structure of employment toward sectors and job categories that use a greater proportion of more educated workers (Katz 1994; OECD 1994b). The share of employment in manufacturing declined everywhere except Japan. In the United States, the manufacturing share of employment dropped by 4.2 percentage points from 1979 to 1989; in OECD-Europe, it fell by 4.1 percentage points. Only Japan's massive export success enabled it to maintain a near constant manufacturing share of employment. Still, even in Japan, changes in technology and the internationalization of economic competition shifted labor demand in favor of more educated workers and against non-college-educated workers.

Differential growth in the supply of workers by level of education, by contrast, contributed to the greater rise in educational wage differentials in the United States than in other countries in the 1980s. In the 1970s, despite shifts in labor demand favoring more educated workers, educational differentials narrowed in all advanced countries at least partially because expansion of higher education systems and high returns to education produced large increases in the supply of highly educated workers. In the 1980s, by contrast, while the educational qualifications of workers trended upward in all countries, the growth of the college-educated workforce decelerated in the United States. Among young American men, the college graduate share of the workforce actually fell over several years.

For differences in the growth of the relative supply of the educated to affect earnings differentials in this manner, it is necessary that changes in their relative supply affect relative wages within countries. The limited time-series evidence available for the United States (Katz and Murphy 1992; Blackburn, Bloom, and Freeman 1990), Canada (Freeman and Needels 1993), Sweden (Edin and Holmlund, chap. 9 in this volume), the Netherlands (Teulings 1992), Britain (Schmitt, chap. 5 in this volume), and South Korea (Kim and Topel, chap. 7 in this volume) shows such a relation. In fact, holding fixed proxies for the growth of demand, the estimates show that a 10 percent increase in the relative supply of educated workers lowers relative pay by 3–7 percent in various countries—as similar a magnitude as one might expect from studies that use various types of data, covering different time periods, and from countries with different wage-setting institutions.

The cross-country pattern of changes in educational wage differentials appears fairly consistent with this interpretation. Countries with at least modest increases in skill differentials by the end of the decade—the United States, the United Kingdom, Sweden, Australia, and Japan—experienced some decline in the rate of growth of the supply of college graduates. Countries whose educational differentials did not expand in the 1980s—France, Germany, and the Netherlands—essentially maintained their 1970s rate of growth of supply of more educated workers into the 1980s (Katz, Loveman, and Blanchflower, chap. 1 in this volume; Abraham and Houseman, chap. 11 in this volume; Teulings 1992; Hartog, Oosterbeek, and Teulings 1992; OECD 1993). Additionally, the continued rapid expansion in Canada helps explain the much more modest increase in educational differentials there than in the United States (Freeman and Needels 1993).

Finally, South Korea provides a striking example of the effect of relative supply changes in determining educational differentials (Kim and Topel, chap. 7). In the 1980s, South Korea saw a huge drop in the advantage of college graduates over less educated workers. Why? A major reason was that South Korea experienced an exceptionally fast growth in the college share of the workforce. Unlike any other developing country or most developed countries, South Korea has moved rapidly toward levels of college education among its young people approaching those found in the United States and Japan.

In sum, the supply-and-demand forces affected educational earnings differentials within countries. Given comparable changes in demand across countries, differences in the growth of relative supply help account for country differences in the growth of skill differentials. Still, they cannot explain the bulk of country differences in levels or changes in inequality. Differences in labor market institutions among countries and changes in those institutions in the 1980s also influenced the pattern of wage inequality.

Wage-Setting Institutions and Changes in Institutions

There are many ways to categorize wage-setting institutions. Most analysts concentrate on the degree of centralization of wage setting, differentiating between countries like the United States, with its highly decentralized labor market, where hundreds of thousands of firms bargain with employees or unions over pay and working conditions with little government intervention, and the more centralized wage-setting systems of Western Europe. But European wage-setting systems differ greatly among themselves. Until recently, for instance, peak-level union confederations and employer federations in Austria and Sweden have historically bargained over national wage settlements that cover much of the workforce but that allow local parties to increase wages above national settlements through "wage drift" (Freeman and Gibbons, chap. 10). In Germany, industry or regional collective bargaining determines basic wages for an area, and the Ministry of Labor often extends those settlements to all workers and firms, including those who did not participate in the bargaining. In France, the minimum wage is important in determining the overall level of wages, and the French Ministry of Labor also extends contracts. In Italy, the *scala mobile,* a form of negotiated wage increase that is designed to compensate for inflation and that is applied effectively to all Italians, increased the pay of low-paid workers faster than that of high-paid workers throughout much of the 1980s (Erickson and Ichino, chap. 8).

Ranking these institutions in terms of the degree to which they centralize wage setting is difficult. Some experts place Germany high on a centralization scale (Bruno and Sachs 1985), others lower (Calmfors and Driffil 1988). Although few view Italy as having highly centralized wage-setting institutions, Italy's *scala mobile* resembles Sweden's peak-level bargaining system. Countries that change wage-setting practices—as Australia did in 1983, when its unions agreed to an accord with the government to limit wage increases so that employment would grow, and as Sweden did when it stepped back from national bargaining in the 1980s—create further classification problems. However, these problems notwithstanding, one thing is clear about international differences in labor institutions: the position of the United States.

No matter which factors one stresses in categorizing countries, the United States ranks low in the role played by institutions in wage setting and high in the role played by market forces. In contrast to European countries or even Canada, whose unions remain strong, the United States has few institutions to augment or alter market wage setting. Unionization is low. Employer federations are weak. The government rarely intervenes to set wages. Since institutional forces tend to dampen inequality, wage inequality ought to be higher in the United States than in most other countries, as it is. By allowing the full brunt of shifts in supply and demand to fall on wages in the 1980s, when those shifts operated against the low skilled and lower paid, the United States could be expected to have especially large drops in the relative earnings of less educated workers, as it did. In Western European countries, by contrast, explicit government and union policies dampened pressures for increased wage differentials in the 1980s.

Finally, there were important changes in wage-setting institutions in OECD countries in the 1980s that affected wage differentials. After growing in the 1970s in many countries (but not in the United States), unionization fell in many countries in the 1980s (OECD 1991). The union share of the workforce dropped precipitously in the United Kingdom, the United States, the Netherlands, and France but held steady in Canada and Germany. Because union membership does not have the same meaning in different labor relations settings, however, even similar declines in density have different effects on the labor market. In the United States and the United Kingdom, reduced union density meant a decreased role for collective bargaining and institutional forces in wage setting. But, in France, falling unionization did not diminish the importance of the national minimum wage in wage setting, and it was accompanied by an increasing number of plant-level collective contracts. Sweden and Austria make another striking contrast. In Sweden, union density has been exceptionally high, whereas density has fallen sharply in Austria. Yet Swedish employers withdrew from peak-level bargaining in 1983, moving to end Sweden's centralized bargaining system, whereas Austria has maintained centralized wage setting throughout the decade. Estimates by the OECD show that the percentage of the workforce covered by collective bargaining contracts, which is presumably the route by which unions affect wages, changed differently than the percentage unionized in many European countries (OECD 1994a).

Weakened unionism and reduced centralization of wage setting contributed to the cross-country pattern of change in wage inequality in the 1980s. In the United Kingdom, the fall in union density accounts for about one-quarter of the growth of wage inequality among males (Schmitt, chap. 5 in this volume)—comparable to the estimated effect of declining density in the United States (Card 1992; Freeman 1993). At the other end of the spectrum, the continued strength of unions in Canada partly explains the smaller increase in inequality in Canada than in the United States. Approximately 40 percent of the difference in wage inequality between the United States and Canada appears to be due to differences in union density (Lemieux 1993). The decentralization of collective bargaining in Sweden helps explain the rise in inequality in that country in the 1980s, although levels of inequality are quite modest indeed by U.S. standards. The unification of East and West Germany moved the East German wage structure toward that of the West (Krueger and Pischke, chap. 12).

This discussion has treated institutional changes as exogenous to the labor market. But institutions are not immune to market forces. Economic forces that raise relative wages are likely to lead to less centralized collective bargaining or a reduction in union influence on wage setting (Freeman and Gibbons, chap. 10). Institutions that go strongly against market forces face a difficult task. That Italy dropped its *scala mobile,* Sweden abandoned peak-level bargaining, and other countries moved toward more plant- or firm-level arrangements in an era when the market moved toward greater differentials is presumably no accident. There is space for institutions to affect outcomes, but that space is limited. The European countries that had small rises in inequality in the 1980s may see greater rises as their institutions either adapt to market forces or are altered by those forces. Still, we expect few if any of these countries, save the United Kingdom, to approach U.S. levels of inequality, as long as they continue to give greater sway to institutional forces in wage setting than does the United States.

Conclusion: Leaning against the Wind

Market incentives for increased investments in education appear to be playing some role in helping ameliorate the huge rise in inequality in the United States. The sharp expansion of the college wage premium in the 1980s has been associated with a large increase in college enrollment rates from 49 percent of new high school graduates in 1980 to over 60 percent in the early 1990s, despite rapidly rising tuition costs (U.S. Department of Education

1994). This change promises accelerated growth of the relative supply of college graduates in the future, which will, in turn, act to offset somewhat continued demand increases favoring the more educated.[6]

Will an increase in the rate of growth of the relative supply of more educated workers be enough to prevent further increases in educational wage differentials and help restore an economic future to less educated American workers? Given continued technological and trade changes favoring the more educated, we doubt that increasing the supply of college graduates and reducing that of less educated workers will by itself undo the rise in inequality of the 1980s. But the experiences of other advanced nations suggest additional ways to lean against the wind of increased inequality and improve the economic well-being of the lower paid.

Two broad strategies were associated with little increase in skill differentials and in overall wage inequality in the 1980s. The first was the European model of greater institutional influence in wage setting through increases in minimum wages and extensions of the terms of collective bargaining agreements to firms not directly involved in such agreements. Strategies of this type succeeded in preventing the wage structures from widening (at least through the mid-1980s) in Italy and France. But by themselves these policies do not deal directly with the changing demand for skills, and they can run into economic difficulties in the long run. Policies that limit market wage adjustments without addressing changed labor market conditions can prevent wage inequality, but they risk stagnant employment growth, persistent unemployment for young workers (as in France), and/or a shift of resources to an underground economy to avoid wage regulations (as in Italy).

The second type of national strategy combines institutional wage setting with education and training systems that invest heavily in non-college-educated workers. Germany and Japan are typically viewed as the exemplar countries here. German and Japanese firms treat college- and non-college-educated workers as much closer substitutes in production than do U.S. or British firms. Technology and trade shocks do not generate as much pressure for wage structure changes in these countries since workers are not sharply differentiated by skill. Germany and Japan appeared fairly successful through much of the 1980s in maintaining the earnings and employment of non-college-educated workers. German institutions constrain wage setting, but they also offer apprenticeships and further training opportunities that try to make supply consistent with wage policies. The Japanese have succeeded with solid

---

6. The small size of cohorts entering the U.S. labor market in recent years has meant that large increases in college enrollment rates have not been associated with a very large acceleration in the rate of growth of the relative supply of more skilled workers. Bound and Johnson (1994) estimate that the relative supply of college-equivalent workers increased only from a 2.9 percent annual growth rate over the period 1979–88 to a 3.2 percent rate over the period 1988–92. In contrast, the annual growth rate was 4.2 percent during the period 1973–79, one of a declining college wage premium.

basic education and much informal firm-based training. Nevertheless, both these economies have run into some (at least transitory) problems during the early 1990s as personified by sluggish employment growth and rising unemployment.

Thus, no nation appears to have found an approach that allows it fully to escape increased labor market difficulties for less skilled workers. But international differences in recent labor market experiences strongly suggest that policies to buffer the earnings of the less educated by institutional wage setting work best when accompanied by institutions that augment those workers' skills as well.

References

Acs, Gregory, and C. Eugene Steuerle. 1993. Trends in the distribution of non-wage benefits and compensation. Washington, D.C.: Urban Institute, August. Typescript.

Bar-Or, Yuval, John Burbidge, Lonnie Magee, and A. Leslie Robb. 1992. Canadian experience-earnings profiles and the return to education in Canada: 1971–90. Working Paper no. 93–04. McMaster University, Department of Economics.

Blackburn, McKinley, David Bloom, and Richard Freeman. 1990. The declining position of less-skilled American males. In *A future of lousy jobs?* ed. G. Burtless. Washington, D.C.: Brookings.

Blank, Rebecca. 1994. *Social protection versus economic flexibility.* Chicago: University of Chicago Press.

Borjas, George. 1994. The internationalization of the U.S. labor market and the wage structure. University of California, San Diego, October. Typescript.

Borjas, George, Richard Freeman, and Lawrence Katz. 1992. On the labor market effects of immigration and trade. In *Immigration and the work force,* ed. G. Borjas and R. Freeman. Chicago: University of Chicago Press.

Bound, John, and George Johnson. 1992. Changes in the structure of wages in the 1980s: An evaluation of alternative explanations. *American Economic Review* 82 (June): 371–92.

———. 1994. What are the causes of rising wage inequality in the U.S.? University of Michigan, October. Typescript.

Bruno, Michael, and Jeffrey Sachs. 1985. *Economics and worldwide stagflation.* Cambridge, Mass.: Harvard University Press.

Calmfors, L., and J. Driffil. 1988. Bargaining structure, corporatism and macroeconomic performance. *Economic Policy* 6 (April): 14–61.

Card, David. 1992. The effect of unions on the distribution of wages: Redistribution or relabelling. NBER Working Paper no. 4195. Cambridge, Mass.: National Bureau of Economic Research, October.

Card, David, and Richard B. Freeman. 1993. *Small differences that matter.* Chicago: University of Chicago Press.

Card, David, and Thomas Lemieux. 1994. Changing wage structure and black-white wage differentials. *American Economic Review* 84 (May): 29–33.

Davis, Steven J., and John Haltiwanger. 1991. Wage dispersion within and between manufacturing plants. *Brookings Papers on Economic Activity: Microeconomics,* 115–80.

Even, William E., and David A. MacPherson. 1994. Why did male pension coverage decline in the 1980s? *Industrial and Labor Relations Review* 47 (April): 439–53.

Freeman, Richard B. 1976. *The overeducated American.* San Diego: Academic.

———. 1993. How much has de-unionization contributed to the rise in male earnings inequality? In *Uneven tides: Rising inequality in America,* ed. S. Danziger and P. Gottschalk. New York: Russell Sage Foundation.

———. 1994. How labor fares in advanced economies. In *Working under different rules,* ed. R. Freeman. New York: Russell Sage Foundation.

Freeman, Richard B., and Karen Needels. 1993. Skill differentials in Canada in an era of rising labor market inequality. In *Small differences that matter,* ed. D. Card and R. Freeman. Chicago: University of Chicago Press.

Gottschalk, Peter, and Robert Moffitt. 1992. Earnings and wage distributions in the NLS, CPS, and PSID: Part I of final report to the U.S. Department of Labor. Brown University. Typescript.

Hartog, Joop, Hessel Oosterbeek, and Coen Teulings. 1992. Age, wage, and education in the Netherlands. University of Amsterdam. Typescript.

Katz, Lawrence F. 1994. Active labor market policies to expand employment and opportunity. In *Reducing unemployment: Current issues and policy options.* Kansas City, Mo.: Federal Reserve Bank of Kansas City.

Katz, Lawrence F., and Kevin M. Murphy. 1992. Changes in relative wages, 1963–1987: Supply and demand factors. *Quarterly Journal of Economics* 107 (February): 35–78.

Lawrence, Robert Z., and Matthew Slaughter. 1993. Trade and U.S. wages in the 1980s: Giant sucking sound or large hiccup? *Brookings Papers on Economic Activity: Microeconomics,* no. 2:161–226.

Lemieux, Thomas. 1993. Unions and wage inequality in Canada and the United States. In *Small differences that matter,* ed. D. Card and R. Freeman. Chicago: University of Chicago Press.

Levy, Frank, and Richard Murnane. 1992. U.S. earnings levels and earnings inequality: A review of recent trends and proposed explanations. *Journal of Economic Literature* 30 (September): 1333–81.

Lynch, Lisa M. 1994. *Training and the private sector.* Chicago: University of Chicago Press.

MacPhail, Fiona. 1993. Has the "great U-turn" gone full circle? Recent trends in earnings inequality in Canada, 1981–1989. Working Paper no. 93–01. Dalhousie University, Department of Economics, January.

Mishel, Lawrence, and Jared Bernstein. 1994. *The state of working America, 1994–95.* Washington, D.C.: Economic Policy Institute.

Murphy, Kevin M., and Finis Welch. 1992. The structure of wages. *Quarterly Journal of Economics* 107 (February): 285–326.

OECD. 1991. *Employment outlook.* Paris.

———. 1993. *Employment outlook.* Paris.

———. 1994a. *Employment outlook.* Paris.

———. 1994b. *The OECD jobs study.* Paris.

Teulings, Coen. 1992. The wage distribution in a model of matching between wages and jobs. University of Amsterdam, October. Typescript.

Topel, Robert. 1993. What have we learned from empirical studies of unemployment and turnover? *American Economic Review* 83 (May): 110–15.

U.S. Department of Education. National Center for Education Statistics. 1994. *The condition of education, 1994.* Washington, D.C.: U.S. Government Printing Office.

I   Cross-Country Studies

1 A Comparison of Changes in the Structure of Wages in Four OECD Countries

Lawrence F. Katz, Gary W. Loveman, and David G. Blanchflower

In the 1970s, the relative earnings advantage of highly educated workers, particularly recent or young university graduates, deteriorated in the United States and most other OECD nations (Freeman 1981). This decline coincided with a pattern of decreasing wage differentials by occupation throughout much of the developed world. The narrowing of skill differentials in the 1970s appears to have been strongly related to dramatic increases in the relative supply of highly educated workers generated by the labor force entrance of baby-boom cohorts and the rapid expansion of higher education. Explicit government and trade union policies aimed at reducing earnings differentials are also likely to have been an important factor in many countries.

In contrast to the experience of the 1970s, wage differentials by education and occupation expanded dramatically in the United States in the 1980s. Over the past ten years, the U.S. wage structure also changed substantially along several other dimensions: wage differentials by experience rose for less educated workers, earnings inequality within education-experience-gender groups increased, and gender differentials narrowed. These changes generated a large increase in overall wage inequality among both men and women and led to a

Lawrence F. Katz is professor of economics at Harvard University and a research associate of the National Bureau of Economic Research. Gary W. Loveman is associate professor of business administration at the Harvard Business School. David G. Blanchflower is professor of economics at Dartmouth College and a research associate of the National Bureau of Economic Research. He is an associate member of the Centre for Economic Performance of the London School of Economics.

The authors thank Rachel Friedberg, David Kotchen, David Lee, and Marian Vaillant for excellent research assistance. They are grateful to Steven Davis, Chinhui Juhn, Karen Lombard, and Kevin M. Murphy for kindly supplying some of the data used in the paper. They have benefited from the comments of Steven Davis, Per-Anders Edin, Richard Freeman, Robert Lawrence, and participants in several seminars and conferences. Generous research support from the Ford Foundation, the National Science Foundation (grant SES-9010759), and the Division of Research of the Harvard Business School is gratefully acknowledged.

particularly sharp deterioration in the relative earnings of young, less educated men.

Many explanations have been offered for recent U.S. wage structure developments. One class of explanations argues that rising education differentials
and narrowing gender differentials reflect shifts in the relative demand for labor
favoring "more skilled" over "less skilled" workers and possibly women over
men. Candidates for shifts in demand favoring more skilled workers include
technological changes associated with the spread of computers and computer-
based technology that reduce the demand for physical labor and increase the
demand for workers able to learn at least cost (Berman, Bound, and Griliches
1994; Krueger 1993; and Mincer 1991); the loss of manufacturing jobs offering
relatively high pay to less educated workers; and the transfer of jobs requiring
relatively routinized tasks to low-wage countries (Reich 1991). Other explanations focus on changes in wage-setting institutions such as the declining influence of unions (Freeman 1993), the erosion of the real value of the minimum
wage (DiNardo, Fortin, and Lemieux 1994), and changes in pay-setting norms
(Mitchell 1989).

Much research attempting to evaluate these alternative explanations for
changes in the U.S. wage structure in the 1980s (e.g., Bound and Johnson
1992; Juhn, Murphy, and Pierce 1993; and Katz and Murphy 1992) has attempted to exploit U.S. time-series information by essentially comparing the
experience of the 1980s with the experiences of the 1970s and the 1960s. Katz
and Murphy (1992) conclude that any consistent explanation of U.S. wage
structure changes since the late 1960s requires a rapid secular growth in the
demand for "more skilled" workers.

U.S. time-series information alone is probably insufficient to distinguish
sharply among competing explanations for recent wage structure changes. A
complementary approach is to collect comparable time-series data for several
countries on wage structure changes and on measures of changes in the supply
of and demand for different labor inputs. Changes in wage structures across
countries not accounted for by demand and supply shifts constitute a residual
category that may be the result of a variety of factors. In particular, an examination of labor market institutions may play an important role in understanding
differences in the evolution of relative wages across countries.[1]

In this paper, we assemble roughly comparable time series of data on
changes in the structure of wages in the United States, Britain, Japan, and
France. These four countries provide useful contrasts since they include two
countries with decentralized wage-setting institutions (the United States and
Britain), one representative of the relatively centralized wage-setting systems
characteristic of continental Europe (France), and a high-growth economy

---

1. Recent studies exploiting broad cross-country comparisons to examine alternative hypotheses
for changing wage structures include Davis (1992), Gottschalk and Joyce (1992), and OECD
(1993).

with strong trade performance (Japan). We examine supply and demand and institutional explanations for the differences in wage structure changes among these countries.

Our major findings concerning similarities and differences among these four countries in patterns of changes in relative wages can be summarized as follows:

1. Trends in overall wage inequality by sex. All four countries share a pattern of rising wage inequality among both men and women in the 1980s, but the magnitudes of the increases differ substantially. Great Britain and the United States both displayed dramatic increases in wage inequality during the 1980s, while the increase in Japan was much more moderate. France experienced declining inequality until 1984 and a moderate increase from 1984 to 1990.

2. Changes in education/occupation differentials. Educational and nonmanual/manual wage differentials narrowed in all four countries in the 1970s. The college wage premium and nonmanual/manual differentials expanded dramatically in the United States and Britain in the 1980s and moderately in Japan. Occupational differentials continued to narrow in France in the 1980s, with a hint of a slight upturn for males after 1985.

3. Within-group inequality. Wage inequality among those with similar education and experience increased for both men and women in the United States and Britain in the 1980s.

We find that simple supply and demand measures go a reasonable distance toward explaining the differences and similarities among these countries in patterns of relative wage movements. Relative labor demand appears to have been rapidly shifting in favor of more educated workers in OECD countries throughout the past twenty years. But the relative supply of college-educated workers grew rapidly enough to drive down skill differentials in all four of our countries during the 1970s. The pace of growth of the relative supply of highly educated workers decelerated substantially in the 1980s in the United States, Britain, and Japan, and each of these experienced rising college wage premiums in the 1980s. An acceleration in the pace of industrial shifts in employment away from sectors that disproportionately employ male manual workers also appears to be an important part of the reason for the tremendous increase in skill differentials in Britain in the 1980s.

Institutional differences across the countries translated the relative demand shifts against less educated workers into similar outcomes of sharply rising inequality in the United States and Britain in the 1980s but a very different outcome in France through the mid-1980s. In France, a high and pervasive minimum wage and contract extensions prevented the relative wages of the unskilled from falling significantly, despite substantial employment declines.

The French experience appears to be consistent with the evidence from other continental European countries, such as Germany and Italy, where significant relative demand shifts did not result in large increases in wage differentials through the late 1980s (Abraham and Houseman, chap. 11 in this volume; Erickson and Ichino, chap. 8 in this volume). Finally, the strength of the Japanese manufacturing sector may partially account for the much smaller magnitude of changes in skill differentials in Japan than in Britain and the United States during the 1980s.

The remainder of the paper is organized as follows. Section 1.1 contrasts changes in overall wage inequality in these four countries over the last twenty-five years. Section 1.2 presents more detailed evidence on changes in the structure of wages in the four countries. Section 1.3 provides supply and demand measures for each country and examines their contribution to changes in the wage structures of the four countries. Section 1.4 provides a speculative discussion of the role played by labor market institutions in explaining the movements in wage differentials not accounted for by demand and supply effects. Section 1.5 concludes.

1.1 Changes in Overall Wage Inequality

We begin by contrasting overall movements in wage inequality in France, Japan, the United Kingdom, and the United States.[2] Figure 1.1 summarizes movements in wage inequality by sex for full-time workers.[3] The figure plots the time series of overall wage inequality for each group as measured by the log wage differential between the ninetieth and the tenth percentiles of the wage distribution for that group. The figure shows large increases in wage inequality in the 1980s in the United States and Britain, a moderate increase in Japan, and a small increase in France starting in 1984. Panel A of figure 1.1 indicates that the 90–10 log wage differential for U.S. males increased substantially in the 1970s (from 1.15 in 1969 to 1.30 in 1979) and even more rapidly in the 1980s (increasing by 0.19 from 1979 to 1989). Wage inequality for U.S. females remained stable in the 1970s and then expanded dramatically in the

---

2. A summary of aggregate labor market developments from 1965 to 1989 in the four countries is presented in appendix table 1A.1.

3. Detailed information on the sources, earnings concepts, and sample selection criteria of all the data sets used to measure wage structure changes in this paper is presented in the data appendix. The wage inequality measures in fig. 1.1 refer to the following earnings concepts and samples: (1) United States: hourly wages (annual earnings divided by the product of weeks worked and usual weekly hours) for full-time workers, eighteen to sixty-four years old, using data from the Annual Demographic Supplements to the March Current Populations Surveys (CPSs); (2) Britain: gross hourly earnings for full-time workers from the New Earnings Survey (NES); (3) France: gross annual earnings adjusted for hours differences for full-time, full-year workers from the Declarations Annuelles de Salaires (DAS); and (4) Japan: monthly scheduled earnings for regular workers from the Basic Survey on Wage Structure.

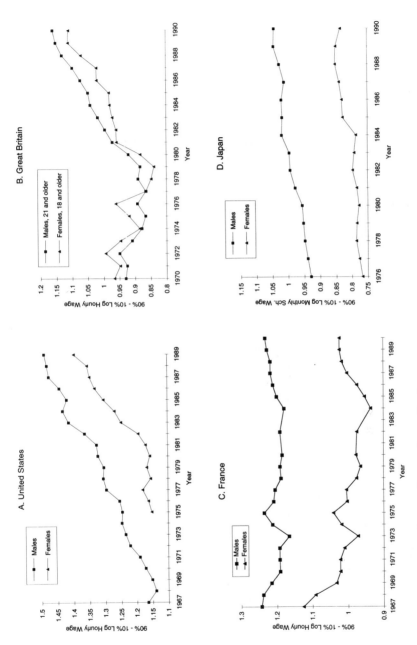

Fig. 1.1 Changes in overall wage inequality by sex

1980s.[4] The figure illustrates a strong similarity in the pattern of sharply rising inequality in the United Kingdom and the United States in the 1980s. In contrast to the U.S. experience, earnings inequality actually narrowed substantially in Britain in the 1970s. Panel C shows that the 90–10 log wage differentials for both men and women narrowed in France from 1967 to 1984 and then show a moderate increase from 1984 to 1990. Finally, panel D indicates a gradual increase in the 90–10 log wage differential of 0.11 for men and of 0.07 for women from 1976 to 1990 in Japan.

France is the only one of the countries that shows no evidence of rising wage inequality in the early 1980s. France's delayed and muted changes in wage structure may reflect labor market institutions that make it difficult to expand skill differentials. A system of minimum wages and contract extensions in France means that unions can have a large effect on wages even with low union density. Smaller increases in wage inequality in Japan than in the United States and Britain may reflect the stability of Japan's manufacturing employment share during the 1980s.

How did the changes in relative earnings documented in figure 1.1 translate into changes in real earnings? Figure 1.2 tries to answer this question by plotting the cumulative log real wage growth of the tenth, fiftieth, and ninetieth percentiles of the wage distributions for men in each country. More precisely, the figure displays the log ratio of each group's real earnings in each year relative to that group's level of real earnings in 1979 (the base year). Panels A and B show fairly similar increases in the 90–10 differential in the 1980s in Britain and the United States but indicate that these increases implied a 0.12 decline in real log earnings from 1979 to 1989 at the tenth percentile in the U.S. wage distribution and a 0.12 increase in real log earnings at the same point of the British distribution. The figure indicates that only in the United States was rising wage inequality in the 1980s accompanied by declining real wages for low-wage males. Even the median U.S. male employee experienced a modest decline in real hourly earnings from 1979 to 1989. Real earnings growth was rapid throughout the earnings distribution in France in the 1960s and 1970s and much more gradual in the 1980s. Panel D shows that real wages have grown rapidly for all groups in Japan over the last fifteen years.

In summary, earnings inequality has increased greatly over the last twenty years in Britain and the United States and fairly moderately in Japan. Over the same period, wage inequality has not changed much in France.

---

4. We do not present estimates of the 90–10 differential for women prior to 1975 because of changes in the CPS between the March 1975 and 1976 surveys. We use imputation procedures for weeks and hours worked for the survey years prior to 1976 developed by Kevin M. Murphy that have been calibrated to fit hours- and weeks-worked distributions for men and not for women. Thus, we are skeptical of hourly earnings distribution estimates for women prior to 1975.

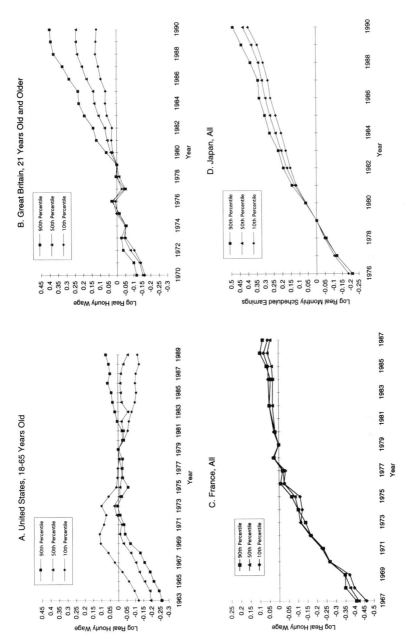

Fig. 1.2   Cumulative real wage growth by decile, males

1.2   Wage Structure Changes in Four Countries

In this section, we turn to a more detailed examination of the patterns of relative wage changes that underlie trends in overall wage inequality in the United States, Britain, Japan, and France. We first separately examine the four countries using the best data available to illustrate each country's wage structure changes. We then summarize the major differences and similarities in patterns of relative wage changes across countries.

1.2.1   Changes in the Structure of Wages in the United States

We examine U.S. wage structure changes over the period 1967–91.[5] Figure 1.3 summarizes relative wage changes for the period 1967–89 using data from all twenty-three Annual Demographic Supplements to the March Current Population Survey (CPS) for survey years 1968–90. The wage measure is hourly earnings computed as annual earnings divided by annual hours (annual weeks worked times usual weekly hours). Table 1.1 provides information on real earnings levels and changes in real and relative earnings by sex-education-experience groups for the period 1979–91 using data from all twelve months of the CPS outgoing rotation groups (ORGs) for 1979, 1987, and 1991. The wage concept used in table 1.1 is the hourly wage measured as usual weekly earnings divided by usual weekly hours. The wage samples used in the figure and the table consist of full-time workers (defined as those who usually work thirty-five or more hours per week).

Panel A of figure 1.3 documents movements in the college/high school log wage ratio for all males (those with one to forty years of potential experience) and for new entrants (those with one to five years of potential experience). The time series of college returns for all males is the fixed-weighted average of the college/high school log wage ratios for workers in forty experience groups (with each group covering a single-year experience interval). The returns for new entrants are a fixed-weighted average of the ratios for corresponding five single-year experience groups. (The weights used in all fixed-weighted averages presented for our U.S. data from the March CPSs are the average shares of the groups in total weeks worked over the entire period 1967–89.) We use fixed-weighted averages to control for changes in the age composition of the different education groups. The figure illustrates that the college wage premium is stable from 1967 to 1971, fell from 1971 to 1979, then rose sharply from 1979 to 1986, and remained at an extremely high level at the end of the 1980s. The swings in education differentials were much larger for new entrants than for older workers in the 1970s and 1980s.

---

5. For a survey of the burgeoning literature examining recent changes in the U.S. wage structure, see Levy and Murnane (1992).

Table 1.1   **Summary of Changes in the U.S. Wage Structure, 1979–91**

Sex	Experience (years)	Education (years)	Estimated Mean Log Hourly Earnings			
			1979	1987	1991	Change, 1979–91
Male	5	10	2.168	1.946	1.874	−.294
		12	2.361	2.155	2.087	−.274
		14	2.440	2.299	2.235	−.205
		16	2.602	2.588	2.536	−.066
	25	10	2.537	2.396	2.304	−.233
		12	2.693	2.612	2.533	−.160
		14	2.811	2.792	2.725	−.086
		16	3.016	2.985	2.937	−.079
Female	5	10	1.909	1.737	1.709	−.200
		12	2.075	1.976	1.930	−.146
		14	2.218	2.170	2.126	−.092
		16	2.377	2.444	2.426	.049
	25	10	2.051	1.964	1.938	−.113
		12	2.197	2.219	2.191	−.006
		14	2.331	2.437	2.422	.092
		16	2.486	2.564	2.583	.097

Note: Each estimate is from a separate cross-sectional regression for full-time workers by sex and year of log real hourly earnings on ten schooling dummies (for fewer than eight, nine, ten, eleven, thirteen, fourteen, fifteen, sixteen, seventeen, and eighteen or more years of schooling), a quartic in experience, interactions of all the experience terms with three broad education-level dummies (fewer than twelve, thirteen to fifteen, and sixteen or more years of schooling), two race dummies, interactions between the race dummies and the broad education-level dummies, and a metropolitan-area dummy. The estimates are predicted values for white, full-time workers, residing in a metropolitan area evaluated at the indicated education and experience levels. Earnings levels are converted to 1991 dollars using the implicit price deflator for personal consumption expenditures from the U.S. national income accounts. The data are from the CPS outgoing rotation groups (ORGs) for 1979, 1987, and 1991. The sample sizes in the regressions ranged from 45,140 to 69,415 observations.

Sharp increases in education differentials are further illustrated in table 1.1. The table presents estimated mean log real hourly wages for men and women at four education levels and two potential experience levels in 1979, 1987, and 1991.[6] These adjusted means of log hourly earnings allow us to control for changes in observed measures of group composition in making inferences concerning real and relative wage changes. Earnings differentials widened among each successive education category for both young workers (those with five

6. The estimates are predicted values from separate log hourly earnings regressions by sex for full-time workers run in each year using data from the CPS ORG samples.

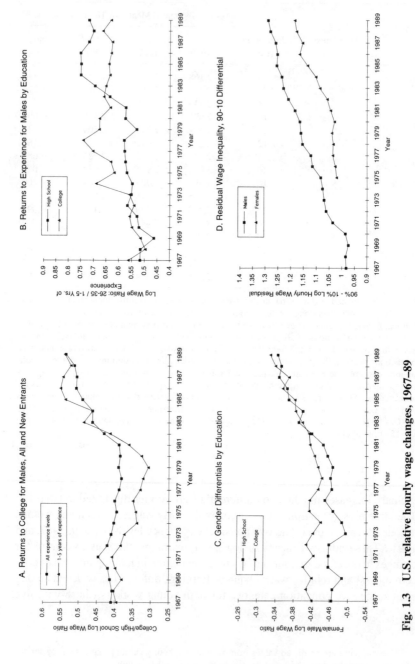

Fig. 1.3   U.S. relative hourly wage changes, 1967–89

years of experience) and prime-age workers (those with twenty-five years of experience) in the 1980s. These relative wage changes in a period of negative average real wage growth for males generated a decline in the real hourly wages of young, less educated males of 25 percent. The earnings differentials between young college graduates and high school graduates increased by approximately 20 percent for both men and women during the 1980s. The pace of increase in educational wage differentials was much slower in the period 1987–91 than in the period 1979–87.

Panel B of figure 1.3 compares movements in the log ratio of the earnings of peak earners (those with twenty-six to thirty-five years of experience) to new entrants for college and high school males. The figure shows that, while experience differentials expanded for both groups from 1967 to 1989, the time patterns of the changes differ substantially. Experience differentials for college graduates expanded from the early 1970s to 1978 and since then have declined. The gap between wages of peak earners and new entrants for less educated males increased sharply from 1979 to 1987 and exhibits a minor decline at the end of the 1980s. Table 1.1 shows similar patterns extending to 1991. The 1980s increase in experience differentials for males with twelve or fewer years of schooling occurred in a period in which the relative supply of less educated new entrants was actually decreasing. The sharp decline in the earnings of less educated young males relative to both college-educated workers and less educated, older workers suggests a sharp shift in demand against less skilled workers, with the bulk of the adjustment falling on younger workers, and older, less educated workers somewhat insulated from external labor market developments by specific human capital and internal labor markets with seniority lay-off rules.

Panel C presents changes in female/male log wage ratios for high school and college workers.[7] Male/female wage differentials in the United States narrowed substantially during the 1980s. The improvement in relative female earnings in the 1980s was slightly greater among high school than among college workers.

The data so far analyzed in this section refer to changes in real wages for groups distinguished by gender, education, and experience. However, given that these factors account for only about one-third of the differences in wages across workers, there is significant room for relative wage changes within these categories as well. We next examine changes in the dispersion of relative wages within our gender by experience by education categories. Empirically, we do this by looking at the distribution of residuals from separate regressions for men and women in each year of log hourly wages on a set of education-level dummies, a quartic in experience fully interacted with broad education-level dummies, race dummies, and interactions of race dummies with broad education-level dummies.

7. The plots are of fixed-weighted averages of the female/male log wage ratios for forty single-year experience groups for both college and high school workers.

Panel D of figure 1.3 plots the time series of the difference in the ninetieth and tenth percentiles of the distributions of residuals from these regressions for men and women. The figure shows that within-group (residual) inequality expanded enormously, with the 90–10 differential in log weekly wages expanding by 0.31 for men over the period 1967–89 and by 0.13 for men and 0.15 for women from 1979 to 1989. Residual inequality started to expand in the early 1970s and continued increasing rather smoothly in the 1980s. This time pattern contrasts sharply with the pattern for education differentials. We conclude from these differences in timing that the general rise in within-group inequality and the rise in education premiums over the period 1963–87 are actually somewhat distinct economic phenomena.[8]

1.2.2   Changes in the Structure of Wages in Great Britain

Data that are reasonably consistent over time on wages by age, gender, occupation, and industry for the United Kingdom are available for 1968 and for every year since 1974 from the New Earnings Survey (NES).[9] The NES is a sample survey of the earnings of employees in employment in Great Britain in April of each year. While individual level data from the NES are not publicly available, published tabulations provide detailed cell means and information on within-group earnings distributions for age, gender, occupation, and industry groups. We examine earnings changes for full-time employees whose pay for the survey pay period was not affected by absence and use gross hourly earnings as our basic wage measure.

Figure 1.4 highlights major changes in relative wages in Great Britain from 1968 to 1991. Panel A plots the nonmanual/manual log hourly wage differential for both males and females. The time series differ from the usual manual/nonmanual differentials presented in many British publications in that they are fixed-weighted averages of the differences in the log of the median gross hourly wages of nonmanual and manual workers in five age groups for both males and females.[10] The figure shows that nonmanual/manual differentials for men and women declined greatly from 1968 to 1974, remained fairly stable from 1974 to 1979, and then increased sharply in the 1980s. The fixed-weighted nonmanual/manual differential increased over the period 1979–91 from 0.32 to 0.46 for males and from 0.22 to 0.43 for females.[11]

---

8. The finding of rising within-group wage inequality in the United States during the 1970s is fairly robust in the March CPS data, but it is not apparent in all other large national household surveys. For example, Mishel and Bernstein (1994) find that rising within-group wage inequality did not emerge until the beginning of the 1980s (or end of the 1970s) in data on hourly earnings from the May CPS data on hourly wage rates and usual weekly earnings and hours.

9. The NES is described in detail in U.K. Department of Employment (1991).

10. The five age categories used are twenty-one to twenty-four, twenty-five to twenty-nine, thirty to thirty-nine, forty to forty-nine, and fifty to fifty-nine years of age. The fixed weights are the average shares in total employment of each age-sex cell in the years 1974, 1979, 1984, and 1989.

11. For a detailed presentation of changes in wages by occupation for males in Great Britain from 1973 to 1986, see Adams, Maybury, and Smith (1988).

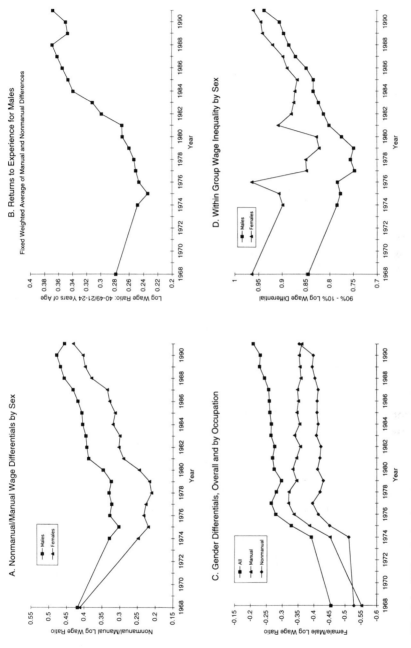

Fig. 1.4 U.K. relative hourly wage changes, 1968–91

Panel B of figure 1.4 shows that experience differentials for males expanded moderately in the second half of the 1970s and quite substantially in the first part of the 1980s. Similar increases in experience differentials are apparent for both manual and nonmanual males. Panel C shows that gender differentials remained fairly steady from 1976 to 1987, after narrowing dramatically under the influence of the Equal Pay Act in the early to mid-1970s. Gender differentials have narrowed a bit more since 1987.

Panel D illustrates that wage inequality within sex–age–broad occupation cells narrowed in the 1970s and then expanded greatly in the 1980s. The figure plots for both men and women the fixed-weighted average in each year of the 90–10 log hourly wage differentials of ten age-occupation cells.[12] In fact, wage inequality increased greatly in the 1980s in Great Britain within both detailed occupations and detailed occupation–industry–gender cells (Katz and Loveman 1990).

While the NES does not provide information on the educational attainment of employees, reasonably comparable individual level data on earnings, demographic characteristics, and educational attainment are available from the General Household Surveys (GHSs) since 1974. The GHS is an annual CPS-style survey of ten to fifteen thousand households.[13] Table 1.2 uses the GHS data to examine the earnings of university graduates relative to individuals with no "educational qualifications" over the period 1974–90. All British children must attend full-time education until the age of sixteen, at which time a large portion of them leave school without earning any educational qualifications. We use the earnings differential between those with university degrees and those with no qualifications as a rough measure of the returns to higher education in Britain. Tabulations for individuals aged sixteen to sixty from the 1989 Labour Force Survey (a much larger household survey than the GHS that unfortunately does not have wage data) indicate that 11 percent of employed males and 7 percent of employed females had a university degree of equivalent qualification while 24 percent of employed males and 31 percent of employed females had no qualifications.

The reported university degree differentials in table 1.2 are the estimated coefficients on a university degree dummy variable in separate regressions for men and women of log gross weekly pay before deductions on thirteen highest educational qualifications dummies, ten region dummies, a race dummy, experience, experience squared, and month dummies.[14] The base education group is those with no qualifications. Thus, table 1.2 compares the earnings of those with university degrees to members of this no qualifications group with the

---

12. The ten cells for each sex involve the combination of five age groups (twenty-one to twenty-four, twenty-five to twenty-nine, thirty to thirty-nine, forty to forty-nine, and fifty to fifty-nine) and two broad occupation categories (manual and nonmanual).

13. For a detailed discussion of earnings and education data in the GHS, see Schmitt (chap. 5 in this volume).

14. The samples for the regressions include full-time employees from sixteen to sixty-nine years of age. Year dummies are included in all the regressions.

Table 1.2   **Log Weekly Earnings Equations, Great Britain, 1974–90**

	1974–75	1978–79	1982–83	1988–90
Males:				
Degree	.6517	.5848	.6204	.6403
	(.0152)	(.0133)	(.0155)	(.0167)
Experience	.0522	.0533	.0534	.0562
	(.0008)	(.0007)	(.0010)	(.0013)
Experience^2	−.0009	−.0009	−.0009	−.0010
	(.00002)	(.00002)	(.00002)	(.00003)
R^2	.4238	.4143	.3569	.3567
N	12,542	12,424	9,010	8,416
Females:				
Degree	.8344	.7530	.7738	.7947
	(.0356)	(.0283)	(.0277)	(.0261)
Experience	.0293	.0279	.0328	.0341
	(.0014)	(.0014)	(.0016)	(.0018)
Experience^2	−.0005	−.0005	−.0006	−.0006
	(.00003)	(.00003)	(.00003)	(.00004)
R^2	.3470	.3271	.3321	.3271
N	5,497	5,615	4,359	4,876

Source: General Household Surveys, 1974–90.

Note: The dependent variable is log gross weekly pay before deductions. Individuals reported their pay the last time they were paid as well as the period covered by this payment. Earnings were then set on a weekly basis. Equations include eleven month dummies, ten region dummies, year dummies, and thirteen qualifications dummies including degree plus a race dummy. The numbers in parentheses are standard errors. The sample is restricted to full-time employees.

same number of years of labor market experience. Regressions are reported for the pooled samples 1974–75, 1978–79, 1982–83, and 1988–90. The estimates indicate that the university earnings premium declined from the mid- to the late 1970s and then increased in the 1980s. The university earnings differential shows a pattern of increase in the 1980s that is similar to but smaller in magnitude than the estimated increases in nonmanual/manual differentials from the NES.

In summary, between- and within-group wage differentials for both men and women narrowed in Britain from the late 1960s to the late 1970s and then expanded tremendously in the 1980s. Our results from the NES concerning overall and within-group changes in inequality for males are quite similar to Schmitt's (chap. 5 in this volume) findings from the GHS for 1974–88.

1.2.3   Changes in the Structure of Wages in Japan

We use data from the Basic Survey on Wage Structure to analyze changes in the Japanese wage structure.[15] These wage data are compiled from wage

---

15. For a further analysis of changes in the Japanese wage structure during the 1980s using data from the Basic Survey on Wage Structure, see Genda (1993).

surveys of nongovernment establishments with ten or more regular workers taken in June of each year. The published wage statistics provide data on mean wages for regular workers by detailed sex-age-education categories and on the tenth, fiftieth, and ninetieth percentile wages of regular workers for sex-age groups. The restriction of the sample to regular workers and the exclusion of small establishments (those with fewer than ten regular worker) means that the Basic Survey on Wage Structure misses a substantial fraction of the Japanese labor force. These exclusions are probably more important for women than for men. We focus on monthly scheduled earnings as our basic wage measure since this is the most readily available measure for education-age cells. Katz and Revenga (1989) and Davis (1992) find that levels of inequality and wage differentials are larger when a more comprehensive measure of earnings that includes overtime earnings and special payments (bonuses) is used but that trends in wage differentials are quite similar for monthly scheduled earnings and total monthly earnings.[16]

Figure 1.5 summarizes basic changes in the pattern of Japanese relative wages from 1967 to 1990. Panel A graphs fixed-weighted averages of log college/high school wage ratios for male age and experience groups.[17] The college/high school wage differential by age group compares the earnings of persons from the same high school class who went on to attain a degree to those who did not. The analogous differential by experience group compares the earnings of college graduates and high school graduates who entered the labor market at the same time. The college log wage premium for those of the same age fell moderately from 0.23 in 1967 to a trough of 0.17 in 1984 and expanded slightly to 0.19 in 1990. The college/high school wage differential by experience group is essentially flat from 1974 to 1990. But panel B of figure 1.5 illustrates that relative earnings of college graduates did improve markedly for new entrants from 1974 to 1990. The log difference between the starting salary of new entrant college graduates and high school graduates increased from 0.15 in 1974 to 0.26 in 1990. The shortage of young workers in Japan since the early 1970s does seem to have created pressures in the labor market favoring young college graduates in the new entrant labor market. This finding is not surprising given the immobility of workers in Japan once they have entered the internal labor market of firms of at least moderate size.

Panel C shows that Japan does have a different pattern of changes in experience differentials than do Britain and the United States. Although experience

16. We have also analyzed changes in wage differentials for men over the period 1967–87 using hourly total earnings. The patterns are quite similar to those for scheduled monthly earnings. We use monthly earnings because we do not have hours data beyond 1987.

17. The age groups are twenty to twenty-four, twenty-five to twenty-nine, thirty to thirty-nine, forty to forty-nine, and fifty to fifty-nine. The experience groups cover workers with approximately one to two, three to seven, eight to twelve, thirteen to seventeen, eighteen to twenty-two, twenty-three to twenty-seven, twenty-eight to thirty-two, and thirty-three to thirty-seven years of potential experience. The fixed weights are the average share of each age (or experience) group in total male employment over the period 1967–90.

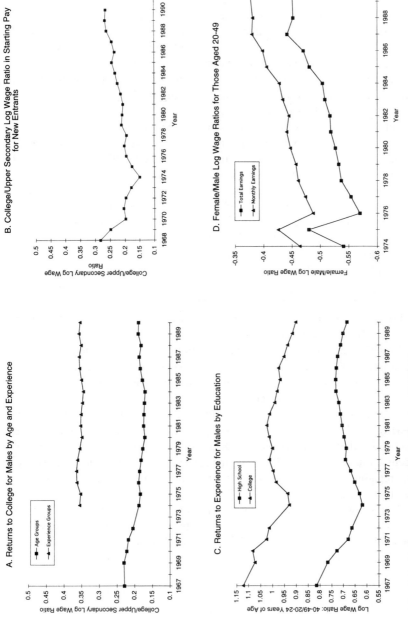

Fig. 1.5 Japan, wage structure changes, 1967–90

differentials increased from the mid-1970s to the early 1980s for males in all three countries, experience differentials declined both in the late 1960s and in the late 1980s in Japan. In fact, Japan is distinct among the countries studied in having a smaller earnings gap between prime age and young males in the late 1980s/early 1990s than in the late 1960s/early 1970s.

Panel D graphs fixed-weighted averages of female/male log wage ratios for six five-year age groups covering workers aged twenty to forty-nine years. The different patterns of educational attainment of men and women in Japan have led us not to adjust for educational attainment in making these comparisons. The figure shows a fairly substantial narrowing of the gender earnings gap among regular workers from 1976 to 1988.

Thus, changes in education and gender wage differentials in Japan in the 1980s are qualitatively similar to but much smaller in magnitude than the analogous changes in the United States. In Japan, education differentials increased slightly overall and moderately for new entrants. The bigger increase in education differentials for young workers is similar to the U.S. pattern. The reversal of a pattern of rising experience differentials to one of shrinking experience differentials by the late 1980s is more extreme in Japan than in the United States. Unfortunately, we do not have data on wage distributions within sex-age-education cells to look at within-group inequality measures in Japan that are similar to those that we can compute for our other countries.

1.2.4 Changes in the Structure of Wages in France

French data on mean wages by gender, occupation, industry, and age come from the Declarations Annuelles de Salaires (DAS), which contains data for full-time workers in all private and semipublic firms. While labor income is measured on an annual basis, it is constructed on the basis of a fixed number of hours so that it has a straightforward transformation into an hourly wage measure. The data have been collected annually for many years but were available in published form from 1967 to 1987.[18] No data collection took place in 1981 or 1983, so these years are missing from the time series. While detailed occupation data are available in the DAS, there was a significant redefinition of occupations beginning in 1984 that makes detailed comparisons problematic. Aggregating occupations into nonmanual and manual categories eliminates nearly all the incompatibilities.

Data on wage distributions by sex and by sex-occupation groups for the periods 1967–82 and 1984–87 are available from two analogous data sets from the DAS. These data sets cover all full-time workers in private and semipublic firms born in October of even-numbered years—roughly 4 percent samples of the covered working population.

Figure 1.6 summarizes between-group changes in the French wage structure for the period 1976–87 and within-occupation changes for the period 1967–87.

---

18. Provisional data for 1987–90 on wages by decile are available from OECD (1993).

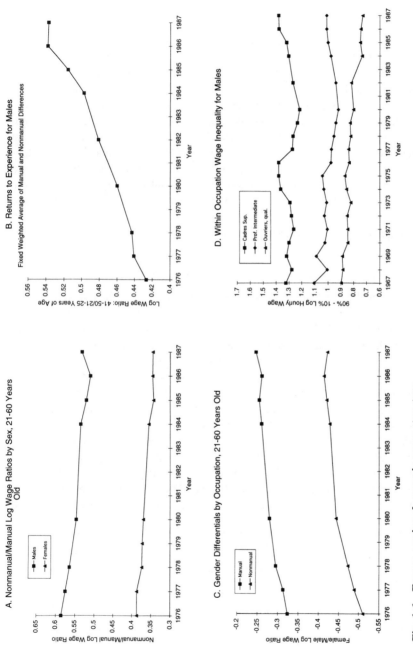

Fig. 1.6 France, major changes in wage structure

Panel A shows movements in the nonmanual/manual differential by sex. The figure graphs fixed-weighted averages of the differences in the log of the mean hourly wages of nonmanual and manual workers in eight age groups for each sex.[19] The nonmanual/manual differential narrows from the mid-1970s through the mid-1980s, with a minor uptick at the end of the sample period. This contrasts with the British experience of a sharply rising nonmanual wage premium throughout the 1980s. But panel B of figure 1.6 shows that the experience differentials for males in France increased in a fashion quite similar to the analogous measure for British males (shown in panel B of fig. 1.4 above). Female/male log wage differentials by broad occupation (as measured by fixed-weighted averages of the female/male log hourly wage ratio for eight age groups) show a narrowing in France of 0.08 for manual and 0.09 for nonmanual workers from 1976 to 1987. Finally, panel D indicates that within-occupation wage dispersion narrowed substantially for males from the late 1960s to 1980. In the 1980s, within-occupation inequality measured by the 90–10 log wage differential expanded for professional and managerial occupations (e.g., *cadres superiores*) and narrowed for manual occupations (e.g., *ouvriers*).

1.2.5   Differences and Similarities in Wage Structure Changes

The qualitative features of wage structure changes over the last twenty years in the United States, Great Britain, France, and Japan are summarized and compared in table 1.3. All four countries shared in the common OECD pattern of declining educational and occupational wage differentials in the 1970s. The pattern of narrowing skill differentials reversed itself in three of the countries by the early 1980s and in France starting in 1984. The magnitude of increases in skill differentials in the 1980s is largest in Britain and the United States.[20]

More generally, Britain and the United States show quite similar patterns of substantial increases in between- and within-group wage inequality in the 1980s. The one exception to this pattern is that experience differentials for more educated workers narrowed in the United States in the 1980s. Japan had moderate increases in inequality in the 1980s, and France is the outlier, with no rise in inequality through 1984. Increased wage inequality in France from 1984 to 1987 suggests that wage structure changes similar to those experienced

---

19. The age groups are twenty-one to twenty-five, twenty-six to thirty, thirty-one to thirty-five, thirty-six to forty, forty-one to forty-five, forty-six to fifty, fifty-one to fifty-five, and fifty-six to sixty. The fixed weights are the average employment shares of each age group over the sample.

20. Differences in education systems mean that the best way to compare the magnitude of skill differential changes in France, Britain, and the United States is to examine changes in analogous occupational wage differentials. Appendix table 1A.2 compares changes in nonmanual/manual wage differentials by age-sex groups in Britain, France, and the United States using as comparable as possible earnings data and occupation classification systems. Differences in the organization of work and similarities in education distributions for males mean that educational earnings differentials are more comparable in the United States and Japan than are occupational wage differentials. Katz and Revenga (1989) compare changes in college/high school wage differentials in Japan and the United States.

Table 1.3   Wage Structure Changes in Four OECD Countries: The Scorecard

	1970s				1980s			
	United States	Britain	France	Japan	United States	Britain	France	Japan
Male:								
Overall inequality	⇈	⇊	⇊		⇈	⇈	↑	⇈
Within inequality	⇈	⇊	⇊		⇈	⇈	↔	
Education/occupation	⇊	⇊	⇊	⇊	⇈	⇈	↔	↑
Experience:								
College/nonmanual	⇈	↔		↑	→	⇈	⇈	⇊
≤ High school/manual	↔	↔		↑	⇈	⇈	⇈	↔
Female:								
Overall inequality	↔	⇊	⇊		⇈	⇈	↑	⇈
Within inequality	↑	⇊	⇊		⇈	⇈	↔	
Education/occupation	⇊	⇊	⇊		⇈	⇈	↔	
Female/male	↔	⇈	↑		⇈	↑	⇈	⇈

Note: ⇈ = increases by a substantial magnitude; ↑ = small increase; ↔ = no change; ↓ = small decrease; and ⇊ = large decrease; a blank space signifies insufficient information.

by the other countries in the early 1980s may be occurring with a lag in France. U.S. males are the only group for whom overall wage inequality was probably already increasing in the 1970s. France and Britain share a pattern of decreasing wage dispersion in the 1970s. Finally, the relative earnings of females improved in all four countries over the last twenty years, although the time patterns of the changes are fairly heterogeneous.

1.3 Supply and Demand Factors

We begin our investigation into the causes of the between-group relative wage changes documented in the previous section using a simple supply and demand framework in which different demographic groups (identified by sex, age, and education) are viewed as distinct labor inputs. We initially abstract from the effects of labor market institutions on wage setting and think of the relative wages of demographic groups in each country as being generated by the interaction of relative supplies of the groups and an aggregate production function with its associated factor demand schedules. To the extent that different demographic groups are imperfect substitutes in production, we can view changes in relative wages as being generated by shifts in relative numbers of workers in each group and shifts in relative demand schedules. Changes in the age structure and educational attainment of the population as well as changes in female labor force participation rates may affect the wage structure by altering the relative supplies of imperfectly substitutable groups of workers. Shifts in the structure of product demand and skill-biased technological change are likely to affect relative labor demands. In this section, we examine the extent to which changes in the relative numbers of workers by education and changes in relative demands associated with industry shifts in employment can help explain cross-country differences in relative wage changes.

1.3.1 Relative Supply Changes

Much research on the U.S. wage structure concludes that substantial secular growth in the demand for "more educated" and "more skilled" workers is necessary to rationalize the persistence of substantial educational wage differentials in the face of a rapid growth in the fraction of highly educated workers in the U.S. labor force (e.g., Bound and Johnson 1992; and Murphy and Welch 1992). Freeman (1981) argues that trend growth in the relative demand for college-educated workers is required to explain patterns of changes in the relative wages and quantities in most OECD economies through the end of the 1970s. Under the stark hypothesis that the relative demand for college graduates grows at a relatively steady trend rate (perhaps because of a steady pace of industrial shifts and technological changes favoring the more skilled), changes in the college wage premium should be inversely related to changes in the rate of growth of the relative supply of college graduates. Katz and Murphy (1992) find that a simple hypothesis of this type does a fairly good job of explaining movements in U.S. educational wage differentials over the last thirty years. This approach suggests that differences in the rate of growth of the supply of highly educated workers in the 1970s and the 1980s may help explain a fairly general pattern of narrowing education differentials in the 1970s and expanding differentials in the 1980s.

Table 1.4 provides summary information on changes in the fraction of the labor force (or adult population) with college educations in the United States, Britain, France, and Japan over the last two decades. The rate of growth of college-educated workers was quite rapid in all four countries in the 1970s. The expansion of the availability of higher education and large baby-boom cohorts fueled the furious pace of relative supply growth over this period. The rate of growth of the relative supply of highly educated workers decelerated substantially in the United States, Britain, and Japan in the 1980s. The relative earnings of university graduates declined in each of these countries during the 1970s, when supply growth was fastest, and expanded in each of these countries in the 1980s, when supply growth was much slower. Relative supply growth slowed down in the 1980s in these three countries both when measured as the annual average change in the log share of college graduates and when measured as the annual average change in the percentage share of college graduates.

Under the assumption that the elasticity of substitution between college-educated and non-college-educated workers in the United States is in Freeman's (1986) preferred one to three range, the slowdown in the rate of growth of college graduates in the United States from the 1970s to the 1980s can explain an increase in the college/high school log wage differential from 1979 to 1989 of 0.06 to 0.20. In fact, the U.S. college/high school log wage ratio for all males (panel A of fig. 1.3 above) increased by 0.14 from 1979 to 1989. If the degree of substitutability of college and other workers is at the low end of existing estimates, then changes in the rate of growth of the relative supply of college workers in the 1980s are sufficient by themselves to explain observed increases in the college wage premium in the United States, Britain, and Japan. Thus, differences in the rate of growth of the relative supply of highly educated workers in the 1970s and 1980s may be an important part of the explanation for declining skill differentials in the 1970s and rising skill differentials in the 1980s.

Table 1.4 further indicates that the one country in which education/occupation differentials do not appear to have expanded in the 1980s, France, is also the country in which the log relative supply growth of college graduates appears to have decelerated the least in the 1980s. The evidence for whether any deceleration at all occurred in the growth of the log relative supply of college workers in France in the 1980s is somewhat ambiguous. One gets different answers for choices of slightly different years and different samples (e.g., the adult population vs. the adult labor force).

Table 1.4   Relative Supplies of College-Educated Workers in Four Countries

Group and Ages	% with College Education			Annual Log Growth Rates	
	1969	1979	1989	1969–79	1979–89
United States:					
Employees:					
Males, 18–64	14.5	21.9	26.6	.041	.019
Females, 18–64	10.4	16.8	23.2	.048	.032
Males & females, 18–64	13.0	19.9	25.1	.043	.023
Population:					
Males, 18–64	13.8	19.8	24.0	.036	.019
Females, 18–64	8.3	13.5	19.2	.049	.035
Males & females, 18–64	10.8	16.6	21.5	.043	.026
	1973	1979	1989	1973–79	1979–89
Britain:					
Population:					
Males, 16–60	9.6	14.5	21.0	.069	.037
Females, 16–60	6.5	9.6	13.9	.065	.037
Males & females, 16–60	8.0	12.0	17.4	.068	.037
Employees:					
Males, 16–60	10.1	15.7	23.9	.074	.042
Females, 16–60	7.7	10.8	17.4	.056	.048
Males & females, 16–60	9.1	13.6	21.0	.068	.037
	1970	1980	1989	1970–80	1980–89
France:					
Population:					
Males, 15+	5.3	8.3	11.8	.045	.039
Females, 15+	5.3	6.9	10.4	.026	.046
	1975	1982	1987	1975–82	1982–87
Labor force:					
Males, 15+	7.8	10.1	13.2	.037	.054
Males & females, 15+	8.3	10.9	14.0	.039	.050
	1970	1979	1990	1970–79	1979–90
Japan:					
Regular employees:					
Males, All	11.1	18.9	25.1	.059	.026
	1971	1979	1987	1971–79	1979–87
All employees:					
Males, 15+	15.1	21.0	25.6	.041	.025
Males & females, 15+	12.0	17.9	22.5	.050	.029

Table 1.4   (continued)

Sources: United States: March Current Population Surveys; Britain: General Household Surveys; France: INSEE, "Tableaux de l'economic francais," various years; Japan: Basic Survey on Wage Structure for regular employees in establishments with ten or more regular employees; Employment Status Survey for all employees.

Note: College-educated workers are defined as follows: United States: college graduates (those with sixteen or more years of schooling); Britain: individuals with post-A-level qualifications (i.e., higher degrees, Higher National Diploma [HND]/Higher National Certificate [HNC], teaching, nursing, and professional qualifications, etc.); France: university graduates (those with higher degrees beyond a baccalauréat); Japan: university graduates for regular employees; those with at least some college including junior college for all employees.

1.3.2   Relative Demand Shifts

It is clear that substantial shifts in relative demand favoring more educated and more skilled workers are necessary to explain patterns of changes in wage structures in most OECD countries over the postwar period. One explanation for patterns of changes in education/skill differentials is that relative demand for more educated workers has grown fairly steadily and that variations in changes in skill differentials across periods are driven by changes in the rate of growth of the relative supply. This explanation is fairly consistent with the observed time series for the United States under the assumption of fairly low substitutability between college and less educated workers. But the 1980s deceleration in the rate of growth of the relative supply of college graduates in many countries is not a sufficient explanation for the observed increases in educational wage differentials if the degree of substitutability is in the high range of plausible estimates. Furthermore, sharp increases in experience differentials for less educated workers in the early 1980s, a period of small entering cohorts of less educated workers, do not seem to fit into a picture of smooth changes in relative skill demands throughout the last twenty years. An alternative set of explanations focuses on an acceleration in the rate of growth of relative demand for more skilled workers possibly arising from an increased pace of technological changes, foreign outsourcing of production jobs, or the decline of the manufacturing sector.

We find it useful to think of relative demand shifts as coming from two types of changes: those that occur within industries (i.e., shifts that change relative factor ratios at fixed relative factor prices) and those that occur between industries (i.e., shifts that change the allocation of labor demand across industries at fixed relative wages). Sources of within-industry shifts include skill-biased technological change, outsourcing, and changes in the prices of nonlabor inputs (e.g., computers). Between-industry shifts may be driven by shifts in product demand across industries, differences across industries in factor-neutral technological change, and shifts in net international trade.

The well-documented finding that the share of employment of college graduates and women increased inside almost every two-digit industry in the

United States over the past three decades despite increases in the relative prices of college graduates and females suggests that important shifts in relative demand have occurred within detailed industries. The rate at which U.S. employment shifted toward more educated and nonproduction workers within detailed industries also appears to have accelerated somewhat (especially in the manufacturing sector) during the 1980s (Berman, Bound, and Machin 1994; Katz and Murphy 1992). Similar changes in factor ratios within broad one-digit industries are apparent in our examination of British data from the Labour Force Survey for the 1980s. Nevertheless, Berman, Bound, and Machin (1994) find that, in contrast to the U.S. experience, the rate of employment shifts from production to nonproduction workers within detailed manufacturing industries actually decelerated somewhat in Britain and Japan from the 1970s to the 1980s. The increased pace of within-sector skill upgrading in a period of rising relative prices of more skilled workers suggests that an acceleration in within-industry relative demand growth favoring the more skilled plays some role in rising U.S. educational/occupational wage differentials in the 1980s. The limited available direct evidence on changes in factor ratios in British and Japanese manufacturing is less consistent with an acceleration in the pace of skill-biased technological change in the 1980s explaining the very different evolution of wage differentials in the 1970s and 1980s.

The effects of between-industry shifts in labor demand on the relative demands for different skill and demographic groups depend on group differences in industrial employment distributions. Shifts in industrial employment will shift relative labor demands if sectors differ in their intensity of use of different types of workers. The data that we have available for the United States, Britain, and Japan all indicate that input coefficients for different education groups and for men and women differ systematically across industries in a similar manner in each country. Less educated workers are overrepresented in agriculture, construction, mining, and many manufacturing sectors. College graduates are overrepresented in professional and related services, finance, insurance and real estate, and some high-technology manufacturing sectors.

Major industrial employment shifts in each country are illustrated in table 1.5. France, the United Kingdom, and the United States all experienced a sharp decline in the share of employment in goods-producing industries (mining, manufacturing, construction, and utilities) in the 1970s and the 1980s. These employment shifts are likely to have led to a shift in relative demand against less skilled workers. The relative decline of employment in goods-producing industries over the entire period was comparable in the United States and France but was significantly larger in the United Kingdom. Japan is an outlier in the other direction: it maintained a stable share of employment in manufacturing throughout the 1970s and 1980s. The shifts illustrated in table 1.5 suggest an acceleration in the pace of between-industry demand shifts against the less skilled in the 1980s in Britain and France. The broad changes in the indus-

Table 1.5   **Sectoral Employment Shares, 1965–89**

	1965	1970	1975	1980	1985	1989
United States:						
Agriculture	6.3	4.5	4.1	3.6	3.1	2.9
Industry	35.5	34.4	30.6	30.5	28.0	26.7
Services	58.2	61.1	65.3	65.9	68.8	70.5
Britain:						
Agriculture	3.8	3.2	2.8	2.6	2.5	2.2
Industry	46.6	44.7	40.4	37.7	31.6	29.3
Services	49.6	52.0	56.8	59.7	65.9	68.5
Japan:						
Agriculture	23.5	17.4	12.7	10.4	8.8	7.6
Industry	32.4	35.7	35.9	35.3	34.9	34.3
Services	44.1	46.9	51.5	52.4	56.4	58.2
France:						
Agriculture	17.8	13.5	10.3	8.7	7.6	6.4
Industry	39.1	39.2	38.6	35.9	32.0	30.1
Services	43.1	47.2	51.1	55.4	60.4	63.5

Source: OECD (1991).

trial distribution of employment in each of the four countries are also likely to have favored women over men.

We next attempt to determine more systematically whether changes in the industrial composition of employment led to an acceleration in the rate of decline in relative demand for less educated workers in the 1980s. We use standard fixed-coefficient relative demand shift indices to measure how changes in the industrial mix of jobs in the United States, Britain, and Japan have affected the relative demand for workers by sex-education categories in the 1970s and in the 1980s. We specify an index of the demand for the labor of the jth group of workers in year t as

$$(1) \qquad E_{jt} = \sum_i \alpha_{ij} E_{it},$$

where E_{it} is total employment in industry i in year t and α_{ij} is the fixed coefficient relating the number of workers in group j to total employment in industry i under fixed technology and fixed relative factor prices. Since we are concerned with changes in relative demands, we normalize both sides of equation (1) by dividing through by aggregate employment at time t (E_t) to yield the index of the relative demand for group j given by

$$(2) \qquad e_{jt} = \sum_i \alpha_{ij} e_{it},$$

where $e_{jt} = E_{jt}/E_t$ and $e_{it} = E_{it}/E_t$. We measure the log change in the relative demand for group j as $\Delta \ln (e_{jt})$. This approach to measuring relative demand shifts arising from sectoral employment shifts can be justified either as a fixed-coefficients "manpower requirements" index (Freeman 1986) or as an approximation to "true" factor demand shifts for more general production functions (Katz and Murphy 1992).

To implement this approach to measuring demand shifts in as comparable a manner as possible in different countries, we divide the economies of each country into nine one-digit industries and divide the labor forces into six to eight sex-education groups. We use separate estimates of the α_{ij}'s for each country. We measure α_{ij} as group j's share of total employment in sector i in a base period.[21] We measure changes in industrial employment shares (changes in e_{it}'s) for each country on a comparable basis using the one-digit industrial employment distributions reported by the OECD (OECD 1991). Although important industrial shifts occurring within one-digit industries are missed by our measure of between-industry demand shifts, this approach does provide a way to gauge differences across countries and time periods in the extent that broad changes in industry mix have affected the relative demands for different groups of workers.

Table 1.6 presents changes in our relative demand shift measures over the periods 1969–79 and 1979–89 for eight demographic groups in the United States and six demographic groups in Britain and Japan.[22] Measured between-industry demand shifts are monotonically increasing for both men and women in all three countries in both time periods. Between-industry shifts also favored women relative to men in every education group for all three countries. The magnitude of demand shifts against less educated workers increased in Britain in the 1980s, appears fairly steady across the two decades in the United States, and decreases in Japan in the 1980s. The large magnitude of the relative demand shifts in Japan in the 1970s is driven by the sharp decline in agriculture's share of employment. Japan's strength in manufacturing in the 1980s meant a smaller between-industry shift in relative labor demand against high school (upper secondary) males in Japan than in Britain or the United States. Overall, the between-industry shifts are consistent with a pattern of trend increases in the relative demand for highly educated workers. The estimates also indicate that the sharp contrast in the labor market performance of less educated young workers in Britain in the 1970s and 1980s may be associated with the particularly sharp acceleration in the pace of deindustrialization in that country in the early 1980s.

Since educational earnings differentials expanded and gender earnings dif-

21. The base period in each country was chosen so that the α_{ij}'s would reflect average production technologies in the 1980s. The base years for each country are 1979, 1984, and 1989 for the United States; 1979, 1983, 1987, and 1989 for Britain; and 1979 and 1987 for Japan. Experimentation with U.S. data indicates that estimated shifts in relative labor demands are not very sensitive to the choice of base year over the period 1967–89. The α_{ij}'s were calculated using data on employment status, industry, education, and sex from household surveys in each country: the CPS ORGs for the United States; the Labour Force Survey for Britain; and the Employment Status Survey for Japan.

22. Unfortunately, we do not have the necessary data to calculate analogous measures for France.

Table 1.6   **Industry-Based Demand Shift Measures, 1969–89**

| | Change in Log Relative Demand | | | |
| | Males | | Females | |
Education Group	1969–79	1979–89	1969–79	1979–89
United States:				
Dropouts	−.044	−.048	−.003	−.009
High school graduates	−.036	−.041	.023	.025
Some college	−.011	−.012	.046	.047
College graduates	.016	.019	.057	.054
Britain:				
No qualifications	−.072	−.097	.028	.000
A-levels, O-levels, etc.	−.039	−.041	.069	.084
College	.026	.059	.102	.119
Japan:				
Lower secondary	−.066	−.057	−.128	−.054
Upper secondary	.035	.007	.032	.028
College	.098	.054	.107	.073

Note: The between-industry demand shift measure for group j is given by $\Delta \ln(e_{jt})$ where $e_{jt} = \sum_i \alpha_{ij} e_{it}$, α_{ij} is group j's share of total employment in sector i in the base period, and e_{it} is industry i's share of total employment in year t. i indexes nine one-digit industries for the United States and Japan and eight one-digit industries for Britain.

ferentials narrowed in each of these countries in the 1980s, the actual between-sector demand shifts that would have occurred at fixed relative factor prices are likely to be greater than those suggested in table 1.6. Additionally, the use of highly aggregate one-digit industry categories is likely to lead us to understate the magnitude of between-industry relative demand shifts. When we use two-digit industry data for Japan and the United States, we find that relative demand shifts across education-gender groups have a similar pattern to the one-digit estimates presented in table 1.6 but are almost twice as large in magnitude.

In summary, simple supply and demand factors appear to go a reasonable way toward explaining differences in changes in the wage structure across time periods and countries. A significant slowdown in the growth rate of the relative supply of college graduates occurred in the United States, Britain, and Japan. This reduction in the pace of the growth of the supply of highly educated workers, combined with steady demand growth favoring such workers, provides a consistent explanation for declining education differentials in the 1970s and a rapid growth of education differentials in the 1980s in Britain and the United States. An acceleration in the pace of between-industry demand shifts also appears in these two countries, with massive increases in wage inequality in the 1980s. The rate of within-industry skill upgrading appears to have accelerated in the United States during the 1980s. France's stable skill differentials may relate to a continuation of a rapid growth of the relative supply of highly educated workers in the 1980s. Nevertheless, the much earlier appearance of rising inequality in the United States than in the other three countries and the extent to which France's wage structure behaved differently than those of the others in the 1980s do suggest that differences in labor market institutions may play a major role in explaining the differential responses of national wage structures to common relative skill demand shifts.

1.4   The Role of Labor Market Institutions

The much different behavior of the pattern of relative wages in France than in the other three countries in the 1980s in a period of substantial industrial employment shifts in France does point to the possibility that French labor market institutions somewhat offset the effects of relative demand shifts on skill differentials. The outstanding features of the French wage data are that differentials across occupation groups failed to increase substantially in the 1980s, wage inequality did not increase significantly overall or within most groups, and real incomes grew substantially, particularly for manual workers.

There are two important and interrelated labor market institutions that may help explain why relative demand shifts led to only quite modest relative wage changes in France: the collective bargaining system and the minimum wage. Collective bargaining in France has taken place mainly at the industry level since 1950, when a law was passed favoring industry-level bargaining between national employers' federations and national unions. Accordingly, the four large unions in France, and a few smaller ones, are organized on an industry basis. There are no majority representation criteria as in the United States. The French unions have the authority to bargain collectively on behalf of the employees in an industry, even though only a small portion of the employees are members of any particular union. Under the terms of the law, industry-level agreements may be extended by the minister of labor to all firms in the industry—even those that are not members of the employers' federation.

French workers are not obliged to join unions to receive the benefits of negotiated agreements. Since dues are collected on an individual basis and are not deducted automatically by the employer, membership statistics are poor, and the unions must make estimates on the basis of total dues revenues. Nonetheless, it is clear that union density has fallen significantly, from roughly 24 percent in the 1970s to less than 15 percent in the late 1980s. The membership of the most militant union, Confederation Generale du Travail, is estimated to have dropped by more than 60 percent from 1976 to 1987 (Bridgford 1990).

The membership figures, however, do not portray union influence accurately. Support for the unions is better measured by their candidates' success in elections for positions on industrial tribunals and enterprise committees.[23] While

23. Industrial tribunals hear claims of unjust and illegal actions by employers against employees. Enterprise committees are responsible for social activities and labor-management consultation.

the percentage of votes cast for union candidates has declined since the 1970s, Bridgford (1990) reports that they still receive nearly 50 percent of the votes for industrial tribunals and nearly 80 percent of the votes for enterprise committees. Moreover, industry-level agreements negotiated by the unions and employer federations are routinely extended to all firms in the industry with the result that unions exert significant influence on the terms and conditions of employment throughout most industries. Data from 1981 show that nearly 80 percent of all firms and nearly 90 percent of all workers were covered by industry-level agreements (Eyraud and Tchobanian 1985; and Caire 1984). The industry-level agreements determine minimum wages for each job category. Companies may, and often do, chose to pay more, especially for the more highly skilled jobs, but the negotiated minima represent a constraint that applies to firms of all sizes throughout an industry.[24]

The second key labor market institution is the legislated minimum wage, or SMIC (*salaire minimum interprofessional de croissance*). The SMIC, which applies to essentially all sectors with few exemptions or abatements, is a very considerable constraint on the wages of the young or less skilled. Begun in 1950 when wartime wage controls were lifted, the SMIC is adjusted automatically for inflation and occasionally changed in real terms by the federal government. Indeed, the legislation enacting the SMIC referred to it, not as a subsistence wage, but rather as a social policy tool intended to help poorly paid workers share in economic growth (OECD 1985). Brazen and Martin (1991) estimate that 12 percent of all wage and salary earners were paid at or below the SMIC in 1987 and that this percentage had risen significantly since the 1970s. Only about 5 percent of all U.S. wage and salary workers were paid at or below the federal minimum wage ($3.35 per hour) in 1988, and this fraction has declined significantly since 1981 (Haugen and Mellor 1990). The SMIC has been at least 60 percent of the mean wage since 1978 and has actually increased significantly since then in terms of the mean wage (Katz and Loveman 1990). Figure 1.7 shows that the SMIC has also increased relative to wages for unskilled workers for the past twenty years. The increase was most dramatic in the early 1980s, when wage differentials were rising sharply in the United States and Britain and starting to rise in Japan. An especially sharp rise in the SMIC in the early 1980s followed the election of the socialists in 1981. The socialist government pursued an economic policy that featured increases in the SMIC as a means of increasing purchasing power for lower-income workers. From July 1980 to July 1984, the government increased the SMIC in real terms by 14 percent, while average real hourly wages rose by just over 6 percent.

These substantial relative increases in the SMIC tightened wage differentials at the lower end of the distribution. Using our data on French earnings distribu-

---

24. Hence, large firms typically cannot significantly reduce labor costs by subcontracting to small producers.

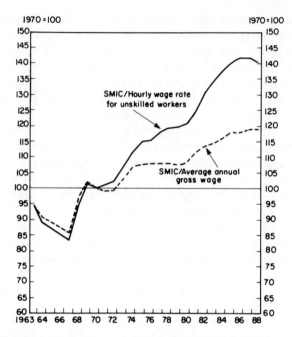

Fig. 1.7   Evolution of statutory minimum wages in France
Source: OECD, *Main Economic Indicators* and *Quarterly National Accounts.*
Note: The statutory minimum wage is the SMIC (*salaire minimum interprofessionnel de croissance*).

tions from the DAS, we estimate that from 1979 to 1987 the SMIC increased from 45.7 to 53.3 percent of the median earnings and from 73.3 to 84.4 percent of the tenth percentile earnings of full-time French male employees. In fact, from 1967 to 1987, the SMIC increased from 75 to 101 percent of the tenth percentile hourly earnings of full-time female workers in the DAS sample. In contrast, the U.S. federal minimum wage remained fixed at a nominal value of $3.35 per hour from 1981 to 1990 and declined in real and relative value throughout the 1980s. We use our March CPS wage samples to estimate that the U.S. minimum wage declined over the period 1979–87 from 40.1 to 30.3 percent of the median and from 82.3 to 69.7 percent of the tenth percentile hourly wage of male, full-time employees in the United States. The SMIC appears to have helped prevent a sharp erosion of real wages at the low end of the French wage distribution.

When the SMIC does not bind on the wages of the less skilled, the industry-negotiated minima do. In some industries, the base (minimum) wage is set equal to the SMIC, while in others, such as metalworking, it is set as a multiple of the SMIC. In either case, changes in the SMIC shift the entire wage distribution. The potential influence of unions and the SMIC on wages in the lower half of the French earnings distribution is highlighted in table 1.7, which shows three measures of overall wage inequality for our four countries for selected years from 1979 to 1989. The table indicates that the bottom half of the French wage distribution for men (as measured by the log wage gap between the fiftieth and the tenth percentiles) is much more compressed relative to the top half (as measured by the log wage gap between the ninetieth and the fiftieth percentiles) than in the other three countries. The 50–10 differential narrowed a bit for both men and women in France in the period of the rapid rise in the value of the SMIC from 1979 to 1984, while the 50–10 gap was rising for both sexes in the United States and Britain and for men in Japan.

While negotiated and legislated minima have maintained the relative wages of the less skilled with jobs, the employment prospects for young, less skilled people deteriorated sharply. In 1984, youth unemployment in France was 26 percent, compared to 15 percent in the seven major industrial OECD countries. Likewise, the duration of unemployment in France was much longer than in Germany, the United Kingdom, and the United States (OECD 1985). While one must be cautious in drawing conclusions concerning the effects of the SMIC on the employment of youths and the less skilled from simple time-series patterns, Brazen and Martin (1991) provide some (weak) evidence suggestive of moderate adverse effects of the SMIC on youth employment in France in the early 1980s.

The DAS wage data suggest that there has been some increase in French wage inequality, both within and between groups, since 1984. The Auroux reforms in 1982 began a process of change in French industrial relations that favors enterprise- or plant-level negotiations over industry-wide negotiations. The reforms require unions and firms to negotiate wages and other matters annually, but they do not require the completion of an agreement. As this legislation matured during the 1980s, negotiations over substantive issues, including wages, have become increasingly decentralized, but agreements remain largely at the industry level. These changes have moved France closer to the U.S. model of low union membership and decentralized negotiations and may have played a role in the modest increases in wage inequality since the mid-1980s.

1.5 Conclusion

This paper has examined similarities and differences in patterns of changes in the structure of wages in the United States, Britain, Japan, and France over the last twenty years. Educational and occupational wage differentials narrowed in all four countries in the 1970s. This pattern reversed itself with increases in skill differentials in the United States, Britain, and Japan in the early 1980s, and a muted but somewhat similar pattern appears to emerge in France starting in 1984.

Reductions in the rate of the growth of the relative supply of college-

Table 1.7   **Alternative Measures of Wage Inequality for Four Countries, 1979–90**

	1979	1984	1987	1990
Males:				
90-10:				
United States	1.23	1.36	1.38	1.40
Britain	.88	1.04	1.10	1.16
France	1.19	1.18	1.22	1.23
Japan	.95	1.02	1.01	1.04
90-50:				
United States	.56	.66	.68	.69
Britain	.51	.61	.63	.67
France	.72	.73	.76	.77
Japan	.49	.52	.51	.55
50-10:				
United States	.67	.70	.69	.71
Britain	.37	.43	.47	.49
France	.47	.45	.46	.46
Japan	.47	.50	.50	.50
Females:				
90-10:				
United States	.96	1.16	1.23	1.27
Britain	.84	.98	1.02	1.11
France	.96	.93	1.00	1.02
Japan	.78	.79	.84	.83
90-50:				
United States	.55	.63	.61	.67
Britain	.50	.58	.59	.64
France	.53	.52	.54	.55
Japan	.43	.45	.50	.49
50-10:				
United States	.41	.53	.63	.61
Britain	.34	.41	.43	.47
France	.44	.41	.46	.48
Japan	.35	.34	.34	.35

Note: 90-10 refers to the log wage differential between the ninetieth and the tenth percentile workers. The 90-50 and 50-10 differentials are defined analagously. The wage inequality measures refer to log hourly wages for the United States, Great Britain, and France and to log monthly scheduled wages for Japan.

educated workers in the face of persistent increases in the relative demand for more skilled labor can explain a substantial portion of the increase in educational wage differentials in the United States, Britain, and Japan in the 1980s. The earlier appearance of rising overall wage inequality in the United States than in Britain may reflect the power of British unions to oppose the apparently market-driven forces that contributed to rising overall wage inequality among males in the United States in the 1970s. The more severe increases in skill differentials in Britain and the United States than in Japan can be partially attributed to an acceleration in the rate of growth of the demand for more skilled workers in the 1980s associated with industrial employment shifts out of manufacturing and within-sector skill upgrading. Similar changes in relative skill demands are likely to have occurred in France, but the effect of such changes on wages has been somewhat offset by a high minimum wage and the ability of French unions to extend contracts even in the face of declining membership.

Data Appendix

United States

Data Source 1. Annual Demographic Files, March Current Population Survey (CPS), 1964–90.

Earnings Concept. Hourly wage (annual earnings divided by annual hours) in the year prior to the survey. Annual hours are given by the product of annual weeks worked and usual weekly hours.

Wage Sample. Full-time workers, eighteen to sixty-four years old. The wage sample excludes those in the military, students, agricultural workers, without-pay workers, those who worked fewer than thirteen weeks in the previous year, wage-salary workers with self-employment income, the unincorporated self-employed, and those with allocated income.

Quantity Sample for Measuring Weeks Worked by Different Groups. Excludes those in the military, students, agricultural workers, and without-pay workers.

Remarks. Adjustments for top coding, bracketed weeks and hours variables, and changes in the CPS imputation procedures in 1976 are as in Murphy and Welch (1992). Potential experience is measured as age at the survey date minus years of completed schooling minus seven. The U.S. data used in figure 1.2 above are from Juhn, Murphy, and Pierce (1993) and cover full-time, male workers, aged eighteen to sixty-five years.

Data Source 2. Outgoing rotation groups (ORGs), CPS, all twelve months, 1979–91.

Earnings Concept. Hourly wage (usual weekly earnings divided by usual weekly hours) at current job.

Wage Sample. Full-time workers, eighteen to sixty-four years old. Excludes the self-employed, workers with allocated (imputed) earnings, and those with reported hourly wages of less than $2.00 or more than $100 in 1991 dollars.

Remarks. Top-coded earnings are adjusted upward by a multiplicative factor of 1.36. Earnings from the unedited usual weekly earnings fields with a higher nominal top code are used to measure weekly earnings for workers with top-coded edited earnings in the 1986–88 surveys.

Great Britain

Data Source 1. New Earnings Survey (NES), published volumes for 1968 and 1970–91.

Earnings Concept. Gross hourly earnings.

Wage Sample. Full-time employees, twenty-one or older for males and eighteen or older for females, whose pay was not affected by absence during the survey period.

Remarks. The NES is a sample survey of the earnings of employees in employment in Great Britain in April of each year. It covers a 1 percent random sample of employees who are members of pay-as-you-earn income tax schemes and is designed to represent all categories of employees in businesses of all kinds and sizes.

Data Source 2. General Household Survey (GHS), 1973–90.

Earnings Concept. Gross weekly earnings.

Wage Sample. Full-time employees, sixteen to sixty-nine years old.

Remarks. A CPS-style household survey of ten to fifteen thousand households per year.

Data Source 3. Labour Force Surveys (LFSs), 1979–90.

Earnings Concept. No earnings information is collected.

Remarks. A large CPS-style household survey that does not collect wage formation but is quite useful for the measurement of relative quantities of different types of workers in total employment and by industry.

Japan

Data Source 1. Basic Survey on Wage Structure, published tabulations, 1967–90.

Earnings Concept. Monthly scheduled earnings.

Wage Sample. Regular workers, eighteen to fifty-nine years old, at nongovernment establishments with at least five to ten regular workers (varies by survey year). Excludes agriculture, forestry and fisheries, private household services, and employees of foreign governments.

Remarks. Seventy thousand to one hundred thousand establishments are surveyed in a typical year. The sample excluded the service sector prior to 1973.

Data Source 2. Employment Status Survey, published tabulations, 1971–87.

Earnings Concept. A continuous individual earnings measure is not available.

Remarks. A large national household survey that is useful for measuring quantities. It covers a broader spectrum of workers than does the Basic Survey on Wage Structure.

France

Data Source. Tabulations from the Declarations Annuelles de Salaires (DAS) for 1967–87. No data are available for 1981 or 1983. Provisional updated data on earnings by decile are used for the period 1988–90.

Earnings Concept. Gross annual earnings adjusted for differences among individuals in annual hours worked.

Wage Sample. Full-time, full-year workers in private and semipublic firms.

Remark. Provisional updated data on wages by decile for 1987–90 are from OECD (1993, 159–61). Changes in the 90–10, 90–50, and 50–10 log earnings differentials for men and women for each year from 1987 to 1990 are derived from the provisional updated data. The level of a wage differential for the period 1988–90 is estimated by adding the provisional change in that differential since 1987 to the 1987 level from the definitive data.

Table 1A.1   **Comparative Overview: The United States, Great Britain, France, and Japan (annual growth rates from preceding to current period)**

	1965	1970	1975	1980	1985	1989
United States:						
Real GNP (1965 = 1)	1	1.16	1.30	1.53	1.72	1.94
		(3.0)	(2.3)	(3.3)	(2.3)	(3.0)
Population, 15–64 years						
(millions)	116.6	127.0	138.9	150.8	158.8	163.9
		(1.7)	(1.8)	(1.6)	(1.0)	(.8)
Civilian employment						
(millions)	71.1	78.7	85.6	99.3	101.2	117.3
		(1.9)	(1.7)	(3.0)	(1.5)	(2.3)
Civilian labor force						
(millions)	74.5	82.8	93.7	106.9	115.5	123.9
		(2.1)	(2.5)	(2.6)	(1.5)	(1.8)
Unemployment rate, all	4.4	4.8	8.3	7.0	7.1	5.2
Unemployment rate,						
16–24 years	9.1	9.9	15.2	13.3	13.0	10.5
Britain:						
Real GNP (1965 = 1)	1	1.13	1.27	1.37	1.49	1.73
		(2.4)	(2.3)	(1.5)	(1.7)	(3.7)
Population, 15–64 years						
(millions)	35.0	35.0	35.2	36.1	37.2	37.5
		(.0)	(.1)	(.5)	(.6)	(.2)
Civilian employment						
(millions)	24.8	24.4	24.7	25.0	24.2	26.0
		(−.3)	(.2)	(.2)	(−.7)	(1.8)
Civilian labor force						
(millions)	25.1	24.9	25.6	26.5	27.5	27.8
		(−.1)	(.6)	(.7)	(.7)	(.3)
Unemployment rate, all	1.2	2.2	3.9	6.5	12.4	6.3
Unemployment rate,						
16–24 years	. . .	2.8	8.7	13.5	21.8	N.A.

(continued)

Table 1A.1   (continued)

	1965	1970	1975	1980	1985	1989
Japan:						
Real GDP (1965 = 1)	1	1.79	2.27	2.95	3.56	4.24
		(11.6)	(4.8)	(5.2)	(3.8)	(4.4)
Population, 15–64 years						
(millions)	66.6	71.6	75.6	78.7	82.3	85.5
		(1.4)	(1.1)	(.8)	(.9)	(1.0)
Civilian employment						
(millions)	47.3	50.9	52.2	55.4	58.1	61.3
		(1.5)	(.5)	(1.2)	(1.0)	(1.3)
Civilian labor force						
(millions)	47.9	51.5	53.2	56.5	59.6	62.7
		(1.4)	(.6)	(1.2)	(1.1)	(1.3)
Unemployment rate, all	.9	1.1	1.9	2.0	2.6	2.2
Unemployment rate,						
15–24 years	1.3	2.0	3.0	3.6	4.8	4.5
France:						
Real GDP (1965 = 1)	1	1.30	1.58	1.86	1.97	2.24
		(5.2)	(3.9)	(3.3)	(1.1)	(3.2)
Population, 15–64 years						
(millions)	30.4	31.6	33.0	34.3	36.3	37.0
		(.8)	(.9)	(.8)	(1.1)	(.5)
Civilian employment						
(millions)	19.5	20.3	20.9	21.3	20.9	21.5
		(.9)	(.6)	(.4)	(−.4)	(.7)
Civilian labor force						
(millions)	19.8	20.9	21.7	22.8	23.4	23.8
		(1.0)	(.9)	(.9)	(.5)	(.4)
Unemployment rate, all	1.5	1.8	3.8	6.0	10.1	9.5
Unemployment rate,						
15–24 years	...	3.2	7.9	15.0	25.6	19.1

Sources: OECD (1991); and OECD, *Quarterly National Accounts.*
Note: N.A. = not available.

Table 1A.2   **Nonmanual/Manual Log Wage Differentials in Three Countries**

	Log Nonmanual/ Manual Wage Ratio			
Sex and Age	1978	1984	1987	1991
United States:				
Male:				
21–24	.143	.268	.298	.352
25–29	.225	.344	.380	.391
30–39	.288	.380	.430	.440
40–49	.305	.392	.428	.496
50–59	.344	.365	.416	.473

Table 1A.2   (continued)

	Log Nonmanual/ Manual Wage Ratio			
Sex and Age	1978	1984	1987	1991
Female:				
21–24	.019	.148	.194	.206
25–29	.101	.198	.261	.320
30–39	.266	.318	.354	.411
40–49	.347	.419	.449	.492
50–59	.385	.426	.467	.545
Britain:				
Male:				
21–24	.063	.116	.155	.222
25–29	.247	.290	.341	.402
30–39	.400	.454	.503	.562
40–49	.464	.536	.581	.647
50–59	.457	.533	.576	.610
Female:				
21–24	.139	.225	.215	.305
25–29	.295	.357	.377	.461
30–39	.301	.435	.460	.578
40–49	.305	.395	.396	.531
50–59	.296	.401	.430	.513
France:				
Male:				
21–25	.153	.159	.146	
26–30	.343	.327	.344	
31–35	.529	.446	.457	
36–40	.666	.598	.563	
41–45	.705	.690	.690	
46–50	.746	.702	.714	
51–55	.776	.726	.717	
56–60	.789	.854	.841	
Female:				
21–25	.224	.215	.194	
26–30	.315	.302	.294	
31–35	.379	.346	.325	
36–40	.413	.401	.368	
41–45	.420	.423	.424	
46–50	.430	.398	.411	
51–55	.449	.410	.403	
56–60	.451	.434	.443	

Note: The reported numbers are the logs of the ratio of the mean hourly wages of full-time non-manual and manual workers in each age-sex group. The U.S. data are from the CPS outgoing rotation groups, the British data are from the NES, and the French data are from the DAS.

References

Adams, Mark, Ruth Maybury, and William Smith. 1988. Trends in the distribution of earnings, 1973 to 1986. *Department of Employment Gazette* 96 (February): 75–82.

Berman, Eli, John Bound, and Zvi Griliches. 1994. Changes in the demand for skilled labor within U.S. manufacturing industries: Evidence from the Annual Survey of Manufactures. *Quarterly Journal of Economics* 109 (May): 367–97.

Berman, Eli, John Bound, and Stephen Machin. 1994. Implications of skill biased technological change: International evidence. Boston University, October. Typescript.

Bound, John, and George Johnson. 1992. Changes in the structure of wages in the 1980s: An evaluation of alternative explanations. *American Economic Review* 82 (June): 371–92.

Brazen, Stephen, and John Martin. 1991. The impact of the minimum wage on earnings and employment in France. *OECD Economic Studies* 16 (Spring): 199–221.

Bridgford, Jeff. 1990. French trade unions: Crisis in the 1980s. *Industrial Relations Journal* 21 (Summer): 126–35.

Caire, Guy. 1984. Recent trends in collective bargaining in France. *International Labour Review* 123 (November/December): 723–41.

Davis, Steven J. 1992. Cross-country patterns of change in relative wages. *NBER Macroeconomics Annual*, 239–92.

DiNardo, John, Nicole Fortin, and Thomas Lemieux. 1994. Labor market institutions and the distribution of wages, 1973–1992: A semi-parametric approach. University of California, Irvine, January. Typescript.

Eyraud, Francois, and Robert Tchobanian. 1985. The Auroux reforms and company level industrial relations in France. *British Journal of Industrial Relations* 23 (July): 241–59.

Freeman, Richard B. 1981. The changing economic value of higher education in developed economies: A report to the OECD. NBER Working Paper no. 820. Cambridge, Mass.: National Bureau of Economic Research, December.

———. 1986. The demand for education. In *Handbook of labor economics,* vol. 1, ed. O. Ashenfelter and R. Layard. Amsterdam: North-Holland.

———. 1993. How much has de-unionization contributed to the rise in male earnings inequality? In *Uneven tides,* ed. S. Danziger and P. Gottschalk. New York: Russell Sage Foundation.

Genda, Yuji. 1993. Skill premiums and Japan's wage structure in the 1980s. Gakushuin University, Tokyo, February. Typescript.

Gottschalk, Peter, and Mary Joyce. 1992. Changes in earnings inequality: An international perspective. Boston College. Typescript.

Haugen, S. E., and E. T. Mellor. 1990. Estimating the number of minimum wage workers. *Monthly Labor Review* 113 (January): 70–74.

Juhn, Chinhui, Kevin M. Murphy, and Brooks Pierce. 1993. Wage inequality and the rise in the returns to skill. *Journal of Political Economy* 101 (June): 410–42.

Katz, Lawrence F., and Gary W. Loveman. 1990. An international comparison of changes in the structure of wages: France, the United Kingdom, and the United States. Harvard University, December. Typescript.

Katz, Lawrence F., and Kevin M. Murphy. 1992. Changes in relative wages, 1963–1987: Supply and demand factors. *Quarterly Journal of Economics* 107 (February): 35–78.

Katz, Lawrence F., and Ana L. Revenga. 1989. Changes in the structure of wages: The United States vs. Japan. *Journal of the Japanese and International Economies* 3 (December): 522–53.

Krueger, Alan B. 1993. How computers have changed the wage structure: Evidence from micro data. *Quarterly Journal of Economics* 108 (February): 33–60.

Levy, Frank, and Richard Murnane. 1992. U.S. earnings levels and earnings inequality: A review of recent trends and proposed explanations. *Journal of Economic Literature* 30 (September): 1333–81.

Mincer, Jacob. 1991. Human capital, technology, and the wage structure: What do time series show? NBER Working Paper no. 3581. Cambridge, Mass.: National Bureau of Economic Research, January.

Mishel, Lawrence, and Jared Bernstein. 1994. *The state of working America, 1994–95.* Washington, D.C.: Economic Policy Institute.

Mitchell, Daniel. 1989. Wage pressures and labor shortages: The 1960s and the 1980s. *Brookings Papers on Economic Activity,* no. 2:191–231.

Murphy, Kevin M., and Finis Welch. 1992. The structure of wages. *Quarterly Journal of Economics* 107 (February): 285–326.

OECD. 1985. *OECD economic surveys: France.* Paris, July.

———. 1991. *Labour force statistics, 1969–89.* Paris.

———. 1993. *Employment outlook.* Paris.

———. Various issues. *Main economic indicators.* Paris.

———. Various issues. *Quarterly national accounts.* Paris.

Reich, Robert B. 1991. *The work of nations.* New York: Vintage.

U.K. Department of Employment. 1991. *New earnings survey, 1991.* Pt. A. London: H.M. Stationery Office. September.

2 International Differences in Executive and Managerial Compensation

John M. Abowd and Michael L. Bognanno

Every spring, as large American companies prepare for their annual share-holder meeting, executive compensation replaces income-tax returns as the topic of conversation around the lunch table and in the business press. The regularity of the phenomenon is related to the annual disclosure, in the proxy statements that accompany the annual reports usually published in March and April, of the compensation package earned by the five highest-paid employees of U.S. corporations. Because these reports must show the cash value of the capital gain associated with the exercise of stock options, they invariably contain some extremely large numbers. Furthermore, because the gains associated with the stock options have often accrued during the five to ten years that preceded the announcements, every year ushers in one or many cases of a chief executive officer (CEO) who has an exceptionally large income in a year in which the company has done poorly. In a book that touched off a firestorm around the issue of U.S. executive pay, Graef Crystal (1991, 1993) argued that the typical American chief executive was grossly overpaid and, worse, got there by the use of complicated long-term incentive compensation, including many

John M. Abowd is professor of labor economics and management at Cornell University and a research associate of the National Bureau of Economic Research. Michael L. Bognanno is assistant professor of economics at Temple University.

This paper was begun while Abowd was a visiting professor at the Institut National de la Statistique et des Etudes Economiques (INSEE) and the Ecole des Hautes Etudes Commerciales (HEC) in Paris. The research was partially supported by the Center for Advanced Human Resource Studies at Cornell University, the National Science Foundation (grant SES 91–11186 to Abowd), the NBER program "Differences and Changes in Wage Structures," and the Ministère de la Recherche et de la Technologie de la République Française. Francis Kramarz, Jean-Louis Lheritier, David Margolis, and Kevin J. Murphy provided helpful comments on earlier versions. The authors did not use confidential data in this paper. The data appendix and references show the authors' private and governmental source publications.

forms of stock options, that shareholders could not properly evaluate.[1] A central thesis of Crystal's book and the recent congressional and regulatory attempts to limit executive compensation is that American executives receive compensation that is far greater than that received by executives in comparable positions around the world.

Several authors, most notably Jensen and Murphy (1990a, 1990b), have argued that the debate over the level of CEO compensation is misguided because the form of the payment, specifically the sensitivity of total compensation to the performance of the firm, is more important than the level of pay. Jensen and Murphy show that U.S. CEO pay is not very sensitive to performance, although they note that the portion of pay delivered as restricted stock and stock options creates a portfolio whose increased value to the CEO is clearly related to the price performance of the firm's stock. In their extensive review of the pay-for-performance literature, Ehrenberg and Milkovich (1987) concluded that very few studies, including studies of CEO compensation, had established a clear statistical link between the structure of compensation and the performance of the firm.[2] While we agree that understanding the relation between compensation system design and firm performance is central to the study of CEO compensation, we also believe that a careful multinational comparison of the level and structure of executive pay and its evolution over time can inform the debate concerning the relative pay of American CEOs. Crystal's book does not contain detailed statistical comparisons. To the best of our knowledge, the only detailed statistical studies comparing executive compensation across many countries are those conducted by the large private compensation consulting firms, specifically the Hay Group, Hewitt Associates, Mercer International, Towers Perrin, and the Wyatt Company. These are our primary sources, and, except for Hewitt Associates, we have used data from each of these sources. Although we make a variety of statistical adjustments, as do the sources before they publish their results, it is clear that American CEOs do earn more than CEOs of comparably sized companies in other countries. It is also clear that the structure of the American CEO's compensation is quite different, being composed of a much larger long-term component. Other American executives, however, do not earn more than comparable executives in comparably sized companies around the world.

A careful international comparison of executive compensation and its rela-

---

1. *In Search of Excess* was originally published in 1991. The paperback edition, published in 1993, contains additional chapters that discuss the critiques of the hardback edition. Crystal was a professional executive compensation consultant before he retired to join the faculty of the University of California, Berkeley, business school as an adjunct professor.

2. Since their review was published, studies by Abowd (1990), Gerhart and Milkovich (1990), and Leonard (1990) and an additional review by Rosen (1990) have appeared. These newer studies estimated both an equation linking executive pay to firm performance and a second equation linking firm performance to the structure of executive pay. Although the results are mixed, these attempts to address both parts of the research question have focused scientific studies on the problem of efficient compensation system design rather than the level of pay.

tion to the compensation of ordinary employees could provide important evidence on the intercountry variation in CEO, high-level manager, and regular employee compensation. The quality of the conclusions drawn from such a comparison rests critically on the comprehensiveness of the compensation information and the thoroughness of the distinction maintained between employer cost and employee value. Comprehensive data are necessary because (1) total compensation costs include all cash disbursements to employees, voluntarily provided benefits, publicly mandated benefits, perquisites, and long-term compensation (multiyear bonus plans and stock-based compensation), (2) in different countries different parts of this compensation package are regulated with regard to funding or benefit formulas, and (3) there is substantial international variation in prices so that components delivered in kind in some countries can have a very different value than if they were delivered in kind elsewhere. Distinguishing between employer cost and employee benefit is necessary because (1) public funding of certain parts of the compensation package creates an explicit tax-and-transfer component to the mandatory benefits that is quite heterogeneous across countries and (2) many long-term compensation plans are worth less to the employee who receives them than they cost the employer to provide.[3]

In section 2.1 of this paper, we use public data from four different consulting firms and from the U.S. Bureau of Labor Statistics to illustrate the real level and evolution of employer total compensation costs for CEOs, top human resource directors (HRDs), and nonsupervisory manufacturing employees (called *operatives* below) for twelve OECD countries (Belgium, Canada, France, Germany, Italy, Japan, the Netherlands, Spain, Sweden, Switzerland, the United Kingdom, and the United States) over the eight-year period from 1984 to 1992. Our findings are (1) that U.S. CEOs rank first in total real compensation cost all through the period, (2) that U.S. HRDs fall in rank from first to tenth between 1984 and 1992, and (3) that U.S. manufacturing operatives not only fall from first to tenth in rank but are the only employees in the survey to decline in total real compensation cost, stated in U.S. dollars. In section 2.2, we use published data from the OECD, national statistical agencies, and multinational accounting and consulting firms to construct a measure of after-tax constant purchasing power income that includes the value of privately consumed services supplied through the public sector. We call this measure the private *replacement value* of the compensation package. Unlike real total compensation costs, which reflect employer costs and vary as a function of both the compensation costs and exchange rates, our constant purchasing power replacement values reflect variation in consumer indirect utility. The two compensation measures, therefore, respond differently to the integration of world

---

3. We refer here to the riskiness of long-term compensation packages, which cannot be diversified like the other parts of executive wealth. Thus, we presume that either a total tax advantage (to the employer and employee jointly) or a productivity gain from the incentive nature of such compensation motivates its use.

markets. Increased integration of world product and capital markets, through factor price equalization, should tend to equalize real total compensation costs across countries for similar employees. On the other hand, increased integration of labor markets, through international migration, is required to equalize purchasing power parity adjusted replacement values. Section 2.3 examines the trends in both of our compensation measures and in the intercountry variation in these measures. We show that there has been a strong tendency toward equalization of the real total compensation costs but that no such tendency is evident for the replacement values.

In section 2.4, we examine some of the tax and institutional differences that may contribute to the American CEO's high total cost. We show that there are enormous differences in marginal tax rates, particularly marginal payroll tax rates, among our sample countries between high-level managers and manufacturing operatives. These high marginal tax rates have a depressing effect on CEO total compensation costs and replacement values but not on the costs or private replacement values of other high-level managers or manufacturing employees. In contrast, the ratio of either CEO or HRD compensation (or replacement value) to the comparable measure for manufacturing employees is very sensitive to differences in the marginal tax rates, indicating that the financing of certain programs through the public sector in some countries and through the private sector in others has a very important distorting effect on the wage structure, particularly at the high end. In this section, we also show that American managerial pay is more sensitive to the size of the company managed than is managerial pay in any of the European countries in our sample (comparable data for Canada and Japan were not available). The tax rate differences and the differential sensitivity of pay to the size of the firm are two important factors in explaining the high pay of American CEOs. Unfortunately, we cannot find an explanation for the big differences in long-term pay between American and other CEOs. We show some evidence that the incidence of stock option compensation is increasing in several of our European countries and that estimates of zero incidence rates for such compensation are probably not correct. We also show that there are no longer serious legal restrictions to stock-based compensation in any of our sample countries and that in some of those countries such compensation enjoys a tax advantage. We cannot explain why only U.S. CEOs seem to have received such large long-term compensation plans, and we speculate that a more integrated world labor market for executives, coupled with the absence of currency and stock ownership regulation, may foster an increase in the stock-based long-term component of non-U.S. executives' compensation.

2.1   Real Total Compensation Costs

Real total compensation cost is the total cost to the firm associated with maintaining an employee, stated in 1990 U.S. dollars. Total compensation consists of the sum of base salary; annual bonus monetary compensation; all bene-

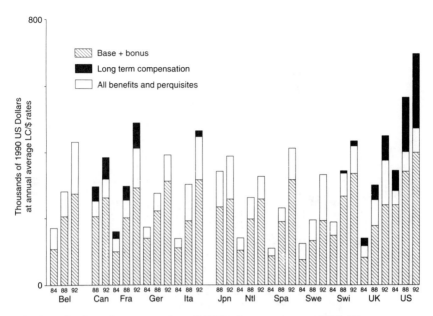

Fig. 2.1   Real total compensation of CEOs, by components, 1984–92

fits, payments in kind, and perquisites; and all long-term monetary compensation. Base salary (or base pay for manufacturing workers) is all cash compensation set in advance and payable throughout the year. The annual monetary bonus is all additional cash compensation based on annual performance evaluations. Benefits, payments in kind, and perquisites consist of all costs associated with providing a service or retirement income to an employee. We distinguish between voluntary benefits, which are provided by an employer but not required by law, and publicly mandated benefits, which are provided either by the employer or by the government and are financed by a tax on employment such as a payroll tax. The cost of voluntary benefits is the employer's expense in providing the benefit. The cost of mandatory benefits is the sum of the employer expense in providing the benefit and the mandatory tax payments. The cost of long-term compensation is the annuity equivalent of the present value of awards that accrue over a period exceeding one year.[4] Forms of long-term compensation include stock-based compensation, such as stock option plans, and multiyear bonus plans.

Figure 2.1 shows the real total compensation cost of the CEO in three components—base salary plus annual bonus, all benefits and perquisites, and long-

---

4. All long-term compensation comes from the Towers Perrin surveys cited in the data appendix. Towers Perrin estimates the present value of long-term compensation on the date of award using a variety of economic models for the cash flows, including option pricing formulas and pro forma business simulation. The annuity equivalent is calculated using the usual interval between awards so that, if a company awards stock options, e.g., every three years, the present value of any given option award is converted to a three-year annuity equivalent.

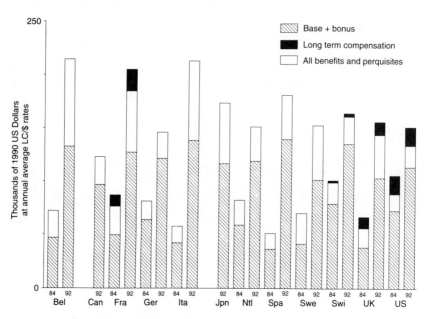

Fig. 2.2   Real total compensation of HRDs, by components, 1984–92

term compensation—for the three years 1984, 1988, and 1992 and for all twelve countries.[5] Compensation is stated in thousands of 1990 U.S. dollars using annual average exchange rates and the U.S. consumer price index. Across countries, an increasing trend in the level of total compensation cost for CEOs is evident. The trend results from general growth in all three compensation components. The total compensation cost of U.S. CEOs is far higher than that of foreign CEOs in each of the three years, in large part because of much higher amounts of long-term compensation, but also because U.S. CEOs receive the highest base salaries and annual bonus payments. We note that U.S. CEOs maintain their absolute edge over foreign CEOs in real total compensation cost despite the weakening of the dollar between 1984 and 1992. The weakening of the dollar vis-à-vis other currencies causes the compensation costs of other countries to rise when expressed in terms of U.S. dollars.[6]

Figure 2.2 shows the real total compensation cost of the top human resource

5. In this section and the next, we present figures comparing our various compensation measures for the years 1984 (the earliest year available), 1988 (the sample midpoint), and 1992 (the latest year available) in all twelve of our countries. The data selected for the figures is a subset of the data used in the statistical analyses of sec. 2.3 below. We tried to minimize problems of comparability by selecting two managerial occupations (CEO and HRD) for which we had reasonably complete data from comparable sources. Thus, the compensation data shown in the figures have not been statistically adjusted to account for differences in sources or average firm size.

6. Although this remark is equally applicable to the real total compensation costs in fig. 2.1, fig. 2.2 below (for HRDs), and fig. 2.3 below (for manufacturing operatives), the real exchange rate effects in figs. 2.2 and 2.3 are much more apparent. Exchange rates provide the correct notion of employer cost; nevertheless, the data appendix provides in figs. 2A.1, 2A.2, and 2A.3 a comparison of total compensation costs adjusted using OECD annual average purchasing power parity rates.

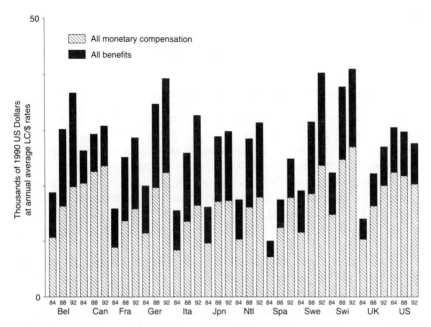

Fig. 2.3   Real total compensation of manufacturing operatives, by components, 1984–92

directors divided into the same three components as for the CEOs. Compensation is again expressed in thousands of 1990 U.S. dollars at annual average exchange rates. The total compensation cost is rising markedly for HRDs between 1984 and 1992 in each country. In contrast to the experience of U.S. CEOs, however, U.S. HRDs fell, relative to the HRDs of the other countries, in total compensation cost from first in 1984 to tenth by 1992. The rate of increase in real U.S. dollar total compensation cost for HRDs was much greater outside the United States.[7]

Figure 2.3 shows the real total compensation cost of a production manufacturing employee in two ways: total monetary compensation and all benefits and perquisites. Long-term compensation (except for pensions, which are included in benefits) is not an important part of manufacturing operative income. Compensation is stated, again, in thousands of 1990 U.S. dollars at annual average exchange rates. We note a strong upward trend in real total compensation costs for all but U.S. manufacturing operatives. A global real exchange rate adjustment of the dollar relative to other currencies, which occurred during the 1980s, is the apparent cause of this trend. Although U.S. CEOs maintained their top ranking in compensation cost and U.S. HRDs fell in ranking but still experienced a real increase in compensation cost, the compensation cost of

---

7. We show results only for the years 1984 and 1992 in fig. 2.2 because none of our data sources provided an estimate for a human resource director in 1988.

U.S. manufacturing operatives declined in rank from first to tenth over the period and actually fell in real terms—the only position and country combination to fall in real total compensation cost in our entire sample.

2.2 Private and Public Compensation at Constant Purchasing Power

Private and public compensation at constant purchasing power, which we call the private replacement value of the compensation package, is the after-tax value to the employee of all privately and publicly provided compensation and benefits stated in 1990 OECD dollars using the OECD annual average purchasing power parity (PPP) exchange rates. Thus, the private replacement value of the compensation package represents the minimum expenditure at international prices required to replace the utility level associated with the goods and services provided publicly and privately to an employee earning the typical compensation package in the country.

We have paid careful attention to the value of benefits whether privately or publicly financed or provided because for international compensation comparisons it is important to account for the significant differences among the countries in the system of financing and delivering benefits. Some countries finance most of the benefit package through a maze of payroll taxes, while consumers purchase the benefits themselves on the open market, and a semipublic agency then reimburses them. In other countries, the employer supplies the benefits as compensation in kind. In still other countries, consumers purchase and finance certain services, considered employment benefits elsewhere, wholly outside the employment relation. In addition to benefits consumed currently by the employees, the countries in our sample differ markedly in their systems for financing and delivering retirement income. In several countries (Belgium, France, Italy, and Sweden, in particular), the public pension system represents both a significant employment cost and a direct public benefit even for CEOs. In order to compare the real after-tax and public benefit incomes of managers and workers in our twelve countries, therefore, we undertook a detailed analysis of the public benefit packages in each country.

We define the private replacement value of a compensation package as the sum of base salary, annual bonus, voluntary benefits, publicly provided (mandatory) benefits, perquisites, long-term monetary compensation, and all public and private pension benefits less employee payroll and income taxes. We then divide this quantity, stated in local currency, by the product of the 1990-based OECD purchasing power parity exchange rates and the OECD index of consumer prices (1990 = 1.00). Thus, our measure controls for local differences in the prices of both publicly and privately supplied goods and services.

We valued base salary, annual bonus, voluntary benefits, perquisites, and long-term monetary compensation at employer cost. Therefore, the before-tax amount is identical to the amount that we used in the employer cost calculations above. We computed the value of publicly provided (mandatory) benefits by taking the sum of a country's expenditures on social protection programs, dividing this sum by the population of the country, and multiplying by four, thus assuming that the employee had a family of four. We valued public and private pension benefits by computing the projected retirement benefit on the basis of survey estimates of the percentage of final salary and bonus paid as a public or private pension at age sixty-five. We computed the present value of the pension at retirement assuming an expected remaining life of fifteen years (at 2 percent real interest). Finally, we converted this sum to an annuity equivalent over a forty-year working life (again at 2 percent real interest). To estimate employee payroll and income taxes, we used survey estimates and direct calculations from simplified summaries of the relevant tax schedules. Income taxes assumed a family of four including two children. For source details, see the data appendix.

For our measure of public benefits, we considered government spending on nine types of social protection, as classified by Eurostat—sickness, invalidism, employment-related injury or disability, maternity, family assistant plans, job training and placement, unemployment benefits, housing subsidies, and miscellaneous social programs. For the countries of the European Community, the social protection expenditure data came directly from Eurostat. We note, for completeness, that Eurostat also reports government current expenditures on old-age and retirement income systems, but we used our own measures of the replacement value of the pension income. For the other countries, we list below the expenditure categories from the country's statistical abstract, which we compared with the Eurostat categories.

For Canada: Sickness included all government health expenditures. Invalidism was included in the category of sickness. Employment injury included provincial workers' compensation. Maternity was included in family assistance. Family assistance included all Canada assistance plans, family allowances, and other provincial welfare programs. Job training and placement included Canada job strategies. Unemployment benefits included federal unemployment insurance. No expenditures were included under housing subsidies. And miscellaneous social programs included registered Indians' and veterans' benefits, vocational rehabilitation of disabled persons, state tax credits and rebates, and municipal social security.

For Japan: Sickness included all medical care expenditures paid directly by the government, the old-age insurance system, or the national insurance system (these expenditures include invalidism expenditures). Employment injury and disability expenditures included the benefit amounts paid for workers' compensation claims. Family assistance included net expenditure on social welfare. No expenditures were included under maternity. Job placement and training included employment services expenditures. Unemployment benefits included total allowances paid under general employment insurance. Housing subsidies included housing aid. And no expenditures were included under miscellaneous.

For Sweden: Sickness included expenditures for sickness and disease. No expenditures were included under invalidism. Employment injury included occupational industry insurance and industrial safety. No expenditures were included under maternity or job training and placement. Family assistance included family and child welfare expenditures. Unemployment benefits included all unemployment insurance system expenditures. No expenditures were included under housing. And miscellaneous included veterans' care.

For Switzerland: Sickness included total public expenses on health care less administrative expenses. Invalidism included total expenses on invalid care less administrative expenses. Employment injury included all expenses, cost of treatment, daily indemnities, invalid premiums, and survival pay. No expenditures were included under maternity. Family assistance included cantonal and federal aid to families. No expenditures were included under job training and placement. Unemployment included total expenses related to unemployment. And no expenditures were included under housing subsidies or miscellaneous social programs.

For the United States: Sickness included federal and state expenditures on Medicare, hospital, medical care, other health and medical programs, and veterans' health and medical programs. Invalidism was included in sickness. Employment injury included state temporary disability insurance. All workers' compensation, state and federal, and state temporary disability insurance. Maternity assistance consisted of maternal and child health programs. Family assistance included public assistance, state and federal; Supplemental Security Income, state and federal; and food stamps. Job training and placement included other state and federal employment training programs and other public employment aid. Unemployment benefits included unemployment insurance; employment services, state and federal; and other railroad unemployment insurance. Housing subsidies included housing expenditures, state and federal. And miscellaneous included all other public welfare programs.

The importance of controlling for differences in publicly provided benefits may not be obvious for a study of executive and managerial compensation. To illustrate the importance of these differences, we selected health care costs, a benefit that is quite significant in U.S. compensation systems, to illustrate the international contrasts. Table 2.1 shows medical and health care expenditures for all OECD countries (the twelve we study and the remaining twelve, for which we have insufficient executive compensation data to use in our other statistical analyses). The table illustrates that, when valued at international prices, U.S. expenditures are higher per capita (col. A) but a lower percentage of GDP (col. C for 1990 and col. D for 1985) than the OECD average. On the other hand, U.S. health care prices are 24 percent above the international average (col. B). Of our sample countries, the French spend the most per capita (in real terms), and the Japanese have the lowest health care prices. For comparison purposes, we include a column (col. E) showing the percentage of health purchases made in the private as opposed to the public sector. Our

Table 2.1   **Medical and Health Care Expenditures in the OECD**

Country	(A) 1990 Real Health Care Expenditures per capita	(B) 1990 Health Price Index	(C) 1990 Health Percentage of GDP	(D) 1985 Health Percentage of GDP	(E) 1990 Private Percentage of Health
Belgium	1,796	79	9.7	9.3	92.7
Denmark	1,153	139	6.0	5.3	15.0
France	2,499	83	12.7	10.0	68.7
Germany	1,799	113	8.7	8.3	95.1
Greece	502	61	6.0	4.8	51.7
Ireland	835	100	6.9	6.1	28.0
Italy	1,526	91	8.4	6.0	54.1
Luxembourg	1,349	87	6.2	5.1	88.1
Netherlands	1,452	93	8.1	7.9	100.0
Portugal	618	58	6.2	4.4	35.3
Spain	820	80	6.2	4.7	45.7
United Kingdom	1,314	75	7.3	6.6	21.6
EEC	1,559	90	8.8	7.4	67.0
Austria	1,544	94	8.2	8.1	32.7
Switzerland	1,554	151	7.2		81.9
Finland	1,280	145	6.8	7.4	30.0
Iceland	1,461	130	7.8		13.5
Norway	1,560	121	8.6	8.3	37.2
Sweden	1,774	127	9.2	11.1	11.9
Turkey	178	34	3.4	2.9	66.3
Australia	1,296	99	7.1	5.8	57.9
New Zealand	1,201	77	7.8	6.6	55.8
Japan	1,722	70	8.6	10.2	93.6
Canada	1,587	99	7.3	3.1	32.8
United States	1,820	124	7.5	7.6	91.5
OECD	1,563	100	8.0		78.0

Sources: Purchasing power parities and real expenditures for 1990 are from Volume 1 EKS Results 1990 (OECD 1992d) Tables 1.1, 1.3 and 1.6. Purchasing power parities and real expenditures for 1985 are from OECD (1987b, table 3).

Note: 1990 real health care expenditures per capita (col. A) are stated in U.S. dollars using the OECD purchasing power parity price indices. The health price index (col. B) is relative to the OECD, which has a value of 100. 1990 and 1985 health percentages (cols. C and D) are stated at OECD average prices. Columns A–D include private and public expenditures.

method of controlling for the public and private benefit packages has the effect of counting as an employment cost the employer's expenditures on health care and the taxes (regardless of statutory incidence) that support the financing of both the private and the public components of the health care expenditures in a given country. Similarly, our method of computing the private replacement value of health care benefits counts the employer's direct expenditures, government reimbursements of private expenditures, and direct public expenditures. Finally, the use of the OECD purchasing power parity exchange rates controls for the enormous differences in local relative prices. Although not as detailed as the health care cost analysis shown here, our benefit valuation method provides essentially the same comprehensive measurement of sources and prices for unemployment insurance, pensions, and other social welfare benefits as the table 2.1 comparison provides for health costs.

Figure 2.4 shows the CEO's private and public compensation package in OECD dollars at average annual OECD purchasing power parity rates. The figure has three components for each year and country entry. The component labeled *private net compensation* is base salary, annual bonus, voluntary benefits, perquisites, and long-term monetary compensation less employee payroll and income taxes; hence, this component is, essentially, after-tax total private compensation. The component labeled *public benefits* is the per capita expenditure on all public benefits except pensions times four, plus the annuity equivalent of the projected public pension. The component labeled *all payroll and income taxes* equals payroll taxes (employer and CEO parts) plus the CEO's personal income taxes.

In the figure, the portion of each bar above zero shows the CEO's replacement value of public and private compensation and benefits in constant purchasing power (at OECD average prices). The two components of the positive part of each bar show the division of the replacement value between private after-tax compensation and public benefits. It is important to notice that, for countries like France, Italy, and Sweden, the public portion of the benefit package is a significant part of the CEO's compensation, as reflected in our measure of the replacement value. The portion of each bar below zero shows the amount of all payroll and income taxes. While the size of public benefits differs across countries, differences in payroll and income taxes, both in absolute size and in proportion to private net compensation, dwarf this variation. Heavier proportional tax burdens are weakly linked to larger public benefits, even for the CEO. The replacement value of public and private compensation and benefits for U.S. CEOs increased in real terms more than that of non-American CEOs. The high and increasing real standard of living of the American CEOs is due to higher before-tax compensation, lower effective taxes, and lower prices for goods and services.

Figure 2.5 shows the top human resource director's private and public compensation package. U.S. HRDs rank first in the replacement value of compensation in both 1984 and 1992. However, the differences between the HRDs are small, especially in comparison to the differences among the CEOs. Although U.S. HRDs rank tenth in compensation costs to their employers in 1992, they rank first in replacement value, by a slim margin, because of low taxes and low relative prices in the United States.

Figure 2.6 shows a manufacturing employee's private and public compensation package for our twelve countries. U.S. manufacturing operatives are near the middle of the pack in the replacement value of their compensation. While low prices in the United States raised the ranking of U.S. manufacturing opera-

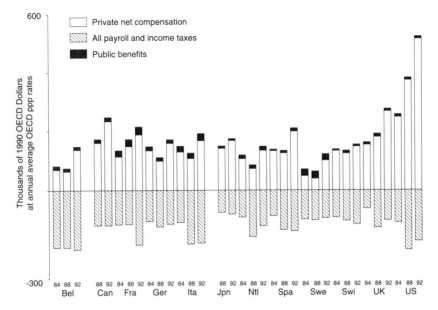

Fig. 2.4   Total taxes, private after-tax compensation, and public benefits for
CEOs, 1984–92

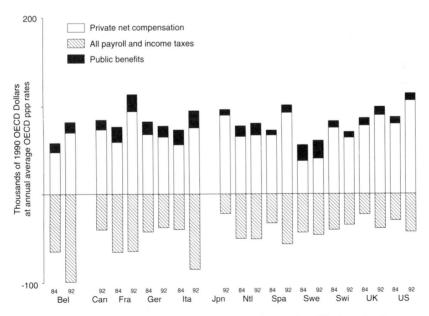

Fig. 2.5   Total taxes, private after-tax compensation, and public benefits for
HRDs, 1984–92

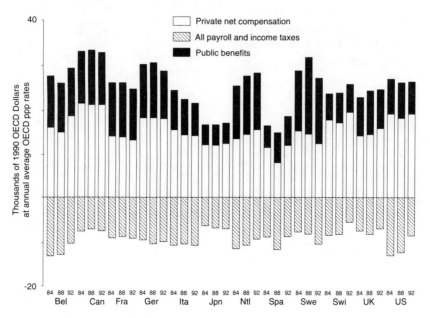

Fig. 2.6   Total taxes, private after-tax compensation, and public benefits for manufacturing operatives, 1984–92

tives from tenth in terms of total compensation cost in 1992 to sixth in terms of replacement value, the lighter tax burdens seen in the case of U.S. CEOs and HRDs are not evident for U.S. manufacturing operatives. Considering all countries together, the manufacturing operatives have not made the gains in replacement value seen among the HRDs and CEOs during the sample period.

2.3   Statistical Analysis of Total Compensation Cost and Replacement Value

In this section, we conduct a variety of statistical analyses using all our executive compensation data to show the basic trends in compensation of CEOs, high-level managers, and manufacturing operatives. We extracted the basic executive compensation data from surveys conducted by Arthur Young, the Hay Group, Towers Perrin, and the Wyatt Company. Survey data apply to the years 1984 and 1988–92. A source had to include information for at least three-fourths of our countries in order to enter the sample. The complete list of compensation sources is given in the data appendix.

Table 2.2 presents a basic regression analysis of the levels of three different compensation measures and two different methods of standardizing across countries. For compensation measures, we considered (a) total compensation, defined as the sum of base salary, annual monetary bonus, voluntary benefits, compulsory benefits (employer payroll taxes), perquisites, and long-term mon-

Table 2.2   Regression Analysis of the Logarithms of Several Real Compensation Measures

Compensation Measure and Independent Variable	Log of Real Measure ($U.S.)			Log of PPP Measure (OECD)		
	CEO	High-Level Manager	Manufacturing Operative	CEO	High-Level Manager	Manufacturing Operative
A. Total compensation						
Overall trend	.125	.011	.085	.025	−.084	−.002
	(.011)	(.047)	(.012)	(.014)	(.055)	(.008)
U.S. incremental effect	.816	.383	.482	.536	.016	.302
	(.139)	(.219)	(.196)	(.180)	(.257)	(.130)
U.S. incremental trend	−.048	−.052	−.087	.022	.026	−.017
	(.023)	(.032)	(.034)	(.029)	(.038)	(.023)
Marginal employee income tax rate + marginal payroll rate	−.339	.244	−.234	−.512	.069	.124
	(.096)	(.169)	(.189)	(.124)	(.198)	(.126)
Marginal corporate income tax rate	.160	.464	.391	−.040	.518	.112
	(.204)	(.316)	(.360)	(.263)	(.370)	(.240)
R^2	.853	.706	.598	.675	.215	.201
Standard error of equation	.150	.208	.550	.193	.243	.135
Error degrees of freedom	73	57	42	73	57	42
B. Replacement value						
Overall trend	.116	.025	.089	−.025	−.070	.002
	(.025)	(.043)	(.016)	(.028)	(.046)	(.012)
U.S. incremental effect	.891	.443	.272	.601	.075	.092
	(.180)	(.202)	(.267)	(.198)	(.216)	(.205)
U.S. incremental trend	−.055	−.063	−.071	.016	.015	−.001
	(.029)	(.030)	(.047)	(.031)	(.032)	(.036)
Marginal employee income tax rate + marginal payroll rate	−.895	−.271	−.272	−1.077	−.445	.087
	(.145)	(.156)	(.258)	(.159)	(.167)	(.199)

(continued)

Table 2.2 (continued)

Compensation Measure and Independent Variable	Log of Real Measure ($U.S.)			Log of PPP Measure (OECD)		
	CEO	High-Level Manager	Manufacturing Operative	CEO	High-Level Manager	Manufacturing Operative
Marginal corporate income tax rate	.193	.398	.432	.060	.453	.153
	(.296)	(.292)	(.491)	(.325)	(.311)	(.378)
R^2	.873	.735	.457	.784	.368	.021
Standard error of equation	.186	.192	.277	.204	.302	.213
Error degrees of freedom	49	57	42	49	57	42
C. Base + bonus or salary						
Overall trend	.141	.023	.091	.041	−.072	.003
	(.019)	(.044)	(.011)	(.013)	(.049)	(.009)
U.S. incremental effect	.741	.334	.630	.461	−.033	.450
	(.137)	(.209)	(.182)	(.167)	(.230)	(.160)
U.S. incremental trend	−.063	−.053	−.094	.008	.025	−.023
	(.023)	(.031)	(.032)	(.027)	(.034)	(.028)
Marginal employee income tax rate + marginal payroll rate	−.380	−.118	−.772	−.553	−.292	−.364
	(.095)	(.161)	(.176)	(.115)	(.177)	(.155)
Marginal corporate income tax rate	.330	.422	−.038	.130	.477	−.317
	(.201)	(.301)	(.335)	(.245)	(.332)	(.294)
R^2	.836	.741	.680	.646	.317	.395
Standard error of equation	.148	.198	.189	.180	.218	.323
Error degrees of freedom	73	57	42	73	57	42

Note: The table shows the estimated coefficients (with standard errors) from ordinary least squares regressions. Regressions for the CEO include variables indicating the data source and the average size of a company. Regressions for the high-level manager include the average size of a company in the survey. Panel C contains regressions analyzing the base plus bonus for the CEO and high-level manager and analyzing cash compensation for the manufacturing operative. The variable labeled *marginal payroll tax* is the employee plus the employer marginal payroll tax rate.

etary compensation, as discussed in section 2.1; (*b*) replacement value, defined as the sum of base salary, annual monetary bonus, voluntary benefits, perquisites, and public benefits (family of four) less employee payroll taxes and personal income taxes (family of four), as discussed in section 2.2; and (*c*) base salary plus annual monetary bonus, a conventional measure. To standardize for price differences we used (1) real U.S. dollars (i.e., compensation stated in local currency divided by the product of the average annual exchange rate [local currency per dollar] and the U.S. consumer price index [1990 = 1.00]) and (2) OECD purchasing power parity dollars (i.e., compensation stated in local currency divided by the product of the OECD purchasing power parity rate [local currency per dollar, 1990 based] and the OECD index of consumer prices [1990 = 1.00]).[8]

Panel A of table 2.2 shows our statistical analysis of total compensation. Real total compensation of CEOs grew rapidly over the eight-year period from 1984 to 1992 (a logarithmic trend of .125 with a standard error of .011). U.S. CEOs were paid more (incremental logarithmic effect of .816 with a standard error of .139), but the U.S. trend was lower than in the other countries (incremental logarithmic trend of −.048 with a standard error of .023). We defer the discussion of tax rate effects until the next section. High-level managers' real total compensation did not grow (an overall trend of .011 with a standard error of .047). For the high-level managers, the U.S. total compensation is insignificantly different from the average, and the incremental trend is negative, meaning that U.S. managers' total compensation grew more slowly than the average of the twelve countries. For manufacturing operatives, real total compensation grew rapidly, but not as fast as for CEOs, over our sample period (overall trend of .085 with a standard error of .012). U.S. manufacturing operatives had higher real total compensation (U.S. incremental effect of .482 with a standard error of .196); however, the U.S. trend for manufacturing operatives was negative and fully offset the overall trend (a U.S. incremental logarithmic trend of −.087 with a standard error of .034). The table also shows these analyses in terms of local purchasing power. Using the OECD purchasing power parity rates, the relative position of U.S. CEOs, high-level managers, and manufacturing operatives is unchanged; however, there are no significant trends, either overall or incrementally for the United States, when the purchasing power parity adjusted measure of total compensation cost is used.

Panel B of table 2.2 shows our statistical analysis of the replacement value of compensation (for the definition, see sec. 2.2). Consider first the purchasing power parity results shown in the rightmost three columns of the table. These results use the OECD deflator that we also used to calculate the replacement values shown in section 2.2. There was no significant overall trend in the replacement value of compensation for any of the three positions during the sam-

---

8. The dollar was chosen as the unit of account for this analysis, but the OECD purchasing power parity rates have the property that they are invariant with respect to the unit of account.

ple period. U.S. CEOs, however, had a higher replacement value than their non-American counterparts (a U.S. incremental effect of .601 with a standard error of .198). Neither high-level managers nor manufacturing operatives in the United States had higher replacement values than elsewhere. The U.S. trend was not different from the overall trend for any of the three positions.

The table also shows the regression analysis of the replacement value of compensation as measured in real (1990) U.S. dollars in the leftmost three columns of panel B. Stated in terms of U.S. dollars, the CEOs and manufacturing operatives both had positive upward trends (overall trends of .116 and .089 with standard errors of .025 and .016, respectively). In addition, measured in 1990 U.S. dollars, both U.S. CEOs and high-level managers had higher replacement values (U.S. incremental effects of .891 and .443 with standard errors of .180 and .202, respectively). On the other hand, measured in U.S. dollars, the U.S. replacement values were declining relative to the other eleven countries for all three positions (see the negative U.S. incremental trend coefficients). One should take caution in drawing conclusions from the replacement value comparisons when stated in 1990 U.S. dollars. Because we used the average annual exchange rate and the U.S. consumer price index in this calculation, comparisons of these replacement values presume that the individual employees could purchase private and public goods and services at U.S. prices, which is clearly not the case. For comparisons of replacement values, we prefer the results based on the OECD purchasing power parity rates.

Panel C of table 2.2 presents the regression analysis of base salary plus annual monetary bonus (cash compensation for the manufacturing operative). This is a commonly used, although flawed, measure of pay. In terms of 1990 U.S. dollars (the leftmost three columns of panel C), we note that the overall trend was positive for CEOs and manufacturing operatives but not for high-level managers. The United States had higher base plus bonus for the same two positions. The U.S. incremental trend, however, was negative, canceling about half the gain for CEOs and all the gain for manufacturing operatives. In terms of OECD purchasing power (the rightmost three columns), CEOs had a slightly positive upward trend, while the overall trend for the other two positions was not significantly different from zero. U.S. CEOs and manufacturing operatives had higher base plus bonus than their non-American counterparts. Finally, in terms of purchasing power, the U.S. incremental trend was not significantly different from zero for any of the positions.

We next consider two hypotheses concerning the integration of the product, capital, and labor markets among our twelve countries. Product and capital market integration alone is sufficient, under very general conditions, to equalize the employer cost of labor. That is, increased product or capital market integration should be associated with smaller intercountry differences in the real total compensation costs. By contrast, integration of the labor markets, including the possibility of intercountry mobility, is required to reduce the differences across countries in the constant purchasing power replacement value of the compensation package. Table 2.3 addresses these questions directly. We compute the adjusted intercountry variance of real total compensation and replacement value at purchasing power parity for each of our sample years.[9] For all three positions (CEOs, high-level managers, and manufacturing operatives), the variance of real total compensation declined substantially over the sample period. Since the period from 1984 to 1992 represented one of increased goods flows between these countries and substantial real exchange rate adjustments, we believe that the decline in the variance of real total compensation costs represents some evidence that the prices of these three types of labor are more similar now than at the beginning of the 1980s, as predicted by factor price equalization. Conversely, there is no downward movement in the variances of replacement value at purchasing power parity over the same time period. Since the labor markets of these countries have not become more integrated over this time period (with the possible exception of the European Community countries), it is not surprising that we find no evidence of the variance reductions that labor mobility might have induced.

Many of the discussions of U.S. CEO pay have focused on the ratio of CEO base plus bonus to manufacturing annual earnings (see, e.g., Crystal 1991). We believe that our two compensation measures (total compensation cost and replacement value) provide a more complete picture of the relative position of CEOs and high-level managers as compared to manufacturing production employees. Figure 2.7 shows the following ratios: CEO total compensation to manufacturing total compensation, CEO replacement value of compensation to manufacturing replacement value, HRD total compensation to manufacturing total compensation, and, finally, HRD replacement value to manufacturing replacement value. Whether measured from the employer or employee perspective, the ratio of American CEO compensation to that of manufacturing operatives is clearly much larger than the ratios in the other eleven countries. For HRDs, however, the American ratios are about average as compared to the ratios in the other eleven countries.

Table 2.4 contains a statistical analysis of these pay ratios. Panel A of table 2.4 analyzes the ratios for total compensation. For CEOs, the overall trend in the ratio of their total compensation to that of manufacturing operatives is positive (a logarithmic trend of .034 with a standard error of .013), while the overall trend for high-level managers is insignificantly different from zero. For both CEOs and high-level managers, neither the U.S. incremental effect nor the U.S. incremental trend is statistically significant. We discuss marginal tax rate effects in the next section. Panel B shows the analysis of replacement values relative to manufacturing employees. None of the overall trends is statistically

9. The regression equation, whose residuals were used to compute these variances, included a complete set of year indicators (for all positions), indicators for the source of the data (CEOs only), and indicators for the position (high-level managers only). A separate equation was fit for each position.

Table 2.3   Trends in the Intercountry Variance of Total Compensation and Replacement Value, 1984–92

	1984	1988	1989	1990	1991	1992
Real total compensation:						
CEO	.0863	.0834	.0614	.0517	.0436	.0378
High-level manager	.0486				.0263	.0256
Manufacturing employee	.0774	.0375	.0332	.0315	.0241	.0252
Replacement value at PPP:						
CEO	.1068	.1970			.1239	.1319
High-level manager	.0204				.0434	.0353
Manufacturing employee	.0415	.0532			.0351	.0328

Note: Reported variance is the average squared residual by year from a regression including a complete set of year indicators (all rows), indicator variables for the source (CEOs only), and indicator variables for the position (high-level managers only).

different from zero. U.S. CEOs, however, had a higher ratio than their counterparts elsewhere (a U.S. incremental effect of .681 with a standard error of .351). The U.S. incremental trend is not statistically different from zero.

To complement our analysis of the compensation levels and ratios, we consider in table 2.5 some differences in the structure of the CEO and HRD compensation for ten of our twelve countries.[10] Consider first the effects of company size. We adjusted our own statistical analyses, discussed above, for differences in the average size of the company responding to the source survey. However, we note that U.S. base salaries are more sensitive to company size than are the base salaries in other countries, as shown in the first two columns of table 2.5.[11] One source of the larger U.S. salaries that appear in unadjusted comparisons is clearly the differential size effect in the United States compared to other countries. Another potential difference between U.S. and other executive compensation systems is the use of stock-based long-term compensation. We consider this in more detail in the next section. We note that, according to Wyatt surveys, stock options, the most common long-term compensation plan in the United States, appear common in Europe. Incidence rates for stock options are shown in the fourth column of table 2.5. There is a problem, however, with using these estimates of the stock option incidence rates. The source for table 2.5 (the Wyatt Company) pools salary responses for U.S. expatriates, other expatriates, and home country nationals in its executive compensation survey.[12] Therefore, the stock option incidence rates in the fourth column are

10. The data in table 2.5 come exclusively from Wyatt sources, which did not contain comparable data for Canadian and Japanese firms.
11. We believe that this statement is also true for total compensation, but we do not have the data with which to confirm this suspicion.
12. Arthur Young, the principal source for 1984, also includes expatriates in its survey. Towers Perrin, the principal source for 1988–90 and one of several sources for 1991 and 1992, includes only home country nationals in its worldwide compensation survey.

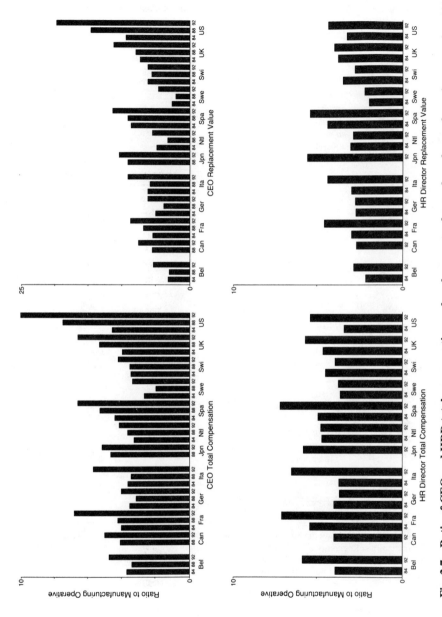

Fig. 2.7 Ratio of CEO and HRD total compensation and replacement value to that of manufacturing operative, 1984–92

Table 2.4   **Regression Analysis of the Ratio of Compensation of Managers to Manufacturing Operatives**

	Log of Compensation Ratio	
Compensation Measure and Independent Variable	CEO	High-Level Manager
A. *Total compensation relative to manufacturing operative*		
Overall trend	.034	.014
	(.013)	(.014)
U.S. incremental effect	.306	−.235
	(.219)	(.268)
U.S. incremental trend	.043	.036
	(.035)	(.040)
Marginal employee tax rate − manufacturing operative marginal rate	−.363	−.403
	(.168)	(.188)
R^2	.518	.181
Standard error of equation	.230	.257
Error degrees of freedom	51	59
B. *Replacement value relative to manufacturing operative*		
Overall trend	.027	.005
	(.021)	(.017)
U.S. incremental effect	.681	.087
	(.351)	(.326)
U.S. incremental trend	.023	.015
	(.056)	(.048)
Marginal employee tax rate − manufacturing operative marginal rate	−.702	−.559
	(.269)	(.229)
R^2	.445	.165
Standard error of equation	.368	.312
Error degrees of freedom	51	59

Note: The table shows the estimated coefficients (with standard errors) from ordinary least squares regressions. Regressions for the CEO include indicators for the data source. Data are for the years 1984, 1988, and 1992 only. The marginal employee tax rate is the marginal personal income tax rate plus the sum of the marginal employee and employer payroll tax rates.

contaminated by the relatively high representation of U.S. expatriates in the sample (shown in the fifth column). One solution to this problem is to estimate the stock option incidence rate for each country assuming that the home country nationals have a zero incidence rate and that the U.S. expatriates have the rate shown in the U.S. row of the table. The final column of the table makes this calculation. In every country except for the United Kingdom, the estimated stock option incidence rate in the final column is lower than the actual survey

Table 2.5   **Some Characteristics of the Wyatt Executive Compensation Sample**

Country	CEO Sales Elasticity	HRD Sales Elasticity	Company Sales ($U.S.)	% CEOs Awarded Options	% American Expatriates	CEOs Options if National Rate = 0 (%)
Belgium	.089	.087	157	22	52	19
France	.108	.084	110	26	63	23
Germany	.093	.070	306	24	33	12
Italy	.104	.166	114	26	56	20
Netherlands	.057	.032	95	30	56	20
Spain	.056	.045	194	24	54	20
Sweden	.157	.150	343	42	68	25
Switzerland	.059	.043	128	30	42	15
United Kingdom	.124	.078	130	23	65	24
United States	.219	.207	511	36		

Source: Wyatt Co. (1992b).

Note: Sales elasticity is from the regression of log base salary on log sales. Comparable data for Canada and Japan were not available.

rate (fourth column), indicating that either U.S. expatriates receive stock options more often than their U.S. counterparts (which is unlikely) or that the foreign national stock option incidence rate is above zero.[13] This conclusion is particularly important for countries like Germany and Sweden where popular discussions of the compensation packages assert that the long-term component of compensation is zero.[14]

2.4 Tax and Institutional Differences between Countries

In the descriptive analyses of sections 2.2 and 2.3, we noted (1) that differences in long-term compensation are very important between the United States and the other countries in our study and (2) that marginal tax rates appear to be related to all our measures of compensation. In this section, we explore these issues in greater detail. With respect to tax effects, we show (1) that top personal marginal income tax rates have become lower and more equal over our sample period, (2) that top marginal payroll tax rates (employer plus employee parts) have remained very unequal, with no change in the level for executives, (3) that marginal income tax and payroll tax rates for manufacturing

13. Charterhouse (1989, 1991) estimates show that U.K. CEOs receive stock options at a rate exceeding the Wyatt estimate and that this rate grew over the 1980s.

14. Our own figs. 2.1 and 2.2 above show no long-term compensation for Belgian, German, Japanese, Dutch, and Swedish executives. The value of the long-term component of compensation in these countries was estimated from Towers Perrin sources. Towers Perrin excludes all expatriates from its *Worldwide Remuneration* surveys. Thus, for the Wyatt and Towers Perrin estimates of long-term compensation incidence rates to be consistent for Germany and Sweden, it must be the case that other European expatriates account for the positive stock option incidence rates in these countries.

employees have increased and become more unequal, and, finally, (4) that marginal overall tax rate differences are strongly related both to the levels of total pay and to the ratios of executive/managerial pay to the pay of manufacturing operatives. With respect to the differences in long-term compensation, we examine both the tax-favored and the non-tax-favored forms of stock-based compensation in all twelve of our countries. Although many countries limit or refuse favorable tax treatment of stock options, they are, nevertheless, legal in all twelve of our countries. Consequently, it is difficult to explain why executives in other countries receive far less of this kind of compensation, especially since the disclosure requirements in other countries are generally not as restrictive as those in the United States.

Define the marginal tax rate on personal income as the tax due from a one-unit increase in taxable personal income. Define the marginal tax rate on corporate income as the tax due from a one-unit increase in taxable corporate income. Let the marginal employer payroll tax rate be the payroll tax due from the employer from a one-unit increase in base salary. Finally, define the marginal employee payroll tax rate as the payroll tax due from the employee from a one-unit increase in base salary.[15] Table 2.6 shows our estimates of these marginal tax rates based on the sources discussed in the data appendix for 1984 and 1992. The columns labeled *both payroll taxes* show the sum of the employer and employee marginal payroll tax. For the executive employees, marginal personal income tax rates declined in every country in the sample (as did top corporate rates, also shown, for most countries). At the same time, marginal personal income tax rates for the manufacturing employees do not show a clear trend between the two years. As regards marginal payroll tax rates, the sum of the employer and employee top marginal rates was virtually unchanged for the executives but rose substantially for the manufacturing employees.

Variability in the marginal personal income tax rates and in the marginal payroll tax rates (sum of employer and employee parts) is not matched by equivalent variability in the level of public benefits provided to executives as opposed to manufacturing employees. The distortion induced in the wage structure of our sample countries from the heterogeneous marginal tax rates coupled with the heterogeneous benefit schedules is evident in the regression analyses shown in tables 2.2 and 2.4 above. In table 2.2, we note that the marginal employee income tax rate plus the marginal payroll rate (sum of employer

---

15. For clarity, we note that *payroll tax* is an American business term. In international English, these are often called *mandatory employer and employee contributions,* which depend on compensation (salary, annual bonus, other cash payments, the taxable part of voluntary benefit packages, the taxable part of perquisites) and not directly on family or personal revenue subject to income tax. A payroll tax is a deductible business expense for the employer and, generally but not always, deductible for the employee. The French terms are *cotisations patronales* (employer) and *salariales* (employee). The German terms are *Gesetzliche Arbeitgeberbeiträge* (employer) and *Arbeitnehmer* (employee). The Italian terms are *contributi obbligatori a carico dell'azienda* (employer) and *dipendente* (employee). The Japanese terms are *kaisha no hōteikyo shukkin* (employer) and *jūgyōin no hōteikyo shukkin* (employee).

Table 2.6   **Summary of Marginal Tax Rates for Corporate Income Tax, Personal Income Tax, and Payroll Taxes in 1984 and 1992**

Year and Country	Corporate Income Tax	Executive Employee		Manufacturing Employee		Difference between Executive and Manufacturing
		Personal Income Tax	Both Payroll Taxes	Personal Income Tax	Both Payroll Taxes	
1984:						
Belgium	.45	.72	.48	.33	.35	.52
Canada	.46	.52	.00	.14	.13	.25
France	.50	.65	.21	.15	.45	.26
Germany	.63	.56	.00	.19	.40	−.03
Italy	.46	.71	.07	.18	.38	.22
Japan	.56	.78	.01	.21	.22	.37
Netherlands	.48	.72	.00	.16	.58	−.02
Spain	.35	.66	.00	.19	.35	.12
Sweden	.52	.70	.36	.15	.30	.62
Switzerland	.31	.46	.10	.21	.21	.14
United Kingdom	.52	.60	.00	.30	.25	.05
United States	.55	.62	.00	.16	.27	.19
Average	.48	.64	.10	.20	.32	.22
1992:						
Belgium	.39	.59	.40	.32	.61	.06
Canada	.44	.49	.00	.26	.19	.04
France	.37	.57	.21	.07	.68	.03
Germany	.59	.53	.00	.19	.57	−.23
Italy	.48	.51	.06	.23	.72	−.39
Japan	.52	.65	.01	.20	.35	.12
Netherlands	.35	.60	.00	.25	.57	−.23
Spain	.35	.53	.00	.23	.46	−.16
Sweden	.30	.49	.36	.34	.51	.01
Switzerland	.31	.50	.12	.06	.31	.24
United Kingdom	.35	.40	.10	.26	.29	−.04
United States	.40	.42	.00	.17	.35	−.11
Average	.40	.52	.11	.22	.47	−.05

Source Note: Corporate marginal income tax rates are for undistributed income as reported by Price Waterhouse (1984, 1992). Marginal tax rates for executives are for the CEO in the Arthur Young (1985) survey using the tax schedules in Price Waterhouse (1984) and the CEO in the Towers Perrin (1992) survey using tax schedules therein. Marginal tax rates for manufacturing employees are for the BLS manufacturing employee using tax schedules in Price Waterhouse (1984) Wyatt (1992a), and Price Waterhouse (1992). The column labeled *difference between executive and manufacturing* is the difference between the sum of the two executive marginal tax rates shown and the two manufacturing rates shown.

and employee parts) is strongly negatively related to CEO compensation regardless of the measure chosen. For the other high-level executives, there is some evidence of a negative relation between marginal employee tax rates and compensation (primarily for the replacement value measures), but not as strong as for the CEO. Conversely, the marginal employee tax rate (including both parts of the payroll taxes) has a significant negative effect on manufacturing compensation only when we use base salary plus annual monetary bonus as the compensation measure. These results suggest that the public financing and supply of benefits serves to depress the compensation of CEOs and, to a lesser extent, high-level executives but serves only to change the form of manufacturing compensation from private to public benefits.

Table 2.4 confirms this conclusion by showing that the ratio of both CEO and high-level manager compensation (either total compensation or replacement value) to manufacturing operative compensation exhibits a strong negative relation to the difference between the marginal employee tax rates (personal income tax rate plus the sum of employer and employee payroll tax rates). The final column of table 2.6 shows that this difference in marginal tax rates declined markedly over our sample period. Consequently, although there is no overall trend toward higher ratios of executive to manufacturing compensation, the strong negative trend in differential marginal tax rates was associated with a pronounced increase in these ratios; that is, the trend toward greater executive to manufacturing operative pay is entirely "explained" by the downward trend in differential marginal tax rates. As it becomes legally possible to deliver higher executive standards of living through the compensation system, it appears that executive pay increases relative to manufacturing pay regardless of the cultural environment.

Turning now from tax effects on total compensation and replacement value to tax effects on long-term compensation, we try to explain why stock-based compensation is less common in all our sample countries as compared to the United States. Unfortunately, the answer is not as apparent as in the case of the effects of changes in the tax structures on total compensation measures. Table 2.7 shows the legal status of tax-favored and non-tax-favored, stock-based long-term compensation plans in all our countries.[16] Such compensation is legal in all twelve countries. In addition, most of the countries have some form of tax-favored scheme, although these schemes are often limited with respect to the size of the tax benefit. Furthermore, plans resembling U.S. nonqualified stock option plans, which were not designed to be tax favored but which do have a tax advantage whenever individual marginal tax rates (the sum of the marginal personal income tax rate, the employer marginal payroll tax rate, and the employee marginal payroll tax rate) exceed corporate marginal income tax rates or whenever individual marginal tax rates are likely to fall in the future, would be similarly tax advantaged in every country we studied except the Netherlands and Sweden. Table 2.6 shows that both the conditions for a tax

16. A compensation plan is tax favored if it results in lower total tax payments, i.e., if the present value of corporate income taxes plus personal income taxes plus all payroll taxes is lower than would result from an equivalent amount of total compensation delivered using salary instead of long-term compensation. The tax-favored status of the plans shown in table 2.7 depends on the deductibility of the compensation expense from taxable corporate income. For all countries shown in the table (except the United States), the expense associated with the stock-based compensation is a legal employment expense and would, thus, be deductible; however, the tax guides do not confirm this directly.

Table 2.7   **Summary of Employee Tax Treatment of Long-Term, Stock-Based Compensation Plans**

Country	Tax-Favored Long-Term Compensation and Restrictions	Ordinary Long-Term Compensation and Recent Legal Changes
Belgium	SOs: G is TE when XN per year does not exceed the lesser of BEF 500,000 or 25% of EE's normal salary. $X \geq S(0)$. $H \geq 2$.	Other SOs: G taxed as EI. Passage of the 1984 Fiscal Recovery Act created tax favored SOs.
Canada	SOs: 25% of G is TE when $X \geq S(0)$, remainder taxed as EI.	Other SOs: G taxed as EI. 1988–89 33% of G was TE, and 50% of G was TE in 1987.
France	SOs: G is TE when $H \geq 1$ and $(R + H) \geq 5$.	Other SOs: G taxed as EI. Restrictions on foreign companies offering SOs to French residents were removed in 1986.
Germany		SOs: G taxed as EI. However, if R $\leq$ 9 months, $G = [S(0) - X]N$.
Italy		SOs: G taxed as EI. Security regulations were relaxed in 1988.
Japan		SOs: G taxed as EI. Japanese firms are generally prohibited from acquiring their own stock. EE stock association groups must be set up to acquire stock in order to permit EEs to exercise their SOs. Although these associations are independent, they are funded by the company and EE contributions.
Netherlands	SOs: 7.5% of $S(0)N$ taxable as EI in year of grant. G is TE if $X \geq S(0)$ and $R \leq 5$. If SO is not exercised, there is no refund of tax at grant.	Other SOs: same tax system applies; however, the percentage of $S(0)N$ that will be taxed as EI in the grant year must be negotiated with Dutch tax authorities.
Spain	SOs: G taxed as CG, which is adjusted for holding period and inflation before the EI rates are applied, if EE was charged for the option.	Other SOs: G taxed as EI if the SO was granted at no charge to the EE, as is typical in an American compensation SO.
Sweden	Convertible debenture: Fair market value of the convertible debenture is $S(0)N$. If EE buys debenture for $S(0)N$, then 60% of the gain at the exercise of the conversion provision, $[S(1) - S(0)]N$, is TE. If EE pays less than fair market value, say, PN, then $[S(0) - P]N$ is taxable immediately as EI, and 60% of	SOs are taxed as EI when granted. Taxable EI is the difference between the fair market value of the SO and the price paid by the EE at the grant, say ZN. At exercise no taxable income is recognized. When the stock is sold, the gain on sale $[S(1) - X]N - ZN$ is taxable as CG. (Note that S(1) refers to the stock

(continued)

Table 2.7   (continued)

Country	Tax-Favored Long-Term Compensation and Restrictions	Ordinary Long-Term Compensation and Recent Legal Changes
	[S(1) − S(0)]N is TE. H ≥ 2. Other variations are possible.	price at sale of the stock and not at exercise in this case.) There are some restrictions on Swedish companies granting stock options that can be circumvented by the use of parent companies and independent stock option funds. Prior to 1989 exchange controls effectively prohibited stock option plans by non-Swedish companies.
Switzerland		SOs: G taxed as EI.
United Kingdom	SOs: G and subsequent stock price appreciation taxed as CG when the shares are sold, not at exercise. 3 ≤ R ≤ 10, minimum 3-year interval between exercises, and the value of shares underlying the SOs must not exceed the larger of 4 times an EE's earnings or £100,000.	Other SOs: G is taxed as EI. If R < 7, taxable income may be recognized on the grant date. Legislation in the late 1970s and early 1980s promoted EE stock ownership.
United States	Incentive stock options (ISOs) are not taxed until the EE sells the shares. If R ≥ 2 and H ≥ 1, G plus the price appreciation on the stock since exercise is taxed as CG. Compensation expense of G is not tax deductible for the employer.	Other SOs: Nonqualified plans have G taxed as EI. ISOs are not automatically tax favored because of the loss of the employer's tax deduction on the compensation expense.

Sources: Primarily William H. Mercer International and Arthur Anderson & Co. (1990), with supplemental information from other tax sources listed in the data appendix.

Note: BEF = Belgian francs. $S(0)$ = market price of share at grant. $S(1)$ = market price of share at exercise. X = exercise price of option. N = number of shares optioned. G = $[S(1) − X]N$. H = number of years shares are held after the exercise of the options. R = number of years the options are held after the grant. SOs = stock options. EE = employee. TE = exempt from employee income and payroll taxes. EI = employment income (called *earned income* in the United States). CG = long-term capital gain.

advantage from non-tax-favored stock option compensation held for all our sample countries except Germany over the period 1984–92. Thus, we might expect that German, Dutch, and Swedish CEOs would have less stock-based compensation for purely tax reasons. For the other countries, however, stock options should have been at least as attractive a form of compensation for CEOs as they were in the United States. We cannot explain why among non-Americans only Canadian, French, Italian, Swiss, and British CEOs have any stock-based compensation. We also cannot explain why the proportion of stock-based long-term compensation is not higher in these countries, although we note that France and the United Kingdom have very strong positive trends for long-term compensation.

2.5   Conclusion

In this paper, we have analyzed the total compensation of chief executive officers, high-level managers, and manufacturing operatives from twelve OECD countries over the period 1984–92. American CEOs are clearly the highest paid whether we measure compensation from an employer cost viewpoint or from an individual replacement value viewpoint. American high-level managers, on the other hand, receive compensation that is on par with their counterparts in the other eleven countries. We identified three important factors related to the higher compensation of U.S. executives. First, the U.S. tax system favored direct compensation as opposed to unmeasured perquisites relative to the compensation systems of the other countries. The negative relation between marginal tax rates and total compensation (either measure) establishes this effect. As marginal tax rates of executives increase as compared to those of ordinary employees, a country's compensation structure becomes more compressed; that is, the ratio of executive compensation to manufacturing operative compensation declines. An international trend toward lower top-end tax rates, therefore, contributed to an increase in executive pay relative to that of manufacturing operatives. The second factor contributing to the difference between U.S. CEOs and others is the large component of long-term compensation that they receive. CEOs in other countries are much less likely to receive stock-based compensation even when the same tax incentives exist to use such remuneration. Although we can document the differences in the institutional environments across our sample countries, we cannot explain why companies outside the United States do not use stock option compensation more extensively. The third factor affecting U.S. executive compensation relative to other countries is the relatively low price of goods and services in the United States as compared to the other OECD countries. Purchasing power adjusted comparisons, particularly using the replacement value of the compensation package, thus, accentuate U.S. differences, whereas exchange rate–adjusted comparisons, particularly over the period 1984–92, tend to ameliorate those differences.

Our compensation comparisons for the executives as well as for the manufacturing production employees are more extensive than most other studies because we considered both total compensation costs from the employer's viewpoint and the replacement value of the compensation package, both public and private components, from the employee's viewpoint. Integration of international goods and capital markets provides an economic mechanism driving total compensation costs to equality across countries. Our evidence suggests that the increased trade in goods and capital has come at the same time as lower intercountry variance in total compensation costs for all three positions studied. This result suggests that factor price equalization may have been an important factor driving changes in wage rates across countries. The integration of world labor markets is required to drive the replacement value of the compensation package to equality across countries. We find no evidence that the intercountry variance in the replacement value of compensation has changed over our sample period.

While one could refine many of the measures used in this paper, we believe that our basic conclusions are sound regarding the relative compensation structures and the correlates of differences across countries in these structures. American CEOs are paid more than their counterparts elsewhere. Whether that higher pay is justified by the economic performance of the firms that these Americans manage is still an open question. Regardless of the answer to this question, it is clear that the American pay advantage is limited to CEOs. American high-level managers and manufacturing production workers are compensated in a manner quite typical of the other developed countries we studied.

Data Appendix

Compensation Data

Sources for CEO Compensation data in 1984 and 1988–92

Arthur Young (1985) includes base plus bonus, estimated personal income taxes, and estimated employee payroll taxes. Employer payroll taxes (compulsory benefits), voluntary benefits, perquisites, and long-term compensation were estimated using the sources listed below. Towers Perrin (1988) includes, for 1988, base plus bonus, compulsory benefits, perquisites, long-term compensation, estimated income taxes, and estimated employee payroll taxes. Voluntary benefits were estimated for 1988 using the sources listed below. Data are for a company with $100 million in annual sales. Towers Perrin (1991) includes voluntary benefits. Data are for a company with $250 million in annual sales. Towers Perrin (1989, 1990) include the same variables as 1988, while Towers Perrin (1992) is comparable to 1991. Wyatt Company (1992b) includes base plus bonus, estimated individual income taxes, and estimated employee payroll taxes. To facilitate comparisons with Towers Perrin, Wyatt base plus bonus estimates were adjusted to represent a company with $250 million annual sales using Wyatt's regression coefficients. Voluntary benefits, compulsory benefits, perquisites, and long-term compensation were estimated using Towers Perrin (1992) and the sources listed below. Wyatt Company (1992c) includes only base plus bonus. All other Japanese compensation components were estimated using Towers Perrin (1992) and the sources listed below. The 1992 Wyatt Japanese base plus bonus data are for a company with 1,000–2,999 employees.

Sources for HRD Compensation in 1984, 1991, and 1992

Arthur Young (1985), Towers Perrin (1991, 1992), and Wyatt Company (1992b, 1992c). All variables are comparable to the CEO variables discussed above from the same source.

Source for Cadre Dirigeant (highest management level) and Cadre Supérieur (senior management) in 1991

Bénichou (1992) reports the results of a specially commissioned study by the Hay Group, giving base plus bonus, estimated individual income taxes, and estimated employee payroll taxes. Voluntary benefits, compulsory benefits, perquisites, and long-term compensation were estimated using Towers Perrin (1991) and the sources listed below.

Sources for Manufacturing Employee Compensation in 1984 and 1988–92

U.S. Department of Labor (1991) includes hourly total compensation costs for a manufacturing production worker from each of our countries in each of our analysis years. We compare the BLS component "pay for time worked," which includes all cash payments made to the workers before any deductions of any kind, to executive base plus bonus. Voluntary benefits are measured as the difference between the BLS "hourly direct pay," which includes the compensation components normally classified as voluntary benefits, and "pay for time worked." Compulsory benefits are measured as the BLS "employer social insurance expenditures," which includes all legally mandated compensation components. We used OECD (1991a, 1992a) to estimate the BLS measures for 1991 and 1992. OECD hourly rates in manufacturing were used to estimate 1991 and 1992 hourly compensation costs by multiplying by the 1990 ratio of BLS hourly compensation costs to hourly pay for time worked. A comparable calculation was used to estimate the voluntary and compulsory benefits components. Annual hours were taken from International Labor Organization (1991). We assumed that no additional perquisites and no long-term compensation were paid to the manufacturing employees. Note that pension costs are included by the BLS in the two benefit measures as appropriate.

Personal Income Tax Rates

Primary Sources for Personal Income Tax Rates for all Executives and Manufacturing Employees in 1984

Deloitte Haskins and Sells (1985), U.S. Department of the Treasury (1984), and OECD (1988).

Primary Sources for CEO Personal Income Tax Rates in 1988–90

DRT International (1991), all countries; the *OECD Economic Surveys,* all countries, various years; and Price Waterhouse, *Doing Business in . . .* , all countries, various years.

Primary Sources for Personal Income Tax Rates for All Executives in 1991–92

Towers Perrin (1991, 1992).

Primary Sources for Personal Income Tax Rates for Manufacturing Employees in 1991 and 1992

Wyatt Company (1992a), Price Waterhouse, *Doing Business in . . .* , all countries, various years.

Corporate Income-Tax Rates

Primary Source for Corporate Income Tax Rates in 1984

Price Waterhouse (1984).

Primary Source for Corporate Income Tax Rates in 1988–92

DRT International (1991), all issues; the *OECD Economic Surveys,* all countries, various years; and Price Waterhouse, *Doing Business in . . .* , all countries, various years.

Social Security and Other Payroll Taxes

Social Security and Other Payroll Taxes for Manufacturing Employees

U.S. Department of Labor (1990, 1991).

Social Security and Other Payroll Taxes for All Executives

Deloitte Haskins and Sells (1985), William M. Mercer International (1987, 1992), Towers Perrin (1988), and Wyatt Company (1992a). Private communication with INSEE Division of Revenue was used for French payroll taxes.

Public Benefits Sources and Expenditure Categories

European Community Countries (Belgium, France, Germany, Italy, the Netherlands, Spain, and the United Kingdom)

Eurostat (1989, 1990, 1991, 1992).

Other Countries

Statistics Canada (1988, 1990, 1992), Japan Productivity Center (1988, 1990), Japan Institute of Labor (1991), Management and Coordination Agency (1991), Statistics Sweden (1992), Central Bureau of Statistics of Norway (1992) (the Norwegian tables contained some comparative data with Sweden), Nordic Statistical Secretariat (1990), Office Fédéral de la Statistique (1989, 1992), U.S. Chamber of Commerce (1991), U.S. Department of Commerce (1989, 1990, 1991), and International Monetary Fund (1991).

Exchange Rates and Purchasing Power Parities and Consumer Prices

Average annual exchange rates are from CITIBASE (1989). Where rates could not be found in CITIBASE (1989), they were taken from U.S. Department of Labor (1991).

For the basis on which the OECD computed purchasing power parities, see OECD (1992d). To compute 1990-based purchasing power parities in the years 1985, 1990, and 1991, we used OECD (1992b). We used changes in consumer prices to put the other year purchasing power parities on the base year 1990 and, thus, to estimate the 1984, 1988, 1989, and 1992 purchasing power parities using OECD (1989a, 1992a).

The U.S. consumer price index is from CITIBASE (1989). The OECD index of consumer prices is from OECD (1990a, 1992b).

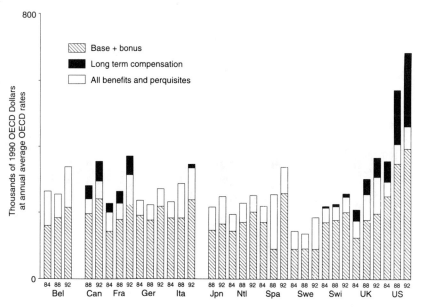

Fig. 2A.1   Total compensation of CEOs at purchasing power parity exchange rates, 1984–92

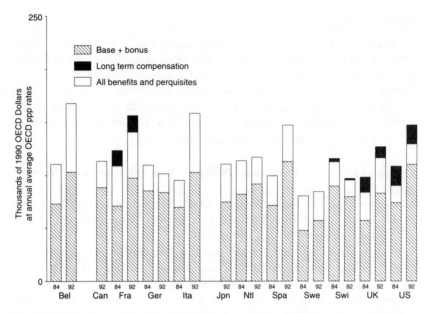

Fig. 2A.2 Total compensation of HRDs at purchasing power parity exchange rates, 1984–92

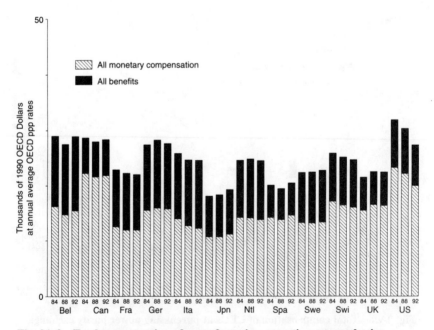

Fig. 2A.3 Total compensation of manufacturing operatives at purchasing power parity exchange rates, 1984–92

References

Abowd, John M. 1990. Does performance-based compensation affect corporate performance? *Industrial and Labor Relations Review* 43, no. 3: 52–73.

Arthur Young. 1985. *Executive compensation international.* New York: Business International Corp.

Bénichou, Paul. 1992. Les cadres français sont-ils bien payés? *Capital* 6 (March): 102–12.

Central Bureau of Statistics of Norway. 1992. *Statistical Yearbook of Norway.* Oslo.

Commission des Communautés Européennes. 1991. *Statistiques de base de la Communauté.* Luxembourg: Office des Publications Officielles des Communautés Européennes.

Charterhouse. 1989. *Top management remuneration, 1988/1989.* Essex: Monks Partnership.

———. 1991. *Board earnings United Kingdom, 1990/1991.* Essex: Monks Partnership.

CITIBASE. 1989. Citibank economic database [machine-readable magnetic data file], 1946–present. New York: Citibank N.A.

Crystal, Graef. 1991. *In search of excess: The overcompensation of the American executive.* New York: Norton.

———. 1993. *In search of excess: The overcompensation of American executives.* 2d ed. New York: Norton.

Deloitte Haskins & Sells. 1985. *Taxation of international executives.* New York: Kluwer Law and Taxation.

U.S. Department of the Treasury. Internal Revenue Service. 1984. *Instructions for preparing form 1040.* Washington, D.C.

DRT International. 1991. *International tax and business guides (Canada, Europe, Japan and United States editions).* New York.

Ehrenberg, Ronald, and George T. Milkovich. 1987. Compensation and firm performance. In *Human resource management and the performance of the firm,* ed. M. Kleiner et al. Madison: IRRA.

Eurostat. 1989. *Basic statistics of the Community.* Luxembourg.

———. 1990. *Basic statistics of the Community.* Luxembourg.

———. 1991. *Basic statistics of the Community.* Luxembourg.

———. 1992. *Demographic statistics.* Luxembourg.

Gerhart, Barry, and George Milkovich. 1990. Organizational differences in executive compensation and firm performance. *Academy of Management Journal* 33 (April): 1–30.

International Labor Organization. 1991. *Yearbook of labor statistics.* Geneva.

International Monetary Fund. 1991. *Government finance statistics yearbook.* Washington, D.C.

Japan Productivity Center. 1988. *Practical handbook of productivity and labor statistics, 1987/1988.* Tokyo.

———. 1990. *Practical handbook of productivity and labor statistics, 1989/1990.* Tokyo.

Japan Institute of Labor. 1991. *Japanese working life profile—labor statistics.* Tokyo.

Jensen, Michael C., and Kevin J. Murphy. 1990a. CEO incentives: It's not how much you pay, but how. *Harvard Business Review* 68, no. 3 (May/June): 138–49.

———. 1990b. Performance-pay and top management incentives. *Journal of Political Economy* 98 (April): 225–62.

Leonard, Jonathan S. 1990. Executive pay and corporate performance. *Industrial and Labor Relations Review* 43, no. 3: 13–29.

Management and Coordination Agency. Statistics Bureau. 1991. *Japan statistical yearbook, 1991.* Statistics Bureau. Tokyo.

Mitchell, Daniel J. B., and Jacques Rojot. 1991. Employee benefits in the context of Europe 1992. Working paper. University of California, Berkeley, March.

Nordic Statistical Secretariat. 1990. *Yearbook of Nordic statistics, 1989/1990.* Copenhagen: Nordic Council of Ministers and Nordic Statistical Secretariat.

OECD. 1985. *1984/1985 OECD economic surveys—Netherlands.* Paris.

———. 1987a. *1986/1987 OECD economic surveys—Netherlands.* Paris.

———. 1987b. *Purchasing power parities and real expenditures 1985.* Paris.

———. 1988. *1987/1988 OECD economic surveys—Japan and Switzerland.* Paris.

———. 1989a. *Economic outlook.* Paris, June.

———. 1989b. *1988/1989 OECD economic surveys—Spain.* Paris.

———. 1990a. *Main economic indicators: Historical statistics.* Paris.

———. 1990b. *1989/1990 OECD economic surveys—Canada, Germany, Japan, Netherlands, Switzerland, United Kingdom, and United States.* Paris.

———. 1991a. *Main economic indicators.* Paris, December.

———. 1991b. *1989/1990 OECD economic surveys—Italy, France, Germany, Italy, Japan, Spain, Sweden, United Kingdom, and United States.* Paris.

———. 1992a. *Economic outlook.* Paris, June.

———. 1992b. *Main economic indicators.* Paris, September.

———. 1992c. *1991/1992 OECD economic surveys—Belgium, France, Germany, Netherlands, and Spain.* Paris.

———. 1992d. *Purchasing power parities and real expenditures 1990.* Paris.

Office Fédéral de la Statistique. 1989. *Annuaire statistique de la Suisse.* Bern.

———. 1992. *Annuaire statistique de la Suisse.* Bern.

Price Waterhouse. 1984. *Capital formation—international survey and analysis.* New York.

———. 1987. *Doing business in . . . (Japan and United States editions).* New York.

———. 1990. *Doing business in . . . (Belgium, Japan, Netherlands, Sweden editions).* New York.

———. 1991. *Doing business in . . . (France, Switzerland, United Kingdom and United States editions).* New York.

———. 1992. *Doing business in . . . (Belgium, Canada, Germany and United Kingdom editions).* New York.

Rosen, Sherwin. 1990. Contracts and the market for executives. NBER Working Paper no. 3542. Cambridge, Mass.: National Bureau of Economic Research, December.

Statistics Sweden. 1992. *Statistical yearbook of Sweden 1992.* Stockholm.

Statistics Canada. 1988. *Canada year book 1988.* Ottawa.

———. 1990. *Canada year book 1990.* Ottawa.

———. 1992. *Canada year book 1992.* Ottawa.

Towers Perrin. 1988. *Worldwide total remuneration, 1988.* New York.

———. 1989. *1989 executive pay update—worldwide total remuneration.* New York.

———. 1990. *1990 executive pay update—worldwide total remuneration.* New York.

———. 1991. *1991 worldwide total remuneration.* New York.

———. 1992. *1992 executive pay update.* New York.

U.S. Chamber of Commerce. Research Center. 1991. *Employee benefits.* Washington, D.C.

U.S. Department of Commerce. Bureau of the Census. 1987. *Statistical abstract of the United States, 1987.* Washington, D.C.

———. 1989. *Statistical abstract of the United States, 1989.* Washington, D.C.

———. 1990. *Statistical abstract of the United States, 1990.* Washington, D.C.

———. 1991. *Statistical abstract of the United States, 1991.* Washington, D.C.

U.S. Department of Labor. Bureau of Labor Statistics. 1990. *International comparisons of hourly compensation costs for production workers in manufacturing, 1975, 1980 and 1982–89.* Report no. 787. Washington, D.C.

————. 1991. *International comparisons of hourly compensation costs for production workers in manufacturing, 1975–90.* Report no. 817. Washington, D.C.

William M. Mercer International. 1987. *International benefits guidelines.* New York.

————. 1992. *International benefits guidelines.* New York.

William M. Mercer International and Arthur Anderson & Co. 1990. *Globalizing compensation extending stock option and equity participation plans abroad.* New York.

Wyatt Co. 1992a. *Benefits report—Europe U.S.A.* Brussels.

————. 1992b. *Top management remuneration—Europe U.S.A.* Brussels.

————. 1992c. *Wyatt-Seikei top management compensation—Japan.* Tokyo.

Wyatt Data Services. 1992. *1992/1993 top management report,* vols. 1–3. Fort Lee, N.J.

3   The Gender Earnings Gap: Some International Evidence

Francine D. Blau and Lawrence M. Kahn

Despite in many cases dramatic reductions in the male-female pay gap since the 1950s, gender differentials persist in all industrialized nations. However, the size of the gender gap varies considerably across countries. Published data suggest that, by the late 1980s, the Scandinavian countries, France, Australia, and New Zealand had female/male hourly pay ratios of 80–90 percent while other countries in Western Europe and the United States had pay ratios of roughly 65–75 percent. The United States was among the countries with the largest differentials. Only Japan, with a ratio as low as 50 percent, had a consistently larger gap (see fig. 3.1). This paper uses micro data to analyze international differences in the gender pay gap among a sample of ten industrialized nations. We particularly focus on explaining the surprisingly low ranking of the United States in comparison to other industrialized countries. An advantage of an international perspective is that countries vary with respect to government policies, women's relative labor market qualifications, and wage-setting institutions. Such variability allows one to infer reasons for differences in the pay gap and, by implication, the effect of alternative government policies.

    Empirical research on gender pay gaps has traditionally focused on the role of gender differences in qualifications and of differences in the treatment of

Francine D. Blau is the Frances Perkins Professor of Industrial and Labor Relations at Cornell University and a research associate of the National Bureau of Economic Research. Lawrence M. Kahn is professor of labor economics and collective bargaining at the School of Industrial and Labor Relations at Cornell University.

    The authors are most grateful to David Blanchflower for his efforts in making the International Social Survey Programme (ISSP) data available to them and to Andrea Ichino for providing the Bank of Italy data. They have benefited from the helpful comments of Richard Freeman, Lawrence Katz, Claudia Goldin, and Pamela Loprest and of participants at the NBER/Ford preconference and the conference "Differences and Changes in Wage Structures" in London, September 1991, and Cambridge, Mass., July 1992, the AEA meetings in New Orleans, January 1992, and the Harvard, University of Chicago, and Princeton Labor Workshops. This research was supported by a grant from the Ford Foundation to the NBER.

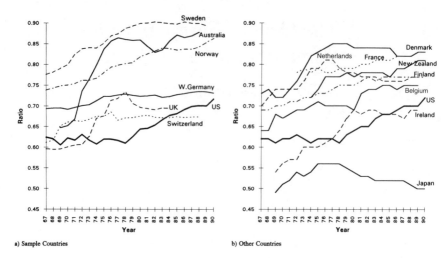

Fig. 3.1   Female/male hourly earnings ratios, nonagricultural workers, 1967–90
Sources: Various issues of OECD, *Labour Force Statistics;* ILO, *Yearbook of Labour Statistics;* and U.S. BLS, *Handbook of Labor Statistics.*

otherwise equally qualified male and female workers (i.e., labor market discrimination). Analyses of trends over time in the gender differential within countries as well as intercountry comparisons of gender earnings ratios have tended to emphasize these types of gender-specific factors. An innovative feature of our study is to focus on the role of wage structure as an additional factor influencing the gender gap. To analyze the effect of wage structure, we adapt a framework developed by Juhn, Murphy, and Pierce (1991) to analyze trends over time in race differentials in the United States. Our findings suggest that labor market institutions that affect overall wage inequality have an extremely important effect on the gender earnings gap.

Wage structure describes the array of prices set for various labor market skills (measured and unmeasured) and rents received for employment in particular sectors of the economy. Research on gender-specific factors influencing the pay gap suggests that men and women tend to have different levels of labor market skills and to be employed in different sectors. This implies a potentially important role for wage structure in determining the pay gap. For example, suppose that, in two countries, women have lower levels of labor market experience than men but that the gender difference in experience is the same. If the return to experience is higher in one country, then that nation will have a larger gender pay gap. Or, as another example, suppose that the extent of occupational segregation by sex is the same in two countries but that the wage premium associated with employment in male jobs is higher in one country. Then, again, that country will have a higher pay gap.

Skill prices can be affected by relative supplies, by technology (e.g., high-tech industries place a premium on highly trained workers), by the composition of demand, or, as emphasized in this paper, by the wage-setting institutions of each country. Specifically, centralized wage-setting institutions, which tend to reduce interfirm and interindustry wage variation and are often associated with conscious policies to raise the relative pay of low-wage workers (regardless of gender), may indirectly reduce the gender pay gap.

The striking finding of this study is the enormous importance of overall wage structure in explaining the international differences, particularly the lower ranking of U.S. women. The higher level of wage inequality in the United States than elsewhere works to increase the gender differential in the United States relative to all the other countries in our sample. Our results suggest that the U.S. gap would be similar to that in countries like Sweden, Italy, and Australia (the countries with the smallest gaps) if the United States had their level of wage inequality.

This insight helps resolve three puzzling sets of facts: (1) U.S. women compare favorably with women in other countries in terms of human capital and occupational status; (2) the United States has had a longer and often stronger commitment to equal pay and equal employment opportunity policies than have most of the other countries in our sample; but (3) the gender pay gap is larger in the United States than in most industrialized countries. An important part of the explanation of this pattern is that the labor market in the United States places a much larger penalty on those with lower levels of labor market skills (both measured and unmeasured). Put differently, our findings suggest that the gender gap in pay in the United States would be far less than it is if U.S. wage-setting processes more closely resembled those in the other countries, as long as U.S. women retained the same level of relative skills.[1]

In addition to having a relatively high level of wage inequality, the U.S. labor market has seen a major increase in inequality and the rewards to skills over the 1970s and 1980s (Katz and Murphy 1992; Juhn, Murphy, and Pierce, 1993). Thus, while American women have increased their relative levels of labor market skills (Blau and Ferber 1992; O'Neill and Polachek 1993), they are essentially swimming upstream in a labor market that has grown increasingly unfavorable to those with below-average skills. The decline in the U.S. gender pay gap in the 1980s becomes all the more impressive in light of this growing overall inequality. Below, we present U.S. data indicating that, over the period 1971–88, rising U.S. wage inequality reduced the potential convergence in the gender pay gap by about one-fourth.

The paper is organized as follows. Section 3.1 presents a brief overview of our findings, highlighting the striking importance of wage structure in explaining the international differences. Section 3.2 summarizes the institutional setting in each country, focusing on gender-specific policies and the degree of

---

1. Of course, under different wage-setting institutions, U.S. women might have different incentives to acquire labor market skills.

centralization of wage-setting institutions. Section 3.3 outlines the basic analytic framework and presents detailed empirical results based on our micro-data files. Section 3.4 examines the effect of rising inequality on the U.S. gender pay gap over the period 1971–88. Finally, section 3.5 presents our conclusions.

3.1   An Overview of the Findings

International differences in gender gaps are summarized in figure 3.2, which gives gender earnings ratios adjusted for hours for ten industrialized countries on the basis of our micro-data files for each country. Data are from the mid-1980s, with the exception of Norway and Sweden, for which the data are from around 1980.[2] (More detailed information about the data and the adjustment process is given below.) Figure 3.2 indicates that Italy, Sweden, Austria, and Australia have the highest gender ratios. The United States ranks toward the bottom of the group, with six of the nine countries (Sweden, Norway, Australia, Austria, Italy, and Germany) having higher gender earnings ratios and only three (the United Kingdom, Hungary, and Switzerland) having lower ratios.

The Italian ratio probably overstates the actual gender ratio in that country. Italy has an especially large proportion of workers who are self-employed or work in an informal sector in which government-mandated benefits are not paid. The self-employed could not be included in computing the gender ratio for Italy because hours worked were not available for them. However, we did ascertain that the gender ratio (not adjusted for hours) in Italy is considerably smaller (.6566) when the self-employed are included than when the sample is restricted to employees (.7431).[3] Further, it is likely that informal sector employment is underreported by the respondents in our survey-based data, possibly also resulting in an understatement of the gender gap. Nonetheless, it is likely that Italy is among the countries with the smallest gender gaps, although not necessarily heading the list, as would be suggested by the data in figure 3.2.

To illuminate the role of wage structure, we present the mean percentile rankings of women in the male wage distribution for each country in figure 3.3.[4] Gender-specific factors, including differences in qualifications and the effect of labor market discrimination, are viewed as determining the percentile ranking of women in the male wage distribution, while the overall wage struc-

2. The country rankings here are similar to those based on published data (when available) or other studies. Note, however, that the ratios for the Scandinavian countries and Australia are below those reported in OECD publications. This discrepancy appears to be due to the OECD data being restricted to manufacturing workers for Sweden and Norway and to nonsupervisory employees for Australia. The magnitudes of the gender ratios that we obtain are consistent with other studies that use micro data for these countries.

3. The gender ratios for the other countries were similar regardless of whether the self-employed were included. Our results include the self-employed for the other countries.

4. That is, we assign each woman in country j a percentile ranking in country j's male wage distribution. The female mean of these percentiles by country is presented in fig. 3.3.

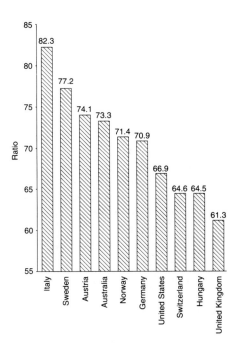

Fig. 3.2   Gender earnings ratios adjusted for hours only (%)

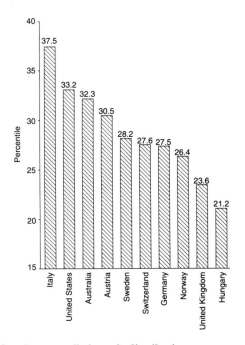

Fig. 3.3   Mean female percentile in male distribution

ture (as measured by the magnitude of male wage inequality) determines the wage penalty or reward associated with this position in the wage distribution. The basic premise is that males at the same percentile ranking as women may be viewed as comparable in the eyes of employers. Thus, the same set of factors will determine the relative rewards of women and of these comparable males, and differences between the rankings of countries in figures 3.2 and 3.3 represent the role of wage structure.

The most striking difference is for the United States. Whereas the United States ranks toward the bottom of the list with respect to the female/male earnings ratios, it ranks near the top in terms of women's percentile ranking. Only Italy ranks higher, and, as noted above, we have most likely overstated Italy's gender ratio. Thus, the relatively high gender pay gap in the United States does not appear to be due to a low ranking of women in the male wage distribution; rather, it is due to the higher level of wage inequality in the United States, which results in an especially large wage penalty for being below average in the distribution.

Also notable in comparing the two figures is the change in the rankings of the Scandinavian countries. Sweden falls from the second highest country in figure 3.2 to the fifth in figure 3.3, while Norway falls from fifth in figure 3.2 to eighth in figure 3.3. This suggests that the relatively more equal wage distribution in the Scandinavian countries is an important reason for the relatively high status of women there. So, for example, while the mean percentile ranking of women in the United States is 33.2, at the U.S. level of male wage inequality this corresponds to a wage that is 66.9 percent of the male mean. In contrast, Swedish women's percentile ranking of 28.2 corresponds to a wage that is 77.2 percent of the male mean, and Norwegian women's ranking of 26.4 corresponds to 71.4 percent of the male mean.

3.2 The Institutional Setting

In this section, we review international differences in gender-specific policies and basic wage-setting institutions. Human capital is also a major determinant of gender pay gaps, and, below, we present some international comparisons of women's relative levels of measured human capital. However, international differences in policies and institutions appear to be more dramatic than those in women's relative human capital levels, at least in our sample. Further, human capital can be affected by such policies and institutions as discussed below. We therefore emphasize the institutional setting in our comparisons of gender-based wage differentials. We first consider what the effect of the policies and wage-setting institutions is expected to be; then we compare each country to the United States across each dimension. We also note findings from previous research that suggest the importance of both gender-specific policies and labor market institutions in reducing the gender pay gap in specific instances.

Gender-specific policies include equal employment opportunity (EEO) and antidiscrimination laws as well as laws and policies governing family leave. The expected positive effect of the former on the earnings ratio is reasonably straightforward, although the effect will most likely depend on the effectiveness of the legislation as well as its provisions. Moreover, evaluating the effect of EEO law changes on women's relative pay in specific instances is complicated by the difficulty of locating an appropriate control group and, as Ehrenberg (1989) has pointed out, the possibility that the change in law was endogenously determined.

In general, it is expected that, given considerable segregation of women by occupation and industry, equal pay laws mandating equal pay for equal work within the same occupation and firm will have a relatively small effect. Laws requiring equal opportunity, hiring preferences, and/or "comparable worth" (i.e., equal pay for work of equal value to the firm, regardless of specific occupational category) have potentially larger effects on the wage differential. In addition, since EEO laws involve occupational shifts, they may require considerable time to have an effect on pay. Thus, the comparable worth approach that provides for immediate increases in relative pay in female-dominated occupations may be expected to have the largest initial wage effect, possibly accompanied by a negative effect on female employment.

The expected effect of family leave (disproportionately taken by women even when it is available to men) is unclear a priori. On the one hand, it is possible that such policies raise the relative earnings of women by encouraging the preservation of their ties to particular firms and hence increasing the incentives of employers and women to invest in firm-specific training. On the other hand, the existence of such policies could increase the incidence and/or duration of temporary labor force withdrawals among women, raising the gender gap for the affected group. Further, the incremental costs associated with mandated leave policies may increase the incentives of employers to discriminate against women.

With respect to wage structure, it seems likely that systems of centrally determined pay entail smaller gender wage differentials for a variety of reasons. First, in the United States, a significant portion of the male-female pay gap is associated with interindustry or interfirm wage differentials that result from its relatively decentralized pay-setting institutions (Blau 1977; Johnson and Solon 1986; Sorensen 1990; and Groshen 1991). Thus, centralized systems that reduce the extent of wage variation across industries and firms are likely to lower the gender differential, all else equal. Second, since in all countries the female wage distribution lies below the male distribution, centralized systems that consciously raise minimum pay levels regardless of gender will also tend to lower male-female wage differentials. Finally, the effect of gender-specific policies to raise female wages may be greater under centralized systems where such policies can be more speedily and effectively implemented.

We now turn to a comparison of the United States with the other countries in our sample along each of these three dimensions. First, with respect to gender-specific discrimination policies, equal employment policy in the United States[5] has consisted of the Equal Pay Act of 1963 (requiring equal pay for equal work), the Civil Rights Act of 1964 (requiring equal employment opportunity), and the executive order implemented in 1968 (which requires government contractors to take "affirmative action" to see that women and minorities are equitably treated). Comparable worth pay policies remain rare in the private sector, although they have been adopted by a number of state governments.

In general, U.S. policies in this area compare relatively favorably on their face to those of the other countries in our sample. All have passed some equal pay and equal opportunity legislation, but, interestingly, the U.S. commitment, particularly to equal employment opportunity, predates that in most of the other countries (see table 3.1). While Italy did mandate equal pay through collective bargaining in the industrial sector in 1960 (predating the U.S. Equal Pay Act by three years), an equal employment opportunity act was not passed there until 1977. The earliest of the other countries, Australia and the United Kingdom, began to implement equal pay in 1969 and 1970. Equal opportunity measures were instituted in 1975 in the United Kingdom and 1978 in Norway. The remainder of the countries passed all relevant legislation in the 1980s. The one country with a clearly stronger intervention than the United States is Australia, the only one to have implemented a national policy of comparable worth through its labor courts (see below). (Although Switzerland incorporated the principle of equal pay for work of equal value into its constitution in 1981 [Simona 1985], there is no indication that it has been implemented as yet.)

There is some econometric evidence that, all else equal, government policy in the 1970s raised the U.S. female/male pay ratio (Beller 1979) and, further, that the portion of the differential attributable to discrimination (as conventionally measured) declined (Blau and Beller 1988). Stronger evidence of the effect of antidiscrimination policies has been obtained for Australia, Sweden, and the United Kingdom. Since the effect of these policies was related to labor market structure, we discuss it below.

The laws governing maternity and parental leave as of 1988 in the various countries are summarized in table 3.2. The United States is the only country in our sample that did not have government-mandated leave at the federal level. (The United States passed legislation mandating up to twelve weeks of unpaid leave in 1993.) However, it was (and continues to be) required in the United States that pregnancy be treated the same as any other medical disability. Thus, leave for the physical aspects of childbearing must be covered under a firm's medical disability plan, if it has one. Further, in the late 1980s, 40 percent of employees of large and medium-size establishments were employed at firms that provided parental leave to women beyond this, the vast majority (92 per-

5. For a summary, see Blau and Ferber (1992).

Table 3.1 Equal Pay and Equal Employment Opportunity Policy

Country	Policy	Principal Implementing Measures		
		Year	Title	Enforcement Machinery
Australia	Equal pay	1969	Major decisions by Conciliation and Arbitration Commission	Conciliation and Arbitration Commission
		1972		
	Equal employment opportunity	1984	Sex Discrimination Act	Sex Discrimination Commissioner
		1984, 1987	Public Service Act Amendments	Public Service Commission
		1986	Affirmative Action Act	Human Rights and Equal Opportunities Commission; Affirmative Action Agency
Austria	Equal pay	1979	Law on Equal Treatment in Employment	Equality Commission
	Equal employment opportunity	1985	(Amended)	Ministry of Labour
Germany	Equal pay	1980	Code of Civil Procedure (§612)	Ministry of Labour and Social Affairs; Labour Courts
	Equal employment opportunity	1949	Basic Law	Ministry of Labour and Social Affairs; Labour Courts
		1980	Code of Civil Procedure (§§611a, 611b, 612a)	
		1986	Directive on professional promotion of women in federal administration	Ministry of Youth, Family, Women and Health
Italy	Equal pay	1960	Equal Pay Agreement of the industrial sector	Collective bargaining parties
		1964	Equal Pay Law for the agricultural sector	Ministry of Labor
	Equal employment opportunity	1977	Act on Equal Employment Opportunities between the Sexes	Labour tribunals; Ministry of Labour
		1983	Ministerial Decree of the Implementation of Equal Employment Opportunities Principles	

(continued)

Table 3.1 (continued)

Country	Policy	Year	Principal Implementing Measures	
			Title	Enforcement Machinery
Norway	Equal pay Equal employment opportunity	1978	Act on Equal Status between the Sexes	Equal Status Council; Equal Status Ombudsman; Equal Status Appeals Board
			Basic Agreement between Employers' and Trade Unions' Confederation	Collective bargaining parties
Sweden	Equal pay	1980	Act on Equality between Men and Women at Work	Equal Opportunity Ombudsman
	Equal employment opportunity	1983–84	Major Equal Opportunity Agreements between Employers' and Trade Unions' Confederation in Private and Public Sector	Collective bargaining parties
United Kingdom	Equal pay	1970 1975 1984	Equal Pay Act (In force) (Amended)	Industrial tribunals
	Equal employment opportunity	1975 1986	Sex Discrimination Act (Amended)	Equal Opportunities Commission (EOC); Industrial tribunals
United States	Equal pay	1963	Equal Pay Act	Equal Employment Opportunity Commission (EEOC)
	Equal employment opportunity	1964 1972	Civil Rights Act, Title VII Equal Employment Opportunities Act	Equal Employment Opportunity Commission (EEOC)
		1968	Executive Order 11375	Office of Federal Contract Compliance Programs

Source: OECD (1988, table 5.11, pp. 167–68).

Table 3.2   **Maternity and Parental Leave as of 1988**

Country	Maximum Length	Paid/Unpaid
Maternity leave:		
Australia	52 weeks	Unpaid[a]
Austria	16 weeks	100%
Germany, Federal Republic	14 weeks	100%
Hungary	24 weeks	100%
Italy	5 months	80%
Norway	20 weeks	100%
Sweden	12 weeks	90%
Switzerland	8–12 weeks	Paid as sickness[b]
United Kingdom	40 weeks	Up to 90%[c]
United States	. . .[d]	. . .
Parental leave:		
Australia	Up to 66 weeks[e]	Mostly unpaid
Austria	Age 1 year	Unpaid (allowance possible)
Germany, Federal Republic	Age 1 year	Paid (fixed allowance)
Hungary	Age 18 months	Paid (child-care benefits)
Italy	6 months	Paid (reduced benefits)
Norway	70 days	Paid (social security)
Sweden	360 days	Paid[f] (social security)
United States	. . .[g]	. . .

Source: International Labour Organization, *Conditions of Work Digest,* vol. 7, no. 2 (February 1988), tables 2 and 3, pp. 20–21.

[a]Provisions for Commonwealth government employees include twelve weeks' paid leave under certain conditions.

[b]Compensation depends on the level of insurance.

[c]Eighteen weeks paid at different rates.

[d]Some states provide unpaid maternity leave. Federal law prohibits employment discrimination based on pregnancy and childbirth.

[e]Applies to some public-sector employees only. Parental leave may encompass maternity leave, adoption leave, etc.

[f]Ninety percent for the first 270 days, then reduced fixed rate.

[g]In some states only. Up to twelve weeks, unpaid.

cent) at firms offering unpaid leave (Hyland 1990). Plans allowed an average of twenty weeks off for unpaid leave. It may be noted that provision for parental leave is particularly generous in Sweden, where nearly a year of paid parental leave is provided after twelve weeks of paid (at 90 percent) maternity leave. While the United States clearly lags behind the other countries in the provision of parental leave, as our discussion above suggests, it is unclear what effect this will have on the pay gap.

Pay setting is considerably less centralized in the United States than in the other countries in this study. The U.S. unionization rates of 20.5 percent for male and 12.5 percent for female workers are considerably lower than elsewhere (see table 3A.2). Further, the collective bargaining process itself is very decentralized in the United States, with an emphasis on single-firm agreements, and the U.S. government intervenes only minimally in wage setting (Flanagan et al. 1989). Wage determination is a mix of centralization and decentralization in Switzerland, where there is no minimum wage legislation, and many collective bargaining agreements do not mention pay, but parties are encouraged to form associations, leaving open the possibility of de facto centralization (Wrong 1987). While we have no explicit information on Hungary, we assume that as a (then) Communist country, albeit a somewhat more market-oriented one, it most likely had relatively centralized wage-determination institutions.

Wage setting is clearly very centralized in the Scandinavian countries, where the great majority of workers (64–80 percent in our micro data) are unionized and the collective bargaining process is very centralized. For example, in Sweden and Norway, the major union federation (LO) signs an agreement with the employers (SAF) covering a major portion of the labor force.[6] Several changes in collective bargaining practices, both gender specific and general, helped reduce the Swedish gender pay gap (Lofstrom and Gustafsson 1991). From 1960 to 1965, labor and management phased out the system of separate wage schedules for men and women that had previously existed in Swedish collective bargaining agreements. In addition, from 1968 to 1974, the LO made a conscious effort to raise the relative wages of lower-paid workers, regardless of gender. Finally, in 1977, the LO and the SAF negotiated a comprehensive package of equal employment provisions, predating the 1980 passage of formal EEO legislation.

German and Austrian wage-determination institutions are also highly centralized, and Austrian pay setting in particular appears to resemble that of Sweden and Norway. While a smaller percentage of Austrian workers are unionized than in Scandinavia (table 3A.2), collective bargaining agreements in Austria in most cases cover an entire industry or group of industries throughout the country. There thus appears to be little room for interfirm differentials in negotiated wages among union workers. Further, the terms of such agreements extend to nonunion workers (Tomandl and Fuerboeck 1986).

While collective bargaining in Germany is less centralized than in Austria, it is undoubtedly more centralized than in the United States. Unlike the U.S. emphasis on single-firm agreements, contracts usually cover all employers in an industry in a state (Kennedy 1982). As in Austria, the terms of such agreements extend to nonunion workers. In contrast to Austria, however, nationwide agreements and interindustry contracts are rare.

While the Australian wage-setting process is also highly centralized, it differs considerably from those of the countries described above. In Australia,

---

6. While wage setting is still far more centralized in these countries than in other European nations, there were some signs that the system was becoming less centralized in the 1980s (Leion 1985; Thorsrud 1985).

minimum wage rates for occupations are set by government tribunals.[7] Currently, nearly 90 percent of employees are covered by tribunal awards. Until World War II, female award rates were set at 54 percent of male rates; in 1950, this was raised to 75 percent. From 1969 to 1972, the concept of equal pay for equal work was implemented, as the female award rate was raised to 100 percent of the male rate for the same job. Finally, in 1972, the federal tribunal moved to the comparable worth concept so that women in female occupations would also be covered by rulings on the minimum male award in other occupations.[8] The raw data in figure 3.1 above as well as some econometric evidence (e.g., Gregory and Daly 1991) suggest that these gender-specific policies implemented by the wage courts have played an important role in lowering the pay gap.

Wage determination in Italy is also a very centralized process and has included explicit attempts to narrow pay differentials in a manner similar to that in Scandinavia. First, while about 40 percent of the Italian labor force in 1985 was unionized (Bean and Holden 1992), labor courts in Italy are empowered to extend the terms of collective bargaining agreements to nonunion workers (Treu 1990), most likely yielding an effective degree of unionization that is considerably greater. Second, and more important for understanding the Italian wage structure, is the operation of the wage indexation system, known as the *scala mobile*. This system, in existence from 1975 to 1992, gave across-the-board lira increases in wages in response to inflation in a conscious attempt to reduced skilled-nonskilled pay differentials (Treu 1990; "Italy" 1992). By 1990, Italian employers claimed that accumulated indexation payments accounted for 40 percent of labor costs.[9]

Wage setting in Britain appears to be less centralized than in the countries reviewed above, but it is most likely more centralized than in the United States. Roughly 40–50 percent of British workers are in unions, suggesting a larger role for unions and the collective bargaining process in Britain. In other respects, the wage-setting process appears similar to that of the United States. In the British private sector in 1980, only 26 percent of all (union and nonunion) workers had their wages set in multiemployer contracts or by wages councils. The rest were covered by single-firm agreements or had wages determined by management (Sisson and Brown 1983). Similarly, government intervention in British pay setting has been largely limited to periods in which incomes policies limited overall wage increases, and reliance on such policies waned in the 1980s (Davies 1983).

In an econometric analysis that controlled for other factors affecting wom-

7. This description of Australian pay setting is based on Gregory and Daly (1991) and Killingsworth (1990).
8. While about 40 percent of workers are covered by federal (as compared to state or other) awards, these other tribunals often follow the federal lead (Killingsworth 1990).
9. See "New Industrial Relations Talks Continue" (1990, 7).

en's relative pay, Zabalza and Tzannatos (1985) found significant effects for the 1970 equal pay legislation. This legislation was implemented through collective agreements (it was not until 1975 that the labor market was more broadly covered). The legislation required not only that differentiated male and female rates be removed but also that, in workplaces covered by collective agreements, women could not be paid at less than the lowest male rate (OECD 1988; Zabalza and Tzannatos 1985). Thus, the effect of the law was in part to raise the minimum for women covered by collective bargaining.

3.3   Earnings Ratios in the Micro Data

Our principal data source for the study of individual countries is the International Social Survey Programme (ISSP) data. The following countries and time periods were used: Austria (1985–87), West Germany (1985–88), Hungary (1986–88), Switzerland (1987), the United Kingdom (1985–88), and the United States (1985–88). The 1985–88 ISSP files lack data on the Scandinavian countries, and preliminary results suggested that the Australian data in the ISSP were inconsistent with other sources and that the Italian ISSP data contained very few observations on women. We therefore supplemented the ISSP with three additional micro-data sets in order to include these countries with very high gender earnings ratios. We used the Class Structure and Class Consciousness (CSCC) data base, originally compiled by Erik Wright, for Sweden (1980) and Norway (1982); the Income Distribution Survey (IDS) for Australia (1986); and a Bank of Italy (BI) survey for Italy (1987).[10] In each case, the sample was restricted to individuals aged eighteen to sixty-five years old.

The specific earnings measures used in the data for each country are described in detail in the appendix. In each case, the earnings figure is expressed on an annual or a monthly basis. The computation of gender wage differentials from these data sets is complicated by the omission from these files of information on annual weeks worked. Weekly hours worked is available, however, allowing for some adjustment of the earnings data for time input.[11] (The adjustment for time input is described below.) In all but two cases, the earnings variable was coded into categories.[12] In the analyses presented below, we arbi-

10. For descriptions of ISSP data, see Blanchflower and Freeman (1992); of CSCC data, Rosenfeld and Kalleberg (1990); of IDS data, Blackburn and Bloom (1991); and of BI data, Erickson and Ichino (chap. 8 in this volume).

11. There is information on weeks worked for Australia and for a subset of the Norwegian data. Analyses correcting for weeks worked yielded very similar results to those reported here, with slightly lower adjusted gender differentials. Lack of information on hours worked for those with multiple jobs forced us to limit the Swedish sample to those with one job only.

12. The Australian earnings data were originally reported as a continuous variable. However, to maintain comparability with the other countries, we recoded the Australian earnings into the ISSP's intervals for Australia. When the analysis was performed for Australia using the original continuous variable, the results were virtually identical to those reported here. The BI data were also continuous but did not match up with the ISSP categories for Italy. We therefore used the continuous earnings variable for Italy. As noted below, Italy's wage distribution had lower residual

trarily coded the top (open-ended) category as 1.2 times its minimum value. However, the gender ratios were virtually identical when we experimented with alternative assumptions for the top category ranging from 1 to 1.5 times its minimum value. Finally, concern for adequate sample size led us to pool years of data for those countries in the ISSP surveyed more than once (see above).

3.3.1   Estimation of the Gender Differentials

Table 3.3 gives estimated gender ratios for log earnings corrected for hours for all workers and by marital status. These estimates were obtained as follows. For each country, the following regression was run separately by sex:[13]

(1) $\ln \text{EARN} = b_0 + b_1\text{PART} + b_2\text{HPART} + b_3\text{HFULL} + B'X + e,$

where ln EARN is the natural log of earnings; PART is a dummy variable for part-time employment (fewer than thirty-five hours per week); HPART and HFULL are interactions of weekly work hours with part- and full-time status; X is a vector of explanatory variables including years of schooling, potential experience and its square, union membership,[14] and industry and occupation dummy variables; and e is an error term. (For the variable means and regression results, see the appendix.) The model allows for both a part-time shift term and different slopes for hours for part- and full-time workers. A detailed adjustment for part-time employment is important in light of the prevalence of part-time work for women in many countries (see below).

The PART, HPART, and HFULL coefficients from (1) were used to adjust each person's earnings for work hours by assuming a forty-hour work week. That is, for each worker i, we have:

(2) $\text{YFULL}_i = \ln \text{EARN}_i - b_1\text{PART}_i - b_2\text{HPART}_i - b_3(\text{HFULL}_i - 40),$

where the coefficients, b_n, are obtained from estimating equation (1) for males and females separately. Gross hours-corrected gender earnings ratios based on the mean of YFULL for the indicated groups were then calculated for each country and are shown in table 3.3.

In the first column are the hours-corrected gender earnings ratios for all workers shown in figure 3.2 above. The last two columns of table 3.3 provide

---

variance than in most of the other countries. Use of earnings categories for these other countries implies that Italy's residual variance would have been even lower relative to the others had earnings categories been used for Italy as well.

13. For countries with more than one year of data, the log earnings variable was obtained by transforming each observation into its 1988 (or end-year) equivalent on the basis of regressions including only gender and year dummy variables. Thus, the dependent variable for each observation on individual i in year t is $\ln \text{EARN}_{it} - \Sigma_t b_t \text{YR}_{it}$, where $\ln \text{EARN}_{it}$ is the observed log earnings for individual i in year t, YR_{it} and b_t are the dummy variable and the estimated coefficient for year t, respectively, and the end year is the omitted year.

14. Union status was not available for Italy or Australia.

Table 3.3   Gender Earnings Ratios Corrected for Hours[a]

| Country | All Workers | | | |
	Own Country Family Composition	U.S. Family Composition[b]	Married Workers	Single Workers
Australia	.7334	.7386	.6756	.9044
Austria	.7407	.7489	.6607	.9170
Germany	.7091	.7248	.6006	.9806
Hungary	.6454	.6631	.6087	.7728
Italy	.8232	. . .	. . .	. . .
Norway	.7138	.7411	.6756	.8958
Sweden	.7724	.7865	.7209	.9435
Switzerland	.6455	.6872	.6140	.8709
United Kingdom	.6133	.6447	.5604	.8251
United States	.6692	.6692	.5672	.8758

[a]YFULL, earnings evaluated at full-time (forty) hours (see eq. [2]). The number of hours is not available for Hungary, but all workers are full-time. Marital status is not available for Italy.
[b]Computed using U.S. proportions of married and single workers.

gender ratios for married and for single workers separately.[15] It is well known that the family division of labor can influence pay gaps by affecting women's (and men's) investments in human capital, accumulation of seniority and experience, and job search strategies.[16] Except for Hungary, for which we have no data on hours, the pay ratio is relatively high among single workers, ranging from .83 to .98.[17] Further, the rankings of the pay gaps for single workers are not always consistent with the overall rankings. In contrast, the pay gap is much larger for married workers and corresponds more consistently to the rankings for the overall labor force. Nonetheless, since the ratios for married workers are always lower than those for single workers, a question may be raised as to whether the overall differences in ratios across countries are simply due to intercountry differences in family composition. This appears not to be the case, however. In the second column of table 3.3, the earnings ratios for all workers are computed using the U.S. proportions of married and single workers. The implied ratios are similar to those for all workers in the first column of the

15. Note that eq. (1), which is used to obtain hours-corrected earnings for each individual, does not control for marital status. This specification was employed because of the complications involved in considering marital status as a productivity indicator for men and women (see our discussion below). We do, however, provide additional results for a subsample of married workers, a strategy that in effect controls for marital status.
16. The division of labor in the home can also of course be affected by women's relative labor market opportunities. Nonetheless, we would still expect the division of labor to have some effect on relative pay.
17. Reasons for the low estimated pay gaps among single workers include the likelihood that they are disproportionately young (the pay gap is lower for young workers [see Mincer and Pola-chek 1974]) and that single males are less productive than married males (see Korenman and Neumark 1991).

table. This similarity suggests that cross-country differences in the family composition of the labor force do not account for the observed differences in relative pay gaps. Rather, as concluded above, it is the intercountry differences in the ratios particularly among married workers that drive the international differences.

3.3.2   Gender Differences in Worker Characteristics

The data presented in table 3.3 suggest that international differences in the gender pay gap are not due to differences in marital status composition. Before providing a formal decomposition of these pay gaps, we briefly examine intercountry differences in other worker characteristics. Such data can reveal at least qualitative differences in the relative labor market skills of women across countries. Overall, we conclude that U.S. women compare favorably with those in other countries when we consider their labor market qualifications relative to those of men.

For all countries except Switzerland and Italy, education and potential experience are similar for men and women (see table 3A.2). In Switzerland, the female labor force is less educated and younger than the male labor force, while, in Italy, women are more highly educated and younger than men. While unfortunately we lack data on actual labor market experience, some indication of labor force commitment may be gained by an examination of the labor force participation (LFP) rates by gender–marital status groups for each country shown in table 3.4. As may be seen in the table, the LFP rate of women in the United States is higher than that of women in any of the other countries except Sweden. The absolute male-female differential in participation rates in the United States is comparable to that in Hungary and lower than that in any of the other countries apart from Sweden.

While the U.S. female population has higher labor force participation than most other countries in the 1980s, this does not necessarily imply that the average employed American woman has more labor market experience. It is possible that, in a country with a high female LFP rate, recent entrants constitute a high proportion of the labor force and thus that women workers have less experience on average than in a country with a low female LFP rate. On the other hand, it is possible that a country's high female LFP rate is due to a more continuous labor force attachment among women (Blau and Ferber 1992; Polachek 1990).

Polachek (1990) in fact finds that, in the 1970s, a growing female LFP rate in the United States was associated with a rising gender gap in actual experience. This finding was due to the low experience levels of the large number of new entrants (or reentrants). However, by the 1980s, rising female LFP rates in the United States were accompanied by rising female relative experience levels. Lacking international data on actual experience, we tentatively conclude that U.S. women are at least as oriented toward market work as women in most other countries.

This conclusion is reinforced by an examination of the incidence of part-

Table 3.4   Labor Force Participation Rates

Country	Men			Women		
	Married	Not Married	All	Married	Not Married	All
Australia	.8933	.8688	.8856	.5624	.6774	.5956
Austria	.7701	.7956	.7784	.3883	.5605	.4444
Germany	.8408	.7047	.7884	.3742	.5759	.4477
Hungary	.8552	.8041	.8423	.6638	.6320	.6562
Italy (1980)	...	...	.7880	...	...	.4390
Norway	.9067	.7790	.8778	.5896	.5960	.5910
Sweden (1988)	...	...	.9000	...	...	.8500
Switzerland	.9679	.8477	.9312	.3949	.8181	.6045
United Kingdom	.9211	.8202	.8930	.5572	.6686	.5886
United States	.9068	.8564	.8873	.6200	.7076	.6614

Sources: Sweden: Lofstrom and Gustafsson (1991). Italy: OECD, *Labour Force Statistics,* (1990, 299).

time work shown in table 3.5. A smaller percentage of employed women in the United States than in any other country work part-time (fewer than thirty-five hours per week). Further, since the incidence of part-time work among men is considerably higher in the United States than in other countries, the gender differential in part-time work is much smaller in the United States than elsewhere. We particularly note the high incidence of part-time work among Scandinavian women. About 46 percent of Swedish and 53 percent of Norwegian employed women work part-time, compared to only 24 percent of employed U.S. women.[18] Finally, while the incidence of part-time work is only slightly higher for Italian than for U.S. women, the Italian female LFP rate is much lower than that in the United States (table 3.4 above).

The commitment of U.S. women to market work is further underscored by the examination of the incidence of part-time work by marital status also shown in table 3.5. In all countries, married women are more likely to work part-time than single women, and single men generally have a higher incidence of part-time work than married men. However, U.S. married women are far less likely to work part-time than those in any other country, while U.S. married men are slightly more likely to work part-time than those elsewhere. In addition, the gap in the incidence of part-time work between married and single women is only about .10 in the United States, while it ranges from .24 to .36 elsewhere.

Tables 3.4 and 3.5 suggest a higher level of relative labor force commitment

18. The high incidence of PART for Scandinavian women may be due in part to the generous family leave policies in these countries. In addition to policies guaranteeing paid parental leave in both Sweden and Norway, since 1979 Sweden has allowed working parents of small children the right to have a six-hour day on demand (Haavio-Mannila and Kauppinen 1992).

Table 3.5   **Means for Married, Spouse Present (MARSP) and Part-Time Work (PART), Employed Sample**

Country	Married (MARSP)		Part-Time (PART)					
			Men			Women		
	Men	Women	All	Single	Married	All	Single	Married
Australia	.6971	.6494	.0457	.0674	.0362	.3740	.2070	.4641
Austria	.6651	.5711	.0218	.0233	.0211	.2821	.1444	.3855
Germany	.6859	.5252	.0170	.0280	.0119	.3455	.1663	.5076
Italy	. . .	. . .	.0573	. . .	. . .	.2613	. . .	. . .
Norway	.8053	.8050	.0697	.0679	.0701	.5251	.2673	.5875
Sweden	.7374	.7177	.0525	.0500	.0534	.4565	.2766	.5272
Switzerland	.7268	.3129	.0232	.0377	.0177	.2517	.1386	.5000
United Kingdom	.7664	.7060	.0366	.0464	.0336	.4485	.2034	.5506
United States	.6366	.5059	.1145	.1800	.0771	.2437	.1915	.2947

Note: PART is defined as employed for fewer than thirty-five hours per week. This variable is not available for Hungary. Marital status is not available for Italy.

among U.S. women, particularly married women, than among women in most other countries. Table 3.6 indicates a lower level of occupational segregation (at the one-digit level of aggregation) for U.S. women than for those in other countries (with the exception of Switzerland).[19] Industrial segregation, again measured at the one digit level, is similar in the U.S. to that in the other countries in the sample. The high levels of occupational and industrial segregation in Scandinavia are especially noteworthy and perhaps understandable in light of the high incidence of part-time work there.

A country's level of occupational segregation is likely to reflect both women's relative training levels and labor force commitment and the effect of employer, government, or union policies (Reskin et al. 1986; Blau and Ferber 1992). To the extent that it reflects training and commitment, we may again conclude that U.S. women's workforce credentials relative to men's exceed those of women in other countries.

3.3.3   Analysis of International Differences in the Pay Gap: The Effects of Skills, the Treatment of Women, and Overall Inequality

Juhn, Murphy, and Pierce (1991) have devised a method that allows us to decompose the international differences in gender pay gaps into a portion due to gender-specific factors and a portion due to differences in the overall level

19. This conclusion regarding the U.S. position largely holds true when the segregation index is calculated using published data from the ILO (Blau and Ferber 1992, 309). Note that our findings for Switzerland must be interpreted with caution given the small size of our sample. A segregation index computed on the basis of ILO data does not indicate a lower level of segregation for Switzerland than for the United States.

Table 3.6   Gender Segregation Indexes by One-Digit Occupation and Industry

Country	Occupation	Industry
Australia	.3807	.3302
Austria	.4020	.3140
Germany	.4216	.3203
Hungary	.4084	.2467
Norway	.4341	.3893
Sweden	.4614	.4263
Switzerland	.3222	.2913
United Kingdom	.4395	.3488
United States	.3568	.3430

of wage inequality. Following their notation, suppose that we have for male worker i and country j a male wage equation:

$$(3) \qquad Y_{ij} = X_{ij}B_j + \sigma_j\Theta_{ij},$$

where Y_{ij} is the log of wages; X_{ij} is a vector of explanatory variables; B_j is a vector of coefficients; Θ_{ij} is a standardized residual (i.e., with mean zero and variance one for each country); and σ_j is the country's residual standard deviation of wages (i.e., its level of male residual wage inequality).

Then the male-female log wage gap for country j is

$$(4) \qquad D_j \equiv Y_{mj} - Y_{fj} = \delta X_j B_j + \sigma_j\delta\Theta_j,$$

where the m and f subscripts refer to male and female averages, respectively; and a δ prefix signifies the average male-female difference for the variable immediately following. Equation (4) states that the country's pay gap can be decomposed into differences in measured qualifications (δX_j) and differences in the standardized residual ($\delta\Theta_j$) multiplied by the money value per unit difference in the standardized residual (σ_j).[20] Note that the final term of (4) corresponds to the "unexplained" differential in a standard decomposition of the gender differential when the contribution of the means is evaluated using the male function.

The pay gap difference between two countries j and k can then be decomposed using (4):

$$(5) \qquad D_j - D_k = (\delta X_j - \delta X_k)B_k + \delta X_j(B_j - B_k) + \\ (\delta\Theta_j - \delta\Theta_k)\sigma_k + \delta\Theta_j(\sigma_j - \sigma_k).$$

20. Note that this formulation is based on a single wage equation for males. That is, one could repeat the analysis starting with a female wage equation. Male-female differences in regression coefficients can reflect either discrimination or sex-correlated measurement errors of variables such as experience. In using the male wage equation for this decomposition analysis, we in effect simulate what the wage equation in a nondiscriminatory labor market would look like (although the elimination of discrimination might change the male as well as the female reward structure). We present both male and female wage equations for each country in the appendix.

The first term in (5) reflects the contribution of intercountry differences in observed labor market qualifications (X) to the gender gap. For example, the pay gap in one country may be less than in another owing to women's higher relative levels of education. The second term reflects the effect of different measured prices across countries for observed labor market qualifications. For example, for a given (positive) male-female difference in schooling, a higher return to education will raise the male-female pay gap.

The third term measures the effect of international differences in the relative wage positions of men and women after controlling for measured characteristics (i.e., whether women rank higher or lower within the male residual wage distribution). That is, it gives the contribution to the cross-country difference in the gender gap that would result if the two countries had the same levels of residual male wage inequality and differed only in their percentile rankings of the female wage residuals. In one country, for instance, the average woman's wage residual may be at the thirty-fifth percentile of the male distribution, while in another it may be at only the twenty-fifth percentile. This percentile ranking may reflect gender differences in unmeasured characteristics and/or the effect of labor market discrimination against women. In the empirical work that follows, we label this term the *gap* effect.

Finally, the fourth term of (5) reflects intercountry differences in residual inequality. It measures the contribution to the intercountry difference that would result if two countries had the same percentile rankings of the female wage residuals and differed only in the extent of male residual wage inequality. Suppose, as is likely, that, controlling for measured characteristics, the female mean log wage is less than the male mean in country j. Then the larger is the intercountry difference in the overall residual inequality in wages $(\sigma_j - \sigma_k)$, the larger difference there will be in the ultimate pay gaps in the two countries. That is, unmeasured deficits in female relative skills or discrimination lower women's position in the male distribution of wage residuals. The larger the penalty a country places on being below average in wages, the larger will be its pay gap. In the empirical work below, we label this the effect of *unobserved prices*.

Following Juhn, Murphy, and Pierce (1991), we estimate the third and fourth terms of (5) empirically using the entire distributions of wage residuals for each country. For example, to compute $(\delta\Theta_j - \delta\Theta_k)\sigma_k$, we first give each woman in country j a percentile number based on the ranking of her wage residual (from the country j male wage regression) in country j's distribution of male wage residuals. We then impute each country j woman's wage residual given her percentile ranking in country j and the distribution of male wage residuals in country k. The difference between the mean of these imputed wage residuals for country j and the actual mean female wage residual for country k is used to find the estimate of $(\delta\Theta_j - \delta\Theta_k)\sigma_k$ (note that the mean male residual is always zero). The fourth term of (5), $\delta\Theta_j(\sigma_j - \sigma_k)$, is obtained analogously.

According to (5), the full effect of gender-specific factors is reflected in the sum of the first and third terms, the effect of gender differences in qualifications and of gender differences in wage rankings at a given level of measured characteristics. Labor market structure is reflected in the sum of the second and fourth terms, the effect of intercountry differences in returns to measured and unmeasured characteristics. Within the framework of a traditional decomposition, the sum of the third and fourth terms represents the effect of intercountry differences in the "unexplained" differential, which is commonly taken as an estimate of discrimination.

The possibility of discrimination complicates the interpretation of the last term of (5). With labor market discrimination, this term in part reflects the interaction between country j's level of discrimination (defined as pushing women down the distribution of wages) and intercountry differences in the overall level of inequality that determine how large the penalty is for that lower position in the distribution (Juhn, Murphy, and Pierce 1991). We will present some indirect evidence that, in the case of the countries compared here, this term at least in part reflects the effect of overall wage setting. The observed price effect may also reflect discrimination if, for example, women are "crowded" by exclusion into certain sectors, lowering relative earnings there even for men (Bergmann 1974).

We implement this decomposition using the Juhn, Murphy, and Pierce (1991) accounting method performed on equation (1). Each country's gross gender differential is expressed in terms of YFULL, hours corrected earnings defined in equation (2). The explanatory variables in X include the traditional human capital variables of education, potential experience and its square, union membership, and one-digit industry and occupation dummy variables.[21] The structural variables may reflect both worker skills and rents received by workers with these characteristics. Unfortunately, the data sets available to us lack information on actual labor market experience. Thus, this remains an important omitted variable in these analyses, although, to some degree, our controls for education, hours, industry, and occupation may pick up some of the effects of such omissions.

We have not controlled for marital status in this analysis, although, as noted above, it may be an important factor influencing the pay gap. An alternative would have been to include marital status as a productivity characteristic. However, such an approach is problematic since this variable appears to measure higher skills for men (Korenman and Neumark 1991) but most likely lower skills for women, especially when data on actual labor market experience are lacking. The approach that we have followed allows us to place a sharper interpretation in the decomposition on the effect of differences in labor market skills. Recognizing the potential importance of marital status, however, we also

---

21. For Hungary, Australia, and Italy, industry and/or occupation differ from those for the rest of the countries. In addition, for the latter two, union membership status is not available. For the purposes of comparing the United States and these countries, we estimated U.S. equations that conformed to the same specification as each country.

perform a decomposition of pay gaps among married workers. Differences in the results for the whole labor force and those for married workers can provide interesting insights in cross-country comparisons. Sample size limitations prevented us from analyzing single workers.

The decomposition for the whole labor force is summarized in table 3.7, and that for married workers (based on eq. [1] estimated for married workers only) is presented in table 3.8 below. Looking first at the results for the whole workforce (table 3.7), we see that, after controlling for measured characteristics, the mean female percentile[22] ranges from 21.2 in Germany to about 37 in the United States, Australia, Sweden, and Italy. It is noteworthy that U.S. (and Italian) women place at the top of the list. The column headed *gap* shows the contribution of each country's female placement in the male residual wage distribution to its relative pay gap. The figure is positive for all countries except Australia and Italy,[23] indicating that these differences in rankings raise the differential relative to the United States, often substantially (the unweighted average effect is .1886). The column headed *unobserved prices* shows that the lower level of residual wage inequality in each of the other countries has a negative effect, often quite considerable, on its gap relative to that in the United States (the unweighted average effect is −.2015).

Table 3.7 also provides estimates of the effect of measured skills and their prices on intercountry differences in the pay gap. The observed X's effect is generally positive, indicating that U.S. women have relatively favorable levels of the measured variables (the unweighted average effect is .0286). The observed prices effect is always negative, indicating that the male returns to the explanatory variables increase the pay gap in the United States relative to other countries (the unweighted average effect is −.0699). However, these observed effects are much smaller in magnitude than the unobserved prices and gap effects.

The last two columns of the lower panel of table 3.7 give the total effect of gender-specific factors and wage structure. The results suggest that U.S. women fare well with respect to gender-specific factors (as measured by the sum of the observed X's and the gap effects). When compared to all countries except Italy, Australia, and Sweden, U.S. women have relatively favorable levels of both productivity characteristics and gender-specific treatment in the labor market. For these three countries, the gender-specific factors (i.e., the observed X's and the gap effects) approximately cancel out. In contrast, the

22. For each country, this is the mean of the percentile ranking of each woman's residual from the male regression (e_{if}) in the distribution of male wage residuals (e_{im}).

23. Although in both table 3.7 and table 3.8 (below) the mean female percentile is highest in the United States, there are a few instances in which the gap effect is negative. This reflects (1) our use of the whole distribution in computing the percentiles and the gap effects that can result in such inconsistencies and (2) our use of alternative specifications for the U.S. wage regression to compare the United States to countries for which we were not able to include the same industry, occupation, or union status variables, which occasionally resulted in a slightly lower percentile for the United States than for the country in question.

Table 3.7   Analysis of Log Wages (YFULL): All Workers

Country	D^a	Female Residual	Mean Female Residual Percentile[b]	Male Residual S.D.	Female Residual S.D.	$D_i - D_{USA}$
Australia	.3100	−.2386	36.8	.5998	.6811	−.0956
Austria	.3002	−.2739	30.4	.3967	.4450	−.1014
Germany	.3437	−.2939	30.5	.3774	.4903	−.0579
Hungary	.4379	−.4115	21.2	.3905	.3667	.0252
Italy	.1946	−.1653	37.3	.3811	.4375	−.1737
Norway	.3371	−.3070	29.5	.4101	.5120	−.0645
Sweden	.2582	−.1985	36.2	.4231	.4551	−.1434
Switzerland	.4377	−.2233	35.1	.4048	.5260	.0361
United Kingdom	.4889	−.3904	24.1	.4084	.4379	.0873
United States	.4016	−.2777	37.3	.6717	.7725	. . .

	Observed X's	Observed Prices	Gap	Unobserved Prices	Sum Gender Specific[c]	Sum Wage Structure[d]
Australia	.0595	−.0737	−.0410	−.0404	.0185	−.1141
Austria	.0679	−.1655	.2283	−.2321	.2962	−.3976
Germany	.0351	−.1091	.2538	−.2376	.2889	−.3467
Hungary	−.0257	−.0351	.5827	−.4967	.5570	−.5318
Italy	.0111	−.0434	−.0133	−.1282	−.0022	−.1716
Norway	.0062	−.0999	.2445	−.2152	.2507	−.3151
Sweden	−.0236	−.0406	.0203	−.0995	−.0033	−.1401
Switzerland	.1008	−.0102	.0020	−.0564	.1028	−.0666
United Kingdom	.0261	−.0514	.4200	−.3073	.4461	−.3587

Note: Regressions include controls for education, potential experience and its square, union status, and occupation and industry dummy variables. The U.S. value used to calculate $D_i - D_{USA}$ for Hungary, Australia, and Italy is based on hours corrections from U.S. regressions that conform to the specifications for each of those countries. However, the U.S. value in the D column is based on the more detailed specification permitted by the ISSP and CSCC data files.

[a]The gender difference in YFULL, earnings evaluated at full-time (forty) hours (see eq. [2]).

[b]The mean female residual percentile in the male distribution of wage residuals.

[c]The sum of the observed X's and gap effects.

[d]The sum of the observed and unobserved prices effects.

U.S. level of inequality (reflected in the sum of observed prices and unobserved prices effects) greatly raises its gender pay gap compared to each of the other countries in the sample. This inequality effect is sufficient or more than sufficient to account for the higher pay gap in the United States than in the six countries with the smaller gaps.

The conclusions for married women (table 3.8) are similar to those for all workers. U.S. women again have the highest percentile ranking, yet the pay gap is larger in the United States than in all the other countries except the United Kingdom.[24] We again find that the U.S. level of inequality raises its

24. Marital status is not available for Italy.

Table 3.8   **Analysis of Log Wages (YFULL): Married Workers**

Country	D^a	Female Residual	Mean Female Residual Percentile[b]	Male Residual S.D.	Female Residual S.D.	$D_i - D_{USA}$
Australia	.4091	−.3629	28.7	.5480	.6887	−.1621
Austria	.4255	−.3966	23.9	.4047	.4751	−.1427
Germany	.5068	−.4817	18.8	.3280	.5225	−.0614
Hungary	.4964	−.4462	18.8	.3811	.3703	−.0700
Norway	.3881	−.3435	25.6	.3735	.5033	−.1801
Sweden	.2839	−.2536	30.2	.3537	.4152	−.2843
United Kingdom	.5789	−.4587	21.0	.3931	.4510	.0107
United States	.5682	−.4650	30.4	.6062	.8450	. . .

	Observed X's	Observed Prices	Gap	Unobserved Prices	Sum Gender Specific[c]	Sum Wage Structure[d]
Australia	.0513	−.0578	−.0958	−.0598	−.0445	−.1176
Austria	.0509	−.1251	.2142	−.2826	.2651	−.4077
Germany	.0145	−.0924	.4740	−.4573	.4885	−.5497
Hungary	−.0281	−.0168	.4997	−.5248	.4716	−.5416
Norway	−.0102	−.0483	.1129	−.2344	.1027	−.2827
Sweden	−.0307	−.0422	−.0279	−.1835	−.0586	−.2257
United Kingdom	.0040	.0130	.3170	−.3233	.3210	−.3103

Note: Regressions include controls for education, potential experience and its square, union status, and occupation and industry dummy variables. The U.S. value used to calculate $D_i - D_{USA}$ for Hungary, Australia, and Italy is based on hours corrections from U.S. regressions that conform to the specifications for each of those countries. However, the U.S. value in the D column is based on the more detailed specification permitted by the ISSP and CSCC data files.

[a]The gender difference in YFULL, earnings evaluated at full-time (forty) hours (see eq. [2]).
[b]The mean-female residual percentile in the male distribution of wage residuals.
[c]The sum of the observed X's and gap effects.
[d]The sum of the observed and unobserved prices effects.

pay gap while gender-specific factors usually lower it. With the exception of Australia and Sweden, higher U.S. inequality (i.e., wage structure) is sufficient or more than sufficient to explain the higher pay gap in the United States compared to the countries with smaller differentials. In the case of Australia and Sweden, U.S. inequality accounts for 72–79 percent of the difference in the married worker pay gap. One interpretation of the moderate difference between these results and the results for all workers (where inequality accounted for 100 percent of the cross-country difference) is that the types of gender-related interventions in Sweden and Australia (discussed above) have had a disproportionate effect on married workers. Parental leave (Sweden) and comparable worth (Australia) may have especially large positive effects on the relative earnings of married women.

An additional point of interest is that, in both tables 3.7 and 3.8, the residual standard deviation of the wage regressions is considerably higher for U.S. men and women than for men and women in other countries (the female residual standard deviation is computed from a female wage regression). Across all the countries in the sample, the correlation coefficient between the male and the female standard deviations is .9344. The fact that the male and female standard deviations seem to move together in this manner adds credibility to our framework in which a country's overall level of inequality is assumed to affect both men and women.[25] Other than the United States, the residual standard deviation is higher for Australia than for the other countries. This occurs despite the Australian tradition of administered wages. This suggests that actual earnings may deviate from award levels, which are intended to be the minimum rates.[26]

The striking finding of tables 3.7 and 3.8 is the importance of wage structure in explaining international differences in the gender gap. However, as noted earlier, what we have labeled *wage inequality* could also reflect the effect of labor market discrimination. What are we thus to conclude about labor market structure? From a number of indirect indicators, we conclude that it is important, even though it may not be possible to estimate its effect precisely.

First, our review of wage-setting institutions in each country strongly suggests that the U.S. system is considerably less centralized than those in other countries, thus making a finding of the importance of wage structure plausible. Second, the United States has had a longer and often stronger commitment to equal pay and equal employment opportunity policies than most other countries in our sample.[27] Further, U.S. women compare favorably to women in other countries in terms of their qualifications and occupational status relative to men. Thus, it is credible that gender-specific factors do not explain the relatively high pay gap in the United States. Third, we found that residual wage variation (and, in results not shown, wage variation) of both men and women in the United States considerably exceeds that of the same gender group in other countries. Similarly, across all countries, female and male wage and residual wage variation were found to be highly correlated. This suggests that the same set of factors—measured and unmeasured prices and wage-setting institutions—affects the wages of both men and women in each country in a similar way. Finally, and perhaps most important, even though the estimated wage inequality effect may include the effect of gender discrimination as it interacts with wage structure, our findings nonetheless suggest an extremely important role for wage inequality in affecting the gender ratio.

25. The standard deviation of gross hours corrected earnings (YFULL) is also higher in the United States than elsewhere (results not shown). Similarly, across all countries, the correlation of the male and female standard deviations is .9647.

26. According to Watts and Mitchell (1990), the Australian wage award system allows for considerable variability in actual earnings. Such variations can be achieved by promotions. In the 1980s, the dispersion in actual earnings appeared to increase, despite the imposition of awards with uniform percentage wage increases.

27. A primary exception is the comparable worth approach pursued in Australia, which might be expected to produce a larger immediate effect on wages.

3.4 Swimming Upstream: U.S. Women and the Male Wage Distribution, 1971–88

Figure 3.1 above shows that, in the 1980s, the gender pay gap in the United States narrowed considerably, following a long period of relative stability. In addition, as noted above, labor market inequality has been increasing in the United States in recent years. The analysis reported above indicated that the high level of U.S. wage inequality has raised its gender pay gap compared to that in other countries. This finding, in conjunction with these time-series features of the U.S. labor market, implies that U.S. women have been swimming against a current of rising inequality. The falling gender gap in the United States becomes even more impressive in light of these recent trends.

To provide some evidence on the degree to which growing inequality has retarded the progress of women's relative pay in the United States, we have included some analyses of wages from the period 1971–88. Specifically, we have examined the log of real weekly wages for full-time workers using data from the 1972, 1982, and 1989 Current Population Surveys. This information refers to earnings in 1971, 1981, and 1988, respectively. Earnings are expressed in 1981 dollars using the consumer price index.

Trends in the pay gap and in the wage distribution for these years are described in the upper panel of table 3.9. During this time, women moved steadily up the distribution of male wages, from an average percentile of 19.53 in 1971 to a figure of 30.41 for 1988;[28] the pace of this upward movement increased in the 1980s. The gender pay differential also fell during both the 1971–81 and the 1981–88 periods, with some acceleration after 1981. (Figure 3.1 shows similar trends.) The declining gender gap reflected a combination of falling male and rising female real wages over the period 1971–88.

Table 3.9 also indicates that the standard deviations of the log of female and the log of male real earnings both rose in the 1980s; from 1971 to 1981, however, only male variability increased. Katz and Murphy (1992) found similar male and female patterns for changes in overall wage inequality. Such results could imply that the wage structure widened for both men and women in the 1980s but only for men in the 1970s, calling into question (at least for the 1970s) our approach based on male inequality. However, changes in the variation in log wages are not the same as changes in the wage structure since the former can be affected by changes in the distribution of productive characteristics as well as in skill prices. Katz and Murphy (1992) in fact found that *residual* wage inequality rose steadily and at similar rates for both men and women in both the 1970s and the 1980s. These findings do suggest that similar pro-

---

28. This latter figure is roughly similar to our results for gross hours corrected earnings from the ISSP (33.2) given in figure 3.3 above, providing further confirmation of the ISSP's representativeness.

Table 3.9   **Analysis of Log Real Weekly Wages for Full-Time Workers, United States, 1971–88 (1981 dollars)**

	1971	1981	1988
Mean-female percentile in male distribution	19.53	24.06	30.41
Ln(wage):			
Males	5.9800	5.8857	5.9003
	(.5123)	(.5493)	(.5891)
Females	5.4360	5.4148	5.5298
	(.4754)	(.4773)	(.5354)
Differential	.5440	.4709	.3705

	Decomposition of Changes		
	Total Change in ln(wage)	Due to Change in Female Percentile	Due to Change in Male Inequality
1971–81	−.0731	−.1143	.0412
1981–88	−.1004	−.1251	.0247
1971–88	−.1735	−.2301	.0566

cesses were at work for both men and women in the United States during this period.[29]

The lower panel of table 3.9 provides a decomposition of changes in the pay gap into portions due to women's movement up the male distribution and portions due to changes in male inequality. The stories for the two subperiods are similar: had the overall degree of inequality not risen, the pay gap would have closed faster than it in fact did. Taking the period 1971–88 as a whole, had male inequality stayed at its 1971 level but women's relative qualifications and/ or treatment improved at their actual rates, then the pay gap would have fallen by .2301 log points. Since the actual fall in the pay gap was .1735 log points, our figures imply that growing inequality in the 1970s and 1980s reduced the convergence in the pay gap by .0566 log points (or about one-fourth—24.6 percent—of the potential decline in the pay gap). The retarding effect of increasing inequality on female gains is also illustrated in figure 3.4, where we see that, had male wage inequality remained at its 1971 level, the gender ratio would have increased from 58.0 percent in 1971 to 73.1 percent in 1988, 4 percentage points higher than the actual 1988 ratio of 69.0 percent.

The results for the U.S. trends imply a moderate but noticeable effect of rising inequality in slowing the convergence in women's relative pay. It is noteworthy that the inequality effect is smaller in table 3.9 than it is in tables 3.7

29. Since in their study of male wage inequality Juhn, Murphy, and Pierce (1993) found that residual inequality grew within as well as between cohorts, they interpret the increase as being due to a rise in skill prices rather than to an increase in the variance of unobserved productivity characteristics.

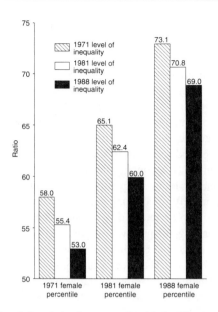

Fig. 3.4 Simulated female/male pay ratios: United States, 1971–88 (%)

and 3.8. That is, the higher U.S. level of inequality compared to other countries has a larger effect on intercountry differences in the gender pay gap than changes in U.S. inequality over time have had on U.S. trends in the pay gap. While there have been major recent changes in the U.S. wage structure, cross-sectional differences between the United States and other countries are even more dramatic.

3.5   Conclusions

In this paper, we have used micro data to examine the gender pay gap in ten industrialized countries. Published data indicate that the gender gap is higher in the United States than in most industrialized countries; and it is higher than in six of the countries in our sample. The striking finding of the paper is the importance of wage structure in explaining the higher U.S. gender gap. The greater level of wage inequality in the United States than elsewhere works to increase the gender differential in the United States relative to all the other countries in our sample. Our results suggest that the U.S. gap would be similar to that in countries like Sweden, Italy, and Australia (the countries with the smallest gaps) if the United States had their level of wage inequality. This suggests that we need to focus both on the supply of and demand for skills (i.e., some of the determinants of skill prices) and on wage-setting institutions to explain this important cause of international differences in the gender pay gap. In a brief review of the institutional setting in each of these countries, we concluded that the wage-determination process in the United States is more decentralized than elsewhere, quite likely contributing to its higher level of wage inequality.

Much attention has been focused on women's growing relative levels of skills and labor force commitment as causes of changes in the pay gap. Our research suggests that, to understand changes in the gender pay gap fully, it would also be fruitful to examine the effect of changes in wage structure. As a preliminary step in that direction, we examined male and female trends in real weekly wages for the period 1971–88 in the United States to determine the degree to which growing U.S. inequality has retarded the growth of women's relative wages. In the face of rising inequality, women's relative skills and treatment have to improve merely for the pay gap to remain constant; still larger gains are necessary for it to be reduced. We found that women were able to counter the effects of rising inequality on their relative earnings through a steady increase in their percentile ranking in the male wage distribution, from 19.53 in 1971 to 30.41 in 1988. The pace of this upward movement quickened in the 1980s, as did the increase in women's relative wages. Our results indicate that increasing inequality reduced women's potential gains in relative pay by about one-quarter during the period 1971–88.

Appendix
Variable Definitions, Means, and Earnings Regression Results by Country

Definitions of the explanatory variables are given in table 3A.1. The earnings definitions for each country are listed below:

Austria. Net monthly income from employment.

Germany and Switzerland. Net income per month after taxes and social insurance.

Italy. Annual labor income.

Britain. Total annual earnings before taxes.

United States. Previous year's earnings from occupation before taxes.

Hungary. Monthly earnings.

Sweden. Income (from all sources) in previous year.

Norway. Annual income from all jobs.

Australia. Annual earnings from all jobs.

Table 3A.1   Definitions of Explanatory Variables

EDUC = years of schooling completed
PEXP = age − EDUC − 6
PEXPSQ = EXP^2
UNION = dummy variable for union membership

Table 3A.1   (continued)

Occupation dummy variable
PROF = professional and technical workers (the omitted category)
MGR = managers, except farm
CLER = clerical workers
SALES = sales workers
CRAFT = craft workers
OPER = operatives
LAB = laborers, except farm
SERVWK = service workers
FARMMGR = farm managers
FARMLAB = farm laborers

Industry dummy variables
AG = agriculture, forestry, and fisheries
MICON = mining and construction
MANDUR = durable goods manufacturing
MANNON = nondurable goods manufacturing
TRANS = transportation, communications, and utilities
WTRADE = wholesale trade
RTRADE = retail trade
FIRE = finance, insurance, and real estate
SERVS = services
GOVT = government (the omitted category)

Industry dummy variables for Hungary
AG (see above)
MINMAN = mining and manufacturing
CONST = construction
TRANS (see above)
TRADE = wholesale and retail trade
SERVS = services, finance, insurance and real estate
GOVT (see above), the omitted category

Occupation dummy variables for Australia
MGR = managers and farm managers
CLER, CRAFT, and OPER (see above)
LAB = laborers and farm laborers
SALESW = sales and service workers
PROF (see above), the omitted category

Industry dummy variables for Australia
AG, TRANS, MINCON (see above)
MANUF = manufacturing
TRADE = wholesale and retail trade
FISERV = finance, insurance, real estate, and services
GOVT (see above), the omitted category

Occupation dummy variables for Italy
BLUE = blue collar
WHITELOW = lower-level white collar
WHITEHI = higher-level white collar, the omitted category

Industry dummy variables for Italy
AG, TRANS, TRADE (see above)
IND = mining, construction, and manufacturing
FIRE, GOVT (see above)
SERVS (see above), the omitted category

Table 3A.2a Means of Explanatory Variables

	Germany		United Kingdom		United States		Austria		Switzerland		Sweden		Norway	
	Men	Women	Men	Women	Men	Women	Men	Women	Men	Women	Men	Women	Men	Women
PART	.017	.346	.037	.449	.115	.244	.022	.282	.023	.252	.053	.456	.070	.525
HPART	.437	7.619	.892	9.233	2.626	5.268	.514	6.284	.585	6.252	1.300	10.526	1.624	10.737
HFULL	44.308	28.212	43.664	21.604	42.459	33.487	45.531	31.502	47.335	33.367	41.151	22.138	41.386	19.280
EDYRS	10.205	10.400	11.291	11.331	13.383	13.265	11.089	10.911	11.335	10.565	10.236	10.460	11.256	10.950
PEXP	22.939	19.613	21.817	20.628	18.843	18.962	20.712	19.138	23.134	18.565	22.746	22.419	22.267	21.473
PEXPSQ	676.298	523.591	642.187	576.875	497.025	513.662	580.379	521.858	664.526	503.707	694.397	685.044	659.995	617.569
UNION	.349	.180	.471	.396	.205	.125	.542	.349	.433	.265	.786	.796	.599	.595
MGR	.104	.069	.157	.066	.187	.141	.145	.062	.180	.095	.055	.018	.102	.039
CLER	.092	.272	.072	.327	.055	.259	.134	.298	.116	.293	.063	.198	.088	.237
SALES	.049	.119	.046	.077	.061	.054	.042	.078	.054	.061	.061	.093	.070	.095
CRAFT	.351	.059	.292	.081	.206	.028	.308	.073	.183	.014	.197	.021	.220	.017
OPER	.095	.015	.119	.032	.124	.071	.101	.037	.090	.027	.269	.087	.190	.060
LAB	.013	.019	.051	.008	.059	.009	.047	.028	.021	.020	.050	.006	.017	.012
SERVWK	.057	.134	.060	.191	.081	.208	.061	.183	.052	.075	.072	.321	.052	.191
FARMMGR	.024	.011	.005	.001	.019	.003	.042	.046	.018	.014	.020	.000	.038	.008
FARMLAB	.009	.007	.005	.003	.009	.002	.014	.014	.003	.007	.009	.006	.010	.008
AG	.031	.021	.015	.007	.041	.013	.056	.050	.031	.020	.048	.006	.056	.019
MICON	.121	.018	.118	.011	.119	.013	.128	.034	.103	.014	.127	.021	.118	.014
MANDUR	.244	.094	.195	.072	.151	.064	.235	.096	.188	.088	.225	.069	.207	.081
MANNON	.111	.098	.129	.107	.092	.066	.103	.147	.152	.129	.094	.084	.034	.056
TRANS	.056	.011	.104	.032	.086	.035	.076	.014	.070	.034	.138	.051	.125	.021
WTRADE	.023	.030	.044	.029	.046	.018	.030	.041	.003	.020	.037	.012	.047	.031
RTRADE	.043	.153	.073	.181	.115	.174	.058	.103	.000	.000	.039	.102	.053	.104
FIRE	.050	.051	.051	.054	.052	.083	.042	.050	.088	.054	.015	.018	.047	.044
SERVS	.089	.248	.202	.439	.218	.471	.112	.317	.111	.122	.230	.565	.299	.606

Table 3A.2b   **Mean of Explanatory Variables**

	Australia		Hungary		Italy	
	Men	Women	Men	Women	Men	Women
PART	.046	.374	. . .	. . .	.057	.261
HPART	.929	7.031	. . .	. . .	1.318	5.733
HFULL	42.370	25.865	. . .	. . .	39.163	29.515
EDYRS	11.010	11.189	11.406	11.026	9.820	11.017
PEXP	19.388	17.161	19.765	19.971	23.917	19.664
PEXPSQ	519.751	431.540	524.690	530.290	732.306	532.517
UNION	. . .	. . .	.636	.762	. . .	. . .
MGR	.114	.030	.059	.051	. . .	. . .
CLER	.093	.348	.072	.242	. . .	. . .
SALESW	.078	.198	.012	.039	. . .	. . .
CRAFT	.241	.038	.252	.080	. . .	. . .
OPER	.116	.033	.270	.076	. . .	. . .
LAB	.157	.149	.110	.179	. . .	. . .
BLUE	. . .	. . .	. . .	. . .	.514	.384
WHITELOW	. . .	. . .	. . .	. . .	.433	.606
SERVWK	. . .	. . .	.041	.107	. . .	. . .
FARMMGR	. . .	. . .	.012	.003	. . .	. . .
FARMLAB	. . .	. . .	.058	.032	. . .	. . .
AG	.034	.013	.233	.132	.034	.035
MICON	.104	.018	. . .	. . .	. . .	. . .
MANUF	.215	.113	. . .	. . .	. . .	. . .
TRANS	.146	.046	.111	.056	.116	.162
TRADE	.163	.194	.042	.116	.112	.035
FISERV	.257	.556	. . .	. . .	. . .	. . .
IND	. . .	. . .	. . .	. . .	.392	.186
FIRE	. . .	. . .	. . .	. . .	.040	.039
GOVT	. . .	. . .	. . .	. . .	.144	.131
MINMAN	. . .	. . .	.316	.280	. . .	. . .
CONST	. . .	. . .	.092	.048	. . .	. . .
SERVS	. . .	. . .	.147	.320	. . .	. . .

Table 3A.3   **Coefficients from Regression Analysis of ln EARN**

| | Germany | | | | United Kingdom | | | |
| | Men | | Women | | Men | | Women | |
Variable	Coeff.	S.E.	Coeff.	S.E.	Coeff.	S.E.	Coeff.	S.E.
INTERCEP	6.0688	.0912	6.3533	.1780	8.0856	.1508	7.7343	.2127
PART	−.5261	.2609	−1.1741	.1773	−1.3979	.2071	−1.8227	.1557
HPART	.0256	.0094	.0358	.0053	.0491	.0078	.0579	.0029
HFULL	.0107	.0013	.0027	.0029	.0045	.0012	.0042	.0035
EDYRS	.0478	.0042	.0535	.0089	.0700	.0096	.0928	.0112
PEXP	.0686	.0032	.0480	.0058	.0529	.0033	.0145	.0040
PEXPSQ	−.0011	.0001	−.0009	.0001	−.0010	.0001	−.0002	.0001
UNION	.0250	.0213	.1033	.0451	.0515	.0236	.0707	.0290
MGR	.0555	.0382	.1125	.0744	.1101	.0397	−.0875	.0623
CLER	−.1775	.0445	−.0363	.0509	−.3158	.0505	−.2251	.0430
SALES	.0277	.0523	−.1492	.0727	−.0606	.0597	−.3541	.0665
CRAFT	−.1860	.0323	−.2051	.0895	−.2253	.0373	−.4172	.0680
OPER	−.2417	.0421	−.0612	.1521	−.3488	.0456	−.5156	.0893
LAB	−.5462	.0908	−.2836	.1307	−.4431	.0577	−.2227	.1524
SERVWK	−.1020	.0481	−.2497	.0620	−.2678	.0535	−.4489	.0467
FARMMGR	−.1357	.1695	−.7794	.2792	−.0177	.1726	−.8178	.4971
FARMLAB	−.2572	.1547	−.2342	.2505	−.3512	.1880	−.6753	.2757
AG	−.2911	.1600	−.0674	.2176	−.2860	.1256	−.1540	.2187
MICON	−.0050	.0384	.0214	.1311	.0208	.0546	.1342	.1323
MANDUR	.0524	.0311	−.0224	.0709	−.0594	.0498	.0971	.0736
MANNON	.0353	.0374	−.1834	.0736	.0077	.0525	.0281	.0701
TRANS	.0676	.0474	.1702	.1618	−.0138	.0548	.1142	.0860
WTRADE	−.0608	.0672	−.0903	.1042	−.0411	.0689	.1811	.0914
RTRADE	−.0994	.0536	−.1338	.0662	−.3327	.0598	−.1362	.0646
FIRE	.1061	.0547	.0097	.0874	.1424	.0643	.0463	.0738
SERVS	−.0300	.0393	−.0808	.0511	−.1782	.0483	−.0674	.0560
SEE	.3774		.4903		.4084		.4379	
R^2	.4582		.3526		.4016		.6521	
Sample size	1,592		874		1,477		1,204	

| | United States | | | | Austria | | | |
| | Men | | Women | | Men | | Women | |
Variable	Coeff.	S.E.	Coeff.	S.E.	Coeff.	S.E.	Coeff.	S.E.
INTERCEP	8.2375	.1770	8.1492	.2507	8.8191	.1507	8.5387	.2357
PART	−.7413	.1763	−1.6344	.1843	−1.4062	.4051	−1.3813	.2189
HPART	.0238	.0062	.0421	.0056	.0549	.0162	.0375	.0067
HFULL	.0085	.0018	.0050	.0029	.0054	.0018	−.0029	.0034
EDYRS	.0695	.0080	.0810	.0117	.0187	.0080	.0484	.0124
PEXP	.0534	.0055	.0333	.0066	.0342	.0053	.0301	.0066
PEXPSQ	−.0008	.0001	−.0004	.0001	−.0005	.0001	−.0005	.0001
UNION	.2222	.0469	.1344	.0704	.0789	.0354	.0761	.0492
MGR	.0757	.0642	.0927	.0838	−.0908	.0755	−.1068	.1151
CLER	−.3257	.0908	−.1161	.0748	−.2499	.0747	−.0954	.0754

Table 3A.3   (continued)

Variable	United States Men Coeff.	S.E.	United States Women Coeff.	S.E.	Austria Men Coeff.	S.E.	Austria Women Coeff.	S.E.
SALES	−.0660	.0917	−.5432	.1189	−.2707	.1085	−.1729	.1159
CRAFT	−.1738	.0681	−.1290	.1575	−.2919	.0668	−.3829	.1136
OPER	−.3292	.0780	−.2162	.1259	−.3266	.0800	−.2741	.1462
LAB	−.5927	.0952	−.5162	.2501	−.3842	.0959	−.3099	.1505
SERVWK	−.3620	.0838	−.4565	.0804	−.2849	.0839	−.3055	.0791
FARMMGR	−.4261	.2119	.4187	.4612	−.7096	.1633	−.6664	.2803
FARMLAB	−.5874	.2447	−.9051	.5658	−.4406	.1587	−.4234	.2150
AG	.1102	.1743	−.5273	.2605	−.0389	.1388	−.0132	.2601
MICON	−.1844	.0884	−.3026	.2211	.0493	.0649	−.1102	.1338
MANDUR	.0177	.0828	.0655	.1378	−.0275	.0588	.0764	.0972
MANNON	−.0550	.0898	−.2454	.1371	.0299	.0667	−.0295	.0975
TRANS	.0403	.0914	.1340	.1507	−.0171	.0734	.0940	.1939
WTRADE	−.2941	.1103	−.2987	.1933	.2073	.1069	.1628	.1249
RTRADE	−.3025	.0864	−.3796	.1089	−.1369	.0894	.0098	.1026
FIRE	.0399	.1056	−.0377	.1214	.2223	.0937	.1295	.1151
SERVS	−.2801	.0759	−.2486	.0973	−.0078	.0683	.0330	.0705
SEE	.6717		.7725		.3967		.4450	
R^2	.3808		.4206		.2883		.3754	
Sample size	1,406		1,194		642		436	

Variable	Switzerland Men Coeff.	S.E.	Switzerland Women Coeff.	S.E.	Sweden Men Coeff.	S.E.	Sweden Women Coeff.	S.E.
INTERCEP	6.2999	.1917	6.2689	.5978	9.4122	.2359	9.6928	.5082
PART	.0939	.5455	−2.1373	.6649	−.7021	.3539	−1.1591	.4648
HPART	−.0008	.0203	.0665	.0164	.0198	.0129	.0307	.0061
HFULL	.0082	.0028	.0021	.0117	.0047	.0028	.0011	.0106
EDYRS	.0548	.0067	.0736	.0172	.0434	.0098	.0426	.0116
PEXP	.0719	.0076	.0543	.0155	.0674	.0063	.0297	.0082
PEXPSQ	−.0010	.0001	−.0008	.0003	−.0010	.0001	−.0004	.0002
UNION	.0292	.0440	.1327	.1135	.1856	.0575	.2828	.0701
MGR	.1735	.0673	−.0985	.1800	.1813	.1060	.2228	.2065
CLER	−.0448	.0831	−.0022	.1503	−.0589	.0980	.0820	.0959
SALES	−.1387	.1082	−.3101	.2676	.0591	.1356	−.0116	.1649
CRAFT	−.2318	.0739	−.1221	.4239	−.0151	.0786	−.1128	.2179
OPER	−.1631	.0921	−.1092	.3465	−.1832	.0750	.1938	.1467
LAB	−.2081	.1578	−.1627	.3438	−.1149	.1272	.0597	.3691
SERVWK	−.2955	.1146	−.3821	.2029	−.2598	.0980	−.0610	.0887
FARMMGR	−1.0129	.2748	−.2577	.7095	−.5679	.2391	.0000	.0000
FARMLAB	.0150	.4585	.1439	.5670	−.1725	.2900	−.5875	.3538
AG	−.0096	.2132	−.2208	.5417	.2624	.1842	.0000	.0000
MICON	.0720	.0823	.2963	.4067	.1777	.1182	.3277	.2192
MANDUR	.1055	.0706	.1037	.1809	.1746	.1123	−.0218	.1572

(*continued*)

Table 3A.3   (continued)

	United States				Austria			
	Men		Women		Men		Women	
Variable	Coeff.	S.E.	Coeff.	S.E.	Coeff.	S.E.	Coeff.	S.E.
MANNON	.0478	.0736	−.0111	.1906	.1167	.1225	−.1237	.1481
TRANS	−.0187	.0986	.4299	.2779	.1508	.1147	.0280	.1517
WTRADE	−.2745	.4206	.3203	.3443	.1869	.1530	.0207	.2764
RTRADE	.0000	.0000	.0000	.0000	.0322	.1748	−.0353	.1762
FIRE	.2721	.0874	.2463	.2221	.5201	.1931	.2367	.2120
SERVS	.0625	.0801	.3602	.1649	.1146	.1065	−.0171	.1109
SEE	.4049		.5236		.4231		.4551	
R^2	.5341		.4294		.4240		.4257	
Sample size	388		147		457		333	

	Norway					Australia			
	Men		Women			Men		Women	
Variable	Coeff.	S.E.	Coeff.	S.E.	Variable	Coeff.	S.E.	Coeff.	S.E.
INTERCEP	10.2470	.1844	11.1202	.3962	INTERCEP	8.9394	.0958	8.8661	.1631
PART	−1.5105	.1818	−2.0945	.3370	PART	−1.5624	.1153	−1.6534	.1397
HPART	.0536	.0066	.0529	.0046	HPART	.0388	.0042	.0472	.0024
HFULL	.0052	.0016	−.0095	.0078	HFULL	.0019	.0014	.0028	.0031
EDYRS	.0453	.0070	.0385	.0119	EDYRS	.0452	.0046	.0410	.0058
PEXP	.0531	.0048	.0099	.0072	PEXP	.0579	.0028	.0295	.0038
PEXPSQ	−.0008	.0001	−.0001	.0001	PEXPSQ	−.0010	.0001	−.0004	.0001
UNION	.0648	.0331	.2091	.0499	UNION	−.0149	.0362	−.1992	.0805
MGR	.0465	.0592	−.0028	.1238	MGR	−.1389	.0380	−.1506	.0410
CLER	−.0051	.0620	−.0582	.0723	CLER	−.1999	.0416	−.2987	.0478
SALES	.0073	.0784	.0232	.1311	SALESW	−.2205	.0328	−.3468	.0742
CRAFT	−.0630	.0552	−.1612	.1977	CRAFT	−.1485	.0394	−.3662	.0862
OPER	−.1419	.0607	−.2354	.1329	OPER	−.2629	.0364	−.4735	.0518
LAB	−.1307	.1281	.0766	.2741	LAB	−.8151	.0595	−.5734	.1231
SERVWK	.0094	.0752	−.2786	.0764	AG	−.0603	.0429	.1726	.1056
FARMMGR	−.5140	.1725	2.1019	.5204	MICON	−.0831	.0376	.0488	.0661
FARMLAB	−.7038	.2001	1.0246	.5229	MANUF	−.0072	.0393	.0739	.0775
AG	.3971	.1934	−1.5774	.4789	TRANS	−.2151	.0400	−.0734	.0610
MICON	−.0478	.1311	−.3251	.2456	TRADE	−.2083	.0366	−.0115	.0544
MANDUR	−.0037	.1273	−.1261	.1755	FISERV				
MANNON	−.2243	.1476	−.2625	.1919					
TRANS	−.0315	.1303	.2525	.2193					
WTRADE	.1342	.1421	−.2353	.1989					
RTRADE	−.0375	.1434	−.3269	.1830					
FIRE	.1425	.1383	−.0611	.1834					
SERVS	−.1339	.1242	−.1704	.1600					
SEE	.4101		.5120			.5998		.6811	
R^2	.4139		.5101			.3135		.4318	
Sample size	832		518			4,556		3,003	

Table 3A.3   (continued)

| | Hungary | | | | | Italy | | | |
| | Men | | Women | | | Men | | Women | |
Variable	Coeff.	S.E.	Coeff.	S.E.	Variable	Coeff.	S.E.	Coeff.	S.E.
INTERCEP	8.1770	.0830	7.7577	.0807	INTERCEP	8.7303	.0783	8.7173	.1579
EDYRS	.0375	.0036	.0463	.0039	PART	−.4825	.1064	−.8566	.1268
PEXP	.0329	.0030	.0319	.0028	HPART	.0205	.0039	.0207	.0030
PEXPSQ	−.0006	.0001	−.0005	.0001	HFULL	.0082	.0012	.0005	.0027
UNION	.0115	.0212	.1027	.0225	ED	.0395	.0022	.0525	.0034
MGR	.0552	.0475	−.1281	.0466	EXP	.0457	.0019	.0377	.0027
CLER	−.1546	.0451	−.1851	.0293	EXPSQ	−.0007	.0000	−.0005	.0001
SALES	−.3007	.0961	−.3734	.0578	BLUE	−.5476	.0330	−.4142	.0950
CRAFT	−.0550	.0358	−.2164	.0419	WHITELOW	−.3783	.0294	−.2420	.0910
OPER	−.0717	.0374	−.1305	.0420	AG	−.1392	.0363	−.6666	.0523
LAB	−.1076	.0453	−.2507	.0357	IND	.0579	.0196	.0102	.0282
SERVWK	−.0977	.0558	−.1862	.0378	TRADE	.0578	.0245	.0299	.0287
FARMMGR	−.0564	.0904	−.8869	.1567	TRANS	.1081	.0243	.0420	.0504
FARMLAB	−.1442	.0545	−.3435	.0630	FIRE	.2218	.0338	.1546	.0481
AG	−.0517	.0455	.0054	.0495	GOVT	−.0162	.0228	−.0415	.0299
MINMAN	.0536	.0428	−.0593	.0439					
CONST	−.0230	.0496	−.0012	.0560					
TRANS	−.0735	.0490	.0197	.0538					
TRADE	−.1243	.0630	−.0216	.0506					
SERVS	.0264	.0447	−.1825	.0427					
SEE	.3905		.3668			.3811		.4375	
R^2	.2059		.2819			.3995		.3741	
Sample size	1,876		1,835			4,152		2,480	

References

Bean, Ron, and Ken Holden. 1992. Cross-national differences in trade union membership in OECD countries. *Industrial Relations Journal* 23 (Spring): 52–59.

Beller, Andrea. 1979. The impact of equal employment opportunity laws on the male/
female earnings differential. In *Women in the labor market,* ed. Cynthia B. Lloyd,
Emily Andrews, and Curtis Gilroy. New York: Columbia University Press.

Bergmann, Barbara R. 1974. Occupational segregation, wages and profits when employers discriminate by race or sex. *Eastern Economic Journal* 1 (April–July):
103–10.

Blackburn, McKinley L., and David E. Bloom. 1991. Changes in the structure of family
income inequality in the U.S. and other industrialized nations during the 1980s. University of South Carolina/Columbia University, June. Typescript.

Blanchflower, David, and Richard Freeman. 1992. Unionism in the U.S. and other advanced O.E.C.D. countries. *Industrial Relations* 31 (Winter): 56–79.

Blau, Francine D. 1977. *Equal pay in the office.* Lexington, Mass.: Heath.

Blau, Francine D., and Andrea Beller. 1988. Trends in earnings differentials by gender, 1971–1981. *Industrial and Labor Relations Review* 41 (July): 513–29.

Blau, Francine D., and Marianne Ferber. 1992. *The economics of women, men, and work.* 2d ed. Englewood Cliffs, N.J.: Prentice-Hall.

Davies, Robert J. 1983. Incomes and anti-inflation policy. In *Industrial relations in Britain,* ed. George S. Bain. Oxford: Blackwell.

Ehrenberg, Ronald G. 1989. Commentary. In *Pay equity: Empirical inquiries,* ed. Robert T. Michael, Heidi I. Hartmann, and Brigid O'Farrell. Washington, D.C.: National Academy Press.

Flanagan, Robert J., Lawrence M. Kahn, Robert S. Smith, and Ronald G. Ehrenberg. 1989. *Economics of the employment relationship.* Glenview, Ill.: Scott, Foresman.

Gregory, R. G., and A. E. Daly. 1991. Can economic theory explain why Australian women are so well paid relative to their U.S. counterparts? In *Womens's wages: Stability and changes in six industrialized countries,* ed. Steven L. Willborn. Greenwich, Conn.: JAI.

Groshen, Erica L. 1991. The structure of the female/male wage differential: Is it who you are, what you do, or where you work? *Journal of Human Resources* 26 (Summer): 457–72.

Haavio-Mannila, Elina, and Kaisa Kauppinen. 1992. Women and the welfare state in the Nordic countries. In *Women's work and women's lives: The continuing struggle worldwide,* ed. Hilda Kahne and Janet Giele. Boulder, Colo.: Westview.

Hyland, Stephanie L. 1990. Helping employees with family care. *Monthly Labor Review* 113 (September): 22–26.

International Labour Organisation (ILO). *Conditions of Work Digest.* 1988. Vol. 7, no. 2 (February).

———. Various issues. *Yearbook of Labour Statistics.*

"Italy." 1992. *European Industrial Relations Review* 223 (August): 9–10.

Johnson, George E., and Gary Solon. 1986. Estimates of the direct effects of comparable worth policy. *American Economic Review* 76 (December): 1117–25.

Juhn, Chinhui, Kevin M. Murphy, and Brooks Pierce. 1991. Accounting for the slowdown in black-white wage convergence. In *Workers and their wages,* ed. Marvin H. Kosters. Washington, D.C.: AEI Press.

———. 1993. Wage inequality and the rise in returns to skill. *Journal of Political Economy* 101 (June): 410–42.

Katz, Lawrence F., and Kevin M. Murphy. 1992. Changes in relative wages, 1963–87: Supply and demand factors. *Quarterly Journal of Economics* 107 (February): 35–78.

Kennedy, Thomas. 1982. *European labor relations.* Lexington, Mass.: Heath.

Killingsworth, Mark. 1990. *The economics of comparable worth.* Kalamazoo, Mich.: Upjohn Institute for Employment Research.

Korenman, Sanders, and David Neumark. 1991. Does marriage really make men more productive? *Journal of Human Resources* 26 (Spring): 282–307.

Leion, Anders. 1985. Sweden. In *Industrial relations in Europe,* ed. B. C. Roberts. London: Croom Helm.

Lofstrom, Asa, and Siv Gustafsson. 1991. Policy changes and women's wages in Sweden. In *Womens's wages: Stability and changes in six industrialized countries,* ed. Steven L. Willborn. Greenwich, Conn.: JAI.

Mincer, Jacob, and Solomon Polachek. 1974. Family investments in human capital: Earnings of women. *Journal of Political Economy* 82, no. 2, pt. 2 (March/April): S76–S108.

New industrial relations talks continue. 1990. *European Industrial Relations Review,* no. 192 (January): 7.

O'Neill, June, and Solomon Polachek. 1993. Why the gender gap in wages narrowed in the 1980s. *Journal of Labor Economics* 11 (January): 205–28.

OECD. 1988. *Employment outlook September, 1988*. Paris.

———. Various issues. *Labour Force Statistics.*

Polachek, Solomon. 1990. Trends in male-female wages: Differences between the 1970s and the 1980s. Paper presented at the meeting of the American Economic Association, December.

Reskin, Barbara, et al. 1986. *Women's work, men's work.* Washington, D.C.: National Academy of Sciences.

Rosenfeld, Rachel, and Arne Kalleberg. 1990. A cross-national comparison of the gender gap in income. *American Journal of Sociology* 96 (July): 69–106.

Simona, Ilda. 1985. Switzerland. In *Women workers in fifteen countries,* ed. Jenny Farley. Ithaca, N.Y.: ILR Press.

Sisson, Keith, and William Brown. 1983. Industrial relations in the private sector: Donovan re-visited. In *Industrial relations in Britain,* ed. George S. Bain. Oxford: Blackwell.

Sorensen, Elaine. 1990. The crowding hypothesis and comparable worth issue. *Journal of Human Resources* 25 (Winter): 55–89.

Thorsrud, Einar. 1985. Norway. In *Industrial relations in Europe,* ed. B. C. Roberts. London: Croom Helm.

Tomandl, Theodor, and Karl Fuerboeck. 1986. *Social partnership.* Ithaca, N.Y.: ILR Press.

Treu, T. 1990. Italy. *Bulletin of Comparative Labour Relations* 19:227–50.

U.S. Bureau of Labor Statistics. Various issues. *Handbook of Labor Statistics.* Washington, D.C. U.S. Government Printing Office.

Watts, Martin J., and William J. Mitchell. 1990. The impact of incomes policy on the male inter-industry wage structure. *Journal of Industrial Relations* 32 (September): 353–69.

Wrong, Gale. 1987. Switzerland. *Bulletin of Comparative Labour Relations* 16:183–201.

Zabalza, A., and Z. Tzannatos. 1985. The effect of Britain's anti-discriminatory legislation on relative pay and employment. *Economic Journal* 95 (September): 679–99.

4   International Wage Curves

David G. Blanchflower and Andrew J. Oswald

This paper uses international microeconomic data to document the existence of an inverse relation between workers' pay and the local rate of unemployment. This relation, or *wage curve,* is estimated for regions using data for Britain, the United States, Canada, Austria, Italy, Holland, Switzerland, and Norway.[1] Evidence of an equivalent relation is presented for industries[2] using data

David G. Blanchflower is professor of economics at Dartmouth College and a research associate of the National Bureau of Economic Research. He is also a research associate of the Centre for Economic Performance, London School of Economics. Andrew J. Oswald is a senior research fellow at the London School of Economics.

This paper draws on work done for a monograph, *The Wage Curve,* to be published by the MIT Press. Richard Freeman, George Johnson, and Larry Katz provided valuable detailed comments. The authors also received suggestions and help from John Abowd, Fran Blau, John Bauer, David Card, Bob Gregory, Alan Gustman, Bertil Holmlund, Richard Layard, John Schmitt, Dennis Snower, Bob Topel, and Steve Venti. Prakash Loungani and Larry Katz generously provided data on variables suitable for instrumenting U.S. unemployment. This work was supported by the Economic and Social Research Council (Swindon, U.K.).

1. Early British results are reported in Blanchflower and Oswald (1990) and Blanchflower, Oswald, and Garrett (1990), which appeal to a bargaining approach without any explicit regional modeling. The papers give cross-sectional results for various U.K. samples and also one small U.S. sample (although they cannot control fully for regional fixed effects) and attempt to summarize previous writings. One notable early paper in this literature is Blackaby and Manning (1987). These authors' later work on the United Kingdom is contained in Blackaby and Manning (1990). Jackman, Layard, and Savouri (1991) offer an interesting model and, using British regional data, obtain results compatible with those presented here; Blanchflower (1991) provides recent U.K. estimates and finds an unemployment elasticity of approximately -0.1; Christofides and Oswald (1992) also obtain a similar estimate of approximately -0.08 using longitudinal Canadian contract data. A number of other authors have recently tested and found some support for wage curves: these include Edin, Holmlund, and Ostros (1992) for Sweden, Groot, Mekkeholt, and Oosterbeek (1992) for Holland, and Freeman (1990), Katz and Krueger (1991a, 1991b), and Blanchflower and Lynch (1994) for the United States. Topel (1986) also studies wage determination in geographic labor markets but examines effects from variables such as the rate of change of employment rather than from the level of unemployment. Holmlund and Zetterberg (1991) find a role for unemployment in industry wage equations for various countries.

2. There is a related literature using micro data that tests for effects from the aggregate level of unemployment. This includes Bils (1985) and Nickell and Wadhwani (1990). Using PSID and

for Korea and Germany (where lack of regional data prevents the same exercise as for the other nations) and for the United States. The estimates suggest that, on average, the unemployment elasticity of pay is approximately -0.1, which implies that a doubling of unemployment leads to a fall in the level of the wage by 10 percent.[3] The empirical work can be viewed as an attempt to trace out the supply half of the scissors that describes labor market equilibrium.

One way to interpret this paper is to see it as establishing, in an atheoretical way, a statistical fact or "law" about labor markets in many countries. High unemployment within a region or an industry is associated, ceteris paribus, with low wages. The relation between the two takes the form of a convex curve with a negative gradient. This curve's structure seems to be qualitatively, and often quantitatively, the same across countries. For example, the estimated responsiveness of pay to unemployment is similar in the United States and Britain.

The paper's evidence for a wage curve also raises theoretical questions. The original empirical research project began in 1987, as an attempt to apply union bargaining models to British cross-sectional data, and gradually took on an international flavor (as it became clear that the main finding held more generally). The original concern was to go beyond time-series methods in order to provide a cross-sectional approach to the calculation of the unemployment elasticity of pay.

During the years of this project, theoretical macroeconomics has begun to change. A generation of models has sprung up in which a wage curve (in this paper's terminology) is the primary distinguishing feature. The exact history of this research current is discussed in Layard, Nickell, and Jackman (1991) and Phelps (1992). Influential contributions include Shapiro and Stiglitz (1984), Layard and Nickell (1986), and the *Scandinavian Journal of Economics* symposium issue "Unemployment-Inflation Trade-Offs in Europe" (1990). A textbook treatment is contained in Carlin and Soskice (1990). The gist of all this work is that, in the 1980s, "a surrogate employment supply curve, or equilibrium wage curve, was born" (Phelps 1992, 1004). A review by Michael Woodford (1992, 396) describes the new theories succinctly: "All of these imply that labor market equilibrium (ie. a state in which expectations are fulfilled and transacting parties correctly understand the aggregate state of the economy) lies at the intersection of the derived labor demand curve with a surrogate labor supply curve that lies to the left of, and is flatter than, the true Marshallian labor supply curve." A recent overview by Lindbeck (1992) adopts the same approach and uses the assumption that there is a Layard-Nickell "wage-setting curve," different from conventional atomistic supply, that slopes upward in

---

CPS data, Beaudry and DiNardo (1991) argue that wages depend, not on current labor market conditions, but on aggregate and industry unemployment rates in earlier time periods when unemployment was low.

3. The early survey by Oswald (1986) argued that an unemployment elasticity of -0.1 was emerging consistently from different kinds of aggregated and disaggregated evidence.

real-wage/employment space. Another new model in which a central part is played by the same general form of wage equation is the fairness approach described in Akerlof and Yellen (1990).

As Shapiro and Stiglitz (1984) and Layard and Nickell (1986) make clear, the novel aspect of these models is not their assumptions about labor demand, which are the standard ones, but rather that the models replace the conventional labor supply curve with a wage-fixing function. This allows the theories to explain, or at least to be consistent with, both involuntary unemployment and the paradoxical fact that real wages fluctuate little over the cycle while the long-run supply of workers appears to be close to vertical.

There are at least two reasons to predict that high unemployment will tend to lead to low pay. The first is that workers have low bargaining power when surrounded by extreme levels of joblessness. This rationale fits well with union and other bargaining theories and, more generally, with Marxist accounts of the role of the reserve army of the unemployed. The second follows efficiency wage models in stressing the role of unemployment as a motivator. In a booming labor market, firms may have to pay well to ensure that individual workers, who know that there are many other jobs open to them, exert enough effort at work.

Although primarily empirical, the paper's secondary purpose is to write down a multiregion efficiency wage model that is consistent with, and offers a possible conceptual framework for the analysis of, the empirical patterns found in the international data. According to this model, even when workers are free to migrate between regions, the contemporaneous cross-sectional correlation between pay and unemployment will be negative rather than, as is sometimes asserted, positive. Within this framework, the paper's estimated wage curve corresponds to a no-shirking condition of the kind in, for example, Shapiro and Stiglitz (1984).[4]

4.1 Background

Three literatures lie behind the empirical work reported in the paper. The oldest is the extensive research into Phillips curves stemming from Phillips (1958). Although similar in its broad concern with the macroeconomic relation between aggregate joblessness and wage setting, the present paper does not study the rate of wage inflation or purport to uncover a disequilibrium adjustment mechanism. It is probably not usefully thought of as an attempt to estimate quasi Phillips curves. A second and related strand of research is the writings of authors such as Layard and Nickell (1986) and, before them, Sargan ([1964] 1984) who use time-series data to estimate the effect of the aggregate unemployment rate on the aggregate level of wages. The present paper can be

---

4. The theoretical papers by Akerlof and Yellen (1990), Bowles (1985), and Phelps (1990) also contain functions very similar to a wage curve.

seen as an attempt to employ microeconomic data to look for what might be described as a cross-sectional version of this relation. The third literature on which the paper builds is the U.S. work initiated by Harris and Todaro (1970) and Hall (1970, 1972) and continued by Adams (1985), Browne (1978), Marston (1985), and Reza (1978). This helped establish the current conventional wisdom that, by a compensating-differential argument, wages and unemployment are positively correlated across geographic areas. The paper tries to show that some aspects of that conventional wisdom are incorrect.

The paper outlines an efficiency wage model of an economy with multiple regions. This model was developed, after examination of the data, as an attempt to find a theoretical structure that is internally theoretically consistent and fits the statistical facts. The present paper does not, and could not, claim that there exist no other models that might be consistent with the estimated wage curves. Other possibilities may include the standard competitive model, contract theory, search theory, and bargaining models. However, competitive theory does not seem to offer a natural way to explain the patterns in the data because it predicts that unemployment—if defined as a disequilibrium surplus of labor supply over demand—will be positively associated with the level of wages. A competitive interpretation would require that later regressions somehow identify a labor supply curve rather than an unemployment effect on wages, and tests reported in a forthcoming monograph shed doubt on such an interpretation. The explanatory power of labor supply and participation variables, for example, is weak. Labor contract theory and search theory also have difficulty generating the correct prediction of a negative correlation between pay and joblessness. A bargaining framework can give the correct general kind of prediction, although the question of how a multiregion model might be constructed has hardly been considered in the literature, but it will not be pursued here. This is partly because one original intention of the paper was to analyze the economy of the United States, where unionism is relatively unimportant, and where choosing a bargaining framework seems correspondingly less appropriate (although not impossible). While important, these issues are taken up more fully in a future monograph and are not the primary focus of the paper.

A central question is that of how the identification of a wage equation is to be achieved if the labor market is to be thought of as a pair of simultaneous equations. At the broadest level, there appear to be three possibilities. First, and most restrictive, the wage curve would be identified if all the random shocks occur on the demand side, namely, through movements in demand shift variables. This is not a plausible exact condition, but it might hold in an approximate way if demand shocks are quantitatively dominant. Second, the wage function would be identified if the system were appropriately recursive. If the pay equation includes lagged unemployment, for example, rather than the contemporaneous level of joblessness, it may be sufficient to treat unemployment as a predetermined variable in the wage equation. Third, if there exist suitable variables that enter the unemployment equation but not the wage equation, then the wage curve could be estimated by conventional instrumental variable methods. If none of these is feasible, OLS estimation is likely to bias upward the coefficient on unemployment in the wage equation, which will make it harder to obtain a significant negative unemployment coefficient in a wage equation.

This project considered the three possibles routes to the identification of the wage equation described above. The most attractive theoretically is the third method, but a practical difficulty is that of finding suitable instruments. Instrumenting unemployment in the U.S. case, for example, by using regional federal expenditure and weather variables makes no difference to the results found with OLS. Instrumenting with military spending and compositional variables (these were generously provided by Larry Katz) increases the estimated unemployment elasticity very marginally. Instrumental variable estimation has to date not changed any of the research project's conclusions. For this practical reason, the approach taken throughout the paper will be to present OLS results and to defer more detailed discussion of simultaneity to a future monograph. In some cases, the estimated equations here could be seen as relying on lags for identification.

An efficiency wage framework suggests that regions with different unemployment benefit levels may have "no-shirking conditions" that differ by a vertical intercept term. This implies that an important addition to wage equations will be controls for regional fixed effects. Such controls will also capture innate differences in the regions' probability distributions of demand shocks. Without including regional fixed-effect terms, an estimated wage equation will tend incorrectly to conflate a no-shirking condition with a Harris and Todaro (1970) zero-migration condition. The latter, loosely speaking, suggests that, in a cross section, the expected unemployment rate may be positively correlated with the expected wage. The former, by contrast, requires that the contemporaneous levels of pay and unemployment be negatively correlated. The model given at the end of the paper shows that these are not incompatible.

4.2   Empirical Evidence for International Wage Curves

Earnings equations were estimated on pooled cross-sectional data for a set of ten countries. Although theory implicitly describes real-wage determination, no consistent regional price data exist for the set of countries, so it is necessary to assume that regional CPI differences are adequately captured by using year and geographic dummies. This method will go wrong only when there are important changes in the relative structure of regions' product prices, which arbitrage should go some way toward preventing. Moreover, Blackaby and Manning (1990) have shown that, in a U.K. sample, the inclusion of regional price deflators makes no substantive difference to the existence of a wage curve, and the industry wage curves that are successfully estimated later in this paper can presumably be seen as immune from the criticism that omitted area price deflators are needed. For these reasons, the lack of geographic prices may not be an insurmountable difficulty.

In most of the regression equations, unemployment at a regional level is included as an explanatory variable within an otherwise conventional form of log earnings equation. Where geographic codes are missing, however, industry unemployment rates are used. Wherever possible, regional and industry dummies are included in the regressions to capture the innate differences among areas. These may correspond to controls for the different utility levels available to those without work: regional unemployment benefit plays the role of a vertical shift variable in the wage curve (or no-shirking) equation. Because of the large number of data sets and space restrictions, no attempt is made here to explain in full the construction of different variables across nations or to give a complete description of the means and summary statistics.[5] Details are available from the authors and in a future monograph. Efforts have been taken, however, to keep the general specifications as similar as possible across the international data sets. Moreover, the estimated unemployment elasticities are not sensitive to either the exact choice of personal control variables or the precise form of the dependent variable (i.e., annual, monthly, weekly, or hourly wages or earnings).

Results for Great Britain begin in table 4.1, which uses the British Social Attitudes (BSA) surveys of 1983–87 and 1989–91 (there was no survey in 1988). Column 1 of table 4.1 estimates a cross-sectional log earnings equation, with approximately eighty-one hundred observations, in which regional unemployment is entered as an explanatory variable. The wage equation explains approximately three-quarters of the variance of pay. It includes sets of personal variables and of year and industry dummy variables. The log of regional unemployment (here there are eleven regions by eight years of data) enters in column 1 with a coefficient of −0.15. Allowing for a set of regional dummies reduces this to approximately −0.11 in column 2. Six other regressions (cols. 3–8) are presented: these disaggregate by union and nonunion status and by private-sector status. The results suggest that the unemployment elasticity of wages is higher in the nonunion sector and in the private sector. For example, the point elasticity in the nonunion column 4 regression is −0.19, whereas that in the union column 3 regression is −0.05. Table 4.2 reveals similar findings, using the General Household Survey (GHS), for the United Kingdom between 1973 and 1977. Including regional dummies to control for fixed effects within regions, the unemployment elasticity of pay is estimated in column 2 at approximately −0.09. It makes little difference whether hourly or weekly earnings are used as the dependent variable: compare columns 2 and 4 of table 4.2.

To guard against the possibility that the standard errors in these kinds of equations are artificially small (a possibility suggested in a series of theoretical

5. Descriptions of some of these data sets are available in Blanchflower (1991), Blanchflower and Freeman (1992), and Blanchflower and Oswald (1989, 1994).

Table 4.1   U.K. Log Earnings Equation with Unemployment Variable (the U.K. wage curve), 1983–87 and 1989–91

	All Employees				Private-Sector Employees			
	(1)	(2)	Union (3)	Nonunion (4)	(5)	(6)	Union (7)	Nonunion (8)
Log unemployment (U_t)	−.150	−.108	−.051	−.190	−.207	−.135	−.093	−.182
	(7.89)	(3.53)	(1.38)	(3.55)	(8.66)	(3.47)	(1.74)	(3.27)
Regional dummies (10)	No	Yes	Yes	Yes	No	Yes	Yes	Yes
$\bar{R}^2$	.732	.737	.734	.737	.731	.736	.727	.733
F	356.43	319.29	201.33	125.11	233.55	209.56	96.18	114.56
DF	8,125	8,116	5,016	3,031	5,336	5,948	2,430	2,828

Source: British Social Attitudes Survey Series.

Note: Unless stated otherwise, the following control variables were included: (1) 41 industry dummies, (2) 10 regional dummies, (3) marital status dummies, (4) nonmanual dummy, (5) supervisor dummy, (6) 2 union dummies, (7) gender dummy, (8) experience and its square, (9) years of schooling, (10) whether employment is expected to rise at the workplace dummy, (11) unemployed in previous 5 years dummy, (12) 7 year dummies plus a constant. The dependent variable is the natural log of gross annual earnings. U_t is the natural log of the regional unemployment rate. Union status is determined on the basis of union recognition at the workplace. *t*-statistics are given in parentheses.

Table 4.2   **The U.K. Wage Curve, 1973–77**

	Weekly Earnings		Hourly Earnings	
	(1)	(2)	(3)	(4)
U_t	−.070	−.090	−.080	−.088
	(10.47)	(4.83)	(12.72)	(5.08)
Regional dummies (10)	No	Yes	No	Yes
Constant	2.890	2.922	−.763	−.743
	(74.01)	(63.04)	(20.79)	(17.10)
$\bar{R}^2$	.598	.601	.435	.438
DF	60,486	60,476	60,186	60,176
F	1,158.21	1,038.12	594.73	535.12

Source: General Household Survey Series.

Note: In all cases, there are 60,565 observations. Unless stated otherwise, the following control variables were included: (1) 24 industry dummies, (2) 10 regional dummies, (3) 5 marital status dummies, (4) 17 qualification dummies, (5) 18 occupation dummies, (6) 4 year dummies, (7) gender dummy, (8) experience and its square, (9) part-time dummy. The dependent variable is the natural log of gross earnings. U_t is the natural log of the regional unemployment rate. *t*-statistics are given in parentheses.

econometrics papers by Moulton [1986, 1987, 1990], Greenwald [1983], and Kloek [1981]), the means of the dependent variable and every independent variable in each region/year cell were calculated. Table 4.3 reports the results of reestimating the BSA regressions using these regional cell means, rather than the individual data themselves, as observations. This satisfies Moulton's condition that the level of aggregation should be the same on both sides of the regression equation. Column 2 of table 4.3 shows that, controlling for regional dummies, the coefficient on the log of unemployment is −0.12, with a *t*-statistic of 1.8. Including a lagged dependent variable raises the *t* very slightly. Although the estimate of the quantitative effect of unemployment on pay hardly changes between tables 4.1 and 4.3, therefore, the level of statistical significance looks considerably lower in the latter. The experiments reported in columns 4–7 suggest that current unemployment has greater statistical power than the lagged rate of unemployment, which is generally weak in this data set.

U.S. results are given in table 4.4, using the March Current Population Surveys (CPSs) from 1964 to 1988, which provides a larger sample than is available for other countries.[6] The unemployment and earnings data used in the

6. After excluding the self-employed and those working without pay, the separate files for each of the years 1964–88 were pooled, giving a data file of over 1.5 million cases. The wage sample includes both full- and part-time workers. Industry and regional unemployment rates were mapped onto the data file for the period 1963–87. Because of changes in industrial classification over the period in question, it was possible uniquely to distinguish only forty-four continuous industry groupings that could be allocated unemployment rates. Analogously, because of changes in the way regions are defined in the 1968–75 CPS, it is possible to identify only twenty-one continuous

Table 4.3   The U.K. Regional Wage Curve, 1983–91

	(1)	(2)	(3)	(4)	(5)	(6)	(7)
U_t	−.157	−.122	−.133	−.134			−.126
	(2.94)	(1.78)	(1.96)	(1.96)			(1.80)
U_{t-1}				−.056	−.009		−.046
				(.34)	(.13)		(.51)
U_{t-2}						.0182	.043
						(.30)	(.44)
U_{t-3}							.013
							(.17)
W_{t-1}			.099	.097			
			(.87)	(.85)			
Regional dummies	No	Yes	Yes	Yes	Yes	Yes	Yes
Constant	4.821	6.271	6.264	6.429	6.013	5.996	6.378
	(7.11)	(9.91)	(5.05)	(4.78)	(9.39)	(9.53)	(9.37)
$\bar{R}^2$	.930	.957	.957	.956	.954	.954	.955
F	73.73	74.67	65.66	62.11	70.90	70.98	64.19
DF	71	61	50	49	61	61	58
N	88	88	77	77	88	88	88

Source: British Social Attitudes Survey Series.

Note: All equations include the same set of controls as included in table 4.1. Because of a shortage of degrees of freedom, industry controls are not included. The dependent variable is log of gross annual earnings. All unemployment rates and the dependent variable (annual income) are in natural logarithms. There are 10 regional dummies. All variables, including the dependent variable, are measured as the mean of all observations in a year/region cell. t-statistics are given in parentheses.

subsequent regressions relate to the respondent's labor market behavior in the year preceding the date of interview. When estimating an earnings equation using, for example, the March 1987 CPS, regional unemployment and industry unemployment rates are mapped in for 1986. In what follows, years relate to the year preceding the survey rather than to the date of the survey. In the above case, for example, estimates from the 1987 CPS would be recorded as being for 1986. The equations in table 4.4 are estimated on regional cell means (derived from the full sample of approximately 1.5 million observations), and, because there are twenty-one regions times twenty-five years, the equations have between 380 and 450 degrees of freedom. These twenty-one regions are each large areas of the United States, such as New York State (see table 4.4), and this choice of aggregation was necessitated by changes in data collection through the period. The included personal control variables, such as experience, schooling, and marital status, are calculated as regional cell means. All the regressions incorporate full sets of (twenty-four) year dummies and (forty-

regional groups over the twenty-five-year period. These area groupings are used to derive the regional dummies that we include in our subsequent regressions. For the 1964–67 and 1976–88 CPSs, unemployment rates are mapped in at the state level. The other years use somewhat broader area definitions. In both cases, there are over one thousand separate unemployment observations.

Table 4.4   The U.S. Regional Wage Curve, 1963–87

	(1)	(2)	(3)	(4)	(5)	(6)	(7)
U_t	−.027	−.048	−.047	−.030			−.026
	(2.78)	(5.56)	(5.81)	(2.87)			(2.53)
U_{t-1}				−.028	−.048	−.024	−.007
				(2.63)	(5.69)	(2.27)	(.59)
U_{t-2}						−.041	−.040
						(3.86)	(3.75)
W_{t-1}			.288	.275	.273	.249	.252
			(8.96)	(8.52)	(8.38)	(7.57)	(7.69)
Regional dummies	No	Yes	Yes	Yes	Yes	Yes	Yes
Constant	5.672	6.611	4.931	5.035	5.109	5.495	5.434
	(25.10)	(29.38)	(16.38)	(16.70)	(16.86)	(17.08)	(16.97)
$\bar{R}^2$	.996	.997	.998	.998	.998	.998	.998
F	1,488.83	2,045.06	2,288.66	2,299.44	2,281.41	2,173.63	2,182.92
DF	445	424	403	402	403	382	381

Source: Current Population Surveys, March tapes.

Note: All equations include full sets of year dummies, region dummies (20), industry dummies (43), plus controls for (1) experience and its square, (2) years of schooling, (3) 4 marital status dummies, (4) 2 race dummies, (5) private-sector dummy, (6) part-time dummy. All unemployment rates and the dependent variable (annual income) are in natural logarithms. All variables, including the dependent variable, are measured as the mean of all observations in a year/region cell. The following 21 regional groupings had to be used: (1) Massachusetts, Maine, New Hampshire, Vermont, Rhode Island; (2) Connecticut; (3) New York; (4) New Jersey; (5) Pennsylvania; (6) Ohio; (7) Indiana; (8) Illinois; (9) Michigan, Wisconsin; (10) Minnesota, Missouri, Iowa, North Dakota, South Dakota, Nebraska, Kansas; (11) Delaware, Maryland, Virginia, West Virginia; (12) Washington, D.C.; (13) North Carolina, South Carolina, Georgia; (14) Florida; (15) Kentucky, Tennessee; (16) Alabama, Mississippi; (17) Arkansas, Louisiana, Oklahoma; (18) Texas; (19) Montana, Arizona, Idaho, Wyoming, Colorado, New Mexico, Utah, Nevada; (20) California; (21) Washington, Oregon, Alaska, Hawaii. *t*-statistics are given in parentheses.

three) industry dummies. Unemployment and earnings are in natural logarithms. Some results for the regressions on individual data, with a total sample of approximately 1.5 million observations, are discussed later.

Table 4.4 shows that the United States has a wage curve and that the elasticity of the curve is not greatly different from that in Britain. Column 1 of table 4.4 reveals a significant and negative effect from regional unemployment: a small coefficient of approximately −0.03 is estimated. Once regional dummies are included, however, this rises in absolute value to approximately −0.05 in column 2 of table 4.4 and, as a long-run equilibrium value, to approximately −0.07 in column 3. The significance of the lagged dependent variable in table 4.4 indicates that wages are mildly autoregressive, with a coefficient on the log of wages a year ago of approximately 0.25. Column 4 incorporates unemployment variables for both the current year and the previous year, and the implied long-run unemployment elasticity of pay is then equal to approximately −0.08.

Columns 6 and 7 of table 4.4 show evidence of fairly long lags, of up to two years, from the level of regional unemployment to wages. The significance in column 7 (table 4.4) of unemployment two years ago might be taken as evidence that movements in joblessness are the cause of, and not predominantly caused by, movements in pay. This argument is based on the idea that unemployment can be treated in such an equation as predetermined and that this helps circumvent simultaneity problems. Lags were considerably weaker in the British regressions.

The same form of exercise, but on U.S. state data from the period 1979–87, is reported as table 4.5. Estimation on cell means now provides 390 degrees of freedom. The first point to be made in this case is that—as in column 1 of table 4.5—when regional fixed effects are ignored there is little or no sign of a negative effect of joblessness on pay. This is effectively the form of inquiry undertaken by Hall (1970) and suggests one reason why his results, which were on a small sample of U.S. cities, reveal no negative slope. To get the negative gradient, column 2 of table 4.5 includes fifty state dummies, and the coefficient on unemployment changes to -0.07 with a t-statistic of 7.3.

Columns 3–8 of table 4.5 include various permutations of lagged unemployment and wage variables. The implied unemployment elasticity of pay in these equations is consistently close to approximately -0.08. The sixth and seventh columns of table 4.5 reveal that the results are robust to the replacement of current unemployment by lagged unemployment.

Further CPS experiments are given in table 4.6. Here the regression is esti-

Table 4.5   The U.S. State Wage Curve, 1979–87

	(1)	(2)	(3)	(4)	(5)	(6)	(7)	(8)
U_t	−.010	−.073	−.088	−.066	−.051			−.065
	(.74)	(7.32)	(7.26)	(4.28)	(3.92)			(4.28)
U_{t-1}				−.033	−.034	−.072	−.055	−.017
				(2.29)	(2.58)	(6.18)	(3.65)	(1.00)
U_{t-2}							−.026	−.026
							(1.78)	(1.77)
W_{t-1}			.009	.002		−.005	−.005	.002
			(.46)	(.13)		(.25)	(.29)	(.11)
State dummies	No	Yes	Yes	Yes	Yes	Yes	Yes	Yes
Constant	6.697	7.576	7.809	8.193	7.639	8.001	8.298	5.434
	(20.56)	(26.28)	(22.11)	(22.11)	(26.63)	(21.93)	(22.03)	(16.97)
$\bar{R}^2$	.938	.983	.980	.980	.983	.979	.979	.980
F	110.32	232.41	171.76	172.82	234.78	164.22	164.60	173.21
DF	390	340	285	284	340	286	285	284

Source: Current Population Surveys, March tapes.

Note: All equations include full sets of year dummies, 50 state dummies (including the District of Columbia), industry dummies (43), plus controls for (1) experience and its square, (2) years of schooling, (3) 4 marital status dummies, (4) 2 race dummies, (5) private-sector dummy, (6) part-time dummy. All unemployment rates and the dependent variable (annual income) are in natural logarithms. All variables, including the dependent variable, are measured as the mean of all observations in a year/state cell. t-statistics are given in parentheses.

Table 4.6 The U.S. Wage Curve, 1963–87

	1963–68		1969–78		1979–87		1963–87		
	(1)	(2)	(3)	(4)	(5)	(6)	(7)	(8)	(9)
Industry U	−.016	−.019	−.079	−.098	−.212	−.212	−.090	−.109	
	(1.39)	(1.68)	(15.45)	(19.33)	(34.64)	(34.75)	(28.82)	(35.19)	
Regional U	.013	−.078	.107	−.045	−.070	−.148	−.002	−.099	−.102
	(1.44)	(5.25)	(20.46)	(5.84)	(15.69)	(24.84)	(.65)	(24.83)	(26.49)
Regional dummies	No	Yes	No	Yes	No	Yes	No	Yes	Yes
Constant	5.985	5.370	6.740	6.617	7.558	7.627	6.312	5.939	5.716
	(195.64)	(132.39)	(333.98)	(296.55)	(368.43)	(351.22)	(462.62)	(444.36)	(485.63)
$\bar{R}^2$	.540	.544	.565	.565	.533	.536	.575	.576	.575
F	5,061.45	3,877.01	11,708.25	9,096.36	12,034.70	9,304.54	25,604.57	20,606.93	20,783.84
N	263,133	263,133	595,138	595,138	675,822	675,822	1,534,093	1,534,903	1,534,093

Source: Current Population Surveys, March tapes.

Note: All equations include full sets of year dummies and industry dummies (43) plus controls for (1) experience and its square, (2) years of schooling, (3) 4 marital status dummies, (4) two race dummies, (5) private-sector dummy, (6) part-time dummy. All unemployment rates and the dependent variable (annual income) are in natural logarithms.

mated on the full micro sample without use of cell means, and both industry and regional unemployment rates—again in logarithms—are entered together as explanatory variables. For the full sample of 1963–87 (cols. 7–9 of table 4.6), when industry and regional dummies are included, the industry unemployment elasticity of pay and the regional unemployment elasticity of pay are each approximately −0.1.

Columns 1–6 of table 4.6 break the time period into different samples as a way of assessing the robustness and stability of the estimates. Column 3 of table 4.6 is especially interesting because it obtains, for the period 1969–78, the Hall (1970) result that wages and unemployment are positively correlated across regions. Column 4, however, reveals that the introduction of regional dummies turns an unemployment coefficient of +0.106 into one of −0.045. Thus, it is omitted regional fixed effects that appear, in this period, to be responsible for the Hall-style finding of a positive relation between a regional wage and regional unemployment. With regional dummies included in the regressions, the regional unemployment elasticity of pay is estimated at −0.08 in 1963–68, −0.05 in 1969–78, and −0.15 in 1979–87. The estimate is −0.1 overall in column 8. It is not easy to understand these variations; they will need eventually to be explained. Nevertheless, the wage curve has a persistently negative gradient and one centered at approximately −0.1. Column 9 suggests that industry and regional unemployment are orthogonal to one another.

Two other points are worth noting. First, a series of U.S. wage equations was estimated for the period 1979–87 replacing regional dummies with "permanent" regional unemployment rates. This permanent unemployment variable was defined as average state unemployment for the period 1960–88. As expected, this variable enters positively and significantly. Although its inclusion improves the performance of the regional unemployment variable, it significantly worsens the overall fit of the equation compared with the specification including regional dummies. Second, a possible objection to noncompetitive interpretations of the estimated wage-unemployment correlation is that unemployment here could be acting as a mismeasured variable for a conventional labor supply curve. In order to test for such a possibility, regressions for the United States were estimated that included the labor force participation rate and, as an alternative, the employment/population ratio. These regressions were estimated on state means for the period 1979–87. When included with the state unemployment rate, these variables were typically insignificant, whereas the coefficient on the unemployment variable remained significant and of the same size as above. Further details on these issues are available on request from the authors.

Separate union and nonunion wage curves are estimated for the United States in tables 4.7 and 4.8. Because of data restrictions, it is necessary to use the March CPSs from 1983 to 1988. As was true in the U.K. case, the union sector of the United States appears to have a less elastic wage curve than the nonunion sector. The coefficient on regional log U is, in table 4.7, approxi-

Table 4.7 **Union and Nonunion Wage Curves, United States, 1982–87**

	All (1)	Union (2)	Nonunion (3)
U_t industry	−.209	−.053	−.234
	(14.58)	(1.89)	(14.27)
U_t region	−.114	−.0697	−.119
	(5.05)	(1.54)	(4.67)
Union dummy	.193	N.A.	N.A.
	(26.23)		
Constant	8.084	8.570	8.090
	(114.87)	(60.13)	(101.63)
$\bar{R}^2$	.533	.376	.531
F	875.19	86.41	715.02
DF	86,379	15,765	70,502
N	86,493	15,878	70,615

Source: Current Population Surveys, March tapes.

Note: All equations include full sets of year, state (50), and industry variables (43) plus controls for (1) experience and its square, (2) years of schooling, (3) 4 marital status variables, (4) two race variables, (5) private sector, (6) part-time status. All unemployment rates and the dependent variable (annual income) are in natural logarithms. *t*-statistics are given in parentheses. N.A. = not available.

Table 4.8 **Union and Nonunion Wage Curves, United States, 1982–87**

	Private Sector			Public Sector		
	All (1)	Union (2)	Nonunion (3)	All (4)	Union (5)	Nonunion (6)
U_t industry	−.222	−.070	−.247	−.034	+.055	−.065
	(14.45)	(2.18)	(14.33)	(.59)	(.63)	(.86)
U_t region	−.122	−.076	−.125	−.088	−.059	−.098
	(4.69)	(1.25)	(4.42)	(1.99)	(.90)	(1.67)
Union	.194	N.A.	N.A.	.194	N.A.	N.A.
	(21.36)			(15.81)		
Constant	8.172	8.712	8.175	7.685	8.210	7.563
	(104.47)	(49.70)	(94.97)	(33.07)	(22.33)	(25.38)
$\bar{R}^2$	.528	.380	.527	.556	.394	.565
F	708.13	57.91	609.07	197.87	39.71	134.81
DF	70,192	10,103	59,979	16,085	5,568	10,422
N	70,304	10,214	60,090	16,189	5,664	10,531

Source: Current Population Surveys, March tapes.

Note: All equations include full sets of year, state (50), and industry variables (43) plus controls for (1) experience and its square, (2) years of schooling, (3) 4 marital status variables, (4) two race variables, (5) private sector, (6) part-time status. All unemployment rates and the dependent variable (annual income) are in natural logarithms. *t*-statistics are in parentheses. N.A. = not available.

Table 4.9   **Public-Sector Wage Curves, United States, 1982–87**

	Federal (1)	Local (2)	State (3)
U_i industry	+.001	−.074	−.234
	(.01)	(.59)	(14.27)
U_i region	+.044	−.143	−.119
	(.47)	(1.92)	(4.67)
Union	.102	.269	.203
	(3.65)	(12.95)	(9.69)
Constant	7.151	8.261	8.478
	(15.50)	(16.40)	(20.59)
$\bar{R}^2$	.533	.376	.571
F	875.19	86.41	80.76
DF	3,603	5,706	5,540
N	3,703	5,801	5,635

Source: Current Population Surveys, March tapes.

Note: All equations include full sets of year, state (50), and industry variables (43) plus controls for (1) experience and its square, (2) years of schooling, (3) 4 marital status variables, (4) two race variables, (5) private sector, (6) part-time status. All unemployment rates and the dependent variable (annual income) are in natural logarithms. *t*-statistics are in parentheses.

mately −0.07 (poorly determined) in union employment and −0.12 in non-union employment. The public/private-sector distinction is examined in tables 4.8 and 4.9. Columns 1 and 4 of table 4.8 suggest that wages are a little more responsive to regional unemployment in the private than in the public sector. Once again, the union sector has a less elastic wage curve. The results reported in table 4.9 are more dramatic (similar findings are given by Katz and Krueger [1991a]); they show that federal sector employees' pay is effectively independent of regional unemployment, with the result that the wage curve is flat.

Although it is not possible to present results in detail, wage curve estimates for Canada, South Korea, Austria, Italy, Holland, Switzerland, Norway, and Germany are summarized in brief form in table 4.10. These use data sets of varying sizes and types (most come from the International Social Survey Programme) but give estimates that are similar. Controlling for region or industry fixed effects, estimates of the unemployment elasticity of wages are distributed around −0.1. They vary from a low of −0.05 for Korea's unemployment elasticity to a high of −0.12 for Austria's and Holland's, which might be interpreted as showing that countries do not differ markedly. The reported results are based on earnings equations of an otherwise conventional cross-sectional kind—the exact specification used does not appear to affect the key findings—into which the log of the unemployment rate has been added. Details of these specifications are available from the authors.

Table 4.10   International Wage Curves

Country	Dependent Variable	Data Set	Coefficient on Log U	t-statistic	Fixed Effects	N
1. Canada	Gross annual earnings	Survey of Consumer Finances, 1986	−.14	9.3	No	31,522
2. S. Korea	Gross monthly earnings	Occupational Wage Surveys, 1983, 1986	−.05*	25.0	Yes	1,168,142
3. Austria	Gross monthly earnings	ISSP, 1985–86	−.16	2.2	No	758
4. Austria	Gross monthly earnings	ISSP, 1985–86	−.12	1.7	Yes	758
5. Italy	Gross monthly earnings	ISSP, 1986–88	−.12	3.8	No	1,532
6. Italy	Gross monthly earnings	ISSP, 1986–88	−.08	2.0	Yes	1,532
7. Holland	Net monthly earnings	ISSP, 1988–89	−.23	2.6	No	1,270
8. Holland	Net monthly earnings	ISSP, 1988–89	−.12	.2	Yes	1,270
9. Switzerland	Net monthly earnings	ISSP, 1987	−.12	3.6	No	645
10. Norway	Gross yearly earnings	ISSP, 1989	−.07	2.1	No	933
11. Norway	Gross yearly earnings	ISSP, 1989	−.09	2.4	Yes	933
12. West Germany	Gross monthly earnings	ISSP, 1986–88	−.02*	.7	No	1,760
13. West Germany	Gross monthly earnings	ISSP, 1986–88	−.08*	2.1	Yes	1,760

Note: Log U is defined as an area unemployment rate at various levels of disaggregation in different countries. Where indicated by an asterisk, unemployment is measured at the industry level. The dependent variable is in natural logarithms. In all cases, personal variables are included as controls (i.e., gender, race, age, schooling, etc.).

4.3   Interpreting the Data

A downward-sloping wage curve is observed in what appears to be a robust way, across various nations, in these microeconomic data sets. The next questions to be tackled are those of why this occurs, of what it implies for labor economics and macroeconomics, and eventually of what it means for government policy. One way to start is to try to write down a model that is internally consistent and makes the correct predictions about the correlation visible in the data.

An intuitive objection to the empirical results is that the wage-unemployment correlation should—by an argument based on compensating differentials—be positive rather than negative. A milder version of such a view is that, at best, the estimated wage curves are likely to be a mixture of downward- and upward-sloping functions and thus that there is an unresolved simultaneity problem. According to this point of view, the estimates conflate the positive Harris-Todaro gradient and the negative gradient of a macroeconomic model such as efficiency wage theory.

This section sets out a model in which a downward-sloping wage curve is derived from optimizing behavior. The reason for the negative gradient is that unemployment frightens workers and that, in consequence, firms find that, in recessions, it is feasible to pay their employees less well. The model is constructed in such a way in that, contrary to Harris and Todaro (1970), wages and unemployment are negatively rather than positively related. To understand why the upward-sloping Harris-Todaro relation is misleading, it is necessary to recall that, in reality, migration is a costly process that takes place in a world with random demand shocks.

The theoretical framework allows workers to migrate across regions but assumes that it is not possible to do so instantly. Unemployed individuals do not immediately attempt to migrate: they migrate only if one region offers a better expected utility than another. This realistic assumption of costly, rational, farsighted migration decisions effectively decouples current pay and current unemployment and so bypasses the positive gradient of the Harris-Todaro relation. A high wage in the current period need not be accompanied in that period by high unemployment; pay and unemployment are positively related (at most) only in expected or long-run terms.

One version of the model goes further: it shows that regions that differ only in nonpecuniary attractions may have the same wage curve and nothing that corresponds to a visible positive wage-unemployment relation. This is possible, for example, if one region is inherently attractive and, to ensure consistency with a zero-migration equilibrium, therefore offers both low pay and high unemployment. Another region, say, pays well and has low unemployment but is an inherently unattractive place. The result is a negatively inclined wage function even in long-run equilibrium.

Consider an economy consisting of two regions. The following assumptions are made about region 1 and, with small modifications, about region 2:

Assumption 4.1. Assume that workers are risk neutral and get utility from income and disutility from effort. Define the wage as w and the level of on-the-job effort as e. Assume that utility equals the difference between income and effort so that (pecuniary) utility is

$$u = w - e.$$

Assumption 4.2. Assume that effort at work, e, is a fixed number determined by technology but that individual employees can decide to "shirk" and exert zero effort. If undetected by the firm, these individuals earn wage w and have

$e = 0$ so that $u = w$. They are then better off than employees who provide effort.[7]

Assumption 4.3. An individual who shirks runs the risk of being detected. Designate as δ the probability of successfully shirking, that is, of escaping detection. Assume that anyone caught shirking is fired and has then to find work elsewhere (at required effort e). Let the expected utility of a fired worker be $\bar{w}$. Define it

$$\bar{w} = (w - e)\, \alpha(U) + b[1 - \alpha(U)].$$

This is a convex combination of $w - e$, the utility from working at the required effort level, and of b, which is defined as the income value of unemployment benefit plus leisure. The function $\alpha(U)$ measures the probability of finding work and how that is affected by the level of unemployment, U, prevailing in the local labor market.

Assumption 4.4. Assume that there is a constant rate of breakup, r, of firms. In steady-state equilibrium, total new hires in the local economy are $\alpha(l - n)$, where l is population, n is employment, and

$$rn = \alpha(l - n).$$

Unemployment is $U \equiv 1 - n/l$, so

$$r = \frac{r}{U} - \alpha.$$

This defines a function $\alpha(U)$ with derivatives

$$\alpha'(U) = -\frac{r}{U^2} < 0,$$

$$\alpha''(U) = \frac{2r}{U^3} > 0.$$

Thus, the probability of finding a job, α, is a convex function of unemployment, U.

Assumption 4.5. Equivalent conditions hold in the second region. The wage there is ω, and the level of unemployment benefit is β. The unemployment rate in the second region is μ.

Assumption 4.6. The second region differs from the first in that both workers and nonworkers enjoy a nonpecuniary benefit, ϕ, from living in the region.

---

7. George Johnson, our discussant, raised the issue of whether this discreteness assumption, of only two effort levels, is necessary to obtain a wage curve. It is not: all that is needed, intuitively, is that workers be frightened by high unemployment. For example, using a version of efficiency wage theory, Phelps (1990, 1992) derives wage curves with a continuous effort function.

Their utility is thus $u = \omega - e + \phi$ when working and $u = \beta + \phi$ when unemployed.

Assumption 4.7. Each region is affected by shocks to the demand for labor. The shock variable is denoted s in region 1, with a density function $g(s)$. The shock variable in region 2 is σ, with density of $h(\sigma)$.

Assumption 4.8. Workers are free, between periods, to choose to live in whichever region they prefer. They cannot migrate during a period.

The assumptions given above describe a form of efficiency wage model. The model's key characteristic is that employers must pay a wage that is sufficiently high to induce employees not to shirk. In equilibrium, workers must be behaving optimally in their effort decisions, and firms must be behaving optimally in their wage setting. Regions differ in their nonpecuniary attractions: one of the two is a nicer place to live than the other. Excluding degenerate equilibria, however, each region must offer workers the same level of expected utility. This condition defines a zero-migration equilibrium.

A number of results can be proved.

Proposition 4.1. Each region has a downward-sloping convex wage curve. If both regions have the same level of unemployment benefit (so $b = \beta$), they have a common wage curve given by the equation

$$w = e + b + \frac{e\delta}{(1 - \delta)[1 - \alpha(U)]}.$$

Proof. For a no-shirking equilibrium, the expected utility from not shirking must equal that from shirking. Thus, in region 1,

(1) $w - e = \delta w + (1 - \delta)\{(w - e)\,\alpha(U) + b[1 - \alpha(U)]\},$

which simplifies, after manipulation, to

(2) $$w = e + b + \frac{e\delta}{(1 - \delta)[1 - \alpha(U)]}.$$

In region 2, in which individuals receive a utility supplement ϕ, the no-shirking condition is

(3) $\omega - e + \phi = \delta(\omega + \phi) + (1 - \delta)\{(\omega - e + \phi)\alpha(U) + (\beta + \phi)[1 - \alpha(U)]\}.$

The ϕ terms cancel from both sides, leaving a wage equation

(4) $$\omega = e + \beta + \frac{e\delta}{(1 - \delta)[1 - \alpha(U)]}.$$

If $b = \beta$, equation (2) is identical to equation (4), and the two regions have the same wage equation. The convexity of this wage curve follows from the convexity of the $\alpha(U)$ function and can be checked by differentiation.

More intuitively, equilibrium necessitates that wages in each region be just enough to dissuade employees from shirking. This requires that the expected utility from shirking be no greater than that from working at effort e. Because the second region's nonpecuniary attractions, ϕ, are available to both the employed and the unemployed, the condition for no shirking is independent of ϕ. Thus, as long as there is no difference in unemployment benefit levels (or, more generally, the utility available to the jobless), each region has the same equation for its no-shirking condition. This common equation traces out a convex negatively sloped locus linking the wage, w, to the unemployment rate, U. When unemployment is low, for example, firms pay high wages to ensure that workers value their jobs sufficiently not to shirk.

Proposition 4.2. Assume that both regions have the same level of unemployment benefit. (i) Then, for a zero-migration equilibrium, they must face different distributions of demand shocks and exhibit different wage/unemployment patterns. (ii) Region 1 has a higher expected wage than region 2.

Proof. For a zero-migration equilibrium, each region must offer the same level of expected utility to workers. The expected utility of a migrant into region 1 is

$$(5) \qquad \int \{(w - e)\alpha(U) + b[1 - \alpha(U)]\}g(s)ds$$

and of a migrant into region 2 is

$$(6) \qquad \int \{(\omega - e + \phi)\alpha(\mu) + (\beta + \phi)[1 - \alpha(\mu)]\}h(\sigma)d\sigma.$$

Given identical unemployment benefit levels $b = \beta$ and identical distributions of demand shocks $g(\cdot) = h(\cdot)$, these two expressions cannot be equal. The difference between them would be $\phi > 0$. In equilibrium, therefore, the regions must exhibit different wage/unemployment patterns, and this establishes the first part of the proposition.

To demonstrate that the expected wage in region 1 is higher than the expected wage in region 2, it is necessary to prove that

$$(7) \qquad \int wg(s)ds > \int \omega h(\sigma)d\sigma.$$

Zero migration requires

$$(8) \qquad \int \{(w - e)\alpha(U) + b[1 - \alpha(U)]\}g(s)ds = \int \{(\omega - e + \phi)\alpha(\mu)$$
$$+ (\beta + \phi)[1 - \alpha(\mu)]\}h(\sigma)d\sigma.$$

The two no-shirking conditions (one for each region) are

(9) $w - e = \delta w + (1 - \delta)\{\alpha(U)(w - e) + [1 - \alpha(U)]b\}$,

(10) $\omega - e + \phi = \delta(\omega + \phi) + (1 - \delta)\{\alpha(\mu)[\omega + \phi - e] + [1 - \alpha(\mu)](\beta + \phi)\}$.

Rearranging, and integrating both sides of each of these equations,

(11) $\int\left(w - \dfrac{e}{1 - \delta}\right)g(s)ds = \int\{\alpha(U)(w - e) + [1 - \alpha(U)]b\}g(s)ds$,

(12) $\int\left(\omega - \dfrac{e}{1 - \delta} + \phi\right)h(\sigma)d\sigma = \int\{\alpha(\mu)[\omega + \phi - e] + [1 - \alpha(\mu)](\beta + \phi)\}h(\sigma)d\sigma$.

By equation (8), the left-hand sides of these must be equal:

(13) $\int\left(w - \dfrac{e}{1 - \delta}\right)g(s)ds = \int\left(\omega - \dfrac{e}{1 - \delta} + \phi\right)h(\sigma)d\sigma$,

which simplifies, noting that the integral of $eg/(1 - \delta)$ equals the integral of $eh/(1 - \delta)$, to

(14) $\int wg(s)ds) - \int \omega h(\sigma)d\sigma = \phi > 0$.

If proposition 4.2(i) were false, the two regions would have identical wage and unemployment outcomes. But, because region 2 is intrinsically attractive (it offers nonpecuniary benefit ϕ), all workers would attempt to migrate there. In equilibrium, therefore, region 2's attractions must be exactly counterbalanced by inferior wage and unemployment combinations.

To illustrate these ideas, figure 4.1 sketches wage curves. Curve I represents the locus along which occur the wage-unemployment combinations for regions with identical unemployment benefit levels. Repeated random shocks produce different points on the curve. To ensure a zero-migration equilibrium, the intrinsically more attractive region 2 must be characterized more often by points in the southeast portion of the wage curve, which implies worse wage and unemployment combinations. Equilibria in the less attractive region 1 must more often occur in the northwest segment of the wage curve—so that workers are willing to live there. This is captured algebraically in proposition 4.2(ii), which states that, because of its inherent disadvantages, the first region must on average offer higher wages than region 2. Equation (14) shows that, in this world of risk-neutral people, the size of the regional gap in expected wages will equal the value of the nonpecuniary difference between the regions.

Proposition 4.3. Assume that the regions have different levels of unemployment benefit. Then the wage curve in the high-benefit region lies vertically above that in the low-benefit region.

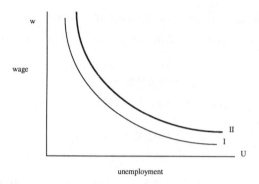

Fig. 4.1   The wage curve
Note: Region II here has a higher level of unemployment benefit than region I.

Proof. Because the no-shirking condition is

(15)
$$w = e + b + \frac{e\delta}{(1 - \delta)[1 - \alpha(U)]},$$

the level of unemployment benefit, b, is a vertical shift parameter in a graph of the wage equation in wage/unemployment space. This result follows from the fact that the level of unemployment benefit (or value of full leisure) is an intercept variable in the no-shirking condition defining equilibrium. As would be expected intuitively, therefore, in a region with higher benefits to those who are unemployed, firms must set higher wage rates if they are to discourage shirking.

Proposition 4.4. The results generalize to models with an arbitrary number of regions.

Proof. A nonshirking condition will hold for each region. Mathematically, the separability of ϕ in the wage equation ensures that, because an equivalent nonshirking condition can be written down for each area, the results generalize to an arbitrary number of regions. The heights of the different wage curves are determined by the size of the different unemployment benefit levels.

An intuitive summary of the model's structure can be given in the following way. In this efficiency wage framework, a high level of regional unemployment is associated with a low level of regional wages: high unemployment makes employees keen to keep their jobs because it will be difficult to find another. Other things constant, therefore, these employees are reluctant to shirk at work, for fear they will be detected and dismissed. Knowing this, firms need pay only low wages to extract the required level of effort from workers. Fear of unemployment then disciplines workers.

If unemployment is low, by contrast, employers have to offer high wages. If they do not, employees are likely to take the risk of shirking at work, realizing that it will be easy to find another job if dismissed. When the unemployment rate is low, high wage rates are necessary to motivate workers.

Because individuals can eventually migrate, this is not the end of the story. First, although actual wage and unemployment combinations will depend on current demand shock variables, the average or expected wage needs to be higher in regions with low nonpecuniary attractions. This is because regions have to offer equal expected utilities: otherwise some will get no workers willing to stay. Second, a region with a relatively high level of unemployment benefit will have a relatively high wage curve (such as the bold curve, labeled II, in fig. 4.1). The intuitive reason for this is that, to ensure that there is no shirking in an area where the utility from being unemployed is relatively great, the employer must pay better than in areas where the utility of the jobless is comparatively low. It is more expensive to motivate workers who have good outside options. Some regions thus have wage curves that lie vertically above those in other regions.

Individuals do not all move to the regions with the highest wage curves or to the regions with the greatest nonpecuniary advantages because those two kinds of regions are areas that more commonly have wage and unemployment outcomes in the southeast segments of their own wage curves (i.e., worse recessions). Probabilistic demand shocks are thus an essential part of a coherent model. Put loosely, intrinsically attractive regions with high unemployment benefits must be characterized, in steady-state equilibrium, by harsher "business cycles" than less favored areas.

According to this multisector model, there can exist a downward-sloping convex function tying together the rate of unemployment in an area and the level of remuneration offered within that location. The intercept in this function depends on the size of the unemployment benefit so that regions have the same wage curve only if they do not differ in the generosity of income paid to (or for exogenous reasons enjoyed by) those out of work.

The purpose of this section has been to offer one way of thinking about the empirical patterns found in the international microeconomic data.[8] The common empirical finding suggests that there is some systematic relation at work across the countries, and it is not easy to see how traditional models could account for it. However, in an efficiency wage framework with random demand shocks, there are reasons to believe that, just as the data show, pay and unemployment will be negatively related. The model has demonstrated why it is

8. At the NBER conference, Richard Freeman favored a "disequilibrium" explanation for the wage curve in which "demand shocks to areas raise wages and lower unemployment." This is exactly the property of the theoretical model, except that we would not use the word *disequilibrium* because it evokes the idea that the wage curve is transitory. Demand shocks hit regions continuously—sliding them left or right along a no-shirking condition.

misleading to expect a positive correlation between regional wage levels and unemployment levels. Because the aim has been to eschew competitive labor market theory, the analysis is necessarily unconventional. It may be that eventually the conceptual framework developed here will be seen to be incomplete or misleading, but at this juncture a multisector efficiency wage model appears to have the right general properties to fit the facts.

4.4   Conclusions

This paper uses a number of microeconomic data sets to study the relation between the level of pay and the level of unemployment. It attempts to demonstrate that there is an empirical regularity (a "wage curve") in international pay and unemployment data, that different countries' estimates of the unemployment elasticity of pay cluster at approximately −0.1, and that conventional wisdom on U.S. regional wage-unemployment patterns needs to be reconsidered.

The paper presents evidence from eight countries for the existence of an inverse relation between employees' pay and the level of regional unemployment and evidence from three countries for the existence of an inverse relation between employees' pay and the level of industry unemployment.[9] Estimates with and without controls for sectoral fixed effects are provided. In the case of the United States, it appears to be important to allow for regional fixed effects: doing so reverses the conventional view that area wages and area unemployment rates are positively correlated.

Although presented here as a kind of statistical fact or uniformity in the data, the estimated wage curve also corresponds to the key element in a new class of macroeconomic models. One example of this class is efficiency wage theory, in which unemployment acts as a discipline device that dissuades employees from shirking on the job: a high unemployment rate allows the firm to pay less in equilibrium. The paper shows how this idea can be incorporated into a model of interregional equilibrium. Its predictions are different from, and in some cases almost the opposite of, those in the tradition of Harris and Todaro (1970) and Hall (1970, 1972). One reason is that this literature has not distinguished as clearly as it could have between, on the one hand, a positive regional correlation between expected pay and expected unemployment and, on the other, a negative regional correlation between contemporaneous pay and unemployment.

The estimated wage curves imply that, averaging across nations, a doubling of local unemployment reduces the level of pay by approximately 10 percent.[10] The size and quality of the international cross-sectional data sets vary, but,

---

9. This does not mean that, as one commentator put it, the unemployment rate in countries with high real wages should be less than it is in those with low real wages or that secularly growing wages will lower unemployment. The model shows that richer countries have (vertically) higher wage curves.

10. This holds true in U.S. data after instrumenting unemployment.

when taken together, the findings suggest that there is a common empirical pattern across nations. It seems that a satisfactory theory of labor market behavior needs to be able to account for the fact that international wage curves exist.

Data Appendix

British Social Attitudes Survey Series, 1983–91

This series of surveys, core funding for which was provided by the Sainsbury Family Trusts, was designed to chart movements in a wide range of social attitudes in Britain and is similar to the General Social Survey carried out by the National Opinion Research Center (NORC) in the United States. The surveys were designed and collected by Social and Community Planning Research (SCPR) and derive from annual cross-sectional surveys from a representative sample of adults aged eighteen or over living in private households in Great Britain whose addresses were on the electoral register. The first three surveys involved around eighteen hundred adults; the numbers were increased to three thousand in 1986. Interviews were also conducted in Northern Ireland for the first time in 1989.

The sampling in each year involved a stratified multistage design with four separate stages of selection. First, in each year, approximately 120 (150 in 1986) parliamentary constituencies were selected, with the probability of selection proportionate to the size of the electorate in the constituency. Then, for each constituency, a polling district was selected also with the probability of selection proportionate to the size of the electorate. Then thirty addresses were selected at a fixed interval on the electoral register. Finally, at each sampled address, the interviewer selected one respondent using a random selection procedure (a Kish grid). The majority of sample errors for each survey lie in the range 1.0–1.5; errors for subgroups would be larger. For further details of the survey design, see, for example, Jowell, Witherspoon, and Brook (1991).

The General Household Survey Series, 1973–77

The General Household Survey is a continuous multipurpose national sample survey based on private households selected from the electoral register. It originated in 1971 as a service to various government departments. Although there is substantial continuity in questions over time, new areas for questioning are introduced, for example, leisure in 1973 and 1977 and drinking in 1978, and the form of questions varies between years.

The sample remained largely unchanged between 1971 and 1974 and was designed to be representative of Great Britain in each calendar quarter. The three-stage sample design involved the selection of 168 local authority areas as the primary sampling units (PSUs) by probability proportional to population size, after first stratifying local authority areas by (*a*) regions, (*b*) conurbations, other urban areas, semirural areas, and rural areas, and (*c*) average ratable value. Each year, four wards (in rural areas, groups of parishes) are selected from each PSU with the probability proportional to the population size. The selected local authority areas are rotated in such a way that a quarter are replaced every three months. Within each ward, twenty or twenty-five addresses are selected. At most, three households are interviewed at each address (and, to compensate for additional households at an address, a corresponding number are deleted from the interviewer's address list). This yielded a total effective sample of 15,360 households in 1973, for example.

Since 1975, in an attempt to reduce the effects of clustering, the sample design has been based on a two-stage sampling procedure with electoral wards as the PSUs. Geographically contiguous wards or parishes are grouped where necessary to provide a minimum electorate of twenty-three hundred before selection. Wards are stratified by (*a*) regions, (*b*) metropolitan and nonmetropolitan counties, and (*c*) percentage in higher or intermediate nonmanual socioeconomic groups, to produce 168 strata. Within these strata, wards are listed by (*d*) percentage of households in owner occupation, before being systematically selected by probability proportional to size. Four wards are used from each stratum each year, with each selected ward in use for three years before being replaced. Selection of addresses within wards remains the same as before 1975, but addresses where there are multiple households are treated somewhat differently. The sample is not representative in each calendar quarter after 1975.

Some households respond only partially; therefore, response rates can be measured in a number of different ways:

1. The minimum response rate, defined as only completely cooperating households—70 percent in 1973.

2. The maximum response rate, which excludes only households where the whole household either refused or was not contacted—84 percent in 1973.

3. The middle response rate, which includes households where information is missing for certain questions but excludes those where information is missing altogether for one or more household members—81 percent in 1973 (the middle response rate therefore includes the 6 percent [in 1973] of households in which information about one or more household members was obtained from someone else in the household [a "proxy"]; certain questions are not asked by proxy, e.g., questions about income, educational qualifications, and opinion).

The data set is based on individuals (i.e., all adults and children in the sample households); that is, the case unit is an individual, not a household. The GHS defines a household as "a group of people living regularly at one address, who are all catered for by the same person for at least one meal a day."

The International Social Survey Series, 1985–89

The International Social Survey Programme (ISSP) is a voluntary grouping of study teams in eleven nations (Australia, Austria, Britain, Holland, Hungary, Ireland, Israel, Italy, Norway, and West Germany). In 1987, a separate Swiss survey was also included. As a condition of membership, each country undertakes to run a short, annual, self-completion survey containing an agreed-on set of questions asked of a probability-based, nationwide sample of adults. The topics change from year to year by agreement, with a view to replication every five years or so. The major advantage of the ISSP is that it produces a common set of questions asked in identical form in the participating countries.

For a description of the technical details of the surveys, see the technical appendix in Jowell, Witherspoon, and Brook (1989).

The Current Population Surveys, 1964–88

The Current Population Survey (CPS) is the source of the official government statistics on employment and unemployment in the United States. The CPS has been conducted monthly for over forty years. Currently, about 56,500 households are interviewed monthly, scientifically selected on the basis of area of residence to represent the nation as a whole, individual states, and other specified areas. Each household is interviewed once a month for four consecutive months in one year and again for the corresponding time period a year later. This technique enables month-to-month and year-to-year comparisons to be obtained at a reasonable cost while minimizing the inconvenience to any one household.

Although the main purpose of the survey is to collect information on the employment situation, a secondary purpose is to collect information on the demographic status of the population, information such as age, sex, race, marital status, educational attainment, and family structure. From time to time, additional questions are included on such subjects as health, education, income, and previous work experience. The statistics resulting from these questions serve to update similar information collected once every ten years through the decennial census and are used by policymakers and legislators as indicators of the economic situation in the United States and for planning and evaluating many government programs.

The CPS provides current estimates of the economic status and activities of the population of the United States. Because it is not possible to develop one or two overall figures (such as the number of unemployed) that would adequately describe the whole complex of labor market phenomena, the CPS is designed to provide a large amount of detailed and supplementary data. Such data are made available to meet a variety of needs on the part of users of labor market information.

Thus, the CPS is the only source of monthly estimates of total employment (both farm and nonfarm); nonfarm self-employed persons, domestics, and unpaid helpers in nonfarm family enterprises; wage and salary employees; and, finally, total unemployment. It provides the only available distribution of workers by the number of hours worked (as distinguished from aggregate or average hours for an industry), permitting separate analyses of part-time workers, workers on overtime, etc. The survey is also the only comprehensive current source of information on the occupation of workers and the industries in which they work. Information is available from the survey not only for individuals currently in the labor force but also for those who are outside the labor force. The characteristics of such people—whether married women with or without young children, disabled individuals, students, older retired workers, etc.—can be determined. Information on their current desire for work, their past work experience, and their intentions as to job seeking are also available.

The March CPS, also known as the Annual Demographic File, contains the basic monthly demographic and labor force data described above plus additional data on work experience, income, noncash benefits, and migration.

The Korean Occupational Wage Surveys, 1983 and 1986

The Occupational Wage Survey is conducted annually by the Korean Ministry of Labor. The survey includes wage, employment, and demographic information on about 5 million workers. The paper makes use of the original tapes with around 600,000 observations that are randomly sampled from the original survey. The sampling units are firms, not individuals. Firms report wage and demographic data on a random sample of their workers, but only firms with ten or more employees are included in the survey. This omits roughly one-third of the nonagricultural workforce in a typical year.

References

Adams, James D. 1985. Permanent differences in unemployment and permanent wage differentials. *Quarterly Journal of Economics* 100:29–56.

Akerlof, George A., and Janet L. Yellen. 1990. The fair wage–effort hypothesis and unemployment. *Quarterly Journal of Economics* 105:255–84.

Beaudry, Paul, and John DiNardo. 1991. The effect of implicit contracts on the movements of wages over the business cycle: Evidence from micro data. *Journal of Political Economy* 99, no. 4:665–88.

Bils, Mark. 1985. Real wages over the business cycle: Evidence from panel data. *Journal of Political Economy* 93, no. 4:666–89.

Blackaby, David H., and Neil D. Manning. 1987. Regional earnings revisited. *Manchester School* 55:158–83.

———. 1990. The north-south divide: Questions of existence and stability. *Economic Journal* 100:510–27.

Blanchflower, David G. 1991. Fear, unemployment and pay flexibility. *Economic Journal* 101:483–96.

Blanchflower, David G., and Richard Freeman. 1992. Going different ways: Unionism in the U.S. and other advanced O.E.C.D. countries. *Industrial Relations* 31, no. 1:56–79.

Blanchflower, David G., and Lisa M. Lynch. 1994. Training at work: A comparison of US and British youths. In *Training and the private sector: International comparisons,* ed. Lisa M. Lynch. Chicago: University of Chicago Press.

Blanchflower, David G., and Andrew J. Oswald. 1989. International patterns of work. In *British social attitudes: Special international report,* ed. Roger Jowell, Sharon Witherspoon, and Lindsay Brook. Aldershot: Gower.

———. 1990. The wage curve. *Scandinavian Journal of Economics* 92:215–35.

———. 1994. *The wage curve.* Cambridge: MIT Press.

Blanchflower, David G., Andrew J. Oswald, and Mario Garrett. 1990. Insider power in wage determination. *Economica* 57:143–70.

Bowles, Samuel. 1985. The production process in a competitive economy: Walrasian, neo-Hobbesian and Marxian models. *American Economic Review* 75:16–36.

Browne, L. 1978. Regional unemployment rates—why are they so different? *New England Economic Review* (July/August), 5–26.

Carlin, Wendy, and David Soskice. 1990. *Macroeconomics and the wage bargain.* Oxford: Oxford University Press.

Christofides, Louis N., and Andrew J. Oswald. 1992. Real wage determination and rent-sharing in collective bargaining agreements. *Quarterly Journal of Economics* 107:985–1002.

Edin, Per-Anders, Bertil Holmlund, and Thomas Ostros. 1992. Wage behavior and labor market programs in Sweden: Evidence from micro data. University of Uppsala. Mimeo.

Freeman, Richard B. 1990. Employment and earnings of disadvantaged young men in a labor shortage economy. NBER Working Paper no. 3444. Cambridge, Mass.: National Bureau of Economic Research.

Greenwald, Bruce. 1983. A general analysis of the bias in the estimated standard errors of least squares coefficients. *Journal of Econometrics* 22:323–28.

Groot, Wim, Eddie Mekkeholt, and Hessel Oosterbeek. 1992. Further evidence on the wage curve. *Economics Letters* 38:355–59.

Hall, Robert E. 1970. Why is the unemployment rate so high at full employment? *Brookings Papers on Economic Activity,* no. 1:369–402.

———. 1972. Turnover in the labor force. *Brookings Papers on Economic Activity,* no. 3:709–64.

Harris, John R., and Michael P. Todaro. 1970. Migration, unemployment and development: A two-sector analysis. *American Economic Review* 60:126–42.

Holmlund, Bertil, and Johnny Zetterberg. 1991. Insider effects in wage determination: Evidence from five countries. *European Economic Review* 35:1009–34.

Jackman, Richard, Richard Layard, and Savvas Savouri. 1991. Labour market mismatch: A framework for thought. Discussion Paper no. 1. Centre for Economic Performance, London School of Economics.

Jowell, Roger, Sharon Witherspoon, and Lindsay Brook, eds. 1989. *British social attitudes: Special international report.* Gower: Aldershot.

———, eds. 1991. *British social attitudes: The 8th report.* Aldershot: Gower.

Katz, Lawrence F., and Alan B. Krueger. 1991a. Changes in the structure of wages in the public and private sectors. In *Research in labor economics,* vol. 12, ed. R. Ehrenberg. Greenwich, Conn.: JAI.

———. 1991b. The effects of the new minimum wage law in a low-wage labor market. *Industrial Relations Research Association Proceedings* 43:254–65.

Kloek, T. 1981. OLS estimation in a model where a microvariable is explained by aggregates and contemporaneous disturbances are equicorrelated. *Econometrica* 49:205–7.

Layard, Richard, and Stephen J. Nickell. 1986. Unemployment in Britain. *Economica* 53:S121–S170.

Layard, Richard, Stephen J. Nickell, and Richard Jackman. 1991. *Unemployment: Macroeconomic performance and the labour market.* Oxford: Oxford University Press.

Lindbeck, Assar. 1992. Macroeconomic theory and the labor market. *European Economic Review* 36:209–36.

Marston, Stephen T. 1985. Two views of the geographic distribution of unemployment. *Quarterly Journal of Economics* 79:57–79.

Moulton, Brent R. 1986. Random group effects and the precision of regression estimates. *Journal of Econometrics* 32:385–97.

———. 1987. Diagnostics for group effects in regression analysis. *Journal of Business and Economic Statistics* 5:275–82.

———. 1990. An illustration of a pitfall in estimating the effects of aggregate variables on micro units. *Review of Economics and Statistics* 72:334–38.

Nickell, Stephen J., and Sushil Wadhwani. 1990. Insider forces and wage determination. *Economic Journal* 100:496–509.

Oswald, Andrew J. 1986. Wage determination and recession: A report on recent work. *British Journal of Industrial Relations* 24, no. 2:181–94.

Phelps, Edmund. 1990. Effects on productivity: Total domestic product demand and incentive wages on unemployment in a non-monetary customer-market model of the small open economy. *Scandinavian Journal of Economics* 92:353–68.

———. 1992. Consumer demand and equilibrium unemployment in a working model of the customer-market incentive-wage economy. *Quarterly Journal of Economics* 107:1003–32.

Phillips, William. 1958. The relation between unemployment and the rate of change of money wage rates in the United Kingdom, 1861–1957. *Economica* 25:283–99.

Reza, Ali. 1978. Geographical differences in earnings and unemployment rates. *Review of Economics and Statistics* 60:201–8.

Sargan, Dennis. 1984. Wages and prices in the United Kingdom: A study in econometric methodology (1964). Reprinted in *Econometrics and quantitative economics,* ed. David Hendry and Kenneth Wallis. Oxford: Blackwell.

Shapiro, Carl, and Joseph Stiglitz. 1984. Equilibrium unemployment as a worker discipline device. *American Economic Review* 74:433–44.

Topel, Robert. 1986. Local labor markets. *Journal of Political Economy* 94:S111–S143.

Unemployment-inflation trade-offs in Europe. 1990. *Scandinavian Journal of Economics,* vol. 92, no. 2 (special issue).

Woodford, Michael. 1992. *Seven schools of macroeconomic thought,* by ES Phelps: A book review. *Journal of Economic Dynamics and Control* 16:391–98.

II Individual Country Studies

5 The Changing Structure of Male Earnings in Britain, 1974–1988

John Schmitt

While many of the changes in the U.S. wage structure during the 1970s and 1980s have been well documented (see, e.g., Blackburn, Bloom, and Freeman 1991; Blackburn and Bloom 1987; Bluestone 1990; Bluestone and Harrison 1988; Bound and Johnson 1989; Juhn, Murphy, and Pierce 1989; Katz and Murphy 1992; Katz and Revenga 1989; and Murphy and Welch 1992), little comparable work exists for Britain.[1] This paper uses data on male, full-time employees from the annual General Household Survey (GHS) to examine developments in the British wage structure during the period 1974–88.

The GHS data indicate that the British wage structure was far from stable during the 1970s and 1980s. Earnings inequality fell slightly during the 1970s, only to rise rapidly in the 1980s. Returns to labor market skills such as education and experience declined dramatically in the 1970s and then recovered in

John Schmitt was a research assistant at the Centre for Economic Performance (CEP), London School of Economics at the time this was written.

The author thanks Daron Acemoglu, Danny Blanchflower, Rebecca Blank, David Card, Richard Freeman, Sarah Gammage, Richard Jackman, Alan Manning, Richard Layard, Steve Machin, Dave Metcalf, Andrew Oswald, Steve Pischke, Andrew Scott, Stephen Trejo, Jonathan Wadsworth, and seminar participants at the CEP, the NBER, University College London, and the Welfare State Programme for helpful comments and discussions. Hilary Beedham, Maria Evandrou, and Jane Falkingham provided invaluable assistance with the General Household Survey (GHS). Material from the GHS, made available through the Office of Population Censuses and Surveys and the Economic and Social Research Council (ESRC) Data Archive, has been used by permission of the controller of H.M. Stationery Office.

1. Three other papers address some of the issues discussed here. Moghadam (1990) examines changes in the returns to education in a much broader analysis of wage determination using data from the Family Expenditure Survey for the years 1978–85. Katz, Loveman, and Blanchflower (chap. 1 in this volume) compare changes in the wage structure in four OECD countries using published data from the New Earnings Survey (NES) and micro data from the General Household Survey for their discussion of the United Kingdom. Bell, Rimmer, and Rimmer (1992) examine the role of age in overall wage inequality among full-time male employees using micro data from the NES.

the 1980s, although not always enough to compensate the earlier losses. Meanwhile, earnings for low-skilled workers increased in real terms over the entire period 1974–88.

The increases in earnings inequality and returns to skills during the 1980s parallel developments in the United States. However, the decline in British earnings inequality and skill differentials through the end of the 1970s—particularly the real earnings successes of low-skilled British workers over both decades—stands in strong contrast to the U.S. experience.

This paper documents some of the key developments of the British wage structure sketched above. It also attempts to explain these changes in the context of a simple relative supply and demand framework that takes into account the role of labor market institutions. It seeks to use the similarities and differences between the United States and Britain to shed light on the forces producing the upheavals in the wage structures of both countries.

The main conclusion is that a simple supply and demand analysis can plausibly explain most of the developments in the British wage structure during the 1970s and 1980s. A large rise in the relative supply of skilled labor during the 1970s drove skill differentials down and indirectly contributed to wage compression. In the 1980s, a large rise in the relative demand for skilled labor forced skill differentials and earnings inequality up despite continued strong growth in the supply of skilled labor. The GHS evidence, however, lends little support to the idea that the cause of the increasing relative demand for skills was a decline in the manufacturing sector in favor of services. Instead, it seems that technological or work-organization-related changes *within* industrial sectors were more likely to be driving the increase in demand for skilled workers.

Labor market institutions, which moderate the workings of the market to a much greater degree in Britain than in the United States, may play an important role in explaining the differences between the two countries. In the United States, low-skilled workers saw absolute declines in real earnings with only moderate rises in relative unemployment; in Britain, the low skilled experienced increases in real earnings and much higher unemployment rates. In the context of a supply and demand model, both countries may have faced the same shift in relative demand. The "free market" in the United States led workers to a "low-wage, high-employment" outcome, while British labor market institutions, particularly trade unions, may have allowed workers to "choose" a "high-pay, low-employment" point on the same relative demand curve. The relative strength of British trade unions, wages councils, and incomes policies may also have delayed the onset of the rise in wage inequality in Britain, relative to the United States.

5.1   The Data

The principle source of data is the annual General Household Survey (GHS) for the years 1974–88. The GHS is a survey of between ten and twelve thousand households in England, Scotland, and Wales conducted continuously throughout the year. It provides detailed, nationally representative information on individuals. Throughout this paper, I analyze a subsample of the GHS comprising males aged sixteen (the legal minimum age for leaving school) to sixty-four (the retirement age for males).[2]

The wage variable is the log of weekly earnings for full-time employees deflated using the appropriate monthly retail price index (RPI) with January 1974 as the base. The questions used to calculate weekly earnings underwent some change between the periods 1974–78 and 1979–88. For the years 1974–78, weekly earnings were derived from all earnings including wages, salaries, tips, bonuses, and commissions in all jobs held in the previous twelve months. To calculate weekly earnings, I divided these total earnings by total weeks worked in the previous twelve months. In the 1979–88 surveys, weekly earnings were estimated as the usual gross earnings including tips and bonuses per pay period from the worker's main job, divided by the usual number of weeks covered in each pay period. These changes may affect comparisons of earnings between the two periods, but no discontinuity is evident, and the GHS weekly earnings data appear to be consistent with data from the New Earnings Survey (NES). Unfortunately, no hourly wage series is available owing to substantial changes in work hours information collected after 1983.

The education variables are based on the highest educational qualification earned by the respondent. The use of qualification-based variables offers two advantages over education measures based on years of schooling. First, the qualification variables outperform years variables in standard human capital equations (see Schmitt 1991). Second, the value of different types of qualifications, particularly vocational as opposed to academic qualifications, may shed more light on the workings of the supply and demand for skills than an undifferentiated years variable.

A complete list and brief description of the education variables appears in table 5.1. The large number of categories reflects the relatively complicated structure of British educational qualifications. All British children must attend full-time education until the age of sixteen, at which point a large portion of them leave school.[3] Those who leave school without earning a qualification join the "no qualifications" (NO QUAL) group. This is by far the largest group in the sample, comprising approximately 54 percent of the male labor force in 1974 and 32 percent in 1988.

---

2. For a detailed description of the GHS, see the annual reports on the GHS published by the Office of Population and Census Surveys. For a detailed description of variables used in this paper, see Schmitt (1992).

3. The school-leaving age was fourteen until 1946 and then fifteen until 1972. This may present some problems with interpretation of the data since the lowest-skilled group does not have a uniform absolute number of years of schooling over time. However, I find no difference in the basic results on skills premiums and earnings dispersion when I conduct the work reported here on a fixed membership subsample defined by year of birth. This cohort approach keeps the composition of absolute years of schooling constant for the group with no qualifications (see Schmitt 1991).

Those who earn qualifications, broadly speaking, follow either a vocational or an academic track. Workers generally earn vocational qualifications while they work, through apprenticeship schemes, part-time study, or relatively short periods of full-time study "sandwiched" between spells of employment, often with the same employer. The vocational qualifications increase in skill from miscellaneous, relatively low-skilled apprenticeships (VOC-OTHER) through incremented, nationally recognized apprenticeships (VOC-LOW, VOC-MIDDLE, and VOC-HIGH). The highest-level vocational qualifications can involve some instruction at what in the United States would be the college level. Some of the qualifications in table 5.1 usually facilitate entry into female-dominated occupations such as teaching, nursing, and clerical jobs (CLERICAL, O-LEV&CLER, NURSING, TEACHING). Few men earn these qualifications.

Schoolchildren following the "academic track" prepare for and take a series of national tests by academic subject. Passing grades on these exams, generally taken at around age sixteen, lead to qualifications that would place individuals in the OTHER, O-LEVEL 1–4, O-LEV&CLER, and O-LEVEL 5+ categories. The "ordinary-level" examination categories distinguish between students who pass between one and four examinations and those who attempt and pass five or more. The distinction is important for some employers and for further study. After "O-levels," some students (usually at around age eighteen) take further national examinations at the "advanced level." For some students, "A-levels" are a terminal qualification; for others, they are only a prerequisite for university admission. The UNIVERSITY category here includes all students who successfully complete the standard three-year university course as well as those who study further. The group with university qualifications represents about 5 percent of the total male labor force in 1974, rising to approximately 11 percent by 1988.

The other principal human capital variable (EXP) measures potential labor market experience, defined in the standard way as age minus age left full-time education.[4] The GHS contains no measure of actual labor market experience, but limiting the sample to males aged sixteen to sixty-four should reduce some of the difficulties associated with using potential rather than actual experience.

A significant drawback of the GHS data is the poor information on workers' industry characteristics. From 1974 to 1980, the GHS reports twenty-four consistent industry classifications. From 1981 to 1988, the industry classification

---

4. The determination of years of full-time education is problematic. The GHS asks respondents their age when they last left full-time education, not the total number of years of full-time education. Each of the fifteen surveys has several hundred (of four to six thousand valid male) respondents who report leaving their last period of full-time education after the age of thirty. The experience definition here assumes that anyone leaving full-time education after twenty-seven has not studied continuously. In these cases, years of schooling is calculated as age minus age left secondary school plus 3.

Table 5.1   **Education Qualification Variables**

Variable	Description
UNIVERSITY	UNIVERSITY: Higher degree (Census Level A), first degree, university diploma or certificate, qualifications obtained from colleges of further education or from professional institutions of degree standard (Census Level B)
VOC-HIGH	HIGHEST VOCATIONAL: Higher National Certificate (HNC) or Diploma (HND), BEC/TEC Higher Certificate or Higher Diploma, City and Guilds Full Technological Certificate, qualifications obtained from colleges of further education or from professional institutions below degree level but above GCE A-level standard
TEACHING	TEACHING: Nongraduate teaching qualifications (Census Level C)
NURSING	NURSING: Nursing qualifications (e.g., SEN, SRN, SCM)
A-LEVEL	A-LEVEL: GCE A-level, Scottish Leaving Certificate (SLC), Scottish Certificate of Education (SCE), Scottish University Preliminary Examination (SUPE) at Higher Grade, Certificate of Sixth Year Studies
VOC-MIDDLE	MIDDLE VOCATIONAL: City and Guilds Advanced or Final, Ordinary National Certificate (ONC) or Diploma (OND), BEC/TEC National, General, or Ordinary
O-LEVEL 5+	FIVE OR MORE O-LEVELS: Five or more subjects at GCE O-level obtained before 1975 or in grades A–C if obtained later, five or more subjects at SCE Ordinary obtained before 1973 or in bands A–C if obtained later, five or more subjects at CSE grade 1 or at School Certificate, SLC Lower, or SUPE Lower
VOC-LOW	LOWER-MIDDLE VOCATIONAL: City and Guilds Craft or Ordinary
O-LEV&CLER	LESS THAN FIVE O-LEVELS WITH CLERICAL OR COMMERCIAL QUALIFICATION: One to four subjects at GCE O-level or equivalent with clerical or commercial qualification such as typing, shorthand, bookkeeping, commerce
O-LEVEL 1–4	LESS THAN FIVE O-LEVELS WITHOUT A CLERICAL OR COMMERCIAL QUALIFICATION
CLERICAL	CLERICAL OR COMMERCIAL QUALIFICATION WITHOUT O-LEVELS
VOC-OTHER	LOWEST VOCATIONAL: Miscellaneous apprenticeships
OTHER	MISCELLANEOUS, NONVOCATIONAL QUALIFICATIONS: Other qualifications including CSE Grades 2–5, plus all remaining qualifications, which consist mainly of local or regional school-leaving certificates and college or professional awards no regarded as "higher education," i.e., not above GCE A-level standard
NO QUAL	NO QUALIFICATIONS: No qualifications including those with no formal schooling

system is reduced to ten one-digit SIC categories, which cannot be matched consistently with the earlier classification. As a result, I have been forced to reduce the industrial categories to only seven groupings in order to find a definition that is consistent over the fifteen-year sample. The seven categories, however, do allow for a distinction between manufacturing (three categories) and services, the two sectors that have featured prominently in much of the discussion of the changing wage structure in Britain and the United States.

5.2   Changes in the British Wage Structure

5.2.1   Earnings Inequality

Earnings inequality in Britain fell slightly during the 1970s, only to rise rapidly during the 1980s. Meanwhile, in the United States, inequality grew continuously over both decades (see, e.g., Juhn, Murphy, and Pierce 1989, table 1 and fig. 3).

The data in panel A of table 5.2 summarize the British earnings distribution at three periods of the GHS sample, 1974–76, 1978–80, and 1986–88. Following much of the work in the United States, the basic measure of inequality in table 5.2 is the difference between the log earnings of workers in different percentiles of the earnings distribution. Table 5.2 also reports the standard deviation of log earnings, another measure of earnings dispersion.

Both measures of inequality paint the same picture. The 90–10 differential (the difference between the log earnings of workers in the ninetieth and the tenth percentiles of the distribution) and the standard deviation of log earnings show a slight decline (0.01 log points) between 1974–76 and 1978–80. Both measures, however, increased by approximately 20 percent between 1978–80 and 1986–88 (the 90–10 differential by 0.22 log points and the standard deviation of log earnings by 0.11 log points). The rise in dispersion in the 1980s does not appear to be simply a phenomenon of the tails of the distribution since the data also indicate a steep rise in the 75–25 differential during the 1980s.

Figure 5.1 makes the same point more dramatically. The figure shows the log point change, relative to 1974, in real earnings for the tenth, fiftieth, and ninetieth percentiles of the earnings distribution. From 1974 to 1980, earnings

Table 5.2		Log Real Weekly Earnings Deciles and Quartiles			
	1974–76 (1)	1978–80 (2)	1986–88 (3)	Change, (2) − (1)	Change, (3) − (2)
A. Raw earnings:					
90-10	.957	.947	1.170	−.010	.223
90-50	.471	.469	.586	−.003	.117
50-10	.486	.479	.583	−.007	.104
75-25	.468	.476	.615	.008	.139
SD	.422	.412	.524	−.011	.112
B. Residual earnings:					
90-10	.753	.750	.888	−.003	.138
90-50	.379	.388	.446	.009	.057
50-10	.374	.362	.442	−.012	.080
75-25	.388	.378	.445	−.009	.067
SD	.318	.313	.378	−.006	.066

Source: General Household Survey.

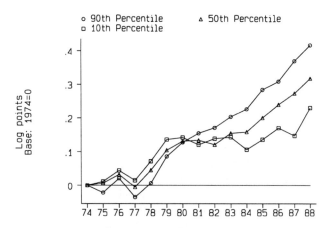

Fig. 5.1   **"Indexed" real weekly earnings**
Source: General Household Survey data deflated by the retail price index, January 1974 = 100.0

of the tenth percentile grew faster than those of the fiftieth and ninetieth percentiles; the earnings of the ninetieth percentile grew at the slowest rate. After 1980, the growth positions reversed, with tenth-percentile earnings remaining flat over most of the rest of the sample and the ninetieth percentile making large gains.

5.2.2   Education and Experience Differentials

A portion of the changes in overall inequality in Britain during the 1970s and 1980s was due to the decline and subsequent recovery of financial returns to labor market skills. Education and experience differentials fell steeply between the mid- and the late 1970s. By 1986–88, however, education differentials had made a strong recovery, and experience differentials had more than made up for ground lost in the previous decade. In the United States, education differentials reached historic lows in the mid-1970s and grew rapidly through the late 1980s (see Blackburn, Bloom, and Freeman 1991, table 2 and fig. 2). Experience differentials in the United States increased steadily after 1970, especially during the 1980s (see Juhn, Murphy, and Pierce 1989, table 3).

To measure the change in returns to labor market skills in Britain, I have estimated identical human capital weekly earnings equations for fifteen consecutive years of GHS data. Each equation explains the log of real weekly earnings as a function of thirteen education qualification dummy variables, their full interactions with years of potential experience and its square, and nine regional dummies. Owing to the omission of ability, family background, and other variables, the human capital equations may yield biased estimates of the *level* of returns to skills in the individual regressions. However, assuming that the effects of these biases are constant over time, the difference in estimated returns from one year to the next should provide a consistent estimate of the *change* in the returns.

The education differentials in panel A of table 5.3 are calculated as the sum of the coefficient for the qualification-specific dummy variable, plus the value of the qualification-specific experience differential evaluated at twenty years of experience, minus the experience differential for a worker with no qualifications also evaluated at twenty years. This formulation of the differential allows a simple yet flexible representation of the returns to a qualification: qualifications can provide a once-and-for-all boost (through the qualification dummy) and a different earnings profile (through the qualification-specific experience terms). The returns to high- and mid-level qualifications (UNIVERSITY, VOC-HIGH, A-LEVEL, VOC-MIDDLE, and O-LEVEL 5+) in table 5.3 all decline between the first and the second periods. In the 1980s, however, the differentials for these qualifications increase strongly, although generally not enough to offset the declines of the 1970s. The returns to the low-level qualifications (VOC-LOW, O-LEVEL 1–4, and VOC-OTHER) manage modest gains in the 1980s, which exceed losses during the 1970s.

Figure 5.2 plots the estimated returns at twenty years' experience for condensed educational qualifications (UNIV, MIDDLE, and LOW) over all fifteen years in the sample.[5] The returns to university and mid-level qualifications fall through 1979–80, rise again until 1984, and then remain approximately constant through the end of the sample.

Panel B of table 5.3 shows the estimated differentials for years of potential experience. The figures reported are the fixed-weighted averages of the experience differentials for all fourteen education categories evaluated at the number of years indicated in the label. The weights used were the average employment shares of the education categories for the period 1974–88. The experience differentials show declines in the 1970s, followed by strong gains in the 1980s. By the late 1980s, experience premiums were well above the levels prevailing in the mid-1970s.

Similar estimates of changes in education and experience differentials for workers aged sixteen to thirty appear in table 5.4. Since younger workers have shorter tenure with the firms where they work, their earnings are likely to be more responsive to market forces changing the earnings structure. In the United States, for example, increases in experience and education differentials were higher among younger workers than among the population as a whole (Blackburn, Bloom, and Freeman 1991). The regression results summarized in table 5.4 show that the rise in skill differentials was also more marked among young British workers.

5. The condensed qualifications are defined as follows: UNIVERSITY is UNIVERSITY; MIDDLE is VOC-HIGH, TEACHING, NURSING, A-LEVEL, VOC-MIDDLE, and O-LEVEL 5+; LOW is VOC-LOW, O-LEV&CLER, O-LEVEL 1–4, CLERICAL, VOC-OTHER, and OTHER; NO QUAL is NO QUAL.

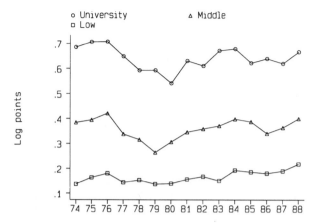

Fig. 5.2   Education differential at 20 years' experience, 16–64-year-olds
Source: General Household Survey using procedure described in notes to table 5.3.

Table 5.3   **Skill Differentials: Sixteen- to Sixty-four-Year-Olds**

	1974–76 (1)	1978–80 (2)	1986–88 (3)	Change, (2) − (1)	Change, (3) − (2)
A. Educational qualifications (20 years' experience):					
UNIVERSITY	.700	.576	.643	−.124	.067
VOC-HIGH	.400	.306	.382	−.094	.076
A-LEVEL	.529	.395	.494	−.134	.098
VOC-MIDDLE	.266	.193	.282	−.073	.089
O-LEVEL 5+	.471	.312	.351	−.160	.039
VOC-LOW	.199	.153	.202	−.046	.048
O-LEVEL 1–4	.312	.285	.331	−.027	.046
VOC-OTHER	.085	.079	.096	−.006	.017
NO-QUAL	.000	.000	.000	.000	.000
B. Years of potential experience:					
0 YEARS	.000	.000	.000	.000	.000
5 YEARS	.219	.192	.258	−.027	.066
10 YEARS	.396	.346	.468	−.049	.121
20 YEARS	.620	.542	.739	−.078	.196
30 YEARS	.674	.588	.813	−.087	.225
40 YEARS	.558	.483	.690	−.075	.207

Source: General Household Survey.

Note: Average values implied by annual regressions of log real weekly pay against 13 education dummies, experience and its square fully interacted with education dummies, and 9 regional dummies. Education differential is the value of the qualification-specific dummy variable, plus the qualification-specific experience differential evaluated at 20 years, minus the experience differential at 20 years for workers with no qualifications. Experience differential is the fixed-weighted average over all education groups. Weights are the average employment share for each qualification over the period 1974–88. All underlying qualification dummies and base-level experience variables are significant at at least the 5 percent level.

Table 5.4   **Skill Differentials: Sixteen- to Thirty-Year-Olds**

	1974–76 (1)	1978–80 (2)	1986–88 (3)	Change, (2) − (1)	Change, (3) − (2)
A. Educational qualifica-tions (5 years' experience):					
UNIVERSITY	.622	.526	.744	−.096	.218
VOC-HIGH	.447	.375	.578	−.072	.203
A-LEVEL	.237	.333	.405	.096	.072
VOC-MIDDLE	.264	.384	.333	.120	−.052
O-LEVEL 5+	.166	.100	.246	−.066	145
VOC-LOW	.127	.307	.158	.180	−.148
O-LEVEL 1–4	−.002	.051	.116	.054	.065
VOC-OTHER	.353	.336	.365	−.017	.030
NO-QUAL	.000	.000	.000	.000	.000
B. Years of potential experience:					
0 YEARS	.000	.000	.000	.000	.000
5 YEARS	.291	.228	.322	−.063	.094
10 YEARS	.581	.456	.643	.125	.187

Source: General Household Survey.

Note: Average values implied by annual regressions of log real weekly pay against 13 education dummies, years of experience fully interacted with education dummies, and 9 region dummies. Education differential is the value of the qualification-specific dummy variable, plus the qualification-specific experience differential evaluated at 5 years, minus the experience differential at 5 years for workers with no qualifications. Experience differential is fixed-weighted average over all education groups. Weights are the average employment share for each qualification over the period 1974–88. Most underlying qualification dummies and base-level experience variables are significant at at least the 5 percent level.

5.2.3   Residual Inequality

Education and experience differentials can explain only a portion of the change in overall inequality in Britain during the 1970s and 1980s. As earnings differentials rose *between* education and experience groups in the 1980s, earnings dispersion was also increasing *within* these same groups. The same is true for the United States, where changes in education and experience differentials can account for only about half the increase in overall inequality since the mid-1970s (see, e.g., Juhn, Murphy, and Pierce 1989, table 4).

The regression residuals from the earnings equations in the previous section clearly establish that changes in education and experience differentials fail to explain most of the rise in overall inequality. Panel B of table 5.2 above summarizes the distribution of these residuals for the three key time periods. The residuals can be interpreted as individual earnings purged of any systematic differences between "groups" defined by the explanatory variables in the regression (education and experience). Were the increase in overall inequality due solely to rising inequality *between* education-experience groups, we would expect the residual distribution to show no tendency toward greater inequality:

the overall inequality would stem from changing endowments or market valuations of human capital that the earnings regression would "remove" from the data. In fact, residual inequality rises considerably. The 90–10 differential for residual earnings grew 0.138 log points between 1978–80 and 1986–88, as opposed to a 0.223-log-point rise for raw earnings. By this crude measure, changes in returns to education and experience can account for only 40 percent of the rise in British earnings inequality during the 1980s. Approximately 60 percent of the increase occurred *within* education and experience groups.

5.2.4 Real Earnings of Low-Skilled Workers

While inequality increased substantially in Britain during the 1980s, the real earnings of employed, full-time, low-skilled workers were also growing. In the United States, on the other hand, inequality increased in large measure because the real earnings of low-skilled workers fell. High school dropouts or workers in the tenth percentile of the U.S. earnings distribution, for example, suffered steady and significant reductions in real annual and weekly earnings after the late 1960s (see, e.g., Blackburn, Bloom, and Freeman 1991, table 1; and Juhn, Murphy, and Pierce 1989, fig. 3).

The median real weekly earnings of British workers with no qualifications increased by approximately 0.30 log points between 1974 and 1988. Since this result stands in such contrast with the experience of the United States, I have made several attempts to check the robustness of the result with different ways of defining low-skilled workers and to confirm the GHS results using other data sources.

While those without educational qualification may be a natural choice to represent "low-skilled" workers, they may not be entirely representative of the low skilled. One important reason is that workers with no qualifications tend to be older than those with qualifications. On average, workers without qualifications may have been able to improve their earnings position by capturing some of the rise in returns to experience during the 1980s. One way to reduce the potential for this experience effect is to choose workers in the tenth percentile of the distribution as a proxy for low-skilled workers. As figure 5.1 above shows, real earnings for workers in the tenth percentile increased by approximately 0.20 log points over the sample period.

At between one-third and half of the total sample in each year, the no-qualifications group is also much larger than the natural low-skilled groupings in the United States such as high school dropouts. It could be that, even as *median* real earnings for the no-qualifications group were rising, the earnings of the less skilled among those without qualifications were dropping. However, by 1988, real earnings for the tenth percentile of the no-qualifications group were approximately 0.15 log points above their level in 1974.

The GHS results are also consistent with other publicly available data on British earnings. Published data from the New Earnings Survey (NES), an annual survey of approximately 1 percent of the British labor force collected through their employers, indicate that the weekly and hourly wages of workers in the tenth percentile of the male earnings distribution both increased by between 10 and 13 percent between 1974 and 1988 (see, e.g., Katz, Loveman, and Blanchflower, chap. 1 in this volume; and Schmitt 1992).[6]

5.2.5 Employment Rates

One of the most striking features of the British wage structure over the period 1974–88 was the large number of people who fell out of it entirely. The unemployment rate quadrupled between the mid-1970s and the mid-1980s—from under 3 percent to over 12 percent. The incidence of unemployment fell much more heavily on the low skilled than on the population as a whole. The unemployment rate for workers with no qualifications exceeded 15 percent in the mid-1980s, with long-term unemployment especially high among those with no qualifications. In the United States, low-skilled workers also bore the brunt of rising unemployment in the 1970s and early 1980s, but the overall and skill-specific unemployment rates there were much lower than in Britain (see, e.g., Blackburn, Bloom, and Freeman 1991, table 3).

To measure the relative unemployment experience of British workers, I have estimated unemployment rates by educational qualification using separate binary probit equations for each of the years of the GHS. Panel A of table 5.5 summarizes the probit-predicted unemployment rates for the three subperiods assuming that all workers were forty years old. The unemployment rates for nearly all qualifications closely track changes in the overall unemployment rate: little change between 1974–76 and 1978–80, followed by large increases through 1986–88. Figure 5.3 graphs the complete unemployment series for the four condensed education categories introduced earlier.

In a world with involuntary unemployment, the return to education has two components—a higher wage while employed and a higher probability of finding and keeping a job. In this simple framework, we can adjust the earlier education differentials to include the differential employment probability associated with a given qualification. Defining the employment probability as one minus the estimated unemployment rate, the relative employment rate for qualification i is then $(1 - u_i)/(1 - u_{\text{NOQUAL}})$. While relative employment rates were low and constant during the 1970s, they rose substantially in the 1980s. Adjusting the changes in education differentials for the changes in relative employment substantially increases the returns to education during the 1980s. Among university graduates, for example, the rise in the education differential

---

6. Meghir and Whitehouse (1992), however, do find a slight decline in real hourly earnings between 1975 and 1986 for the tenth percentile of the distribution of nonunion, full- and part-time, manual male employees aged twenty-two to fifty-six using data from the Family Expenditure Survey (see their fig. 6). But, even in this fairly disadvantaged segment of the British labor market, the twenty-fifth percentile managed to hold its own between 1975 and 1986. Furthermore, as Meghir and Whitehouse note, the variables that they use to divide their sample into union and nonunion sectors are only indirect measures of union status and may not be completely consistent over time.

Table 5.5   **Unemployment and Relative Employment Rates**

	1974–76 (1)	1978–80 (2)	1986–88 (3)	Change, (2) − (1)	Change, (3) − (2)
A. Estimated unemployment rate:					
UNIVERSITY	.014	.013	.027	−.001	.014
VOC-HIGH	.010	.009	.028	−.001	.019
A-LEVEL	.020	.014	.050	−.007	.037
VOC-MIDDLE	.006	.017	.042	.011	.025
O-LEVEL 5+	.011	.016	.040	.005	.024
VOC-LOW	.014	.021	.054	.007	.033
O-LEVEL 1–4	.017	.019	.049	.002	.030
VOC-OTHER	.026	.036	.085	.010	.049
NO QUAL	.041	.055	.131	.014	.077
B. Employment/population ratio:					
UNIVERSITY	.928	.941	.912	.012	−.029
VOC-HIGH	.961	.957	.924	−.004	−.033
A-LEVEL	.786	.752	.779	−.034	−.027
VOC-MIDDLE	.971	.957	.895	−.014	−.063
O-LEVEL 5+	.834	.835	.764	.001	−.071
VOC-LOW	.960	.939	.889	−.021	−.051
O-LEVEL 1–4	.909	.878	.855	−.031	−.023
VOC-OTHER	.942	.908	.796	−.034	−.112
NO QUAL	.886	.845	.704	−.040	−.142

Source: General Household Survey.

Note: Unemployment rates implied by probit regression of employment status against 9 education dummies, age and its square, and 9 region dummies. The 9 qualifications are the 8 here plus an "other" category not shown. Predicted rates evaluated at age 40. Employment/population ratio calculated as GHS sample share of all 16–64-year-old males in full- or part-time employment.

between 1978–80 and 1986–88 increases from 0.067 to 0.113 log points after factoring in the change in employment probabilities over the period.[7]

Given the large drop in labor force participation rates among working-age males during the 1980s, the unemployment rates in panel A of table 5.5 tell only part of the story of the decline in employment rates. Panel B of table 5.5 lists the sample employment/population ratios calculated from the raw GHS data. They show an even sharper drop in relative employment probabilities than implied by the unemployment rates. Except for A-LEVEL and O-LEVEL 5+, employment/population rates in the period 1974–76 clustered around 90

7. To calculate the change in the employment probability–adjusted differential, multiply the average university differential from tables 5.3 and 5.4 for the period 1978–80 by the relative university employment probability $(1 - u_{\text{UNIV}}/(1 - u_{\text{NOQUAL}}))$ for the same period $(1.044 \times 0.576 = 0.601)$; do the same for 1986–88 $(1.120 \times 0.643 = 0.720)$; and then subtract the first from the second $(0.720 - 0.601 = 0.113)$.

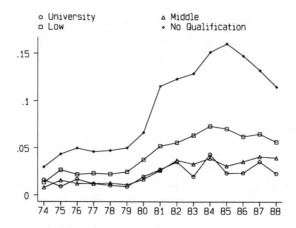

Fig. 5.3   Unemployment rate
Source: General Household Survey using procedure described in notes to table 5.5.

percent.[8] By 1986–88, employment/population rates fell off by a few percentage points for highly skilled workers and plummeted by 14 percentage points for workers with no qualifications.

5.3   Supply, Demand, and Labor Market Institutions

Simple models of the relative supply of and demand for workers of different skill levels have been quite successful in explaining changes in skill differentials in the United States (see, e.g., Freeman 1976; Bound and Johnson 1989; Blackburn, Bloom, and Freeman 1991; Katz and Murphy 1992; and Murphy and Welch 1992). A relative supply and demand model also seems a natural benchmark for an analysis of British skill differentials. In this section, I examine the market for skilled labor in Britain, taking into account the evolving role of several British labor market institutions.

5.3.1   Relative Supply of Skills

In Britain, the rise in the supply of workers with educational qualifications during the 1970s and 1980s was dramatic. A breakdown of the male labor force by educational qualifications for the three subperiods of the GHS sample appears in table 5.6. In 1974–76, workers with no qualifications constituted over half the male labor force. By 1986–88, they were less than one-third of the total. Over the same period, workers with university degrees more than doubled from about 5 to 11 percent of the total labor force. Interestingly, the share of workers with the highest levels of vocational qualifications (VOC-

---

8. A-levels are normally a prerequisite for university admission; students taking A-levels generally have five or more O-levels. Therefore, the large expansion in university education in the 1970s and 1980s probably explains the low employment rates among individuals with these qualifications.

Table 5.6   **Relative Supply of Skills**

	1974–76 (1)	1978–80 (2)	1986–88 (3)	Change, (2) − (1)	Change, (3) − (2)
A. Relative supply of males, 16–64:					
UNIVERSITY	.048	.079	.109	.030	.031
VOC-HIGH	.044	.065	.097	.022	.032
A-LEVEL	.030	.021	.045	−.015	.024
VOC-MIDDLE	.042	.043	.076	.001	.033
O-LEVEL 5+	.058	.066	.043	.008	−.023
VOC-LOW	.048	.046	.063	.002	.017
O-LEVEL 1–4	.051	.058	.085	.008	.027
VOC-OTHER	.095	.100	.071	.006	−.029
NO QUAL	.517	.464	.323	−.053	−.141
B. Ratio of females to males, 16–64:					
UNIVERSITY	.272	.314	.455	.041	.142
VOC-HIGH	.107	.139	.172	.032	.033
A-LEVEL	.584	.574	.819	−.010	.245
VOC-MIDDLE	.062	.083	.252	.021	.169
O-LEVEL 5+	.971	1.045	1.446	.074	.401
VOC-LOW	.114	.135	.311	.021	.176
O-LEVEL 1–4	.701	.827	.828	.126	.001
VOC-OTHER	.095	.119	.143	.024	.024
NO QUAL	.812	.852	.857	.040	.005

Source: General Household Survey.

Note: Columns in panel A do not total to one owing to the exclusion of workers with qualifications not shown.

HIGH and VOC-MIDDLE) also doubled over the three periods. Only two of the education groups failed to increase their share of the labor force over the full sample: five or more O-levels (O-LEVEL 5+) and the lowest vocational qualification (VOC-OTHER). Given the fall in workers with no qualifications, these declines probably reflect decisions by individuals not to end their education after achieving these qualifications but instead to use them to gain access to further education.

In a competitive labor market with constant relative demand, an increase in the relative supply of skilled labor would reduce the relative wages of skilled labor. The large increase in the relative supply of skilled labor is consistent with the observed decline in returns to education in Britain during the 1970s but makes a coherent explanation of the recovery of education differentials in the 1980s more difficult. The coincident rise in supplies of and differentials for skilled workers during the 1980s strongly suggests that the relative demand for skilled workers must have grown substantially over the decade.

One of the major developments of the postwar period in both Britain and the United States was the enormous increase in female participation in the paid workforce. New female workers may have competed disproportionately with low-skilled male workers, thus helping widen skill differentials. Panel B of table 5.6 reports the ratio of females to males by educational qualification for the three subperiods. In 1974–76, there was approximately one female graduate for every four male graduates. By 1986–88, the ratio had doubled to nearly one female graduate for every two male graduates. In comparison, the ratio of females to males among workers with no qualifications increased from 81 to 86 percent in the same period. The rise in female participation, therefore, led to a disproportionate rise in competition for qualified workers.[9] The rise in female participation actually makes it more difficult to explain widening differentials in the 1980s.

The large growth in the relative supply of skilled labor may lie behind the decline in skill differentials and inequality in the 1970s. In the absence of new sources of competition, the declining relative share of male low-skilled workers may also help explain the rise in absolute earnings for low-skilled workers over both decades. However, relative supply movements clearly make the rise in differentials in the 1980s a more puzzling phenomenon.

5.3.2   Relative Demand for Skills

The supply analysis implies an important role for relative demand changes in the 1980s. Most previous research on the U.S. economy has usefully divided relative demand changes into two categories: "between-industry" factors, which affect product demand (and thus labor demand) across industries (e.g., the rise in services as opposed to manufacturing or the rise in foreign as opposed to domestic sources for manufacturing goods), and "within-industry" factors, which affect the valuation of skills independently of changes in product demand (e.g., skills-biased technological innovations or organizational developments favoring skilled workers). While the debate in the United States generally agrees on the importance of demand shifts, no clear conclusions have been reached about these two, not necessarily competing explanations.

Given international trade in goods and production technology, the demand shifts hypothesized in the United States are also likely to have been operating in Britain. The dramatic decline in the share of manufacturing employment in total employment evident in figure 5.4 certainly makes a case for a careful examination of the role of between-industry effects in the growth of inequality during the 1980s. While the relatively poor range of industrial variables makes the GHS data set less than ideal for analyzing relative demand shifts, I have nevertheless conducted some crude tests of the principal demand shift hypotheses. The GHS data do allow us to distinguish workers in three separate manu-

9. Unless females with educational qualifications substituted for males with no qualifications. However, given the employment structure and occupational gender segmentation in Britain during the sample period, this is probably not an important factor.

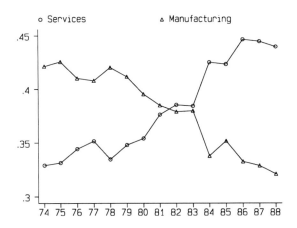

Fig. 5.4   Share in total employment
Source: General Household Survey.

facturing categories from workers in agriculture, services, and two other generally nontraded sectors (transport and communications; construction). I use
these simple categories to attempt to estimate the effect of the general decline
in domestic manufacturing on skill differentials and overall earnings inequality.

Following Blackburn, Bloom, and Freeman (1991), I use two methods to
estimate the role of industrial shifts in the rise in skill differentials between
1978–80 and 1986–88. The first is a shift-share decomposition of the change
in education differentials between the two periods. The second is a regression-
based decomposition of education and experience differentials.

The shift-share decomposition divides the change in education differentials
into three components: (1) the portion due to between-industry changes in the
distribution of employment by qualification; (2) the portion due to within-
industry changes in the earnings of workers with different qualifications; and
(3) the interaction of these two effects.

The decomposition involves several stages of calculations. First, the raw
earnings data are used to calculate education differentials, d_{qst}, for each qualification (q) within each industrial sector (s) in each year (t):

(1) $$d_{qst} = \overline{\ln w_{qst}} - \overline{\ln w_{0st}},$$

where w refers to real wages, 0 is the base group with no qualifications, and a
bar indicates a sample mean. Second, the qualification differentials in each
sector are used to produce an economy-wide "raw differential," d_{qt}, for each
qualification as a weighted average of the qualification differential in each of
the sectors:

(2) $$d_{qt} = \sum_{s} d_{qst} \cdot x_{qst},$$

where x is the proportion of all workers with qualification q working in industry s at time t. Third, the between-industry effect is removed from the differential by reestimating d_{qt} using the average employment share for the period 1974–88:

$$(3) \qquad \hat{d}_{qt} = \sum_s d_{qst} \cdot \bar{x}_{qs}.$$

Fourth, in a similar way, the within-industry effect is removed from the differential by reestimating d_{qt} using the average industry-specific differential for each qualification over the full sample:

$$(4) \qquad \hat{d}_{qt} = \sum_s \bar{d}_{qs} \cdot x_{qst}.$$

Finally, the changes in the three differentials are calculated for the three subperiods. The interaction of the between- and within-industry effects is defined as the signed difference between the change in the raw differential and the sum of the changes of the two "controlled" differentials.

The results of this shift-share decomposition for the 1980s appear in panel B of table 5.7. The first column shows the actual change in the education differentials. Note that these estimates differ slightly from earlier ones since the differentials here are calculated using the raw data without controlling for compositional effects. The shifts in employment from manufacturing to the other sectors make only a negligible contribution toward the rise in differentials during the 1980s (see col. 2 of panel B). The within-industry component of the change in differentials (col. 3 of panel B) accounts for nearly all the rise in the overall education differentials.

The second decomposition technique attempts to measure the effect of manufacturing-to-service employment changes using a modified human capital earnings equation. To implement this decomposition, I pooled the GHS samples for 1978–80 and 1986–88 (and, separately, 1974–76 and 1978–80) and used the data to estimate an equation of the form

$$(5) \qquad \ln w_i = a + b_1 S_i + b_2 Q_i + b_3 (D_i Q_i) + b_4 R_i + b_5 (D_i R_i) + e_i,$$

where S is a vector of six industrial sector dummy variables; Q is a vector of educational qualification dummy variables and their complete interactions with experience and experience squared; R is a vector of nine region dummies; D is a dummy variable equal to one if the observation belongs to the later subperiod; e is an error term; and a and b are parameters to be estimated. In this specification, the coefficients, b_3, represent the change between the first and the second periods in the differential associated with each of the educational qualifications. We can measure the effect of between-industry employment changes by comparing the estimates of b_3 in a regression like (5) with estimates of b_3 in an identical regression that excludes the industry-sector dummies.[10] If the decline in relative earnings for the low skilled is due to their

---

10. The qualification differentials are constructed exactly as in tables 5.3 and 5.4.

Table 5.7   **Industry-Based Shift-Share Decomposition**

| | | Change in Differential Due To: | | |
	Change in Raw Differential	Between Industry Shifts	Within Industry Shifts	Interaction
A. 1974–76 to 1978–80:				
UNIVERSITY	−.074	.006	−.078	−.002
VOC-HIGH	−.109	−.003	−.105	−.001
A-LEVEL	.161	.004	.166	−.008
VOC-MIDDLE	.040	.000	.040	−.001
O-LEVEL 5+	−.194	−.022	−.174	.001
VOC-LOW	.128	.001	.128	−.001
O-LEVEL 1–4	.004	.006	.003	−.005
VOC-OTHER	−.003	−.001	−.003	.001
B. 1978–80 to 1986–88:				
UNIVERSITY	.080	.001	.074	.004
VOC-HIGH	.048	.004	.042	.002
A-LEVEL	−.068	.005	−.075	.003
VOC-MIDDLE	−.053	.004	−.061	.004
O-LEVEL 5+	.161	.036	.128	−.003
VOC-LOW	−.139	−.003	−.132	−.004
O-LEVEL 1–4	.016	.007	.005	.004
VOC-OTHER	.008	−.002	.009	.001

Source: General Household Survey.

increasing concentration outside the manufacturing sector, then the estimated change in differentials (b_3) should be smaller in the regression that controls for industrial sector. The difference between the b_3 coefficients in the regressions with and without the industry controls, therefore, should give an estimate of the importance of industry shifts.

Panel B of table 5.8 reports results of the regression decomposition of the industry shift for the 1980s. Column 1 presents the estimated increase in the differential in a regression like (5) that excludes industrial sector controls. These differentials are nearly identical to those in column 2, estimated using six industry dummies. The resulting estimated cross-industry effects in column 3 are tiny, reinforcing the conclusions from the shift-share analysis.[11]

The evidence from both decompositions suggests that the decline in the manufacturing employment share was probably not the main source of widening skill differentials. This is not entirely surprising given that the manufactur-

---

11. While the two decompositions are related, it is important to be clear about how they differ. The shift-share decomposition does not control for compositional effects due to experience or region, but it does allow for education differentials to vary across sectors. The regression decomposition controls for compositional effects but imposes the restriction that education differentials are identical across industries.

Table 5.8   **Industry-Based Regression Decomposition**

	Change in Regression Estimated Differential		Estimated Industry Effect
	No Industry Controls	6 Industry Controls	
A. 1974–76 to 1978–80:			
UNIVERSITY	−.121	−.113	−.008
VOC-HIGH	−.090	−.098	−.008
A-LEVEL	−.142	−.138	−.004
VOC-MIDDLE	−.071	−.064	−.007
O-LEVEL 5+	−.168	−.174	.006
VOC-LOW	−.052	−.052	.001
O-LEVEL 1–4	−.025	−.020	−.005
VOC-OTHER	−.009	−.012	.003
B. 1978–80 to 1986–88:			
UNIVERSITY	.066	.063	−.003
VOC-HIGH	.077	.075	.002
A-LEVEL	.106	.099	.007
VOC-MIDDLE	.084	.083	−.001
O-LEVEL 5+	.046	.050	−.004
VOC-LOW	.052	.053	−.002
O-LEVEL 1–4	.050	.041	.010
VOC-OTHER	.013	.018	−.005

Source: General Household Survey.

ing employment share was falling in the 1970s as skill differentials and earnings inequality were also dropping.

The decomposition results point strongly toward within-industry factors. Data on the breakdown of skill-group employment by industrial sector in tables 5.9 and 5.10 indicate that the pattern of labor demand within industries including manufacturing changed significantly over the sample period. The share of manufacturing employees with a university degree (see panel A of table 5.9) almost tripled from 3.0 to 8.6 percent between 1974–76 and 1986–88. The share of university graduates in services (see panel B) did not quite double over the same period. These numbers suggest a sharp rise in demand for skilled workers *within* manufacturing, one that in relative terms was actually greater than in services.

The employment share of university graduates, however, may not reflect a rise in demand so much as the greater abundance of university graduates by the end of the sample. Jobs that had been filled by workers with less than a university education in 1974–76 may have been filled by university graduates in 1986–88 simply because more workers had university degrees. In this respect, the occupational employment shares in table 5.10 argue more persuasively that production methods changed within manufacturing in ways that favored highly skilled workers. Nonmanual employment (defined by job classification, not a worker's personal characteristics) increased from approximately 26 percent of total manufacturing employment in 1974–76 to 36 percent in 1986–88—with all the increase stemming from a higher share of professional employees.

A comparison of the 90–10 differentials in manufacturing and services provides a final piece of evidence supporting the importance of within-industry effects. Over the entire period 1974–88, the 90–10 differential for services was on average about 0.30 log points larger than in manufacturing. All else constant, the shift in employment from manufacturing to services would have contributed to a rise in inequality. However, the 90–10 differential for manufacturing grew faster than in services over the 1980s—a 0.200-log-point rise versus 0.178—a phenomenon that the between-industry hypothesis cannot explain.

To summarize the importance of relative supply and demand factors, I have regressed the log of the university differential against the log of the relative supply of university graduates and a quadratic trend term (to proxy shifts in

Table 5.9   **Skills Distribution by Industry: Education**

	1974–76 (1)	1978–80 (2)	1986–88 (3)	Change, (2) − (1)	Change, (3) − (2)
A. Manufacturing:					
UNIVERSITY	.030	.051	.086	.021	.035
VOC-HIGH	.043	.068	.128	.026	.059
A-LEVEL	.016	.009	.028	−.007	.019
VOC-MIDDLE	.056	.046	.090	−.010	.044
O-LEVEL 5+	.039	.056	.029	.016	−.027
VOC-LOW	.052	.046	.070	−.006	.023
O-LEVEL 1–4	.044	.049	.079	.005	.030
VOC-OTHER	.120	.130	.093	.010	−.037
NO QUAL	.546	.483	.324	−.063	−.160
B. Services:					
UNIVERSITY	.096	.154	.179	.058	.025
VOC-HIGH	.058	.078	.097	.021	.019
A-LEVEL	.056	.028	.071	−.028	.044
VOC-MIDDLE	.030	.029	.067	−.001	.038
O-LEVEL 5+	.100	.090	.065	−.010	−.025
VOC-LOW	.034	.030	.047	−.004	.018
O-LEVEL 1–4	.068	.079	.095	.011	.017
VOC-OTHER	.057	.061	.043	.004	−.018
NO QUAL	.404	.358	.238	−.046	−.120

Source: General Household Survey.

Note: Skills shares within each industry grouping do not total to one owing to exlusion of workers with qualifications not listed.

Table 5.10   **Skills Distribution by Industry: Occupation**

	1974–76 (1)	1978–80 (2)	1986–88 (3)	Change, (2) − (1)	Change, (3) − (2)
A. Manufacturing:					
Nonmanual:					
Professional	.136	.150	.243	.013	.093
Other	.119	.114	.112	−.004	−.003
Manual:					
Skilled	.519	.518	.459	−.002	−.058
Semiskilled	.191	.185	.159	−.007	−.026
Unskilled	.033	.033	.027	−.000	−.006
B. Services					
Nonmanual:					
Professional	.337	.328	.378	−.009	.050
Other	.325	.329	.287	.004	−.042
Manual:					
Skilled	.203	.208	.206	.006	−.002
Semiskilled	.083	.077	.071	−.006	−.006
Unskilled	.035	.038	.034	.004	−.004

Source: General Household Survey.

Note: Skills shares within each industry grouping do not total to one owing to exclusion of workers in "personal services" occupation.

relative demand and other factors affecting the differential). Estimating the equation using ordinary least squares on the sample period 1974–88 gives an estimate of −0.29 for the elasticity of the university differential with respect to the relative supply of university graduates.[12] This supply elasticity can help predict what might have happened to differentials during the 1980s in the absence of a continued expansion of supply. Restricting relative supplies of university graduates to their average level over the period 1974–88, and using the estimated supply elasticity, yields an estimate of the differential under the assumption that relative supplies were constant through the 1980s. Under these assumptions, the differential would have increased by 0.207 log points (vs. 0.067) between 1978–80 and 1986–88. An alternative interpretation is, of course, that relative demand shifts during the 1980s must have been very large to make their effects felt despite large increases in relative supplies.

5.3.3   Labor Market Institutions

Labor supply and demand shifts can explain many of the similarities in the development of the U.S. and British wage structures. However, supply and demand are less illuminating when it comes to explaining differences. Labor

---

12. The standard error of the supply elasticity is 0.093, making it significant at the 1 percent level; the R^2 is 0.456; and the Durbin-Watson statistic is 1.64 (critical value $d^L = 0.95$ and $d^U = 1.54$), providing no indication of serial correlation.

market institutions may be in a better position to account for the divergences, especially in the experiences of low-skilled workers and the timing of the rise in inequality. I therefore now examine the role of several British labor market institutions: the extensive use of incomes policies in Britain during the 1970s; the industry- and occupation-specific minimum wages set by national wages councils; the unemployment benefit system; and trade unions.

Incomes Policies of the 1970s

Five incomes policies were in effect during the first five years of the GHS sample. Two of these limited pay increases to a uniform nominal amount (the same, fixed pounds-per-week ceiling applicable to workers at all pay levels); a third policy prescribed proportional increases that may have impeded any underlying tendency toward wage dispersion. In an analysis that pays particular attention to wage differentials, Ashenfelter and Layard (1983) conclude that the incomes policies of the 1970s achieved some of their implicit wage compression targets and probably prevented dispersion from increasing as fast as it would have in the absence of such policies. The effects, however, are difficult to quantify, and incomes policies in the 1970s probably tell us little about the period of widening inequality in the 1980s.

Wage Councils

Britain did not have a statutory national minimum wage in force at any time during the period 1974–88. However, approximately 10 percent of the national labor force worked in industries covered by wages councils, which set minimum pay rates by occupation for workers under their jurisdiction. Anecdotal evidence suggests that a serious erosion in the scope, enforcement, and "bite" of wages council minimums took place after the election of the Conservative government in 1979. By the time the Wage Act of 1986 restricted councils to setting a single minimum for all occupations within a covered industry and removed workers under the age of twenty-one from councils' jurisdiction, wages councils had lost a great deal of their previous influence on wages.

In a broader study of the effects of minimum pay rates on employment, Machin and Manning (1992) examined the effect of wages councils on hourly wage dispersion. Their estimates suggest that the decline in wages council minimums relative to industry averages resulted in an 8 percent increase in the coefficient of variation of wages for covered workers.[13] Since this estimate excludes the effects of reduction in coverage and enforcement, it is probably an underestimate of the effect of the decline in councils on dispersion.

The demise of wages councils during the 1980s may have played an important role in rising inequality during the 1980s. Nevertheless, the disman-

---

13. For the decline in the industry minimum relative to the industry average, see their fig. 4. For wage dispersion, see their fig. 5. The dispersion-to-elasticity figure is based on their table 2, cols. 3 and 4.

tling of wages councils, which disproportionately protect the wages of low earners, makes it more difficult to explain the rise in real earnings for low-skilled workers.

Unemployment Benefits

Real earnings for the low skilled may have increased in Britain over the sample because the benefit system placed an ever-rising floor on earnings. A rise in the real value of benefits could account for the simultaneous increase in low-skilled earnings and unemployment.

A careful analysis of the effect of the complex British benefit system on low-skilled workers over the fifteen-year period of the sample is well beyond the scope of this paper. As a quick check on the possible effects of benefits on low-skilled earnings, I have graphed the indexed value of real unemployment benefits and the real earnings of workers in the tenth percentile over the sample years in figure 5.5. Unemployment benefit is an unemployment insurance program covering most unemployed workers in the first year of unemployment. The benefit data graphed in figure 5.5 are the log of the real statutory level of unemployment benefits for a single man with no children (see Department of Social Security 1992, table C1.01). Figure 5.5 suggests that the absolute value of unemployment benefits grew slightly over the sample period. However, unemployment benefits failed to keep pace with rises in earnings of workers in the tenth percentile of the full-time earnings distribution.

In absolute terms, the unemployment benefit system was not much more generous in 1988 than it was in 1974. However, in relative terms, it was actu-

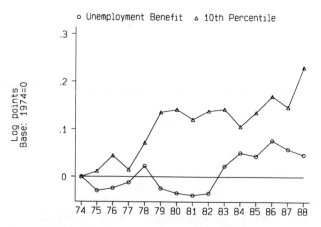

Fig. 5.5   "Indexed" unemployment benefit and earnings
Sources: Weekly unemployment benefit for single male with no children from Department of Social Security (1992, table C1.01, pp. 133–34). Weekly earnings for the tenth percentile of full-time male employees from the General Household Survey. Both series deflated using the retail price index, January 1974 = 100.0.

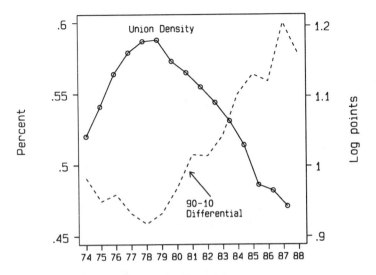

Fig. 5.6   Union density and earnings dispersion
Sources: For union density, see notes to table 5.11. Log weekly earnings differential for full-time male employees from General Household Survey as in table 5.2.

ally less generous. While the analysis is far from complete, the idea that the benefit system pushed the real earnings of low-skilled workers up in absolute terms over the 1970s and 1980s does not appear to be consistent with evidence on unemployment benefit.

Trade Unions

Perhaps the most striking institutional difference between Britain and the United States is the much higher degree of unionization in Britain. In Britain, union membership grew rapidly during the 1970s to a historic peak of just under 60 percent of the workforce in 1979. Union density in the United States, on the other hand, declined steadily in the 1970s, falling below 20 percent by the end of the decade. In the 1980s, both countries experienced drops of about 10 percentage points in union density.

Figure 5.6 shows a strong inverse relation between trade union density and overall earnings dispersion in Britain. While the figure cannot establish causation, the striking association suggests that the decline in unionization played a crucial role in the development of the British wage structure during the 1980s. In this respect, it may be telling that the continuous decline in union density in the United States coincided with a continuous rise in earnings inequality there.

Following Freeman (1991, table 2), table 5.11 estimates the contribution of the decline in union membership to the change in skill differentials from 1978–80 to 1986–88 using micro data from the GHS. Column 1 presents cross-sectional estimates of the union differential from the GHS data for 1983 (the only year where the GHS asks workers about their union affiliation). As in the

Table 5.11   Unions and Skill Differentials, 1978–80 to 1986–88

	Union Differential (1983)	Change Union Membership	Effect on Earnings	Change Skill Differential	Share of Change Explained
A. Education differentials:					
UNIV	.031	−.103	−.003		
NO QUAL	.170	−.103	−.018		
Total			.014	.067	.21
B. Occupational differentials:					
Nonmanual	.078	−.103	−.008		
Manual	.227	−.103	−.023		
Total			.014	.110	.13

Note: Union differentials for 1983 estimated using GHS data with the model from table 5.3, augmented by a trade union membership dummy variable and its interaction with relevant skill categories. The change in union membership is the change in overall union membership. For membership data for 1974–78, see Central Statistical Office (CSO), *Social Trends* 18 (1988), table 11.8, p. 172; and for 1979–88, see Bird, Stevens, and Yates (1991, 337). The working population is employees in employment in June of each year from the *Department of Employment Gazette.* Change in university differential from table 5.3. Change in nonmanual differential from OLS regressions of natural log of real pay against a dummy variable for nonmanual job, experience and experience squared and their interactions with the nonmanual dummy, and 9 region dummies.

United States, union differentials are small for skilled workers and much larger for less skilled workers. Since no estimates of British union membership by education or occupation exist for the skill groups and time period in table 5.11, column 2 uses the change in union membership in the whole economy (-10.3 percentage points) to estimate the decline in union membership in each skill group. Multiplying the change in membership by the union differential for each skill group gives an estimate of the effect of union decline on the earnings of each skill group. A comparison of these union earnings effects across complementary skill groups yields an estimate of the total effect of union decline on the corresponding skill differential. On this basis, union membership losses account for about 21 percent of the rise in the university differential and 13 percent of the rise in the nonmanual differential during the 1980s.[14]

As with wages councils, the decline in union membership does not make it any easier to account for the rise in low-skilled earnings. However, it may be that the divergent earnings experiences of low-skilled workers in the United

14. These estimates lie very close to the 25 percent figure for the United States given by Freeman (1991). Table 5.11 makes two assumptions that bias the estimates in different directions. The assumption that declines in membership were uniform across skill groups probably significantly reduces the union effect. Declines in membership were almost certainly much greater among low-skilled workers. In the United States, e.g., unionization rates among college graduates fell 3 percentage points between 1978 and 1988, while those for high school graduates dropped 12 percentage points (Freeman 1991, table 2). On the other hand, the assumption of a constant union markup probably inflates the union effect, given some evidence that the union differential fell slightly in Britain during the 1980s. Using plausible values for both missing numbers suggests that table 5.11 probably underestimates the union effect on differentials.

States and Britain have less to do with *changes* in institutions within the two countries over time and more to do with cross-country differences in the *levels* of influence of the institutions. Skill differentials and overall inequality may have increased in Britain because of the weakening of some labor market institutions, but low-skilled workers may have been able to protect absolute earnings more effectively in Britain than in the United States owing to the much greater level of influence exerted by the British institutions. Freeman (1991) finds some evidence for this institutional "levels" effect in cross sections of OECD countries. Countries with high union density have lower variances of earnings. They also experienced smaller changes in earnings differentials between 1978 and 1987 (Freeman 1991, tables 8 and 9, pp. 36–37).

5.4 Some Conclusions

The 1970s and 1980s were tumultuous times for the British earnings structure. The GHS data indicate that skill differentials and overall earnings inequality fell slightly during the 1970s and then rose sharply in the 1980s.

A simple relative supply and demand framework can explain many of these developments. Large increases in supplies of skilled labor helped narrow skill differentials during the 1970s. During the 1980s, a strong rise in the demand for skilled labor led to widening skill differentials despite a continued expansion in the relative supply of skilled labor. The GHS data provide little support for the hypothesis that the decline in British manufacturing employment lies behind changing relative demand for labor or the increase in inequality. The GHS data, however, do support the view that a rise in demand for skills within industries—including manufacturing—has made an important contribution to the rise in inequality.

Labor market institutions also appear to have played an important role in the changing earnings structure. Incomes policies may have checked an underlying tendency toward wage dispersion during the mid-1970s and delayed the onset of rising inequality until the late 1970s. The declining importance of wages councils, and especially trade unions, also probably allowed for greater inequality during the 1980s.

What does the evidence from the 1970s and 1980s say about the 1990s? Despite a British institutional framework that attenuates the effects of supply and demand changes to a much greater degree than in the United States, the same market forces that led to widening differentials during the 1980s could act to close them in the 1990s. The rising differentials are providing a strong financial incentive for individuals to acquire formal education and skills training. The number of new graduates, for example, increased steadily from approximately 95,000 in 1980 to over 120,000 in 1988 (*Highly Qualified People* 1990). Particularly if wages councils and unions avoid further declines in influence, continuing supply responses could conceivably undo many of the developments of the 1980s.

References

Ashenfelter, O., and R. Layard. 1983. Incomes policy and wage differentials. *Economica* 50:127–43.

Bell, D., R. Rimmer, and S. Rimmer. 1992. Earnings inequality in Great Britain, 1975–90: The role of age. Mimeo.

Bird, D., M. Stevens, and A. Yates. 1991. Membership of trade unions in 1989. *Department of Employment Gazette* (June), 337–43.

Blackburn, M., and D. Bloom. 1987. Earnings and income inequality in the United States. *Population and Development Review* (December), 575–609.

Blackburn, M., D. Bloom, and R. Freeman. 1991. The declining economic position less-skilled American males. In *A future of lousy jobs?* ed. Gary Burtless. Washington, D.C.: Brookings.

Bluestone, B. 1990. The impact of schooling and industrial restructuring on recent trends in wage inequality in the United States. *American Economic Association Papers and Proceedings* 80, no. 2:303–7.

Bluestone, B., and B. Harrison. 1988. The growth of low-wage employment: 1963–86. *American Economic Association Papers and Proceedings* 78, no. 2:124–28.

Bound, J., and G. Johnson. 1989. Wages in the United States during the 1980s and beyond. University of Michigan. Mimeo.

Department of Social Security. 1992. *Statistics 1991.* London: H.M. Stationery Office.

Freeman, R. 1976. *The overeducated American.* New York: Academic.

———. 1991. How much has de-unionization contributed to the rise in male earnings inequality? NBER Working Paper no. 3826. Cambridge, Mass.: National Bureau of Economic Research.

Highly qualified people: Supply and demand. [report of an interdepartmental review]. 1990. London: H.M. Stationery Office.

Juhn, C., K. Murphy, and B. Pierce. 1989. Wage inequality and the rise in returns to skill. University of Chicago. Mimeo.

Katz, L., and K. Murphy. 1992. Changes in relative wages: Supply and demand factors. *Quarterly Journal of Economics* 107, no. 1:35–78.

Katz, L., and A. Revenga. 1989. Changes in the structure of wages: The United States versus Japan. *Journal of the Japanese and International Economies* 3:522–53.

Machin, S., and A. Manning. 1992. Minimum wages, wage dispersion and employment: Evidence from the U.K. wages councils. Centre for Economic Performance, London School of Economics. Mimeo.

Meghir, C., and E. Whitehouse. 1992. The evolution of wages in the U.K.: Evidence from micro data. Institute for Fiscal Studies. Mimeo.

Moghadam, R. 1990. Wage determination: An assessment of returns to education, occupation, region and industry in Great Britain. Discussion Paper no. 8. Centre for Economic Performance, London School of Economics.

Murphy, K., and F. Welch. 1992. The structure of wages. *Quarterly Journal of Economics* 107, no. 1:285–326.

Schmitt, J. 1991. Changing returns to education and experience for British males, 1974–88. Working Paper no. 122. Centre for Economic Performance, London School of Economics, rev. April 1992.

———. 1992. Creating a consistent time-series of cross-sections from the General Household Survey, 1974–88. Working Paper no. 227. Centre for Economic Performance, London School of Economics.

6   Real Wages, Employment, and Wage Dispersion in U.S. and Australian Labor Markets

Robert G. Gregory and Francis Vella

There are a number of reasons why a comparison of Australian and U.S. labor markets might improve our understanding of the large changes in relative earnings that are occurring in the United States.[1] First, it would be interesting to know whether the economic forces generating those changes are so powerful and internationally pervasive that the same earnings outcomes can be observed in very different institutional settings. The Australian labor market is a good comparison for such an inquiry because, unlike the relatively free and flexible U.S. labor market, it is dominated by direct trade union coverage and a strong centralized wage-fixing institution, the Industrial Relations Commission, which sets awards rates of pay and delivers trade union conditions to almost 90 percent of the Australian workforce.[2]

Second, perhaps the comparison can help us form rough judgments as to the way in which shocks affect relative employment and wages differently in different labor markets. It is widely believed that Australian relative award wages

Robert G. Gregory is professor of economics and head of the Division of Economics and Politics, Research School of Social Sciences, Australian National University. Francis Vella is assistant professor of Economics at Rice University. During 1992 he was a visiting fellow in the economics program, Division of Economics and Politics, Research School of Social Sciences, Australian National University.

Steve Davis, Peter Sheehan, and Eva Klug provided helpful comments and assistance. Earlier versions of the paper were presented by R. G. Gregory as the 1992 Chris Higgins Memorial Lecture, Economic Society of Australia (Canberra Branch), May 1992, and as "Aspects of Australian Labour Force Living Standards: The Disappointing Decades, 1970–1990," the Copeland Oration, Twenty-first Conference of Economists, Melbourne, July 1992.

1. Davis (1992) compares U.S. outcomes with those of a number of OECD countries. Levy and Murnane (1992) survey the existing U.S. literature.

2. Awards set the same rate of pay and working conditions for approximately nine thousand separate job classifications throughout the country. There is provision for overaward and more market-orientated payments, but these are confined to about 2–3 percent of wage and salary earners.

are fairly inflexible across enterprises, skill categories, and industries and that most adjustment to micro shocks takes the form of relative *employment* responses. This contrasts with the U.S. labor market, where relative employment *and* wages seem to change considerably.

Of course, the U.S. experience prompts a range of questions about the Australian labor market. For example, will the rigid relative wage system begin to break down if exposed to the same labor demand and supply shifts that are occurring in the United States? Will wage rigidity in Australia give rise to exaggerated relative employment changes and increases in structural unemployment? These questions become more pointed within the Australian income policy regime that has operated during most of the 1980s.

The paper is divided into three sections. In section 6.1, the performance of the Australian and the U.S. labor markets is compared. The section begins with a description of the macro history of each country from 1950 to 1992, with the emphasis being placed on average wage changes. The histories are very similar, except for a brief period between 1969 and 1976 when Australian real wages increased by about one-third relative to those in the United States, the relative employment/population ratio fell about 10 percent, and the unemployment rate increased from typically one-third of U.S. levels to exceeding them. The changes of this period have remained in place, and during the 1980s the two countries have again shared a similar history.

Since 1970, and after adjusting for population growth, one in four male full-time jobs has disappeared in Australia.[3] In the United States, the full-time job loss among males has been minor, one in twelve. Is this very different employment history only a response to the Australian average real wage shock of the mid-1970s, or is it also related to the interaction of the Australian system of rigid relative wages and the forces generating changes in the earnings-employment dispersion in the United States?

This question is addressed by directing attention toward employment changes within different ranges on the earnings distribution rather than adopting the approach of other papers in this volume that emphasize changes in earnings at different points on the employment distribution. To do this, we take 1976 as the base year, rank full-time earnings for male wage and salary earners, and divide the earnings distribution into quintiles. The earnings boundaries of each quintile are expressed as a ratio of median earnings and applied to the median of each subsequent year. Then, to 1990, we follow the changing distribution of employment. There will be a close correspondence between changes in employment and earnings. A widening dispersion of employment implies a widening dispersion of earnings.

We find almost identical patterns of employment changes across the two countries. Male employment growth is overwhelmingly among high- and low-

---

3. A job loss of this magnitude has never occurred before in Australian history. From peak employment in 1927–28 to the depth of the depression in 1931–32, the employment/population ratio for males fell 18 percent; approximately two-thirds of the fall in the male full-time employment/population ratio occurred between 1970 and 1983.

paying jobs, and employment in the middle 60 percent of the weekly earnings distribution is disappearing at an astounding rate. After adjusting for population growth over the period 1976–90, employment in the middle three quintiles has fallen by around 33 percent in Australia and 18 percent in the United States. These findings give rise to a number of conjectures. For example, since changes in relative earnings and employment seem independent of the different average real-wage histories, the large across-the-board shock of average wages in Australia does not seem to have made a significant contribution to the change in relative earnings. In addition, the earnings dispersion appears to be widening at the same rate in both countries, and there is no evidence that the more compressed Australian distribution of earnings is converging toward the U.S. pattern. This section concludes with the observation that, unlike in the United States, the widening earnings dispersion in Australia has not been accompanied by an increase in the rate of return to education.

Section 6.2 discusses changes in the Australian employment-earnings distribution in more detail. We show that in Australia there is not a close correspondence between employment growth in different quintiles of the employment distribution and employment growth in different occupations. As in the United States, the widening dispersion of employment is largely occurring within occupations. The loss of male employment in the middle of the income distribution may be related to the rapid rate of growth of female employment, although the effect is not large. Middle-pay jobs are disappearing in both the public and the private sectors, and in the private sector it seems clear that the loss of middle-pay jobs has not been significantly affected by a move toward a more centralized wage system and the adoption of an income policy regime. The Prices and Incomes Accord between the trade union movement and the Labour government may have had some influence in the public sector, where the growth of high-earnings jobs has been subdued. Brief concluding comments are offered in section 6.3.

6.1   The Australian-U.S. Comparison

6.1.1   The Macro Background

At the beginning of 1993, the unemployment rate in Australia was around 11 percent, the highest level since the 1930s. The average unemployment rate had increased from 1.8 percent over the 1960s, to 3.6 percent for the 1970s, to 7.2 percent over the 1980s. It is widely believed that the average for the 1990s will continue to trend upward.

Although this unemployment trend is not unique to Australia, not all countries have fared as badly.[4] In the United States, the average unemployment rate

4. Most of OECD Europe has experienced similar unemployment increases to Australia's, but, viewed on a decade-by-decade basis, Australia's deteriorating unemployment performance is among the worst, along with France, Germany, and the United Kingdom. The change in average

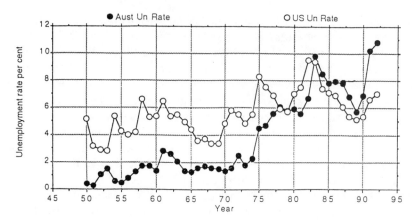

Fig. 6.1   Unemployment rate, United States and Australia, 1950–92
Sources: Foster and Stewart (1991); EconData Pty Ltd (OECD *Economic Outlook* diskette)

for each subsequent decade since the 1960s has been higher than the one before—4.6, 6.0, and 7.1 percent, respectively—but by Australian standards the increases have been small (fig. 6.1). Australian unemployment has quite clearly changed from low rates—which were typically a third of those in the United States during the 1950s and 1960s—to rates that typically exceed those of the United States. Most of this change occurred quite quickly over a four- to five-year period during the mid- to late 1970s.

To explain the relative increase in unemployment in Australia, a simple macro neoclassical model would look first to average real-wage changes, relative to labor productivity. Real wages increased at about the same rate as in the United States between 1950 and 1970, by just under 70 percent (fig. 6.2). Then, beginning in the early 1970s, four remarkable things happened.

First, after two and a half decades of steady increase, average real wages in the United States began to fall from a 1973 peak and today have just returned to levels prevailing two decades earlier. Second, between 1973 and 1975, Australia gained exceptional real-wage increases of around 20 percent. Based on the average experience of the 1960s, this change would have taken about seven years to accrue.

Third, since 1976, Australian real wages have varied little, increasing in the labor market deregulation period of 1980–83, and falling between 1983 and 1990 under the Prices and Incomes Accord. Recently, real wages have increased marginally and are now just above 1976 levels. The labor markets of both countries, which operate under very different institutional arrangements,

---

unemployment from the 1960s to the 1980s for each of these countries is 1.5–9.0 percent for France, 0.8–6.9 percent for Germany, and 1.6–9.5 percent for the United Kingdom. For an analysis of unemployment across most of the OECD, see Madsen (1992).

have not been able to generate significant real-wage increases for at least fifteen years in Australia and twenty years in the United States.

Fourth, primarily as a result of changes between 1973 and 1975, the long-term relation between U.S. and Australian real wages has changed in a fundamental and dramatic way (fig. 6.3). Between 1966 and 1975, Australian real wages increased by approximately 40 percent relative to those in the United States, or by about $12,000 per annum in terms of 1992 U.S. wage levels for full-year, full-time workers. This change is equivalent to about two-thirds of the average real-wage increase in the United States since 1950. It is a very large shift in relative living standards for employed workers in two mature developed countries over such a short period of time.

The large change in relative wages between the two countries occurs primarily in the two years immediately preceding the increase in relative unemployment, as would be predicted by a macro neoclassical model. Between 1950 and 1975, the variations in employment levels were similar; then relative employment seemed to respond quickly to the relative real-wage change of 1973–75 (fig. 6.3). Between 1976 and 1979, the Australian employment/population ratio fell 3.5 percent and that of the United States increased 5.5 percent (fig. 6.4). This is the only sustained period within the forty-year data span when the employment/population ratios of the two countries moved in opposite directions. Since 1979, variations of the employment/population ratio have been similar.

The changes in relations between U.S. and Australian labor markets during the 1970s were very large. If U.S. unemployment had maintained its 1960s

Fig. 6.2   Real wages, United States and Australia, 1950–92
Sources: Foster and Stewart (1991); EconData Pty Ltd (OECD *Economic Outlook* diskette)
Note: Real wages are measured as the ratio of compensation of employees adjusted for changes in consumer prices and divided by the number of wage and salary earners. 1950–88: Foster and Stewart (1991, tables 6.15, 6.23). 1989–92: EconData.

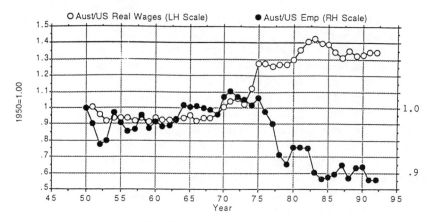

Fig. 6.3   Relative employment and real wages, United States and Australia, 1950–92

Sources: Real wages: see fig. 6.2 Employment/population ratios: Foster and Stewart (1991, table 6.12); EconData Pty Ltd (OECD *Economic Outlook* diskette). *Economic Report of the President* (Washington, D.C.: U.S. Government Printing Office, February 1991).

Note: Employment is measured as employment divided by the population sixteen years and older.

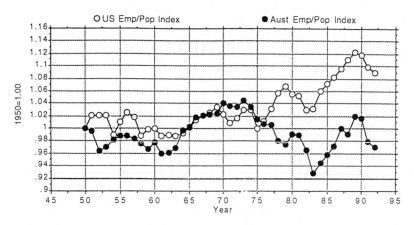

Fig. 6.4   Employment-population indices, United States and Australia, 1950–92

Sources: See fig. 6.3.

relation with that of Australia, the average unemployment rate would have been 18.4 percent during the 1980s rather than 7.1 percent.[5] If, from 1975, the U.S. employment/population ratio had increased at the same rate as it did in Australia, 13.8 million employment opportunities would have been lost in the United

---

5. This is calculated by applying to the U.S. unemployment rate of the 1960s the Australian percentage increase in average unemployment from the 1960s to the 1980s.

States. This is approximately two times the current number of unemployed people. A United States with 12 percent fewer people at work, an average unemployment rate of 18.4 percent,[6] and a real wage 30–40 percent higher would possess a very different allocation of living standards among the population.

This macro comparison suggests that Australian labor markets can deliver large real-wage changes and keep them in place, but not without affecting employment. It also suggests that real-wage increases are not fully offset by employment losses. The elasticity of demand appears to be about 0.3 so that the real-wage increase leads to a significant increase in the share of income being directed toward labor.[7]

6.1.2   The Disappearing Group of Middle-Wage Earners

The macro history of the previous section conceals two important labor market trends. First, between 1970 and 1991, there has been a strong bias against full-time jobs in Australia: 47 percent of Australian employment growth has been in part-time jobs. The equivalent U.S. ratio is 22 percent. Second, in both countries, there has been a similar bias toward female jobs, despite very large real-wage increases for Australian women.

Since 1970, these biases have been associated with a 25 percent reduction in Australian male full-time employment, adjusted for population growth (fig. 6.5). The contrast with the United States, where the male full-time employment/population ratio has fallen 10 percent, is starkly evident. Between 1966 and 1975, the male full-time employment series for both countries fell together, but, after 1975, following the change in the average wage relativity across the two countries, they diverged markedly. If the United States had matched the Australian proportionate job loss, then 7.8 million male full-time jobs would have disappeared between 1976 and 1991, approximately twice the 1991 average number of unemployed men in the United States.

To investigate the loss of male full-time jobs, attention is first directed toward job growth at different earnings levels in each country. There are no comprehensive and consistent Australian wage data for individuals extending back throughout the 1950s and 1960s, but since the mid-1970s the Australian Bureau of Statistics has been collecting two series of employee weekly earnings that are useful for our purposes. One is from a large sample of employers[8] (the May survey), and the other is from the sample of households included in the

---

6. These illustrative calculations do not allow for labor force responses to either the real-wage increase or the reduced level of employment opportunities.

7. For a range of estimated labor demand elasticities, see Russel and Tease (1991).

8. *Distribution and Composition of Employee Earnings and Hours,* Australian Bureau of Statistics (ABS), Catalogue no. 6306.0. For 1987, the sample extended to approximately ninety-one hundred employers and seventy-three thousand employees. The sample for 1976–81 differs from that for 1983 on. The data were not collected for 1982 and 1984. These data are referred to as the *May survey.*

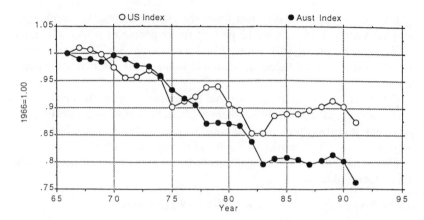

Fig. 6.5   Male full-time employment-population indices, United States and Australia, 1966–91

Sources: Australia: *The Labour Force,* ABS Catalogue no. 6203.0, various issues (August). United States: *Handbook of Labor Statistics* (Washington, D.C.: U.S. Department of Labor, Bureau of Labor Statistics, August 1989); *Employment and Earnings* (Washington, D.C.: U.S. Department of Labor, Bureau of Labor Statistics).

Note: Population is measured as male population sixteen years and older.

regular Labour Force Survey[9] (the August survey). The U.S. data are weekly earnings of full-year, full-time wage and salary earners taken from the March CPS tapes of 1977 and 1991.[10]

To identify where the job loss is occurring in each country, the weekly earnings distribution of male full-time workers in 1976 is ranked by earnings levels and then divided into quintiles and each boundary earnings level calculated as a proportion of median earnings. These boundaries are then applied to the median male full-time wage for 1990 and full-time male employment falling within each category counted and expressed as a proportion of the total. This places the emphasis on the changing employment distribution over fixed intervals of the earnings distribution. The alternative method, adopted in other papers, is to document changes in relative earnings at fixed points on the employment distribution. Each approach is measuring the same phenomenon, but the method adopted here seems more natural when the focus is to account for such large employment losses.

Columns 1–3 of table 6.1 list the 1976 dividing boundaries for each employment quintile expressed as a fraction of median earnings. They show quite clearly, as suggested by many other authors,[11] that the Australian earnings dis-

---

9. *Weekly Earnings of Employees (Distribution) Australia,* ABS, Catalogue no. 6310.0. These data are collected from two-thirds of 1 percent of the population and are referred to as the *August survey.*

10. We wish to thank Larry Katz for processing the U.S. data.

11. This compression has been discussed and documented in Hughes (1973), Norris (1986), and Gregory and Daly (1991).

Table 6.1   **The Distribution of Male Full-Time Earnings in 1976 and Employment Changes by Earning Quintiles, United States and Australia, 1976–90**

	Earning Boundaries, Ratio of 1976 Male Median Full-Time Earnings			Employment Distribution, 1990 (%)		
	United States:	Australia		United States:	Australia	
Earning Quintiles	Full-Time Wage and Salary Earners (1)	Full-Time Nonmanagerial Employees (2)	Full-Time Wage and Salary Earners (3)	Full-Time Wage and Salary Earners (4)	Full-Time Nonmanagerial Employees (5)	Full-Time Wage and Salary Earners (6)
First	.62	.82	.78	23	27	25
Second	.88	.99	.92	18	16	17
Third	1.15	1.07	1.07	17	15	17
Fourth	1.50	1.28	1.35	14	19	18
Fifth				27	23	24

Sources: United States: Weekly earnings of full-year, full-time wage and salary earners from the March Current Population Survey, 1977 and 1991. Australia: Full-time wage and salary earners: *Weekly Earnings of Employees (Distribution) Australia,* Australian Bureau of Statistics (ABS) Catalogue no. 6310.0 (August survey); full-time nonmanagerial employees: *Distribution and Composition of Employee Earnings and Hours,* ABS Catalogue no. 6306.0.

tribution is more compressed than the U.S. earnings distribution. The compression is quite significant, especially at low earnings. For example, in 1976, male full-time earnings in the United States at the twentieth employment percentile were about one-quarter less than in Australia. In terms of 1992 wage levels, this difference is equivalent to about U.S. $6,000 and, in proportionate terms, is equivalent to all the increase in U.S. male average earnings over the last thirty years. At the eightieth employment percentile, U.S. male full-time earnings were 11–17 percent more than in Australia.[12] These are comparisons of gross earnings, and the disparities between the two countries are widened when allowance is made for taxes and transfers.

The changes in the employment distribution between 1976 and 1990 are presented in columns 4–6. The pattern is remarkable, and the first impression is that the change seems almost identical in each country. The proportion of employment at low and high weekly earnings has increased in both countries by about 25 percent. The proportion of employment in the middle three quintiles has fallen by about 18 percent. The Australian data are consistent for both the August Labour Force Survey, which in terms of data-collection method and data definition is directly comparable to the U.S. data, and the more restricted sample collected from employers in the May survey. The sec-

12. Data taken from the two Australian series, full-time nonmanagerial (May survey) and all wage and salary earners (August survey), are very similar, but, as expected, the earnings dispersion is greatest among full-time wage and salary earners, for two reasons. First, the data include managers. Second, data reported by individuals from a household survey tend to be more variable than data reported by firms.

ond impression is that, in the high-growth areas at the extremes of the distribution, Australian employment, relative to that in the United States, is growing faster at the bottom but more slowly at the top.

These results suggest the following comments. First, the evidence from table 6.1 does not support the conjecture that both countries are moving toward the same earnings distribution. Although the earnings distributions and the quintile cutoff points are so very different in each country—the gap between the bottom and the top quintile is almost twice as great in the United States—the pattern of job change is approximately the same. Despite compressed wage relativities, Australia has not been subject to a greater hollowing out of middle-level jobs. The forces bringing about change are altering the earnings distributions in the same proportionate way, but they are *not* acting to equalize the earnings distributions across the two countries.

The lack of an equalization tendency can be seen in table 6.2, where U.S. quintile divisions have been applied to Australian data in 1976 and 1990. As mentioned earlier, the Australian earnings distribution is more compressed: in 1976, 33.5 percent of Australian male earnings lie in the middle quintile of the U.S. earnings distribution and only 8.1 percent in the lowest quintile (August survey). The Australian distribution, however, has moved toward the U.S. 1976 earnings distribution, as the middle quintile has fallen to 28.0 percent of employment and the bottom quintile increased to 11.2 percent. This change would have represented an equalizing tendency across the two countries except that the U.S. distribution has also changed and become less equal. The net result is that the two distributions have moved further apart.[13]

Second, we have shown elsewhere that the difference in the earnings distributions between the two countries cannot be explained by human capital variables, as conventionally measured, and that the compression of employment in Australia is institutionally determined (Gregory and Daly 1991). It is perhaps surprising, therefore, that, on an employment basis, Australian institutions are able to *maintain* relativities between U.S. and Australian earnings distributions but not *offset* the trends for the earnings distribution to widen. It is puzzling that the rate of change should be so similar in the two countries when one is perceived as having a flexible labor market (in which relative employment and earnings change) and the other an inflexible labor market (in which relative employment changes but relative earnings are fairly inflexible).

Third, and perhaps even more surprising, the change in the employment distribution is approximately the same in both countries despite the fact that,

13. A measure of the difference between the two distributions, after applying the U.S. boundaries to the Australian data, is calculated as follows. The percentage point difference between the two countries in the employment proportions in each quintile is calculated and then averaged, ignoring the signs. The average percentage point difference across the two countries in the 1976 distributions, calculated by ignoring the signs, was 7.5 percentage points (August survey). This had narrowed to 5.5 percentage points between Australia in 1990 and the United States in 1976, but, because of the U.S. change since 1976, the average difference between the two countries in 1990 had widened to 9.9 percentage points.

Table 6.2   **Employment Shares Calculated from U.S. 1976 Employment Quintiles**

| | Australian Employment Share (%) | | | | U.S. Employment Share (%) | |
| | August Survey | | May Survey | | | |
Quintile	1976	1990	1976	1990	1976	1990
First	8.1	11.2	2.3	3.4	20.0	23.1
Second	25.3	25.8	27.8	31.7	20.0	18.0
Third	33.5	28.0	39.0	30.4	20.0	17.7
Fourth	18.7	18.9	21.1	22.7	20.0	14.2
Fifth	14.4	16.1	9.8	11.8	20.0	26.9

Sources: See table 6.1.

since 1970, and adjusting for population growth, Australia has lost 25 percent of its male full-time jobs and the United States only 8 percent. Given the large wage increases in Australia in the mid-1970s, and given the fact that the unemployed are drawn disproportionately from those with lower earnings, it might have been expected that employment at the bottom of the earnings distribution would not have grown so much in Australia.

Fourth, as the pattern of change is so similar across the two countries, it appears as though the change in relative earnings and employment can be regarded as independent of the different macro history. In other words, the large change in Australian average wage levels, relative to those in the United States, does not seem to have affected relative employment at different earning levels.

6.1.3   Education and Disappearing Employment at Middle-Level Earnings

The changes in the employment distribution in table 6.1 above are so similar that they suggest common forces generating U.S. and Australian changes. Most commentators on U.S. earnings distribution changes believe that the increasing demand for better-educated workers, not matched by an increase in supply, has been important (Burtless 1990; Blackburn, Bloom, and Freeman 1990). What has been the Australian experience?

Table 6.3 documents educational attainment and income for Australian full-year, full-time male workers from 1968–69 to 1989–90. Before the mid-1970s, the change in the rate of return to education is similar to that in the United States. The ratio of average earnings of degree holders to those who left school at fourteen or fifteen years fell 23 percent between 1968–69 and 1978–79, and the earnings relativity for those with a diploma fell 19 percent. Since 1978–79, when the earnings dispersion widened, the change in the education return has been quite different across the two countries. In Australia, the rate of return appears to have been constant, while, in the United States, it has increased substantially. The failure of the education return to increase in Australia since the mid-1970s might be explained by the greater increase in the supply of

Table 6.3   **Full-Year, Full-Time Workforce in Australia: Ratio of Average Earnings by Educational Attainment to the Average Earnings of Those Who Left School at Age Fourteen or Fifteen, 1968–69 to 1989–90 (average earnings of those who left school at age fourteen or fifteen = 100)**

Educational Attainment	1968–69	1973–74	1978–79	1981–82	1985–86	1989–90
Males with postschool qualifications:						
Degree	238	202	183	173	170	179
Diploma/certificate (nontrade)	160	147	135	135	143	135
Trade certificate	115	111	111	107	114	112
Other	N.A.	132	121	122	114	121
Males without postschool qualifications:						
Left school at 17	109	105	104	101	104	106
Left school at 16	102	100	97	104	99	102
Left school at 13 or under	95	96	96	98	96	95

Sources: 1968–69: *Income Distribution, 1968–69: Consolidated and Revised Edition,* ABS Catalogue no. 6502.0, table 63. 1973–74: *Social Indicators no. 3, 1980,* ABS Catalogue no. 4101.0, table 6.8. 1978–79: *Income Distribution, Australia, 1978–79: Supplement to Social Indicators no. 3,* ABS Catalogue no. 4108.0, table 8. 1981–82: *Social Indicators no. 4, 1984,* ABS Catalogue no. 4101.0, table 6.8. 1985–86: *1986 Income Distribution Survey, Persons with Earned Income, Australia,* ABS Catalogue no. 6546.0, table 11. 1989–90: *1990 Survey of Income and Housing Costs and Amentities, Persons with Earned Income, Australia,* ABS Catalogue no. 6546.0, table 11.

Note: N.A. = not available.

Table 6.4   **Full-Year, Full-Time Male Workforce in Australia by Educational Attainment, 1968–69 to 1989–90 (%)**

Educational Attainment	1968–69	1973–74	1978–79	1981–82	1985–86	1989–90
With postschool qualifications:						
Degree	3.6	4.5	8.1	9.1	10.7	13.4
Diploma/certificate (nontrade)	8.6	10.2	13.1	13.6	12.0	14.0
Trade certificate	15.6	18.4	26.1	27.0	28.4	28.2
Other	N.A.	2.7	3.6	1.7	1.9	0.1
Total	27.8	35.8	50.9	51.4	53.0	56.3
Without postschool qualifications:						
Left school:						
Over 17 years	4.2	10.9[a]	3.7	4.3	5.3	6.0
17 years	5.9		6.4	7.3	7.8	8.1
16 years	11.1	11.2	9.8	10.6	10.3	10.4
14 or 15 years	40.0	34.2	23.8	21.3	19.4	16.0
13 years or under	11.0	7.9	5.1	4.9	4.1	3.0
Total	72.2	64.2	49.1	48.6	47.0	43.7

Source: See table 6.3.

Note: N.A. = not available.

[a]Includes both over 17 years and 17 years.

better-educated workers, especially in the earlier period (table 6.4). Between 1968–69 and 1989–90, the proportion of full-year, full-time male workers with postschool qualifications increased from 27.8 to 56.3 percent and those with degrees from 3.6 to 13.4 percent.[14]

Even though the different experience of rate of return changes may be easily explained, there are still a number of potential difficulties. First, given that the earnings-employment distribution changes are so similar since 1976, why is the change in the return to education so different?[15]

Second, can the relative stability of the education return in Australia be reconciled with the evolving employment growth pattern? It is surprising, perhaps, that declining employment in the middle of the earnings distribution and rapid growth of employment at low weekly earnings have not affected the education return.

Third, what can be said as to the rate of return to education for the economy as a whole? Since 1976, the average number of years of schooling has increased by one year from 11.6 to 12.5 years. However, average real wages have not increased, and 71 percent of *all* new jobs are in the bottom quintile of the male earnings distribution. The disjuncture between the rapid growth of the average level of education and new jobs being created primarily at the bottom of the earnings distribution suggests that the additional government investment in education may not yet be paying off.

6.2   The Australian Story in More Detail

6.2.1   The Demand for Different Occupations

To comment on the relation between changes in the dispersion of employment at different levels of earnings and shifts in occupational employment re-

14. The relation between the rate of return to education and the changing stock of educated workers is not clear-cut. For example, the increase in degree holders since 1978–79 has been substantial, but the increase in those with some postschool qualifications is not very significant. The increase in those with degrees and diplomas—this aggregation might be equivalent to those with degrees in the United States—does not seem sufficient to explain why the increase in the rate of return experienced in the United States is not found in the Australian data. It is obvious that considerably more work needs to be done in this area. For the latest Australian research, see Maglen (1991).

15. The data from table 6.3 above are not standardized for labor force experience, but a more careful analysis does not suggest an increasing rate of return to education over the data period analyzed. Borland (1992), e.g., has processed the available unit record data from the Income Distribution Surveys for 1982, 1986, and 1990. He confined his analysis to wage and salary earners and those full-year, full-time workers earning more than $60.00 a week. After standardizing for a quadratic in experience, his results show that the education differentials increase marginally between 1982 and 1986 and then narrow between 1986 and 1990. Borland suggests that, in the Income Distribution Survey data, the differential across education categories has not expanded as rapidly in Australia as in the United States but that wage differentials across experience categories appear to have widened by a larger amount. The change to the return for experience seems surprising and is not consistent with the published data, which include the self-employed. Borland also provides a wide range of earnings statistics from each of the available data sources.

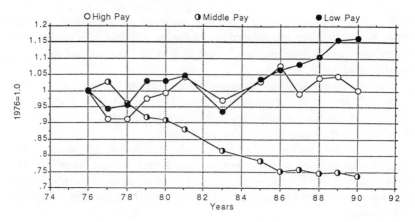

Fig. 6.6   Male employment indices for high-, middle-, and low-paying earnings, Australia, 1976–90

Source: Distribution and Composition of Employee Earnings and Hours, ABS Catalogue no. 6306.0.

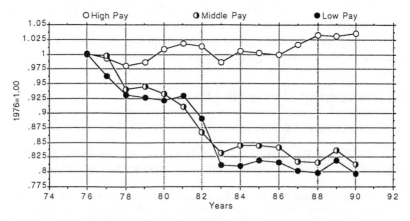

Fig. 6.7   Male employment indices for high-, middle-, and low-paying occupations, Australia, 1976–90

Sources: The Labour Force Survey, ABS Catalogue no. 6203.0, various issues (August); *Distribution and Composition of Employment Earnings and Hours,* May 1983, ABS Catalogue no. 6306.0.

quires matching different data sets.[16] Changes in occupational employment from the Labour Force Survey can be compared to employment growth in different quintiles of weekly earnings from the May survey. To do this, male full-

16. There are few data series available over a long time period that allow a detailed analysis of wage changes within occupations. The data sources that could be used include the Income Distribution Surveys for 1968–69, 1973–74, 1978–79, 1982, 1986, and 1990, but individual level data are available on tape only since 1982. The 1976, 1981, and 1986 census data are available on tape, but unit record data are available only for 1981 and 1986.

time employment from the Labour Force Survey is divided into three fixed occupation groups to approximate employment from the highest weekly earnings quintile, the middle three quintiles, and the lowest quintile taken from the May survey.[17] In 1976, high- and low-paying occupations each accounted for 28 percent of all employment.[18] The occupation classification available does not allow a closer approximation of employment proportions to the quintile groups.

Employment growth in the high weekly earnings quintile, figure 6.6, and in high-paying occupations, figure 6.7, is similar and matches the population growth rate. Employment growth in the middle-earnings quintiles and middle-pay occupations is also similar but declines strongly. It appears that the 25 percent employment loss in the middle quintiles of the earnings distribution could be "explained" by the 25 percent employment loss in middle-level occupations.[19] But there is an evident puzzle when we turn to the low-earnings group. An explanation of the disappearance of middle-paying jobs cannot be based on changing demands for occupations. For low-paying occupations, there has been a 25 percent *decrease* in the employment/population ratio, but employment in the low-earnings quintile has *increased* 15 percent. Across each earnings group, therefore, there is not a precise mapping of employment changes by occupation onto employment changes by earning levels. Employment growth at low weekly earnings cannot be explained by employment growth in low-paying occupations, and, as a result, employment declines at middle-level earnings cannot be explained by employment declines in middle-level occupations.

It also appears that the loss of middle-paying jobs is not related to a fall of average earnings in middle-paying occupations relative to low-paying occupations. High-paying occupations have experienced a real earnings increase of 5

---

17. The employment data are taken from the *The Labour Force*, ABS Catalogue no. 6203.0, August issues. Relative wages of occupations are taken from the *Distribution and Composition of Employment Earnings and Hours, May 1983*, ABS Catalogue no. 6306.0. It is not a straightforward matter to allocate full-time employment to occupations. Employment classified by occupation is not divided into full- and part-time employment, but this is not a serious problem for the male labor market over this period as part-time employment never accounts for more than 8 percent of all male employment. Before 1985, low-paying occupations are defined as laborers not elsewhere classified, other clerical workers, storemen, toolmakers, and metalworkers. The high-paying occupations are all professionals and managers. Middle-paying occupations are the residual. After 1985, the classification changes. Low-paying occupations are laborers, machine operators, drivers, sales assistants, tellers, miscellaneous sales, vehicle trades, and horticulturists. High-paying occupations are managers, professionals, and paraprofessionals. The series are spliced on the assumption that the employment distribution did not change between 1985 and 1986.

18. Within the high-paying occupation group, employment of professionals has grown quite strongly, but employment of managers has not. For some purposes, it would be useful to disaggregate the data further.

19. The question now becomes, Why is employment disappearing in middle-level occupations? It should be easy to make progress on this question because occupations can be matched to the changing demand for industry output and different patterns of international trade to discover whether imports are a factor. Alan Powell of Monash University has begun to do this; see also the new research project of Falvey, Forsyth, and Tyers (1992).

percent over the period 1976–90. Real earnings for low- and middle-paying occupations have fallen steadily and at a similar rate until 1987, something on the order of 4–5 percent. Since earnings in low- and middle-paying occupations have fallen at the same rate, the Australian experience is consistent with U.S. results that indicate that most of the changing earnings dispersion is occurring within and not across occupations.

6.2.2   The Employment of Women

A disproportionate share of the exceptional real-wage growth in Australia during the early 1970s was accounted for by women. Had their real-wage increase been constrained to that of men, the average aggregate real-wage increase between 1969 and 1975 would have been about 8 percent less, and the average aggregate wage increase relative to the United States over this period would have been reduced from about one-third to one-quarter.

The real earnings increase for Australian women between 1968–69 and 1975–76 was approximately 65 percent, while that of U.S. women was around 4 percent. Despite this extraordinary earnings increase in Australia, the employment of women continued to increase relative to that of men. For example, the number of adult women employed as full-time nonmanagerial employees (the May survey) increased 39 percent between 1976 and 1990, while male employment increased 7 percent. Among *all* new jobs, women employed full- and part-time have accounted for seven of every ten.[20] This rapid growth of female employment naturally prompts the question as to the relation between their employment growth and the distribution of male jobs. Perhaps better-educated women have been filling some of the missing male middle jobs.

Table 6.5 refers to full-time nonmanagerial employees (the May survey). Column 1 allocates the male employment change between 1976 and 1990 to each quintile from table 6.1 above. The absolute employment loss in the middle quintiles is clearly evident. Column 2 allocates women employed full-time to the same quintiles to see where their employment growth lies in the male earnings distribution. The dispersion of additional employment for women since 1976 is more even,[21] but once again job growth is greatest at levels of weekly earnings equivalent to the bottom 20 percent of male workers. Women have done absolutely and relatively better than men in obtaining employment in the middle of the male pay distribution, and, in this sense, there has been some employment substitution. The extent is slight, however. Had all additional employment of women been allocated to men, there would still be a disappearing middle, and the growth rate of low-paying jobs would have been even greater than before.

---

20. For a further analysis of the effect of female employment growth on the Australian labor market, see Gregory (1990).

21. Women have done particularly well in the fourth quintile, where they filled eight of every ten new jobs.

Table 6.5   **Australian Employment Growth by Earning Quintiles, 1976–90 (thousands)**

Quintile	Full-Time Nonmanagerial Employees				All Employees (5)
	Male (1)	Female (2)	Public Total (3)	Private Total (4)	
First (lowest)	176	114	111	178	983
Second	−51	24	29	−60	4
Third	−82	54	−4	−25	10
Fourth	15	104	89	30	139
Fifth (highest)	94	50	35	117	243
Total	152	347	260	240	1,379

Source: Distribution and Composition of Employee Earnings and Hours, ABS Catalogue no. 6306.0.

Finally, we look at *all* new jobs created since 1976, extending the sample to include managers and part-time workers.[22] The data presented in column 5 are extraordinary: 71 percent of all additional employment created in Australia between 1976 and 1990 is in the bottom 20 percent of the male full-time weekly earnings distribution; a further 18 percent of employment is in the top quintile. Australia is losing middle-level employment at an astounding rate, to be replaced primarily by employment at weekly earnings at the bottom of the earnings distribution.

6.2.3   The Accord

Australian data provide an opportunity to measure the effect of income policies on the changing distribution of employment at different levels of weekly earnings. Beginning in 1983, the newly elected Labour government and the trade union movement adopted a Prices and Incomes Accord that was to act as a general means to coordinate and centralize wage changes. The objective was to limit real and nominal wage increases so that a larger proportion of economic growth could be directed toward additional employment. As with most moves toward centralized wage fixing, the accord process was expected to compress wage relativities and thus might also be expected to increase employment in the middle and reduce employment growth in the bottom and top quintiles. There was also another period (1976–79) during which wage changes were also largely controlled and centralized by the Industrial Relations Commission.

Figure 6.8 presents the proportion of male employment in the aggregate of the middle three quintiles for both surveys. Although it has been suggested by King, Rimmer, and Rimmer (1992) that the accord widened the earnings

22. The ratio of managers to nonmanagers has not changed over the data period. Part-time employment, however, has grown quickly.

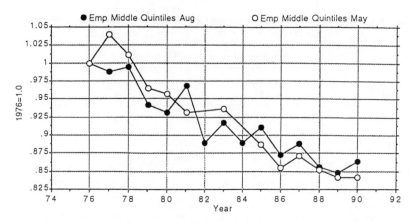

Fig. 6.8   Male employment indices for middle three quintiles, Australia, 1976–90, May and August surveys
Sources: Distribution and Composition of Employee Earnings and Hours, ABS Catalogue no. 6306.0 (May survey); *Weekly Earnings of Employees (Distribution) Australia,* ABS Catalogue no. 6310.0 (August survey).

dispersion, the effects of this are not obvious in a break in the trend toward greater employment dispersion. A significant accord effect on the time trend is difficult to discern. There is a suggestion in the data, however, that the rate of decline of the disappearing middle has moderated in recent years.

It might be expected that the effects of the accord will differ in magnitude in the public and private sectors and that middle-level jobs will disappear at a faster rate in the private sector, but in both sectors the employment series are again trend dominated.[23] It is also apparent that the rapid growth of low-paying jobs is approximately the same in both sectors, and the trend has not been interrupted by the accord (fig. 6.9). There is no marked accord effect on low-earnings employment. It is the rapid growth of employment at high earnings in the private sector that distinguishes the two sectors. If there is an obvious and significant accord effect, it is to be found in the lower employment growth at high wages in the public sector.

The comparison between sectors prompts the following conjectures. First, as the rapid rate of employment growth at the bottom of the earnings distribution is approximately equal in the two sectors, the economic forces generating the growth of low-earnings employment may be similar. This may suggest that the growth of low-earning jobs and the decline in the middle of the earnings distribution are not just the result of a private-sector decline in manufacturing or of unusual private-sector profit squeezes. Second, as there has been steady

23. The sample frame was changed in 1983 in response to the changing distribution of firms, and this may explain the unusual 1983 observation in the private-sector data. As 1983 is the beginning of a new sample frame, it raises difficulties in discriminating between the effects of the sample change, the 1982 recession, and the beginning of the accord.

employment growth at low weekly earnings in both sectors and the effects of moving toward and away from a centralized wage-setting system are not obvious, perhaps it is the change in employment growth at different levels of earnings that is important rather than changes in relative wages for existing jobs. This conjecture is further supported by the observation that middle-level jobs have also disappeared in the public sector, even though the wage system is more rigid there.

6.2.4   Real Earnings at the Top and Bottom

Other papers in this volume focus on changes in real wages at different points on the employment distribution. To facilitate comparisons, we conclude this section by presenting real weekly earnings for male full-time, nonmanagerial employees at the tenth and ninetieth percentiles.

There are marked but consistent differences across sectors (fig. 6.10). In the public sector, which employs approximately one-third of adult male full-time, nonmanagerial employees, real wages paid to the top and bottom 10 percent have moved closely together, as might be expected from a rigid-wage public-sector system that generally does not make overaward payments. Nevertheless, there is a widening earnings gap of about 4 percentage points. Employees at both extremes of the wage distribution have experienced significant real wage reductions since 1985, and, in 1991, real wages are 2–5 percent below 1976 levels. It is interesting to note that the loss of middle-paying jobs and the contrast between rapid employment growth in the bottom quintile and slow employment growth in the top quintile do not translate into significant changes in the relation between real wages at the tenth and ninetieth percentiles in the public service.

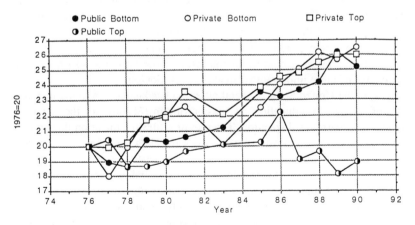

Fig. 6.9   Male employment indices for top and bottom quintiles, Australia, 1976–90, public and private sectors
Source: Distribution and Composition of Employee Earnings and Hours, ABS Catalogue no. 6306.0 (May survey).

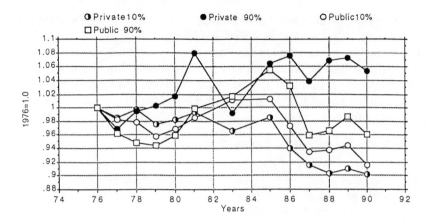

Fig. 6.10   Male real wages, Australia, 1976–90, public and private sector at the tenth and ninetieth percentiles
Source: See fig. 6.9.

It is in the private sector that the earnings gap has widened most. Real earnings for the top 10 percent have increased 6 percentage points since 1976, and real wages for the bottom group have fallen 10 percent. The real-wage gap has opened by 16 percentage points, a very large increase indeed.

6.3   Concluding Remarks

Perhaps the most important result that flows from the U.S.-Australian comparisons is the similarity of changes in employment dispersion across the two countries. Both are losing middle-income jobs and creating employment at the extremes of the distribution. The employment-earnings distribution appears to be widening at the same rate in each country, but there is no evidence of convergence. The gap between the countries has not narrowed. The similarity of the change raises a number of interesting questions that still need to be resolved. The more important seem to be the following.

First, in the United States, special attention has been given to the increased rate of return to education as a contributing factor to the widening employment-earnings dispersion. The rate of return to education does not appear to have increased in Australia, but the same change in earnings dispersion is observed.

Second, although the Australian earnings dispersion is more compressed than that in the United States, the earnings distributions are not moving closer together as international trade and the links between the two countries increase. The loss of middle-paying jobs appears to be increasing at much the same rate in both countries.

Third, the change in the earnings dispersion in Australia is occurring in both the public and the private sectors, and it does not seem to have been retarded to any significant degree by income policy regimes. As it is generally thought that income policy regimes compress the earnings distribution, the Australian experience is particularly interesting and raises the question as to whether the change in the earnings distribution would have been even greater without the income policy regime. If so, then the Australian employment distribution may have shown clear signs of converging toward the U.S. distribution.

Fourth, the macro history of the two countries has been very different. Australian male employment has fallen 25 percent, after adjusting for population growth, and U.S. male employment has fallen 8 percent. Our analysis suggests that the very large increase in real wages in Australia during the 1970s is an important part of the explanation for falling employment, increasing unemployment, and the loss of male full-time jobs but seems not to be an important explanation of job growth at low earnings and the disappearance of middle-level jobs. All dispersion effects are subject to strong trend influences rather than the sudden response that might be expected from the mid-1970s real-wage shock.

References

Blackburn, M., D. Bloom, and R. Freeman. 1990. The declining economic position of less skilled American men. In *A future of lousy jobs: The changing structure of US wages,* ed. G. Burtless. Washington, D.C.: Brookings.

Borland, J. 1992. Wage inequality in Australia. Paper presented at a National Bureau of Economic Research conference, April.

Burtless, G. 1990. Introduction. In *A future of lousy jobs: The changing structure of US wages,* ed. G. Burtless. Washington, D.C.: Brookings.

Davis, S. J. 1992. Cross country patterns of change in relative wages. University of Chicago, May. Mimeo.

Falvey, R., P. Forsyth, and R. Tyers. 1992. Chronic unemployment and the distribution of income in Australia: The implications of Asia's export boom. Australian National University. Mimeo (first draft).

Foster, R. F., and S. E. Stewart. 1991. Australian economic statistics, 1949–50 to 1989–90. Occasional Paper no. 8. Sydney: Reserve Bank of Australia.

Gregory, R. G. 1990. Jobs and gender: A lego approach to the Australian labour market. *Economic Record* 667:S20–S40.

Gregory, R. G., and A. Daly. 1991. Who gets what? Institutions, human capital and black boxes as determinants of relative wages in Australia and the US. In *Long-run perspectives of the New Zealand economy: Proceedings of the sesquicentennial conference of the New Zealand Association of Economics,* vol. 2. Wellington.

Hughes, B. 1973. The wages of the weak and the strong. *Journal of Industrial Relations* 15:1–24.

King, J. E., R. Rimmer, and S. Rimmer. 1992. The law of the shrinking middle: Inequality of earnings in Australia, 1975–1989. *Scottish Journal of Political Economy* 39, no. 4:391–412.

Levy, F., and R. J. Murnane. 1992. US earnings levels and earnings inequalities: A review of recent trends and proposed explanations. *Journal of Economic Literature* 30, no. 3:1333–81.

Madsen, J. 1992. Unemployment in the OECD: A macroeconomic study. Ph.D. diss., Division of Economics and Politics, Research School of Social Sciences, Australian National University.

Maglen, L. R. 1991. The impact of education expansion on the distribution of earnings in Australia. *Australian Bulletin of Labour* 17, no. 2:132–59.

Norris, K. 1986. The wages structure: Does arbitration make any difference? In *Wage fixation in Australia,* ed. J. Niland. Sydney: Allen & Unwin.

Russel, B., and W. Tease. 1991. Employment output and real wages. *Economic Record* 67:34–45.

7   Labor Markets and Economic Growth: Lessons from Korea's Industrialization, 1970–1990

Dae-Il Kim and Robert H. Topel

7.1   Introduction and Summary

This paper studies the evolution of labor markets in the Republic of Korea (henceforth, Korea) during an episode of extraordinary economic growth and structural change. Real per capita income in Korea roughly tripled between 1971 and 1986. This was accompanied by a transformation of the Korean labor market from a largely rural base—agriculture accounted for half of total employment in 1970 but less than 20 percent in 1990—to one in which manufacturing's share of total employment (25 percent) is now larger than it is in the United States. This industrialization has been fueled by dramatic productivity growth and by a fourfold increase in exports' share of national output. By these measures, Korea underwent a greater industrial transformation in the twenty-five years following 1965 than Britain did in the seventy-five years following 1780.

While studying the evolution of the Korean labor market is interesting in its own right, our motives are somewhat broader. First, we think that Korea's rapid industrialization offers a unique laboratory in which to gauge the way decentralized labor markets adjust to structural change. After all, in what other important market did labor productivity triple in only fifteen years, fueling a wholesale shift of the workforce from agriculture to urban manufacturing? What other country has upgraded the skills of its workforce so rapidly that the proportion of high school and college graduates increased by 30 percentage

Dae-Il Kim is assistant professor of Economics at Rice University. Robert H. Topel is the Isidore Brown and Gladys J. Brown Professor in Urban and Labor Economics at the University of Chicago and a research associate of the National Bureau of Economic Research.

The authors are grateful to the Ford Foundation, the Bradley Foundation, and the National Science Foundation for financial support and to Larry Katz, Richard Freeman, Bill Dickens, Ann Case, and conference participants for valuable comments. Jeff Williamson, the discussant, provided extraordinarily useful written comments.

points since 1972? The changes that we observe in developed economies are glacial, and minor, by comparison.

Our second motive is to provide new evidence relevant to long-standing debates in the development literature. How do wage inequality and income inequality change during economic development? Do rapid changes in educational attainment have important labor market effects? Do manufacturing exports drive wage and income growth? How do government policies, including so-called industrial policies, affect labor markets? How mobile is labor, and what is the role of urban-rural migration in development?

7.1.1   Main Results

We address these issues by drawing on a number of data sources, including both published series and individual earnings and employment records for large samples of Korean men.[1] Our findings can be grouped into five main areas, as follows.

1. Productivity, trade, and employment. Korea's small share of world markets implies that demands for tradable manufactured goods are highly elastic, so productivity growth increases the demand for labor. Yet productivity growth was unevenly distributed among industries, which means that labor demand growth was too. Looking across industries, we find that both exports and employment expanded in proportion to productivity gains. We take this as evidence that advancing productivity drove the transformation of the Korean labor market.

2. Sectoral neutrality of aggregate wage growth. While government policies aimed at controlling wage growth appear to have been effective in the early 1970s, wages were determined by market forces during most of the period under study. Aggregate labor demand expanded rapidly, drawing millions of workers from rural to urban labor markets and tripling the aggregate real wage. Yet, in spite of wide differences among sectors in rates of employment growth, we find that sectoral changes in wages and employment are unrelated. In other words, aggregate wage growth was neutral among sectors. This comports with related evidence for the United States (see Murphy and Topel 1987a, 1987b; and Dickens and Katz 1987) and suggests that there is "one labor market" in Korea.

3. Sectoral mobility of workers. The growth of manufacturing and related sectors was accompanied by a wholesale shift of employment out of agriculture. Workers of all ages left the farm. Yet we find scant evidence that manufacturing drew on agriculture or any other sector as a source of labor supply. Instead,

---

1. We plan to analyze women in a paper that compares Taiwan and Korea.

virtually all of manufacturing's growth was accomplished by hiring ever larger numbers of new entrants to the labor force, who then stay in the sector over their careers. In the manufacturing sector, there was virtually no net hiring of workers older than age twenty-five. In a sort of "musical chairs" process, migrants from agriculture entered the nonmanufacturing sector, replacing the young workers who were hired into manufacturing.

4. High labor turnover. Japan's model of lifetime jobs does not apply to Korea. While industrial expansion has been accompanied by increased durability in employment relationships, job spells remain very short by the standards of developed countries. Even today, the average job in progress has lasted only about four years, compared to about nine years in the United States. In the growing manufacturing sector, 60 percent of all new jobs end in the first year, and turnover is much *higher* in manufacturing than in the rest of the economy. To square this finding with the virtual absence of net mobility from manufacturing as a whole, there must be very high interfirm mobility within that sector.

5. Inequality. Simon Kuznets's 1955 presidential address to the American Economic Association introduced a now-famous hypothesis about changes in wage inequality during economic development. Kuznets argued that the initial stages of industrialization would cause wage inequality to rise. This relation has been dubbed the *Kuznets curve* by development economists, yet subsequent research has shown only weak evidence in its favor.[2]

Our results for Korea do not support Kuznets's conjecture. Korea is a prominent example of rapid industrialization combined with sharply declining wage inequality. In 1970, wage inequality (as measured by the spread between the ninetieth and the tenth percentiles of the wage distribution) was 40 percent greater in Korea than in the United States. The 90-10 differential fell by 20 percent over the next fifteen years, and by 1986 wages were *more* equally distributed in Korea than in the United States.

One explanation for declining inequality is the rapid expansion of manufacturing, perhaps driven by purposeful industrial policies favoring that sector. These policies might have increased the demand for less skilled workers. But we find no evidence of this: sectors that employ relatively unskilled workers did not expand more rapidly than others. Instead, the data point to improvements in human capital as the major force that narrowed wage differences. In 1972, over 60 percent of Korean workers had only a grade school education, a figure that fell to 30 percent by 1989. We find important changes in relative wages that were driven by these changes in factor ratios: as high school and college graduates became more plentiful, their relative wages fell by more than half.

---

2. See the discussion in Little (1982) and the references therein.

7.1.2   The Data

We analyze data from a variety of sources. Employment data are drawn from the *Annual Reports on the Economically Active Population* (*EAP*), published by the Economic Planning Board, which is a census-style sample of the Korean labor force. The main source for wages, job tenures, and other job-related statistics is the Occupational Wage Survey (OWS), conducted annually by the Korean Ministry of Labor. This survey includes wage, employment, and demographic information for about 5 million workers per year, which makes it much larger than typical sources of micro data in the United States and other countries.[3] For the most part, we rely on published cross-tabulations of these data, although we also make use of original files, in tape form, for 1971, 1983, 1986, and 1989.[4]

The OWS has its drawbacks. The sampling units are firms, not individuals. Firms report wage and demographic data for a random sample of their workers, but only firms with ten or more employees are included in the survey. This omits roughly one-third of the nonagricultural labor force in a typical year. Since manufacturing firms are larger than those in other sectors and they employ younger workers, this has the effect of giving greater weight to young workers who work in manufacturing. At this stage, we have not tried to reweight the data to reflect these limitations. Readers are advised to keep this in mind.

7.2   The Setting: Growth, Institutions, and Policy in Korea, 1970–90

7.2.1   Trade, Income, and Productivity Growth

Table 7.1 compares per capita income growth in South Korea and other countries since 1970. Over this period, Korea grew more than twice as fast as did Japan and roughly three times faster than the United States and the remaining OECD countries. By 1990, per capita income in Korea was $5,584, up from $1,023 in 1970. For comparison, this is 30 percent of the U.S. level, which stood at $18,482 in 1990.

The evident sources of Korean growth are rapid advances in labor productivity coupled with open markets for exports of manufactured products. Figure 7.1 shows the evolution of average hourly wages and manufacturing productivity in Korea since 1971.[5] There are two noteworthy points about the figure.

3. A similar survey is conducted by the Japanese Ministry of Labor (see, e.g., Hashimoto and Raisian 1985).
4. These data were kindly provided by John Bauer. Each of these tapes has about 600,000 observations that are randomly sampled from the original survey.
5. Alternative measures of labor productivity give substantially different estimates of productivity growth in Korea. The Korean Productivity Center (KPC) index of output per *production worker* is based on survey responses of Korean manufacturers. From a base of one hundred in 1975, this index rises to nearly four hundred by 1987! Measured output per hour worked by all employees, calculated by us, shows less dramatic growth. We are suspicious of the survey data and uncomfortable with the survey's focus on production workers, so calculated productivity is shown in fig. 7.1.

Table 7.1   **Growth Rates of Real per Capita GNP, Selected Countries, 1970–88**

Country	1970–88	1970–75	1975–80	1980–85	1985–88
South Korea	7.3	7.1	5.1	7.3	11.4
	(7.4)	(7.4)	(5.6)	(7.4)	(10.6)
United States	2.0	1.5	2.5	1.6	2.6
	(2.0)	(1.4)	(2.3)	(1.6)	(2.9)
Japan	3.6	3.3	4.1	3.4	3.6
	(3.4)	(3.3)	(4.0)	(3.2)	(3.1)
Canada	2.5	3.7	1.8	1.6	3.2
	(2.4)	(3.6)	(1.9)	(1.4)	(3.0)
Germany	2.3	1.7	3.6	1.4	2.5
	(2.3)	(1.7)	(3.6)	(1.5)	(2.7)
United Kingdom	2.1	1.8	1.7	1.8	3.8
	(2.0)	(2.0)	(1.7)	(1.6)	(3.5)

	1960–68	1968–73	1973–79	1979–87
OECD	3.9	3.4	1.8	1.8

Sources: Calculations are from World Bank, *World Tables* (Baltimore: Johns Hopkins University Press, 1970–88). The data for OECD are from United Nations, *National Accounts Statistics* (New York: 1960–87).

Note: Growth rates for real per capita GDP are in parentheses.

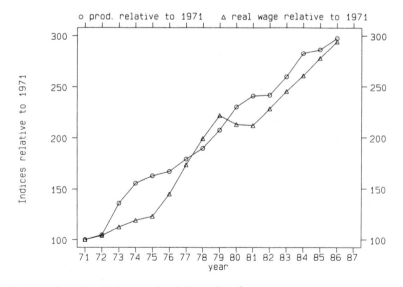

Fig. 7.1   Growth of labor productivity and real wage

Source: Economic Planning Board, *Korean Statistical Yearbook* (various years).

Note: Labor productivity is calculated as output per worker in manufacturing.

First, over the long term, wage growth and productivity growth are identical. Both indices tripled in a period of only sixteen years. The obvious message is that advancing labor productivity fueled wage and income growth in Korea. More generally, the close correspondence between productivity and wages points to the widely discussed emergence of manufacturing as the engine of Korean economic development.

The second point is timing. Real-wage growth in the early 1970s lagged behind productivity growth, but the gap closed after 1975. As we will indicate below, government efforts to suppress wage growth—at least for less skilled workers—seem to have been successful in the early 1970s. At least from the middle 1970s on, market forces play a dominant role in wage determination.

Later we will argue that productivity growth in particular industries fueled a transformation of the Korean labor market, creating export opportunities and huge shifts in the sectoral composition of employment. For now, figure 7.2 shows the growth in aggregate foreign trade since 1970. The real value of manufactured exports grew sevenfold in only fifteen years. As a proportion of total output, exports grew from about 10 percent of GNP in 1970 to over one-third of GNP in 1985. For comparison, the corresponding figures for the United States are 7.2 percent and 10 percent, respectively.

7.2.2   Industrial Policies Affecting the Composition of Output[6]

Like other developing countries in East Asia (except Japan), Korea's rapid development coincides with a shift in policy from import substitution to active export promotion. As in Taiwan, which began its shift in policy in the early 1950s, export promotion was achieved by dismantling macroeconomic policies that had restricted exports and by instituting policies that actively favored them.

The 1960s were a turning point for Korean economic policy. Until then, the government's policy of import substitution had controlled all imports. Imports were restricted to those on a "permissible" list that included only 207 commodities before 1965. This system was reversed in 1967 so that only specified commodity imports were prohibited. As a result, the import liberalization ratio (automatically approved/total importable) jumped from 12 to 59 percent (Collins and Park 1989).[7]

Export incentives took various forms, including direct cash subsidies for exported products, preferential tax treatment of income from exports, interest rate subsidies, tax exemptions on intermediate inputs, and tariff exemptions on imported raw materials used for export production. During the 1970s, preferential interest rates and tax and tariff exemptions accounted for more than 90 percent of gross subsidies per dollar of exports. Interest subsidies were abolished in 1982.

---

6. The discussion in this section draws on Collins and Park (1989), Kim (1990), and Song (1990b).

7. This ratio remained fairly stable until 1978, after which it grew to 88 percent by 1985.

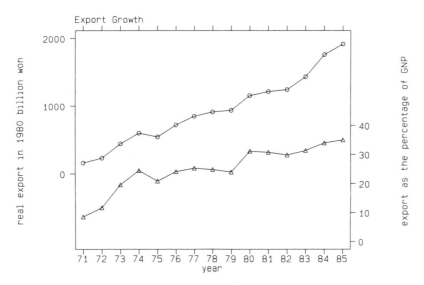

Fig. 7.2   Real export growth, Korea, 1971–85
Source: Economic Planning Board, *Korean Statistical Yearbook* (various years).

Rising prices of raw materials and labor, together with the emergence of other Asian producers of labor-intensive products in the early 1970s, undermined Korea's comparative advantage in light manufacturing. This led to the reestablishment of import substitution policies in 1973. These policies coexisted with export incentives for the rest of the decade. This explicit industrial policy—which came to be known as the "Big Push"—sought to expand Korea's industrial base and to shift its emphasis from light manufacturing to particular heavy and defense-related industries. Policy instruments included quantitative restrictions on imports of particular products, financing and tax incentives for targeted industries, and restrictions on foreign direct investment.

These industrial policies remained in place until 1980, when rising oil prices and a poor rice crop contributed to a 4.9 percent contraction in real GNP. Following the coup of 1979, a reevaluation of policy alternatives led to greater emphasis on market mechanisms and trade liberalization. The import liberalization ratio climbed from 69 percent in 1979 to over 90 percent by 1986, and import tariffs fell by roughly half. Restrictions on foreign direct investment were also reduced, along with government control and regulation of the financial sector.[8] Interestingly enough, heavy industry continued to grow more rapidly than light manufacturing during the subsequent expansion of the 1980s.

---

8. Rationing of interest-subsidized loans favored large firms and those in targeted industries during the Big Push from 1973 to 1979. Subsequent liberalization of the financial sector reduced the between-industry variance in borrowing costs from 21 percent in 1979 to 6 percent in 1984.

7.2.3 Labor Market Policies

Korean governments have intervened in labor markets with varying degrees of success. Our reading of government policy and its effects leads us to believe that wages and employment were mainly determined by market forces during the period under study, although there is some evidence that the government was successful in capping wage growth in the early 1970s.

This is not to say that governments took a hands-off approach to labor markets. Two aspects of these policies are noteworthy. First, as noted by Song (1990a, 1990b), legal restrictions on collective bargaining have been an important component of Korean industrial policies. Perhaps because of this, union members of all kinds have accounted for a very small portion of total employment. Figure 7.3 shows that union membership (including company unions) peaked at about 8 percent of total employment in 1979, which corresponds to about 13 percent of nonagricultural employment. At its peak in the late 1970s, union membership may have accounted for 18 percent of total manufacturing employment. The post-1986 upturn in union coverage reflects a relaxation of government restrictions on collective bargaining, as indicated below.

Emergency provisions enacted in 1971 prohibited collective bargaining by broad labor organizations. This sharply reduced the power of the Korean Headquarters of Unions (KHU) and industrial unions, which had grown in the 1960s. At least until 1974, these organizations lost effective control over firm-level unions. The result of this policy was to strengthen the role of decentralized wage setting, which seems to have been a goal of government policies throughout the period under study. Even when unions were involved in wage setting, it was generally as a party to a bilateral negotiation between an individual company and its union. Strikes and other forms of collective action were also banned at this time.

Korean governments also attempted to limit wage growth in key sectors. Under the threat of withdrawing government subsidies and support, employers were directed to keep nominal wage growth below an upper limit established by the Economic Planning Board (EPB). Roughly speaking, the allowable limit on any firm's nominal wage growth was 80 percent of the sum of inflation and aggregate productivity growth. While there is little evidence that the limit was enforced, circumstantial evidence suggests that the policies were fairly successful in the early 1970s. Figure 7.1 above showed that aggregate wage growth lagged behind productivity growth at that time. More specifically, figure 7.4 shows the correspondence between actual nominal wage growth and the government targets set by the EPB. Nominal wage growth exceeded government targets by huge margins after 1975. This was a period of substantial price inflation and, as figure 7.3 above showed, of some resurgence in union coverage. Indeed, KHU and industrial unions reentered the wage negotiation process in 1975.

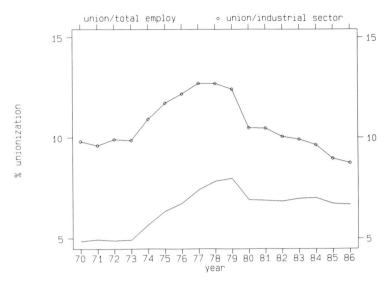

Fig. 7.3   Union membership as percentage of total and nonagricultural employment, Korea, 1970–88
Source: Economic Planning Board, *Korean Statistical Yearbook* (various years).

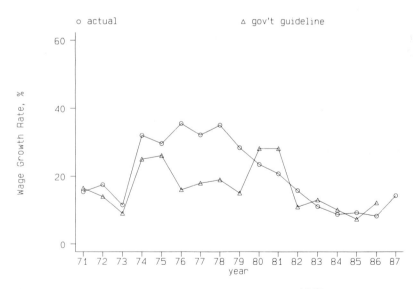

Fig. 7.4   Nominal wage growth, actual vs. government guideline
Source: Song (1990b).

Following the coup of 1979, KHU and industrial unions were again prohibited from participating in wage negotiations. Authority for industrial relations—including wage negotiations—was placed in mandated labor-management committees, which further eroded the importance of unions. These policies coincide with the decline of union coverage up through 1986 and—because inflation was brought under control—with nominal wage increases that were in line with government targets (fig. 7.4). Actual wage growth kept pace with productivity in this period, however. Restrictions on collective bargaining were relaxed in 1986. This led to another resurgence of union power and a sharp increase in organizing and strike activities.

7.3   Labor Market Performance in Korea

7.3.1   Productivity, Employment, and Exports

We argued above that sustained productivity growth has been the fulcrum of Korea's economic development. Our interpretation of the labor market effects of rising productivity is straightforward. Coupled with open markets for manufactured exports, increases in total factor productivity raise the demand for labor in the manufacturing sector. With fixed aggregate labor supply, this causes net migration of labor to manufacturing and support industries and rising aggregate wages. Consistent with this, figure 7.5 shows that manufacturing's share of total Korean employment doubled between 1971 and 1986. This relative growth has been fed by a steady decline in agricultural employment.

Large-scale migration from agriculture is certainly consistent with rising relative demand for nonagricultural labor. With a rising supply price of migrants, this might widen the rural-urban income gap in the short run. While the unemployment rate of nonfarm households fell steadily over the period, Tcha (1992) shows that rural incomes rose relative to urban ones until 1975 and actually exceeded urban incomes from 1973 to 1978.[9] There is some evidence in Tcha's data for declining relative incomes of rural workers after 1975. Overall, however, his data indicate rough parity between urban and rural incomes during the period of our data.[10] This is weak evidence against the relevance of Todaro (1969)–style models of segmented labor markets, where urban wages are held above those in rural areas. Given the magnitude of the migration that took place, these data are superficially consistent with highly elastic labor supply from rural areas.

International trade is a key element of this scenario. With prices of manufac-

9. The data for unemployment rates are from the Economic Planning Board (EPB), *Monthly Statistics of Korea,* 1988, and *Annual Report of the Economically Active Population,* various issues.

10. Tcha's data are fairly tentative. They are adjusted for differences in costs of living between rural and urban areas, which he finds to be quite large. Further, Tcha's adjustment to income *levels* is based on government data from 1980 alone, so time-series changes in the cost of living are not captured in his estimates.

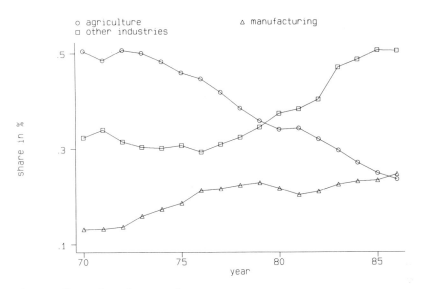

Fig. 7.5   Sectoral employment shares
Source: Economic Planning Board, *Korean Statistical Yearbook* (various years).

tured goods fixed on international markets, productivity growth in a small open economy raises the demand for factors because increased output can be sold abroad. This means that exports will account for a rising proportion of total output, which is what happened. At a more disaggregated level, it also means that rapidly growing sectors—in terms of output and employment—should be those with the greatest productivity growth. In turn, these should also be the sectors with the largest increases in exports. Figures 7.6–7.8 below provide direct evidence on these points.

Figure 7.6 shows patterns of export growth among manufacturing industries between 1978 and 1985.[11] Exports grew most rapidly in fabricated metals, where they nearly quadrupled in seven years, while the real value of exports actually declined in wood products. Table 7.2 shows the corresponding values for labor productivity after 1971. While productivity grew dramatically in all industries, the range of growth rates is fairly wide. Output per worker grew by a factor of four in fabricated metals and machinery—an annual rate of nearly 10 percent—but by less than 50 percent in wood products.

The relations among productivity growth, employment growth, and exports are shown in figures 7.7 and 7.8. Figure 7.7 plots rates of employment growth against rates of productivity growth for manufacturing industries between 1978 and 1985.[12] The correlation between them is .85. Figure 7.8 is a conform-

11. Data from earlier years were not available.
12. A corresponding figure for growth rates from 1971 to 1985 shows the same relation. We focus on 1978–85 to be consistent with fig. 7.8. Export data by industry were available to us only for this period.

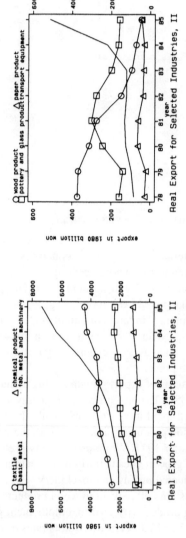

Fig. 7.6 Exports of manufacturing industries, 1978–85
Source: Economic Planning Board, *Korean Statistical Yearbook* (various years).

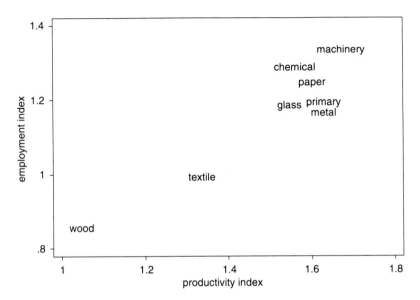

Fig. 7.7   Employment and productivity, 1985 vs. 1978

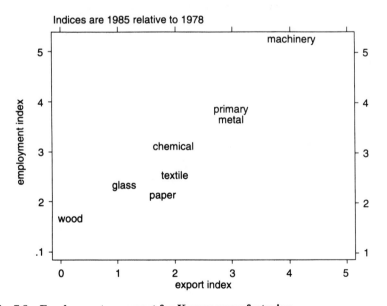

Fig. 7.8   Employment vs. export for Korean manufacturing

Table 7.2   Productivity Indices within Manufacturing Measured as Output per
                     Worker, Korea, 1971–86

Year	Entire Mfg.	Sectors within Manufacturing							
		(1)	(2)	(3)	(4)	(5)	(6)	(7)	(8)
1971	100.0	100.0	100.0	100.0	100.0	100.0	100.0	100.0	100.0
1972	104.7	105.2	113.8	93.2	100.4	101.4	110.8	117.8	108.4
1973	135.8	128.3	149.8	113.6	138.2	116.4	128.9	185.3	148.9
1974	155.6	138.6	151.2	118.2	163.2	156.1	157.1	205.5	179.3
1975	162.6	168.5	165.8	124.1	147.0	176.0	184.7	159.7	171.6
1976	166.8	180.8	174.7	123.3	157.5	164.6	184.5	198.0	189.4
1977	179.1	198.5	178.2	131.5	175.6	172.7	214.1	194.0	218.0
1978	189.7	208.9	187.7	137.3	188.6	181.4	198.0	115.2	223.3
1979	207.4	204.0	202.1	157.9	205.4	207.7	234.7	223.4	248.2
1980	230.1	217.6	216.4	145.6	228.0	261.9	261.2	251.0	237.5
1981	240.7	233.5	216.3	137.8	241.2	274.8	244.9	281.7	271.3
1982	241.7	251.0	204.5	138.5	237.2	260.3	248.3	288.0	289.0
1983	259.7	256.0	213.9	143.6	276.9	276.6	289.1	302.6	324.0
1984	282.5	266.0	243.2	149.8	300.2	294.6	301.9	325.2	362.3
1985	286.3	268.5	252.1	144.4	302.6	283.5	307.3	332.2	370.3
1986	297.6	278.3	282.4	146.4	337.2	247.7	346.8	345.1	409.4

Source: Calculations are from *Korean Statistical Yearbook* (Seoul: Economic Planning Board, 1971–86).
Note: (1) Food and beverages, (2) textiles, (3) wood products, (4) paper products, (5) chemical product, (6) pottery and glass, (7) primary metals, and (8) fabricated metals and machinery.

able graph of employment growth against export growth for the same period; the correlation between these is .62. The data suggest a strong causal link running from productivity growth to exports and employment.

7.3.2 Industry Growth, Productivity, and Wages

The preceding data indicate that important changes in relative labor demands have caused large shifts in the sectoral composition of employment in Korea. If expanding industries require specific talents subject to rising supply price, then the speed of these shifts should cause conformable changes in relative wages. We find scant evidence of this. Instead, we find that the dramatic real-wage growth documented in figure 7.1 above is mainly neutral across manufacturing industries. To a first approximation, there is one big labor market in Korea, at least in the nonagricultural sector.

To investigate these issues, we regressed industry values of log wages, productivity, and employment on fixed industry effects and common year effects, as in

$$(1) \qquad W_{it} = a_i + B_t + w_{it},$$

where W_{it} is the log of average hourly earnings for workers in industry i at time t. Call the residuals from these regressions w_{it}, p_{it}, and e_{it} for wages, productivity, and employment, respectively. To demonstrate the relation between employment and productivity growth rates, figure 7.9*a* shows results from re-gressing e_{it} on p_{it} for the eight manufacturing industries listed in table 7.2 above. As above, the data clearly indicate that greater productivity growth in-creases labor demand; on average, productivity growth that is 10 percent greater than average generates employment growth that is 6 percent greater than average.

There is slight evidence of a positive relation between productivity growth and wages, shown in figure 7.9*b*. A 10 percent increase in relative productivity growth is associated with about a 1 percent increase in relative wages. Our estimates cannot control for changes in the quality of the workforce, but we take this as some evidence that skill upgrading raised measured productivity in some sectors.

Finally, figure 7.9*c* shows the estimated relation between wage growth and employment growth. There isn't one. These data indicate that differences in relative growth rates have had no measurable effect on relative wages. In other words, while differences in productivity growth strongly influence labor de-mand and output, there is no evidence that growing sectors faced a rising sup-ply price of labor over this period.[13]

7.3.3   Sectoral Reallocation of Labor

The neutrality of wage growth in spite of large shifts in relative demands suggests that sectoral wage differentials are arbitraged by labor mobility and the growing supply of skilled workers. While our data do not allow for a de-tailed investigation of mobility among manufacturing industries, we can use the *EAP* data to investigate patterns of mobility among broader industry aggre-gates. We find that almost all intersectoral mobility occurs among young work-ers and new entrants to the labor force. They account for virtually all the growth in manufacturing employment, and it appears that their numbers are large enough to arbitrage intersectoral wage differences. Later we will show that the wages of young workers have risen through time, but it seems that this can be attributed to a decline in their relative supply (a baby bust) rather than to an increase in demand in any particular sector.

Evidence on sectoral mobility is in table 7.3, which shows how the sectoral composition of employment has changed within labor market cohorts. We know from earlier evidence that employment has shifted from agriculture to manufacturing and trades. The table demonstrates the pace with which this transformation of the labor market has taken place. As late as 1975, the modal job among new entrants (twenty to twenty-five years old) was in agriculture, which accounted for nearly a third of all young workers' jobs. By 1989, that figure had fallen to 6 percent, while nearly half of all new entrants worked in

---

13. This does not mean that supplies of different skill groups were perfectly elastic at each point in time. As the education data suggest, supply curves of skill groups were also shifting during this period.

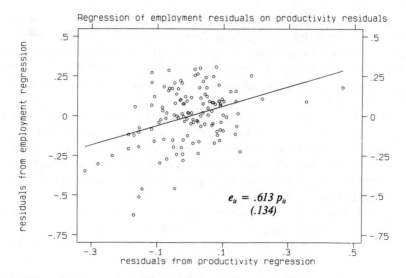

Fig. 7.9a   Employment and productivity within manufacturing

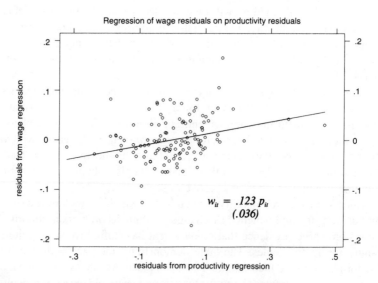

Fig. 7.9b   Neutrality in wage growth within manufacturing

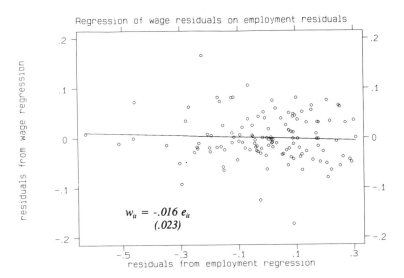

Fig. 7.9c   Neutrality in wage growth within manufacturing

manufacturing. The corresponding figure in 1970 was only 23.7 percent. For comparison, by 1985 less than one-fifth of labor force entrants in the United States began their careers in manufacturing (Murphy and Topel 1987a).

Surprisingly, in spite of the rapid growth of manufacturing, there is little evidence of *within-cohort* migration to that sector. For example, among workers who were twenty-five to twenty-nine years old in 1970, the proportion who work in manufacturing remained stable at roughly 17 percent for twenty years.

This pattern occurs in all cohorts, which implies that the growth of manufacturing employment was accomplished by allocating ever larger proportions of new entrants to that sector. This is illustrated in figure 7.10, which simply plots the shares of successive age cohorts that work in manufacturing. The within-cohort shares are basically flat lines; indeed, there is some evidence of within-cohort *outmigration* from manufacturing between 1975 and 1985. The figure shows that all the growth in manufacturing's average share—shown as the bold line—is due to rapidly increasing shares at the margin, that is, of new entrants. It appears that workers who start in manufacturing stay there, with little net migration in or out at older ages.

While there is no evidence of within-cohort migration to manufacturing, inspection of table 7.3 does show that agricultural workers were leaving the farm, albeit at faster rates among the young. They were absorbed by the non-manufacturing sector, especially by wholesale and retail trade. This pattern suggests a sort of "musical chairs" interpretation of the sectoral reallocation of labor in Korea. During Korea's industrialization, agriculture declined, and manufacturing grew, but agricultural workers did not migrate to manufacturing. Instead, it appears that manufacturing draws on the urban young, who

Table 7.3   **Employment by Sector and Cohorts, Korea, 1970–89**

Age Cohorts	1970	1975	1980	1985	1989	Sectors
20–24 in 1989					6.0	(1)
					44.6	(2)
					20.1	(3)
					29.3	(4)
20–24 in 1985				13.2	8.5	(1)
				38.8	38.4	(2)
				20.7	21.1	(3)
				27.3	32.0	(4)
20–24 in 1980			25.6	14.8	11.1	(1)
			36.6	30.7	31.8	(2)
			14.3	22.2	23.2	(3)
			23.5	32.3	33.9	(4)
20–24 in 1975		31.8	23.6	17.4	14.9	(1)
		22.6	28.1	25.6	26.7	(2)
		9.4	17.9	24.5	25.0	(3)
		36.2	30.4	32.5	33.4	(4)
20–24 in 1970	40.4	36.7	25.5	20.7	18.1	(1)
	23.7	22.0	23.1	21.4	23.2	(2)
	11.6	14.9	20.5	25.7	25.5	(3)
	24.3	26.4	30.9	32.2	33.2	(4)
25–29 in 1970	40.7	38.3	32.6	28.0	26.9	(1)
	17.1	17.7	17.7	17.6	17.8	(2)
	13.7	16.9	20.9	25.0	24.4	(3)
	28.5	27.1	28.8	29.4	30.9	(4)
30–34 in 1970	44.3	45.8	41.8	37.3	37.1	(1)
	13.3	13.0	13.3	13.2	14.6	(2)
	14.1	16.4	18.7	22.2	18.9	(3)
	28.3	24.8	26.2	27.3	29.4	(4)
35–39 in 1970	48.9	52.1	50.2	44.6	47.0	(1)
	10.5	9.8	10.0	10.1	11.4	(2)
	14.7	15.8	16.4	20.2	17.3	(3)
	25.9	22.3	23.4	25.1	24.3	(4)

Source: Annual Reports on the Economically Active Population (Seoul: Economic Planning Board, 1970, 1975, 1980, 1985, 1989).

Note: (1) Agriculture, (2) manufacturing, (3) trades, (4) all others.

develop skills that bind them to that sector. Their places in nonmanufacturing industries are taken by agricultural migrants of varying ages.[14]

Why this occurs is something of a mystery. One explanation is the nature of secondary school training in Korea, which emphasizes vocational skills for

14. It is possible, although improbable, that substantial intersectoral mobility *within* a cohort would leave manufacturing's share constant. This would be more plausible were manufacturing's overall share of employment stable. It is hard to believe that new cohorts enter manufacturing in ever mounting numbers while offsetting gross flows for older cohorts leave their shares of manufacturing employment unchanged.

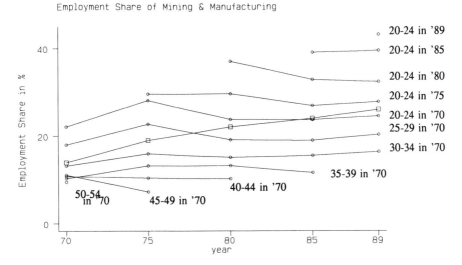

Fig. 7.10   Employment shares in mining and manufacturing, by cohort and year, 1970–89
Source: Economic Planning Board, *Annual Reports on the Economically Active Population* (1970, 1975, 1980, 1985, 1989).

students who are not college bound. Rural schools emphasize agricultural skills, while urban ones provide mechanical training that is more suited to manufacturing employment. This difference makes the urban young a natural source of manufacturing employment and may account for the mobility patterns shown in table 7.3.

7.3.4   Interfirm Mobility

Within-cohort stability of manufacturing's share, combined with the overall growth of that sector, might suggest that the Korean labor market is moving toward "lifetime" employment relations reminiscent of Japan. In fact, average job durations have risen substantially over time, yet our data suggest that turnover rates remain remarkably high, especially in manufacturing.

Figure 7.11 shows that the average duration of job spells in progress has risen over time. Since the average age of the labor force has also been rising, the estimates in the figure are regression adjusted to reflect average job tenures for the mean age (thirty-three) during the sample period. In spite of the fact that average job durations have risen by about 1.5 years, job duration in Korea remains much shorter than in other industrialized countries. The average duration of an (incomplete) job in Korea—now slightly more than four years—is less than half as long as the average job in the United States (nine years; Aker-

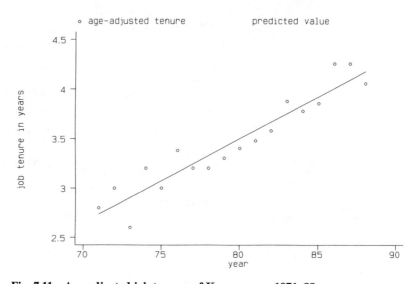

Fig. 7.11   Age-adjusted job tenures of Korean men, 1971–88
Note: The values shown in the figure are average incomplete job tenures, adjusted for changes in the age composition of the workforce.

lof and Main 1980).[15] Job durations in Japan were longer still (Hashimoto and Raisian 1985).

The tenure data indicated that long-term employment relations are less important in Korea than in the United States or Japan. To get closer to this issue, we obtained data on the raw number of separations at various job durations during the 1980s. We then combined these data with OWS estimates of the number of workers at each tenure level, yielding turnover rates by job tenure for manufacturing and nonmanufacturing jobs. These "employment hazards" are shown in table 7.4. They show the usual pattern of declining mobility with job tenure. More important, they also indicate a sharp decline in turnover rates during the 1980s, especially for workers with more than one year of job seniority.

Interestingly, turnover rates are much *higher,* and job durations correspondingly lower, in manufacturing than in other sectors. This is the opposite of what is found in most other industrialized countries, and it suggests that firm-specific skills are less important in Korea than elsewhere. This surprising result also stands in contrast to our earlier findings on net sectoral mobility, which showed virtually no within-cohort mobility to and from the manufacturing sec-

---

15. The OWS survey also records "task tenure," which can exceed job tenure if workers move among firms but remain in the same occupation. Task tenures have also risen over time, indicating increased specialization of the workforce. Even so, average task tenures were only 5.5 years for the mean age at the end of the 1980s. Even among workers aged fifty to fifty-four in manufacturing, average job durations were only about seven years in the mid-1980s.

Table 7.4   **Job Separation Rates, Korea, 1982–88**

Year	Years of Job Tenure						Expected Tenure
	<1	1–2	3–4	5–9	10+	Total	
A. Manufacturing sector:							
1982	64.1	23.4	11.0	7.0	7.0	25.1	3.77
1983	74.4	21.0	10.5	5.5	4.8	24.4	3.33
1984	84.2	26.9	13.3	7.1	4.3	30.5	2.44
1985	68.0	20.8	9.8	5.8	4.7	23.6	3.70
1986	69.1	17.8	9.7	5.1	4.4	21.0	3.72
1987	55.7	17.3	8.4	4.9	3.7	19.8	4.34
1988	61.0	16.8	8.4	4.9	3.3	20.8	4.15
B. Nonagricultural sector:							
1982	26.6	10.1	5.2	3.2	2.8	10.4	5.35
1983	32.4	9.6	5.2	2.8	2.2	10.4	5.26
1984	37.8	8.0	6.4	3.4	2.6	13.0	5.13
1985	30.7	10.1	5.1	2.9	2.1	10.2	5.28
1986	31.2	8.9	5.0	2.7	2.0	9.2	5.30
1987	26.8	8.6	4.6	2.5	1.8	8.7	5.41
1988	27.9	8.1	4.4	2.4	1.7	8.9	5.40

Source: Authors' calculations from *Reports on Occupational Wage Survey* (Seoul: Ministry of Labor, 1982–89) and *Annual Reports on the Economically Active Population* (Seoul: Economic Planning Board, 1982–89).

Note: For the group with more than ten years of tenure, the distribution of job tenure is assumed to decline linearly until it reaches zero at thirty years of tenure for the calculation.

tor. This implies that *within-sector* mobility is very high in manufacturing. Evidently, the human capital that binds workers to the manufacturing sector is industry, rather than firm, specific.[16]

7.4 Wage Differentials and Inequality

While wages of workers in different industries have moved together, there is strong evidence of changing relative wages along observable and unobservable dimensions of skill. We analyze the determinants of changing returns to schooling and age and draw implications for the determinants of changing overall wage inequality in Korea.

7.4.1 Wage Inequality and Changing Skill Premiums

Overall wage inequality fell dramatically during Korea's industrialization. On the basis of our micro-data files for 1971, 1983, 1986, and 1989, table

---

16. In an economy as dynamic as Korea's, recorded job separation numbers may be heavily influenced by births and deaths of firms. We have been unable to obtain any evidence on this.

Table 7.5   **Wage Inequality among Korean Men, 1971, 1983, 1986, 1989**

Percentile Difference	1971	1983	1986	1989
A. Log wage:				
90-10	1.683	1.410	1.289	1.219
90-50	.800	.700	.657	.605
50-10	.883	.710	.642	.614
SD	.663	.550	.517	.484
B. Log wage residuals:				
90-10	1.066	.801	.762	.739
90-50	.511	.372	.307	.360
50-10	.555	.429	.375	.379
SD	.438	.327	.300	.305

Source: Calculations from OWS microdata files, Ministry of Labor, Korea.

Note: Wage measure is by log monthly earnings deflated by the consumer price index provided by the Economic Planning Board of Korea. Regressors for panel B estimates are three education dummies, an experience quartic, a quadratic in years with current employer, years at current job (task), dummies for one-digit occupation and one-digit industry.

7.5 summarizes changes in the distribution of wages among Korean men. The difference in log wages between men in the ninetieth and tenth percentiles of the wage distribution fell from 1.68 in 1971 to 1.22 in 1989, a narrowing of forty-six log points. The comparable statistic for the United States *increased* during this period from 1.16 to 1.46 (Goldin and Margo 1992). Indeed, these data indicate that overall wage inequality is now *greater* in the United States than in Korea.[17] The lower panel of the table shows the change in "residual inequality" after controlling for a vector of observed worker characteristics. The 90-10 spread in unobserved determinants of wages fell by thirty-three log points over this period, which is about three-quarters (33/46) of the overall change in wage inequality.

There are several hypotheses about why inequality narrowed. One is that changes in the educational composition of the labor force caused a narrowing of *opportunities,* which could directly reduce wage dispersion. Figure 7.12 shows the raw labor force shares of schooling groups in the OWS data. The main message of the figure is the large decline in the relative supply of less educated workers, reflecting the extraordinary increase in school enrollments following World War II. The labor force share of elementary school graduates was halved in only eighteen years, from 60 to 30 percent. Two-thirds of this decline is due to a rising share of high school graduates, indicating that overall inequality of education levels declined.

17. Keep in mind that these statistics are based on the OWS data, which exclude small firms. As in other countries, there is every reason to believe that small firms employ disproportionate numbers of less skilled workers (Brown and Medoff 1989), so overall inequality in Korea is likely to be understated.

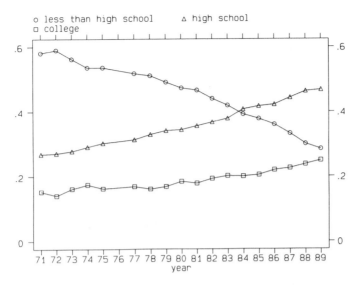

Fig. 7.12   Employment shares by education: Korean men, 1971–89

Somewhat surprisingly, this change in inequality of opportunities had almost no direct effect on overall wage dispersion. We calculated predicted inequality measures for each year, fixing the wage distributions within each education category at their 1971 values but allowing the labor force shares of the categories to vary over time. In this way, relative prices of both observed and unobserved skills are held constant at their 1971 levels, so changes in inequality can be directly attributed to changes in the distribution of education. We found that the predicted measures of inequality were virtually identical to their 1971 values. Narrowing inequality of educational opportunities did *not* cause overall wage dispersion to fall.

How can this be? While it is true that the declining share of elementary graduates gives reduced weight to low-wage workers, it turns out that within-group inequality is substantially greater for high school and college graduates, whose labor force shares are increasing. These effects are offsetting in the data, so predicted inequality remains stable.

Coupled with the estimates in table 7.5, these findings suggest that declining inequality was driven by changes in the relative "prices" of observed and unobserved dimensions of skill, not simply by changes in the composition of skills in the labor force. More direct evidence on this point is shown in figures 7.13 and 7.14 below.

Figure 7.13 plots raw returns to schooling between 1971 and 1989. The upper curve shows the difference in average log wages between college and high school graduates, while the lower curve records the same information for indi-

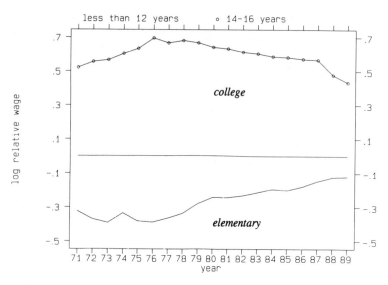

Fig. 7.13   Log relative wage by education

viduals with fewer than twelve years of schooling.[18] The main message of the figure is that wage inequality between schooling groups greatly declined. From its peak in 1976, the college–elementary school wage differential fell by nearly fifty log points in thirteen years. The college–high school differential fell by twenty-five log points over the same period. Notice that the inverted U shape of the college–high school curve is the opposite of what is observed in the United States over this period. In fact, by the end of the 1980s, the return to a college education in Korea was only two-thirds as large as in the United States. It had been double the U.S. return in 1979.

Age-earnings profiles also flattened, which is another dimension of declining inequality in wages. Figure 7.14 plots the relative wages of "young" (aged twenty to twenty-nine) and "old" (fifty to fifty-nine) men from 1977 to 1989.[19] From 1977 to 1987, the wages of young men drifted upward by about five points relative to those of men aged thirty to thirty-nine. Then they rose by another 10 percent in only two years. Similarly, the relative wage of older men drifted downward and fell by about 10 percent in 1987–89. Among older workers, age-earnings profiles were essentially flat by 1989, when twenty years of experience was associated with only 10 percent premiums.

18. Given rapidly changing education levels in Korea, trends in fig. 7.12 could partly reflect changes in average years of schooling within the reported categories. Our understanding is that dropouts from the different levels of the Korean education system are rare. For example, individuals who begin high school rarely fail to obtain a degree. Thus, the three-way categorization used in fig. 7.12 is a fairly good description of wage changes.

19. Published tabulations of the OWS do not break out age categories for earlier years.

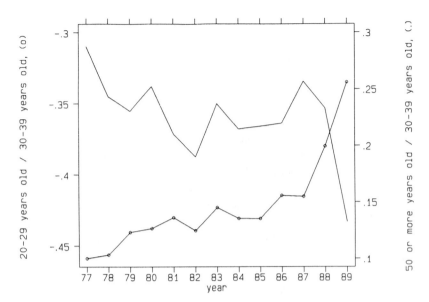

Fig. 7.14 **Relative wages of young (20–29) and old (50–59) Korean men, 1977–89**

7.4.2   Determinants of Changing Wage Premiums[20]

Changing wage inequality can be driven by (at least) three factors. First, changes in relative supplies of different skill groups can change their relative wages. For example, a decline in the relative supply of less educated workers could raise their relative wage, which is consistent with the trends shown in figures 7.12 and 7.13 above. Second, expanding industries may be intense users of some worker types, which raises the relative demand for those workers. For example, manufacturing may employ disproportionate numbers of less skilled workers, so expansion of the manufacturing sector would benefit them. Finally, the pace of technical change may favor certain worker types, thus shifting relative labor demands over time.

We analyze these forces in a simple, equilibrium model of labor demand. We think of "skill" groups—defined by education, age, or other measures—as representing separate inputs to production in industry production functions. We ignore capital and assume that production in industry j is homothetic in its labor inputs, x^j:

$$(2) \qquad\qquad y^j = \theta^j F^j(x^j t^j),$$

---

20. Katz and Murphy (1992) use models similar to ours to study relative wage fluctuations in the United States. Rhee and Kwark (1991) also applied a similar model to Korean data. Our analysis follows Topel (1994).

where θ^j represents total factor productivity and the parameters $t^j = (t_1^j, t_2^j, \ldots)$ represent factor-augmenting technical change for each input in industry j. Given (2) and output prices p^j, the factor demand equations are of the form

$$(3) \qquad \dot{x}_i^j = E_i^j \dot{w} + \beta^j(\dot{p}^j + \dot{\theta}^j) - \dot{\phi}_i^j,$$

where $\dot{x}_i^j \equiv d \log x_i^j / dt$ etc., and $w = (w_1, w_2, \ldots, w_n)$ is the vector of market wage rates for inputs $i = 1, 2, \ldots, n$. In (3), E_i^j is the row vector of compensated demand elasticities for input i in industry j, and $\dot{\phi}_i^j$ indexes biased technical change affecting the demand for input i. Notice that factor-neutral technical change raises the demand for all inputs because price, p^j, is fixed. The terms $\beta^j(\dot{p}^j + \dot{\theta}^j)$ are unobserved but common to all inputs in industry j. They can be eliminated by imposing the homogeneity condition that a cost share–weighted sum of demand elasticities is zero, which is equivalent to removing fixed effects within industry j. Letting k_i^j be the cost share of input i, subtract

$$(4) \qquad \dot{z}^j = \sum_i k_i^j \dot{x}_i^j$$

from each demand equation (3), yielding the deviations model for factor i in industry j:

$$(5) \qquad \dot{x}_i^j - \dot{z}^j = E_i^j \dot{w} - \dot{\phi}_i^j.$$

In (5), the term $\dot{x}_i^j - \dot{z}^j$ represents the rate of change in the factor ratio for input i, which is determined by pure substitution effects of relative wage changes, E_i, and by factor-biased technical change.

In market equilibrium, the set of factor demand equations (5) must solve

$$(6) \qquad \dot{x}_i = \sum_j s_i^j \dot{x}_i^j,$$

where $\dot{x}_i$ is the market-wide rate of change in supply of input i, and where s_i^j is the share of input i that is employed in industry j. Substitute (5) in the equilibrium condition (6), yielding the *market* demand equation for each input i:

$$(7) \qquad \dot{x}_i - \dot{z}_i = E_i \dot{w} - \dot{\phi}_i, \quad i = 1, 2, \ldots, n,$$

where $E_i = \sum_j s_i^j E_i^j$ is a weighted sum of within-industry demand elasticities for input i. In (7), the term $\dot{z}_i = \sum_j s_i^j \dot{z}^j$ can be thought of as a relative demand index for input i; expansion of industries ($\dot{z}^j$) that use input i intensively (s_i^j) raises the relative demand for input i.

Finally, we can invert the demand system (7) to obtain a system of linear equations for the determinants of equilibrium relative wages:

$$(8) \qquad \dot{w} = \underline{C} \, [\dot{x} - \dot{z}] + c\dot{\phi}.$$

According to (8), changes in relative wages are determined by (i) changes in the "relative net supply" of inputs, $\dot{x}_i - \dot{z}_i$, and (ii) biased technical changes that shift the relative demands for inputs. The coefficients in these models,

$C \equiv E^{-1}$, are output-constant "elasticities of complementarity" that measure the effect of net relative supplies of factors on relative wages. The terms $\dot{x}$ and $\dot{z}$ involve only observable quantities (employment and wages), so (8) can be used to study the determinants of wages in Korea.[21]

7.4.3 Factors Affecting the Returns to Schooling

We use model (8) to estimate the determinants of the returns to schooling and age, which changed substantially during the period under study. For schooling, we categorize individuals into three groups: college graduates (c), high school graduates (h), and those with only elementary school training (e). We estimate models of the general form

$$(9) \qquad \log(w_c/w_e) = c_{11}(x_c - z_c) + c_{12}(x_H - z_H) + \lambda_c(\text{trend}) + \varepsilon_c,$$

$$(10) \qquad \log(w_H/w_e) = c_{21}(x_c - z_c) + c_{22}(x_H - z_H) + \lambda_H(\text{trend}) + \varepsilon_H,$$

where $c_{11} < 0$, $c_{22} < 0$, and the trend terms are meant to control for biased technical change over time.

Before proceeding to the estimates, it is instructive to decompose the relative net supply of type i workers as

$$(11) \qquad x_i - z_i = (x_i - x) - (z_i - x),$$

where x is the log of total employment. The first term in (11) is simply the log share of type $i(= c, h, e)$ workers in the labor market. Smaller values of $x_i - x$ mean reduced relative *supply* of type i workers, which should increase their relative wage. This is consistent with the declining share of elementary graduates in figure 7.12 above, whose relative wages were rising. The second term in (11) indexes growth in *demand* for type i workers relative to total employment. For example, the returns to schooling will fall if rapidly growing manufacturing industries are intense users of less educated workers.

It turns out that almost all the variation in $x_i - z_i$ is accounted for by changing employment shares, $x_i - x$. This is demonstrated in figure 7.15, which plots calculated values of $x_i - z_i$ and $x_i - x$ for the three schooling groups. For each group, the series are almost indistinguishable.[22] This means that differences in industry growth rates had *no appreciable effect* on relative demands for skill.[23]

---

21. To calculate the cost shares, k_j^i, we use average values of wages over the full period of our data.

22. The R^2 values from regressions of net relative supply on the corresponding employment share for each group are .99, .99, and .93 for elementary, high school, and college graduates, respectively. In fig. 7.14 above, there is minor evidence that industrial shifts reduced the demand for college graduates in the late 1980s.

23. The net supply indexes, $x_i - z_i$, are constructed using data on men only, which means that changes in female labor force participation are ignored. Inclusion of women in the analysis is unlikely to change our conclusions since they are typically employed in less skilled jobs. Further, because most agricultural workers are excluded from the OWS, we ignore agriculture in constructing the demand indexes z_i. Since agriculture is the least education-intensive industry, our

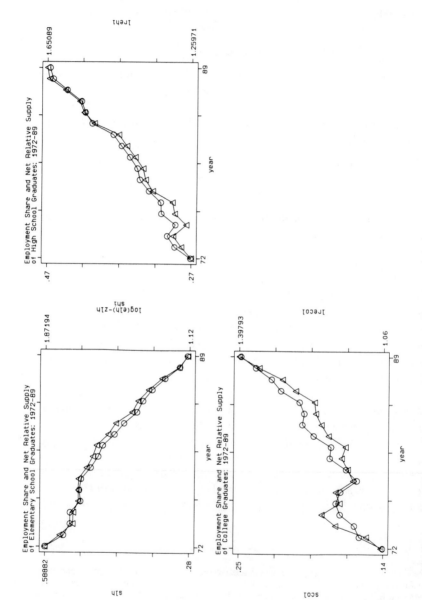

Fig. 7.15   Employment shares and net relative supplies for schooling groups, 1972–89.
Note: See text and eq. (11) for definitions.

This finding is important. We had expected that rapid growth of manufacturing was the link between industrialization and declining inequality in Korea. Instead, the data indicate that any effects of industry growth rates on the demand for skills are swamped by the very rapid upgrading of the educational quality of the Korean workforce. If there is a story to be told, it comes from the supply side—changing the stock of human capital via education—rather than from industry shifts that could change the relative demands for skills.

This brings us to estimates of models (10) and (11), which are reported in table 7.6. For each group, the first reported model includes only the "own effect" of a change in the net relative supply $(x_i - z_i)$ of the group whose wage is modeled. For both high school and college graduates, the estimates indicate that increasing relative supply reduces relative wages. For these specifications, the elasticities of complementarity are approximately the inverse own-price elasticities of demand. The estimates indicate that the long-run demand for high school graduates is more elastic than the corresponding demand for college graduates. And the implied elasticities of demand do not seem unreasonable.

Figures 7.16 and 7.17 plot the predicted and actual values of relative wages for high school and college graduates on the basis of the "own effects" models in column 1 of table 7.6 above. For high school graduates, the overall fit of the model is quite good—virtually all the 30 percent long-run decline in their relative wage is explained by increased relative abundance in the labor force. The model does somewhat less well for college graduates, mainly because of a poor fit in the early 1970s. Then, the rising relative supply of college graduates was accompanied by rising relative wages (see figs. 7.12 and 7.13 above), which is inconsistent with the observable parts of the model. Keep in mind that this was a period in which the government was apparently more successful in controlling wage growth as part of an industrial policy of remaining competitive in traded goods. We conjecture that these policies may have had a smaller effect in the market for college graduates, although we can offer no proof at this time.

The remainder of table 7.6 shows variants on the basic model of wage determination. Column 2 adds a linear trend, allowing for slowly moving, biased technical change that affects relative wages. Not surprisingly, this causes a substantial decline in the estimated elasticities of complementarity, especially for college graduates. Column 3 adds cross-effects. The only noteworthy aspect of these estimates is that the relative quantity of high school graduates has more explanatory power for college wages than do college graduates themselves. This is not surprising in light of the perverse movements in college wages and quantities in the early 1970s, mentioned earlier. Finally, column 4 includes both cross-effects and trend.

results may miss a component of declining demand (increasing net supply) for less skilled workers. Since we find that the net supply of less skilled workers actually fell, this omission is unlikely to affect our conclusions.

Table 7.6   Net Relative Supply and Relative Wages for Education Categories, 1972–89: Elasticities of Complementarity

	High School Relative Wage				College Relative Wage			
	(1)	(2)	(3)	(4)	(1)	(2)	(3)	(4)
High school relative quantity	-.692	-.396	-.784	-4.78			-.992	-1.880
	(.045)	(.219)	(.091)	(.227)			(.214)	(.498)
College relative quantity			.167	.172	-1.460	-.573	-.196	-.213
			(.144)	(.138)	(.239)	(.396)	(.336)	(.304)
Trend		-.007		-.008		-.016		.024
		(.005)		(.005)		(.006)		(.012)
Intercept	1.250	1.430	1.180	1.370	2.620	2.860	2.420	1.840
	(.065)	(.143)	(.087)	(.151)	(.287)	(.263)	(.204)	(.331)
R^2	.936	.944	.941	.949	.701	.794	.866	.898
N	18	18	18	18	18	18	18	18

Source: Authors' calculations from *Reports on Occupational Wage Survey* (Seoul: Ministry of Labor, 1972–89).

Note: Dependent variable = log monthly earnings relative to workers with fewer than twelve years of schooling. Standard errors are in parentheses.

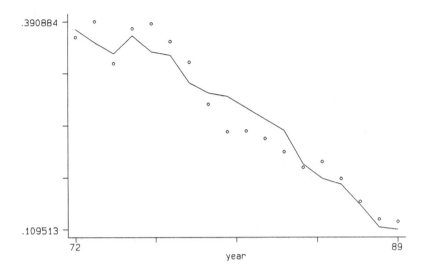

Fig. 7.16 Predicted and actual high school relative wage model (1): own effects only

Note: The figure shows actual and predicted values of the high school–elementary school wage differential, based on the estimates in table 7.7.

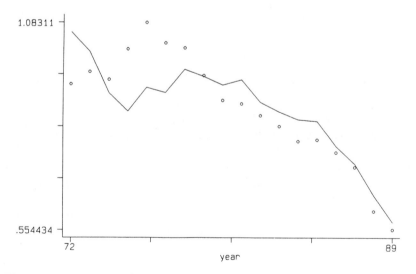

Fig. 7.17 Predicted and actual college wage model (1): own effects only
Note: See note to fig. 7.16.

A Caveat

Our estimation strategy has taken changes in the educational composition of the Korean labor force at face value. Specifically, we assumed that the average "qualities" of high school and college graduates did not change when their numbers increased. Given the scale and speed of educational upgrading in Korea, this assumption may not be satisfied. For example, expansion of high schools and colleges may have diluted the quality of education, at least at the margin, and drawn in less able students. This would reduce the relative wage of educated workers and cause us to overstate the substitution effects of changes in labor force shares.

Some suggestive evidence on this point is presented in figure 7.18. Using data from the 1984 OWS, the figure graphs the ratio of high school to elementary school graduates at each age (left scale) and the ratio of their average wages (right scale). For recent (aged twenty-five) entrants to the labor market, high school graduates are fourteen times more plentiful than elementary graduates, and they earn about fourteen percent more. Compare this to the cohort aged twenty-five in 1967 (forty-two in 1984), which entered the labor market just before the education boom. In that cohort, high school graduates are only twice as plentiful as elementary school graduates, but they earn about 40 percent more. Of course it is possible that this pattern reflects substitution effects—greater relative quantities reduce relative wages at each age—but the magnitudes shown in the figure make us suspect that the relative quality of high school graduates was diluted. In light of this, extra caution is warranted in interpreting the substitution effects shown in table 7.6. Even so, it is worth emphasizing that changing relative qualities cannot be the whole story. Changes in the return to schooling conform to the reduction in overall wage inequality, which cannot be explained by composition.

7.4.4   Net Supply and Shapes of Age-Earnings Profiles

We next apply the model to changes in relative wages across age groups, which were shown in figure 7.14 above. We choose our aggregates on the basis of observed relative wage changes. Thus, we treat workers aged twenty to twenty-nine as a separate input. Wages rose for this group, which could be generated by a decline in their net relative supply or by technical change that favored young workers. Similarly, relative wages of workers aged fifty and older have fallen, which could be generated by an increase in their net supply.

Figure 7.19 shows time series for aggregate employment shares and estimated net relative supply for these two age groups since 1977. We do not have data on wages and employment by age groups before then. As we found for schooling groups, the figures imply that differential rates of employment growth across industries had only minor effects on relative labor demands. Virtually all the variation in these series is caused by changes in labor force shares. Indeed, the data indicate that Korea experienced something of a "baby bust"

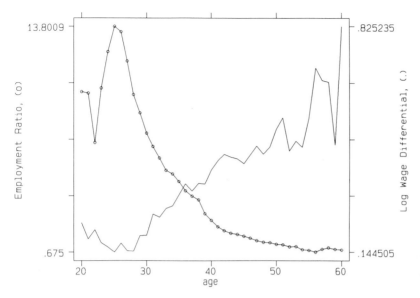

Fig. 7.18   Employment and wage for each age, 1984: 12 years vs. 9 years of education

in the 1980s, with the employment share of young workers falling by about seven points. Similarly, the share of older workers rose by about 3.5 points.[24]

Estimated elasticities of complementarity for young and old workers are shown in table 7.7. Since we have only thirteen observations for these regressions, we concentrate on "own effects" in estimating the model, along with possible effects of technical change as represented by simple trends.

For young workers, the estimates imply that reduced relative supply—the baby bust—raised wages. Figure 7.20 plots actual and predicted values of the log relative wage for young workers, generated from model (1) in the table. The model fits the general shape of the series, although it underestimates the very sharp increase in wages at the end of the period. The results are similar for older workers. As also indicated in figure 7.20, the simplest model fits the general shape of the series, although we underestimate the very sharp (and perhaps suspicious) decline in relative wages of older workers in 1989.

7.4.5   Interpretation

While changes in productivity and overall labor demand have had an undeniable effect on wages in Korea, we are struck by the absence of demand shifts in affecting *relative* wages. Wages converged over various observable dimen-

---

24. The lack of data for years before 1977 is unfortunate because the later years do not have a significant turning point in cohort size; the share of young workers basically falls after 1978.

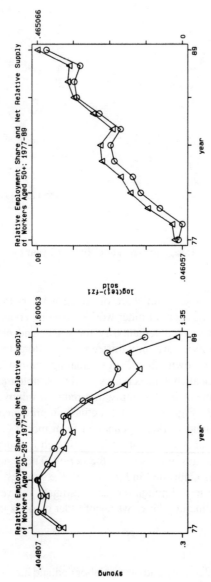

Fig. 7.19 Employment shares and net relative supplies of men aged 20–29 and 50+, 1977–89

Table 7.7   **Net Relative Supply and Relative Wages for Age Groups, 1977–89**

	Relative Wages			
	Young,[a] 20–29 Years Old		Old,[b] 50+ Years Old	
	(1)	(2)	(1)	(2)
Own relative quantity	−.377	−.239	−.225	−.271
	(.066)	(.148)	(.046)	(.202)
Trend		.033		.002
		(.003)		(.007)
Intercept	.149	−.307	.122	.001
	(.101)	(.452)	(.012)	(.523)
R^2	.745	.770	.683	.685
N^2	13	13	13	13

Source: Authors' calculations from *Reports on Occupational Wage Survey* (Seoul: Ministry of Labor, 1977–89).

Note: Standard errors are in parentheses.

[a]Dependent variable = log monthly earnings relative to thirty to thirty-nine years old.

[b]Dependent variable = log monthly earnings relative to forty to forty-nine years old.

sions of skill—schooling and age—but relative demand shifts played a trivial role. Instead, it appears that changes in relative supplies of different skill groups reduced wage inequality in Korea.

This gives an interesting interpretation to the relative roles of industrial policy and education in affecting wages. We have shown that most of the advances in average education were accomplished at lower schooling levels. Successive cohorts contained ever larger proportions of high school graduates, which raised the average level of education in the workforce and reduced educational inequality. This alone might have reduced overall wage inequality because there are more high school graduates and fewer elementary school ones. Yet we found no evidence for this effect. Instead, the data show that substitution effects raised the relative wages of shrinking groups. In true Ricardian fashion, the least skilled benefited from the educational investments of others because their own skills became more scarce. How much of the overall narrowing of the wage distribution is caused by improvements in overall human capital and consequent substitution effects? We are unable to say, but these results suggest that the effects may be quite large.

In contrast, we noted that shifts in the industrial composition of labor demand had trivial effects on relative wages. That surprised us. At the outset, we expected that Korea's large and evidently purposeful shift toward manufacturing and exports would raise the relative demand for less skilled workers and so help explain the narrowing wage inequality that accompanied development. What we found is that industrial policies, which may have nurtured particular

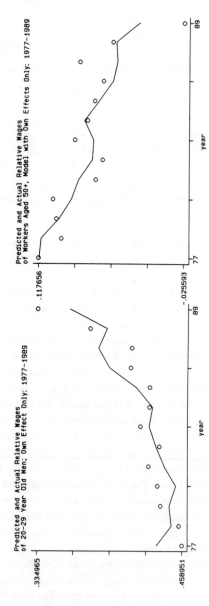

Fig. 7.20 Predicted and actual relative wages for Korean men aged 20–29 and 50+, 1977–89

Note: The figure shows actual and predicted values of the indicated relative wages, based on model (1) of table 7.7

industries, did not appear to benefit any particular group of workers relative to others.

7.5 Conclusions

We have analyzed labor market performance in Korea during a period of extraordinary growth and structural change. Driven mainly by rapid productivity growth in tradable goods, the demand for industrial labor increased dramatically between 1970 and 1990. Real wages tripled, as did productivity and the share of exports in GNP. To supply this expansion, workers left the farm in droves. The share of agriculture in total Korean employment fell by 30 percentage points in fewer than twenty years. Yet we find no evidence that agricultural workers migrated to manufacturing. Instead, the growth of manufacturing employment was accomplished solely by hiring new entrants to the labor force, who tend to stay in that sector over their careers.

Despite this apparent stability of manufacturing employment, it does not appear that employment relations in Korea are evolving toward the form taken by those in Japan. Turnover is high and job durations short, especially in the manufacturing sector. The implied mobility of the labor force may be a boon to development and structural change, especially on the scale that these have occurred in Korea.

We found no evidence for a "Kuznets curve" in Korea. Wage inequality fell during the period under study. Indeed, our estimates indicate that wages are now more equally distributed in Korea than in the United States. Given the large shifts that occurred in the sectoral composition of employment, it is tempting to conclude that this convergence was related to government policies that fostered the growth of certain industries, perhaps raising the relative demand for less skilled workers. But we can find no support for this idea; differences in industrial growth rates had negligible effects on the relative demands for skill groups. Changes in relative supply did matter. The rapid growth of education has caused a convergence of schooling levels, which reduced inequality. The labor force share of unskilled workers fell, which raised their relative price.

None of this is to say that government policies did not matter to labor market outcomes. At certain times, especially in the early 1970s, it appears that the government successfully capped wage growth as a means of maintaining comparative advantage in international markets. Union participation in wage determination has been severely limited at various times. And, overall, industrial policies ranging from subsidies to protection seem to have benefited certain industries. But we find that these policies had little effect on relative wages, measured either across industries or across identifiable skill categories of the workforce. Growth of demand in certain industries raised aggregate wages, while relative wages changed because of shifting relative supplies.

References

Akerlof, George A., and Brian G. M. Main. 1980. Unemployment spells and unemployment experience. *American Economic Review* 70 (December): 885–93.

Brown, Charles, and James Medoff. 1989. The employer size-wage effect. *Journal of Political Economy* 97 (October): 1027–59.

Collins, S. M., and W. Park. 1989. External debt and macro-economic performance in South Korea. In *Developing country debt and economic performance,* vol. 3, ed. Jeffrey D. Sachs and Susan M. Collins. Chicago: University of Chicago Press.

Dickens, William T., and Lawrence F. Katz. 1987. Inter-industry wage differences and industry characteristics. In *Unemployment and the structure of labor markets,* ed. Kevin Lang and Jonathan S. Leonard. New York: Blackwell.

Economic Planning Board. 1970–89. *Annual reports on the economically active population.* Seoul.

———. 1971–89. *Korean statistical yearbook.* Seoul.

———. 1980–89. *Monthly statistics of Korea.* Seoul.

Goldin, Claudia, and Robert A. Margo. 1992. The great compression: The wage structure in the United States at mid-century. *Quarterly Journal of Economics* 107 (February): 1–34.

Hashimoto, Masanori, and John Raisian. 1985. Employment tenure and earnings profiles in Japan and the United States. *American Economic Review* 75 (September): 721–35.

Katz, Lawrence F., and Kevin M. Murphy. 1992. Changes in relative wages, 1963–87: Supply and demand factors. *Quarterly Journal of Economics* 107 (February): 35–78.

Kim, K. 1990. Import liberalization and its impact in Korea. In *Korean economic development,* ed. Jene K. Kwon. Westport, Conn.: Greenwood.

Kuznets, Simon. 1955. Economic growth and income inequality. *American Economic Review* 45, no. 1 (March): 1–28.

Little, I. M. D. 1982. *Economic development.* New York: Basic.

Ministry of Labor. 1971–89. *Reports on Occupational Wage Survey.* Seoul.

Murphy, Kevin M., and Robert H. Topel. 1987a. The evolution of unemployment in the United States: 1968–1985. *NBER Macroeconomics Annual,* 11–58.

———. 1987b. Unemployment, risk, and earnings: Testing for equalizing differences in the labor market. In *Unemployment and the structure of labor markets,* ed. K. Lang and J. Leonard. London: Blackwell.

Rhee, C., and S. Kwark. 1991. Educational wage differentials in Korea. University of Rochester. Typescript.

Song, H. 1990a. Government and labor policy in authoritarian Korea, 1970–1987. In *Labor and inequality* (in Korean), ed. Ho-Geun Song. Nanam.

———. 1990b. *Labor policy and market in Korea.* Seoul. Nanam.

Tcha, M. 1992. Altruism and migration in developing countries. University of Chicago. Typescript.

Todaro, M. P. 1969. A model of labor migration and urban unemployment in less-developed countries. *American Economic Review* 59, no. 1 (March): 138–48.

Topel, Robert H. 1994. Wage inequality and regional labor market performance in the United States. In *Labor market and economic performance: Europe, Japan, and the USA,* ed. Toshiaki Tachibanaki. New York: St. Martin's.

United Nations. 1960–89. *Yearbook of national account statistics.* New York.

———. 1982–89. *National account statistics: Analysis of main aggregates.* New York.

World Bank. 1970–88. *World tables.* Baltimore: Johns Hopkins University Press.

8   Wage Differentials in Italy: Market Forces, Institutions, and Inflation

Christopher L. Erickson and Andrea C. Ichino

During the 1970s, Italy experienced an impressive compression of wage differentials, similar to the better-known situation in Sweden. Most evidence suggests that this compression came to a stop around 1982–83, coincident with a major institutional change (in the form of the escalator clause in Italian union contracts), a major economic change (the slowdown in inflation), a major technological change (industrial restructuring and the computer revolution), and a major political change (the loss of support for unions and their egalitarian pay policies). There is some slight evidence of a reopening of differentials since then, but the evidence is uneven, and, even where a reopening is apparent, the degree of inequality is still generally below the level of the early- to mid-1970s.

In this paper, we analyze the evolution of wage differentials across skill and occupation levels and individual characteristics in Italy for workers employed in the regular sector of the economy: workers who are not self-employed, have

Christopher L. Erickson is assistant professor at the Anderson Graduate School of Management at the University of California, Los Angeles. Andrea C. Ichino is ricercatore at Bocconi University and IGIER (Innocenzo Gasparini Institute for Economic Research).

The authors thank Lawrence Katz and Richard Freeman for providing comments on earlier drafts as well as seminar participants at the NBER conferences in September 1991 and July 1992, FIEF (Trade Union Institute for Social Research) Stockholm, and the Swedish Institute for Social Research. Pietro Ichino spent much time in long and insightful discussions. They also thank Ignazio Visco, Giuseppe Presutto, and Franco Santarelli for giving them access to the Bank of Italy, Assolombarda, and Federmeccanica data sets, respectively. Luigi Cannari, Paolo Sestito, and Luigi Guiso of the Bank of Italy were extremely patient in answering many questions on the Bank of Italy data set. Andrea Fioni was similarly helpful with the Assolombarda data set. Mark Jerger and Federica Zagari were very dedicated research assistants; the latter was occasionally helped by Patrizia Canziani. Roberto Benelli, Marco Bolandrina, Davide Lombardo, Marco Reverdito, Roberto Torresetti, and, in particular, Francesca Nieddu and Carlo Tognato worked on inputting the Italian data sets. During the period this research was conducted, Erickson was supported in part by the UCLA Institute of Industrial Relations, and Ichino was supported in part by IGIER and Assicurazione Generali and benefited from the hospitality of FIEF.

"above-ground" jobs, and are not covered by special low-wage training contracts. The evidence that we provide is consistent with the view that unions were able to push for institutional reforms that compressed wage differentials in the 1970s and that this egalitarian trend has been only partially, if at all, reversed in the 1980s. While we cannot definitively distinguish among the relative influences of institutions, market forces, technology, and politics on the evolution of earnings inequality in Italy, our analysis of skill-level differentials and our comparison at the individual level with the more laissez-faire system of the United States suggest that both inflation and egalitarian wage-setting institutions have importantly influenced Italian wage outcomes.

In section 8.1, we describe the stylized evidence on the recent evolution of wage differentials across industries, occupation levels, and individuals. We then briefly lay out, in section 8.2, the institutional setup of wage determination in Italy. We also examine the evolution of the compensation structure and its effects on wage differentials across skill levels in metal-manufacturing, concentrating in particular on the effects of inflation. Our primary findings here are that the main "market" portion of wages (the individually contracted part) and the main "institutional" portion (the escalator payments) largely serve to cancel each other out but that inflation did have a significant effect on wage compression before 1983, less so recently. In section 8.3, we examine the determinants of annual wage and salary income and the degree of inequality at the individual level, comparing raw inequality and earnings regressions from a representative sample of Italian households with the U.S. Current Population Survey; we find a more compressed compensation structure in Italy along almost all dimensions and a weak trend toward less inequality, in marked contrast to the situation in the United States. Finally, in the concluding section, we examine the possible effects of this compression on self-employment, the underground economy, and low-wage training contracts, three mechanisms that may have increased overall inequality in Italy but are not captured in our quantitative analysis of the regular sector of the economy.

8.1   Raw Evidence on Italian Earnings Inequality

The main focus of this paper is on earnings inequality across skill and occupation categories within sectors and across individual characteristics. First, however, we examine some aggregate data on differentials across sectors. Figure 8.1 displays the coefficient of variation of blue-collar hourly wages across industries from 1974 to 1985 (after which the series was discontinued). The figure indicates a clear compression of differentials until 1982; after 1982, the dispersion of blue-collar wages increased somewhat but remained below its 1974 level in 1985. Again, this measure of inequality is not our primary interest, but it goes back the furthest and is consistent with the view that differentials have not significantly widened recently.

Figure 8.2 presents the ratio between average white-collar and average blue-

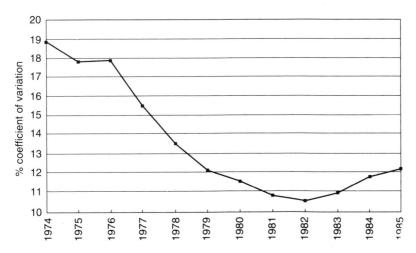

Fig. 8.1   Dispersion of blue-collar hourly wages across industries
Source: Ministry of Labor.

collar monthly wages within the metal-manufacturing sector. Two series are presented here: the Assolombarda series, consisting of metal-manufacturing firms in the Milan area, and the Federmeccanica series, consisting of metal-manufacturing firms nationwide.[1] Once again, we observe an unambiguous compression until 1983, followed by no clear trend in the Assolombarda series and some evidence of a widening of differentials in the Federmeccanica series, but not to the level of the mid-1970s by the beginning of the 1990s.

Finally, table 8.1 displays the standard deviation of the logarithm of annual earnings from employment from a survey conducted for the Bank of Italy over the period 1977–87 (excluding 1981 and 1985).[2] At this individual level, we find a continuing downward trend in inequality; in section 8.3 below, we analyze this downward trend and the determinants of individual labor income.

Overall, then, we do not see a clear trend toward a *significant* widening of wage inequality in these findings, although the aggregate evidence does seem to indicate a leveling off of wage compression around 1982–83. In the next section, we will see what the institutional setup of wage determination can tell us about the trends that we observe here.

1. These data sets have been previously analyzed in ASAP (1986–91) and Carniti Commission (1988). They are described in greater detail in the data appendix, along with the other data sets used in this paper.
2. The number given is the standard deviation of the log of earnings from employment for full-time, full-year, nonagricultural, non-self-employed workers between the ages of eighteen and sixty-five. This data set is further explained and analyzed in sec. 8.3 below and in the data appendix.

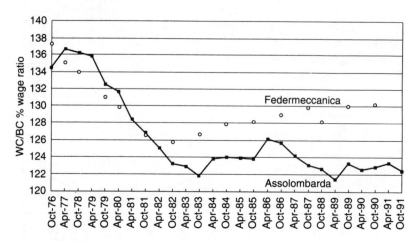

Fig. 8.2   White-collar/blue-collar monthly wage differential in metal-manufacturing
Sources: Assolombarda, Milan; Federmeccanica, nationwide.
Note: The Federmeccanica data refer to December in each year.

8.2   Institutional Framework and Wage Differentials: Descriptive Evidence from the Metal-Manufacturing Sector

8.2.1   The Actors

Three major unions (CGIL, CISL, UIL) have represented workers in Italy during the postwar period.[3] These unions had their origins at the beginning of the cold war with the splitting of a unified union under government and U.S. pressures aimed at isolating the Italian Communist Party (PCI). The three unions were initially, and to some extent still are, characterized by different political inspirations, more or less related to the three main strains of Italian politics: Communist, Christian Democratic, and Social Democratic, respectively. The political pressures to split the Italian labor movement were, however, not entirely successful, given that, after a decade and for most of the remaining postwar period, the three unions have acted together, following a unified strategy, particularly in pursuing egalitarian compensation policies. As we shall see below, it is only recently that they have disagreed on some major substantive issues, in particular on the reform of the indexation system.

It should be noted that CGIL, CISL, and UIL are confederations of sectoral unions. The extent to which bargaining strategies are coordinated across sectors is not, however, immediately clear. Yet some sectors seem to have played a leading role in the bargaining process; this is particularly true for the metal-manufacturing sector, on which we focus our analysis in this section. Contracts

---

3. For more extensive English-language analysis of Italian industrial relations history and structure, see Neufeld (1960), Giugni (1984), and Locke (1992).

Table 8.1   **Dispersion of Individual Annual Labor Income**

	1977	1978	1979	1980	1982	1983	1984	1986	1987
SD of logarithms	.46	.44	.44	.41	.42	.41	.39	.38	.37

Source: Bank of Italy.

in metal-manufacturing cover a vast array of industries, including all metal transformation activities: industrial, electrical, and transportation machinery, computers, other precision instruments, and several smaller metal and machinery industries.[4] Unions have traditionally had their strongholds in these industries, and, therefore, metal-manufacturing contracts have often been the first to introduce significant pro-worker rules later extended to other sectoral bargaining units. On a few occasions, metal-manufacturing contracts have even been translated into law.

All private industrial employers are represented by a single association (Confindustria) that has traditionally played the leading role in bargaining. Other similar associations represent employers in the other main sectors (trade, other services, artisans, agriculture), and an important role is also played by the association of companies that are partially owned by the government (Partecipazioni Statali) but operate under market rules. Finally, the role of the public administration as an employer has become increasingly important, particularly in recent years, during which, in contrast to the past, industrial relations outcomes in the public sector have started to influence the private sector.[5]

The relative strength of workers' unions and employers' associations and the extent to which they have been able to achieve their bargaining goals have gone through quite substantial swings in the postwar period; we identify three major phases here. The 1950s and 1960s were a period of relative weakness for unions, although some initial steps were undertaken toward the construction of the strongly pro-worker legislation that now characterizes Italian industrial relations.[6] The *Autunno Caldo* (Hot Autumn) of 1969 was the first important turning point: a period of widespread social unrest and acute class conflict that gave unions enormous popular support and bargaining power. The result was a tremendous pro-worker shift in legislation and bargaining outcomes: the most important example is the Statuto dei Lavoratori (Charter of workers rights) that

4. Metal-manufacturing workers accounted for approximately one-third of all non-self-employed industrial workers and one-tenth of all non-self-employed workers in 1990; we say *approximately* because it is not possible to know exactly how many workers are covered by the terms of the metal-manufacturing contract. Metal-manufacturing production accounted for 38 percent of total industrial production. Source: Confindustria.

5. Particularly important was the wave of contract renewals in public administration in the late 1980s that granted large wage increases to public-sector workers and apparently caused a ratchet effect on private-sector workers.

6. For example, laws on layoffs and firing, on the protection of female workers, and on the prohibition of gender- and region-based contractual pay differences.

provided the world-famous Italian workers' protection against firing as well as other significant labor market regulations that heavily constrained the freedom of employers in the labor market.

During the 1970s, the achievement of an egalitarian distribution of income was one of the focal objectives of unions, and, given their relative strength during this period, they were able to induce a strong compression of wage differentials. Several collective contracts in the early 1970s granted equal contractual increases to all workers, and in 1975 a new indexation system, to which we return below, provided for equal increases to all workers for each percentage point of inflation. The slogan "equal pay for all work" would have been subscribed to by most union leaders during this period, and it is difficult to doubt that a large part of the compression of wage differentials observed in the 1970s (discussed above) was caused by the unions' successful pursuit of egalitarian pay policies.

The march against unions by forty-thousand high-level white-collar workers in Turin (the location of Fiat) in the fall of 1980 may be considered the second turning point. The compression of wage differentials had reached a threshold of unacceptability for high-skilled workers, and their opposition to egalitarianism, probably latent in the previous years, came explicitly to the surface. In the meantime, the process of heavy plant restructuring, spurred by the oil shocks and begun in the late 1970s, had extended to a large part of the industrial sector, resulting in major layoffs in the industrialized regions. The unions progressively began to lose members and public support, owing in no small measure to their inability to protect less skilled workers from layoffs and the opposition of the highly skilled workers to egalitarianism.

Table 8.2 presents some illustrative figures on this recent diminution of union strength. The first two columns report measures of strike activity for the national industrial sector and for the Lombardy metal-manufacturing sector, respectively: both series display a significant decrease in the number of hours lost to labor conflicts after 1983.[7] The last column reports union membership for the metal-manufacturing sector in the Milan area. Different definitions of *Milan area* in the publications from which these numbers were taken cast doubt on the exact comparability of these numbers across years. We are, nevertheless, confident about the basic message that can be taken from this column: union membership has been steadily falling since the mid-1970s, with a significant drop at the beginning of the 1980s.

The result of these trends was a loss of bargaining power from which the three traditional major unions do not seem to have recovered. Furthermore,

7. An additional interesting fact concerning the significant reduction of strike activity in 1978 is that that was the year of the kidnapping of the Christian Democratic leader Aldo Moro by the Red Brigades. A government of national solidarity against terrorism and the economic crisis, with the external support of the PCI, was put in power on that occasion. The general feeling of national solidarity against the Red Brigades, shared by the PCI, contributed to the decrease in strike activity.

Table 8.2   **Labor Conflicts and Union Membership, 1974–90**

Year	Average Number of Hours Lost to Strikes per Month (entire industrial sector)[a]	Total Number of Hours Lost to Strikes per Year (metal-manufacturing, Lombardy)[b]	CGIL, CISL, and UIL Members (metal-manufacturing, Milan area)[c]
1974	6,516		196,022
1975	8,424	19,930	200,288
1976	10,653	29,553	193,738
1977	4,138	17,598	191,108
1978	2,604	7,773	184,721
1979	9,685	28,947	183,486
1980	11,859	18,549	179,434
1981	4,067	10,872	115,340
1982	4,369	25,267	102,524
1983	6,216	19,035	91,568
1984	800	5,676	78,574
1985	1,276	4,531	72,717
1986	1,182	2,894	67,854
1987	642	2,705	42,819
1988	1,161	1,190	40,366
1989	622	2,271	
1990	1,953		

Source: These data were collected at the FLM historical archive in Milan.

[a]Average of the January, April, July, and October number of hours lost to strikes in millions, from the Bank of Italy.

[b]Total number of hours lost in each year in thousands, from the Instituto Nationale di Statistica's *Annuario di statistiche del lavoro.*

[c]Number of members of the FLM (federation of metal-manufacturing workers); this is the confederation that jointly organizes CGIL, CISL, and UIL workers in metal-manufacturing.

new corporative unions representing small groups of workers in crucial positions have acquired substantial power, particularly in public-sector services, exacerbating the current weakness of the traditional Italian labor movement. All this adds up to a labor movement with a diminished ability (and perhaps willingness) to push through egalitarian pay policies.

8.2.2   The Bargaining Structure and the *Inquadramento*

On the basis of an extensive interpretation of the Constitution, and in the absence of rules concerning unions' certification, collective contracts signed by the three main unions have erga omnes validity as far as compensation is concerned (i.e., they apply to all workers regardless of union status).[8] Therefore, in Italy, union membership may differ dramatically from union coverage: the latter is always virtually 100 percent within each unit for which a collective

8. The literature on the Italian bargaining structure and on the *inquadramento* is large; we draw in particular on Carinci (1987) and Ichino (1992).

contract is signed. Furthermore, collective contracts have on a few occasions been translated into law. Hence, the influence of unions has reached those parts of the economy that the unions have not directly organized.

Bargaining takes place at the national, sectoral, provincial, and firm levels. Essentially, all aspects of labor relations may be a subject of negotiations, as long as the bargaining outcome is at least as favorable for the workers as what is implied by the law. Bargaining at the national or provincial level can be characterized as a state-contingent process in the sense that it usually occurs when specific issues of general relevance need to be discussed; as far as compensation differentials are concerned, the most important issue discussed at the national level has been the indexation system. In contrast, sectoral and firm-level bargaining are better characterized as time-contingent processes. Typically, sectoral contracts last approximately three years, and, after the signing of each sectoral contract, bargaining at the firm level begins. The sectoral contract provides a wage floor for the firm level, but bargaining does not necessarily occur at the firm level. Indeed, during the early 1980s, Confindustria often advised its members not to bargain on wages at the firm level; moreover, in many firms at that time unions did not have enough strength to push the discussion of wage increases beyond those granted by the sectoral contract.

Many of the outcomes of collective agreements are differentiated across workers according to a skill ranking system. The law first divides non-self-employed workers into four categories: blue-collar workers, white-collar workers, *quadri,* and managers. The nature of the occupation, whether manual or intellectual, traces the borderline between blue-collar workers and the other categories, while the amount of directive responsibilities traces the distinctions among the higher categories. High-level white-collar workers with directive responsibilities, known as the *quadri,* were first recognized by the law as a separate category in 1985. However, after the march of the forty thousand in 1980, collective contracts and employers acting independently from the contracts had already started to grant them some preferential treatment. The process that led to the recognition of the *quadri* as a separate category was one of the many signs that the compression of differentials achieved in the 1970s had gone too far for the unions' constituencies and the public at large.

Within the ranks of the nonmanagerial workers, collective contracts at the sectoral level further subdivide workers into several quasi skill categories called *inquadramento* levels. Wages and working conditions are attached to these levels, and contracts establish which types of workers are in which level; instead of job descriptions, there are *inquadramento* descriptions.

In the 1950s and 1960s, there were different *inquadramento* levels for blue-collar and white-collar workers, while the *quadri* category did not yet exist. The distinction between blue-collar and white-collar workers was, however, in evident contrast to the egalitarian goals of the unions. Therefore, during their period of strength in the early 1970s, the unions tried to push, through collective bargaining, for the *inquadramento unico:* a single ranking structure for blue-collar and white-collar workers. The goal was to make explicit the equivalence of the skill content of manual and intellectual work. The attempt was, however, only partially successful, with blue- and white-collar workers ranked together only in the bottom half of the *inquadramento* and only white-collar workers ranked in the upper half.

In the metal-manufacturing sector, for example, there are eight *inquadramento* levels.[9] All blue-collar workers are ranked in the first five levels; some blue-collar workers with directive responsibilities are called *intermediates* and are ranked in the fourth and fifth levels. White-collar workers are ranked in all levels but the first. Finally, the *quadri* are ranked in the seventh level. Thus, despite the egalitarian gains of the unions, it is possible to identify fifteen different skill ranks of workers in metal-manufacturing: five blue-collar levels, two intermediate levels, seven white-collar levels, and one level for the *quadri.*

Our analysis in this section is based on the average monthly wages for these categories of workers for samples of firms from two data sets. The Assolombarda data set is collected by the Lombardy section of Confindustria from questionnaires sent to metal-manufacturing firms in the Milan area. This data set provides fairly disaggregated information on the components of the compensation package. The Federmeccanica data set is collected by the metal-manufacturing section of Confindustria and is based on firms in the whole country, but it provides more limited information on components of the compensation package.[10]

First, we believe that it is important to get a sense of the extent of the homogeneity of these fifteen categories across firms, in terms of monthly compensation. From the Assolombarda data set, we have access to the average monthly wages paid by each firm to the workers in each of the fifteen categories for the years 1983–90. The *inquadramento* level of the workers explains approximately 80–90 percent of the total variance of average monthly wages across *inquadramento* levels and firms. Furthermore, the (employment-weighted) within-*inquadramento* coefficient of variation of the average monthly wages paid across the firms in the sample is never above 10 percent (i.e., the standard deviation is never larger than 10 percent of the mean).

Looking separately at blue-collar and white-collar workers, there is the most homogeneity within the central ranks of each of the two groups. It should be kept in mind, however, that very few firms in the Assolombarda data set rank workers in the lowest blue-collar and white-collar levels, so the coefficients of variation are not very significant for these two levels. In the rest of our analysis based on the Assolombarda data set, we will drop these two levels. Intra-*inquadramento* pay for white-collar workers seems to be on average less homogeneous than for blue-collar workers, and for high white-collar levels the coef-

9. The levels are numbered from 1 to 7, but an additional category called *5-super* has been added between the fifth and the sixth levels.
10. Further descriptions of these two data sets are provided in the data appendix.

ficient of variation is significantly larger. There is, then, apparently less pay homogeneity across firms at high *inquadramento* levels.

Since we do not have access to individual wages in these data sets, we have little to say about within-firm variability. Limiting ourselves to differences across firms, we take the above as evidence that *inquadramento* levels explain a large part of the variability of monthly compensation. In other words, workers in a given level seem to receive fairly similar wages in different firms, although this is less true the higher the skill level. If one is willing to believe that wage homogeneity reflects skill homogeneity, and in the absence of better measures, *inquadramento* levels can then be considered as fairly satisfactory proxies for skill ranks.

The distribution of workers across *inquadramento* levels has undergone interesting changes in recent years. The Federmeccanica data set contains information on the proportion of workers in each level that is comparable across years. Between 1976 and 1991, the proportion of blue-collar workers in the nonmanagerial metal-manufacturing labor force decreased from 75.8 to 63.5 percent. This decrease seems to have been mainly due to a decrease in the proportion of workers in the three lowest *inquadramento* levels; since relatively few workers are ranked in the first two levels, most of the decrease in the blue-collar fraction of the labor force comes from the third level. As for white-collar workers, the increase in their proportion of the labor force is almost entirely due to an increase in the proportion of workers ranked in the two highest levels. These trends are particularly evident between 1976 and 1987.

This evidence suggests that the metal-manufacturing sector underwent a significant change in the composition of its labor force across *inquadramento* levels between 1976 and 1987. There are two principal interpretations of this change in composition. First, inasmuch as the *inquadramento* levels reflect skill levels, there may have been a shift away from lower skills and toward higher skills. Unfortunately, with our data, we have no way of measuring how much of this shift was due to labor demand forces and how much to labor supply forces.

Second, these trends may simply be the result of internal promotions during a period in which employment growth in the metal-manufacturing sector was minimal. In centralized bargaining systems, upgrading is a typical response to market forces pushing for more wage dispersion, resulting ultimately in an implicit form of wage drift. Again, however, with our data we cannot disentangle the extent to which these trends in the composition of the labor force reflect technological shifts toward more skill-intensive production and the extent to which they represent a form of wage drift. While reading the succeeding sections, however, keep in mind that, on top of the wage drift that we will explicitly measure (as the non–collectively contracted portion of the compensation package), wage drift is also likely to have taken place implicitly through promotions.

Table 8.3   **The Structure of the Typical Compensation Package**

Contractual minimum (sector)

+

Scala mobile component (sector, nation, or law)

= Contractual compensation
  + Collective superminimum (firm)
  + Individual superminimum (individual)
  + Seniority increase (sector)
  + Production premium (sector/firm)

  = Base monthly compensation
    + Extraordinary pay (sector, law)
    + Overtime payments (sector, law)

    = Monthly compensation × 12
      + 13th–14th months, etc. (sector/law)
      + Other annual bonuses (sector/firm)

      = Total annual compensation
        + Severance pay (law)

        = Total compensation

Note: The bargaining level at which the component is discussed, or whether it is determined by law, is in parentheses.

8.2.3   The Compensation Structure and Compensation Differentials

The structure of the typical compensation package for an Italian industrial worker is detailed in table 8.3.[11] The contractual minimum is determined at the sectoral bargaining level; the indexation system (*scala mobile,* "escalator"), regulated by sectoral bargaining or by law, is thought of as protection for the purchasing power of the contractual minimum. These two components make up the contractual compensation. Bargaining at the firm level adds to this floor a wage increase called the *collective superminimum* and a component called the *production premium;* the latter component originally had an incentive function that was abandoned in the 1970s under union pressure, although it still remains in the compensation package. More recently, annual bonuses, sometimes in the form of profit sharing, and plant-level incentive components have also been introduced into firm-level bargaining; seniority increases, in contrast, have always been determined at the sectoral level. The individual superminimum is the last component of the so-called base monthly compensation; it is determined by the employer outside any direct influence by unions—as we

11. The data sets on which this section is based have been used by several previous researchers. This section owes a great deal to that literature, particularly ASAP (1986–91), Carniti Commission (1988), Biagioli (1985, 1988), Frey (1988), Bordogna (1988), and Lucifora and Presutto (1990).

will see, because of this feature, it has played a significant role in the determination of wage differentials.

Adding some minor extraordinary payments and overtime payments,[12] we get to the total monthly compensation. The annual compensation is not just equal to twelve monthly installments, however, because, in addition to the annual bonuses mentioned above, at least one (by law), or two, or in some cases up to four additional "months" are added according to the sectoral contracts. Finally, severance payments are granted by law in any case of job separation.

Not all these components are equally important, particularly as far as wage differentials are concerned. As shown in table 8.4, the contractual minimum, the cumulated *scala mobile* payments,[13] and the individual superminimum accounted for between 80 and 90 percent of the total monthly wage in 1991 in each *inquadramento* level, although their relative weights varied, as will be discussed below. Furthermore, because overtime payments, severance payments, and thirteenth-month (and above) installments depend on the base monthly compensation, the behavior of these three components essentially shapes the behavior of the entire compensation package. In the remainder of this subsection, we describe the evolution and the determinants of these three key components.

The Contractual Minimum

As previously mentioned, the floor of the entire wage structure is the contractual minimum, established at the sectoral bargaining level. For each *inquadramento* level, and for each year of the contract, a minimum wage is agreed on. As shown in table 8.4, this component amounted to approximately 30 percent of the total monthly wage in each *inquadramento* level in 1991.

With the exception of a few contracts in the early 1970s, contracted minimum increases have always displayed some differentiation across *inquadramento* levels. Nevertheless, the compression of differentials for contracted levels continued until the end of the 1970s. For metal-manufacturing in the Milan area, these trends are shown in figure 8.3.[14] In 1976, the contracted minimum for white-collar workers in the seventh level was 80 percent more than for blue-collar workers in the second level. This percentage fell to 60 percent in 1979 and then grew more or less steadily up to 1991: in this year, the highest contracted minimum was almost twice the lowest.

Figure 8.3 also shows the same dispersion measure for total monthly com-

12. The minor extraordinary payments are payments for missions or compensating payments for specific job characteristics, e.g. overtime payments are not included in the monthly compensation data that we use in the rest of this section.

13. Here and elsewhere in the figures and tables, we refer to *scala mobile* payments cumulated since 1981.

14. Each point in this figure represents a compensation ratio between the seventh white-collar level and the second blue-collar level, with the exception of the upper observations on monthly compensation after 1987 (see n. 15 below).

Table 8.4   **Main Components of the Monthly Wage as a Percentage of the Total, Milan Area Metal-Manufacturing Sector, 1991**

Inquadramento Level	Contractual Minimum	Scala Mobile	Individual Supermin.	Collective Supermin.	Other
BC2	31.47	58.38	.51	2.67	6.96
BC3	31.62	53.12	1.30	2.95	11.01
BC4	31.76	49.91	3.27	4.01	11.05
BC5	32.35	45.62	3.54	3.96	14.53
IN4	31.19	49.06	6.75	2.60	10.40
IN5	30.35	42.80	12.10	4.54	10.20
WC3	31.54	53.00	3.04	4.44	7.97
WC4	31.22	49.08	4.83	5.86	9.01
WC5	31.53	44.47	9.92	5.18	8.90
WC5S	30.28	39.56	14.37	4.15	11.63
WC6	30.18	35.57	21.48	5.16	7.62
WC7	29.47	27.91	30.06	4.22	8.34
QU7	26.15	23.11	38.59	4.16	7.98

Source: Assolombarda.

pensation.[15] This differential is larger than the contracted one in every year and is U shaped, with a minimum in 1983; this minimum occurs four years after the minimum of the contracted differential. In other words, despite the fact that contracted differentials began to widen in the late 1970s, total differentials continued to compress. If the contracted minimum plus the *scala mobile* component is considered (the third series displayed in fig. 8.3), the max/min ratio for this series also keeps decreasing until 1983. This evidence suggests that, in conjunction with the indexation system, inflation bore major responsibility for the compression of monthly wage differentials between 1979 and 1983.

The Scala Mobile

Indexation has a long and conflict-ridden history in Italy, full of consequences for the evolution of wage differentials.[16] The first escalator (*scala mobile*) was introduced in bargaining at the national level immediately after the war. For each unit increase in the price index, equal wage increases (called *punti di contingenza* = points) were paid to workers in all sectors and *inquadramento* levels, but the increases were differentiated by region (lower in the

15. After 1987, the figure reports two max/min rations for total compensation. The upper one uses the average wage of the *quadri* as the *max*. This should not necessarily be interpreted as a widening of differentials with respect to previous years since the category of the *quadri* was created by splitting the seventh white-collar category. As discussed above, the *quadri* started being treated differently long before this split. The figure indicates, however, that the differential treatment of the *quadri*, hidden in the seventh level before 1987, was indeed significant.

16. For additional information on the debate concerning the *scala mobile* and on its history, see D'Apice (1975), Quarchioni (1979), CNEL (1981), Alleva (1986), Faustini (1987), and Mariani (1991).

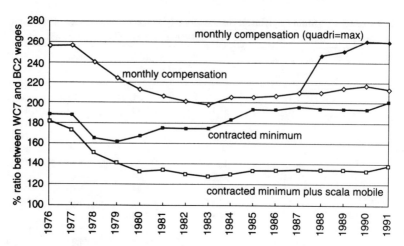

Fig. 8.3   Max/min ratios across *inquadramento* levels, Milan area metal-manufacturing sector
Source: Assolombarda.

south), gender (lower for women), and age (lower for young workers). A reference basket of goods was established that remains essentially unchanged today. The agreement, initially proposed by Confindustria, was explicitly interpreted by the parties as an exchange of indexation for social peace.

The provision of equal *scala* payments for all workers (which ensured 100 percent coverage for the mean worker's contracted wage in 1946) clearly induced a compression of wage differentials. It also essentially provided zero coverage for subsequent contracted wage increases; yet, on the other hand, since the *punti di contingenza* were paid for each unit increase in the price index (rather than for each percentage point drop in the mean worker's real wage, e.g.), this system accelerated the reaction of wages to inflation. Such a system, therefore, requires periodic adjustments, first to provide coverage for subsequent contracted wage increases, and second to reduce the built-in acceleration of the wage-price spiral.

The compression of differentials caused by this indexation system, in conjunction with the high postwar inflation, soon led to calls for the elimination of the egalitarian aspects of the escalator. The system was slightly changed in 1951: the new system was still based on points, but the escalator increases were differentiated to provide 100 percent coverage for each *inquadramento* level and to maintain inter-*inquadramento* differentials on a 100–239 scale from the lowest blue-collar level to the highest white-collar level. All other aspects remained unchanged, including zero coverage for future wage increases and the built-in accelerator.

The *scala mobile* maintained this same basic structure until the mid-1970s, with periodic readjustments to provide coverage for interim contracted wage increases and to reduce the reaction speed of the escalator. One major change, concerning not only the indexation system but also contracted wages, was the elimination by law of *scala mobile* payments and contracted wage differentiation by gender, age, and region. The escalator, originally introduced in bargaining, was extended by law to the entire industrial sector in 1960. With few exceptions (the financial sector, e.g.), it was extended through contracts to the rest of the economy, although its nontrivial drawbacks in terms of coverage and the wage-price spiral were already evident.

Then, when union strength increased dramatically after the *Autunno Caldo,* the unions sought changes in the system. Most obviously, the egalitarian aspirations of the early 1970s clashed with the differentiation of *scala mobile* payments across *inquadramento* levels; in addition, given the large contracted wage increases of the early 1970s, and despite the periodic readjustments, the coverage provided by the system had decreased. Finally, the first appearance of oil shock inflation suggested to the unions the need for better protection of real wages.

At the unions' request to Confindustria, a return to a fully egalitarian escalator was negotiated in 1975: the parties agreed on a two-year transition to a system where all workers would receive, at a quarterly frequency, equal escalator increases for each point increase of the price index in the previous quarter (i.e., similar to the 1945–46 system, but without differentiation by region, gender, and age).[17] The *scala* point was set equal to the highest point of the previous system (upward equalization). In addition, a quite substantial fixed sum was paid to all workers as compensation for the lack of full coverage of interim wage increases under the old system. A 1977 law prohibited escalator systems more favorable to workers than the escalator negotiated in 1975; this implied de facto legal extension of the industrial sector escalator to the entire economy.

Somewhat surprisingly, the two major drawbacks of the previous system (zero coverage of subsequent contracted increases and acceleration of the wage-price spiral) remained in place, while the potential for dramatic compressionary effects on wage differentials in a country already facing double-digit inflation was built in. In addition, the average coverage was dramatically raised by the upward equalization of the *punti,* increasing real rigidities potentially incompatible with the consequences of the oil shocks.

Indeed, between 1975 and 1983, while inflation fluctuated between 10 and 20 percent (fig. 8.4), the potential for wage compression became a reality, as shown by the evidence presented in the first section and in figure 8.3 above: the dispersion of all the measures that we consider (except the contracted minimum alone), and in particular the contracted plus *scala mobile* component of the compensation package, displays a continuing compression until 1982–83.

17. Note the similarity of this system to the escalator clauses in many U.S. union contracts: in the automobile and aerospace industries, e.g., cost-of-living clauses often specify across-the-board cents-per-hour wage increases for given increases in the consumer price index.

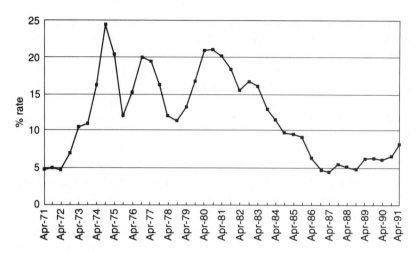

Fig. 8.4   Annual inflation in Italy
Source: Bank of Italy.

Despite increasing opposition by highly skilled workers to wage compression, unions remained attached to the egalitarian nature of the *scala mobile.* They also opposed any attempts to cut the degree of coverage and the reaction speed of the escalator.

On these latter issues, however, the three unions came to fundamental disagreement after many years of unified action. In 1983, CISL and UIL joined in an agreement with employers (spearheaded by the government) that implemented a 15 percent downward adjustment in the degree of coverage, followed in 1984 by a predetermined cap on *scala* payments. The Communist majority within the CGIL opposed the agreements, and together with the PCI they pushed for a referendum against the 1984 agreement. The referendum, held in 1985, acquired a political importance that went far beyond the relevance of the money involved: it became a referendum on the *scala mobile.* The result was a defeat for the PCI and the CGIL that signaled the end of the old indexation system.

On the wave of the referendum results, Confindustria was strong enough to reject the old indexation system as a whole. However, the bargaining process over a new system between Confindustria and the unions came to a dead end. The government was therefore compelled to intervene directly in order to avoid social unrest, doing so in 1986 with a law on indexation that imposed a new public-sector escalator on the entire economy. The point-based system was abandoned for something analogous to a progressive tax system: 100 percent coverage for a portion of the contracted compensation (equivalent to the contractual minimum of a medium-level worker), with the remainder up to the total contractual compensation (contractual minimum plus *scala mobile:* see table 8.3 above) indexed at 25 percent. All other compensation components were uncovered. The average overall degree of indexation was approximately 50 percent for blue-collar workers and 40 percent for white-collar workers.

The law expired in 1990 and was extended for one year in the hopes that the parties would reach a solution. In December 1991, the parties decided to suspend the existing indexation system (begun in 1986) and to open, in June 1992, a new bargaining round aimed at a comprehensive reform of the entire compensation system, including indexation. The trade unions, the employers, and the government came to a first agreement at the end of July 1992. Despite the strong opposition of the Communist left in the CGIL, the July agreement brought the death of the *scala mobile:* in exchange for the elimination of the indexation system, Italian workers were to receive monthly lump-sum payments beginning in January 1993 equal, for everyone, to slightly more than 1 percent of the monthly wage of the lowest-level blue-collar worker in 1990. In addition, bargaining at the firm level was suspended by the July agreement until the end of 1993.[18]

This agreement clearly has the flavor of a large concession from workers to employers, and in fact it generated much opposition among some union members. In addition, the subsequent exchange rate crisis of the lira, initiated in September 1992 and followed by a stabilization program proposed by the government, made the July agreement even more difficult for the unions' base constituency to accept: the devaluation generated a widespread fear of growing inflation in the absence of indexation, while the stabilization program (more taxes and fewer social expenditures) contradicted some of the commitments made in July by the government.

Returning to the 1986 reform, it apparently did not induce very much differentiation across *inquadramento* levels: figure 8.3 above indicates that the max/min ratio of the contracted minimum plus *scala mobile* component increased only slightly in the late 1980s, although the differential for the contracted increase shows a more marked upward trend. We see in table 8.4 above that, in 1991, the portion of total compensation accounted for by the *scala mobile* payments cumulated since 1981 still shrinks as we move to higher *inquadramento* levels; during the 1980s, the indexation system did not fully protect the wages of highly skilled workers. Table 8.4 seems, however, to suggest that the third main component of the compensation package, the individual superminimum, has at least partially compensated the highly skilled workers for the low coverage provided by the *scala mobile* system.

The Collective and the Individual Superminima

Bargaining at the firm level has clearly influenced wage differentials. The main portion of the compensation package that is determined at this level is the collective superminimum (see table 8.3 above). The ratio between the high-

---

18. As for the comprehensive discussion of the entire compensation structure, the agreement mentions only a generic commitment of the parties to discuss the issue in future bargaining rounds.

est and the lowest *inquadramento* levels for the cross-firm average of this wage component (from the Assolombarda data set) ranged from 233 in 1976 to 339 in 1991, while for the contracted minimum the ratio ranged from 187 to 201 over the same time period; however, the collective superminimum ratio is still relatively small if we compare it to the ratio for the individual superminimum, which ranged from 3,670 in 1976 to 12,708 in 1991.

The individual superminimum is the part of the monthly wage that is determined by the employer specifically for each worker and, therefore, is the only component of the compensation package that is not regulated by collective bargaining or by the law. As shown in table 8.4 above, this component is practically insignificant at low *inquadramento* levels but grows to almost 40 percent of the compensation package at the highest white-collar level. All together, this evidence suggests that the individual superminimum is the main instrument by which individual employer-worker bargaining influences wage dispersion.

Some interesting descriptive evidence on the role of this component is provided in table 8.5. This table, based on Federmeccanica data, displays the following decomposition of the annual increase in monthly compensation:

$$\log\left(\frac{\text{WT}_t}{\text{WT}_{t-1}}\right) = \log\left(\frac{\text{WCS}_t}{\text{WT}_{t-1}}\right) + \log\left(\frac{\text{WT}_t}{\text{WCS}_t}\right),$$

where WT = total monthly compensation, WCS = contracted minimum wage plus cumulated *scala mobile,* and t indexes years. That is, the total percentage monthly wage increase between two years can be decomposed into the sum of the percentage increase due to the *scala mobile* and the contract, plus the log of the ratio between the total wage and the contracted plus *scala mobile* portion. This last term is known in the literature as the *drift rate* (see, e.g., Hibbs and Locking 1991). Table 8.5 presents, for each *inquadramento* level, the averages of these three terms for the periods 1976–82 and 1983–90. This data set does not offer separate information on the individual superminimum, and therefore we can examine only the overall drift. We know, however, from the evidence presented above that, as far as differentials are concerned, the individual superminimum is the most important component of the drift.

Looking at total wage growth in the different *inquadramento* levels, the compression of wage differentials in the first subperiod and the expansion in the second appear evident.[19] But what is most striking in this table is the existence of a scissor between the drift rate and the increase due to the contract plus the *scala mobile,* which grows larger as we move across *inquadramento* levels. Notice also that, in the second subperiod, the size of the scissor clearly widens, particularly in the higher white-collar levels. Combining the evidence provided by this table and by figure 8.3 above, it seems that the disequalizing effect of the drift rate became greater in the second subperiod, when inflation

---

19. Keep in mind that, while white-collar *inquadramento* levels are listed after blue-collar levels in the table, blue- and white-collar workers in the same level are comparable in terms of the contracted portion of the compensation package.

Table 8.5   **Decomposition of the Total Monthly Wage Increase in the Nationwide Metal-Manufacturing Sector**

Inquadramento Level	1976–82 Averages			1983–90 Averages		
	Total Wage Growth	Drift	Contract Plus *Scala*	Total Wage Growth	Drift	Contract Plus *Scala*
BC1	18.50	13.71	4.79	7.54	12.07	−4.53
BC2	17.61	16.33	1.28	7.43	14.31	−6.88
BC3	17.18	19.49	−2.32	7.90	19.40	−11.51
BC4	16.90	20.77	−3.87	7.96	21.52	−13.56
BC5	16.57	22.29	−5.72	8.20	24.81	−16.60
IN4	16.51	28.32	−11.81	8.01	27.69	−19.68
IN5	15.60	33.89	−18.28	8.27	31.08	−22.81
WC2	17.87	13.79	4.08	6.93	10.12	−3.18
WC3	17.55	20.45	−2.90	7.05	17.81	−10.75
WC4	17.04	25.20	−8.16	7.07	21.92	−14.85
WC5	15.64	29.48	−13.84	7.88	29.75	−21.87
WC5S	15.06	33.35	−18.28	7.98	34.01	−26.04
WC6	13.92	41.00	−27.08	8.59	45.92	−37.33
WC7	14.91	62.11	−47.20	10.08	73.36	−63.29

Source: Federmeccanica.

was lower, but that this component has acted primarily to offset the equalizing effect of the escalator.

8.2.4 Inflation and Wage Dispersion

Given the evidence presented above, it can be argued that inflation affected wage differentials through two interrelated channels, one direct and one indirect. The direct channel worked through the egalitarian indexation mechanism and generated a compressionary effect on the wage distribution. The indirect channel worked instead through the drift: the higher inflation, the greater is likely to have been the extent of the use of the drift on the part of employers to offset the compression caused by the *scala mobile;* this second channel generated an expansionary effect on the wage distribution.

Since the percentage increase in total wage dispersion is a function of changes in the dispersion due to the escalator and to the drift, one can estimate the reduced-form overall effect of inflation on the change in total wage dispersion and thus get a sense of which of these two channels prevailed. The results of this reduced-form estimation are contained in the following equation, estimated over the period 1976–90 on Federmeccanica data:

$$\log\left(\frac{\text{VWT}_t}{\text{VWT}_{t-1}}\right) = \underset{(0.06)}{0.19} \quad - \underset{(0.41)}{1.57 \cdot \text{INFLATION}}$$

$$+ \underset{(0.04)}{0.01 \cdot \text{CONTRACT}} - \underset{(0.05)}{0.06 \cdot \text{QUADRI},}$$

where VWT is the variance of the log of monthly wages across *inquadramento* levels (excluding the *quadri*), CONTRACT is a dummy variable that takes the value one in the years in which a contract is signed, and QUADRI is a dummy variable that takes the value one for the years in which the *quadri* were separated from the seventh white-collar level. Inflation, through the *scala mobile* and the drift, clearly had a strong negative and significant effect on the percentage change in wage dispersion. Therefore, the disequalizing effect of the wage drift was not strong enough to offset completely the compression of differentials caused by the indexation system.

On the other hand, when we distinguish between the two subperiods analyzed in table 8.5, we obtain the following result:

$$
\log\!\left(\frac{\text{VWT}_t}{\text{VWT}_{t-1}}\right) = \underset{(0.08)}{0.07} - \underset{(0.52)}{0.96} \cdot \text{INFLATION1} - \underset{(1.13)}{0.23} \cdot \text{INFLATION2}
$$
$$
+ \underset{(0.04)}{0.03} \cdot \text{CONTRACT} - \underset{(0.04)}{0.05} \cdot \text{QUADRI},
$$

where INFLATION1 (INFLATION2) is equal to inflation for the years 1976–82 (1983–90) and zero otherwise, and the other variables are defined as above. Here we see that inflation significantly compressed wages only until 1982. After 1982, inflation does not seem to have affected wage differentials, despite the persistently egalitarian nature of the escalator. This suggests that, in the second subperiod, the disequalizing effect of the drift became relatively stronger and capable of practically offsetting the effect of the escalator.

What we have found, then, is that a large part of the compression generated by twenty years of inflation and egalitarian institutions seems still to be present. We next see what we can learn from individual data and a comparison with the United States, where egalitarian wage-setting institutions clearly play a much less significant role.

8.3 Individual Characteristics and Earnings Inequality: A Comparison of Italy and the United States

We now turn to an analysis of individual level data on the determinants of annual wage and salary earnings in Italy, using the United States as a benchmark. We first describe the trends in educational attainment and the age structures of our samples of workers in the two countries over the period under study, 1978–87, finding roughly similar age structures and a higher average level of educational attainment in the United States but a trend toward more educated workforces in both countries. We then examine returns to schooling and experience and measures of overall earnings inequality in the two countries. Our main findings here are that overall inequality and returns to skill (as measured by the variability of actual and residual log earnings and the return to a college degree) are unambiguously higher in the United States than in

Italy and that, while inequality has clearly increased in the United States, the pattern is less clear in Italy—indicating, if anything, a trend toward a less unequal distribution.

8.3.1 Data

The Italian data source is a representative household survey collected by a private company for the Bank of Italy over the period 1978–87, excluding 1981 and 1985; we refer to this data set as the *BDI*.[20] For the United States, we use the March Current Population Survey (CPS). Several data limitations for the BDI require discussion. First, the earnings variable is annual earnings from employment net of taxes, which does not have an exact equivalent in the CPS; we use CPS annual gross wage and salary earnings.[21] Schooling and age are not continuous in the BDI, but they are segmented into five and six categories, respectively (schooling categories: no schooling, completed elementary, completed junior high, completed high school, and college or higher degree; age categories: under twenty-one, twenty-one to thirty, thirty-one to forty, forty-one to fifty, fifty-one to sixty-five, and over sixty-five); for our comparative regressions, we similarly segment the CPS data, making the schooling categories none = completed grade 0–5; elementary = completed grade 6–8; junior high = completed grade 9–11; high school = completed grade 12–15; and college+ = completed grade 16+. Note that the BDI does not contain information on the worker's *inquadramento* level.

Finally, we restrict our samples to full-time, full-year nonagricultural workers between the ages of eighteen and sixty-five who are not self-employed. Earnings are not top coded in the BDI; we impute top-coded CPS annual earnings at 1.45 times the annual top-code amount (following Katz and Murphy 1992). We conduct all our analyses separately for men and women.[22]

8.3.2 Age and Educational Composition of the Labor Forces

First, we examine the levels and changes of the age and occupational structures in the two countries. Table 8.6 presents the sample proportions for the five schooling and five age categories in the two countries for men and women in 1978 and 1987. Note in particular the generally higher level of schooling in the United States and the rough similarity of the age distributions. From the beginning of this period to the end of this period, the proportion of Italian men

20. These data were previously analyzed in Cannari, Pellegrini, and Sestito (1989) and Sestito (1990), who estimated earnings functions for Italy and examined the residual variance, concluding that there has been no significant increase in inequality. We thank them for their insights and the Bank of Italy for providing the data. The survey was conducted in 1981, but the data in that year deviate from the adjacent years along enough dimensions to be highly suspect; we exclude it. No survey was conducted in 1985.

21. We discuss the Italian tax system and its possible effects on earnings inequality below.

22. The male/female earnings differential is greater in the United States than in Italy and is dropping faster in the United States. For an analysis of the gender earnings gap in Italy and elsewhere, we refer the reader to Blau and Kahn (chap. 3 in this volume).

Table 8.6   **Sample Percentages of Age and Education Categories, Italy and the United States, 1978 and 1987**

	Men		Women	
	1978	1987	1978	1987
Education: Highest level completed				
None:				
Italy	4.0	1.2	3.0	1.2
United States	2.2	1.3	1.2	.7
Elementary:				
Italy	31.0	21.3	24.0	14.0
United States	7.7	4.5	5.5	2.7
Junior High:				
Italy	31.7	36.8	28.5	27.7
United States	12.0	9.0	10.8	6.6
High School:				
Italy	25.2	30.0	33.8	40.8
United States	56.0	57.8	64.9	66.0
College+:				
Italy	8.1	10.6	10.7	16.2
United States	22.1	27.4	17.7	24.0
Age category				
18–20:				
Italy	3.6	1.6	7.1	2.6
United States	2.9	1.9	4.2	2.2
21–30:				
Italy	23.5	21.0	34.9	27.7
United States	27.3	27.3	31.7	30.4
31–40:				
Italy	26.7	29.3	27.5	33.4
United States	26.7	32.1	22.1	30.4
41–50:				
Italy	23.5	27.5	21.0	25.1
United States	21.2	21.0	20.4	20.7
51–65:				
Italy	22.8	20.6	9.5	11.2
United States	21.9	17.8	21.7	16.2
Experience				
Italy	25.7	25.3	19.9	20.9
United States	22.0	20.7	21.2	19.8

Sources: Bank of Italy, U.S. Current Population Survey.

Note: For education and age categories, the number given is the percentage of the particular gender's total sample of full-time, full-year nonagricultural workers who are not self-employed, aged 18–65, accounted for by particular category. Highest level of education completed in United States: none = completed grade 0–5, elementary = 6–8, junior high = 9–11, high school = 12–15, college+ = 16+. Experience = mean of age category minus years to completion of schooling category minus six.

in this sample who had not completed high school fell 11 percent (from 66.7 to 59.3 percent), while the proportion of their American male counterparts who had not completed high school fell 32 percent (from 21.9 to 14.8 percent); the proportion of Italian men with college degrees rose 31 percent, and the proportion of American men with college degrees rose 24 percent. For Italian women, the proportion who had not completed high school fell 23 percent, and the proportion with college degrees rose 51 percent; the corresponding numbers for American women in the CPS sample are −43 percent and 36 percent. In both countries, then, there was a trend toward greater educational attainment among full-time workers over this period.[23] We return to these findings and their possible roles in explaining the trends in overall inequality.

8.3.3 Educational Earnings Differentials

We now examine differences and changes in the return to human capital characteristics. Looking first at the raw evidence on the influence of schooling on earnings, significant cross-country differences appear to exist in education-earnings profiles. Table 8.7 presents raw (completed high school)/(did not complete high school) and (college degree)/(completed high school) average earnings ratios for men and women in each country for four age groups (combining the youngest two in table 8.6 above to create the eighteen to thirty category). Both ratios rise in every age-gender group from the beginning of the period to the end of the period among Americans, and the college/high school gap rises in all groups but one in Italy (men forty-one to fifty). Yet the high school/(less than high school gap was smaller in 1987 than in 1978 in six of the eight age-gender groups in Italy (except age thirty-one to forty for both men and women). By 1987, the ratios for Americans were greater than or equal to the corresponding ratios for Italians in every age-gender group.

Differences also seem to exist in the shape of the raw education-earnings profiles. In most cases, the college/high school gap is greater than the high school/less than high school gap in the United States, but the opposite is often true in Italy, particularly among the older cohorts and in the later years. This suggests that education-earnings profiles tend to be convex in the United States and concave in Italy.

---

23. We can use these five age and five schooling levels to create twenty-five age-schooling categories, the finest division possible for the Italian sample along the dimensions of schooling and experience. For Americans, both men and women in both 1978 and 1987, the largest age-education categories are always high school aged twenty-one to thirty and thirty-one to forty. The largest age-education categories in 1978 for Italian men were junior high aged twenty-one to thirty and elementary aged fifty-one to sixty-five and in 1987 junior high and high school aged thirty-one to forty. In 1978 the largest categories for Italian women were high school and junior high aged twenty-one to thirty and in 1987 high school aged twenty-one to thirty and thirty-one to forty (as in the United States). Apart from the generally higher level of schooling in the United States, the two countries look reasonably similar in terms of the distribution of age cohorts within schooling categories, and all the distributions seem to be moving toward older and more educated populations (although the share in the oldest category, fifty-one to sixty-five, drops for everyone but Italian women).

Table 8.7 **Education/Earnings Ratios by Age Groups, Italy and the United States, 1978–87 (excluding 1981 and 1985)**

	1978	1979	1980	1982	1983	1984	1986	1987
Men								
18–30:								
Italy [A]	1.13	1.14	1.23	1.21	1.16	1.14	1.20	1.11
Italy [B]	1.25	1.18	1.24	1.13	1.22	1.25	1.29	1.38
United States [A]	1.27	1.27	1.24	1.22	1.31	1.32	1.31	1.35
United States [B]	1.26	1.24	1.23	1.29	1.33	1.35	1.43	1.48
31–40:								
Italy [A]	1.18	1.27	1.22	1.23	1.16	1.18	1.15	1.19
Italy [B]	1.14	1.02	1.07	1.06	1.25	1.08	1.08	1.27
United States [A]	1.31	1.34	1.35	1.41	1.37	1.35	1.41	1.40
United States [B]	1.29	1.27	1.24	1.26	1.31	1.34	1.41	1.41
41–50:								
Italy [A]	1.36	1.51	1.31	1.30	1.29	1.30	1.29	1.23
Italy [B]	1.24	1.01	1.25	1.21	1.19	1.24	1.07	1.19
United States [A]	1.32	1.30	1.30	1.35	1.43	1.38	1.40	1.40
United States [B]	1.43	1.43	1.44	1.41	1.45	1.45	1.49	1.49
51–65:								
Italy [A]	1.51	1.36	1.33	1.39	1.31	1.44	1.34	1.36
Italy [B]	1.28	1.45	1.33	1.12	1.33	1.29	1.32	1.31
United States [A]	1.33	1.32	1.32	1.32	1.38	1.32	1.36	1.36
United States [B]	1.56	1.51	1.51	1.50	1.56	1.56	1.59	1.58
Women								
18–30:								
Italy [A]	1.24	1.22	1.14	1.16	1.10	1.21	1.18	1.17
Italy [B]	1.06	1.02	1.23	1.14	1.28	1.13	1.28	1.30
United States [A]	1.24	1.24	1.22	1.33	1.31	1.33	1.38	1.30
United States [B]	1.31	1.33	1.35	1.38	1.37	1.38	1.45	1.51
31–40:								
Italy [A]	1.20	1.32	1.15	1.24	1.38	1.24	1.23	1.24
Italy [B]	1.01	1.05	1.01	1.06	1.04	1.08	1.04	1.03
United States [A]	1.35	1.23	1.29	1.35	1.43	1.39	1.40	1.46
United States [B]	1.44	1.46	1.43	1.37	1.40	1.41	1.42	1.48
41–50:								
Italy [A]	1.39	1.30	1.33	1.37	1.19	1.32	1.26	1.27
Italy [B]	1.08	1.05	.98	1.06	1.10	1.09	1.08	1.11
United States [A]	1.33	1.27	1.29	1.34	1.36	1.33	1.41	1.46
United States [B]	1.44	1.47	1.43	1.39	1.46	1.44	1.47	1.50
51–65:								
Italy [A]	1.46	1.61	1.38	1.38	1.43	1.37	1.38	1.40
Italy [B]	.91	1.01	1.20	1.06	1.21	1.08	1.06	1.06
United States [A]	1.34	1.36	1.34	1.39	1.42	1.32	1.34	1.41
United States [B]	1.42	1.43	1.50	1.37	1.40	1.52	1.50	1.46

Sources: Bank of Italy, U.S. Current Population Survey.

Note: Italy[A] and United States[A] = completed high school/did not complete high school average earnings ratio. Italy[B] and United States[B] = college degree or more/completed high school average earnings ratio. Earnings = annual wage and salary earnings, full-time, full-year nonagricultural workers who are not self-employed, aged 18–65. Before tax in United States, after tax in Italy.

We investigate these education-earnings relations further by comparing the coefficients from logarithmic earnings functions estimated separately for men and women in the two countries. Tables 8.8 and 8.9 present the coefficients on experience (defined as the mean of the age category occupied by a given observation minus the years to completion of the schooling category minus six), experience squared, and three schooling levels (up to completed elementary, completed junior high, and college degree plus; completed high school is the excluded category) for the years 1978–87 for men and women, respectively.

There are several interesting results from these regressions. First, judging by the adjusted R^2's, the explanatory power for the regressions are roughly comparable across the two countries within gender groups. Second, while the returns to high school as well as college are clearly rising for both men and women in the United States, the trend is much less clear in Italy—indicating, if anything, a weak trend toward lower returns to high school (relative to those with elementary or less in particular) and higher returns to college.[24]

Third, making within-gender comparisons across the two countries, in each period the returns to high school and college are higher and the experience-earnings profile steeper for American men than for Italian men (excepting the return to completing high school relative to completing junior high in 1982). While Italian women begin with steeper experience-earnings profiles and a greater earnings deficit at the lowest education category compared to American women, these relations are reversed by the end of the period after the greater growth in returns to education and experience among American women (the return to a college degree is much greater for American women than for Italian women throughout, but the gap is larger at the end of the period).

Finally, making within-country comparisons across the genders, American men and women have roughly similar returns to high school and college, while Italian women have a greater return to a high school degree than Italian men when the comparison group is elementary or less, and Italian men have a somewhat greater return to college.

8.3.4 Overall Earnings Inequality

The trends in overall inequality are shown in table 8.10, which displays five measures of earnings inequality for men and women: the 90-10 log earnings differential, the 90-50 log earnings differential, the 50-10 log earnings differential, the standard deviation of log earnings, and the standard deviation of log earnings residuals from separate regressions by gender-year-country cells (i.e., the regressions presented in tables 8.8 and 8.9 above) as well as the standard deviation of log earnings for men in industry in Italy and manufacturing in the United States. In all cases but the 50-10 differential for women in the earlier

---

24. Note the large jump in returns to college for men in 1983. This jump comes primarily from those employed in public administration; the return for those employed in industry actually falls slightly.

Table 8.8   Earnings Function Coefficients for Men in Italy and the United States, 1978–87 (excluding 1981 and 1985)

	1978	1979	1980	1982	1983	1984	1986	1987
Experience (divided by 10):								
Italy	.39	.41	.34	.36	.36	.35	.34	.27
	(.03)	(.04)	(.03)	(.02)	(.03)	(.02)	(.02)	(.02)
United States	.45	.43	.42	.43	.45	.44	.48	.46
	(.01)	(.01)	(.01)	(.01)	(.01)	(.01)	(.01)	(.01)
Experience squared (divided by 1,000):								
Italy	-.55	-.56	-.50	-.50	-.49	-.48	-.46	-.36
	(.05)	(.05)	(.05)	(.04)	(.04)	(.04)	(.03)	(.03)
United States	-.70	-.65	-.63	-.63	-.66	-.64	-.69	-.67
	(.02)	(.02)	(.02)	(.02)	(.02)	(.03)	(.02)	(.03)
Elementary or less:								
Italy	-.35	-.39	-.36	-.37	-.34	-.34	-.34	-.32
	(.02)	(.03)	(.02)	(.02)	(.02)	(.02)	(.01)	(.02)
United States	-.39	-.41	-.41	-.41	-.46	-.42	-.47	-.47
	(.01)	(.01)	(.01)	(.01)	(.01)	(.02)	(.02)	(.02)
Junior high:								
Italy	-.21	-.24	-.23	-.26	-.23	-.23	-.23	-.19
	(.02)	(.03)	(.02)	(.02)	(.02)	(.02)	(.01)	(.01)
United States	-.23	-.24	-.25	-.25	-.28	-.26	-.29	-.31
	(.01)	(.01)	(.01)	(.01)	(.01)	(.01)	(.01)	(.01)

College+:								
Italy	.22	.14	.18	.15	.27	.21	.16	.26
	(.03)	(.04)	(.03)	(.03)	(.03)	(.03)	(.02)	(.02)
United States	.35	.32	.32	.33	.37	.39	.43	.43
	(.01)	(.01)	(.01)	(.01)	(.01)	(.01)	(.01)	(.01)
$\bar{R}^2$:								
Italy	.23	.24	.25	.26	.29	.23	.27	.23
United States	.23	.22	.19	.21	.22	.19	.22	.23
No. of observations:								
Italy	1,767	1,637	1,610	2,201	2,250	2,019	3,766	3,192
United States	22,391	22,827	27,324	23,566	22,244	22,640	23,955	23,692
Average earnings ($US):								
Italy	6,436	7,442	8,975	7,978	7,913	7,888	10,861	13,819
United States	15,991	17,186	18,595	22,145	23,578	24,419	27,070	28,237

Sources: Bank of Italy, U.S. Current Population Survey.

Note: Dependent variable = log of annual wage and salary earnings, full-time, full-year nonagricultural workers who are not self-employed, aged 18–65, before tax in United States, after tax in Italy. Excluded education category = completed high school; all regressions also contain a constant. Standard errors are in parentheses.

Table 8.9   Earnings Function Coefficients for Women in Italy and the United States, 1978–87 (excluding 1981 and 1985)

	1978	1979	1980	1982	1983	1984	1986	1987
Experience (divided by 10):								
Italy	.30	.27	.23	.24	.19	.20	.28	.18
	(.04)	(.04)	(.04)	(.04)	(.04)	(.03)	(.03)	(.02)
United States	.21	.22	.23	.22	.25	.25	.27	.30
	(.01)	(.01)	(.01)	(.01)	(.01)	(.01)	(.01)	(.01)
Experience squared (divided by 1,000):								
Italy	-.50	-.45	-.39	-.33	-.25	-.29	-.43	-.24
	(.09)	(.08)	(.08)	(.08)	(.08)	(.06)	(.05)	(.05)
United States	-.34	-.36	-.36	-.36	-.42	-.42	-.44	-.50
	(.03)	(.02)	(.02)	(.03)	(.03)	(.03)	(.03)	(.03)
Elementary or less:								
Italy	-.44	-.50	-.43	-.49	-.43	-.44	-.42	-.39
	(.04)	(.04)	(.05)	(.04)	(.04)	(.04)	(.03)	(.03)
United States	-.37	-.35	-.40	-.40	-.40	-.38	-.42	-.45
	(.02)	(.02)	(.02)	(.02)	(.02)	(.02)	(.02)	(.02)
Junior high:								
Italy	-.22	-.21	-.13	-.17	-.20	-.21	-.21*	-.20
	(.04)	(.04)	(.03)	(.03)	(.03)	(.03)	(.02)	(.02)

	(1)	(2)	(3)	(4)	(5)	(6)	(7)	(8)
United States	−.25	−.22	−.23	−.27	−.28	−.25	−.29	−.31
	(.01)	(.01)	(.01)	(.01)	(.02)	(.02)	(.02)	(.02)
College+:								
Italy	.08	.08	.13	.15	.18	.13	.12	.14
	(.05)	(.05)	(.05)	(.04)	(.04)	(.03)	(.03)	(.02)
United States	.36	.36	.38	.36	.38	.39	.43	.45
	(.01)	(.01)	(.01)	(.01)	(.01)	(.01)	(.01)	(.01)
$\bar{R}^2$:								
Italy	.16	.21	.15	.17	.17	.20	.19	.21
United States	.16	.16	.15	.15	.15	.14	.16	.18
No. of observations:								
Italy	838	820	829	1,104	1,101	1,073	1,991	1,797
United States	12,204	12,999	16,055	14,886	14,981	15,547	16,493	16,807
Average earnings ($U.S.):								
Italy	4,787	5,683	7,072	6,216	6,321	6,129	8,395	10,684
United States	9,242	10,051	10,936	13,198	14,397	15,265	17,226	18,128

Sources: Bank of Italy, U.S. Current Population Survey.

Note: Dependent variable = log of annual wage and salary earnings, full-time, full-year nonagricultural workers who are not self-employed, aged 18–65, before tax in United States, after tax in Italy. Excluded education category = completed high school; all regressions also contain a constant. Standard errors are in parentheses.

Table 8.10   **Measures of Inequality of Log Earnings, Italy and the United States**

Year	90-10 Differential	90-50 Differential	50-10 Differential	SD	SD of Residuals	SD in Industry
Italian men						
1978	.827	.470	.357	.402	.353	.409
1979	.742	.336	.405	.410	.358	.420
1980	.742	.377	.365	.367	.319	.377
1982	.762	.405	.357	.373	.320	.387
1983	.724	.361	.363	.370	.311	.364
1984	.693	.379	.314	.374	.328	.333
1986	.729	.419	.310	.337	.288	.317
1987	.734	.446	.288	.355	.311	.371

						SD in Manufacturing
American men						
1978	1.206	.533	.672	.531	.466	.471
1979	1.216	.549	.668.	.535	.473	.512
1980	1.261	.565	.696	.578	.522	.509
1982	1.257	.564	.693	.564	.502	.520
1983	1.348	.606	.742	.586	.516	.518
1984	1.379	.598	.781	.632	.570	.543
1986	1.409	.629	.780	.638	.563	.575
1987	1.452	.631	.821	.627	.549	.582
Italian women						
1978	.916	.336	.580	.447	.408	
1979	.869	.256	.613	.437	.388	
1980	.787	.288	.500	.435	.400	
1982	.867	.342	.525	.447	.407	
1983	.860	.314	.547	.427	.388	
1984	.693	.241	.452	.371	.330	
1986	.818	.268	.550	.398	.358	
1987	.693	.251	.442	.343	.305	
American women						
1978	1.082	.548	.535	.484	.443	
1979	1.124	.568	.556	.472	.433	
1980	1.054	.543	.511	.514	.473	
1982	1.099	.560	.539	.510	.471	
1983	1.161	.571	.591	.532	.491	
1984	1.204	.580	.624	.548	.507	
1986	1.253	.616	.636	.556	.509	
1987	1.322	.629	.693	.564	.511	

Sources: Bank of Italy, U.S. Current Population Survey.

years, inequality is greater for Americans than for their Italian gender counterparts. In all but one case, there is evidence of an increase in inequality in the United States and somewhat weaker evidence of a decrease in inequality in Italy—the exception is the 90-50 log earnings differential for men in Italy, which increases steadily after 1979.[25]

We do not have a conclusive explanation for the lack of a U shape in Italian individual level inequality that we see in the aggregate sectoral data presented in the previous two sections. One possible explanation is that the composition of our sample of individuals may lead to results that do not reflect the changes in metal-manufacturing inter-*inquadramento* inequality or the other measures of interindustry and interoccupational inequality presented above. Less than 50 percent of the BDI sample (substantially less for women) is employed in industry, and, when we analyze this sector separately, we do find a rise in the standard deviation of log earnings for men in 1987 to a level above that in 1983,[26] although it still drops from 1983 through 1986 (see the final column of table 8.10). Another possibility is that "industry" contains sectors that had a different experience than metal-manufacturing; unfortunately, we cannot separate out these other sectors in this data set.

8.3.5   Possible Explanations for the Divergent Trends in Overall Inequality in Italy and the United States

We recognize that there are many conceivable explanations for these divergent results on the coefficients in the earnings functions and the dispersion of earnings in the two countries. These range from differences in technology (or the relation of earnings and productivity within individual firms), to differences in the imbalances between the supply of and the demand for skills (including the effect of the price of education on labor supply, college being virtually free in Italy), to the possibility of different methods of non–price rationing in the labor markets (including various types of discrimination), to the changing influence of taxes (which are netted from the Italian but not the U.S. data).

We certainly cannot distinguish definitively among these alternatives at this point. Yet, because we find the difference in the trends of inequality to be so striking, we close this section by examining some possible explanations for the movement toward rising inequality in the United States and stable to falling inequality in Italy, as displayed in table 8.10. An explanation that is logically possible involves the distribution of skills in the two countries: the results reported above might be consistent with a sharper trend toward higher educational attainment among fully employed workers and thus toward greater over-

---

25. This suggests that, for men, Italian labor market institutions may have succeeded in keeping up wages at the bottom but not in preventing substantial wage drift at the top. The same does not seem to be true for women. Note as well that the 90–50 differential is greater for Italian men than for Italian women, perhaps reflecting the greater returns to a college degree for men in Italy, while most other measures of inequality are greater for Italian women than for Italian men.

26. The sample of women in industry is too small to be reliable.

all inequality in the United States. Recall, however, from the discussion above (table 8.6) that, while the average levels of education are higher in the United States, the trends in educational attainment seem to be going in the same basic directions in the two countries—in fact, the proportion of fully employed workers with college degrees or more has increased more sharply in Italy than in the United States for both men and women.[27]

The findings on the trends in inequality could also be consistent with differential changes in the occupational or industrial structures in the two countries. In fact, the share of blue-collar workers has been falling and the share of white-collar workers rising for both men and women in the Italian sample: the share of blue-collar workers among men fell from 59 percent in 1978 to 49 percent in 1986, while the share of white-collar workers rose from 41 to 51 percent; among women, the share of blue-collar workers fell from 49 percent in 1978 to 40 percent in 1986, and the share of white-collar workers rose from 50 to 60 percent.[28] As for the industrial distribution, the category industry is the largest among men but has dropped over this period from 48 percent of the workers in 1978 to 39 percent in 1986, while the categories public administration and the residual category have been growing. Among women, public administration has always been the largest category (rising from 33 percent of the workers in 1978 to 43 percent in 1986) and has also grown relative to industry; trade is the third largest category among women, as compared to transportation and communications among men.[29]

Overall, then, there has been a shift away from blue-collar and industrial jobs and a shift toward white-collar and public administration jobs among both men and women in Italy over this period. The industry and occupation categories are not strictly comparable with those in the CPS, so we do not present a direct comparison, but these results suggest that Italy has been undergoing a deindustrialization similar to that experienced by other Western countries, indicating that the explanation for the divergence of the trends in inequality will probably not be found here.

Furthermore, when we calculate the effects of between-industry shifts in labor demand on the relative demands for different skill and gender groups in Italy (using the methodology of Katz and Murphy [1992] and Katz, Loveman, and Blanchflower [chap. 1 in this volume], who find evidence of shifts toward more educated workers in the United States and elsewhere) on the basis of six industries and six gender-skill groups, we find a shift against workers with less than a high school degree, a slight shift in favor of workers who completed

27. On the other hand, a given increase in the proportion of college-educated workers might be expected to produce more overall inequality in the United States, given the generally higher returns to schooling.
28. This is consistent with the findings for the metal-manufacturing sector presented in sec. 8.2 above.
29. Note that we use 1986 for the ending date here because the industrial and occupational classification systems changed in 1987.

high school, and a much greater shift toward workers with a college degree or more for both men and women.[30] We conclude that the fall in returns to high school, the less than dramatic rise in the returns to college, and the drop in overall inequality in Italy are not due to between-industry shifts in labor demand away from more educated workers.[31]

The influence of taxes, which are netted from the Italian but not from the U.S. data, is another candidate explanation for the observed trends in inequality in Italy and the United States. The Italian tax system is effectively progressive because of both the structure of marginal tax rates and the lump-sum nature of deductions. While before-tax earnings have been found to be more unequal than after-tax earnings, the progressivity of the tax system seems to have decreased between 1982 and 1987 (see Nardecchia and Patriarca 1992; Ricciardelli 1992; and Di Bella and Parisi 1992). This suggests that, while the influence of taxes might contribute to the difference in the level of inequality in the two samples, it probably does not drive the difference in the trends; if anything, we would expect a bias toward *increasing* inequality in Italian after-tax earnings from the decreasing progressivity of the Italian tax structure over this period.

One additional possibility that we find appealing is that differences in the nature and evolution of labor market institutions in the two countries have contributed to the low and falling inequality in Italy and the high and rising inequality in the United States—specifically, labor market institutions (union contracts and relatively centralized bargaining structures, e.g.) act to narrow earnings inequality to a greater extent in Italy and have not been deregulated or otherwise dismantled to the extent that they have been in the United States. This final interpretation is consistent with the generally lower returns to a college degree and the less steep experience-earnings profiles in Italy as well as the general thrust of the evidence provided in section 8.2 above on the metal-manufacturing sector.

---

30. The six industries are industry, public administration, trade, public transport and communication, banking, and other. The six gender-skill groups are did not complete high school, completed high school, and college degree for men and women. We use 1978 as the base year and 1986 as the ending year owing to the change in the occupational classification system in 1987. The value of the shift away from men who did not complete high school, as measured by the difference in the logarithms of the indexes of relative demands from 1978 to 1986, is $-.132$, toward men who completed high school .095, toward men with a college degree .158, away from women who did not complete high school $-.003$, toward women who completed high school .172, and toward women with a college degree .253.

31. The evidence on the growth of education categories within industries is somewhat more mixed: while the share of workers with a high school degree or above rises or remains stable between 1978 and 1986 in every industry except the residual other, the share with a college degree actually falls slightly in three industries: public administration, banking, and other. This suggests that there may not have been increases in the demand for skilled workers within these industries; keep in mind, however, that public administration and banking are both relatively politically controlled and that their hiring practices may therefore be driven by concerns other than the technological needs for skills (political patronage, e.g.).

8.4   Conclusions: Mechanisms outside the Regular Economy Influencing Overall Italian Wage Inequality

The overall picture of Italy presented in this paper is of a country with a compressed wage structure that is not yet undergoing the rapid decompression experienced elsewhere during the 1980s. The decline of inter-*inquadramento*, interindustry, and blue-collar/white-collar differentials during the 1970s came to a stop and was slightly reversed during the 1980s, but these differentials did not rise back to pre-1980s levels despite the reforms of the mid-1980s. Over the period 1978–87, measures of individual level earnings inequality indicate, if anything, a trend toward a less unequal distribution. This trend is in marked contrast to the experience in the United States, where inequality clearly increased during the 1980s.

There seem to have been three important determinants of this evolution of wage differentials in Italy over the last twenty years. First is the *egalitarian ideology* of Italian unions, which in times of union strength such as the 1970s led to the institutionalization of equalizing practices such as low contracted wage differentials and egalitarian escalator clauses. Second is the dynamic of *inflation* in conjunction with the different escalator regimes that Italy has experienced during this period. Third is the evolution of *technology, productivity differentials,* and related *skill shortages* in the labor markets, which most likely primarily influenced the individually contracted portion of total compensation.

One might have expected that the clear break in the evolution of wage differentials around 1982–83 would have offered the chance to evaluate the relative importance of these factors. However, the simultaneous nature of these processes makes such a task impossible with the available information: the years when the compression of wage differentials came to a stop, or at least to a slowdown, were also the years in which major discontinuities occurred in the evolution of the three factors identified above: union strength, as measured by strike activity and by membership, significantly weakened; inflation, after the explosion of the 1970s, started a downward trend that lasted until the late 1980s; and, finally, the process of industrial restructuring induced by the oil shocks and by the computer revolution likely caused changes in the demanded skill composition of the labor force, not necessarily and not immediately matched by changes in the composition of supplies.

Nevertheless, the evidence provided by the comparison with the United States suggests that the continuing compression in the regular sector likely cannot be attributed to market forces. Both countries appear to have experienced the sort of trend toward a more educated and more heavily white-collar workforce that accompanies deindustrialization. In addition, the analysis of between-industry labor demand shifts provides no evidence of a shift away from more educated workers in either country. Despite these similar labor supply and labor demand indicators, measured inequality has been relatively high and increasing in the United States and low and decreasing in Italy. Thus, there seems to be room enough for alternative explanations for the Italian case.

It is difficult to deny that egalitarian institutions, and in particular the *scala mobile,* bore a large measure of responsibility for the wage compression of the 1970s. We cannot say how much of that compression was actually expected in 1975 when the *scala mobile* payments were first equalized across all workers; most likely, the probability of many years of inflation in double figures was underestimated at that time.[32] Indeed, the fact that contracted differentials started to increase in 1979, leaving indexation as the primary factor causing compression through 1983, suggests that unions might have realized that the compression was becoming excessive. Yet the 1975 system was not modified until 1983, and only in 1986 was its egalitarian nature substantially changed. The fact that it took so long to reform the *scala mobile* leads to the suspicion that the implied compression was not too far from what the market could bear. On the other hand, episodes like the march of the forty thousand in 1980 and the referendum against the *scala mobile* in 1985 suggest that the compression had already reached the threshold of sustainability by the early 1980s, and indeed in subsequent years the system was changed.

Before the reform of the *scala mobile,* the individual superminimum was the escape valve through which the parties could make bearable the compression caused by inflation. One might even suspect that the disequalizing effect of the drift was part of some kind of implicit agreement between employers and unions to control the compression caused by unexpectedly high inflation. Unions might have been attached to the egalitarian *scala mobile* for internal political reasons, allowing the drift to correct for the unexpected effects. However, we do not have evidence on the validity of these speculations, and, if they were true, one would be left with the question, Why wasn't the excessively egalitarian nature of the escalator system reformed before the mid-1980s if even the majority within the unions may have been dissatisfied with it?

Indeed, had the system been modified by giving more weight to contracted increases, as, for example, in Sweden (see Edin and Holmlund, chap. 9 in this volume), unions might have acquired more control over wage determination and wage dispersion. But precisely the comparison with the Swedish experience suggests that the instrument through which compression is achieved (escalator in Italy, contracted increases in Sweden) is probably irrelevant: what matters is the extent to which compression can be imposed, and in both countries the sustainable threshold was reached around the same period.

---

32. Franco Mattei, one of the Confindustria experts who bargained the 1975 agreement, wrote afterward, "The compression effect of the new system was perceived, but it was considered as justified in the short period emergency [to protect low wages from the oil shock inflation]. Even myself, looking back at my notes, in November 1974 I did not expect that we would have had an inflation rate around 20% for so many years. I thought that we were at a peak of inflation but that inflation was soon going to be eliminated" (Mattei 1981, 141).

Why, then, were employers unable to undo the compression? For employers, individual superminima were not a costless instrument for controlling wage compression: given the compensation increases granted by the contracts and by the *scala mobile* to low *inquadramento* levels, larger superminima at high levels implied a greater growth in total labor costs. Therefore, the disequalizing potential of individual superminima was somewhat limited by constraints on total labor cost increases. These constraints were likely to have been particularly binding during the period of high inflation, and this might explain why the individual superminima did not fully offset the effect of the *scala mobile* before 1983. Yet the puzzle remains as to why wage inequality did not increase back to its levels of the early 1970s after inflation slowed down, particularly when technological changes probably required, if anything, a more marked trend toward larger compensation differentials across skills, as occurred in the United States and elsewhere.

A credible partial explanation to this puzzle is that other remedies to wage compression, perhaps less costly to employers, seem to have proliferated in the nonregular areas of the economy, not covered by our empirical analysis above. For example, Italy is among the developed countries with the greatest levels and highest recent growth rates of self-employment: nonagricultural self-employment as a proportion of total civilian employment grew from 18.9 percent in 1979 to 22.3 percent in 1990 (OECD 1992).[33] Italian self-employment may be a consequence of the presence of restrictive labor market regulations imposed by unions, in particular hiring and firing costs (Bertola 1990). It is also possible that the compression of wage differentials for non-self-employed workers might have spurred the diffusion of self-employment: some of the highly skilled workers who saw their earnings limited by the egalitarian union policies may have offered themselves as freelancers (perhaps even to the same firms that were previously hiring them as employees) with the aim of getting better returns to their skills. Although we are not aware of any explicit quantitative evidence on this link between wage compression in the unionized sector and self-employment, it seems to be a credible hypothesis, consistent with anecdotal evidence. If this is the case, then the egalitarian efforts of unions have been only partially successful: wages of regular employees may have been compressed, but an increasing number of workers could have avoided the compression by becoming self-employed.

Italy is also well known for having a large underground economy, and, almost by definition, the underground economy is something over which official

---

33. As a point of comparison, the share of self-employed workers grew from 7.1 percent in 1979 to 7.6 percent in 1990 in the United States. The United Kingdom seems to be the country with the greatest growth of the proportion of self-employed, from 6.6 percent in 1979 to 11.6 percent in 1990. The share of self-employed workers in the complete Bank of Italy survey rises from 17.5 percent in 1978 to 23 percent in 1987; we do not use these observations for the wage inequality calculations in sec. 8.3 above because we have no way of distinguishing full-time self-employed from part-time.

wage-setting institutions and unions have no legal control and minimal influence. As in the case of self-employment, one is tempted to attribute the size of the underground economy to the existence of labor market and fiscal regulation that employers view as burdensome. Indeed, the available estimates of the underground economy for Italy are larger than most estimates for other Western countries, where labor market regulations are generally less restrictive (Dallago 1988, 1990).[34] In line with this view, the compression of wage differentials in the unionized sector could be a stimulant for the underground economy: if some of the compression is achieved by raising low wages (a hypothesized effect of the *scala mobile*), it becomes difficult for employers to profitably maintain "overground" activities involving less skilled workers. Although hiring less skilled workers into underground activities not controlled by unions may not be feasible for large companies, the reader should keep in mind that the Italian productive structure is constituted in large part by very small firms.

Yet, in contrast to self-employment, it is difficult to find any reliable evidence of a significantly increasing trend in the underground economy in Italy in recent years. While the lack of reliability is no doubt in large part inherent in any attempt to measure underground activities, the official statistics that do exist (a revised series of Italian GNP from the central statistical office, ISTAT) show that the nonexplicitly measured portion of national product went from 15.3 percent in 1980 to 17.7 percent in 1985 and then slightly decreased to 16 percent in 1986 (Dallago 1988, 73–75).[35] It thus seems more difficult than in the situation of self-employment to build a prima facie case for a link between the trend in the compression of wage differentials and possible diffusion of the underground economy.

Another manner in which a de facto wider wage distribution may have been achieved despite the compression documented above involves the so called *contratti di formazione e lavoro:* special labor contracts for workers between fourteen and twenty-nine years of age. Permanently introduced by law in 1984 after several previous experiments, they require employers to provide some training in return for lower wages and social contributions. In contrast to standard jobs, the contracts are temporary (twenty-four months); at the expiration of the contract, the employer can decide whether to hire the worker for a lifetime position without having to consider other unemployment queues, and financial incentives for transitions into permanent contracts are provided by the government. The number of young workers hired under these contracts grew from 10,694 in 1984 to 529,297 in 1989. The biggest jump was between 1986

34. Dallago (1988) reports that recent estimates of the Italian underground GDP as a proportion of total GDP range from 6 to 30.1 percent, with most estimates in double figures. For the United States, the analogous estimates range from 2.6 to 33 percent, with very few estimates in double figures. For further discussion of the Italian underground economy, see also Deaglio (1984) and Rey (1985).

35. Note, however, that only a part of this change can be attributed to the actual growth of the underground economy; the rest is due to a revision in statistical techniques.

and 1987, when the number of hirings grew from 229,126 to 402,586; this jump was influenced by a modification to the law providing employers with larger wage and social contribution savings. The number of new *contratti di formazione e lavoro* has started to decline slightly only recently, down to 469,050 in 1990.[36] The available data indicate that approximately 50 percent of these contracts (40 percent in the south) are eventually transformed into permanent contracts (Ministero del Lavoro 1988–91).

The popularity of these contracts among both young workers and employers is consistent with the view that a less compressed wage distribution is welcomed by both groups (possibly at the expense of unemployed older workers, who would have to be hired under standard permanent contracts), particularly given the often-stated charge that these employment relationships do not really serve their official function of providing young workers with meaningful special training. From the employers' point of view, the advantages are fairly obvious, but these contracts are likely to represent a desirable alternative to unemployment or to employment in the underground economy for the young workers as well. Youth unemployment has been relatively high in Italy in recent years: the percentage of total unemployment constituted by job seekers between the ages of fourteen and twenty-four fluctuated around 61–62 percent between 1978 and 1983, declining thereafter to 54 percent in 1987 and to 48 percent in 1990 (OECD 1978–90). Most likely, many of these young workers have been finding jobs in the underground economy. But, even if the amount of underground employment hidden in the official youth unemployment figures is significant, the basic conclusion that we draw from this evidence is unchanged: it seems that, by imposing their egalitarian aspirations on the regular sector of the economy, Italian unions may have ended up limiting the size of this sector.

The evidence that we present in the first three sections of this paper indicates that wage differentials have indeed been compressed in the regular sector of the economy. Yet this concluding section suggests that this very compression may well have contributed to the flight away from the regular sector at both ends of the skill distribution: highly skilled workers may have left to seek the unrestricted returns to self-employment, while less skilled entrants were induced to accept lower-paying training contracts, were forced into the more precarious underground economy, or remained unemployed. These mechanisms may well, in turn, have contributed to a greater overall degree of inequality than is apparent in our analysis of wage differentials in the regular sector of the Italian economy.

---

36. This amounts to approximately 3 percent of the total nonagricultural paid workforce.

Data Appendix

Assolombarda

Assolombarda is the association of private employers in the Lombardy region. The data set is based on a survey of the associated firms in the Milan area. The survey has been taken in October and April of each year since 1976, but not all the surveys are available, particularly at the beginning of the sample. For each firm and *inquadramento*-level cell, the survey provides the average of each compensation component received by the workers in that cell; individual firms cannot be identified, however. In 1988, there was a change in the design of the survey, but, for the metal-manufacturing sector (the one we analyze), previous data have been readjusted by Assolombarda to ensure comparability across years. We are, however, less than fully confident about the consistency of these readjustments since some apparent discontinuities have not been eliminated; therefore, we use cross-time comparisons in this data set only when the regularity of the data seems acceptable.

We have access to firm-level information only for the October surveys from 1983 through 1990. For the other years we rely on the published averages across firms for each *inquadramento* level.

Bank of Italy

The Bank of Italy survey of Italian households was first collected in 1977. The survey was not conducted in 1985, and the data for 1981 are not considered to be sufficiently representative by the experts at the bank. After 1987, the survey has been conducted biannually.

Data are collected on a representative cross section of Italian households by a private company for the Bank of Italy. The survey has been mainly designed to provide information on consumption and savings behavior; therefore, the information available for the estimation of earnings functions, and in general the information available for labor market research, is somewhat limited.

See also Bank of Italy, "I bilanci delle famiglie Italiane," in *Supplementi al bollettino statistico: Note metodologiche e informazione statistiche* (various years), and "Le indagini campionarie sui bilanci delle famiglie italiane," *Contributi all'analisi economica* (special issue, 1986).

Federmeccanica

Federmeccanica is the national association of private metal-manufacturing firms. This data set is based on a sample of the associated firms and provides, for each *inquadramento* level, the cross-firm average total monthly compensation and the cross-firm average contractual plus *scala mobile* compensation. It also provides the proportion of workers in each *inquadramento* level. Data are available from 1976 through 1990.

Ministry of Labor

This data set is based on a survey of eleven thousand plants and is sponsored by the Ministry of Labor. Until 1977, only firms with more than five employees were included. After 1977, the survey is limited to firms with more than fifty employees.

The data used in figure 8.1 above is the average hourly blue-collar and trainees' compensation, computed as the total monthly base compensation paid to these workers divided by the total number of hours. The series was discontinued in 1985. A new series was started in 1986, but the data are not yet available.

National Accounts

We have used the new series (1970–89) of the national accounts data published by ISTAT (Istituto Nazionale di Statistica, Rome), in *Collana di informazione,* vol. 10 (1990).

References

Alleva, P. G. 1986. Legislazione e contrattazione collettiva nel 1985–1986. *Giornale di diritto del lavoro e di relazioni industriali* 31:611–64.
ASAP Unita' Studi. 1986–91. *Rapporto sui salari.* Milan: Franco Angeli.
Bertola, G. 1990. Job security, employment, and wages. *European Economic Review* 34:851–86.
Biagioli, M. 1985. Contrattazione aziendale e differenziali retributivi. *IRES Papers* 1:1–61.
———. 1988. I differenziali retributivi interprofessionali e intercategoriali. In *Il sistema retributivo verso gli anni '90.* Naples: Jovene.
Bordogna, L. 1988. Differenziali retributivi, sindacalizzazione e rincorse salariali. In *Il sistema retributivi verso gli anni '90.* Naples: Jovene.
Cannari, L., G. Pellegrini, and P. Sestito. 1989. Redditi da lavoro dipendente: Un'analisi in termini di capitale umano. Temi di discussione del Servizio Studi, Banca d'Italia (Bank of Italy discussion paper), no. 124. Rome.
Carinci, F. 1987. L'evoluzione storica. *Quaderni di diritto del lavoro e delle relazioni industriali* (Turin) 1 (special issue, "Inquadramento dei lavoratori"): 12–39.
Carniti Commission. 1988. *I salari in Italia negli anni ottanta.* Venice: Marsilio.
Consiglio Nazionale per l'Economia e il Lavoro (CNEL). 1981. *Inflazione e scala mobile.* Quaderni di documentazione CNEL (CNEL discussion paper). Rome.
Dallago, B. 1988. *L'economia irregolare.* Milan: Franco Angeli.
———. 1990. *The irregular economy.* Dartmouth: Dartmouth.
D'Apice, C. 1975. *La scala mobile dei salari.* Rome: Editrice Sindacale Italiana.
Deaglio, M. 1984. *Economia sommersa e analisi economica.* Turin: Giappichelli.
Di Bella, G., and V. Parisi. 1992. Il prelievo fiscale e la redistribuzione del reddito nel lavoro dipendente. In *Retribuzione, costo del lavoro, livelli della contrattazione: Analisi quantitative,* ed. R. Brunetta. Milan: Etas Libri.
Faustini, G. 1987. A new method of indexing wages in Italy. *Labour* 1:71–91.

Frey, L. 1988. Differenziali retributivi e "job evaluation." In *Il sistema retributivo verso gli anni '90.* Naples: Jovene.

Giugni, G. 1984. Recent trends in collective bargaining in Italy. *International Labour Review,* vol. 123, no. 5.

Hibbs, D., and H. Locking. 1991. Wage compression, wage drift, and wage inflation in Sweden. Stockholm: FIEF. Mimeo.

Ichino, P. 1992. *Il lavoro subordinato: Definizione e inquadramento, Artt. 2094–2095.* Milan: Giuffre'.

Katz, L., and K. Murphy. 1992. Changes in relative wages, 1963–1987: Supply and demand factors. *Quarterly Journal of Economics* 107: 35–78.

Locke, R. 1992. The demise of the national union in Italy: Lessons for comparative industrial relations theory. *Industrial and Labor Relations Review* 45, no. 2:229–49.

Lucifora, C., and G. Presutto. 1990. Retribuzioni lorde e nette. In *Occupazione e retribuzioni.* Milan: Assolombarda.

Mariani, I. F. 1991. Profili storici della disciplina della scala mobile. In *Scala mobile: Storia e prospettive.* Rome: Notiziario di Giurisprudenza del Lavoro.

Mattei, F. 1981. Comment. In CNEL (1981).

Ministero del Lavoro e della Previdenza Sociale. 1988–91. *Labour and employment policies in Italy: Annual report.* Rome: Istituto Poligrafico e Zecca dello Stato.

Nardecchia, L., and S. Patriarca. 1992. Il prelievo fiscale sulle retribuzione negli anni 80: L'incidenza formale. In *Retribuzione, costo del lavoro, livelli della contrattazione: Analisi quantitative,* ed. R. Brunetta. Milan: Etas Libri.

Neufeld, M. 1960. *Italy: School for awakening nations.* Ithaca, NY: ILR Press.

OECD. 1978–90. *Quarterly labor force statistics.* Paris.

———. 1992. *Employment outlook.* Paris, July.

Quarchioni, R. 1979. *Storia della scala mobile e valori dell'indennita di contingenza nel settore industriale dal 1954 al 1979.* Milan: Pirola.

Rey, G. M. 1985. Influenza del sommerso sulla formazione del prodotto interno lordo. In *Il sommerso: Realt ed influenza dell'economia irregolare.* Novara: Europma.

Ricciardelli, M. 1992. Il prelievo fiscale sulle retribuzione negli anni 80: L'incidenza effettiva. In *Retribuzione, costo del lavoro, livelli della contrattazione: Analisi quantitative,* ed. R. Brunetta. Milan: Etas Libri.

Sestito, P. 1990. Empirical earnings functions in a decade of turbulence: The Italian experience. Servizio Studi, Banca d'Italia (Bank of Italy discussion paper), no. 135. Rome.

9   The Swedish Wage Structure: The Rise and Fall of Solidarity Wage Policy?

Per-Anders Edin and Bertil Holmlund

Wage inequality in Sweden declined precipitously during the 1960s and the 1970s. There was a sharp reduction in overall wage dispersion and in the relative earnings advantage of highly educated workers, a marked narrowing of wage differences between men and women, and a trend increase in youth relative wages. There was also a substantial narrowing of wage differentials among workers within broad occupation and education groups.

The trend decline in wage inequality was broken in the 1980s. Wage differentials have widened along several dimensions from the mid-1980s to the early 1990s. There has been a modest rise in overall wage inequality and some increase in educational wage differentials, and the trend increase in youth relative wages has been reversed. Wage inequality within manual as well as nonmanual occupations has widened.

The pattern of decreasing wage differentials during the 1970s and expanding differentials during the 1980s is not a feature that is unique to the Swedish labor market. Wage differentials by education and occupation declined during the 1970s in a number of countries, whereas the 1980s have seen rising inequality, notably in Britain and the United States (see, e.g., Bound and Johnson

Per-Anders Edin is associate professor of economics at Uppsala University and a research economist of the National Bureau of Economic Research. Bertil Holmlund is professor of economics at Uppsala University.

Maria Fornwall, Peter Fredriksson, and Thomas Östros have provided excellent research assistance. The authors are grateful to Anders Björklund, Nils Elvander, Anders Forslund, Richard Freeman, Lawrence Katz, Henry Ohlsson, Claes-Henric Siven, Robert Topel, and Johnny Zetterberg for useful comments on an earlier draft. Comments from participants at seminars at FIEF (Fackföreningsrörelsens Institut för Ekonomisk Forskning), KI (Konjunkturinstitutet), Uppsala University, and NBER conferences in London and Cambridge, Mass., are also acknowledged. This research has been partly financed by the Ford Foundation, Jan Wallander's and Tom Hedelius's Research Foundation, and the Council for Research on Higher Education.

1992; Davis 1992; and Katz, Loveman, and Blanchflower, chap. 1 in this volume).

Much of the Swedish discussion has taken it for granted that the pay compression has been driven by the egalitarian ambitions of strong and coordinated trade unions. Indeed, the period of narrowing wage differentials coincides with the heydays of the "solidarity wage policy," the deliberate attempt by the main union confederations to reduce wage dispersion. The years of widening wage differentials coincide with a period when centralized bargaining loses its edge. A conclusion that movements in wage inequality can be traced to institutional forces lies therefore close at hand. Our analysis of the Swedish wage structure suggests that institutions are only part of the story. We show that conventional demand and supply factors can go a substantial way toward explaining some key relative wage movements in Sweden.

The plan of the paper is as follows. We begin in section 9.1 with a brief overview of the institutional background. Section 9.2 turns to a comprehensive documentation of the changes in the Swedish wage structure that took place from the 1960s on. By means of estimated wage equations for several different years we decompose the changes in wage dispersion into changes in individual characteristics and in returns to these characteristics and into residual changes. Section 9.3 discusses alternative explanations of the observed patterns. To what extent have sectoral shifts affected the relative demand for skilled labor? Are the movements in the wage dispersion driven by changes in the relative supply of skilled labor? Is there any evidence that changing institutional conditions in the labor market, in particular the breakdown of centralized wage bargaining, have influenced wage behavior? Section 9.4 examines whether pay compression has resulted in a deterioration of the labor market for youths, and section 9.5 looks at the relations between the returns to schooling and the demand for higher education. Section 9.6 concludes.

Our main findings can be summarized as follows:

1. The sharp pay compression that took place during the 1960s and the 1970s has been partly reversed during the 1980s. Wage compression was mainly due to narrowing age and education differentials as well as decreasing wage differentials between males and females. The recent widening of wage differentials is largely an increase in within-group dispersion.

2. The returns to higher education decreased sharply from the late 1960s and up to the mid-1980s, followed by a rebound during the second half of the 1980s. The main source of these fluctuations appears to be fluctuations in the relative supply of university-educated labor.

3. Youth relative wages increased continuously over the 1970s and up to the mid-1980s, with a slight trend reversal in the period thereafter. These movements are largely consistent with fluctuations in the relative supply of young and older workers.

4. Youth employment has shown substantial responsiveness with respect to

fluctuations in the size of the youth population. It is not obvious that pay compression has resulted in severe distortions in the youth labor market.

5. School enrollment among twenty- to twenty-four-year-olds has been highly responsive to the returns to university education. The demand for higher education declined as the university wage premium decreased. This led to a deceleration in the rate of growth of university-educated labor, which in turn resulted in a rebound of the university wage premium in the late 1980s.

9.1 The Institutional Setting

9.1.1 Industrial Relations in Sweden

Sweden has a reputation for peaceful labor relations.[1] This reputation is based on Sweden's experience after World War II, where labor conflicts have been rare events. Labor relations in previous decades were much less peaceful, however. The number of annual workdays lost owing to conflicts typically amounted to one or several millions during the interwar period; the corresponding figures during the 1950s and the 1960s were typically fewer than 100,000 days.

An important turning point is the "Basic Agreement" from 1938 between LO (the Swedish trade union confederation) and SAF (the Swedish employers' federation). This agreement—commonly referred to as *Saltsjöbadsavtalet*— defined a set of rules for conflict resolutions, which together with previously introduced legislation formed a basis for more peaceful labor relations. The legislation included a law on collective agreements from 1928, which made conflicts illegal after a contract had been signed. A labor court was also introduced in 1928 to handle disputes over contracts.

LO was founded in 1898 and is still the largest union confederation, with a membership over 2.2 million and twenty-three affiliated unions. LO organizes blue-collar workers in both the private and the public sectors. White-collar union confederations were formed just after World War II, and their membership figures have been gradually increasing during the postwar period. TCO— the central organization for salaried employees—is the largest white-collar confederation with over 1.2 million members among twenty affiliated unions. The third major organization is SACO—the Swedish confederation of professional associations—with 330,000 members and twenty-five unions. SACO is almost exclusively an organization for employees with a university education.

By international standards, a very high share of the Swedish workforce is unionized. According to the labor force surveys, 81 percent of employees were union members in 1991, and unionization rates show negligible variations

---

1. The section draws primarily on Calmfors and Forslund (1991), Elvander (1988), Hibbs (1990), Meidner (1974), Nilsson (1993), and Ullenhag (1971).

across broad education and occupation groups. For example, employees with a university education have union membership rates close to the average. Union membership rates are higher in the public sector than in the private; in 1990, the figures were 90 and 74 percent, respectively (Statistics Sweden 1992).

Union density has fallen sharply in many countries over the past decade. Sweden has so far experienced very little of this decline, although the number of union members fell in 1987 for the first time since the 1930s. There has been a slight decrease in unionization rates since 1987, mainly due to decreasing membership rates among young workers.

The growth of the public sector, in conjunction with increasing union membership rates among white-collar workers, has gradually eroded LO's dominant position among the union confederations. LO accounted for 80 percent of the total union membership in 1950 but less than 60 percent in 1990. Public-sector unions increased their share of the total number of union members from 26 to 42 percent during the same period.

The growth of public-sector and white-collar unions has reduced the relative importance of LO and SAF in the wage rounds. LO and SAF were the two key players in the heydays of "the Swedish model," when their wage agreements for the private sector worked as guideposts for the rest of the labor market. This has become an increasingly less accurate description of the Swedish wage negotiation system. A new private-sector player was formed in the early 1970s, a negotiation cartel (PTK) comprising private-sector employees from primarily TCO and SACO. (TCO and SACO do not as central organizations take direct part in the wage negotiations.) SAF and PTK struck several central agreements during the 1970s and the 1980s.

In 1965, public-sector employees were given the right to bargain over wages, including the right to strike. Employer organizations for the central and local governments have since then regularly negotiated with public-sector unions, with substantial coordination on both sides of the bargaining table. Private-sector wage agreements have in general been struck before public-sector agreements. Statistical studies of intersectoral wage linkages confirm this pattern; wage increases in the private sector have typically preceded ("Granger caused") public-sector wage increases (Holmlund and Ohlsson 1992).

9.1.2 Coordination and Solidarity: Theory and Practice

The term *solidarity wage policy* was coined in the late 1930s, but egalitarian ideas have a long history in LO. Demands for wage equalization among different groups within LO were regularly voiced during the LO congresses, typically closely related to demands for a more centralized bargaining structure within LO. LO had in fact little influence over its constituent unions during its early history. For example, no central negotiations between LO and SAF took place during the period 1909–36.

The year 1936 seems to have been one of takeoff for the solidarity wage policy. In that year the metalworkers' union placed a motion before the LO congress recommending a "socialist wage policy, with the emphasis on solidarity." The motion recognized, however, that LO had limited possibilities of pursuing such a policy in practice. The idea that *coordination* was a necessary prerequisite for *solidarity* was developed and refined in a number of articles and LO reports during the following decade. Of particular importance in this regard were the writings of the LO economists Gösta Rehn and Rudolf Meidner. (For an account of this discussion, see Turvey [1952].)

Rehn and Meidner argued that coordination should be seen not only as a device to achieve a wage policy of solidarity but also as a means to promote growth and structural change in the economy. The guiding principle should be "equal pay for equal work," irrespective of the ability to pay among particular firms or industries. The principle might be viewed as an attempt to use the centralized union's visible hand to achieve a wage structure that would appear in a competitive labor market. The Rehn-Meidner program did not rule out wage differences among workers with different skills or working conditions, only differences based on firms' profitability. The program did recognize, however, that a wage policy of this kind might put pressure on weak firms and ultimately cause unemployment in certain industries or regions. The solidarity wage policy should therefore be combined with an *active labor market policy* to facilitate the relocation of workers made redundant in less efficient firms.

A solidarity wage policy and an active labor market policy—two basic ingredients of what has been referred to as "the Swedish model"—were gradually initiated in practice during the 1950s. The first centralized wage round between LO and SAF took place in 1952, but coordination did not become a permanent feature of such negotiations until 1956. In fact, LO participated in the 1952 wage round reluctantly, SAF this time being the eager supporter of coordination. This SAF policy seems to have originated in the view that centralization might be conducive to wage moderation by preventing excessive leapfrogging.

Recent econometric work suggests that wage differentials in Sweden reflect industry rents to a much smaller extent than wages in the United States do (Holmlund and Zetterberg 1991; Edin and Zetterberg 1992). This finding is clearly consistent with the objectives of the solidarity wage policy. Equal pay for equal work is only one facet of solidarity wage policy, however. Another, based on strong ideological convictions among the union leaders and the membership at large, is *wage equalization.* There has always been a tension between these two facets of the solidarity wage policy. To some extent pay compression could be justified as establishing equal pay for equal work; an example is wage hikes for female workers and the abolition of special female wage scales. In other cases it was not at all clear what the operational content of equal pay for equal work really was. Attempts to achieve some consensus on wage differentials through elaborate job evaluation schemes have not been very successful. Solidarity wage policy from the late 1960s up to 1983 has therefore to a large extent been equivalent to pay compression.

The wage-bargaining process during the period 1956–83 took place at three levels: a central framework agreement between LO and SAF (or PTK and SAF), a number of national industry negotiations, followed by local negotiations at the plant level. There have been sixteen central LO-SAF agreements between 1956 and 1983, with contract lengths of one, two, or three years. Despite this centralized bargaining structure, "wage drift" has been a pervasive phenomenon. For example, wage drift among private-sector blue-collar workers—conventionally measured as the difference between actual wage increases and wage increases agreed on at the industry level—has on average accounted for close to 50 percent of total wage increases.

The egalitarian ambitions of the wage policy were manifested in the central LO-SAF agreements, but similar egalitarian ambitions seem to have dominated among white-collar unions within TCO. The frame agreements typically included a common wage increase specified in absolute terms (Swedish öre) rather than as a percentage. Other ingredients were special low-wage provisions, wage-drift guarantees to compensate workers without wage drift, and cost-of-living adjustments. It was possible to implement deviations from the frame agreement's distribution profile at the industry-level negotiations, but only if the parties could agree. The distribution rules in the frame agreement became binding if the parties at the industry level failed to agree on other distribution plans.

The pay compression face of solidarity wage policy has been caricatured as equivalent to "equal pay for all work." This is certainly an exaggeration, but the radical egalitarianism of the wage policy is one factor that has been put forward to explain the ultimate breakdown of centralized wage bargaining in Sweden. The employers' organization in the engineering industry (Verkstadsföreningen) had for years been critical of the central negotiations, arguing that the frame agreements allowed too little flexibility at the industry and local levels. Verkstadsföreningen and other critics of wage equalization argued in favor of pay systems that would allow higher remuneration of skilled workers. The turning point came in 1983, when Verkstadsföreningen was able to side-step LO and SAF and negotiate a separate agreement with the metalworkers' union. The wage negotiations after 1983 have primarily involved industry-level rather than national bargaining, although three notional central frame agreements were struck during the second half of the 1980s.

The period 1991–93 is a special case, entailing government-promoted voluntary incomes policies in conjunction with a sharp disinflation policy. Despite all the noise that SAF had made about the costs of central negotiations, the organization was quite anxious to follow suit when the government called for coordinated national efforts to achieve deceleration of wage inflation. The degree of coordination in the wage rounds of the early 1990s has been extreme, involving virtually all employer organizations and most of the unions.

There is a common presumption that the period 1991–93 is an interlude that will be followed by something similar to the industry-level negotiations that took place in the wake of the breakdown of centralization in 1983. The exact shape of Sweden's future wage-bargaining system is, however, very much an open question. SAF seems to have ambitions to prevent any return to the old system of nationwide coordination, and some employer representatives argue in favor of decentralization all the way down to the firm and plant levels. On the union side, there are signs of emerging cooperation between blue-collar and white-collar workers, a development that may be unavoidable as the sharp borderlines between traditional blue- and white-collar jobs begin to disappear.

9.2   Changes in the Swedish Wage Structure

9.2.1   Basic Facts

Sweden has experienced dramatic changes in its wage structure over the past three decades. Data from a variety of sources indicate that substantial pay compression took place from the mid-1960s to the early 1980s. As in many other countries, this trend was reversed from around 1980–85 on; the data at hand show a modest increase in the dispersion of wages and salaries during the second half of the 1980s and up to the early 1990s.[2]

Table 9.1 displays the standard deviation of log hourly earnings from two representative samples of the Swedish population (see Eriksson and Åberg 1987; and Klevmarken and Olofsson 1993). For 1968, 1974, and 1981, we have data from the Level of Living Survey (LNU); for 1984, 1986, 1988, and 1991, we use the Household Market and Nonmarket Activities Survey (HUS). We have restricted the samples to eighteen- to sixty-five-year-old employees (excluding the self-employed). The three LNU samples and HUS 1984 are constructed in an identical fashion. The later HUS samples are somewhat different. This is due to the household panel construction of HUS.[3] The earnings data from LNU and HUS are comparable in the sense that they are measured in essentially the same way. Respondents are asked to report, among other things, current (before-tax) wage or salary as well as normal hours of work; hourly earnings for those who are not paid on an hourly basis are calculated as the ratio between weekly (monthly) pay and hours worked. These two surveys are our main data sources for the analysis in this section.

---

2. The trend decline in wage dispersion has been discussed by, among others, Björklund (1986, 1987), Jonsson and Siven (1986), and Hibbs (1990). The development during the late 1980s is less well documented, an exception being Hibbs (1990).

3. The 1984 sample was reinterviewed in the later surveys. New individuals have been added to the sample through an additional sample in 1986 and through interviews with young individuals leaving their parents and new adult members of existing households in 1986 and 1991. For these new individuals we construct the independent variables in the same way as above. For the panel samples of HUS 1986, 1988, and 1991, however, we have information only on events taking place between the surveys. Since we did not have access to spells of employment for the 1991 sample or to changes in educational attainment as formulated above, we constructed these variables in a different way. For experience we used the initial values and assumed that the individual had been working until the survey in question. For education we used the initial level of education.

Table 9.1   The Swedish Wage Dispersion, 1968–91 (standard deviation of log hourly earnings)

	1968	1974	1981	1984	1986	1988	1991
LNU	.456	.359	.311	. . .	. . .	. . .	. . .
	(2,957)	(3,009)	(3,431)				
HUS	. . .	. . .	. . .	.305	.341	.368	.356
				(1,637)	(1,854)	(1,561)	(1,365)
HINK	. . .	. . .	.406	.343	.365	.391	.383[a]
			(1,000)	(1,004)	(1,889)	(1,779)	(1,746)

Note: The number of observations is given in parentheses. The samples cover 18–65-year-olds, excluding the self-employed. The HINK samples refer to individuals with no income from the public social insurance system (*Försäkringskassan*).
[a]Refers to 1990.

The picture that emerges from table 9.1 is quite striking. Between 1968 and 1981, we observe a decrease in the standard deviation of log hourly earnings of 32 percent (from .46 to .31). From 1984 to 1991, there is instead an increase in the dispersion by about 17 percent. Most of this increase seems to have occurred between 1984 and 1986. The dispersion in the early 1990s is of the same order of magnitude as the dispersion in the middle of the 1970s. This general pattern is confirmed by annual data from the Household Income Survey (HINK), 1981–90, reported in the bottom row of table 9.1. The earnings data in this survey are based on annual labor income, obtained from tax returns, divided by annual hours of work, as reported in a complementary survey.[4] These figures suggest that the drop in wage dispersion between 1981 and 1984 may be understated in the LNU-HUS comparison. The development after 1984 is very similar in the HINK and HUS samples, however.

Alternative measures of changes in wage dispersion are presented in figure 9.1 in terms of log wage differentials between different percentiles of the wage distribution. We report the log(P90/P10), where P_i is percentile i. The overall pattern of changes is the same as in table 9.1, with a substantial wage compression until the early 1980s and a tendency toward increasing wage dispersion thereafter. Decomposing the 90-10 differential into a 90-50 and a 50-10 differential illustrates that wage compression occurred at both the top and the bottom of the wage distribution. The wage dispersion is higher at the top, however. Furthermore, the 75-25 wage differential shows that the changes that we observe are not confined to the tails of the distribution.

The overall measures of wage dispersion reported here reveal that overall wage inequality in Sweden is small when viewed from an international perspective (see Davis 1992). Katz, Loveman, and Blanchflower (chap. 1 in this

---

4. Unfortunately, the earnings data also include sick pay and some other social insurance payments; it is possible to deduct these payments in a direct way only after 1985.

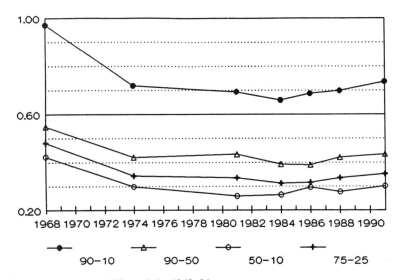

Fig. 9.1   Log wage differentials, 1968–91
Source: LNU and HUS.

volume) report that the 90–10 log wage differential for U.S. males was 1.36 in 1984. The corresponding figure for Sweden was 0.68 (0.66 including females). Thus, according to this measure, wage dispersion was about twice as high in the United States as in Sweden in 1984. The Swedish figure was also much lower than those for the other three countries examined in the Katz, Loveman, and Blanchflower study, namely, Britain (1.04), France (1.18), and Japan (1.02).

The general pattern of changes in wage dispersion in LNU and HUS, shown in table 9.1 and figure 9.1, is confirmed by statistics on wages and salaries obtained from SAF.[5] The data at our disposal are in the form P90/P10 or P75/P25. Data on individual hourly wages for blue-collar workers in the private sector are available since 1970. The message from figure 9.2 is clear; there is a fall in the wage dispersion by 15 percent between 1970 and 1983, followed by a rise of 6 percent from 1983 to 1990. The 90–10 wage differential in the early 1990s is of the same order of magnitude as the corresponding ratio in the mid-1970s.

Data on individual salaries for full-time, private-sector, white-collar workers are available since the late 1950s. Figure 9.3 reveals a pronounced pay compression during most of the 1960s and the 1970s, followed by an increase in the dispersion during the 1980s. Pay compression has been particularly strong

5. These data cover all workers whose employers are members of SAF. We are grateful to Douglas Hibbs and Håkan Locking for providing data on blue-collar workers and to Birgitta Preussner, SIF, for data on white-collar workers.

Fig. 9.2   Log wage differentials for private-sector blue-collar workers, 1970–90
Source: SAF.

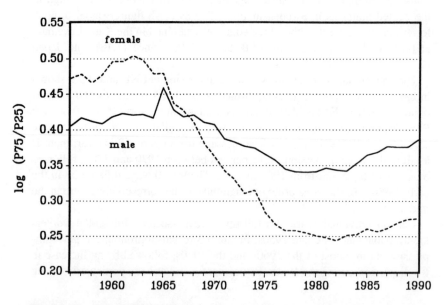

Fig. 9.3   Log wage differentials for private-sector white-collar workers, males and females, 1956–90
Source: SAF.

for female workers. Note that both figure 9.2 above and figure 9.3 show that wage compression started to lose its edge in the late 1970s and that the minimum wage dispersion occurs earlier than was implied by table 9.1 above.

Public-sector employees have also experienced widening wage differentials from the mid-1980s, again a clear reversal of the trends that prevailed during the 1970s and the early 1980s (see Statistics Sweden 1987, 1991). The 90–10 ratio for central government employees fell by some 20 percent between 1973 and 1985 and has increased during the second half of the 1980s. The data for local government employees show a similar picture. Computations based on LNU from 1974 and 1981 shown in Zetterberg (1988) reveal a decrease in the standard deviation of log wages by over 20 percent between 1974 and 1981 for local government employees; the corresponding change for central government employees was 16 percent. The period after 1984 involves a gradual increase in the 90–10 ratio for white-collar local government employees organized in TCO and SACO (Statistics Sweden 1991). The development in wage dispersions for blue-collar workers in the local public sector is more erratic, but the general trend is clearly consistent with the basic patterns for other groups (Statistics Sweden 1991).

9.2.2   Accounting for Changes in Wage Dispersion

In this section, we use the LNU and HUS micro data to investigate changes in the wage dispersion over the period 1968–91. We are interested in the extent to which changes in productive characteristics and changes in returns to these characteristics can account for the observed changes in wage dispersion. A similar exercise using the first four of our samples (LNU 1968, 1974, and 1981 and HUS 1984) is found in Björklund (1987); consequently, he dealt with the decline in wage dispersion. Hibbs (1990) used the first five of the samples to investigate whether changes in measured human capital characteristics could explain the changing wage dispersion among LO workers. He found that changes in human capital variance were much smaller than changes in earnings variance.

To address the question of changes in wage dispersion, we start by estimating simple human capital–type wage equations for each sample. We regress the log of hourly earnings on gender, a quadratic in experience, and years of schooling. The construction of hourly earnings is described above. Years of work experience is obtained from a direct question. Schooling is represented by dummy variables for each year of schooling above nine years, which corresponds to the compulsory schooling limit of the current system. (The schooling variable is truncated at eighteen years.) This choice was dictated by differences in the definition of schooling degrees obtained across the two surveys.[6]

---

6. The difference is in the definition of a university degree. The LNU samples apply a more strict definition of a university degree and do not include some degrees from the new *Högskola*, which were given university status in 1977. These degrees are counted in the HUS samples.

Table 9.2   **Estimated Wage Equations**

	1968	1974	1981	1984	1986	1988	1991
Const.	1.936	2.594	3.307	3.403	3.609	3.721	3.926
	(.020)	(.018)	(.016)	(.026)	(.031)	(.041)	(.040)
Female	−.262	−.205	−.148	−.125	−.128	−.129	−.135
	(.014)	(.011)	(.009)	(.013)	(.014)	(.017)	(.017)
Exp.	.037	.028	.023	.022	.019	.019	.024
	(.002)	(.001)	(.001)	(.002)	(.002)	(.003)	(.003)
Exp.^{2}/100	−.065	−.047	−.036	−.028	−.023	−.026	−.037
	(.004)	(.003)	(.003)	(.004)	(.005)	(.006)	(.006)
Years of schooling:							
10	.189	.088	.095	.071	.089	.114	.088
	(.022)	(.019)	(.017)	(.022)	(.026)	(.031)	(.034)
11	.189	.077	.104	.149	.122	.193	.140
	(.028)	(.019)	(.015)	(.020)	(.024)	(.028)	(.028)
12	.292	.164	.142	.162	.133	.167	.154
	(.033)	(.022)	(.016)	(.023)	(.026)	(.031)	(.030)
13	.452	.221	.216	.198	.197	.264	.216
	(.039)	(.024)	(.019)	(.024)	(.027)	(.031)	(.031)
14	.571	.277	.268	.302	.236	.279	.276
	(.041)	(.026)	(.021)	(.025)	(.029)	(.034)	(.035)
15	.669	.398	.274	.313	.335	.336	.346
	(.047)	(.031)	(.026)	(.026)	(.032)	(.039)	(.041)
16	.878	.449	.346	.358	.371	.384	.411
	(.057)	(.036)	(.028)	(.035)	(.037)	(.045)	(.046)
17	.975	.616	.400	.367	.400	.468	.399
	(.076)	(.045)	(.031)	(.038)	(.045)	(.048)	(.045)
18+	.920	.614	.414	.446	.421	.541	.431
	(.058)	(.035)	(.025)	(.034)	(.041)	(.046)	(.046)
N	2,957	3,009	3,431	1,629	1,818	1,537	1,323
R^2	.405	.348	.283	.352	.234	.225	.246
σ_ε	.353	.291	.264	.246	.301	.326	.306

Note: Standard errors are in parentheses. 18–65-year-olds excluding the self-employed. The 1968, 1974, and 1981 results refer to the LNU sample, and 1984, 1986, 1988, and 1991 are from the HUS sample. Definitions of the variables are given in the text.

Table 9.2 shows the estimates for the seven samples. We see that the absolute values of the estimated coefficients decrease in most cases between 1968 and 1984. This is consistent with the strong tendencies toward wage compression during this period. The gender wage differential is almost halved during this period, the experience profiles become much more flat, and the returns to education fall. The picture after 1984 is much less clear-cut. There are some tendencies toward increasing differentials, but these changes are relatively small. Note also that the explanatory power of the wage equation, measured in terms of R^2, falls markedly after 1984. It is also worth noting that the standard deviation of the residual follows the same time pattern as overall wage dispersion.[7]

Before turning to a decomposition of the overall changes in wage dispersion, we take a closer look at wage differentials by education and age. These dimensions of wage inequality will receive additional attention in subsequent sections. Figure 9.4 shows the returns to higher education in terms of the university-gymnasium (college–high school) log wage premium, calculated from table 9.2 above as the wage differential between workers with sixteen and twelve years of education. Our estimated wage equations imply dramatic changes in the returns to education. The estimates show a sharp decrease in the return to a university degree between 1968 and 1974 and a continued fall until 1984; after 1984 there is a slight recovery. A similar pattern is found if the model is estimated with dummies for education levels instead of dummies for years of schooling.[8] We also plot the university-gymnasium wage differential from another data source. This series refers to monthly salaries for male, full-time, white-collar workers in mining, manufacturing, and construction. This series confirms the basic pattern from our wage equations. Using the wage difference between fifteen and twelve years of schooling from table 9.2 above as our measure of the university wage premium, we obtain a series that closely follows the "manufacturing" data.

Table 9.2 also revealed a substantial flattening of the experience-earnings profile. This profile is of course closely related to the age-earnings profile. Table 9.3 reports some results from estimations of wage equations where the experience variables are replaced by age dummies. The table gives the estimated log wage differentials for different groups, along with the corresponding wage ratio, relative to prime-age workers (aged thirty-five to forty-four years). The relative wage of eighteen- to nineteen-year-olds increased dramatically from about 55 percent of prime-age wages in 1968 to almost 80 percent in 1986. After 1986 there is a moderate drop in the relative wage of eighteen- to nineteen-year-olds by about 6 percentage points. The relative wage of twenty- to twenty-four-year-olds has been much more stable around 80 percent, with a minor increase between 1968 and 1974.

To what extent can changes in productive characteristics and changes in returns to these characteristics account for the observed changes in wage dispersion? In table 9.4, we use the estimated equations in table 9.2 above to generate

---

7. One might argue that changes in the wage structure should be more visible for workers who have recently entered the labor market. Therefore, we have estimated similar wage equations for workers twenty-five to thirty-four years old. These estimates show a similar development over time, but the estimates are in general much less precise, especially in 1986, 1988, and 1991. (The estimates are available from the authors on request.)

8. As a check for quality changes among university graduates, we estimated the seven wage equations separately for the cohort aged twenty-five to thirty-four years in 1968. These estimates show the same basic patterns as the full samples, thus providing no evidence for substantial quality changes.

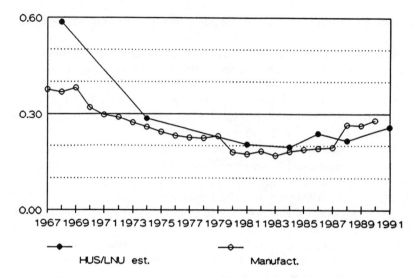

Fig. 9.4   University-gymnasium log wage differentials, 1967–91
Sources: Calculations based on table 9.2 (16 vs. 12 years of education) and Statistics Sweden.

the dispersion in predicted wages. The first panel shows that changes in the *characteristics* of the samples, weighted by the 1968 wage equation, are unable to account for the changing pattern of wage dispersion over time. If anything, the changes in sample characteristics would have produced *increasing* wage dispersion between 1968 and 1984, that is, during the period when the actual wage dispersion was dramatically reduced. In the second panel, we find that the changing *returns* to different characteristics produce a strong trend decline in dispersion (using characteristics of the 1968 sample as weights).[9] The standard deviation of predicted log wages falls from 0.29 in 1968 to 0.16 in 1981 and stays roughly constant thereafter. This decrease corresponds to almost 88 percent of the overall decrease in wage dispersion between 1968 and 1981 of 14.5 log points.[10]

In conclusion, then, we have shown that the substantial pay compression that took place during the 1960s and 1970s has been partly reversed during the second half of the 1980s. Wage compression in the earlier period was mainly due to decreasing dispersion between gender-experience-education groups, while the recent increase in dispersion has to a larger extent taken place within

9. The results are qualitatively the same if we use the 1991 characteristics and wage equations as weights.

10. A similar pattern is found for the young worker sample, with more than a 50 percent decrease in wage dispersion from 1968 (0.231) to 1981 (0.108). Also in this case we see a break in the trend after 1981; in fact, there is an *increase* in the standard deviation of predicted log wages during the 1980s. The predicted wage dispersion of young workers is almost as high in 1991 as in 1974 if we use the 1968 sample as weights. However, given the small number of observations (and low precision) in the young worker sample, these figures should be interpreted with caution.

groups. We have also shown that the earnings of young workers rose dramatically until the mid-1980s and that the return to higher education has changed sharply over time, closely mimicking the trends in overall wage dispersion.

9.3 Alternative Explanations

9.3.1 Demand and Supply Factors

Why have wage differentials in Sweden been reduced from the mid-1960s up to the early 1980s, and why are they widening from the mid-1980s? We

Table 9.3   Youth Wage Differentials (vs. 35–44 years)

	18–19		20–24		25–34	
	$\hat{\beta}$	Ratio	$\hat{\beta}$	Ratio	$\hat{\beta}$	Ratio
1968	−.605	.546	−.274	.760	−.073	.930
	(.035)		(.023)		(.020)	
1974	−.575	.563	−.224	.799	−.070	.932
	(.032)		(.020)		(.015)	
1981	−.396	.673	−.199	.820	−.105	.900
	(.031)		(.017)		(.013)	
1984	−.406	.663	−.220	.802	−.121	.886
	(.071)		(.026)		(.017)	
1986	−.229	.795	−.221	.802	−.052	.949
	(.056)		(.030)		(.020)	
1988	−.272	.762	−.186	.830	−.093	.911
	(.059)		(.036)		(.023)	
1991	−.303	.738	−.215	.806	−.077	.926
	(.087)		(.040)		(.028)	

Note: The estimates are based on wage equations with dummies for education, gender, and age (18–19, 20–24, 25–34, 45–54, 55–65). Ratio is the relative wage calculated as $\exp(\hat{\beta})$. Standard errors are in parentheses.

Table 9.4   Standard Deviation of Predicted Log Wages

	$\hat{\beta}_{68}$			X_{68}
X_{68}	.290		$\hat{\beta}_{68}$	.290
X_{74}	.314		$\hat{\beta}_{74}$	.200
X_{81}	.328		$\hat{\beta}_{81}$	.163
X_{84}	.351		$\hat{\beta}_{84}$	.179
X_{86}	.346		$\hat{\beta}_{86}$	.164
X_{88}	.349		$\hat{\beta}_{88}$	.165
X_{91}	.353		$\hat{\beta}_{91}$	.171

Note: The left panel shows the standard deviation of predicted log wages using the 1968 estimates for all samples, while the right panel shows the standard deviation when estimates for different years are applied to the 1968 sample.

begin our investigation by examining how far conventional demand and supply factors can explain movements in wage differentials by education and age. We make use of a variety of data sources that provide time-series variation in relative wages as well as potential explanatory variables, including the seven micro-data sets that were used in the previous section.

A simple theoretical framework is illustrated in figure 9.5. Consider two types of workers, for example, young (y) and adult (a) workers. The number of potential labor force participants in the two categories is denoted L_y and L_a, respectively. Effective supply is lower than potential supply because of frictional unemployment and other kinds of nonparticipation. Let effective supply be given as $N_y = v L_y W_y^\eta$ and $N_a = \mu L_a W_a^\eta$, where W_y and W_a are real-wage rates. Effective relative supply is then obtained as $N_y/N_a = (v/\mu)(L_y/L_a)(W_y/W_a)^\eta$. As drawn, the figure implies $\eta = 0$. The downward-sloping curve represents a relative demand schedule that is compatible with a production function of the CES variety. Equilibrium obtains where relative demand (D_r) equals effective relative supply (S_r).

Suppose that wages are flexible, and consider an increase in the potential relative supply of young workers. If the effective relative supply is independent of the relative wage, as implied by figure 9.5, we obtain a relative wage response to the increase in relative supply as given by the elasticity $-1/\sigma$, where σ is the (constant) elasticity of substitution between young and adult workers. The relative employment response is in this case equal to one, implying that

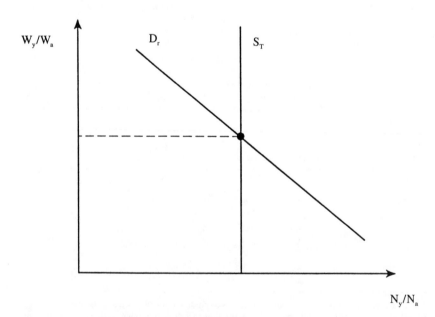

Fig. 9.5   The determination of relative wages

employment–to–labor force ratios remain constant. These wage and employment responses are modified when the relative supply depends on the relative wage. Suppose that the effective relative supply is wage elastic, with η denoting the (constant) elasticity. The market-clearing wage response to an exogenous increase in the potential supply is then given by the elasticity $-1/(\sigma + \eta)$, whereas the employment elasticity is given as $\sigma/(\sigma + \eta)$.

We apply this simple framework to an analysis of wage differentials by education and age categories. The key exogenous variable on the supply side is potential relative supply. We take relative labor force shares as exogenous in the analysis of education wage differentials. (The results are almost identical if relative population shares are used instead of relative labor force shares.) Participation decisions among youths are, however, sensitive to labor market conditions and schooling opportunities, so relative labor force shares may fail to be exogenous with respect to relative wages. Relative population shares are therefore taken as exogenous in the analysis of age-earnings differentials.

Educational Wage Differentials

We have documented a substantial fall and a subsequent partial rebound of the university wage premium, that is, the relative wage differential between university and high school graduates. Movements in the university wage premium can usefully be interpreted as the outcome of shifts in the relative supply of and relative demand for highly educated workers or—to use the terminology of Tinbergen (1975)—the "race" between education and technology. To the extent that market forces have been of importance in forming the Swedish wage structure, the market for university graduates should have been particularly responsive. The direct influence of union egalitarianism has most likely been least pervasive at the upper end of the wage distribution.

There is a common presumption that technological progress is associated with a steady increase in the relative demand for highly educated labor. Direct evidence on this matter is meager, however. We have confined ourselves to examining the role of sectoral shifts in employment by making use of simple "fixed manpower requirements" models. (For similar applications, see Freeman 1980; and Katz and Murphy 1992.) The two data sets at hand are far from ideal, but they both tell a similar story. One data set is based on the labor force surveys and captures the whole economy but has little industrial detail (only seven sectors including the public sector). The other data set describes mining and manufacturing, with a disaggregation into forty-four industries. Education by sector data are available in the labor force surveys from 1971 on; for mining and manufacturing we have education by industry data for 1970 and 1985. We use four education categories: (i) primary education (education levels below gymnasium); (ii) secondary education (gymnasium one to three years); (iii) some university (one to two years); and (iv) university (three years or more). The basic formula yielding the relative demand for education category k at time t is

(1) $$D_{kt} = \sum_{j} a_{kj}(N_j/N)_t,$$

where N_j is employment in sector j, N is total employment, and $a_{kj} = N_{kj}/N_j$ is the fixed labor skill coefficient calculated as the ratio of the number of workers in education k and industry j to total employment in industry j. For mining and manufacturing we compute the labor skill coefficients as averages of the coefficients for 1970 and 1985. For the whole economy we make use of three years—1971, 1984, and 1991—to obtain measures of skill coefficients.

The results of these computations, expressed as annualized percentage changes, are displayed in table 9.5. The basic pattern is that the relative demand for highly educated workers grows at a *slower* pace during the late 1980s than during the 1970s and the early 1980s. This pattern differs from what has been observed in Britain and the United States, where skill-biased demand shifts are of the same order of magnitude in the 1980s as in the 1970s (see Katz and Murphy 1992; and Katz, Loveman, and Blanchflower, chap. 1 in this volume). Our results thus suggest that sectoral shifts offer little help in explaining the observed movements in the university wage premium. Measured changes in the allocation of labor among industries seem to have been *less* favorable to more educated workers during the period of rising returns to university education. This is clearly inconsistent with a simple demand-side explanation of the changes in the university wage premium.

Turning next to the supply side, two distinct patterns in the data are required in order to explain observed movements in the wage differentials (absent obvious explanatory power from the demand side). There must be a trend increase in the relative supply of highly educated workers during a period lasting roughly from the 1960s to the early 1980s; the sharp fall in the university wage premium would otherwise be difficult to explain by conventional market forces. There must also be a pronounced *deceleration* in this relative supply growth in order to explain the rebound of the returns to higher education since the mid-1980s. In fact, both these patterns do appear in the data.

Table 9.5   Demand Shift Indices, 1970–91

	Mining and Manufacturing (44 sectors)		All Industries (7 sectors)	
	1970–84	1984–90	1971–84	1984–91
Primary education	−.18	−.01	−.56	−.32
Secondary education	.20	.04	.05	.14
Some university (1–2 years)	.61	−.01	1.13	.36
University (3 years or more)	.83	−.22	1.44	.43

Sources: Own computations based on eq. (1) using unpublished tables from Statistics Sweden (mining and manufacturing) and the labor force surveys (all industries). The table shows annualized percentage changes in relative demand.

Figure 9.6 displays the labor force shares of three main categories of education—primary, secondary, and higher education—over the period 1971–91. The period is clearly characterized by a steady increase in the level of education. Those with only primary education constitute less than 30 percent of the labor force in the early 1990s. The fraction with higher (at least some university) education has more than doubled since the early 1970s.

A closer look at the relative supply changes is provided by table 9.6 and figure 9.7. The labor force share of university graduates (with university education for at least three years) has increased steadily up to the mid-1980s; the share stays roughly *constant*, however, during the second half of the 1980s and up to the early 1990s.

The decline and subsequent rebound of the university wage premium thus seems consistent with a simple explanation emphasizing relative supply movements. The ratio between the number of labor force participants with a university degree and the number with (three years of) gymnasium stood at 0.48 in 1971 and reached 0.90 in the mid-1980s; by 1991 the ratio had declined to 0.80. The university wage premium, obtained from the estimated wage equations in table 9.2 above, is negatively correlated with the relative supply of university graduates. The negative relation between relative wages and relative supplies appears consistent with a simple model with stable relative demand and fluctuating relative supply. There are only seven data points, however, and one would like to see corroborating evidence from other sources. This leads us

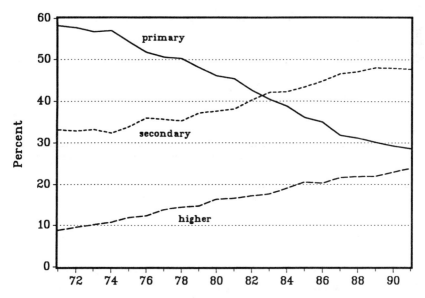

Fig. 9.6   Education in the Swedish labor force, 1971–91
Source: The labor force surveys, Statistics Sweden.

Table 9.6   **Relative Supply Changes by Education, 1972–91**

	1972–74	1975–80	1981–84	1985–91	1972–91
Primary	−.39	−1.82	−1.82	−1.46	−1.48
	(−.67)	(−3.55)	(−4.30)	(−4.37)	(−3.56)
Some gymnasium (1–2 years)	−.47	.91	.80	.50	.54
	(−2.19)	(3.89)	(2.89)	(1.59)	(1.97)
Gymnasium (3 years)	.20	−.04	.35	.28	.19
	(1.74)	(−.38)	(2.93)	(2.06)	(1.46)
Some university (1–2 years)	.23	.53	.18	.57	.43
	(6.09)	(9.62)	(2.38)	(5.77)	(6.29)
University (3 years or more)	.43	.42	.48	.11	.33
	(7.36)	(5.38)	(4.81)	(.99)	(4.02)

Source: The labor force surveys, Statistics Sweden.

Note: The figures are mean annual changes of labor force shares, multiplied by 100; the parentheses show mean annual changes of *log* shares, multiplied by 100.

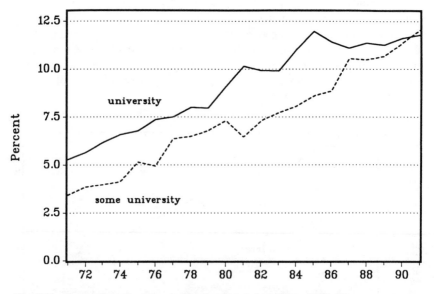

Fig. 9.7   University education in the Swedish labor force, 1971–91
Source: The labor force surveys, Statistics Sweden.

to an examination of movements in the university wage premium within Swedish industry (mining, manufacturing, and construction).

Statistics on private-sector, white-collar workers' salaries, disaggregated by education, are available in official statistics from the late 1960s (see fig. 9.4 above). There is a pronounced decline in the university wage premium from the late 1960s to the early 1980s followed by a rise in the late 1980s, similar to the pattern found in our micro data. We take the private-sector university wage premium as a proxy for the corresponding economy-wide differential and apply the simple relative demand–relative supply framework, including a time trend to allow for shifts in relative demand. Table 9.7 displays the regression results. The simple model is remarkably successful in explaining the relative wage movements. The estimated elasticity with respect to relative supply in column 2 suggests an elasticity of substitution between university and high school graduates of 2.9 (assuming wage-inelastic relative supply). Available evidence from other countries suggests elasticities of substitution between highly educated and less educated workers of between one and two (see Freeman 1986). It is noteworthy that the regressions in the last two columns, based on only seven data points, produce estimates of the relative supply effect that are of a similar order of magnitude. The positive trend coefficients in columns 2 and 3 suggest that secular demand shifts have favored highly educated workers.

Youth Relative Wages

Our estimated wage equations have revealed a substantial fall in the returns to experience from the late 1960s. This has implied rising relative wages

Table 9.7   **The University Wage Premium and Relative Supply: Dependent Variable, $\ln(W_u/W_g)$**

| | Industry | | | All Sectors (68, 74, 81, 84, 86, 88, 91) | |
| | 1971–90 | | 1972–90 | 16–12 Years | 15–12 Years |
	(1)	(2)	(3)	(4)	(5)
Constant	.179	.024	−.026	.144	.124
	(13.40)	(.73)	(.72)	(4.50)	(7.08)
$\ln(L_u/L_g)$	−.143	−.350	−.251	−.429	−.259
	(4.16)	(7.33)	(4.33)	(5.73)	(6.29)
$\ln(L_u/L_g)_{-1}$			−.155		
			(2.45)		
Time		.008	.011		
		(4.93)	(5.88)		
$\bar{R}^2$	.462	.765	.790	.842	.865
SE	.031	.020	.018	.055	.030
D-W	.49	2.27	2.35		

Note: Absolute *t*-values are in parentheses. The dependent variable in cols. 1–3 is the university/ gymnasium log wage differential among male white-collar workers in mining, manufacturing, and construction. The dependent variables in the last two columns are the estimated university/ gymnasium log wage differentials obtained from table 9.2, 16 vs. 12 years and 15 vs. 12 years of schooling. $L_u(L_g)$ is the number of labor force participants with university (gymnasium) education. The relative supply figure for 1968 is imputed by using the figure for 1971 and assuming that the change in L_u/L_g over the period 1968–71 is the same as the observed change over the period 1971–74.

among youths in the labor market, as is evident from table 9.3 above. The relative wage improvement is particularly striking for teenagers; the wage of eighteen- to nineteen-year-olds relative to thirty-five- to forty-four-year-olds rose from 55 percent in 1968 to 80 percent in 1986, with some decline over the following years.

To what extent can these movements in youth relative wages be explained by relative supply changes, assuming smooth and possibly nonneutral demand shifts? The youth labor market in postwar Sweden, as well as in many other countries, has been exposed to substantial demographic shocks (cf. Freeman and Bloom 1986). The timing of the baby boomers' impact is illustrated in figure 9.8 by the number of eighteen- to nineteen-year-olds. The size of this age group peaked in the mid-1960s and decreased substantially between 1965 and 1980. The second wave of large youth cohorts entered the labor market in the mid-1980s, and there are noticeable fluctuations in the number of youths over the late 1980s and up to 1991.

The marked fluctuations in the size of the youth cohorts translate into substantial changes in relative population ratios. The period of rising youth relative wages coincides with a trend decline in the relative youth population. The ratio of eighteen- to nineteen-year-olds relative to thirty-five- to forty-four-year-olds declined from .25 to .19 over the period 1968–86. By regressing the estimated log wage differentials in table 9.3 on the corresponding log relative population ratios, we obtain for the eighteen- to nineteen-year-olds an estimated coeffi-

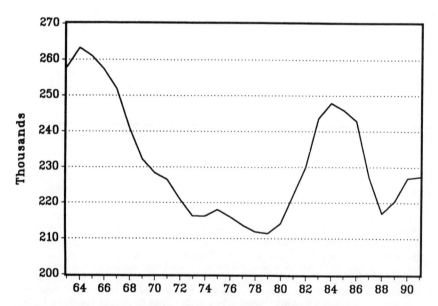

Fig. 9.8   The number of 18–19-year-olds in the population, 1963–91
Source: The labor force surveys, Statistics Sweden.

cient on the relative supply variable of -0.96 with a t-value of 6.2. For twenty- to twenty-four-year-olds the corresponding relative supply elasticity is -0.12 with a t-value of 2.5. These estimates have the reasonable implication that twenty- to twenty-four-year-olds are closer substitutes to prime-age workers than eighteen- to nineteen-year-olds are. The results are encouraging and suggest that explorations of other data sources may be worthwhile.

We make use of time series on youth relative wages in mining and manufacturing over the period 1970–88.[11] In these data, youths are identified as those aged eighteen to twenty-four, whereas adults are those aged twenty-five to forty-nine. Table 9.8 presents the results of simple models with only two explanatory variables; the population ratios capture relative supply, and the trend captures everything else with a trend component, including relative quality changes and nonneutral demand shifts. For three of the four groups we obtain sizable negative estimates of the relative supply effect. The exception is young female blue-collar workers, whose relative wages have shown a continuous upward trend over the whole period.

Our examination of wage differentials by age thus leads to the same basic conclusion as the analysis of educational wage differentials: relative wage fluctuations seem to be driven by fluctuations in relative supply. It is clear, however, that the estimated models have been extremely simple and allowed only for "own effects" in the quantity-to-wage link. This means that the particular estimates are unlikely to survive a more elaborate modeling of factor demand systems. The magnitudes of the estimated relative supply effects are plausible, however, and usually not very different from estimates obtained in other studies.

Gender Wage Differentials

From 1968 to 1981 we also observe a remarkable increase in the relative wage of females. This has occurred simultaneously with a large increase in the female labor supply (table 9.9). After 1981 the gender wage gap has been more or less stable at the same time as the growth of female relative supply has gone down. There are several factors that may help explain these movements in relative wages and relative supply, such as the abolishment of separate female wage scales by SAF and LO in the early 1960s, the introduction of separate taxation for spouses between 1965 and 1971, the changing rules and benefits for maternity leave, and the increasing supply of public day care. We will not go into details about the possible explanations, however. It will be sufficient here to highlight one factor, namely, demand. Applying the fixed manpower requirements model, and calculating the relative demand for females for the whole economy (using seven sectors), we get the demand changes reported in table 9.9. Measured relative demand for females increased sharply between 1968 and 1981. During the 1980s, in contrast, we find no changes in

11. We are grateful to Per Skedinger for providing these data. For details, see Skedinger (1990).

Table 9.8   **Youth Relative Wages and Relative Population Ratios (18–24 vs. 25–49 years), 1970–88: Dependent Variable, $\ln(W_y/W_a)$**

	Blue-Collar Workers			White-Collar Workers			
	Males		Females	Males		Females	
	(1)	(2)	(3)	(4)	(5)	(6)	(7)
Constant	−.397	−.507	−.124	−.805	−.778	−.763	−.801
	(9.95)	(3.25)	(3.45)	(10.34)	(4.47)	(10.61)	(6.32)
$\ln(P_y/P_a)$	−.201	−.291	−.028	−.241	−.215	−.378	−.407
	(5.71)	(2.28)	(.89)	(3.52)	(1.47)	(5.97)	(3.78)
Time	.003	.003	.002	.002	.003	−.0009	−.0008
	(6.99)	(3.42)	(4.91)	(2.91)	(2.09)	(1.15)	(.72)
$\bar{R}^2$	.945	.947	.788	.811	.819	.760	.745
SE	.007	.006	.006	.014	.012	.012	.012
D-W	1.03	1.95	1.44	1.02	1.47	1.24	1.82
AR(1)	No	Yes	No	No	Yes	No	Yes

Note: For details on the wage variables, which refer to mining and manufacturing, see Skedinger (1990). The population series refer to both males and females and are obtained from the labor force surveys. Absolute *t*-values are in parentheses.

Table 9.9   **Changes in Female Relative Wages, Relative Demand and Supply**

	$\Delta \ln (W_f/W_m)$	$\Delta \ln D_f$	$\Delta \ln (L_f/L_m)$
1968–74	.057	.084	.152
1974–81	.057	.069	.170
1981–84	.023	.018	.039
1984–91	−.010	−.012	.041

Note: $\Delta \ln (W_f/W_m)$ is the change in the standardized female relative wage, as implied by table 9.2. $\Delta \ln D_f$ is the measured change in relative demand for female labor, applying eq. (1) to data from the labor force surveys, and using the average weights (a_{kj}) for 1968, 1981, and 1991. $\Delta \ln (L_f/L_m)$ is the change in female/male shares of the labor force from the labor force surveys.

relative demand. This development is partly driven by the rapid growth of public-sector employment during the 1970s and the subsequent deceleration of public-sector expansion during the 1980s. The demand pattern is strikingly similar to the relative wage pattern of females. Clearly, relative demand shifts for female labor is a factor that cannot be overlooked in an investigation of gender wage differentials in Sweden.

9.3.2   Institutional Factors

Egalitarianism became a pervasive ingredient of LO's solidarity wage bargaining from the mid-1960s through the 1970s. The policy was implemented through central framework agreements with low-wage provisions. TCO's egalitarian ambitions were always less explicit than LO's, but there is little doubt that the unions within TCO adhered to wage policies that were largely similar to those of LO.

Wage bargaining within the LO-SAF area from 1956 to 1983 took place at three levels, namely, the national, the industry, and the local plant levels. The central frame agreement typically involved three components: (i) a common flat rate amount specified in öre; (ii) a wage-drift guarantee with the purpose of compensating workers who received no or only small pay rises in excess of the contractual increase; and (iii) a low-wage adjustment amount targeted at workers whose actual hourly wages were lower than a specified reference level (the low-wage boundary). In addition, cost-of-living adjustments, typically on a flat rate basis, were negotiated in some of the frame contracts.

Hibbs (1990) has simulated the wage distribution implied by complete implementation of the frame agreement in the LO-SAF area. His main finding is that the trend decline in the actual dispersion from the early 1970s to the early 1980s is closely tracked by the frame dispersion. The frame always implied a more compressed wage structure than the actual outcome, however; on average, around 80 percent of the frame compression was achieved. Hibbs's results are striking, but they give no information on whether the frame agreements were compatible with the fundamental demand and supply forces. For example, we have seen that the market environment during the 1970s favored rising youth relative wages, which surely explains part of the decline in overall dispersion among LO workers.

We have not attempted any detailed examination of the sources of the reduced wage dispersion among LO workers to ascertain to what extent the wage agreements have conformed to demand and supply factors. It seems implausible, however, to rule out any independent role for egalitarian union wage policies. Solidarity wage bargaining is closely linked to coordinated wage negotiations, and centralized wage negotiations were effectively dismantled from 1983 on. If the changes in the wage-bargaining system are more substance than form, we should expect to find significant changes in wage behavior over the second half of the 1980s.

We address the issue of institutional changes by offering a brief analysis of wage determination at the industry and regional levels. One issue is whether the breakdown of centralized wage bargaining has made industry wages more responsive to industry-specific factors. Earlier work has indicated that industry-specific factors such as output prices or productivity have a negligible effect on industry wages in Sweden (Holmlund and Zetterberg 1991; Forslund 1992, 1994). If centralization matters, one would expect to see more scope for rent sharing as the system becomes more decentralized.

We have estimated simple industry wage equations to explore whether sectoral variables become more important after 1983. We make use of pooled time-series and cross-sectional data for twenty-eight industries within Swedish manufacturing, covering the period 1963–89.[12] The hourly wage rate pertains to blue-collar workers. The basic idea is to view the industry wage as shaped by a blend of industry-specific variables and general labor market variables as in studies by, among others, Blanchflower, Oswald, and Garrett (1989), Nickell and Wadhwani (1990), Holmlund and Zetterberg (1991), and Forslund (1992, 1994). We expect that the shift to more decentralized wage bargaining has increased the importance of the industry-specific variables, here captured by (lagged) profits per employee. The general labor market variables are captured by time dummies.

Table 9.10 presents the results of estimations of error correction type specifications, where the change in the log wage rate of the industry ($\Delta \ln W_{it}$) is explained by the lagged dependent variable, the lagged wage *level,* as well as the lagged profit variable. The latter is defined as $R_{it} = (\text{VA}_{it} - \text{WT}_{it})/E_{it}$, where VA is value added, WT is the total wage bill in the industry, and E is the total number of employees. (WT and E include both blue- and white-collar workers.) The second column includes dummy interaction terms to test the hypothesis that sectoral variables have become more important as a result of the shift to industry bargaining. There is some evidence in favor of the hypothesis. The coefficient on the lagged profit variable is significantly larger during the period 1983–89 than during the earlier years, suggesting an increasing albeit small role for rent sharing during the latter part of the 1980s.

A more decentralized wage-bargaining system may also make regional wages more responsive to regional labor market conditions. Some evidence on this matter can be obtained from a different data source pertaining to regional wages. We use pooled cross-sectional and time-series data for twenty-four regions (*län*) over the period 1966–89 (see Jansson and Östros 1991). We allow for regional fixed effects as well as time dummies. The major difference compared to the industry wage equations is that we include a measure of regional labor market tightness, the difference between the vacancy rate and the unemployment rate $(V - U)$ in the region (as a percentage of the labor force). Measures of firms' performance are not available, however. Table 9.11 gives the results. Regional wages do respond to changes in tightness, but the effect is quantitatively small. There is no evidence that wages have become more responsive after 1983, as is clear from column 2 in the table.

The basic message that emerges from these analyses of industry and regional wage behavior is that the changes in the wage-bargaining system have so far had only weak effects on wage behavior at the sectoral level. The effect that can be identified suggests an increasing role for rent sharing, as should be expected.

One piece of evidence that may indicate that the wage policy has been important is the behavior of residual wage dispersion. As was observed in connection with table 9.2 above, residual dispersion followed a time pattern that was

---

12. This is an updated version of the data set used in Holmlund and Zetterberg (1991).

Table 9.10   **Industry Wage Equations, 1965–89: Dependent Variable, $\Delta \ln W_{it}$**

	(1)	(2)
$\ln W_{i,t-1}$	−.222	−.248
	(7.97)	(8.66)
$\Delta \ln W_{i,t-1}$	−.271	−.263
	(7.01)	(6.85)
$\ln R_{i,t-1}$	.005	.001
	(1.17)	(.34)
D8389 · $\ln R_{i,t-1}$		.009
		(3.42)
$\bar{R}^2$	.605	.611
SE	.020	.020

Note: Absolute *t*-values are in parentheses. D8389 is a dummy for the period 1983–89. Full sets of time dummies and industry dummies are included. There are 700 observations.

Table 9.11   **Regional Wage Equations, 1966–89: Dependent Variable, $\Delta \ln W_{it}$**

	(1)	(2)
$\ln W_{i,t-1}$	−.138	−.138
	(7.50)	(7.48)
$\Delta(V - U)_{i,t-1}$	.002	.002
	(3.16)	(3.18)
$(V - U)_{i,t-1}$	.002	.002
	(2.24)	(2.25)
D8389 · $\Delta(V - U)_{i,t}$		−.001
		(.72)
D8389 · $(V - U)_{i,t-1}$		−.0002
		(.17)
$\bar{R}^2$	.883	.882
SE	.009	.009

Note: Absolute *t*-values are in parentheses. D8389 is a dummy for the period 1983–89. Full sets of time dummies and regional dummies are included. U and V are measured in percentages. There are 576 observations.

similar to overall dispersion. We do not have obvious candidates for supply shifts that can explain this fact. Other studies indicate that a substantial part of this decreasing within-group dispersion was associated with decreasing wage differentials between industries (Arai 1991; Edin and Zetterberg 1992).

9.4   The Performance of the Labor Market for Youths

Economists and other observers have expected to see a deterioration in youth labor market performance as a response to institutionally driven increases in youth relative wages. Our analysis, however, suggests that movements in wage differentials by age are largely consistent with a simple demand and supply framework with flexible wages. The trend increase as well as the subsequent modest decline in youth relative wages can be accounted for by changes in the relative supply of young workers. This view also implies that youth relative *employment* should adjust to changes in the relative size of the youth population. This section examines this hypothesis, along with other aspects of youth labor market performance. The evidence that emerges is somewhat mixed, but severe distortions are difficult to establish.

We have noted sharp increases in youth relative wages over the 1970s and the 1980s (see table 9.3 above). The relative wage increases have been particularly strong for eighteen- to nineteen-year-olds, whereas the relative wages of twenty- to twenty-four-year-olds have increased only modestly. If youth relative wages can be explained by demand and supply forces, we should also expect youth relative employment shares to be highly responsive to movements in youth relative population shares. Youth relative employment should in fact be unit elastic with respect to relative population if relative supply is wage inelastic. If the youth labor market is characterized by rigid relative wages, perhaps owing to negotiated minimum wages, we should on the other hand expect only weak employment responses to population changes. These responses should in that case be particularly weak among eighteen- to nineteen-year-olds as relative wage increases have been most dramatic for this group.

Table 9.12 presents results of relative employment regressions of the form

(2) $$\ln(N_y/N_a) = \alpha + \beta \ln(P_y/P_a) + \gamma U + \varepsilon,$$

Table 9.12   **Youth Relative Employment and Relative Population Ratios, 1964–91: Dependent Variable, $\ln(N_y/N_a)$**

	Males 18–19		Males 20–24		Females 18–19		Females 20–24	
	(1)	(2)	(3)	(4)	(5)	(6)	(7)	(8)
Constant	−.675	−.848	−.469	−.486	.307	.914	.912	−.163
	(.99)	(1.61)	(8.05)	(5.45)	(.33)	(1.97)	(.142)	(1.19)
$\ln(P_y/P_a)$	.859	.730	.768	.754	1.225	1.310	.825	.766
	(3.51)	(3.28)	(19.47)	(11.99)	(3.72)	(6.66)	(5.86)	(7.32)
	[.58]	[1.21]	[5.95]	[3.57]	[.68]	[1.57]	[1.24]	[2.23]
U	−.065	−.060	−.030	−.030	−.053	−.065	−.022	−.026
	(4.37)	(4.12)	(6.09)	(5.97)	(2.74)	(3.73)	(2.42)	(3.06)
Time		−.007		−.0003		−.013		−.012
		(1.52)		(.24)		(4.77)		(8.42)
$\bar{R}^2$	.941	.944	.986	.985	.973	.978	.985	.989
SE	.032	.031	.011	.011	.043	.038	.022	.019
D-W	2.31	2.15	1.32	1.32	2.50	1.94	2.69	1.82

Note: All estimations allow for first-order autocorrelated errors. Absolute *t*-values are in parentheses and brackets; tests for coefficients equal to unity are in brackets. The unemployment rate (U) is measured in percentages.

Table 9.13   **The Youth Labor Market, 1968–91 (%)**

		Unemployment Rate				Employment/Population			
		Males		Females		Males		Females	
	All, 16–64	18–19	20–24	18–19	20–24	18–19	20–24	18–19	20–24
1968	2.2	5.8	3.0	4.6	3.0	62.4	75.3	61.3	61.7
1974	2.0	4.3	2.7	7.4	3.2	64.9	78.5	60.6	68.3
1981	2.5	7.6	4.8	9.9	4.7	62.1	79.5	62.2	78.8
1984	3.1	5.0	6.2	3.9	6.6	57.3	77.7	61.8	74.8
1986	2.7	4.2	6.3	4.1	6.2	58.6	76.4	61.5	75.8
1988	1.6	2.3	3.3	3.3	3.4	60.8	81.4	64.5	78.0
1991	2.7	7.5	6.7	6.8	5.8	53.0	77.2	59.1	73.8

Source: The labor force surveys, Statistics Sweden.

Note: The figures are not adjusted for the changes in measurement techniques introduced in 1987.

where N_y/N_a is relative youth/adult employment, P_y/P_a is relative population, and U is the aggregate unemployment rate. P_a is represented by the number of twenty-five- to forty-nine-year-olds. If the labor market is competitive and relative supply is wage inelastic, we expect $\beta = 1$. The alternative extreme case involves complete wage rigidity and $\beta = 0$. The unemployment rate is included to capture the possibility that the cyclic variability of the ratio of effective to potential supply varies among age groups.

The results displayed in table 9.12 show substantial employment responsiveness to population changes. The point estimates of β are typically lower than unity, but in most cases we cannot reject the hypothesis of complete employment adjustment, that is, $\beta = 1$. The exception is male twenty- to twenty-four-year-olds. There is no support for the hypothesis that teenage employment is particularly rigid with respect to population changes.

There is, however, some evidence indicating a deterioration in youth labor market performance. From the mid-1960s to the early 1980s there is a trend increase in youth unemployment rates and also a trend increase in youth relative to adult unemployment (tables 9.13 and 9.14). Youth participation in labor market programs has also increased, particularly during the mid-1980s. For example, over 10 percent of sixteen- to nineteen-year-olds were engaged in public employment programs in 1984.

Employment/population ratios among sixteen- to nineteen-year-olds have shown a trend decline since the 1960s (table 9.14). This is mainly due to a rise in school enrollment, however. There is a strong trend increase in school enrollment among teenagers, reflecting in part an expansion of the senior high school to provide (usually two years of) vocational training. School enrollment among sixteen- to nineteen-year-olds—measured as the number of full-time students as a percentage of the population—stood at 30 percent in the mid-

Table 9.14   Labor Market Activities and School Enrollment among
                    16–19-Year-Olds (%)

	U	LFPR	N/P	S/P	R/P	M/P	(N + S)/P	(N − R + S)/P
1968	5.7	54.6	51.4	32.8			84.2	
1974	6.6	55.2	51.6	32.7			84.3	
1981	9.4	49.7	45.1	41.3	1.5	1.8	86.4	84.9
1984	4.9	45.3	43.1	44.5	10.1	1.3	87.6	77.5
1986	4.1	45.0	43.2	47.3	7.3	.7	90.5	83.2
1988	3.1	47.3	45.9	49.3	4.0	.5	95.2	91.2
1991	6.7	44.7	41.7	51.2			92.9	

Source: The labor force surveys, Statistics Sweden, and the Swedish Labor Market Board.
Note: U = unemployment rate; LFPR = labor force participation ratio; P = population; N = employment; S = school enrollment; R = relief jobs (including youth jobs and youth teams); M = manpower training (including vocational introduction programs); N is inclusive of R; and S is inclusive of M.

1960s and had risen to 50 percent in the early 1990s. Column 7 of table 9.14 shows that the fraction of teenagers in employment or school has increased from 84 percent in 1968 to over 90 percent in the early 1990s. A similar picture emerges if employment is confined to "regular" employment by excluding workers in public employment programs (col. 8).

The evidence on the performance of the youth labor market is thus mixed. There is some increase in youth relative unemployment and/or youth participation in labor market programs. There is, however, also a trend rise in the proportion of teenagers engaged in "productive activities," that is, an increase in the share engaged in employment or education. Rising school enrollment has made the labor force participants among teenagers an increasingly selected group with relatively low educational attainment; this contributes to higher relative youth unemployment. Other institutional changes have worked in the same direction. There have, for example, been marked changes in the availability and levels of unemployment benefits; the Swedish unemployment insurance system was much more generous in the 1980s than in the 1960s (Björklund and Holmlund 1991). Labor market regulations, in particular the legislation on employment protection, may also have contributed to some increase in youth unemployment by making firms less likely to hire workers with little previous labor market experience.

9.5   The Returns to Education and School Enrollment

We have documented a sharp fall and a subsequent modest rebound of the university wage premium. How has the demand for higher education been affected by these movements? It should be noted that the university wage premium is an imperfect measure of the private gains from university education. The private internal rate of return is also affected by the progressivity of the tax system, by tuitions, and by the availability and generosity of student loans and stipends. The Swedish tax system became gradually less progressive in the late 1980s; a new comprehensive tax system was introduced in 1990–91 with roughly 50 percent as the top marginal tax rate on labor earnings. Swedish university students have had access to stipends and subsidized loans since the early 1960s. A new student loan system was introduced in 1989. A university student receives a monthly tax-free sum of approximately 70 percent of a blue-collar worker's average after-tax earnings; one-third of this sum is a pure stipend, and the remainder is a loan.

Accounting for taxes and subsidized student loans has a substantial effect on calculations of the private internal rate of return to university education. We have undertaken calculations based on the standard procedure of computing internal rates of return from a single cross section, thus ignoring general economic growth. We consider a man aged twenty who has left gymnasium and contemplates four years of university education. The estimated wage equations are used to calculate lifetime income profiles for the two alternatives assuming that retirement takes place at age sixty-five; the discount rate that equalizes the two paths is the private internal rate of return to university education. Any direct costs of education are ignored; tuition is essentially zero in Sweden, and other direct costs (books etc.) are probably offset by access to low-priced housing, drinking, and dancing. The first column of table 9.15 shows the rate of return unadjusted for taxes, and the second column accounts for taxes. The progressive tax system sharply reduced the return in the 1970s and early 1980s, while increasing wage differentials and lowered tax rates have increased the returns during recent years.

The calculations reported in table 9.15 do not account for stipends, which of course will lead to an underestimate of the returns to education. (We cannot compare the old and the new student loan systems in a meaningful way without making explicit assumptions about inflation.) For 1991 we have calculated the return to education assuming forward-looking expectations concerning·infla-

Table 9.15   **Internal Rates of Return to Higher Education, Males, 1968–91, Static Expectations (%)**

	Without Taxes	With Taxes
1968	15.7	11.9
1974	6.9	3.6
1981	4.3	.5
1984	3.9	1.7
1986	5.3	3.3
1988	4.7	2.7
1991	6.0	4.5

Note: The calculations are based on the estimated wage equations in table 9.2. The tax system that prevails in a particular year is assumed to remain intact over the individual's life cycle. The calculations do not account for stipends.

Table 9.16   **Internal Rates of Return to Higher Education, Males, 1991, Forward-Looking Expectations (%)**

	Without Taxes	With Taxes
No stipends or loans	7.0	6.6
Stipends and loans (8 percent interest rate)	9.8	11.0

Note: The calculations are based on the estimated wage equations in table 9.2. The 1991 tax system is assumed to remain intact over the individual's life cycle. The calculations are based on the assumptions of 4 percent annual nominal wage increases and a 3 percent rate of inflation.

tion and general economic growth. This allows for *shifts* of the cross-sectional age-earnings profiles as well as movements *along* a given profile. We assume 4 percent nominal wage increases and 3 percent inflation. The 1991 tax system is assumed to prevail during the full life cycle. This produces a 7 percent return to university education in the absence of taxes and stipends (table 9.16). The after-tax and after-stipend rate of return in 1991 is over 11 percent.[13]

To what extent can movements in the rates of return to education explain fluctuations in school enrollment? School enrollment among young adults has shown marked fluctuations, and there is a marked upward trend in the female enrollment rate (fig. 9.9). Enrollment peaked around 1968–71, declined during most of the 1970s, and started to rebound in the 1980s. Other data sources, capturing the number of students registered at the universities, show a similar pattern (see Fredriksson 1992). There is also a trend increase in school enrollment among prime-age individuals, presumably to a large extent driven by legislation permitting leaves of absence for education reasons.

It is tempting to relate fluctuations in the enrollment rate among young adults to our estimated rates of return to education. If the male enrollment rate is regressed on the after-tax rate of return (RoR), we obtain

$$\ln(\text{enrollment rate}) = 2.19 + 3.36 \cdot \text{RoR},$$
$$(5.33)$$

where RoR is given by the second column of table 9.15 above (divided by 100). The rate of return coefficient is highly significant ($t = 5.33$), and R^2 is 0.82. This is clearly consistent with the conventional wisdom that the demand for education is responsive to the prospective rates of return. It would be premature, however, to place much confidence on the particular estimate obtained from a crude specification using only seven data points. We have therefore also exploited another data source, namely, the time series on private-sector wage

13. The income tax system of 1991 has essentially two brackets. There is a large segment with a tax rate of roughly 30 percent. The marginal tax rate increases to 50 percent beyond a certain threshold. This threshold is indexed to inflation. It is also increased annually to prevent tax hikes owing to general economic growth (expected to be 2 percent per year). The rate of return would fall to 9 percent were the "real wage protection" rule of the tax system abolished.

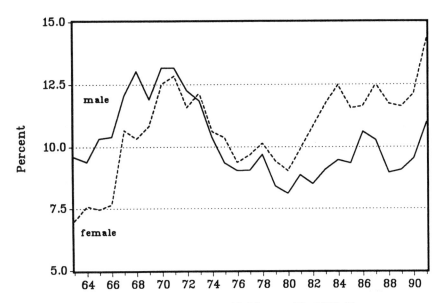

Fig. 9.9   School enrollment rates among 20–24-year-olds, 1963–91
Source: The labor force surveys, Statistics Sweden.

differentials between male university and high school graduates. The basic specification applied is

$$
(3) \qquad \ln(\text{enrollment rate}) = \alpha + \beta \ln\left[\frac{(1 - U_u)W_u(1 - \tau_u)}{(1 - U_g)W_g(1 - \tau_g)}\right] + \varepsilon,
$$

where U is the unemployment rate, W the monthly salary, and τ the average tax rate; the subscripts u and g denote university and gymnasium, respectively. The independent variable can be thought of as the expected after-tax university wage premium. A higher unemployment risk among university graduates reduces the expected returns to higher education; a higher unemployment rate among gymnasium graduates increases the relative attractiveness of higher education. Unemployment among university graduates is represented by the unemployment rate in the unemployment insurance fund of university graduates (*Akademikernas arbetslöshetskassa*), whereas unemployment pertaining to the gymnasium category is represented by the unemployment rate among male twenty- to twenty-four-year-olds according to the labor force surveys.

The dynamic specification of equation (3) was chosen after a few experiments that suggested that the relative after-tax wage should be lagged one year. Table 9.17 gives the results of alternative regressions for the period 1968–91, where the restrictions implied by equation (3) are successively relaxed. The model fits very well and conforms to our priors. The most restrictive specification in column 1 is only marginally improved on by relaxing the restrictions.

Table 9.17   **Male School Enrollment and the Returns to Higher Education: Dependent Variable, ln(enrollment rate)**

	(1)	(2)	(3)
Constant	1.939	1.879	1.598
	(57.11)	(36.67)	(4.66)
$\ln\left(\dfrac{1 - U_u}{1 - U_g}\right)_t + \ln\left[\dfrac{W_u (1 + \tau_u)}{W_g (1 - \tau_g)}\right]_{t-1}$	1.901		
	(11.57)		
$\ln\left[\dfrac{W_u (1 + \tau_u)}{W_g (1 - \tau_g)}\right]_{t-1}$		1.968	
		(11.91)	
$\ln\left(\dfrac{1 - U_u}{1 - U_g}\right)_t$		3.240	2.942
		(3.67)	(2.74)
$\ln W_{u,t-1}$			2.081
			(7.20)
$\ln W_{g,t-1}$			-2.049
			(7.51)
$\ln\left(\dfrac{1 - \tau_u}{1 - \tau_g}\right)_{t-1}$			2.242
			(4.08)
$\bar{R}^2$	.852	.861	.853
SE	.058	.056	.058
D-W	1.68	1.81	2.01

Note: The estimation period is 1968–91. Absolute *t*-values are in parentheses.

In fact, the data accept the restrictions imposed in column 2 relative to the least restrictive form in column 3. The enrollment elasticity with respect to the relative wage is around two, very similar to estimates obtained in studies based on data from other countries (see Freeman 1986).

The demand for higher education thus seems highly responsive to the returns to university education. The higher the university wage premium, the larger the fraction of twenty- to twenty-four-year-olds enrolled in education. The higher the degree of tax progressivity, the lower the demand for education. The late 1980s and the early 1990s have seen an increase in the returns to higher education through a rise in the university wage premium and via marked reductions in top marginal tax rates. Those changes will all contribute to a rising demand for higher education over the next few years. This scenario presupposes of course that the education system is responsive enough to increased demand for higher education. Restricted entry is as usual conducive to the emergence and persistence of rents in the labor market.

9.6 Conclusions

Our analysis of Swedish wage differentials over the past twenty-five years or so has identified two largely distinct periods. The period of pay compression, lasting from the late 1960s and up to the early 1980s, involved dramatic changes in wage differentials across gender, experience, and education categories. The (standardized) female/male wage ratio increased by 10 percentage points, and the returns to schooling and experience fell by 50 percent. The period of pay compression is followed by a period of widening wage differentials, including a rebound of the returns to higher education.

Swedish discussions of the causes and consequences of pay compression have typically been centered around union wage policies in general and solidarity wage bargaining in particular. Alternative plausible explanations have largely been ignored, however, and this may be a serious omission. Our analysis suggests that a simple demand and supply framework can account for movements in educational wage differentials as well as fluctuations in youth relative wages. The fall in the university wage premium is, according to our story, driven by the rapid growth of university graduates in the labor force, assuming a smooth trend relative demand growth. The rise in the university wage premium is then explained by the fact that the growth of the supply of more educated workers stops in the mid-1980s. Changes in youth relative wages are analogously explained by fluctuations in the relative supply of young workers. It should be recognized, however, that we do not have much direct evidence on the nature of relative demand shifts.

We do not offer formal models that are able to quantify the relative importance of market forces as opposed to union compression push. We find the compression push story plausible for the LO-SAF area but seriously incomplete as an explanation of movements in the educational wage differentials. Suffice it to say that white-collar unions organizing workers with intermediate schooling levels could pursue successful pay compression policies because the market conditions favored wage moderation at the top end of the earnings distribution. The breakdown of centralized wage bargaining and the retreat from radical egalitarianism occur during a period where the market winds blow in favor of more educated workers.

Fluctuations in the relative supply of more educated workers are determined by past school enrollment decisions, and the latter in turn are influenced by the prospective returns to higher education. The sharp fall from the mid-1980s in the rate of growth of university graduates can be viewed as a lagged response to falling returns to higher education. The rising returns in the late 1980s and the early 1990s reflect a higher university wage premium as well as policy decisions on taxes and subsidized student loans. The increase in the returns to investment in higher education is likely to further increase school enrollment and subsequently depress educational wage differentials.

References

Arai, M. 1991. Essays on non-competitive wage differentials. Ph.D. diss., Swedish Institute for Social Research, Stockholm University.

Björklund, A. 1986. Assessing the decline in wage dispersion in Sweden. In *IUI yearbook, 1986–87: The economics of institutions and markets.* Stockholm: Industriens Utredningsinstitut.

———. 1987. A comment on "The wage structure and the functioning of the labor market." In *Unemployment in Europe,* ed. C.-H. Siven. Stockholm: Timbro.

Björklund, A., and B. Holmlund. 1991. The economics of unemployment insurance: The case of Sweden. In *Labour market policy and unemployment insurance,* ed. A. Björklund, R. Haveman, R. Hollister, and B. Holmlund. Oxford: Oxford University Press.

Blanchflower, D., A. Oswald, and M. Garrett. 1990. Insider power in wage determination. *Economica* 57:143–70.

Bound, J., and G. Johnson. 1992. Changes in the structure of wages in the 1980's: An evaluation of alternative explanations. *American Economic Review* 82:371–92.

Calmfors, L., and A. Forslund. 1991. Wage formation in Sweden. In *Wage formation and macroeconomic policy in the Nordic countries,* ed. L. Calmfors. Stockholm: Studieförbundet Näringsliv och Samhälle; Oxford: Oxford University Press.

Davis, S. J. 1992. Cross-country patterns of changes in relative wages. *NBER Macroeconomics Annual,* 239–92.

Edin, P. A., and J. Zetterberg. 1992. Inter-industry wage differentials: Evidence from Sweden and a comparison with the United States. *American Economic Review* 82:1341–49.

Elvander, N. 1988. *Den svenska modellen* (The Swedish model). Stockholm: Publica.

Eriksson, R., and R. Åberg. 1987. *Welfare in transition.* Oxford: Clarendon.

Forslund, A. 1992. *Arbetslöshet och arbetsmarknadspolitik* (Unemployment and labor market policy). Stockholm: Allmänna Förlaget.

———. 1994. Wage setting at the firm level—insider versus outsider forces. *Oxford Economic Papers* 46:245–61.

Fredriksson, P. 1992. Lönsamhetsförändringar och efterfrågan på högre utbildning (Changes in the returns to and the demand for higher education). Department of Economics, Uppsala University. Mimeo.

Freeman, R. 1980. An empirical analysis of the fixed coefficient "manpower requirements" model, 1960–1970. *Journal of Human Resources* 15:176–99.

———. 1986. Demand for education. In *Handbook of labor economics,* vol. 1, ed. O. Ashenfelter and R. Layard. Amsterdam: North-Holland.

Freeman, R., and D. Bloom. 1986. The youth labor market problem: Age or generational crowding. In *OECD economic outlook.* Paris: OECD.

Hibbs, D. A. 1990. Wage dispersion and trade union action in Sweden. In *Generating equality in the welfare state: The Swedish experience,* ed. I. Persson. Oslo: Norwegian University Press.

Holmlund, B., and H. Ohlsson. 1992. Wage linkages between private and public sectors in Sweden. *Labour* 6:3–17.

Holmlund, B., and J. Zetterberg. 1991. Insider effects in wage determination: Evidence from five countries. *European Economic Review* 35:1009–34.

Jansson, M., and T. Östros. 1991. Regionala arbetsmarknadsdata (Regional labor market data). Department of Economics, Uppsala University. Mimeo.

Jonsson, L., and C.-H. Siven. 1986. *Varför löneskillnader?* (Why wage differentials?). Stockholm: SAF.

Katz, L., and K. Murphy. 1992. Changes in relative wages, 1963–1987: Supply and demand factors. *Quarterly Journal of Economics* 107:35–78.

Klevmarken, A., and P. Olofsson. 1993. *Household market and nonmarket activities.* Stockholm: Industriens Utredningsinstitut.

Meidner, R. 1974. *Co-ordination and solidarity: An approach to wages policy.* Stockholm: Prisma.

Nickell, S., and S. Wadhwani. 1990. Insider forces and wage determination. *Economic Journal* 100:496–509.

Nilsson, C. 1993. The Swedish model: Labour market institutions and contracts. In *Labour market contracts and institutions: A cross-national comparison,* ed. J. Hartog and J. Theeuwes. Amsterdam: North-Holland.

Skedinger, P. 1990. Unemployment, real wages, and labor market programs: A disaggregative analysis. Working Paper no. 1990:15. Department of Economics, Uppsala University.

Statistics Sweden. 1987. *Löneutvecklingen, 1973–85* (The development of wages, 1973–85). Information om arbetsmarknaden (Labor information), no. 1987:3. Stockholm.

———. 1991. *Löner i Sverige, 1982–1989* (Wages in Sweden, 1982–1989). Stockholm.

———. 1992. *Facklig anslutning* (Trade union membership). Information i prognosfrågor (Forecasting information), no. 1992:1. Stockholm.

Tinbergen, J. 1975. *Income distribution: Analysis and policies.* Amsterdam: North-Holland.

Turvey, R., ed. 1952. *Wages policy under full employment.* London: Hodge.

Ullenhag, J. 1971. *Den solidariska lönepolitiken i Sverige* (The solidarity wage policy in Sweden). Stockholm: Läromedelsförlagen.

Zetterberg, J. 1988. *Lönestruktur i privat och offentlig sektor* (Wage structure in the private and the public sector). Nationalekonomiska studier (Economic studies), no. 1988:2. Uppsala: Uppsala University.

10   Getting Together and Breaking Apart: The Decline of Centralized Collective Bargaining

Richard B. Freeman and Robert S. Gibbons

> The centralized system is a catastrophe. LO cannot deliver wage restraint. We'll go for anything else wherever it leads.
> —SAF EMPLOYER ASSOCIATION REPRESENTATIVE, 1990

> Provided it is given the opportunity [the traditional system] will continue to serve both sides . . . for years to come
> —LO UNION REPRESENTATIVE, 1987

From the 1970s through the mid-1980s, many economists extolled the virtues of centralized bargaining arrangements. Crouch (1985), Tarantelli (1986), Bruno and Sachs (1985), Olson (1990), Calmfors and Driffil (1988), and Soskice (1990) among others stressed that centralized bargaining can internalize the negative externalities of sectoral union-management bargaining such as inflationary wage and price increases or unemployment. Empirical studies of macroeconomic responses to the 1970s oil shocks found that centralized systems had better unemployment-wage trade-offs and unemployment and inflation outcomes than systems where unions operate as limited special interest groups and at least as good outcomes as highly decentralized systems.[1] Some countries with decentralized union movements, such as Australia, sought to centralize labor relations. Analysts in other countries, such as the United Kingdom, suggested that their country would do better with a more centralized mode of wage setting (Layard 1991). The International Labour Organisation endorsed tripartite national agreements as a mode of addressing labor market problems.

Richard B. Freeman holds the Herbert Ascherman Chair in Economics at Harvard University. He is also director of the Labor Studies Program at the National Bureau of Economic Research and executive programme director for comparative labour market institutions at the London School of Economics' Centre for Economic Performance. Robert S. Gibbons is professor of economics at the Johnson Graduate School of Management at Cornell University and a research associate of the National Bureau of Economic Research.

Part of the research in this paper is based on fieldwork at FIEF. The paper has benefited from detailed discussions with many specialists from Swedish labor and management organizations, including LO, SIF, Metall, SAF, and SVF, and with academic researchers.

1. For studies finding better performance for centralized systems, see Bruno and Sachs (1985) or Crouch (1985). For studies showing that centralized systems yield better outcomes than systems with local bargaining or considerable state intervention in wage setting and similar outcomes to decentralized systems, see Calmfors and Driffil (1988) and Freeman (1988).

Despite the reputed virtues of centralized bargaining, however, many centralized arrangements fell into disarray in the 1980s. Country after country moved toward more decentralized bargaining (Katz 1993). Italy abandoned the *scala mobile,* which had been the major centralizing force in its wage-setting system. New Zealand introduced legislation that greatly weakened its collective bargaining system. In France, there was a huge increase in plant-level agreements. Australian unions and employers sought more company and plant negotiations. Perhaps most striking, Sweden abandoned the peak-level wage-bargaining system that had served it since the 1950s. In 1983, the Swedish metalworkers and Volvo withdrew from centralized negotiations, and bargaining lurched thereafter toward the company and sector level. The central union and management groups alternated between increasingly weak central agreements and complete abandonment of peak negotiations.

What explains the retreat from the centralized bargaining that seemed so fruitful in the 1970s? Are centralized wage-setting arrangements intrinsically less stable than decentralized bargaining? Did the costs of centralized arrangements rise relative to their benefits? What determines whether labor and firms "get together" or "break apart" in peak-level negotiations?

This paper examines these questions, paying particular attention to the decline in peak-level bargaining in Sweden. We develop a model of centralized bargaining among independent unions and firms that treats the costs as well as the benefits of centralization. Our analysis stresses that central negotiators have neither the instruments nor the information needed to tailor national agreements to the particular circumstances of individual industries or enterprises and thus must allow for some "wage drift" to maintain flexibility. But drift opens the door for defection by local bargaining pairs, which threatens the viability of centralized arrangements. We argue that the more variegated the economic environment, the greater is the equilibrium level of wage drift, and the stronger is the incentive for some local pair to defect. We attribute the decline in centralized bargaining in the 1980s to two forces that increased the dispersion of the local conditions covered by the central bargain—growing unionization of new groups, such as white-collar workers, and market forces favoring greater wage differentials—and to the decline in the threat of inflation, which was an initial motivation for centralized bargaining.[2] While simple, our model captures some of the major elements of the decay in peak-level

---

2. We recognize that the paper falls short of giving a "complete" model of centralized bargaining, in which several unions voluntarily give the right to bargain to a union federation and determine a bargaining stance for the federation; several employers voluntarily give the right to bargain to an employer federation and determine a bargaining stance for the employers' group; the union confederation and employer federation reach a centralized agreement; and the local parties concur or defect from the central agreement. Developing such an analysis is extremely difficult (for the problems of trying to capture too much, see Elster [1989]) and risks losing insights in a full "general equilibrium"–type story. Our goal is the more limited one of laying out selected themes that illuminate some forces that contribute to the decline of centralized bargaining.

bargaining in Sweden and, we hope, illuminates the decentralization of collective bargaining elsewhere.

10.1   The Basic Framework: Centralization versus Flexibility

Most analyses of centralization stress the benefits of treating externality problems in wage determination (such as inflationary wage-price spirals) through peak-level bargaining arrangements (e.g., Flanagan 1987; Calmfors 1987; Calmfors and Driffil 1988; Calmfors and Forslund 1990; Calmfors and Horn 1986; and Horn and Wolinsky 1988a, 1988b). What is less stressed in the literature is that centralized arrangements cost an economy flexibility and require that the center monitor and police settlements reached by independent bargaining pairs that have information unavailable to the center. If central bargainers had the same information as local bargainers, centralization should increase social well-being by leading to an efficient solution. With full information, local parties would give negotiating rights to the center, which would set wages, just as might an omniscient wage- or price-control agency. Deviations from the settlement would be instantly detected and potentially punished, for instance, through fines. Centralized bargaining would be a superior way to restrain aggregate wages, compared to macroeconomic policies that operate largely through unemployment.

The problem is that central bargainers never have the same information as do local bargainers and thus cannot be certain whether any wage (or price) change that deviates from the central agreement does so because of local market conditions unknown to the center or because local bargainers defected from the agreement. In one state of the world, for example, the market might require a 0 percent wage increase for efficiency so that a 2 percent increase in sector A would reflect defection from a central agreement that had, say, a 0 percent wage inflation goal. In another state, however, a 2 percent increase might be needed for efficient production so that a 0 percent increase would be an inflexibility that would reduce output by failing to induce workers to move to sector A (or to work hard, or to invest in skills, or the like), for reasons unknown to and not verifiable by the center. These considerations yield the following:

Basic Point 1. An ideal central wage-setting system must allow deviations from the frame agreement so that local parties can take account of conditions unknown to the center.

This is commonly done in centralized bargaining with a multilevel system of wage setting. For simplicity, we consider two levels. At the first level, central bodies determine appropriate aggregate wage changes on the basis of national economic conditions. For example, in Sweden during the heyday of centralized bargaining, the main union federation (LO, Landsorganisationen) and employers' association (SAF, Svenska Arbetsgivareforeningen) reached peak-level agreements that set the frame for lower-level industry and firm bargaining. Once the frame is set, local unions cannot strike, and firms cannot lock out workers to obtain a wage settlement that differs from the frame, but the two sides can agree to further wage changes on the basis of local conditions, producing wage drift. What distinguishes drift from other negotiated wage changes is that it arises from a Pareto-improving agreement by the local union and employer. In essence, the central agreement determines the threat point in local bargaining and guarantees that negotiated drift will benefit both sides, as neither can use economic force (such as a strike) to gain a bigger share of the pie. In Sweden and other countries with centralized wage arrangements, a substantial proportion of wage changes normally consisted of positive wage drift.

Unfortunately for the center, there are two ways in which both local parties can benefit by wage drift. They can agree to market-efficient wages that raise output and joint surplus. Or they can bargain for inflationary wage (and price) gains that redistribute income from the rest of society to them. Changes in wages in any sector i (W_i) thus consist of three parts: the common frame wage inflation (W); deviation or drift due to market conditions (DM_i); and drift due to defect strategies (DD_i). In an ideal world, one could imagine that the common frame agreement should be set so that $E(DM_i) = 0$: some sectors would increase wages by more than the frame, while others would increase wages by less owing to their particular market conditions, balancing out to zero net drift. Furthermore, in this ideal world, DD_i would be zero: no one would defect. If local parties chose only economically efficient drift, then centralization would yield a first-best optimum—the optimal aggregate wage inflation and the optimal change in relative wages.

Knowing that some drift is likely to be efficient and other drift likely to reflect defection, the center must develop a strategy of "allowable" drift. If the center does nothing to penalize deviations, the incentive to defect is likely to be high, leading to a breakdown of the agreement and the loss of the benefits of centralization. At the other extreme, if the center prevents all deviations, the economy loses from inflexibility. Figure 10.1 depicts the problem. The horizontal axis measures centralization on a scale from zero to one, where a value of 0 represents a totally decentralized wage-setting system, while a value of 1 represents a totally centralized system. Intermediate values reflect differences in the leeway given local bargainers to deviate from the frame agreement because the center either imposes different penalties for deviation or allocates different amounts of resources (from moral suasion to side payments) to reduce deviation. The vertical axis measures the benefits and costs from centralized wage setting. Benefits are a rising parabola on the assumption that inflation costs follow a quadratic loss function. Costs fall with increasing centralization until point M, then rise. The fall reflects the possibility that some centralization may be necessary to control monopoly or monopsonistic wage setting or inefficient "rent sharing" between profitable firms and their workers. The rise rep-

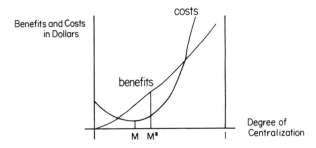

Fig. 10.1   Benefits and costs of centralization

resents the fact that high degrees of centralization extract a large cost in terms of lost flexibility. Absent any costs of flexibility, optimal centralization is 1 since it minimizes wage inflation. Absent inflation costs, optimal centralisation is M (= 0 if there are no dangers of inefficient rent sharing). Given a trade-off between the benefits of centralization and the loss of flexibility, optimal centralization is $M^* > M$. The wider the gap between the benefit and cost curves, the more beneficial and stable will centralized wage setting be, given "random" shifts in those curves.[3]

This framework sets the stage for analyzing the three elements of centralized wage setting: the benefits of centralization from internalizing the externalities of local agreements; the costs of centralization due to lost flexibility; and the process of controlling or limiting defection from a frame agreement.

10.2   The Benefits of Centralization

Why should local unions or firms voluntarily give the right to bargain to a higher-level organization? The most widely mentioned reason invokes a prisoner's dilemma (or other externality) model of wage settlements: lower-level bargaining pairs choose between socially desirable restraint in wage setting or inflationary settlements.[4] Absent centralization, they end up at a noncooperative inflationary outcome. By internalizing the costs of inflationary settlements, centralized bargaining should, by contrast, produce the cooperative settlement.

3. The curves in the exhibit reflect two underlying relations: (i) the effect of centralization on wage inflation/inappropriate wage structures and (ii) the welfare costs of each. Thus, the curves will shift whenever centralization becomes more/less effective in altering the outcomes or when the outcomes become more/less costly to the economy.

4. Centralization has other potential benefits as well. It can reduce labor disputes by bringing the costs of third parties to bear on the disputees. It can minimize the inefficiency costs of local monopoly union wage setting or monopsonistic employer wage setting. Also, it insures workers against wage losses due to negative shocks, and ensures that firms benefit from positive shocks, because wages do not respond. Regressions show that industry wage changes are uncorrelated with changes in value added per worker in Sweden but highly correlated in the United States and that Swedish wages are only modestly correlated with such things as firm size, profitability, etc. (Holmlund and Zetterberg 1989).

The major benefit of centralization is presumably reductions in wage inflation, but any gain due to internalizing an externality can demonstrate how forming a central organization can produce benefits in collective bargaining. Since we do not want to develop a full macro model to assess the costs of inflation, we briefly analyze the externality created by wage settlements that result from an unemployment benefit system.

Consider the following two-sector, two-union model. Labor is the only factor of production, and union i is the monopoly supplier of labor to firm i. Union i has N_i members and seeks to maximize its members' income (or indirect utility, more generally), which depends on wages, W_i, the probability members work in the sector, $P(W_i)$, and the unemployment benefit they get, b.

Decentralized bargaining proceeds as follows: unions choose wages separately; firms choose prices and employment; and workers get W_i or b. Bargaining under a union federation differs only in the first stage: unions bargain between themselves over a wage vector; firms choose prices and employment; and workers get W_i or b. In brief, we model centralization *not* as a change in the parties' preferences (such as union i suddenly caring about members of union j) but rather as a change in the game the parties play (bargaining with each other first rather than individually with firms). This modeling strategy parallels Grossman and Hart's (1986) observation that the best way to model changes in vertical integration is to analyze how they affect the structure of interactions between parties rather than their preferences.

To keep things simple, this model is based on monopoly-union behavior. In both the decentralized and the federation cases, given wages from the first stage we solve the last two stages of the model by backward induction. In the decentralized case, the first-stage wages are then given by the Nash equilibrium of the wage-choice game between the unions, whereas in the federation case these wages are given by the Nash bargaining solution. Since in this model the union federation has the instruments that the individual unions have (namely, one wage per sector), both unions are better off in the federation case. The externality in the decentralized case is the cost of b paid by nonmembers of each union. To see this, contrast a union whose members pay no taxes to the unemployment benefit fund with a union that has a fully experience-rated fund, where workers pay the full cost.

If all unemployment benefits come from taxes on other workers, the union maximizes $pW + (1 - p)b$. It ignores the tax burden created by b. The first-order condition is $W = b - p/p'$. If, by contrast, the unemployment benefit system is fully funded by its members, the union maximizes the after-tax income received by members, $(1 - t)pW + (1 - p)b$, subject to the budget constraint that taxes paid by those working equals the unemployment benefits received by jobless members, $tpW = (1 - p)b$. This calls for maximizing pW, yielding the standard revenue-maximizing result: $W = -p/p'$; that is, the union raises wages until the elasticity of labor demand, $-Wp'/p$, equals one.

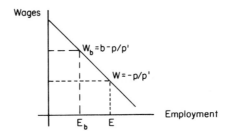

Fig. 10.2   The effect of a union federation

Figure 10.2 shows how the choice of wages in these two cases affects employment (output). In the free-rider case, the union chooses the wage $W_b = b - p/p'$, and the firm chooses E_b; in the fully funded case, the union chooses W, and the firm chooses E. The lost output is the trapezoid $W_b WEE_b$. It is larger the greater the level of b and the more elastic the demand curve. The magnitude of the gain from internalizing funding of the unemployment system through a union federation can be sizable since centralization reduces unemployment.

Extending the analysis to a case where a percentage of the tax burden of financing own-member unemployment is paid by union i's members is simple and makes clear that changing the structure of bargaining from decentralized firm-union pairs to a central union federation is beneficial because it forces each union to internalize the cost of unemployment benefits.

10.3   The Costs of Inflexibility

There are two ways in which inflexibility in wage setting can reduce economic well-being. First, it can lead to a misallocation of labor between expanding and contracting sectors. For simplicity, consider a two-sector economy that is in full employment. Each sector faces an upward-sloping labor supply schedule, owing to heterogeneity among workers in the costs of mobility, preferences, or skills. The elasticity of demand in sector A is h, while the elasticity of supply is e. When demand shifts upward by X', as in figure 10.3a, the wage should rise by $X'/(e + h)$, inducing an increase in employment of W'_a. But centralized bargaining does not allow sector A to raise its wage. The result is that neither employment nor output in the sector increases. Instead of E' persons working in sector A, E work in the sector. The social loss is a standard welfare triangle set by the gap between the value of adding additional workers to sector A and their reservation wage/the opportunity value of their time for working in B. Too many people remain in sector B, and too few (none) move to sector A. Misallocation losses of this sort are usually viewed as being of second-order importance compared to the costs of lost output due to unemployment or the costs of wage inflation.

a

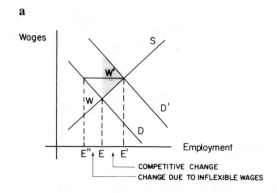

b

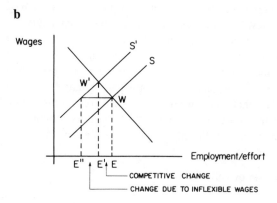

Fig. 10.3   The costs of inflexibility

But inflexibility in wage setting can also produce "first-order" effects in the form of wasted resources that show up in unemployment or possibly inadequate work effort that reduces output just as does unemployment. Consider, for example, what happens when demand for labor falls in sector A from D' to D (see fig. 10.3a). With rigid wages, employment will drop from E' to E'' rather than to E, as it would in a flexible wage regime. Thus, $E'' - E'$ more workers are displaced from the sector because of inflexible wages. Since wages are fixed in sector B, these workers will end up unemployed, barring macroeconomic changes that might alter the real cost of labor in both sectors. Inflexible relative wages produce inflexible real wages and joblessness that would have been avoided had sector A been free to reduce pay in the face of the decline in demand or had sector B been able to reduce wages to hire those displaced from A.

Inflexibility in wages can also have first-order effects on an economy by altering work effort and preventing the appropriate adjustments in efficiency wages. Consider again an economy that has full employment and the "right" wage structure. Let work requirements change in a particular sector so that the supply of labor shifts from S to S', as in figure 10.3b: individuals want a higher wage in the sector because the work has become more difficult, work conditions have eroded, and so on, relative to other sectors. The market-clearing wage is W', and the market-clearing employment is E', but with inflexible wages the sector can pay only W and will obtain only E'' workers. If wages are rigid elsewhere and unemployment is less desirable than working, the loss in labor supply is likely to take the form of reduced effort rather than of an actual reduction in employment. Relabel the horizontal axis to refer to effort. At the "right" wage W' a given workforce would offer E' units of effort, whereas at W it will offer just E''. The loss to the economy is the difference in effort levels E'' and E'.

While we have not "proved" that inflexibility in wages has sizable first-order effects on economic performance, our discussion suggests that it is reasonable to treat the costs of inflexibility on employment or effort on a par with the costs that come from free-riding on the unemployment benefit system in figure 10.2 above.

10.4   The Centralized Bargaining Game

Consider next a centralized bargaining system with three players: the center, a union, and a firm. The center's actions represent peak-level bargaining between union and employer federations, and the firm's and the union's actions represent lower-level bargaining at the industry or enterprise level. The maximands of the three players are the following:

Union. $U = w_0 - c(a) + g(w - w_0)$, where w_0 is the wage floor set by the center, $c(a)$ is the cost of activity level a (such as effort or investing in skills) to workers, w is the wage (so $w - w_0$ is the amount of drift), and g is the rate at which the union values wage drift. (Economically it might seem that g should equal one so that the union cares only about the realized wage w, but politically there may be a difference between wage gains granted from on high, w_0, and wage drift resulting from bargaining between ongoing players at the local level.)

Firm. $\pi_f = rv(a) - w_0 - h(w - w_0)$, where $v(a)$ is the revenue function, r is a shift parameter known to the firm and union that affects the value of production (perhaps a productivity or price shock), and h is the rate at which wage drift costs the firm. (Again, h may differ from one for political reasons.)

Center. $\pi_c = [rv(a) - c(a)] - kw_0 - m(w - w_0)$, where $rv(a) - c(a)$ is social output in the sector, k is the rate at which a high central wage settlement harms the center, and m is the additional cost to the center of the modeled sector's wage drift. (If the center cares only about realized wages, then $m = k$.)

Some comments on this structure:

1. The parameter r measures the private information about local conditions held by the firm and union but not by the center. It may seem strange that the firm and union observe r but that the center does not since the center is the amalgam of a federation of firms and a federation of unions. One interpretation is that r is realized after the center has determined w_0. Another interpretation is that political processes within federations (not modeled here) lead firms or unions to keep r private information.

2. The variable w_0 is a wage floor so that deviations from the frame involve higher wages only. We assume this because it would be politically difficult for a union to settle for less than was recommended by higher-level bargainers. In the "no-drift" model that follows, w_0 is a wage ceiling as well, but in the "full-drift" model the firm and union can negotiate a Pareto-improving increase in the wage.

3. While the firm and union payoffs are standard, the center's deserves explanation. We assume that the center cares about (i) the efficiency of production, as measured by $rv(a) - c(a)$, but not (directly) about its division between the parties; (ii) the cost of inflationary central agreements, as reflected by the parameter k; and (iii) the extent of wage drift from the frame wage w_0 as reflected by the parameter m. To keep things simple, we assume hereafter that $m = k$, but in a richer model it might be valuable to distinguish between these effects. (For example, m might vary across sectors.) Likewise, we hereafter assume $g = h = 1$.

We consider two extreme models: one in which the center can impose such severe penalties that there is *no drift* in the economy, and one in which it cannot impose any penalties so that there is *full drift*. We then offer conjectures about a model of *partial drift* that compromises between these extremes. In all three models, the basic sequence of decision making is as follows: the center chooses w_0; observing r, the firm and the union negotiate $w \geq w_0$; and, given w, the firm and the union negotiate an activity level, a. In the no-drift case, the firm and the union have no choice but to settle on $w = w_0$; in the full-drift case, any $w \geq w_0$ is allowed. In the partial-drift case, the center chooses not only w_0 but also a parameter d representing the maximum allowable percentage wage drift: the firm and the union must negotiate a wage w from the interval $[w_0, (1 + d)w_0]$.

In all three cases, we think of the negotiation(s) over activity level as occurring over the life of the contract and hence after the negotiation over wage at the start of the contract. Negotiations over activity level depend (in part) on grassroots political forces on the shop floor, whereas firm-union negotiations over wage depend (in part) on the character, credibility, and charisma of individual union leaders. It therefore seems plausible that the union's bargaining power differs in these two negotiations. We use the (generalized) Nash bargaining solution to solve each negotiation but allow the union's bargaining power over wages (q) to differ from that over activity level (p), where $0 \leq p$, $q \leq 1$.

In the final stage of each model, when the firm and the union negotiate an activity level, we assume that, if no settlement is reached, the firm shuts down, yielding payoffs of zero to each party. Thus, given the realization of the productivity parameter r and a wage w, the Nash bargaining solution (generalized to arbitrary rather than symmetric bargaining power) solves

$$\max_{a}[w - c(a)]^p[rv(a) - w]^{1-p},$$

subject to the constraints that $w - c(a) \geq 0$ and $rv(a) - w \geq 0$. We denote this negotiated activity level by $a_N(r, w)$.

To (help) ensure that such a Nash bargaining solution exists, we impose conventional regularity conditions: $v(0) = c(0) = 0$, $v'(0) > 0 = c'(0)$, $v'' < 0 < c''$, and $a \geq 0$, as illustrated in figure 10.4. Even with these assumptions, however, no solution exists if w is too large: w must not exceed the cost $c(a)$ at the activity level where $rv(a) = c(a)$, else the firm cannot afford to remain in business. (Again, see the figure.) Given such a nonbankrupting value of w, the negotiated activity level depends on the parties' bargaining powers, p and $1 - p$. The highest possible negotiated activity level earns the union no surplus ($w - c[a] = 0$); naturally, this occurs when the union has no bargaining power, $p = 0$. Similarly, the lowest possible negotiated activity level earns the firm no surplus ($rv[a] - w = 0$); this occurs when $p = 1$. For an arbitrary p, the Nash bargaining solution $a_N(r, w)$ solves the first-order condition

$$pc'(a)[rv(a) - w] = (1 - p)rv'(a)[w - c(a)],$$

as illustrated for a small value of p in the figure.

Given this negotiated activity level in the final stage, we can now work back-

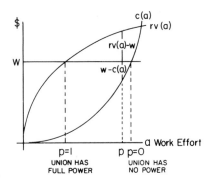

Fig. 10.4   Nash bargaining between firm and union

ward to the wage negotiation in the second stage, taking each of the three cases in turn.

10.4.1   Model I: No Drift

In the no-drift case, we assume that the penalties at the center's disposal are sufficiently great that there is never any drift: $w - w_0 = 0$. In effect, the center has a fully enforced wage-control system. This simplifies the payoffs to $\pi_c = [rv(a) - c(a)] - kw_0$ to the center, $\pi_f = rv(a) - w_0$ to the firm, and $U = w_0 - c(a)$ to the union. Since the intermediate stage of the model (in which the firm and the union negotiate over wages) is irrelevant, in the first stage the center chooses the wage w_0 to solve

$$\max_{w_0} E_r\{rv[a_N(r, w_0)] - c[a_N(r, w_0)]\} - kw_0.$$

Even in this no-drift case, the center's optimal wage floor reflects a compromise between the center's two goals: efficient production and wage discipline. Efficient production requires a positive wage increase, while wage discipline requires a 0 percent increase. (Here and below, we allow ourselves to use the language of *wage increases* and *inflation* even though the model concerns wage levels.) For example, if the center knew r, then setting $w_0 = 0$ would yield an inefficiently low activity level.

To compute the optimal wage floor w_0^*, the center considers the effect on the subsequent activity-level negotiation of variations in w_0. Implicitly differentiating the first-order condition for the negotiated activity level (or inspecting fig. 10.5a) shows that $a_N(r, w)$ increases with the wage. (The bold and solid vertical lines are, respectively, the firm's and the union's surpluses at the wage w. The bold dotted and the dotted vertical lines are the analogous surpluses at the wage w'.) Roughly speaking, keeping the activity level constant, a higher wage benefits the union and harms the firm, so the Nash bargaining solution redresses this imbalanced distribution of surplus by increasing the activity level.

The complementary analysis (fig. 10.5b) shows that the negotiated activity level *decreases* with the productivity parameter r. Here, an increase in r (to r', in the figure) benefits the firm but has no effect on the union, so the Nash bargaining solution reallocates surplus by decreasing the activity level. Unfortunately, this response runs directly counter to efficiency considerations: the efficient activity level—$a^*(r)$, which maximizes $rv(a) - c(a)$—increases with r. The reason the negotiated activity level behaves in this perverse fashion is that in this no-drift case the firm is unable to compensate the union for higher activity levels, no matter how badly the firm would like to achieve such levels.

This discordance between the negotiated and the efficient activity levels motivates the center to allow wage drift, as we explore below. Alternatively, if the center persists in enforcing the present no-drift case (presumably because k is large), the firm and the union may consider breaking away from centralized bargaining. In a full analysis of this possibility, the center would appreciate

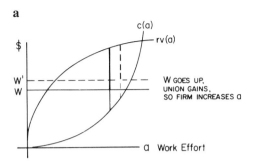

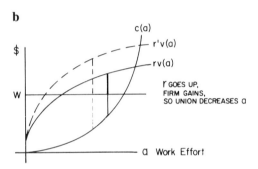

Fig. 10.5   Comparative statics of Nash bargain

that the sector might break away and so might modify the choice of w_0 to discourage such behavior. We conduct only an initial analysis of the sector's incentive to break away, under the assumption that the center chooses w_0^* as described above.

To keep things simple, suppose that there are only two values of r, $H > L$. Figure 10.5*b* implies that, given the centrally determined wage w_0^*, the negotiated activity level for high-productivity (H) firms will be less than that for low (L), and figure 10.5*a* implies that both these activity levels increase with w_0^*. Thus, if w_0^* is very large, then it could be that both efficient activity levels are less than both negotiated activity levels,

$$a^*(L) < a^*(H) < a_N(H, w_0^*) < a_N(L, w_0^*),$$

while, if w_0^* is very small, then it could be that both efficient activity levels are greater than both negotiated activity levels,

$$a_N(H, w_0^*) < a_N(L, w_0^*) < a^*(L) < a^*(H).$$

It seems likely that the center typically will prefer an intermediate value of w_0 so that neither of these extreme cases arises. For large enough values of k (relative to the difference in the efficient social surplus for H vs. L), however, the center will prefer the latter extreme over the former since the latter offers a much lower wage. This suggests that for sufficiently large k the high-productivity sectors will operate most inefficiently and so have the greatest incentive to break away from centralized bargaining.

Basic Point 2. If the center is sufficiently dedicated to wage discipline, then a sector's incentive to abandon the system increases with the value of the sector's production.

10.4.2   Model II: Full Drift

The polar opposite to central control with no drift is a situation in which the firm and the union tailor the wage and the activity level to the realized value of the productivity parameter r, without any penalty from the center. This reinvigorates the intermediate stage of the game: the firm and the union bargain over the wage, subject to the constraint that $w \geq w_0$, taking into account the subsequent negotiation over the activity level.

In this wage negotiation, we assume that, if no settlement were reached, then the central agreement w_0 would be imposed, after which the firm and the union would proceed to negotiate over the activity level as described above. Thus, the parties' threat payoffs are

$$U_0 = w_0 - c[a_N(r, w_0)]$$

and

$$\pi_0 = rv[a_N(r, w_0)] - w_0.$$

The Nash bargaining solution in the wage negotiation therefore solves

$$\max_{w \geq w_0} \; \{w - c[a_N(r, w)] - U_0\}^q \{rv[a_N(r, w)] - w - \pi_0\}^{1-q},$$

subject to the constraints that $w - c[a_N(r, w)] \geq U_0$ and $rv[a_N(r, w)] - w \geq \pi_0$, where q is the union's bargaining power over wages. We denote this negotiated wage by $w_N(r, w_0)$.

The first-order condition for the negotiated wage is

$$q(rv - w - \pi_0) - (1 - q)(w - c - U_0) + a'[(1 - q)(w - c - U_0)rv' - q(rv - w - \pi_0)c'] = 0,$$

where a' denotes the partial derivative of $a_N(r, w)$ with respect to w. Note that the term involving a' is reminiscent of the first-order condition for the negotiated activity level,

$$pc'(a)[rv(a) - w] - (1 - p)rv'(a)[w - c(a)] = 0.$$

More specifically, if $q = p$ and $U_0 = \pi_0 = 0$, then the term involving a' is zero, so the first-order condition for $w_N(r, w_0)$ becomes $p(rv - w) = (1 - p)(w - c)$, or

$$w = prv + (1 - p)c.$$

The first-order condition for $a_N(r, w)$ then becomes

$$p(1 - p)c'(a)[rv - c] - p(1 - p)rv'(a)[rv - c] = 0,$$

or $rv' = c'$, which defines the efficient activity level $a^*(r)$.

To summarize, we have just shown that, if the union's bargaining power over wages is equal to its bargaining power over activity levels ($q = p$), and if the payoffs to the union and the firm from abiding by the center's wage frame w_0 are both zero, then the full-drift model yields the efficient activity level (for every realization of r). Unfortunately (from the perspective of efficient production), these sufficient conditions are also necessary. More precisely, we show in the appendix that the full-drift model yields the efficient activity level for every realization of r only if $p = q$ and $w_0 = 0$ (where the latter implies $U_0 = \pi_0 = 0$). Thus, if p differs from q, then there is no way for full drift to achieve efficient production. This gives us a result in the spirit of the Coase theorem.

Basic Point 3. Full drift yields the first best micro-efficient outcome only if the unions and management have similar bargaining power in wages and in the choice of activity level; differences in bargaining power over the two outcomes can produce inefficiency in the same manner as transactions costs.

When p differs from q, the center's optimal choice of w_0 involves subtle considerations. The wage floor influences the parties' threat payoffs, U_0 and π_0. Since the center dislikes high wages but likes efficient production, the center would like to choose a wage floor that favors π_0 over U_0, anticipating that the parties' choice of an activity level will be influenced by efficiency considerations but that negotiated wages will have to be relatively low to accommodate the firm's high threat payoffs.

When $p = q$, on the other hand, it seems likely that $w_0 = 0$ will be the center's optimal wage floor in this full-drift model—since lower wage floors seem likely to lead to lower negotiated wages, in which case the center can achieve efficient production while keeping wages as low as full drift will allow them to be kept. The center would be even better off, however, if a little production inefficiency could be traded for still lower wages. To explore this possibility, we turn next to the partial-drift model.

10.4.3   Model III: Partial Drift

The timing of moves in the partial-drift case is identical to that in the full-drift case, except that the center's move in the first stage now involves two actions rather than one. Whereas in the no-drift and full-drift cases the center chose only a wage floor w_0, now the center also chooses a wage-drift parameter d. Specifically, if the center chooses w_0 and d, then the bargaining between the firm and the union in the second stage is constrained to produce a wage no less than w_0 but no greater than $w_0(1 + d)$. Thus, d is the maximum percentage drift that the center will allow. The no-drift and full-drift cases are limits of this partial-drift case ($d = 0$ and $d = \infty$, respectively).

We think of the partial-drift case as a one-shot game in which the center can commit to any value of d it chooses, but we intend this to be a reduced form for a repeated-game analysis in which the center cannot constrain the firm's and the union's current behavior but can later punish a firm-union pair that exceeds the current limit on drift. When the Swedish system was in its heyday, such punishments were available. For example, both LO and SAF had large strike funds that could be used to reward members that stayed within the guidelines for drift but could also be withheld to punish members who strayed outside.

In a world in which partial drift operates, the inefficiencies of both the no-drift and the full-drift models will likely reappear, albeit in muted fashion. The center can trade off the wage discipline/grossly inefficient activity levels from the no-drift case against the more efficient production/uncontrolled wages from the full-drift case. But this trade-off will not produce fully efficient production with tightly controlled wages.

It seems reasonable to conjecture that the center will find it optimal to allow more wage drift if production inefficiencies become more important, such as would occur if the population distribution of r increased in variance. Section 10.5 describes (among other things) the growth (and eventual explosion) of wage drift that preceded the decline of centralized bargaining in Sweden. The fact that even full drift may not yield efficient production (say, because p differs from q) seems consistent with the Swedish experience: if production efficiency becomes sufficiently important (and controlling wages sufficiently unimportant), then the institution of centralized bargaining may be unable to persist. To conclude this section, we elaborate on this and other implications of our three models.

10.4.4   Implications of the Analysis

In our model, three things create problems for a centralized wage-setting system:

1. An increase in the dispersion of desired outcomes across existing sectors. This will take the form of a greater dispersion in r across sectors. High-r sectors have an incentive to opt out of the system.

2. An increase in the heterogeneity of groups covered by the agreement, through the addition of new groups. In our framework, this also takes the form of a greater dispersion in r. The more heterogeneous the groups covered by the central agreement, the more likely some groups will have relatively high values of r and thus consider a defect strategy.

3. A reduction in the importance of controlling inflation through centralized negotiations. A decline in the benefits curve in figure 10.1 above makes centralized bargaining less valuable. In our models, this takes the form of a reduced value of wage discipline (k).

Our analyses suggest that decentralization could take the form of a growth of drift in a centralized system or of bargaining pairs opting out of the system if the center does not allow enough drift. These considerations seem to be relevant to the ongoing decentralization of centralized bargaining in the OECD. The widening of wage differentials in the United States and the United Kingdom, the countries that give greatest leeway to the market in wage setting, implies that developed-country economic conditions favor an increase in dispersion of labor market outcomes. The increased organization of white-collar and public-sector workers in unions in Europe in the 1970s created greater heterogeneity of interests in the organized sector. The worldwide drop in inflation meant that the gains from controlling inflation through centralized wage setting had fallen. If this analysis is correct, countries with greater market pressures for wage differentiation, with greater growth of organization of nontraditional union groups, and facing the least threat of serious wage inflation were likely to have moved furthest down the decentralization path. Rather than comparing different countries, however, our empirical analysis examines changes in the country that has moved most dramatically toward decentralized bargaining: Sweden.

10.5   Does the Model Illuminate the Swedish Case?

With the highest union density in the OECD and extensively organized employers' associations, Sweden has long been viewed as the archetype of centralized collective bargaining, ranked at or near the top in corporatism rates. The explicit consideration that LO and SAF gave national economic conditions made Sweden the leading example of the all-encompassing unionism that can deliver socially desirable outcomes (Olson 1990). But, from the early 1980s through the early 1990s, employers refused to enter into peak-level negotiations, and even sought to decentralize the industry negotiations, giving much greater leeway for decentralized wage setting. Even in this traditional exemplar of corporatism, centralized bargaining was not what it had once been.

Does our model capture essential features of the Swedish experience? In this section, we give a schematic description of Sweden's peak-level bargaining system and its evolution over time and then examine this bottom-line question.

10.5.1   The Traditional Centralized Bargaining System

Following other analysts (Ahlen 1989; Swenson 1989; Elster 1989; Martin 1984, 1992; Lundberg 1985; Nilsson 1993) we identify two major players in Sweden's traditional peak-level bargaining system. The first is LO, a strong central federation dominated by private-sector blue-collar workers, to which major unions gave a mandate to negotiate. The second is SAF, the private employer's association, with the mandate to negotiate for firms. However, we also note that Sweden's union movement now contains two other major federations divided along skill lines: TCO, which organises white-collar workers; and SACO/SR, which covers professional workers.

Table 10.1 gives a brief chronology of the development of the traditional system through its decay in the 1980s. The 1940s set the stage for centralization. In 1938, following considerable labor turmoil, LO and SAF reached the Saltsjobaden agreement to cooperate to resolve labor disputes. LO strengthened its authority over member unions by restricting their rights to strike without LO approval, allowing the LO executive board to participate in member unions' contract negotiations and to intervene in proposed settlements, and making union leaders rather than members the final authority in negotiations and dispute strategy. In 1944, LO founded TCO, the white-collar workers' union, to bring these weakly unionized workers into the labor movement. SAF and LO reached agreements on workplace rules and wage setting, and LO supported wage freezes as part of the Social Democrats' wartime economic policy.

In the 1950s, fearful that interindustry rivalry would produce a wage explosion harmful to the country's trade position, SAF pressed for centralized negotiations. It refused to allow its members to negotiate separately with unions until a central agreement was struck, forcing LO unions to give the right to bargain to LO, although many preferred local bargaining. Union support for centralization grew as leaders realized that it offered a mechanism for solidaristic wage policies beneficial to low-wage workers, reduced labor disputes, and lowered the risk of inflationary settlements that endangered full employment and would harm the union-allied Social Democrats. Both LO and SAF seemed to have sufficient tools to make central agreements effective. Under the rules of LO, the leaders of unions (who are on the LO executive council) rather than union members had the authority to confirm agreements. The leaders gave the federation a mandate to make "frame agreements" with SAF that set the parameters for lower-level bargaining. Unions engaged in disputes outside the frame faced the highly organized employers on their own, whereas workers on approved strikes received essentially full pay from individual union and federation strike funds. On the employer side, centralization was nominally stronger. Member firms and employer associations gave SAF the right to negotiate an agreement on their behalf. SAF had to approve lower-level agreements and lockouts and could fine firms that violated the central agreement, although it rarely did. SAF raised a large insurance fund available for firms that were struck or engaged in an approved lockout. Strengthening the importance of the central agreement, Sweden's labor courts treated the LO-SAF agreement as the legal norm: "In practice, unorganized employers thus are dependent on the agreements made by the large organizations" (Skogh 1984, 150).

Most analysts view the 1960s as the heyday of the centralized system. LO and SAF signed two- and three-year central agreements that dominated wage setting. Wage drift was moderate. LO's wage-solidarity policy reduced differentials noticeably (Hibbs and Locking 1991). Two events, however, portended future problems: 1966 legislation that granted the right to strike to public em-

Table 10.1   **Decadal Chronology of Industrial Relations Development**

1938–1940s: Development of cooperative arrangements
- Saltsjobaden Agreement (1938) establishes procedures for settling disputes
- SAF-LO set national wage agreements for war period; reach cooperative agreements on works councils, time and motion studies, etc.
- LO establishes greater control over member unions; founds TCO in 1944

1950s–1960s: Successful centralized negotiating system
- SAF pushes for centralized wage setting in 1950s; few strikes and limited wage drift
- Public-sector workers given right to strike in 1966
- Earnings development guarantee in LO contracts in 1966
- LO pushes wage solidarity; reduces differentials
- Miners wildcat strike for higher differentials, better conditions in 1969

1970s: Centralized system under pressure
- Volvo workers strike for wages above central agreement; wage drift rises
- LO uses legislation to win role at workplace it cannot gain in bargaining: employee participation legislation requires provision of information, right to strike on codetermination issues, 1976; bitter dispute over proposed wages fund
- In 1971, government emergency legislation imposes settlement on professional workers in public sector within central agreement
- Oil shock produces massive wage inflation in 1974–75; devaluations needed to restore competitiveness
- White-collar union cartel (PTK) strikes in 1976

1980s: System lurches toward decentralization
- Massive 1980 lockout/strike viewed as "investment for future" by employers
- SAF-LO-PTK 1982 agreement on local level efficiency and participation, strengthening local unions
- Strikes and lockouts by white-collar and public-sector workers: 1981 PTK strike opposed by LO; TCO massive public-sector strike in 1985; additional public-sector strikes to maintain guarantees in 1986; SIF strikes VIF to gain greater union influence on local pay in 1988
- LO weakens solidarity wage policy in 1987 to favor differentials at top
- Private sector led by VF moves to decentralize private-sector bargaining; VF does not give mandate to SAF in 1983, bargains separately with white-collar unions; no central bargain in 1988; SAF refuses to bargain centrally in 1990
- Public-sector decentralizes: police gain higher settlement in 1989; SACO-SAV agree to individual negotiations for top civil servants; SAV decentralize negotiations for teachers and nurses
- Government seeks bigger role in wage setting: 1984–85 Rosebund meetings; 1989 failure to impose national price-wage freeze/no strike central agreement

1990s: Decentralized collective bargaining
- No central agreement in 1990
- Rehnderg Commission secures national wage settlement
- Industry agreements allow greater discretion for lower-level parties to differentiate wages even absent drift

ployees, strengthening their unions, and a 1969 wildcat strike by miners in the state-owned mining company owing to miners' opposition to central settlements that restricted local union independence (and that lowered their pay relative to other blue-collar workers and to white-collar workers in mining).

In the 1970s, illegal strikes and the oil price increases placed centralized bargaining under great stress. Volvo workers struck in 1970 and gained an 11 percent wage increase (compared to 3 percent in the SAF-LO agreement), lower wage differentials within the company, and other benefits. High demand for labor and a limited supply of workers for production jobs made Volvo unwilling to weather a labor dispute for the sake of the central agreement. Workers struck other profitable companies for a share of "excess profits" and then struck less profitable companies to restore relativities. The centralized system forced only one group into line, university graduates working for the state. It did this by enacting emergency legislation in 1971 that imposed a modest wage settlement on these workers over the opposition of their unions. While some Swedish observers cite this as demonstrating the ability of the centralized system to enforce the frame agreement, in fact it was an isolated instance in a period when most wildcat strikes succeeded.

One might expect centralized bargaining to be ideally suited to deal with the 1970s supply-side oil price explosion, but the Swedish system did not fare well. Wage drift produced huge wage increases in 1974 despite a moderate central settlement; the frame agreement and wage drift combined to produce even larger nominal increases in 1975. Wage inflation was greater than in any other advanced OECD country save Japan. A wave of wildcat strikes swept the country in 1974. Reflecting the failure of the central agreement to cap wage increases, industry and local bargaining pairs wrote earnings guarantees and cost-of-living adjustments into contracts. (Earnings guarantees are clauses assuring workers with little opportunity for drift that, if, say, Volvo workers earned 5 percent over the negotiated settlement, they would get the same.) Union rivalry was increasingly important in wage setting.

A different set of problems surfaced in the mid-1970s when LO pressed the Social Democrats for legislation opening company books to unions and establishing codetermination at workplaces. Employers fought against a union proposal for wage-earner funds to be paid by taxes on profits. Employers felt that LO's use of political muscle to gain benefits they could not win in bargaining violated the spirit of Saltsjobaden for cooperative agreements between the "social partners."

Finally, in the 1980s, the centralized bargaining system began to disintegrate. In 1980, there was a massive national lockout and strike that the head of SAF labeled "an investment in the future" for reducing the power of LO. Substantial wage increases in 1981–82 required a devaluation of the currency to restore competitiveness on world markets and company profitability. No longer deferring to the central agreement, white-collar and public-sector unions battled employers in major labor disputes. Public-sector workers struck unsuccessfully in 1986 to maintain earnings guarantees in contracts. In 1988, the private-sector clerical union, SIF, struck unsuccessfully for three weeks against major multinationals to gain a greater influence in local wage setting (a key to union power because of wage drift). Led by the large multinationals of the engineering employers' association (VF), employers started to decentralize the bargaining system. In 1983, VF met separately with white-collar unions and Metall, sidestepping the central agreement. SAF negotiated no central bargain in 1988. State efforts to rejuvenate centralized bargaining in 1989 failed when the municipal employees union rejected a government-sponsored price-wage freeze/no-strike agreement that LO and some large employers had worked out. In 1990, SAF disbanded its negotiating division and announced the end of centralized bargaining. In the public sector, the university graduates' union pushed for more decentralized bargaining and individual negotiations for top civil servants. The policemen's union won a favorable contract and threatened to leave TCO because the federation had not supported their demands. In 1990, SAV stopped negotiating centrally with the teachers' and nurses' unions, and bargaining authority devolved to local governments. In 1993, employers insisted that industry bargaining would leave greater leeway to local parties to determine the allocation of changes in aggregate wages, effectively decentralizing a greater part of the wage bargain, even absent drift.

In contrast to some other centralized wage-setting systems, such as that of Austria, Swedish unions, firms, or sectoral employers' associations voluntarily chose to bargain at the peak level rather than separately. This meant that LO and SAF had to develop goals and reach agreements acceptable to member unions and firms, creating a coordinated bargaining structure: An institutional arrangement through which unions (and firms) could arrive at and carry out a common policy (Martin 1992, 49; 1995). In addition, since white-collar and public-employee unions bargain separately, LO and SAF had to consider how these groups would respond to the central agreement; these two second-movers created great problems as their sizes increased. In principle, the key players in the LO-SAF bargaining arrangement were the major export employers and their blue-collar workers. The Swedish model envisaged central bargainers setting wages to maintain competitiveness on world markets, with unions and employers in protected sectors and white-collar workers following the lead of the major private LO union, Metall, and the associated employers' association, VF. Our analysis stresses that the group most likely to want to pull out of a central agreement that imposes "too much" wage discipline is a sector with high r. This appears to be the case in Sweden, with Metall and VF leading the breakup of the centralized system.

Our analysis also stresses that the growth of new organizations (more precisely, an increase in the heterogeneity of the population of bargainers) makes centralized bargaining arrangements more difficult. Table 10.2 measures labor and management organization in Sweden from 1950 to 1988/89. Row 1 documents Sweden's extraordinary rate of unionization, which grew from 50 percent of the workforce in 1950 to peak at 88 percent in 1980, after which it began to fall gradually. Row 2 gives the distribution of union members among the major labor federations: LO, TCO, and SACO/SR. The marked fall in LO's share of unionized workers reflects the successful organization of white-collar workers in the 1950s and 1960s and to a lesser extent the declining blue-collar share of the overall workforce. Row 3 shows a major change in the composition of the workforce in LO, from private-sector employees to public-sector workers, as employment growth in the public sector and increased unionization made the union of central government employees and the union of local government employees major players within LO. By 1989, the union of local government employees had more members than the leading industrial workers union, Metall. Row 4 summarizes the changing shares of the workforce by union status in terms of LO-associated private-sector unions, LO-associated public-sector unions, and SACO/SR-associated unions. It shows that the LO private share of the workforce was as large in 1988/89 as in 1950, which highlights the fact that it was the growth of other organized groups, not any decline in LO private unionization, that reduced the LO private union importance in the organized labor market.

The next part of table 10.2 turns to the employer side of the market. Row 5 estimates the percentage of all workers working for firms affiliated with an employers' federation: a remarkable 82 percent. Row 6 gives the percentage of private-sector workers in SAF-associated firms: the figures in the 1980s were on the order of 55 percent. Because LO does not represent white-collar workers, however, only a third of private-sector workers are directly covered by SAF-LO bargaining. Nearly a quarter are covered by bargaining between white-collar unions, who bargain together in the PTK bargaining consortium, and SAF. An additional 15 percent of private employees work in firms that are members of other associations, notably banking, newspapers, and consumer cooperatives. In total, roughly 80 percent of private workers are employed in firms who are members of employer associations. Row 7 shows the percentage of public-sector workers whose employers are members of associations. Here, membership is universal for workers employed by the central government, whose agencies form the employers' federation SAV, and extremely high (81 percent) for workers employed in public bodies associated with the association of local and county employers. Finally, row 8 gives the estimated share of workers in the various employer-union bargaining pairs. In 1988/89, only 28 percent of the workforce was covered by LO-SAF bargaining, compared to 34 percent of the workforce covered by local public-sector bargaining. This contrasts sharply with the situation in the 1950s and 1960s. By the 1970s, LO and SAF could no longer dominate the organized sector. Instead of a single leading bargaining pair and a large fringe of followers, Swedish collective bargaining expanded to include important white-collar and public-sector bargaining groups.

We speculate that centralized bargaining dominated by LO private-sector unions and SAF potentially contributed to Sweden's unionization of white-collar and public-sector workers through "defensive unionization." This reduced the stability of the centralized wage system. Shifts in bargaining power

Table 10.2   **Percentage of Workers, by Union Confederation and Employer Association in Sweden, 1950–89**

	1950	1960	1970	1980	1988/89
Union confederation					
1. Percentage of all workers who are unionized	51	60	75	88	85
2. Percentage of union members who are:					
LO (blue collar)	80	76	66	62	59
TCO (white collar)	17	20	30	31	33
SACO/SR (professional)	3	4	5	7	8
3. Percentage of LO members who are:					
Private	80	80	76	66	63
Public	20	20	24	34	37
4. Percentage of all workers who are:					
LO private sector	33	36	38	32	33
LO public sector	7	9	11	19	20
Non-LO union	10	14	26	35	35
Employer association					
5. Percentage of all workers in firms who are members of employers' associations	...	...	...	...	82
6. Percentage of private-sector workers in firms in SAF	...	...	...	56	54
Wage earners (LO)	...	...	...	33	31
Salaried (PTK)	...	...	...	23	23
7. Percentage of workers in units in associations:					
Central government (SAV)	...	...	...	...	100
Local association	...	...	...	...	81
Bargaining areas					
8. Percentage of workers in major bargaining areas, by group:					
Private wage (LO-SAF)	...	...	...	...	28
Salaried (PTK-SAF)	...	...	...	...	21
Public central (All-SAV)	...	...	...	...	17
Public local	..	...	...	...	34

Sources: Swedish Statistical Yearbook (Statistisk Arsbok för Sverige); Nilsson (1993).

toward white-collar and skilled workers and employers due to market forces further eroded the economic rationale of wage-solidarity policies. The result was that frame bargaining delivered neither the noninflationary wage settlements that are the sine qua non of centralized arrangements nor economically appropriate wage differentials.

Appendix

We show here that the full-drift model yields the efficient activity level for every realization of r only if $p = q$ and $w_0 = 0$. First, recall that the first-order condition for the negotiated activity level $a_N(r, w)$ is

(A1) $$pc'(a)[rv(a) - w] = (1 - p)rv'(a)[w - c(a)]$$

and that the first-order condition for the efficient activity level $a^*(r)$ is $rv'(a) = c'(a)$. Thus, to achieve $a_N(r, w) = a^*(r)$ for every r, we must have $w = prv[a^*(r)] + (1 - p)c[a^*(r)]$.

Now recall that the first-order condition for the negotiated wage $w_N(r, w_0)$ is

(A2) $$q(rv - w - \pi_0) - (1 - q)(w - c - U_0) +$$
$$a'[(1 - q)(w - c - U_0)rv' - q(rv - w - \pi_0)c'] = 0,$$

where a' denotes the partial derivative of $a_N(r, w)$ with respect to w. Substituting $w = prv[a^*(r)] + (1 - p)c[a^*(r)]$ and $rv'[a^*(r)] = c'[a^*(r)]$ into (A2) yields

(A3) $$\{q[(1 - p)(rv - c) - \pi_0] -$$
$$(1 - q)[p(rv - c) - U_0]\}(1 - a'c') = 0.$$

Computing a' from (A1), and substituting $w = prv[a^*(r)] + (1 - p)c[a^*(r)]$ and $rv'[a^*(r)] = c'[a^*(r)]$ into the expression for a' shows that $1 - a'c' > 0$, so (A3) becomes

(A4) $$(q - p)(rv - c) = q\pi_0 - (1 - q)U_0$$

for every r. Since $U_0 = w_0 - c[a_N(r, w_0)]$ and $\pi_0 = rv[a_N(r, w_0)] - w_0$, (A4) becomes

(A5) $$(q - p)\{rv[a^*(r)] - c[a^*(r)]\} = qrv[a_N(r, w_0)] - w_0 +$$
$$(1 - q)c[a_N(r, w_0)]$$

for every r.

The argument thus far establishes a first interesting result. Stated formally, there is no interval of values of w_0 such that the full-drift model achieves efficient production for every realization of r (because the right-hand side of equation (A5) varies with w_0 but the left does not). Stated informally, it is not true that there is a (positive) critical value of w_0 such that, if the center chooses any wage floor below the critical value, then the wage floor is irrelevant in the sense that for any value of r the parties renegotiate the wage and achieve the efficient activity level.

We show next that (A5) holds for every r only if $p = q$ and $w_0 = 0$. Since the efficient activity level $a^*(r)$ approaches zero as r approaches zero, the left-hand side of (A5) approaches zero as r approaches zero, so w_0 must equal zero because $rv[a_N(r, w_0)]$ and $c[a_N(r, w_0)]$ approach zero as r approaches zero. But, if $w_0 = 0$, then $v[a_N(r, w_0)]$ and $c[a_N(r, w_0)]$ are zero, so the right-hand side of

(A5) is zero for every r, so we must have $p = q$. An informal discussion of this result is given in the text.

References

Ahlen, Kristina. 1989. Swedish collective bargaining under pressure: Inter-union rivalry and incomes policies. *British Journal of Industrial Relations* 27, no. 3 (November): 330–46.

Bosworth, Barry P., and Alice M. Rivlin, eds. 1987. *The Swedish economy.* Washington, D.C.: Brookings.

Bruno, Michael, and Jeffrey Sachs. 1985. *The economics of worldwide stagflation.* Cambridge: Harvard University Press.

Calmfors, Lars. 1987. Efficiency and equality in Swedish labour markets: Comment to Flanagan. In *The Swedish economy,* ed. Barry P. Bosworth and Alice M. Rivlin. Washington, D.C.: Brookings.

Calmfors, Lars, and John Driffil. 1988. Bargaining structure, corporatism and macroeconomic performance. *Economic Policy* 6 (April): 13–62.

Calmfors, Lars, and Anders Forslund. 1990. Wage formation in Sweden. In *Wage formation and macroeconomic policy in the Nordic countries,* ed. Lars Calmfors. Oxford: Oxford University Press.

Calmfors, Lars, and Henrik Horn. 1986. Employment policies and centralised wage-setting. *Economica* 53:281–302.

Crouch, Colin. 1985. Conditions for trade union restraint. In *The politics of inflation and economic stagnation,* ed. L. Lindberg and C. S. Maier. Washington, D.C.: Brookings.

Elster, Jon. 1989. *The cement of society: A study of social order.* Cambridge: Cambridge University Press.

Flanagan, Robert. 1987. Efficiency and equality in Swedish labor markets. In *The Swedish economy,* ed. Barry P. Bosworth and Alice M. Rivlin. Washington, D.C.: Brookings.

Freeman, Richard. 1988. Labour market institutions and economic performance. *Economic Policy* 6:64–80.

Grossman, S., and O. Hart. 1986. The costs and benefits of ownership: A theory of vertical and lateral integration. *Journal of Political Economy* 94:691–719.

Hibbs, Douglas A., Jr., and Håkan Locking. 1991. Wage compression, wage drift, and wage inflation in Sweden. Working Paper no. 87. Stockholm: FIEF (Trade Union Institute for Economic Research), May.

Holmlund, Bertil, and Johnny Zetterberg. 1989. Insider effects in wage determination: Evidence from five countries. Working Paper no. 72. Stockholm: FIEF (Trade Union Institute for Economic Research), October.

Horn, Henrick, and Asher Wolinsky. 1988a. Bilateral monopolies and incentives for merger. *Rand Journal of Economics* 19, no. 3 (Autumn): 408–19.

———. 1988b. Worker substitutability and patterns of unionisation. *Economic Journal* 98 (June): 484–549.

Katz, Harry C. 1993. The decentralization of collective bargaining: A literature review and comparative analysis. *Industrial Labor Relations Review* 47, no. 1 (October): 3–22.

Layard, Richard. 1991. *Why abandon the Swedish model?* Stockholm: FIEF (Trade Union Institute for Economic Research).

Lundberg, Erik. 1985. The rise and fall of the Swedish model. *Journal of Economic Literature* 23 (March): 1–36.

Martin, Andrew. 1984. Trade unions in Sweden: Strategic responses to change and crisis. In *Unions and economic crisis: Britain, West Germany, and Sweden,* ed. P. Gourevitch, A. Martin, G. Ross, C. Allen, S. Bornstein, and A. Markovits. London: Allen & Unwin.

———. 1985. Wages, profits, and investment in Sweden. In *The politics of inflation and economic stagnation,* ed. L. Lindberg and C. S. Maier. Washington, D.C.: Brookings.

———. 1992. *Wage bargaining and Swedish politics: The political implications of the end of central negotiations.* Stockholm: FIEF (Trade Union Institute for Economic Research).

———. 1995. The Swedish model: Demise or reconfiguration? In *Employment relations in a changing world economy,* ed. T. Kochan, R. Locke, and M. Piore. Cambridge: MIT Press, forthcoming.

Nilsson, Christian. 1993. The Swedish model: Labour market institutions and contracts. In *Labour market contracts and institutions: A cross-national comparison,* ed. J. Hartog and J. Theeuwes. Amsterdam: North-Holland.

Olson, Mancur. 1990. How bright are the northern lights? Some questions about Sweden. Craaford Lectures 3, Institute for Economic Research, Lund University.

Skogh, Goran. 1984. Employers associations in Sweden. In *Employers associations and industrial relations: A comparative study,* ed. J. P. Windmuller and A. Gladstone. Oxford: Clarendon.

Soskice, David. 1990. Wage determination: The changing role of institutions in advanced industrialised countries. *Oxford Review of Economic Policy* 6:1–23.

Swedish statistical yearbook (Statistisk arsbok för Sverige). Various editions. Stockholm: Statistiska centralbyran.

Swenson, Peter. 1989. *Fair shares: Unions, pay, and politics in Sweden and West Germany.* Ithaca, N.Y.: Cornell University Press.

Tarentelli, Ezio. 1986. *Economica politica del Lavora.* Turin: UTET.

Udden-Jondal, Eva. 1993. Wage formation in a unionised economy. Ph.D. diss., Stockholm School of Economics.

11   Earnings Inequality in Germany

Katharine G. Abraham and Susan N. Houseman

A number of recent studies have documented the growth of earnings inequality in the United States during the 1980s (see, e.g., Juhn, Murphy, and Pierce 1993; Katz and Murphy 1992; Blackburn, Bloom, and Freeman 1990; and Bound and Johnson 1992). The most salient characteristics of the growth in earnings inequality in the United States are (1) the increase in the relative earnings of more educated workers, (2) the pronounced increase in the earnings of older workers relative to younger workers among those without college degrees, and (3) the increase in earnings inequality within education and age groups. Some recent studies have shown an increase in earnings inequality along similar dimensions in other industrialized countries (Gottschalk and Joyce 1992; Katz, Loveman, and Blanchflower, chap. 1 in this volume; Davis 1992; Green, Coder, and Ryscavage 1992).

In this paper, we examine trends in earnings inequality in the former West Germany. Although we do not present new evidence on earnings trends in the United States, we make frequent reference to findings from other researchers' analyses of U.S. data in an effort to understand the notable differences between the trends that we document for Germany and those that have been documented for the United States.

Most research by German scholars on the structure of wages has focused on intersectoral and interregional wage differentials, although there has been some

Katharine G. Abraham is professor of economics at the University of Maryland and a research associate of the National Bureau of Economic Research. Susan N. Houseman is a senior economist with the W. E. Upjohn Institute for Employment Research.

The authors are indebted to Lutz Bellman for his assistance in obtaining the German social security data used in the paper, to Carolyn Thies for outstanding research assistance, and to Claire Vogelsong for her help both with data entry and in the preparation of the manuscript. Lawrence Katz, Steve Pischke, Michael Piore, and the participants at the conference for which the paper was prepared provided useful comments on an earlier draft.

analysis of earnings differentials across industrial workers in different broad occupation groups. There is clear evidence that wage differentials along all these dimensions narrowed between 1950 and the mid-1960s but that wage differentials generally remained stable or even increased slightly between the mid-1960s and the late 1970s or early 1980s (Thiehoff 1987; Franke 1983; Vogler-Ludwig 1985). Analyses of the relative incomes of workers with different qualifications include Blossfeld (1984) and Bellman and Buttler (1989). Both postulated that the expansion of higher education in Germany beginning in the early 1970s might have led to a fall in the relative earnings of highly educated workers. Their findings concerning trends in the relative incomes of labor market entrants with different qualifications are generally consistent with this hypothesis.

Our study is modeled on the analyses that have documented the growing inequality of earnings in the United States during the 1980s and sought explanations for that growth. In contrast to recent trends in the United States, and in contrast to the conclusions drawn from much sketchier data by Davis (1992) and Green, Coder, and Ryscavage (1992), we find virtually no evidence of growth in earnings inequality in Germany in recent years.[1] Our analysis of two micro-data sets shows that the overall dispersion of earnings in Germany instead has narrowed somewhat, primarily because earnings differentials among workers in the bottom half of the earnings distribution have narrowed. We find little evidence of widening earnings differentials across skill groups, rough stability in the relative earnings of more and less educated workers, no evidence of a general widening of differentials across age groups, and no consistent evidence of widening differentials within either education or age groups.

In trying to explain the widely divergent trends in earnings inequality in Germany and the United States, we consider the effects that various factors may have had. Institutional differences between the German and the U.S. wage-setting processes probably contributed to the quite different trends in earnings inequality in the two countries. We conclude, however, that German wage-setting institutions, which we suspect do tend to limit earnings differentials across groups of workers, cannot on their own explain the different pattern of wage changes in Germany compared with the United States. Different trends in the supply of more highly educated workers in the two countries may help explain why the returns to education grew dramatically in the United States during the 1980s but narrowed in Germany over that period. In addition, institutional differences in the two countries' education systems may have contributed to the different trends in wage inequality that have been observed. German youths who do not attend college arguably receive better general training than their U.S. counterparts, with the result that shifts in relative demand and supply

---

1. The numbers reported for Germany by both Davis (1992) and Green, Coder, and Ryscavage (1992) come from the Luxembourg Income Study (LIS) and refer only to 1981 and 1984. Different surveys underlie the 1981 and 1984 LIS numbers. In addition, it turns out to be misleading to extrapolate from changes in the distribution of income observed over the period 1981–84.

produce smaller changes in relative marginal products, and thus relative wages, in Germany than in the United States.

The remainder of the paper is organized as follows. Section 11.1 presents evidence on trends in earnings inequality in Germany in recent years. Section 11.2 examines the potential influences of wage-setting institutions, demand and supply factors, and the structure of the education system on trends in German earnings inequality. Our findings and conclusions are summarized in section 11.3.

11.1   Trends in Earnings Inequality in Germany

We draw from several different data sources in our analysis of trends in wage inequality in Germany. The first is an establishment survey that collects information for the industrial sector on the compensation of workers in each of seven occupation groups. We also make extensive use of micro data from social security earnings records and from the German Socioeconomic Panel, both of which are described in greater detail below.

The Survey of Compensation in Industry and Trade (Verdiensterhebung in Industrie und Handel) is of interest primarily because it provides the longest available time series on the relative earnings of workers in different skill groups. The survey yields data for blue- and white-collar workers employed at establishments with ten or more employees in manufacturing, mining, construction, and utilities. Employers responding to the survey report earnings separately for men and women in each of three blue-collar and four white-collar job categories. The job categories for which data are reported and their approximate shares of covered employment in 1986 are as follows: unskilled blue-collar jobs (BC1), 12 percent; semiskilled blue-collar jobs (BC2), 24 percent; skilled blue-collar jobs (BC3), 35 percent; white-collar positions requiring no vocational training (WC1), 1 percent; junior supervisory staff positions (WC2), 5 percent; foremen's or supervisory positions (WC3), 14 percent; and middle-management positions (WC4), 10 percent (Fels and Gundlach 1990). Data for top executives are not reported, and respondents are asked to report earnings in each of the included occupation categories only for full-time workers who are not apprentices.[2] We use tabulations of mean weekly (blue collar) or monthly (white collar) earnings by sex and occupation group from this survey published by the Federal Statistical Office (Statistisches Bundesamt).[3]

---

2. Data from another survey, the 1978 Wage and Salary Structure Survey (Gehalts- und Lohnstrukturerhebung 1978), indicate that the excluded top management category accounts for only about 1 percent of industrial employment. Part-timers account for about 5 percent of industrial employment.

3. The individual establishment reports from this survey are not available for use by researchers. Data on blue-collar workers come from Statistisches Bundesamt, *Fachserie 16: Löhne und Gehälter, Reihe 2.1: Arbeiterverdienste in der Industrie* (Wiesbaden) and data on white-collar workers from *Fachserie 16: Löhne und Gehälter, Reihe 2.2: Angestelltenverdienste in Industrie und Handel* (Wiesbaden).

Figure 11.1 shows trends in the relative earnings of blue- and white-collar workers by skill group over the period 1964–89. Figure 11.1*a* displays trends in relative earnings for men; figure 11.1*b* displays trends for women.[4] Particularly for men, the ratio of white-collar to blue-collar earnings appears somewhat cyclically sensitive, rising during recessions and falling during upturns. This reflects the cyclic sensitivity of blue-collar workers' weekly hours. Since the late 1970s, again particularly among men, the earnings of white-collar workers have increased somewhat relative to the earnings of blue-collar workers. These changes in relative earnings are, however, not large; only the earnings of the most skilled male white-collar workers were notably higher relative to the earnings of men in other groups in 1989 than they had been in 1975.

A major limitation of the Verdiensterhebung in Industrie und Handel is that only average earnings for workers in broadly defined occupational groups are collected. In order to draw a more detailed picture of recent trends in the distribution of earnings across individual workers in Germany, we use two microdata sets. The first contains social security data housed with the Federal Employment Service (Bundesanstalt für Arbeit). The social security data cover all workers included in the social security system; the major exclusions are government workers and the self-employed. These exclusions are of some significance because a large share of highly educated Germans work in the public sector. The share of all dependent employees covered by the social security system is close to 90 percent, but comparisons between data from the German Mikrozensus (a household survey) and data from social security records reported by Clement, Tessaring, and Weisshuhn (1980) indicate that only about one-third of employed university (*Hochschule*) graduates and two-thirds of employed technical college (*Fachhochschule*) graduates were in covered employment in 1978. Social security records include information on gross earnings subject to the social security tax, gender, educational qualifications, and birth date. They also contain information on whether an individual worked full-time or part-time and on the share of the year that the individual worked.

The Bundesanstalt für Arbeit generally does not allow outside researchers direct access to the social security data. We were given special tabulations based on a longitudinal sample used by researchers there. This longitudinal data set was constructed by sampling randomly from the population of men who paid social security taxes in any year from 1976 through 1984 and includes a record for each selected man for each year in which he held a covered job.[5] Our tabulations report the number of persons with annualized social security earnings in thousand-deutsche-mark (DM) increments for full-time (al-

---

4. To calculate the reported white-collar/blue-collar ratios, the weekly earnings of blue-collar workers were multiplied by 4.3 to make them comparable to the monthly white-collar earnings.

5. The method used to construct the longitudinal data file is such that the sample of records for each year should be representative of all men in covered employment in that year. Because of an unspecified problem with the 1984 earnings data, we were not sent tabulations for that year.

Fig. 11.1   Relative earnings trends

though not necessarily full-year) male workers, by education and age.[6] The sample size in each year is about fifty-five thousand persons. These tabulations allow us to approximate earnings by education and age at various percentiles of the earnings distribution.[7]

The major limitation of the social security data is that reported earnings are truncated at the social security taxation threshold. The earnings cutoff varies from year to year. Except in 1976 and 1977, fewer than 10 percent of sampled workers have censored earnings, but censoring is more of a problem for the most educated and the oldest subgroups in the data set. In most years, more than half of *Hochschule* graduates had earnings in excess of the social security maximum, and we were therefore unable to approximate median earnings for

6. Annualized earnings were created by dividing a person's total social security earnings during a year by his days of employment in that year, then multiplying the resulting daily earnings figure by 365.

7. We approximated the median by interpolation as E1 + [(0.50 − P1)/(P2 − P1)] × (E2 − E1), where E1 is the level of earnings at the lower boundary of the cell containing the median, E2 is the level of earnings at the upper boundary of the cell containing the median, P1 is the share of persons with earnings in cells below the cell containing the median, and P2 is the share of persons with earnings either in the cell containing the median or in a lower cell. Similar calculations were made to identify the ninetieth percentile and the tenth percentile of earnings.

this group. For the same reason, we were unable to approximate the 1976 median earnings of *Fachhochschule* graduates. In addition, it was impossible to construct an estimate of earnings at the ninetieth percentile of the earnings distribution for *Fachhochschule* graduates, *Hochschule* graduates, persons aged forty to forty-nine, persons aged fifty to fifty-nine, or persons aged sixty and older in any year.

The second micro-data set that we use is the German Socioeconomic Panel (GSOEP), which is similar to the Panel Study of Income Dynamics. A 95 percent sample drawn from the data set is available to non-German researchers. The panel was begun in 1984 and covers about five thousand households. We report data on average monthly earnings for the years from 1983 (interview year 1984) through 1989, the year prior to German reunification, and the sample used for this paper covers only households in the former West Germany.[8] Foreigners are oversampled relative to their share of the population. We therefore used sample weights when calculating basic summary statistics with these data. The GSOEP includes information on average gross monthly earnings, other pay such as thirteenth- and fourteenth-month pay and holiday allowances,[9] gender, nationality, birth year, type of secondary education, and university or occupation qualification. The earnings measure that we report for the GSOEP is average monthly earnings plus one-twelfth of any thirteenth-month pay, fourteenth-month pay, or holiday allowances received during the calendar year preceding the survey interview.[10] All our analysis has been replicated using pay in the month prior to the survey interview in place of the earnings measure just described. None of our results is sensitive to the earnings measure used. Unlike the social security earnings measure, the GSOEP earnings measures are neither reported by intervals nor truncated at an upper threshold. Furthermore, whereas the social security data are limited to full-time, covered employment but include part-year employees, the GSOEP sample that we study is not restricted to employment covered by the social security system but includes only full-time, full-year workers. For these reasons, figures from the social security data and the GSOEP data are not strictly comparable.

Table 11.1 presents trends in the overall distribution of German earnings from the social security and the GSOEP data. The reported numbers based on the social security data, which appear in the table's top panel, show the ratios

---

8. We have updated our analysis of the GSOEP data on households in the former West Germany through 1991. The basic trends in the GSOEP data documented for the 1980s also are apparent in the early 1990s.

9. It is common practice for German employers to give their employees a lump-sum payment in the amount of one to two months' pay at the end of the calendar year. This pay is termed *thirteenth-month* or *fourteenth-month pay,* as appropriate. The amount of such pay commonly is specified in the applicable collective bargaining agreement.

10. Persons with implausibly low earnings (less than DM 500 per month) or implausibly high earnings (anyone in the upper tail of the earnings distribution whose average monthly earnings were grossly out of line with the average monthly earnings reported by the same individual in other years) were excluded from the sample. In all years, these exclusions reduced the size of our sample by less than 1 percent.

Table 11.1   **Trends in the Distribution of Earnings in Germany**

	Earnings Ratios for Male Full-Time Workers[a]		
	90th/10th Percentile	90th/50th Percentile	50th/10th Percentile
1976	...	...	1.49
1977	...	...	1.52
1978	2.24	1.48	1.51
1979	2.19	1.46	1.50
1980	2.18	1.46	1.49
1981	2.18	1.46	1.50
1982	2.19	1.50	1.46
1983	2.23	1.52	1.47
	Earnings Ratios for Male Full-Time, Full-Year Workers[b]		
1983	2.62	1.72	1.52
1984	2.60	1.71	1.52
1985	2.50	1.73	1.45
1986	2.53	1.73	1.47
1987	2.45	1.73	1.41
1988	2.43	1.69	1.44
1989	2.41	1.72	1.40
	Earnings Ratios for All Full-Time, Full-Year Workers[b]		
1983	2.80	1.72	1.63
1984	2.99	1.73	1.73
1985	2.72	1.73	1.57
1986	2.63	1.71	1.54
1987	2.61	1.73	1.51
1988	2.53	1.68	1.51
1989	2.58	1.72	1.50

[a]Authors' calculations using social security earnings data. The underlying numbers are annualized earnings for all men who worked full-time for any part of the year. In both 1976 and 1977, the ninetieth percentile of the distribution of annualized earnings fell above the maximum earnings subject to social security tax and thus was not observed in these data.

[b]Authors' calculations using German Socioeconomic Panel data. The underlying numbers are average monthly earnings for either the male or the total population of full-time, full-year workers.

of the ninetieth/tenth, the ninetieth/fiftieth, and the fiftieth/tenth percentile levels of earnings for full-time male workers over the period 1976–83. As already indicated, we were unable to calculate the ninetieth percentile level of earnings for either 1976 or 1977. The numbers in the table's bottom two panels are based on the GSOEP data and show the same ratios for male full-time, full-year workers and for all full-time, full-year workers over the period 1983–89.

The most striking finding to emerge from this table is the absence of increased dispersion in the overall distribution of earnings over either the 1978–83 or 1983–89 period. In the social security data for 1978–83, the ratio of the earnings of males at the ninetieth percentile of the earnings distribution to the earnings of males at the fiftieth percentile rose slightly, and the ratio of the earnings of males at the fiftieth percentile to the earnings of males at the tenth percentile fell slightly, leaving the 90–10 differential essentially unchanged. The GSOEP numbers suggest that, both for males and for males and females combined, the 90–50 differential was roughly constant between 1983 and 1989 but that the 50–10 differential fell by about 8 percent so that the differential between the ninetieth and the tenth percentiles of the earnings distribution also fell.

Our finding of narrowing differentials at the bottom of the earnings distribution is similar to that reported for France in Katz, Loveman, and Blanchflower (chap. 1 in this volume) and is in striking contrast to trends in the United States in the 1980s. In the United States, the earnings of those at the bottom of the distribution fell both in absolute real terms and relative to the rest of the workforce. In Germany, the real earnings of all groups were rising, and the least-well-paid workers were gaining on the rest of the workforce.

In the United States, the dramatic rise in earnings differentials across education groups is an important part of the overall growth in earnings inequality. Before looking at trends in earnings differentials by education group in Germany, we provide a brief description of the basic structure of the German education system. As shown in figure 11.2, German youths enter school at age six and typically spend four years at a *Grundschule* or neighborhood primary school. At age ten, they must choose to attend one of three types of secondary school: a *Hauptschule,* a *Realschule,* or a *Gymnasium.*

The *Hauptschule* curriculum generally takes about five years to complete and prepares students for apprenticeships in the trades, semiskilled office work, retail sales, or domestic services. The typical apprenticeship lasts three years, with apprentices spending roughly a day a week at a *Berufschule* or part-time vocational school. The *Realschule* curriculum takes about six years to complete and prepares students either for further vocational secondary schooling or for apprenticeships in higher-level occupations. Those who graduate from a full-time vocational secondary school, in turn, may qualify for attendance at a *Fachhochscule. Fachhochschulen* offer curricula similar to those in applied fields at U.S. universities. Those who successfully complete the nine-year course of study and subsequent examinations at a *Gymnasium* receive an *Abitur,* a certificate that qualifies them for enrollment at a *Hochschule* or university. It is possible to obtain a *Hochschule* degree in as little as five years, although the typical student takes longer. While most of those who receive the *Abitur* enroll in postsecondary education, a significant and growing minority choose instead to enter an apprenticeship.

In the social security data that we use to examine trends in relative earnings over the period 1976–83, workers are classified into five qualification groups.

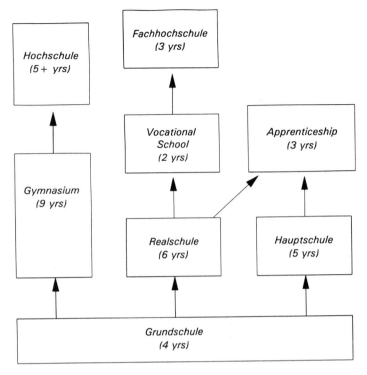

Fig. 11.2   The German education system
Source: Adapted from Teichler and Sanyal (1982).

Because of data limitations, we use earnings information for only three of these groups in our by-education-level analysis: (1) persons with no occupational qualification, a group that includes *Hauptschule* and *Realschule* graduates who did not complete an apprenticeship or graduate from a full-time vocational secondary school; (2) persons with an occupational qualification, which might be either a completed apprenticeship or graduation from a full-time vocational secondary school; and (3) *Fachhochschule* graduates.[11] Our tabulations of GSOEP data for the period 1983–89 make use of earnings information for three groups: (1) persons with no occupational qualification; (2) persons with an occupational qualification, most typically completion of an apprenticeship; and (3) persons who graduated from either a *Fachhochschule* or a *Hochschule*.[12]

11. The remaining two groups were *Hochschule* graduates and persons holding an *Abitur* but having no other qualification. The earnings of *Hochschule* graduates frequently exceeded the social security maximum and thus were truncated; the number of people holding an *Abitur* but possessing no other qualification is small.

12. The survey questionnaire contains more detailed questions concerning respondents' educational and training background, but sample sizes for more disaggregated groups were too small to

Table 11.2 presents trends in German earnings by education from the social security and GSOEP data. The ratios presented in this table were calculated using the median earnings for each education group. As already noted, we were unable to calculate the median earnings for *Hochschule* graduates for most years covered by the social security data, and we were also unable to compute 1976 median earnings for *Fachhochschule* graduates. Because those with *Hochschule* and *Fachhochschule* degrees are grouped together in the tabulations based on the GSOEP data, we would have preferred to report social security medians for *Fachhochschule* and *Hochschule* graduates together, but, because of the truncation problems already discussed, the median for this combined category could be approximated for only three years.

Table 11.2 shows no general widening of earnings differentials across education groups since the mid-1970s. The social security data in the top panel of the table indicate that, over the period 1977–83, the relative earnings of those with a *Fachhochschule* degree rose slightly relative to both those with no qualification and those with an occupational qualification, but the GSOEP data in the second and third panel indicate that these trends were at least partially reversed during the period 1983–89. The social security data suggest that there was a slight decline in the earnings of those with an occupational qualification relative to those with no qualification between 1976 and 1983; the relative earnings of workers in these two groups also declined between 1983 and 1989.

Another prominent feature of the growth in earnings inequality in the United States has been the widening of experience- and age-related earnings differentials. The German figures reported in table 11.3 show no comparable widening of differences in earnings across age groups. Although the social security data reveal some increase in the earnings of workers aged forty and older relative to workers aged twenty to twenty-nine over the period 1976–83, the GSOEP data suggest that this increase was largely reversed during the mid-1980s. The earnings of persons aged thirty to thirty-nine rose at the same pace as the earnings of those aged twenty to twenty-nine between 1976 and 1983, but the earnings advantage of thirty- to thirty-nine-year-olds was eroded between 1983 and 1989. If any general conclusion can be drawn from the evidence on median earnings by age group, it is that age-related earnings differentials in Germany have been relatively stable or have narrowed since the mid-1970s.

While widening education and age differentials are important features of the growth in overall inequality observed in the United States, the dispersion of earnings within education and age groups has also widened there. Perhaps not surprisingly, given the patterns of change in the distribution of German earnings that we have already documented, there does not appear to have been a comparable widening of within-group dispersion in earnings in Germany. Ta-

---

support meaningful analyses. Sample size considerations also dictated grouping *Hochschule* and *Fachhochschule* graduates. Persons with an *Abitur* but no other qualification were assigned to a fourth category that does not appear in our by-education-level tabulations.

Table 11.2	**Trends in Earnings by Education in Germany**

	Earnings Ratios for Male Full-Time Workers[a]		
	Fachhochschule/ No Qualification	Occupational Qualification/ No Qualification	*Fachhochschule/* Occupational Qualification
1976	. . .	1.18	. . .
1977	1.67	1.18	1.42
1978	1.70	1.17	1.45
1979	1.66	1.17	1.42
1980	1.68	1.17	1.44
1981	1.68	1.17	1.44
1982	1.70	1.15	1.48
1983	1.73	1.15	1.50

	Earnings Ratios for Male Full-Time, Full-Year Workers[b]		
	Fachhochschule/ No Qualification	Occupational Qualification/ No Qualification	*Hochschule* or *Fachhochschule/* Occupational Qualification
1983	1.98	1.19	1.66
1984	1.99	1.20	1.66
1985	1.93	1.19	1.62
1986	1.90	1.15	1.66
1987	1.98	1.19	1.67
1988	1.95	1.18	1.66
1989	1.92	1.17	1.64

	Earnings Ratios for All Full-Time, Full-Year Workers[b]		
	Hochschule or *Fachhochschule/* No Qualification	Occupational Qualification/ No Qualification	*Hochschule* or *Fachhochschule/* Occupational Qualification
1983	2.06	1.26	1.64
1984	2.02	1.22	1.65
1985	2.00	1.22	1.64
1986	2.07	1.24	1.67
1987	1.91	1.21	1.58
1988	1.97	1.19	1.65
1989	1.91	1.17	1.63

[a]Ratios of median earnings for each of the two indicated education groups, based on authors' calculations using social security earnings data. The underlying numbers are annualized earnings for all men who worked full-time for any part of the year. In 1976, the median of the distribution of annualized earnings for *Fachhochschule* graduates exceeded the maximum earnings subject to social security tax and thus was not observed in these data.

[b]Ratios of median earnings for each of the two indicated education groups, based on authors' calculations using German Socioeconomic Panel data. The underlying numbers are average monthly earnings for either the male or the total population of full-time, full-year workers.

Table 11.3   Trends in Earnings by Age Group in Germany

Earnings Ratios for Male Full-Time Workers[a]

	30–39/20–29	40–49/20–29	50–59/20–29	60+/20–29
1976	1.24	1.22	1.20	1.09
1977	1.23	1.21	1.19	1.08
1978	1.26	1.24	1.20	1.10
1979	1.24	1.23	1.19	1.13
1980	1.25	1.25	1.20	1.13
1981	1.25	1.26	1.20	1.16
1982	1.25	1.27	1.21	1.21
1983	1.25	1.29	1.23	1.19

Earnings Ratios for Male Full-Time, Full-Year Workers[b]

	30–39/20–29	40–49/20–29	50–59/20–29	60+/20–29
1983	1.35	1.45	1.34	1.35
1984	1.30	1.41	1.31	1.30
1985	1.30	1.38	1.26	1.36
1986	1.28	1.35	1.29	1.35
1987	1.25	1.40	1.24	1.27
1988	1.26	1.42	1.27	1.29
1989	1.22	1.40	1.28	1.20

Earnings Ratios for All Full-Time, Full-Year Workers[b]

	30–39/20–29	40–49/20–29	50–59/20–29	60+/20–29
1983	1.36	1.43	1.39	1.36
1984	1.36	1.42	1.38	1.38
1985	1.33	1.39	1.33	1.47
1986	1.36	1.43	1.36	1.45
1987	1.27	1.40	1.26	1.33
1988	1.29	1.44	1.30	1.32
1989	1.25	1.38	1.29	1.28

[a]Ratios of median earnings for each of the two indicated age groups, based on authors' calculations using social security earnings data. The underlying numbers are annualized earnings for all men who worked full-time for any part of the year.

[b]Ratios of median earnings for each of the two indicated age groups, based on authors' calculations using German Socioeconomic Panel data. The underlying numbers are average monthly earnings for either the male or the total population of full-time, full-year workers.

ble 11.4 reports annual values of the 90–10 differential for selected education groups; table 11.5 reports the same statistic for selected age groups. These differentials exhibit no consistent trend over the period 1976–83 and, if anything, have fallen over the period 1983–89.

One question that might be raised about the figures presented thus far is whether the patterns that they reveal are an artifact of changes in the composition of particular education or age groups. One way to address this question would be to prepare similar tabulations for groups defined using information on a larger number of characteristics (e.g., both education and age). Our ability to do this is limited. We have, however, used the GSOEP to fit a set of standard earnings regressions, one for each year, that allow us to examine how the returns to various individual characteristics have changed over time. In table 11.6, we report the results of this analysis only for the odd-numbered years in order to conserve space.[13] In these regressions, the dependent variable is the log of average monthly earnings (including one-twelfth of thirteenth-month, fourteenth-month, and holiday pay). The models include two sets of education and training dummies, one intended to capture an individual's occupational preparation and the other to capture his or her secondary school background. The first set of education and training measures includes dummy variables for *Hochschule* and *Fachhochschule* graduates, for those with an occupational qualification, and for those with some other educational qualification; the omitted category includes those with no occupational qualification. The second set includes dummies for completion of the *Abitur,* graduation from a vocational secondary school, graduation from a *Realschule,* graduation from a *Hauptschule,* and completion of some other secondary curriculum (this involves mostly foreigners); the omitted category includes persons with no completed secondary education. The model also includes age and age squared along with a dummy variable for females, interactions between the female dummy and the age terms, and a dummy variable for foreigners.

While the coefficient on the dummy variable for *Hochschule* or *Fachhochschule* degree remains fairly constant over time, the coefficient on the dummy variable for those with a vocational qualification drops by over 40 percent between 1983 and 1989. The implied decline in the return to having a vocational qualification is consistent with the tabulations reported in table 11.2 above, and also with the narrowing of earnings differentials in the bottom half of the earnings distribution between 1983 and 1989 shown in table 11.1 above.[14] Consistent with the findings reported in table 11.3 above, the results of table 11.6 also imply that age-related earnings differences declined over this period.

11.2 Alternative Explanations

One possible explanation for why earnings differentials have not grown in Germany as they have in the United States is that the solidaristic wage policies

13. The coefficients from earnings regressions for the even-numbered years depict trends similar to those reported.

14. The coefficient on the "other occupational training" dummy variable also drops dramatically, although it is hard to interpret this finding. The sample in this category is small, and the drop may be due to a change in the composition of workers in it.

Table 11.4   **Trends in the Distribution of Earnings for Selected Education Groups in Germany**

	Ratios of the 90th to the 10th Percentile of Earnings for Male Full-Time Workers[a]		
	No Qualification	Occupational Qualification	*Fachhochschule*
1976	2.05	1.98	. . .
1977	2.07	2.00	. . .
1978	2.06	2.04	. . .
1979	2.06	2.03	. . .
1980	2.02	1.99	. . .
1981	2.00	2.02	. . .
1982	1.94	2.03	. . .
1983	1.95	2.04	. . .

	Ratios of the 90th to the 10th Percentile of Earnings for Male Full-Time, Full-Year Workers[b]		
	No Qualification	Occupational Qualification	*Hochschule* or *Fachhochschule*
1983	2.01	2.18	2.00
1984	2.03	2.12	1.91
1985	1.83	2.10	2.12
1986	2.13	2.12	1.94
1987	1.77	2.12	1.97
1988	1.82	2.00	1.94
1989	1.80	2.02	2.12

	Ratios of the 90th to the 10th Percentile of Earnings for All Full-Time, Full-Year Workers[b]		
	No Qualification	Occupational Qualification	*Hochschule* or *Fachhochschule*
1983	2.32	2.36	2.26
1984	2.34	2.25	2.03
1985	2.03	2.25	2.18
1986	2.04	2.21	2.01
1987	1.99	2.23	2.27
1988	1.96	2.10	2.07
1989	2.10	2.12	2.29

[a]The reported ratios are based on authors' calculations using social security earnings data. The underlying numbers are annualized earnings for all men who worked full-time for any part of the year. Ratios are not reported for cases in which earnings at the ninetieth percentile of the earnings distribution exceeded the maximum earnings subject to social security tax and thus were not observed in these data.

[b]The reported ratios are based on authors' calculations using German Socioeconomic Panel data. The underlying numbers are average monthly earnings for either the male or the total population of full-time, full-year workers.

Table 11.5   **Trends in the Distribution of Earnings for Selected Age Groups in Germany**

	Ratios of the 90th to the 10th Percentile of Earnings for Male Full-Time Workers[a]		
	Aged 20–29	Aged 30–39	Aged 40–49
1976	1.91	. . .	. . .
1977	1.91	. . .	. . .
1978	1.94	1.97	. . .
1979	1.95	1.96	. . .
1980	1.90	1.91	. . .
1981	1.95	1.90	. . .
1982	1.96	1.94	. . .
1983	1.97	1.98	. . .
	Ratios of the 90th to the 10th Percentile of Earnings for Male Full-Time, Full-Year Workers[b]		
1983	2.26	2.21	2.31
1984	2.16	2.21	2.36
1985	1.84	2.13	2.49
1986	1.87	2.19	2.43
1987	1.89	2.12	2.33
1988	1.79	2.16	2.18
1989	1.74	2.22	2.35
	Ratios of the 90th to the 10th Percentile of Earnings for All Full-Time, Full-Year Workers[b]		
1983	2.29	2.33	2.61
1984	2.38	2.39	2.62
1985	2.08	2.26	2.66
1986	2.02	2.26	2.60
1987	2.00	2.26	2.44
1988	1.96	2.21	2.30
1989	1.91	2.30	2.51

[a]The reported ratios are based on authors' calculations using social security earnings data. The underlying numbers are annualized earnings for all men who worked full-time for any part of the year. Ratios are not reported for cases in which earnings at the ninetieth percentile of the earnings distribution exceeded the maximum earnings subject to social security tax and thus were not observed in these data.

[b]The reported ratios are based on authors' calculations using German Socioeconomic Panel data. The underlying numbers are average monthly earnings for either the male or the total population of full-time, full-year workers.

Table 11.6   Trends in the Returns to Education and Age in Germany: Dependent Variable, log (avg. monthly earnings)

	1983	1985	1987	1989
HOCHSCHULE/FACHHOCHSCHULE DEGREE	.289	.305	.273	.286
(Yes = 1)	(.027)	(.030)	(.033)	(.036)
VOCATIONAL QUALIFICATON (Yes = 1)	.115	.088	.078	.064
	(.012)	(.014)	(.015)	(.017)
OTHER OCCUPATIONAL TRAINING (Yes = 1)	.186	.080	.056	−.027
	(.048)	(.055)	(.058)	(.061)
GYMNASIUM/ABITUR (Yes = 1)	.266	.216	.244	.214
	(.031)	(.032)	(.035)	(.037)
VOCATIONAL SECONDARY SCHOOL	.249	.174	.209	.221
(Yes = 1)	(.034)	(.036)	(.037)	(.042)
REALSCHULE (Yes = 1)	.114	.068	.076	.081
	(.020)	(.019)	(.019)	(.022)
HAUPTSCHULE (Yes = 1)	−.014	−.056	−.066	−.068
	(.016)	(.014)	(.014)	(.016)
OTHER SECONDARY EDUCATION (Yes = 1)	.016	.026	.050	.036
	(.065)	(.066)	(.079)	(.083)
AGE	.076	.057	.052	.050
	(.003)	(.004)	(.004)	(.004)
AGE SQUARED[a]	−.083	−.060	−.056	−.054
	(.004)	(.005)	(.005)	(.005)
FEMALE	.078	−.165	−.417	−.331
	(.120)	(.126)	(.127)	(.142)
FEMALE · AGE	−.015	−.001	.010	.004
	(.007)	(.007)	(.007)	(.008)
FEMALE · AGE SQUARED[a]	.013	.004	−.014	−.006
	(.008)	(.009)	(.009)	(.010)
FOREIGN	−.086	−.128	−.125	−.123
	(.012)	(.011)	(.011)	(.012)
Intercept	6.309	6.847	7.040	7.186
	(.069)	(.073)	(.074)	(.086)
N	4107	3684	3586	3212

Note: Standard errors are in parentheses.
[a]Coefficients and standard errors are multiplied by 100.

pursued by German trade unions constrain the behavior of relative wages. A second hypothesis is that the very different evolution of relative earnings in the two countries reflects differences in demand and supply conditions. Finally, the relative stability of earnings differentials in Germany might reflect the stronger general training received by German youths who do not attend college, which arguably makes workers with different levels of education and experience closer substitutes in Germany than in the United States. We consider these explanations in turn.

11.2.1 Wage-Setting Institutions

Differences in German and U.S. wage-setting institutions offer an appealing potential explanation for the divergent trends in earnings inequality in the two countries.[15] German unions generally have pursued what has been termed a *solidaristic* wage policy. At times, they have sought to narrow the gap between highly paid and less highly paid workers. More typically, they have sought uniform percentage increases in wages for all workers. In a period when market forces would dictate growing differentials in wage rates by skill level, these policies seem likely to limit any increase in the dispersion of wages that would otherwise occur.

Because of the importance of the collective bargaining system in Germany, union wage policies are likely to have a substantial impact on the overall structure of German wages. Most German workers are covered by collective agreements. In contrast to the highly decentralized process by which U.S. workers' wages are determined, German wages are determined by fairly centralized collective bargaining between unions and employers' associations. Between 35 and 40 percent of German workers are union members. Unlike the situation in the United States, union representation in Germany has not fallen over the past two decades (see Freeman 1989). Moreover, roughly 90 percent of workers are employed by firms that belong to an employers' association. Collective agreements most typically cover workers in a particular industry and *Land* (state).[16]

Nonunion members employed in a company that belongs to an employers' association also are likely to benefit from collective bargaining. Although the terms of a collective bargaining agreement between a union and an employers' association are binding only with respect to the wages and working conditions offered to union members employed by members of the employers' association, employers almost universally choose to treat union members and nonmembers alike.

Even workers in companies that do not belong to an employers' association may be covered by a collective agreement. If a contract covers at least half the workforce in a particular sector and region, and if the minister of labor and social affairs determines that there is a compelling public interest that the contract be generally binding, the contract may be extended to cover employers who are not members of the employers' association. Although only about 4 percent of all pay agreements are extended (see Lindena and Höhmann 1989),

---

15. The following discussion of German wage-setting institutions draws heavily on both Brandes, Meyer, and Schudlich (1991) and Paque (n.d.), both of which provide further details. The interpretation of the likely consequences of these institutions that we offer is ours, not theirs.

16. Contracts in some industries are national in scope, while others cover geographic areas smaller than a *Land*. In addition, there are many single-employer bargaining units, although most are small; these units together account for only about 6 percent of covered workers.

virtually all employers choose to comply with the terms of the contract in their industry and region. This may reflect, in part, the threat of a formal contract extension.

Unlike collective bargaining agreements in the United States, German agreements set only a floor on wages and working conditions. Any employer is free to pay more than is specified in the contract, and many choose to do so. Unfortunately, it is extremely difficult to measure the size of the gap between actual wages and contractual wages. Published statistics on actual and contractual wages are not comparable either conceptually or with respect to the skill groupings employed.[17] One recent employer survey that asked directly about this gap concluded that only about 15 percent of employers paid exactly the negotiated rate, while on average actual pay exceeded negotiated pay by 14 percent (Brandes, Meyer, and Schudlich 1991).

The fact that many employers choose to pay in excess of the negotiated rate does not imply, of course, that the terms of the collective agreement have no effect on what these employers pay. At least some employers deliberately choose to pay in excess of the negotiated rate as part of a "high-wage" policy; increases in the negotiated rate of pay are likely to lead these employers to raise their pay rates as well, even though they are not bound to do so. Anecdotal evidence also suggests that payments in excess of the negotiated wage are much more common for highly skilled workers than for workers at the bottom of the skill ladder.

In light of the importance of collective bargaining coupled with the solidaristic wage policy of unions, we would expect that any pressures toward greater wage inequality would be muted in Germany. Our finding that wage inequality in Germany did not grow during the 1980s is thus consistent with what an examination of German wage-setting institutions would have led one to expect. The finding that differences in earnings at the bottom of the wage distribution declined during this period while differences in earnings at the top of the distribution were more stable is also consistent with the structure of German wage-setting institutions, insofar as contractual wage floors are more likely to have been binding for the less skilled groups whose relative market wages we might have expected to have fallen.

11.2.2   Demand and Supply

Many researchers have suggested that shifts in the industrial composition of employment have contributed to the growth in earnings differentials across education groups in the United States. In particular, it is argued that the decline of manufacturing has resulted in the loss of many high-paying jobs for low-skilled workers. Table 11.7 shows the distribution of employment by broad

---

17. The most important conceptual difference between the two sorts of numbers is that the actual pay statistics include payments for overtime as well as other special payments, whereas the contractual pay statistics refer only to the hourly rate for a set of jobs.

Table 11.7   **Distribution of Employment by Industry (%)**

	1969	1979	1989
Germany			
Agriculture	1.4	1.1	.9
Mining	1.6	1.5	.8
Manufacturing	44.6	37.8	34.0
Utilities	.9	1.1	1.0
Construction	8.8	7.8	6.6
Trade, restaurants and hotels	12.9	13.6	14.7
Transport, storage, and communication	6.5	6.5	6.2
Fire, insurance, and real estate; business services	4.2	5.7	7.4
Community, social, and personal services	19.0	25.0	28.2
United States			
Agriculture	4.7	3.6	2.9
Mining	.7	.9	.6
Manufacturing	27.3	22.7	18.5
Utilities	1.2	1.1	1.1
Construction	6.2	6.5	6.5
Trade, restaurants and hotels	19.8	21.5	22.1
Transport, storage, and communication	6.0	5.7	5.4
Fire, insurance, and real estate; business services	6.5	8.2	11.3
Community, social, and personal services	27.5	29.7	31.6

Source: OECD, *Labour Force Statistics, 1969–1989* (Paris, 1991).

sector in 1969, 1979, and 1989 for Germany and the United States. Although the manufacturing sector is relatively more important in Germany than in the United States, the two countries have experienced comparable declines in the manufacturing sector's share of employment. Similarly, both countries have experienced large relative increases in service-sector employment, particularly employment in finance, insurance, real estate, and business services, and in community, social, and personal services.

To assess more formally the effects of changes in the industrial mix of employment on the demand for workers by education level, we constructed an index of demand using a shift-share analysis like that in Freeman (1975). Construction of this sort of index requires information both on the educational composition of employment by sector for some base period and on changes in the sectoral composition of employment over time. We used data from a special tabulation of the 1985 Mikrozensus on the share of workers in each of three education categories—those who had graduated from a *Hochschule* or *Fachhochschule,* those with an occupational qualification, and those in a residual category including both persons with no occupational qualification and persons not reporting their educational attainment—for each of fifty-three sectors of the economy. These proportions were then applied as weights to total annual employment in each of the fifty-three sectors over the period 1960–89 to construct a derived demand for each category of worker for each year. Specifically, this measure of demand for workers with education i in year t is calculated as

$$\sum_{j=1}^{53} w_{ij} E_{jt},$$

where j indexes the industry, w_{ij} is the proportion of workers in industry j with education i in the base year, and E_{jt} is total employment in industry j in year t.[18] Changes in this measure between any two years represent changes in the demand for a particular education group attributable to changes in the sectoral composition of employment.

Table 11.8 reports the rate of growth in this measure of demand by education level over the period 1960–89 and various subperiods. In all periods, there has been much more rapid growth in demand stemming from industrial changes for *Hochschule* or *Fachhochschule* graduates than for workers with an occupational qualification; demand for workers with no occupational qualification has actually fallen. The differences in the rate of growth of demand for the most educated and the least educated workers appear to have fallen somewhat from the 1970s to the 1980s. Although these numbers should be taken as fairly rough approximations, a slowing of the relative growth in demand for more educated workers might help explain why earnings differentials widened slightly along certain dimensions between 1976 and 1983, then narrowed between 1983 and 1989.

The demand index numbers in table 11.8, of course, capture only shifts in demand stemming from shifts in the industrial composition of employment. Econometric work by some researchers suggests that the introduction of new technology biased toward more highly educated workers is an important factor underlying the widening earnings differentials in the United States (Bound and Johnson 1992; Katz and Murphy 1992). It is difficult to get hard evidence at an aggregate level on the labor market effects of new technology. There is no obvious reason to believe, however, that either the rate of introduction of new technology or the nature of its bias has been significantly different in the German than in the U.S. economy.

One hypothesis about the widening of wage differentials across age groups in the United States also relates to the changing industrial structure of employment. Younger workers have been more adversely affected by the shifting of

18. Data on the proportion of workers by education level by industry came from Schoer (1986), 868. Data on employment by industry came from Statistisches Bundesamt, *Fachserie 18: Volkswirtschaftliche Gesamtrechnungen, Reihe S9: Ergebnisse für Wirtschaftsbereiche* (Wiesbaden). We would have liked to have had information on the proportion of industry employment by education for a year closer to the start of our period, but we were unable to locate this information for any year other than 1985.

Table 11.8   **Indices of Demand Growth by Education due to Changes in the**
Industrial Mix of Employment

	Hochschule and *Fachhochschule* Graduates	Occupational Qualification	No Occupational Qualification
1960–89	1.42	.25	−.22
1960–70	1.65	.23	−.40
1970–89	1.30	.26	−.12
1970–80	1.55	.22	−.28
1980–89	1.03	.30	.05

Note: The numbers reported are annual rates of growth in the demand for workers of the specified types attributable to changes in employment by industry using a shift-share analysis. Details are given in the text.

employment from the high-paying manufacturing sector toward the low-paying service sector in the United States. Owing to inverse seniority layoff rules, particularly in union settings, and to laws against age discrimination in employment, older workers enjoy greater job security than younger workers. In addition, young cohorts entering the workforce have found few vacancies in the high-paying manufacturing sector (see Levy and Murnane 1992, 1361).

Although Germany experienced a similar shift of employment from manufacturing to services, the effect on wage differentials across age groups likely was muted by wage-setting institutions, dismissal laws, and early retirement policies. Wage differentials across industries are much narrower in Germany than in the United States.[19] These relatively small interindustry wage differentials dampen the effect of shifts in the industrial structure of employment on earnings inequality by age. Furthermore, German dismissal laws make it difficult to lay off younger as well as older workers. To hasten workforce reductions in the 1980s, many companies instituted early retirement programs that were subsidized by the German government. Thus, younger workers were somewhat more protected against shifts in the industrial structure of demand in Germany than in the United States.

Trends in relative wages by skill group and by age are also likely to be affected by trends in the relative supply of workers of different types. There have been important changes in the German education system over the past twenty years, with an increasing number of students attending the higher secondary school tracks and an increasing number going on to university. In the early 1950s, more than 70 percent of fourteen-year-old students were enrolled in what would today be termed a *Hauptschule;* by the early 1980s, only about half of secondary school students attended a *Hauptschule,* with roughly a quarter attending a *Realschule* and a quarter attending a *Gymnasium.* In addition,

19. This fact probably reflects strong unions in the German service sector. For documentation and a discussion of German interindustry wage differentials, see Burda and Sachs (1987).

changes were introduced that made it easier for students in the *Realschule* track or even the *Hauptschule* track to switch to a *Gymnasium* or otherwise earn an *Abitur* (Hamilton 1990). *Hochschule* enrollments also grew dramatically during the 1970s and early 1980s, reflecting both an increase in the share of young persons choosing to enroll and the growth in the size of the youth population (Hamilton 1990; Teichler and Sanyal 1982). These changes have translated with some lag into increases in the level of educational attainment of the working-age population.

Tables 11.9 and 11.10 below present information on the supply of working-age Germans by education level over the period 1976–89. Data on educational attainment for the entire population, the employed, the unemployed, and those not in the labor force are collected for selected years in the annual German Microzensus, a household survey, and published by the Statistisches Bundesamt.[20] Although tables 11.9 and 11.10 report only figures for the population as a whole, the same basic trends are apparent in figures based on employment and the labor force.

Table 11.9 shows trends in the percentage of the German population aged twenty to sixty and aged twenty-five to thirty that followed each of the most important secondary education tracks. Because schooling tends to last longer in Germany than in the United States and German university or college students often do not graduate until they are aged twenty-five years or older, we selected twenty-five- to thirty-year-olds to represent new entrants to the labor force.[21] Both for the population as a whole and for the new entrants, the percentage who had attended *Hauptschule,* the lowest secondary school track, fell dramatically between 1976 and 1989, from 74.2 percent to 58.5 percent for the German population aged twenty to sixty and from 68.4 percent to 44.1 percent for the population aged twenty-five to thirty. At the same time, the proportion of the population completing both *Realschule,* the technical vocational high school, and the *Abitur,* the entrance exams required for university attendance, rose dramatically. The growth in the proportion of the population with an *Abitur* reflects both the growing share of German youths in the *Gymnasium* track and institutional changes in the German education system made in the 1970s that make this qualification more accessible to students in other tracks. From 1976 to 1989, the proportion of the working-age population as

20. Statistisches Bundesamt, *Fachserie 1: Bevölkerung und Erwerbstätigkeit, Reihe 4.4.2: Beruf, Ausbildung und Arbeitsbedingungen der Erwerbstätigen* (Wiesbaden). Data on a consistent basis are not available prior to 1976.

21. Even among twenty-five- to thirty-year-olds, a significant share of those who have chosen to attend *Fachhochschulen* or *Hochschulen* have not yet completed their degrees. In 1980, e.g., 10.2 percent of twenty-five- to thirty-year-olds had completed one of these degrees; by 1985, the percentage of the same cohort, now aged thirty to thirty-five, that had completed one of the two degrees had risen to 14.2 percent. None of our qualitative conclusions concerning trends in educational attainment is affected, however, by the decision to treat twenty-five- to thirty-year-olds, rather than thirty- to thirty-five-year-olds, as the new entrant group.

Table 11.9   **Percentage of the German Working-Age Population by General Education Track Completed**

	Hauptschule	Realschule	Gymnasium/ Abitur
Aged 20–60			
1976	74.2	15.4	9.7
1977	73.0	15.6	10.2
1980	71.9	15.5	12.1
1982	69.2	17.3	12.8
1985	64.1	19.1	15.6
1987	62.0	20.2	16.6
1989	58.5	21.7	18.7
Relative changes[a]			
1976–89	−1.8	2.6	5.0
1976–82	−1.2	1.9	4.6
1982–89	−2.3	3.2	5.4
Aged 25–30			
1976	68.4	17.4	13.5
1978	66.0	17.8	14.8
1980	62.8	18.2	18.6
1982	57.5	21.0	20.9
1985	50.9	23.6	24.5
1987	48.3	25.9	24.9
1989	44.1	27.9	27.1
Relative changes[a]			
1976–89	−3.4	3.6	5.4
1976–82	−2.9	3.1	7.3
1982–89	−3.8	4.1	3.7

Note: Figures are authors' calculations based on German Microzensus data.

[a]Calculated as the log difference in the percentages divided by the number of years in the period. This number equals the rate of growth in the population with a particular educational attainment less the rate of growth in the total population.

well as the population aged twenty-five to thirty with an *Abitur* roughly doubled.

Table 11.10 shows trends in the population classified by their highest occupational qualification. The omitted category in this table includes those with no occupational qualification as well as those who did not respond to the question.[22] The percentage of the population in almost all the occupation-education categories has grown. Particularly notable is the expansion of the percentage receiving vocational training (typically an apprenticeship).

Overall trends in the supply of workers by education level have been similar in Germany and the United States, in the sense that in both countries the supply

22. According to numbers presented in Clement, Tessaring, and Weisshuhn (1980), nonrespondents represented about 20 percent of the residual category in 1976.

Table 11.10   **Percentage of the German Working-Age Population by Vocational or University Training**

	Vocational Training (A)	Technical School Degree (B)	*Fachhochschule* Degree (C)	*Hochschule* Degree (D)	Sum (A)–(D)
Aged 20–60					
1976	49.7	5.3	1.9	4.1	61.0
1978	50.7	5.3	2.1	4.4	62.5
1980	. . .	5.9	2.5	4.8	. . .
1982	52.8	5.6	2.4	5.0	65.8
1985	53.3	6.2	2.9	5.4	67.8
1987	54.5	6.0	3.1	5.6	69.2
1989	56.3	6.5	3.2	6.2	72.2
Relative changes[a]					
1976–89	1.0	1.6	4.0	3.2	1.3
1976–82	1.0	.9	3.9	3.3	1.3
1982–89	.9	2.1	4.1	3.1	1.3
Aged 25–30					
1976	55.8	4.8	2.5	5.7	68.8
1978	56.5	5.0	2.6	6.2	70.3
1980	. . .	5.8	3.2	7.0	. . .
1982	58.3	4.9	3.3	6.9	73.4
1985	58.8	5.6	3.7	6.1	74.2
1987	60.3	5.2	3.7	5.4	74.6
1989	61.6	5.7	3.5	5.4	76.2
Relative changes[a]					
1976–89	.8	1.3	2.6	−.4	.8
1976–82	.7	.3	4.6	3.2	1.1
1982–89	.8	2.2	.8	−3.5	.5

Note: Figures are author's calculations based on German Microzensus data.

[a]Calculated as the log difference in the percentages (multiplied by 100) divided by the number of years in the period. This number equals the rate of growth in the population with a particular educational attainment less the rate of growth in the total population.

of more educated workers has risen dramatically relative to the supply of workers without any occupational qualification (in Germany) or with twelve or fewer years of schooling (in the United States). Katz and Murphy (1992), however, have argued that the deceleration in the growth of the highly educated labor supply in the United States in the 1980s may explain the rise in returns to education in the 1980s. If, as Katz and Murphy hypothesize, the relative demand for more highly educated workers has shifted out steadily over time, this deceleration in the growth of the highly educated labor supply may explain why returns to education fell during the 1970s in the United States but grew during the 1980s.

Tables 11.9 and 11.10 also present rates of growth of the German population by educational attainment over the period 1976–89 and over the subperiods 1976–82 and 1982–89. Looking first at the trends in secondary education reported in table 11.9, one can see that the growth in the relative supply of workers graduating from the higher tracks has accelerated over time, in contrast to the situation in the United States. Because the type of secondary school that a person attends is imperfectly related to the occupational qualification ultimately obtained, figures on occupational qualifications arguably are more relevant. These figures, which are reported in table 11.10, tell a somewhat different story. There was an acceleration in the growth of the relative supply of persons with certain vocational qualifications but a deceleration in the growth of the relative supply of persons with others. The last column in table 11.10 shows the percentage of the population with any vocational qualification. For the working-age population overall, there has been no change in the rate of growth of the relative supply of workers with some vocational qualification.

Clearly, differences in the trends in educational earnings differentials in Germany and the United States may be consistent with a simple demand and supply story, if the magnitudes of the shifts in the relative demand and supply of more highly educated workers in the two countries differ in the appropriate fashion. One hypothesis concerning the different trends in education differentials in the two countries during the 1980s is that relatively more rapid growth in the supply of more educated workers in Germany, together with slower or comparable growth in the demand for more highly educated individuals, has resulted in some narrowing of earnings differentials there, while slower supply growth and comparable or more rapid demand growth in the United States has resulted in a widening of earnings differentials. Although this hypothesis seems generally consistent with the available evidence, we cannot conclusively identify differences in the magnitude of the relevant demand and supply shifts.

It is more difficult to tell a similar story concerning the contrasting trends in by-age-group differentials in Germany and the United States. Given that the share of young workers was falling in the United States during the 1980s, it seems reasonable to interpret the increases in age-related earnings differentials

Table 11.11   **Percentage of the German Working-Age Population by Age Group**

	< 20	20–29	30–39	40–49	50–65
1970	10.5	19.8	22.9	20.4	26.4
1972	10.6	19.8	23.8	20.0	25.8
1974	11.1	19.7	24.0	19.7	25.5
1976	11.9	20.3	22.5	20.3	25.0
1978	12.5	20.5	21.4	20.9	24.6
1980	13.0	20.6	20.1	21.8	24.5
1982	12.9	20.8	18.8	22.3	25.1
1984	12.0	21.7	18.3	22.0	25.8
1986	11.0	23.4	19.6	20.0	26.7
1988	9.4	23.9	19.9	19.6	27.2
1989	8.6	24.0	20.3	19.5	27.5

Source: Authors' calculations based on German Mikrozensus data.

there as the consequence of demand-side forces. The German baby boom lagged that in the United States by almost a decade. Table 11.11 reports the share of the German population by age group for the years 1970–89. The share of the German population aged twenty to twenty-nine rose steadily beginning in the mid-1970s, with most of the growth observed in the mid- to late-1980s. A similar pattern is observed in data for the labor force. One would think that this growth in the relative supply of young workers should have reinforced the effects of any relative demand shifts favoring more experienced workers, leading to large increases in age-related earnings differentials during the 1980s. Instead, as was documented earlier, age-related earnings differentials appear, if anything, to have narrowed during this period.

11.2.3   Education and Training of Non-College-Bound Youths

A final possible explanation for the stability of relative wages in Germany lies with that country's unique system of apprenticeship training, which is widely credited with providing German industry with a highly skilled and flexible workforce. Companies recruit apprentices at age sixteen or seventeen and train them for two to three years. About two-thirds of all teenagers currently participate in the system (Münch 1991, 41). Apprenticeships are offered in all sectors of the economy, in white-collar as well as blue-collar jobs.

Apprenticeship training in Germany is often referred to as the *dual system* because apprentices receive both on-the-job and classroom training. The system is jointly managed by the employers' associations, the unions, and the government. Apprentices must pass written and oral examinations. To maintain uniform standards, the curriculum for a particular apprenticeship is set at the federal level, and examinations are conducted by local industry chambers. The dual system emphasizes general training that is intended to provide the foundation for a career in an occupation. Observers of the system also have stressed that it socializes teenagers to a working environment, teaching them the importance of punctuality and reliability.

The cost of apprenticeship training is shared by companies and by the state and federal governments. Large companies often supplement apprenticeship training in state-supported vocational schools with their own classroom training. State governments typically help support the cost of in-class training provided by companies. Smaller companies often send apprentices to training centers that are jointly funded by local chambers of commerce and the Federal Ministry of Education and Science. The relatively high degree of coordination between employers and the government associated with the apprenticeship system makes it possible to adjust the mix of apprenticeships offered as the relative demand for different types of workers changes.

There is a consensus among German trade unions and employers that the apprenticeship system is important for maintaining German industry's competitiveness in world markets. Germany is highly dependent on exports; during the early 1980s, about a third of output in the manufacturing sector was exported. Because its workforce is highly paid, Germany relies on "quality rather than price-competitive products, and . . . [thus needs] a highly skilled and reliable work force as well as a cooperative relationship between management and labour on the shop floor" (Streeck 1987, 5).

Some observers have also argued that, because apprenticeship programs are designed to provide a workforce that possesses a broad set of skills, they provide an important degree of labor flexibility to employers, facilitating the redeployment of workers within the company to accommodate changes in demand. By the same token, the broad general training received by the majority of German workers should facilitate the substitutability of different groups of workers. Because workers lacking a college degree nonetheless have received extensive general training, they may be more readily substitutable for college graduates in the production process than is true of U.S. workers who lack a college education. In addition, because new entrants to the labor market typically have received intensive on-the-job training during their first two to three years of work, they may be better substitutes for more experienced workers than is true of new entrants to the U.S. labor market. The German apprenticeship system thus might well have the effect of muting the effects of shifts in relative demand on relative wages across both education and age groups.

11.2.4   Distinguishing among the Competing Explanations

Unfortunately, it is difficult to draw a firm conclusion concerning the relative importance of each of the influences just described. Data on relative unemployment rates by education and age group should be of some value for this purpose. If German wage-setting institutions have compressed wage differentials and limited their responsiveness to changes in the relative demand for workers of different types, one would expect to observe an increase in the relative unemployment rates of less educated and younger workers. In contrast, if relative wages have been fairly stable in Germany either because demand and supply for workers of different types have moved in tandem or because workers of different types are readily substituted for one another, we would not expect the relative unemployment rates of less educated or younger workers to have risen disproportionately during the 1980s.[23]

Table 11.12 presents evidence on whether less skilled workers have experienced a disproportionate increase in their unemployment rates. The table shows the evolution of unemployment rates for workers in five education categories over the period from 1976 to 1989, constructed from the Mikrozensus data on employment and unemployment by level of educational attainment described earlier in the paper. The period covered by these data was generally one of rising unemployment. While unemployment rates for all groups rose,

---

23. Soltwedel et al. (1990) are among those advancing the argument that relative wage rigidities have contributed to excessive unemployment in Germany, although others, such as Franz (1987), have argued that the structure of relative wages is unlikely to be responsible for the growth in unemployment in Germany during the 1980s.

Table 11.12   Unemployment Rates by Educational Group

	Hauptschule	Realschule	Gymnasium/ Abitur	No Qualification/ No Answer[a]	Vocational Training	Technical School Degree	Fachhochschule Degree	Hochschule Degree
1976	3.7	2.7	2.8	5.1	2.9	1.9	2.8	1.7
1977	3.6	2.4	2.6	5.3	2.8	1.4	2.1	1.4
1980	2.9	1.9	2.2	8.2	2.1	1.4	1.5	1.6
1982	5.9	3.8	4.6	8.5	4.5	2.3	3.0	3.0
1985	9.0	6.1	6.9	13.1	6.9	3.3	4.4	4.9
1987	9.3	5.5	5.8	12.7	7.0	3.6	4.2	4.3
1989	8.3	5.1	5.7	11.6	6.2	3.6	4.0	4.8

Note: All unemployment rates were calculated using information on employment and unemployment by level of educational attainment based on the German Mikrozensus and published by the Statistisches Bundesamt.

[a]The "no qualification" category includes persons who did not answer the Mikrozensus question concerning their level of educational attainment.

those for the least well qualified rose substantially more in absolute terms and typically somewhat more in relative terms as well. Between 1976 and 1987, for example, the unemployment rate for *Hauptschule* graduates rose by 5.6 percentage points (a 250 percent increase), while that for persons with an *Abitur* rose by only 3.0 percentage points (a 207 percent increase). Over the same period, the unemployment rate of persons in the no qualification/no response group grew by 7.6 points (a 249 percent increase), while that for all persons with an occupational or educational credential rose by 3.6 percentage points (a 233 percent increase).

The data in table 11.12 are consistent with the hypothesis that the German wage-setting process prevented the relative wages of the least-skilled workers from falling to the level that would have been dictated by market forces, thereby increasing the gap between their unemployment rates and those of more highly skilled workers. Examination of trends in relative unemployment rates in the United States, however, suggests that differences in wage-setting institutions cannot fully explain the different German and U.S. trends in earnings inequality. Relative wages in the United States generally are considered to be highly responsive to changes in market conditions, yet an increase in the relative unemployment rates of less educated workers has been observed there as well. Overall unemployment in the United States fell slightly between 1979 and 1989 from 5.8 to 5.3 percent. Over this period, however, the unemployment rate for persons with less than a high school education rose from 8.9 to 10.0 percent while that for those with some college fell from 4.8 to 4.3 percent and that for college graduates fell from 2.6 to 2.4 percent.[24] The similarity of movements in relative unemployment rates in Germany and the United States leads us to believe that the stability of the German wage structure reflects a better matching of demand and supply and/or the more ready substitution of different types of workers in the production process in addition to any constraints imposed by the German wage-setting process.

Table 11.13 depicts trends in unemployment rates by age in Germany. If the demand for more experienced, and hence older, workers has increased relative to that for inexperienced, younger workers, and if German wage-setting institutions limit the responsiveness of wages to changes in relative demand, we would expect, all else the same, that the unemployment rate of younger workers would have risen relative to that of older workers. The same outcome also would be expected if younger workers in Germany have been disproportionately affected by the decline in employment in manufacturing and wages in service have been insufficiently flexible to absorb the influx of workers looking for employment there.[25]

---

24. The overall U.S. unemployment rates cited for 1979 and 1989 are official statistics. The unemployment rates by education level were calculated using files from the outgoing rotation groups of the Current Population Survey.

25. Burda and Sachs (1987) expound the hypothesis that the rise in the overall unemployment rate in Germany has been caused by wage inflexibility in the service sector.

Table 11.13   Unemployment Rates by Age Group

	15–20	20–30	30–40	40–50	50–55	55–60	60+
1976	7.1	4.7	2.8	2.6	2.6	3.4	1.8
1978	6.4	4.5	3.0	2.5	2.6	3.3	1.5
1980	4.9	3.5	2.4	1.9	2.0	3.2	2.0
1982	9.1	7.6	5.0	3.8	3.9	5.2	3.5
1985	12.8	10.5	8.0	6.0	6.1	8.5	3.3
1987	10.0	9.3	8.0	6.6	6.9	9.9	4.9
1989	8.1	7.4	7.3	5.8	6.1	11.7	5.7

Note: All unemployment rates were calculated using information on employment and unemployment by age based on the German Microzensus and published by the Statistisches Bundesamt.

The figures in table 11.13, however, show that, while young German workers have experienced substantial increases in unemployment, German workers over age fifty-five have experienced much larger absolute and relative unemployment rate increases. Although the pattern provides no support for the hypothesis that unresponsive wage-setting institutions are the principal reason for the absence of growing differentials in earnings across age groups in Germany, the large increase in the unemployment rate for workers aged fifty-five to sixty relative to that for younger workers largely can be explained by another institutional factor. Under German law, older workers are allowed to collect unemployment benefits for an extended period of time, and, if they have been unemployed for at least fifty-two weeks out of the last year and a half, they can retire at age sixty and receive a government pension. Thus, many companies officially fired workers in their late fifties, providing them with supplemental benefits, in order to use the unemployment insurance system to help fund early retirement schemes.[26]

11.3 Conclusion

Since the mid-1970s, earnings inequality has fallen in Germany. Evidence from German social security data and the German Socioeconomic Panel data show that earnings differentials overall have narrowed, particularly in the bottom half of the distribution. While occupation differentials have risen slightly,

26. We discuss the use of the German unemployment insurance system to subsidize early retirement programs at greater length in Abraham and Houseman (1993). We have also examined trends in German unemployment rates by education level by age. These figures show that, within narrowly defined age groups, the unemployment rate of less educated workers has risen relative to that of more highly educated workers. In addition, the unemployment rate of older workers relative to that of younger workers has risen primarily among those who are less educated. Finally, we have analyzed trends in the employment/population ratio by level of education and age for Germany and the United States. Trends in the employment/population ratio reflect trends in both unemployment and labor force participation. Our analysis of employment/population ratios leads to conclusions consistent with those drawn from our analysis of unemployment rates.

differentials across education groups have remained relatively constant, and differentials in earnings by age group generally have remained stable or narrowed.

These trends in Germany stand in striking contrast to trends in earnings inequality in the United States. One potential explanation for the different trends in the two countries rests on differences in wage-setting institutions. German wage setting is far more centralized than that in the United States. Moreover, German unions have fought for a narrowing of wage differentials or at least for uniform percentage wage increases for all workers. Thus, even during periods when there were market pressures to widen wage differentials, one might still observe stable or even narrowing earnings differentials in Germany. The growing relative unemployment rate of workers with no occupational qualification is consistent with this interpretation, but the fact that similar increases in the relative unemployment rates of less educated workers have been observed in the United States suggests that other factors contributed to the different trends in the two countries. In addition, there is no strong indication that the unemployment rates of younger German workers have risen especially rapidly.

A second potential explanation for the different German and U.S. trends in earnings inequality is that demand and supply conditions in the two countries have differed. In both countries, the demand for more educated workers has been increasing over time, but so too has the supply of more educated workers. In Germany, however, the increase in the relative supply of more educated workers accelerated or at least remained stable during the 1980s, while the growth in the relative supply of more educated workers in the United States slowed considerably. Assuming that the relative demand for more educated workers has not grown more rapidly in Germany, these differences in the relative supply of more educated workers may help explain the widely divergent trends in earnings inequality in Germany and the United States. The timing of the German baby boom, however, makes it more difficult to tell a demand and supply story about the behavior of age-related earnings differentials in Germany during the 1980s.

A final, and related, explanation for the stability of the German earnings distribution is that the German education and training system simply does a better job of supplying workers with an appropriate mix of skills. This might be true both because employers have more direct influence over the kind of training received by new entrants to the labor market and because apprenticeship training gives German workers a good general foundation that makes it easier for them to learn new tasks so that workers with different backgrounds are more easily substitutable for one another.

On the whole, the different development of wage inequality in Germany and the United States cannot be readily attributed to the existence of fundamentally different demand and supply side forces in the two countries, although we should stress that the evidence on this point is far from conclusive. Rather, it appears that institutional factors played an important role in mitigating pressures for greater wage inequality in Germany. German wage-setting institutions probably have helped limit increases in earnings inequality. Moreover, the German education and training system, which many believe provides a better match between demand and supply than the U.S. system, likely has lessened the downward pressures on wages for less educated, younger workers.

References

Abraham, Katharine G., and Susan N. Houseman. 1993. *Job security in America: Lessons from Germany.* Washington, D.C.: Brookings.
Bellman, Lutz, and Friedrich Buttler. 1989. Lohnstrukturflexibilität—Theorie und Empirie der Transaktionskosten und Effizienzlöhne. *Mitteilungen aus der Arbeitsmarkt- und Berufsforschung* 22, no. 2:202–17.
Blackburn, McKinley L., David E. Bloom, and Richard B. Freeman. 1990. The declining economic position of less skilled American men. In *A future of lousy jobs? The changing structure of U.S. wages,* ed. Gary Burtless. Washington, D.C.: Brookings.
Blossfeld, Hans-Peter. 1984. Die Entwicklung der Qualifikationsspezifischen Verdienstrelationen von Berufsanfängern zwischen 1970 und 1982. *Köllner Zeitschrift für Soziologie und Sozialpsychologie,* no. 2:293–322.
Bound, John, and George Johnson. 1992. Changes in the structure of wages in the 1980's: An evaluation of alternative explanations. *American Economic Review* 82, no. 3 (June): 371–392.
Brandes, Wolfgang, Wolfgang Meyer, and Edwin Schudlich. 1991. ILO research project on pay classification systems in industrialized countries: National monograph for Germany. Universität/Gesamthochschule Paderborn/Universität Hannover/Institut für Sozialforschung.
Burda, Michael C., and Jeffrey D. Sachs. 1987. Institutional aspects of high unemployment in the Federal Republic of Germany. NBER Working Paper no. 2241. Cambridge, Mass.: National Bureau of Economic Research, May.
Clement, Werner, Manfred Tessaring, and Gernot Weisshuhn. 1980. Zur Entwicklung der qualifikationsspezifischen Einkommensrelationen dur Bundesrepublik Deutschland. *Mitteilungen aus der Arbeitsmarkt- und Berufsforschung* 13, no. 2:184–212.
Davis, Steven J. 1992. Cross-country patterns of change in relative wages. NBER Working Paper no. 4085. Cambridge, Mass.: National Bureau of Economic Research, June.
Fels, Joachim, and Erich Gundlach. 1990. More evidence on the puzzle of interindustry wage differentials: The case of West Germany. *Weltwirtschaftliches Archiv* 126, no. 3: 544–60.
Franke, Siegfried Franz. 1983. Der Einfluss von Lohnhöhe und Lohnstruktur auf Beschäftigungsvolumen und -struktur. *Wirtschaftsdienst* 1:29–34.
Franz, Wolfgang. 1987. Beschäftigungsprobleme auf Grund von Inflexibilititäten auf Arbeitsmärkten? Discussion Paper no. 340–87. University of Stuttgart.
Freeman, Richard B. 1975. Overinvestment in college training? *Journal of Human Resources* 10, no. 3 (Summer): 287–311.
———. 1989. The changing status of unionism around the world: Some emerging patterns. In *Organized labor at the crossroads,* ed. Wei-Chiao Huang. Kalamazoo, Mich.: W. E. Upjohn Institute for Employment Research.

Gottschalk, Peter, and Mary Joyce. 1992. Is earnings inequality also rising in other industrialized countries? Working paper. Boston College, March.

Green, Gordon, John Coder, and Paul Ryscavage. 1992. *International comparisons of earnings inequality for men in the 1980s.* Studies in the Distribution of Income, Current Population Reports, Consumer Income, P60–183. Washington, D.C.: Bureau of the Census, U.S. Department of Commerce, October.

Hamilton, Stephen F. 1990. *Apprenticeship for adulthood.* New York: Free Press.

Juhn, Chinhui, Kevin M. Murphy, and Brooks Pierce. 1993. Wage inequality and the rise in returns to skill. *Journal of Political Economy* 101, no. 3 (June): 410–42.

Katz, Lawrence F., and Kevin M. Murphy. 1992. Changes in relative wages, 1963–1987: Supply and demand factors. *Quarterly Journal of Economics* 107, no. 1 (February): 35–78.

Levy, Frank, and Richard J. Murnane. 1992. U.S. earnings levels and earnings inequality: A review of recent trends and proposed explanations. *Journal of Economic Literature* 30 (September): 1333–81.

Lindena, Bodo, and Helmut Höhmann. 1989. Allgemein-verbindlichkeit und Publizität von Tarifverträgen. *Der Arbeitgeber* (March, special issue), 3–23.

Münch, Joachim. 1991. *Vocational training in the Federal Republic of Germany.* Berlin: European Centre for the Development of Vocational Training.

Paque, Karl-Heinz. N.d. Labour market contracts and institutions: The case of Germany. University of Kiel. Typescript.

Schoer, Karl. 1986. Bruttolöhne und -gehälter 1975 bis 1985. *Wirtschaft und Statistik,* no. 11 (November): 861–71.

Soltwedel, Rudiger et al. 1990. *Regulierungen auf dem Arbeitsmarkt der Bundesrepublik.* Tübingen: Mohr.

Streeck, Wolfgang. 1987. Industrial relations in Germany: Agenda for change. Discussion Paper no. IIM/LMP 87–5. Berlin: Wissenschaftszentrum für Sozialforschung.

Teichler, Ulrich, and Bikas C. Sanyal. 1982. *Higher education and the labour market in the Federal Republic of Germany.* Paris: Unesco Press.

Thiehoff, Rainer. 1987. *Lohnnivellierung und qualifikatorische Arbeitslosigkeitstruktur.* Baden-Baden: Nomos.

Vogler-Ludwig, Kurt. 1985. Flexibilisierung der Lohnstrukturen. *IFO-Schnelldienst* 16:18–31.

12

A Comparative Analysis of East and West German Labor Markets: Before and After Unification

Alan B. Krueger and Jörn-Steffen Pischke

The unification of East and West Germany provides a unique natural experiment to study a Soviet-style labor market undergoing a dramatic and rapid transition. Furthermore, the demise of the Communist regime in East Germany has for the first time enabled researchers to obtain large quantities of data collected during the Communist era. The availability of these data sets permits a detailed comparison of the operation of the labor market under different economic systems. In this paper, we use several large micro-data sets to compare the labor markets in East and West Germany before and after unification.

Specifically, we address the following questions: How did the income distributions compare in East and West Germany just before the collapse of East Germany? What factors determined wages in these countries? How has the transformation to a market-based economy affected the income distribution in eastern Germany? How do former East Germans who commute to work in west Germany or migrated to west Germany perform in the labor market? To provide another point of comparison for the wage structures, we also examine data for the United States.

A number of observers have noted that East German physical capital is of little or no value. The main asset acquired by West Germany from unification is human capital. We therefore devote a great deal of attention to comparing education levels and the economic value of education in East and West Germany.

Alan B. Krueger is the Bendheim Professor of Economics and Public Policy at Princeton University and a research associate of the National Bureau of Economic Research. Jörn-Steffen Pischke is assistant professor of economics at the Massachusetts Institute of Technology.

The authors thank Matt Downer, Ondraus Jenkins, Gabi Reiss, and Kainan Tang for outstanding research assistance. They are also grateful to seminar participants at the NBER conference on "Differences and Changes in Wage Structures," at the Universities of Cologne, Konstanz, Mannheim, and Yale, and at the Center for European Economic Research (ZEW), and to Rebecca Blank, Richard Freeman, Jennifer Hunt, Lawrence Katz, and Robert Topel for helpful comments.

Our main conclusion is that East Germans were well educated and received a substantial payoff to their education. Indeed, despite greater wage compression in East Germany, the rate of return to education was about the same in East and West Germany in 1988. After unification, the return to education fell slightly in eastern Germany. East Germans who commute to work in the west have performed fairly well in the capitalist economy. German unions have tried to impose a wage structure and bargaining structure on eastern Germany that mimics the western model. Although it is very early in the transition process, we find that the wage structure of the former East Germany is approaching that of West Germany. Most significantly, wage dispersion has increased in eastern Germany, especially at the right tail of the distribution, and interindustry wage differentials now more closely resemble those in the west.

The transition to a market-based economy will probably occur much more quickly in East Germany than in the other East-bloc countries because of the great deal of financial and technical assistance provided by West Germany. Thus, East Germany's experience to date provides unique insights into the transition process.

The remainder of the paper is organized as follows. Section 12.1 presents a brief summary of relevant institutional features of the East and West German labor markets and education systems. Section 12.2 describes changes in wage-setting institutions in East Germany since 1989. Section 12.3 offers some theoretical observations on expected changes in the East German labor market due to unification. Section 12.4 describes the data sets we use. Section 12.5 presents a comparison of the wage structures in East Germany, West Germany, and the United States, with particular emphasis on comparing the rate of return to schooling. Section 12.6 examines changes that have taken place in the eastern German labor market since unification.

12.1 Labor Market Institutions

12.1.1   West Germany (FRG)

Collective bargaining is an essential labor market institution in West Germany.[1] German unions are generally organized nationwide along industry lines. The largest German labor union is the Deutscher Gewerkschaftsbund (DGB), which is an umbrella organization that includes seventeen industry unions. Roughly 80 percent of all unionized workers are members of the DGB. Employers either bargain with the DGB member unions individually or are members of a nationwide employer association that bargains on their behalf. The employer associations are also organized along industry lines. Although wage contracts are ultimately negotiated at the *Land* or plant level, the national

---

1. Our description of collective bargaining in West Germany draws heavily on Schmidt (1991) and Burda and Sachs (1988).

unions publicize their wage demands, which then become a standard for other negotiations. The public-sector and metalworkers' unions are widely considered important pattern setters.

A significant feature of the West German system is that it is possible for collective bargaining agreements to become "generally binding" for all employees and enterprises in an industry, regardless of whether they belong to the labor union or employer association. Either party to a collective bargaining agreement may petition the labor minister in the *Länder* to extend the contract to nonunion enterprises if more than half the employees in the relevant industry are employed by firms that were a party to the negotiated contract. Although only about one-third of German workers are union members, collective bargaining may affect as many as 90 percent of German workers because of contract extensions and spillovers. Burda and Sachs (1988) note that the process of contract extension compresses regional wage differences.

Because a great many nonunion employees are covered by collective bargaining agreements, and because there is a good deal of spillover even to nonunion workers who are not covered by legal contracts, the union-nonunion distinction is not particularly relevant in West Germany. As a consequence, researchers have found only a small wage differential between union and nonunion members in West Germany, typically ranging between 0 and 5.5 percent (see Schmidt 1991; and Blanchflower and Freeman 1992). Owing to the large role played by unions, one would expect more wage compression and emphasis on seniority in West Germany than in a country with plant-level bargaining and weak unions, such as the United States.

12.1.2   East Germany (GDR)

There was a great deal of centralization in the labor and product markets in East Germany.[2] All firms were owned by the state, and an elaborate plan directed the allocation of inputs, the distribution of outputs, wage levels, and prices. Only six broad compensation groups existed for production workers. Wage levels for these groups, however, varied by industry. But even within the wage groups there was extensive variation. According to Stephan and Wiedemann (1990), this variation was quite large and cannot be explained by the official wage norms, with the result that to some extent individual enterprises were able to deviate from the planned targets. Much of the "unplanned" variation comes from bonuses, which accounted for 6 percent of compensation, on average, in East Germany. Enterprises had more discretion over bonuses than over the base wage. East German workers were free to work for whichever firm they chose, but rationed housing may have frequently limited mobility.

East German plants were typically much larger than West German plants. Vortmann (1985) contends that East German enterprises used their discretion-

---

2. For a discussion of the GDR economy and of the restructuring effort under way, see Siebert and Schmieding (1992).

ary power to attract the workers they needed. If an industry was at a disadvantage owing to the wage targets specified in the government plan, firms could often circumvent the plan. Thus, the East German wage structure *should* exhibit some features that are common in Western economies. Nevertheless, the Communist system operated like a large internal labor market, with rules and party membership playing an important role in the allocation of jobs and wages.[3]

12.1.3   The Education Systems in Germany

Unlike the United States, the German education systems are characterized by a multitude of different kinds of schools, many of them offering alternative routes to a similar degree. Despite their common history, the education systems in East and West Germany have diverged significantly, making direct comparisons difficult. Figures 12.1*a* and 12.1*b* contain tree diagrams outlining the education systems in East and West Germany. The systems are described in detail in the appendix.[4]

For our purposes, the main difference between the education systems is that the average time to completing a higher degree is longer in West Germany than in East Germany. For example, a university degree requires roughly seven years of study in West Germany but only four years of study in East Germany. On the other hand, there were no education fees in either East or West Germany. And both countries had an elaborate apprenticeship system that was tied to public schools and widely used. Although East German elementary and secondary schools did devote some time to Communist ideology, the level of instruction was generally considered to be comparable to that in the west.

12.2   The Eastern German Labor Market in Transition

The wage-setting institutions in eastern Germany have undergone a rapid and dramatic transformation. At midnight on 30 June 1990, formal monetary union took place. At this time, East German wage contracts were converted to West German marks at a rate of one for one, and the legal, tax, and social insurance systems in the two Germanies were harmonized. In the months following monetary union, the East German economy sunk into a deep depression, with industrial output quickly falling to roughly half its 1989 level (see Akerlof et al. 1991). Since the collapse of East Germany in late 1989, employment fell from 9.2 million in 1989 to 7.1 million in July 1991.[5] Unemployment increased from around 1 percent of the labor force to over 10 percent of the labor force. And even these numbers understate the extent of employment ad-

3. This analogy has also been made by Večerník (1991) in reference to Czechoslovakia.
4. For extensive descriptions of the education systems, see also Waterkamp (1987) on East Germany and Führ (1989) on West Germany.
5. An estimated 400,000 workers migrated to the West or commute to work in the West. They are not included in these figures.

justment because a substantial number of employed workers were put on short-time hours (*Kurzarbeit*), early retirement, and public works jobs (see Bellman et al. 1992).

Even before monetary union, West German unions aggressively organized East German workers. In early 1990, the West German unions achieved remarkable success in organizing East German workers, in part because the old East German Communist unions were completely discredited. The structure of unions in eastern Germany is now similar to that in the west: unions organize and bargain along *Land*/industry lines, although some contracts are being negotiated for all new *Länder* simultaneously. The first round of bargaining in the summer of 1990 yielded mostly lump-sum wage increases. However, in some industries (e.g., chemical), large percentage base wage increases were negotiated. The construction industry immediately tied wages in the east to about 60 percent of the western level. Contracts were generally written for short time periods. As in the west, the eastern unions have sought to prevent contract wages from varying with the performance of individual firms.

The second round of negotiations was held in the winter of 1990–91. In this round, many sectors agreed to tie wages to a specified proportion of the western level, and schedules were set so as to gradually achieve parity with the west in 1994 or 1995. There was tremendous variance in the east/west wage ratio across industries at this time. For example, cleaning services in East Berlin paid 100 percent of the West Berlin level, while the eastern textile industry paid 43 percent of the western level. Most contracts set base wages at 50–60 percent of the western level. This exaggerates the relative size of take-home pay in the east, however, because bonuses and fringe benefits were much lower or nonexistent in the east. Furthermore, work hours are longer in the east and vacation time shorter. Bispinck and WSI-Tarifarchiv (1991) calculate that metalworkers in Saxony earned 44.8 percent of the hourly wage of Bavarian metalworkers during the first half of 1991, although the base wage was formally set at a 58.6 percent level.

Many general contracts (*Manteltrarifverträge*) were also written in 1991. These contracts set general wage structures for a handful of skill levels. Workers were thereby classified into skill groups, causing some friction. Notably, in the public sector, unions initially negotiated a contract that completely eliminated seniority pay. Workers went on strike against this contract, and it was subsequently modified. We also note that several firms are believed to deviate from negotiated contract rates.

Another critical development in the east is the process of privatization, carried out by the Treuhand. As of November 1991, the Treuhand had sold about 25 percent of eastern German companies to private concerns and was subsidizing a sizable proportion of the remainder (see *Economist,* 21 March 1992, 71). The Treuhand closed down only about 6 percent of east German companies. Akerlof et al. (1991) contend that managers of Treuhand-operated firms have had little incentive or ability to resist union wage demands, a situation that is partly responsible for the fast growth of eastern wages.

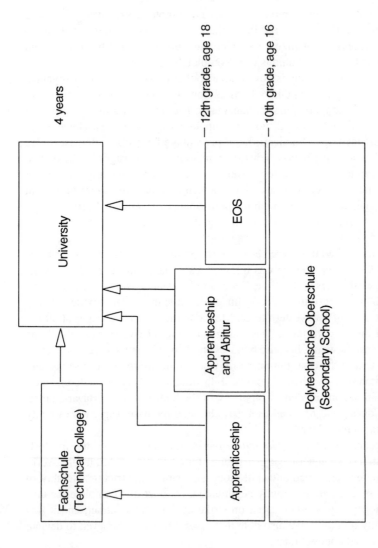

Fig. 12.1a The education system in East Germany

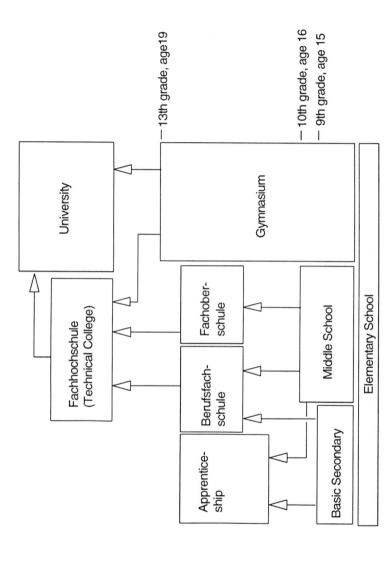

Fig. 12.1b The education system in West Germany

12.3   Theoretical Framework

The wage-setting institutions in East Germany under communism are expected to compress wage dispersion greatly. The Communist ideology stressed uniformity in outcomes, irrespective of individual differences in ability or effort. Nevertheless, the East German system clearly allowed firms some discretion in wage setting, which should lead the wage structures in East and West Germany to have some similarities. Moreover, wage incentives were used by the government to induce individuals to invest in training and attain higher levels of education. Given the importance of unions in West Germany, we expect wage dispersion to be lower there than in the United States but still greater than in East Germany.

After unification, we expect there to be widescale revaluation of individual characteristics in the former East Germany. Our guiding theoretical principle is that we expect the wage structure in the former East German labor market gradually to approach that in West Germany. We expect the two wage structures to approach each other because there are now free flows of capital and labor between the two lands. Absent rigidities, differences in wage structures should eventually be arbitraged away. Moreover, German unions have vigorously pursued a policy of imposing the West German wage structure on eastern Germany. Because the East German population is only about one-quarter as big as the West German population, and because East Germany's GDP was only about 10 percent as big as West Germany's, we expect that unification will lead to far greater changes in East Germany than in West Germany.

We also expect that younger workers will make the transition to a market-based economy more easily than older workers. In particular, firms and the government have a greater incentive to invest in younger workers because there is a longer period to recoup the investment. This suggests that experience profiles will flatten out initially in East Germany. The effect of unification on the return to education is ambiguous. On the one hand, the market-based economy is expected to reward human capital more generously, which would increase the return to education. On the other hand, the education acquired under the Communist regime may not be very valuable in a capitalist economy. In any event, we expect wage variation to increase eventually in the east, as those at the top of the income distribution are free to increase their position and those at the bottom are no longer so vigorously propped up by the government.

Capital and labor flows take time. Workers are reluctant to move far away from their families and friends to find new jobs, and firms are loath to invest large sums of money in new capital until they are certain of the quality of the workforce and existing capital stock. We should stress that our analysis focuses on the early stage of the transition process and that the East German labor market is most likely still in a state of disequilibrium. Nevertheless, the changes in the East German wage structure that we can detect will give us an indication of the extent of labor market restructuring that has taken place and of the distance that remains to be traveled.

12.4   Data Sets

12.4.1   East Germany

The East German micro data used in this study come from the Survey on Income of Blue- and White-Collar Households in the GDR (Einkommens-stichprobe in Arbeiter-und Angestelltenhaushalten). This is a cross-sectional survey that was conducted every two or three years by the Statistical Office of the GDR. The survey was intended to contribute "reliable information on the level and change of the incomes of blue- and white-collar households and about other aspects of the standard of living" in East Germany (Statistisches Amt der DDR 1990). Aggregate results from the survey are published in the *Statistical Abstract* of the GDR and in other official publications. We were able to obtain an IBM standard label tape containing the survey conducted in September 1988 from the former Statistical Office of the GDR. The survey was conducted in the year before the collapse of the GDR, and it is the last such survey taken before German unification. The survey contains data on seventy-nine thousand individuals in twenty-eight thousand households, or roughly 0.5 percent of the total population of the GDR. Krause and Schwarze (1990) provide an extensive description of the data set.

The survey contains detailed questions on various categories of income of individuals and households. In addition, the survey provides basic demographic and labor force information about each household member. Finally, a set of questions is asked about the households' ownership of cars and household appliances, such as televisions and dishwashers. A household is defined as an economic unit sharing income and would include a household member who contributes to the household income but lives separately.

The sampling design of the survey is sufficiently different from typical household surveys conducted in Western countries to warrant some elaboration. The basic sampling unit is not the residence of the household; it is the employer. Firms were selected by the central Statistical Office to participate in the sample to achieve a representative distribution across regions and industries. Within a selected firm, a random sample of employees was drawn from payroll records. The household of the selected employee became a target household for the sample. The target respondent was contacted early in September 1988. At that time, the respondent received a record sheet similar to the questionnaire to prepare for the interview. The interviews took place at the end of September, and the respondent provided the information on all the members of the household (i.e., proxy responses). Earnings for the respondent, however, were supplied by the payroll office of the firm. The interviewer was supposed to have verified the firm-reported income amounts with the respondent and to supplement the payroll data if necessary.[6] Note that the individual who was interviewed may be someone other than the household head.

The firms selected for the sample are all state-owned enterprises, state-owned farms, and certain cooperatives in the trade sector. Excluded are other cooperatives, private enterprises, and joint ventures. Individuals working in such firms can still be part of the sample if they are members of the household of a target individual. A target household drawn within a sample firm was excluded from the sample if any one of the household members was currently a member of the armed forces or state security or was a full-time employee of the party organization or other mass organizations like unions. A household was also excluded if the target respondent was an apprentice or working in her own home.

The sampling design leads to a number of problems. First, a household is more likely to be drawn for the sample if it has more earners. Thus, the sample is not representative of the households in the GDR and cannot be used for analyses of household characteristics. Second, the exclusion of certain sectors distorts the distribution of workers across industries. Despite these problems, we show below that the sample is reasonably representative of the employed population in East Germany.[7]

To the extent possible, the income variables in the sample refer to monthly income during August 1988. Vortmann (1985) claims that this leads to some distortions in the income measure because August is unrepresentative with respect to sick time. Some sources of income, like employment bonuses and interest, accrue only on an annual basis. Respondents were asked to report annual income for 1987 for such categories, which we converted to monthly amounts by dividing by twelve.

12.4.2 West Germany

For West Germany, we use the 1988 wave of the Socioeconomic Panel (SOEP). The SOEP is a longitudinal survey of about six thousand households that has been conducted annually since 1984. All household members sixteen years old or older are interviewed directly; the survey follows sample members if they leave their original household. Proxy interviews are utilized only in rare cases. The panel deliberately oversampled about sixteen hundred households with foreign-born individuals. We exclude this subsample from our analysis.

---

6. The variance of earnings does not differ between self-respondents and proxy respondents in the survey. Returns to education are slightly lower for proxy respondents, however. Vortmann (1985) claims that the income levels for proxy respondents are underreported.

7. It is interesting to note that there are no missing values in the data set because individuals refused to respond to certain questions. However, the Statistisches Amt der DDR (1990) points out that the survey was voluntary. While the guidelines for the selection of respondents make provisions for the fact that complete refusals will occur, the Statistical Office does not provide statistics on the response rates.

Owing to attrition, there were about thirty-seven hundred households left in 1988, with seventy-six hundred interviewed individuals. The interviews for the panel are conducted mainly in March and April of each year. Most interviews were conducted in person (about 60 percent); the remainder were conducted by mail and to a lesser extent by telephone.

The survey consists of a household questionnaire and separate question-naires for each individual in the household. The questionnaires include a con-stant set of items asked in each wave. For the household, these are questions concerning living quarters, household income and assets, and noninterviewed children. For the individuals, information is collected on basic demographics, education, labor market participation, unemployment, earnings, taxes and so-cial security contributions, time use, satisfaction with various aspects of life, health, and political preferences. In addition, there are topical modules on each wave.

12.4.3   Eastern Germany in Transition

In 1990, the SOEP initiated a special survey of the former East Germany, the so called SOEP-East. The first wave of the SOEP-East was conducted (mostly) in June 1990, just before monetary union, and a follow-up survey was conducted (mostly) between March and May 1991. The first wave also in-cluded retrospective information on earnings in 1989. The sample consists of households drawn at random from the Central Register of Population. A total of 2,179 households with 4,453 people over age sixteen participated in the survey. Importantly, individuals were included in the follow-up survey even if they had moved to the western section of Germany. Although the SOEP-East was recently made available, the SOEP-West was not available for 1990 and 1991 at the time of writing. We use the SOEP-East to examine the preliminary effects of the transition of the eastern German labor market.

12.4.4   United States

We use the March 1989 Current Population Survey (CPS) to estimate basic wage regressions and to describe income distribution in the United States. The CPS contains information on individuals in a sample of 56,500 households, one-quarter of which are asked questions about weekly earnings and union status. Weekly wages are examined for the United States and monthly wages for the Germanies. We suspect that wage dispersion in the United States would be even greater were monthly instead of weekly earnings used because of vari-ation in weeks worked. In some of our analysis, we also analyze CPS outgoing rotation group files for various years.

12.5   Distribution of Earnings and Returns to Education

We created samples of eighteen- to sixty-five-year-old full-time, nonagricultural workers in East and West Germany and the United States.[8] For West Germany and the United States, we also excluded self-employed workers. There are no self-employed workers in the East German data set. To the extent possible, we have defined the variables to be comparable. Table 12.1 reports means and standard deviations of the variables for each country. Mean earnings in East Germany were about M 1,200. The spread of the earnings distributions can be compared by looking at the standard deviations of log earnings and the interquartile ranges. Not surprisingly, East Germany has the tightest distribution of earnings.[9] However, there is a significant spread in the distribution. The interquartile range of log earnings is 40 percent in East Germany, 50 percent in West Germany, and 75 percent in the United States. The standard deviation of log earnings just for unionized workers in the United States is about the same as for all West Germany (.41 vs. .44). Relatively tight earnings distributions are a feature of both parts of Germany. Figure 12.2 presents a graph of Kernel density estimates of the earnings distributions of male household heads. To make units comparable, all distributions have been shifted so that the median worker earns the same amount in East German marks in all countries. The West German and U.S. distributions exhibit greater positive skewness than the East German one.

Some caution should be exercised in comparing income distributions between the three economies.[10] First, the income measures are gross of taxes. The income tax system in East Germany was only moderately progressive, with a maximum average tax rate of 20 percent for incomes above M 15,120. West Germany, on the other hand, has a highly nonlinear tax schedule, with an increasing marginal tax rate up to a maximum income of DM 130,032 in 1988. Thus, the tax system is progressive, and the net income distribution would be quite a bit tighter. We do not attempt to calculate net incomes since the tax system makes it hard to attribute taxes to husbands and wives in multiple-earner families.

A second difficulty is due to nonpecuniary benefits of employment. Ac-

---

8. We focus on full-time workers because our earnings data for the Germanies pertain to the monthly wage, and hours worked will greatly affect the amount of monthly income for part-time workers.

9. Atkinson and Micklewright (1992) and Večerník (1991) find that the wage distributions were more compressed in the socialist economies of Czechoslovakia, Hungary, Poland, the Soviet Union, and Yugoslavia than in the United Kingdom, West Germany, and Austria in the late 1980s. They also find significant differences in the wage structures among East-bloc countries and different trends over time. The East German wage structure is compressed even by East-bloc standards. For earlier analyses of wage structures in Soviet-style economies, see Bergson (1984) and Brown (1977).

10. Hauser (1991) presents a careful discussion of problems in making distributional comparisons between East and West Germany.

Table 12.1   **Descriptive Statistics (means with standard deviations in parentheses)**

Variable	East Germany (1)	West Germany (2)	United States (3)
Earnings[a]	1,179.14[b]	3,814.11[c]	425.54[d]
	(359.04)	(1,798.46)	(242.16)
Log earnings	7.026	8.154	5.914
	(.315)	(.438)	(.527)
Interquartile range of log earnings	.389	.492	.751
Net monthly family income[e]	1,970.38[b]	3,579.78[c]	3,340.57[d]
	(746.20)	(2,009.90)	(1,889.06)
Standard deviation of log family income	.402	.421	.648
Years of school	13.06	12.32	12.94
	(1.78)	(2.72)	(2.68)
10th grade or less	.051	.137	. . .
	(.219)	(.343)	
Completed apprenticeship	.594	.617	. . .
	(.491)	(.486)	
Master craftsman	.056	.087	. . .
	(.229)	(.282)	
Technical school	.189	.062	.222
	(.391)	(.241)	(.416)
University	.111	.098	
	(.314)	(.297)	
Age	38.35	39.01	37.64
	(11.30)	(11.57)	(11.57)
Experience	19.31	20.69	18.71
	(11.35)	(11.79)	(12.02)
Female	.463	.288	.471
	(.499)	(.453)	(.499)
Married	.748	.641	.612
	(.434)	(.480)	(.487)
White collar	.493	.481	.560
	(.500)	(.500)	(.496)
Public servant	. . .	.136	. . .
		(.343)	
Shift work	.188	. . .	. . .
	(.390)		
Sample size	43,532	2,496	8,118

Note: Data for East Germany are from the 1988 Survey of Blue- and White-Collar Households, for West Germany from the 1988 wave of the Socioeconomic Panel, and for the United States from the March 1989 CPS. Samples consist of nonagricultural, full-time employed men and women. For West Germany and the United States, self-employed workers are deleted.

[a]Earnings refers to gross earnings in the month prior to the interview plus one-twelfth of annual bonuses for the previous year for both German data sets. For the United States, earnings is gross weekly earnings on the main job.

[b]East German marks.

(*continued*)

Table 12.1   (continued)

cWest German deutsche marks.
dU.S. dollars.
eFamily income is total net monthly family income for August 1988 plus one-twelfth of total annual income for the previous year for the East German data, formed as the sum of the separate income categories. For West Germany it is the answer to the question, "What was the net income of your household last month." For the United States it is gross total family income for 1988 divided by 12.

cording to anecdotal evidence, one means of transferring additional resources to individuals favored by the East German regime was through greater access to goods. For example, a physician who was regarded as important would be given a house far below the normal cost. Valuing such transfers is difficult because often there was no market for comparable goods. Transfers in kind are not captured by our data, and their inclusion probably would increase the right tail of the income distribution.[11] Nonpecuniary benefits are also omitted in our analysis of the west.

The third difficulty involves relative prices. Necessities were substantially subsidized in East Germany. For example, rent for a one-bedroom apartment was some seventy-five marks a month (6 percent of the average salary), a local bus ticket twenty pfennigs, etc. On the other hand, luxuries were comparatively expensive; for example, a Czech Skoda car cost M 25,000. Therefore, in terms of real consumption possibilities, earners at the lower end of the distribution spent relatively more of their budget on necessities and were comparatively better off in East Germany than in the Western economies. The opposite is true for the rich. Hence, the "real" income distribution in East Germany was much tighter than suggested by our measures of nominal income.

This last difference between the Germanies, which should be the most important concern, has evaporated with the monetary union beginning in July 1990. Since wage contracts were converted to West German marks at a rate of one to one, the 1988 income distribution would have approximately characterized the situation at the beginning of the transition process. With the major exceptions of rents, the prices and availability of goods changed quickly after monetary union. Hence, thinking of the distributions as characterizing the situation in the Germanies on the eve of political union in October 1990 is a plausible exercise. (The average exchange rate in 1991 was DM 1.66 per U.S. dollar.)

Return to table 12.1. The similarities between the Germanies are even more striking when comparing the family income distributions. The table reports log standard deviations for total family income. They are computed for the families in the sample with at least one full-time worker. This is the only group for

11. We have estimated Engle curves for cars and other consumer durables in East Germany. These results indicate that, despite rationing, income was an important determinant of consumption.

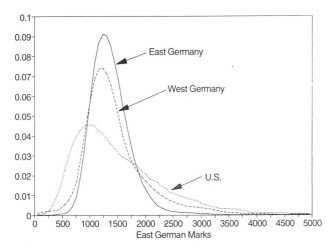

Fig. 12.2   Distribution of earnings: Working male household heads

Sources: Data for East Germany are from the 1988 Survey of Blue- and White-Collar Households, for West Germany from the 1988 wave of the Socioeconomic Panel; and for the United States from the March 1989 CPS. Samples consist of nonagricultural, full-time employed male household heads. Self-employed workers are deleted for West Germany and the United States.
Note: Kernel density estimates.

which the East German data are roughly representative. The estimates indicate that family incomes in the two Germanies have a very similar level of dispersion. West Germany stands out as the only country where family income is less variable than individual earnings. Apparently, incomes between spouses there are strongly negatively correlated. Importantly, female labor force participation in West Germany is quite low (49.6 percent in 1988) compared to the United States (59.2 percent) and especially East Germany (81 percent).

12.5.1   Rate of Return to Schooling

Table 12.1 reports the distribution among five education categories. The results for East Germany correspond closely to the counts from the Labor Markets Monitor, the first labor market survey conducted in the new states after unification (see Bielinski and von Rosenbladt 1991). As described in detail in the appendix, we constructed a continuous years of schooling variable using information on individuals' highest degree and postsecondary training. We present evidence below that our linearization works well in practice.

According to our continuous education measure, on average, workers in East Germany spend slightly more years in school than their counterparts in West Germany. This is primarily due to the importance of *Fachschulen* (technical schools), which were attended by 19 percent of East German workers, whereas only 6 percent of West Germans attended comparable *Fachhochschulen*. The somewhat surprising finding that a larger fraction of the East German population has technical or academic training has also been observed by others. Scheuer (1990) attributes this to the fact that one trains for occupations like nurses at the East German *Fachschulen*. Since we included them in the West German count for the "technical school" category, we can discard this explanation. Enrollment in higher education grew rapidly in East Germany after World War II but leveled off in the 1970s and 1980s; enrollment in higher education in West Germany grew considerably in the 1970s and 1980s, surpassing the East German level.

We estimated standard ordinary least squares log earnings regressions using either the unrestricted education dummies or the linear years of schooling variable. The results are shown in table 12.2. Surprisingly, the estimated rate of return to a year of schooling is the same in both parts of Germany: 7.7 percent higher earnings per year of schooling. This is in contrast to Schwarze (1991a, 1991b), who reports a much lower return to education for men in East Germany (about 5.6 percent using this data set). Lower returns to higher education in East Germany than West Germany are also reported by Stephan and Wiede-

Table 12.2   Returns to Education: Men and Women (standard errors in parentheses)

Independent Variable	East Germany		West Germany		United States
	(1)	(2)	(3)	(4)	(5)
Intercept	5.927	6.717	6.786	7.521	4.494
	(.009)	(.006)	(.040)	(.030)	(.029)
Years of schooling	.077	. . .	.077	. . .	.093
	(.001)		(.002)		(.002)
Completed apprenticeship	. . .	.139	. . .	.190	. . .
		(.005)		(.020)	
Master craftsman	. . .	.274	. . .	.350	. . .
		(.007)		(.029)	
Technical school	. . .	.361	. . .	.491	. . .
		(.006)		(.032)	
University	. . .	.489	. . .	.734	. . .
		(.006)		(.028)	
Experience	.020	.019	.045	.041	.032
	(.000)	(.000)	(.002)	(.002)	(.001)
Experience squared (/100)	−.035	−.033	−.077	−.071	−.048
	(.001)	(.001)	(.005)	(.006)	(.003)
Female	−.234	−.232	−.251	−.250	−.302
	(.002)	(.002)	(.015)	(.015)	(.010)
R^2	.414	.410	.457	.432	.329
σ_ε	.241	.242	.323	.331	.432
Sample size	43,532	43,532	2,496	2,496	8,118

Note: Dependent variable is log monthly earnings for East and West Germany and log weekly wage for the United States. For additional details on the samples, see the notes to table 12.1.

mann (1990) in a study of payroll data for 1988. Notice that our unrestricted dummy variable specifications (cols. 2 and 4) also find a lower return to post-secondary education in East Germany.

How can these seemingly conflicting results be reconciled? Most important, higher education in West Germany takes longer than in the east. The higher education groups—technical school and university—are the groups that have the most pronounced differences in relative earnings between the east and the west. Our conclusion is that the higher returns to these degrees in the west are just due to longer schooling, not to higher returns per year of schooling. Schwarze (1991a), on the other hand, mechanically assigns the same number of years of schooling to similar groups for both the east and the west. His results therefore have to reflect our dummy variable results.

We consider the continuous schooling measure more informative. For East and West Germans alike, a year of schooling means a year of forgone earnings, so in this respect the schooling coefficient is a measure of the return on a comparable investment.[12] From this perspective, young Germans faced similar budget constraints in both parts of the country. The structure of the East German labor market apparently did not provide major disincentives for higher education, which is also borne out by the finding of similar mean years of education.

Furthermore, we provide some evidence in figure 12.3 that the earnings-schooling relation is indeed approximately log linear in both parts of Germany. The figure displays the coefficients on dummy variables for each possible value that the schooling variable can take.[13] The graph also shows the lines corresponding to the OLS regression estimates for the continuous schooling measure. The linear specification reflects the unrestricted earnings-education relation rather well.

Finally, the continuous schooling measure allows a comparison with the United States, which is shown in column 5 of the table. The rate of return to schooling in the United States was greater than 9 percent in 1989, almost 2 percentage points above the Germanies. The payoff to a year of education was unusually high in the United States in the late 1980s, but even in more typical years the payoff to education was probably higher in the United States than in the Germanies. Given the high cost of college tuition in the United States, it is not surprising that the payoff to a year of education is greater in the United States than in the Germanies, where education is free.

That we observe more schooling on average for the East German sample than for the West German sample, of course, does not mean that the East Germans are necessarily better educated. The results may, for example, reflect the

---

12. This is one of Mincer's (1974) essential insights.

13. There are nine points shown for East Germany despite the fact that education is coded only in six separate levels. This is because additional values were created for university graduates under thirty. We also separate out physicians since medical school requires an additional year of study. For other details, see the appendix.

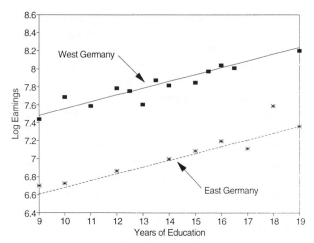

Fitted Regression Lines for Continuous Education Measure Shown

Fig. 12.3   Unrestricted log earnings-education relations
Sources: 1988 Survey of Blue- and White-Collar Households and 1988 wave of the Socioeconomic Panel.

fact that formal education has been more important in the east while there is more upgrading of skills on the job in the west. This is consistent with the much higher return to experience in West Germany (4 percent in the first year compared to 2 percent in the east). Notice, however, that the experience profiles in West Germany are also steeper than they are in the United States.

Figure 12.4 presents a plot of unrestricted age-earnings profiles estimated on the basis of dummy variables for three-year age groups in the two Germanies. Profiles for unskilled workers and university graduates are shown separately. Especially for unskilled workers, the East German profile is essentially flat. Figure 12.5 presents age-earnings profiles for men in the Germanies and the United States. Again, the much lower returns to work experience in East Germany are apparent.

The R^2's of the regressions in table 12.2 are higher for West Germany than for the United States. This is not surprising since there seems to be more emphasis on formal educational attainment and seniority compared to individual performance in the German compensation systems. But the R^2 is highest for West Germany, around 45 percent, compared to 41 percent for the east. Thus, even in East Germany, there is a good deal of earnings variation left over after accounting for the standard human capital factors. The system apparently left enough room for firm- and/or individual specific factors to influence compensation significantly.

It is useful to summarize this information with the ANOVA table for the models in columns 1, 3, and 5 of table 12.2 that is shown in table 12.3. Although the total log earnings variance in West Germany is twice that of the

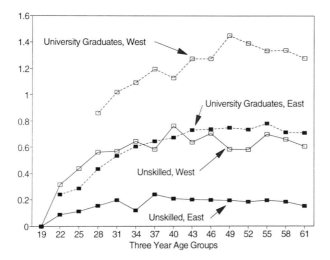

Fig. 12.4   Age-earnings profiles
Sources: 1988 Survey of Blue- and White-Collar Households and 1988 wave of the Socioeconomic Panel.

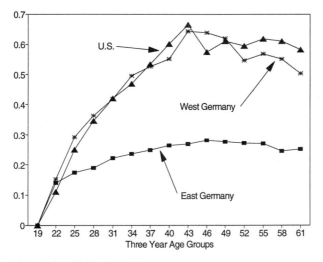

Fig. 12.5   Age-earnings profiles: Men
Sources: 1988 Survey of Blue- and White-Collar Households, 1988 wave of the Socioeconomic Panel, and March 1989 CPS.

east, the same pattern emerges. Slightly less than half the variance is explained by standard human capital factors. This contrasts with the United States, where the human capital variables explain about the same amount of earnings variance as in West Germany. The larger total variance in the United States is entirely due to the higher residual variation.

Table 12.3   **ANOVA for Simple Earnings Regressions**

	East Germany	West Germany	United States
Total variance	.099	.192	.278
Explained variance	.041	.088	.091
Residual variance	.058	.105	.187

Table 12.4   **Returns to Education: Men (standard errors in parentheses)**

Independent Variable	East Germany		West Germany		United States
	(1)	(2)	(3)	(4)	(5)
Intercept	6.008	6.759	6.767	7.497	4.473
	(.012)	(.009)	(.042)	(.034)	(.037)
Years of schooling	.071	. . .	.075	. . .	.085
	(.001)		(.003)		(.002)
Completed apprenticeship	. . .	.106	. . .	.153	. . .
		(.008)		(.024)	
Master craftsman	. . .	.226	. . .	.303	. . .
		(.009)		(.031)	
Technical school	. . .	.321	. . .	.515	. . .
		(.009)		(.038)	
University	. . .	.419	. . .	.699	. . .
		(.009)		(.032)	
Experience	.020	.019	.049	.046	.042
	(.001)	(.001)	(.003)	(.003)	(.002)
Experience squared (/100)	−.036	−.035	−.083	−.079	−.061
	(.001)	(.001)	(.006)	(.006)	(.004)
R^2	.305	.300	.419	.394	.310
Sample size	23,382	23,382	1,778	1,778	4,297

Note: Dependent variable is log monthly earnings for East and West Germany and log weekly wage for the United States. For additional details on the samples, see the notes to table 12.1.

Table 12.2 above also includes a dummy indicating gender; women receive 25–30 percent lower earnings than men in all three countries, other things held constant. Table 12.4 above and table 12.5 report separate wage regressions for men and women. The estimated return to education is greater for women than men in all three countries.

Experience profiles differ little for men and women who work full-time in East Germany: they are flat in both cases. This contrasts sharply with the Western countries, where women's profiles are flatter than men's. Thus, although the average male-female wage gap is about the same in both parts of Germany (25 percent), the gap varies substantially depending on education and experience, being much greater at high levels of experience in the United States and

West Germany than in East Germany. One may suspect that this pattern is related to the fact that the labor force attachment of women is much greater in East Germany than in West Germany. On the other hand, the United States has a female labor force participation rate that is much higher than West Germany's but even greater expansion in the male-female wage gap with experience.

Table 12.6 reports regression results with additional explanatory variables. Columns 1 and 3 add dummy variables for marital status and marital status interacted with gender. There is little effect of marital status on the earnings of either men or women in East Germany, while both West Germany and the United States have a large earnings differential between married men and women.

In column 2, we add a number of additional variables available on the East German data set. White-collar employees earn just 4 percent more than blue-collar workers. This contrasts with the large effects for the Western countries (on the order of 20 percent) and is probably a reflection of Communist ideology, which was biased against white-collar labor. Additionally, we find a 15 percent premium for workers who work on late shifts in East Germany. Such a positive premium has proved difficult to find with cross-sectional micro data

Table 12.5   **Returns to Education: Women (standard errors in parentheses)**

	East Germany		West Germany		United States
Independent Variable	(1)	(2)	(3)	(4)	(5)
Intercept	5.589	6.448	6.523	7.298	4.177
	(.014)	(.009)	(.083)	(.051)	(.044)
Years of schooling	.085	. . .	.082	. . .	.103
	(.001)		(.006)		(.003)
Completed apprenticeship	. . .	.162	. . .	.232	. . .
		(.008)		(.039)	
Master craftsman	. . .	.357	. . .	.446	. . .
		(.016)		(.083)	
Technical school	. . .	.394	. . .	.430	. . .
		(.008)		(.062)	
University	. . .	.582	. . .	.770	. . .
		(.010)		(.063)	
Experience	.019	.019	.042	.036	.023
	(.001)	(.001)	(.005)	(.005)	(.002)
Experience squared (/100)	−.033	−.032	−.075	−.064	−.037
	(.001)	(.001)	(.011)	(.011)	(.005)
R^2	.294	.292	.283	.252	.270
Sample size	20,150	20,150	718	718	3,821

Note: Dependent variable is log monthly earnings for East and West Germany and log weekly wage for the United States. For details on the samples, see the notes to table 12.1.

Table 12.6   Additional Earnings Regressions (standard errors in parentheses)

	East Germany		West Germany		United States
Independent Variable	(1)	(2)	(3)	(4)	(5)
Intercept	5.912	5.855	6.770	6.802	4.589
	(.009)	(.011)	(.039)	(.040)	(.029)
Years of schooling	.077	.077	.076	.069	.073
	(.001)	(.001)	(.002)	(.003)	(.002)
Experience	.020	.021	.042	.042	.025
	(.000)	(.000)	(.002)	(.002)	(.001)
Experience squared (/100)	−.036	−.038	−.075	−.074	−.040
	(.001)	(.001)	(.005)	(.005)	(.003)
Female	−.203	−.195	−.174	−.244	−.220
	(.005)	(.005)	(.022)	(.022)	(.015)
Married	.009	.014	.081	.075	.162
	(.004)	(.004)	(.019)	(.018)	(.014)
Married females	−.043	−.044	−.136	−.118	−.175
	(.005)	(.005)	(.030)	(.030)	(.019)
White collar	...	.040	...	.188	.203
		(.003)		(.015)	(.011)
Civil servant	...	...	...	.025	...
				(.027)	
Public sector	...	...	...	−.036	...
				(.017)	
Federal	...	...	...	...	.088
					(.023)
State and local	...	...	...	...	−.079
					(.014)
Late shift	...	.143	...	...	...
		(.003)			
Union	...	...	...	...	.221
					(.012)
Black	...	...	...	...	−.092
					(.015)
Other nonwhite	...	...	...	...	.009
					(.024)
Sample size	43,532	43,532	2,496	2,496	8,118
R^2	0.415	0.443	0.462	0.502	0.391

Note: Dependent variable is log monthly earnings for East and West Germany and log weekly earnings for the United States. For further dteails on the samples, see the notes to table 12.1.

for Western countries and may reflect the emphasis on rules in the socialist system.

In summary, these regressions document several differences between the East German, West German, and U.S. wage structures. Nevertheless, the results support Brown's (1977, 43) conclusion, which is based on casual evidence: "The white-collared apart, the most remarkable feature of the comparison between Soviet-type and Western pay structures is their extent of similarity." We would add, however, that the lower level of residual wage dispersion in East Germany is also a striking feature of the Soviet-type pay structure.

12.6 Analysis of the East German Labor Market in Transition

One question that immediately arises in studying the economic transformation of the East German labor market is, How should the East German labor market be defined after unification? We choose to define the labor market on the basis of geographic location. Thus, former East Germans who migrated west or commute to work in the west are not included in our sample of eastern Germany. As a practical matter, this is of little significance because migrants and commuters make up only about 0.5 percent of our sample.[14] On the other hand, it is instructive to study separately former East Germans whom we observe working in the western part of Germany. These workers provide a rough indication of how former East Germans would fare in the West German labor market, although one must be concerned about selective migration and commuting.

Since so many east German workers were placed on short-time hours (18 percent of our sample in 1991), we include short-time workers in our analysis. The German government subsidized short-time workers, who earned 63–68 percent of their previous pay. Firms were supposed to add another 22 percent to their pay, bringing short-time workers' pay up to 85–90 percent of their previous level. In our sample, workers on short time worked 32.8 hours per week, on average, compared to 43.1 hours for workers on regular-time hours.

12.6.1 Wage Growth and Dispersion

We turn first to the growth of wages, which Akerlof et al. (1991) and others identify as the main source of the eastern German depression. Table 12.7 summarizes the rise in earnings in East Germany since 1988. The table is based on the Survey of Blue- and White-Collar Households for 1988, retrospective earnings data from the SOEP-East for 1989, and current wage reports from the SOEP-East for 1990 and 1991. In spite of splicing together different wage series, the 1988 and 1989 data (both years before unification) are remarkably similar, suggesting that the data are comparable. East German wages grew rapidly between 1989 and 1991. (The CPI increased by about 6 percent between 1988 and March 1991, so these wage changes can be thought of as mostly real

14. If we include the commuters and migrants in a log wage regression using 1990 data, when they were observed in eastern Germany, their average residual is 0.12. Given the small number of commuters and migrants, this finding suggests that they would not have a large influence on the estimated regression had they remained in eastern Germany.

Table 12.7   **Summary of Monthly Earnings in Eastern Germany, 1988–91**
                    (standard deviations are in parentheses)

Year	Average Monthly Earnings Measured In:		Coefficient of Variation: DM
	Logs	DM	
1988	7.03	1,179.1	.30
	(.32)	(359.0)	
1989	7.02	1,182.3	.32
	(.37)	(382.8)	
1990	7.15	1,331.4	.31
	(.29)	(410.4)	
1991	7.35	1,635.2	.35
	(.32)	(568.9)	

Note: Data for 1989 have been inflated by 6 percent to adjust for bonus payments. The average bonus payment was 6 percent of total compensation in 1988 and 1990. Workers placed on short-time hours are included in 1989–91. 1991 figures exclude east Germans who migrated west or commute to work in the west; if these individuals are included, the mean of log earnings is 7.38 and the standard deviation .35.

changes.)[15] Between 1989 and 1990 the average monthly wage increased by 12.5 percent, and between 1990 and 1991 it increased by another 22.8 percent. Over the period 1989–91 wages grew by 38.3 percent. This growth is even more impressive in view of the fact that nearly one-fifth of workers were placed on short-time hours.

In spite of dramatic growth, wages in the east were still only about 40 percent of the west German level in 1991. Nevertheless, the east German real-wage growth stands in marked contrast to that of other former East-bloc countries. For example, in the last quarter of 1991, real wages were lower by 43 percent in Bulgaria, 26 percent in Czechoslovakia, 8 percent in Hungary, 0.2 percent in Poland, and 20 percent in Romania relative to their 1990 level (see Boeri and Keese 1992). Although there was strong *nominal* wage growth in these countries, extremely high rates of inflation eroded real earnings. The unique relation between eastern and western Germany has clearly cushioned the transition to a market-based economy for East Germany.

For the subsample of individuals who were working in both 1990 and 1991, earnings grew by 24 percent. Wage growth was exceptionally high for individuals who changed jobs. Using longitudinal data from the SOEP-East, we can decompose the variability in individuals' log wage growth between 1990 and 1991 according to the type of job change using the formula

15. One cautionary note is that, although the average CPI was relatively stable between 1988 and 1991, there were wide differences in the rate of inflation for many goods. For example, rental costs jumped 58 percent in January 1991, while food prices increased 15 percent, clothing and shoe prices decreased 30 percent, and furniture prices decreased 20 percent between 1989 and January 1991. The rapidly changing prices of consumer goods are likely to have distributional consequences that go beyond changes in the wage structure.

$$\sigma^2 = \sum_i [p_i\sigma_i^2 + p_i(\mu_i - \mu)^2],$$

where σ^2 is the total variance of the change in log wage, σ_i^2 is the variance of the change in log wage for group i, p_i is the fraction of the sample belonging to group i, μ_i is the mean wage change for group i, and μ is the change in the grand mean.

Table 12.8 contains the results of this decomposition. The overall variance in log earnings growth for individuals in East Germany (.056) during this period of dramatic transformation is lower than the level that Abowd and Card (1989) report for the United States (over .12) but higher than the typical level that we find for West Germany using the SOEP for 1984–89 (.036).[16] (In terms of standard deviations, the figures are .24 for eastern Germany, .35 for the United States, and .19 for West Germany.)

Nearly 85 percent of employed East Germans in 1990 and 1991 remained employed by the same firm, and 77 percent remained on the same job. Ten percent of east German workers reported changing jobs without any intervening unemployment. Over two-thirds of the total variance in log earnings growth is due to individuals who remained on the same job. Job changers who did not suffer intervening unemployment contributed 20 percent of the total variance.

Looking cross-sectionally, it is clear from table 12.7 above that earnings variability increased in eastern Germany following unification. The variance of the level of monthly earnings (in deutsche marks) increased each year since 1988 and was 150 percent greater in 1991 than in 1988. Notice also that the coefficient of variation of earnings increased from .30 to .35, in spite of the large increase in mean earnings. However, the standard deviation of log monthly earnings, which was .32 both in 1988 and in 1991, shows no clear trend. The level of wage dispersion in eastern Germany still has a long way to go before it reaches the West German level. In West Germany, the coefficient of variation of monthly earnings was consistently around .44 between 1984 and 1989.

Table 12.9 gives the ratio of various percentiles of the earnings distribution relative to the median for eastern Germany, West Germany, and the United States in selected years. The wage distribution in eastern Germany was notably stable between 1988 and 1990, but the top 20 percent of wage earners gained significantly on the median earner in 1991. The increase in earnings dispersion in East Germany occurred mainly at the upper tail of the wage distribution. On the other hand, the wage structure in West Germany was conspicuously stable in the 1980s, especially compared to the United States.

To explore changes in the east Germany wage structure further, Figure 12.6 presents a graph of earnings growth between 1988 and 1991 for each percentile of the earnings distribution. That is, the figure gives the percentage wage increase for a worker occupying each percentile of the wage distribution in 1991

---

16. The U.S. figure is based on log annual earnings.

Table 12.8 **Variance Decomposition for Change in Log Wage, Eastern Germany, 1990–91**

Group	% of Sample (p_i)	Mean (μ_i)	Variance (σ_i^2)	$[p_i(\mu_i - \mu)^2]/\sigma^2$ (%)	$(p_i\sigma_i^2)/\sigma^2$ (%)
New job with intervening unemployment	1.1	.106	.068	.4	1.4
New job without intervening unemployment	9.6	.350	.097	1.9	16.7
Same employer under new ownership	5.9	.240	.047	.0	5.0
Changed job within firm	6.7	.279	.038	.1	4.6
No job change	76.8	.228	.051	.4	69.8
Total	100.0	.245	.056	2.7	97.3

Note: Data set is SOEP-East. Sample size is 1,443.

Table 12.9 **Various Percentiles of the Earnings Distribution as a Percentage of the Median**

	Percentile in the Earnings Distribution				
	10th	25th	50th	75th	90th
A. East Germany					
1988	68.08	82.10	100	121.12	141.91
1989	65.45	81.82	100	118.18	142.73
1990	70.01	83.32	100	120.90	143.84
1991	69.63	82.89	100	123.83	159.40
B. West Germany					
1984	62.49	79.37	100	129.99	171.00
1985	62.15	79.02	100	130.62	173.44
1986	62.31	78.40	100	130.17	173.94
1987	61.25	77.44	100	130.33	175.94
1988	62.49	78.25	100	129.68	173.08
1989	62.31	79.19	100	130.50	171.88
C. United States					
1979	51.04	66.67	100	141.67	191.67
1984	49.22	67.06	100	150.00	203.13
1991	48.54	67.96	100	149.27	218.45

Note: Data for East Germany are from the Survey of Blue- and White-Collar Households for 1988 and from the SOEP-East for 1989–91. 1989 figures for East Germany exclude bonuses. Data for West Germany are from the Socioeconomic Panel. Data for the United States are outgoing rotation group files from the Current Population Survey; earnings refer to usual weekly earnings.

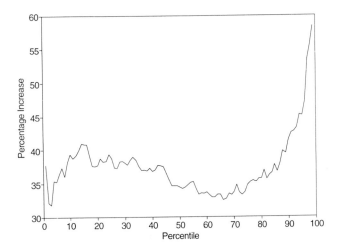

Fig. 12.6   Wage increases between 1988 and 1991 by percentile
Sources: 1988 Survey of Blue- and White-Collar Households and 1991 wave of the Socioeconomic Panel–East.

relative to a worker occupying the same percentile of the distribution in 1988. It is quite clear that the increase in earnings variability occurred primarily because of an expansion of the right-hand tail of the distribution: the top decile had extraordinary income growth. Recall that figure 12.2 above showed that the right-hand tail of the East German wage distribution in 1988 was unusually short compared to West Germany and the United States.

The left-hand tail of the eastern German wage distribution experienced about average wage growth after unification. This finding is significant because one may suspect that the Communist government in East Germany artificially raised the earnings of low-income workers and that the move to a market economy would have had a greater effect on the low-wage earners. There are two explanations for why the low-wage earners were not especially hurt by unification. First, figure 12.2 indicates that there was not a great disparity in the left-hand tails of the wage distribution between East and West Germany just before unification. Second, after unification, union contracts and government policies may be maintaining low-skill workers' wages above their equilibrium level in eastern Germany. As shown below, the fact that the unemployment rate is now much higher for less educated workers in eastern Germany suggests that there may be some merit to this view.

Table 12.10 investigates the extent of year-to-year mobility in workers' earnings in eastern and western Germany.[17] Workers are cross-classified by quintile

---

17. The period between 1988 and 1989 coincided with an expansion in West Germany. Mobility was only slightly higher between 1984 and 1985, which was a recessionary period in West Germany.

Table 12.10   **Transition Matrix by Quintile of the Earnings Distribution**

	Eastern Germany, 1990–91: Earnings in 1991				
	Bottom	Second	Third	Fourth	Top
Earnings in 1990:					
Bottom	.581	.210	.114	.066	.028
Second	.256	.369	.239	.107	.031
Third	.107	.234	.308	.276	.072
Fourth	.045	.117	.242	.314	.255
Top	.010	.069	.097	.210	.614
	West Germany, 1988–89: Earnings in 1989				
Earnings in 1988:					
Bottom	.790	.167	.024	.011	.007
Second	.158	.625	.171	.045	.000
Third	.042	.181	.601	.172	.004
Fourth	.007	.027	.196	.650	.120
Top	.002	.000	.007	.123	.869

Note: Data are from the Socioeconomic Panels and refer to full-time employed men and women. Earnings are gross monthly earnings plus one-twelfth of annual bonuses.

of the earnings distribution each year. There is greater earnings mobility in eastern Germany than western Germany, especially for workers in the middle of the earnings distribution. In 1991, nearly 40 percent of the top fifth of wage earners in eastern Germany were not in this income class in the preceding year, whereas in West Germany only about 13 percent of workers joined the top 20 percent in a typical year.

In table 12.11 we summarize the characteristics of the top 10 percent of wage earners in eastern Germany in 1991, the group that has undergone the most significant change in relative earnings since unification.[18] Compared to the rest of wage earners, the top 10 percent is much more likely to hold professional or executive positions, to have higher education, to work in private firms, to live in a large city (e.g., Berlin, Leipzig, Dresden), to be self-employed, and to work in a newly founded firm. By and large, these are characteristics that are associated with top wage earners in the west. About half the workers in the top 10 percent of the wage distribution in 1991 were in the top 10 percent of the wage distribution in 1990, and the average percentile ranking was almost in the top 20 percent. Earnings grew by over 50 percent between 1990 and 1991 for the top 10 percent of earners, compared to 25 percent for all others. Since the top 10 percent of wage earners still have some distance to go until they are as relatively successful in the east as in the west, the evolution of this group will be especially interesting to track in the future.

18. We included self-employed workers in table 12.11 because of interest in entrepreneurship. Self-employed workers are excluded from all other results.

Table 12.11   **Means of Selected Characteristics of Top 10 Percent and Bottom 90 Percent of Wage Earners, Eastern Germany, 1991**

Characteristic	Top 10%	Bottom 90%
Gross monthly earnings	2,972	1,502
	(757)	(359)
% of compensation due to bonus	1.96	1.59
Average percentile rank in 1990 distribution	78.8	46.8
Earnings growth, 1990–91 (%)	52.2	25.7
	(73.8)	(31.1)
Weekly hours	49.5	41.8
	(10.9)	(8.2)
Female (%)	21.7	47.9
Age	43.0	38.5
	(9.6)	(10.5)
Years of tenure	12.3	10.8
	(12.1)	(10.4)
Years of schooling	14.4	12.5
	(1.7)	(2.2)
Technical school (%)	32.2	17.5
University (%)	30.7	10.1
Short time (%)	4.8	18.1
White collar (%)	72.0	48.9
Professional (%)	47.6	14.1
Executive (%)	9.5	0.5
Self-employed (%)	12.2	3.3
Private firm (%)	68.8	54.9
Works in newly founded firm (%)	9.5	3.1
Firm size > 200 (%)	51.3	53.2
City > 100,000 (%)	48.7	27.7
Sample size	189	1,684

Note: Standard deviations are in parentheses. Except for firm size and tenure, the difference between the top 10 percent and the bottom 90 percent is statistically significant at the 1 percent level for each characteristic.

12.6.2   Wage Regressions for Eastern Germany

Table 12.12 presents simple wage regressions using each cross section of the SOEP-East survey. For comparison, the first column reports estimates for East Germany in 1988 and the second column estimates for West Germany in 1988. The 1988 East German survey yields coefficient estimates and an R^2 that are very close to the SOEP-East for 1989, again suggesting that the 1988 East German survey is reasonably representative of the workforce.[19]

There are a number of interesting changes in the wage structure in East Germany between 1988 and 1991. First, the rate of return to education fell

19. Oddly, the experience profile is steeper in 1989 than in 1988. On further investigation, we found that this result is due to a few outliers with low experience. The other coefficients are not greatly affected if these outliers are deleted.

Table 12.12   Earnings Equations before and after Unification (standard errors are in parentheses): Dependent Variable, Log Monthly Earnings

Independent Variable	East Germany, 1988	West Germany, 1988	East Germany, 1989[a]	East Germany, 1990	Eastern Germany, 1991	Easterners in West, 1991[b]
Intercept	5.927	6.786	5.777	6.216	6.481	7.151
	(.009)	(.040)	(.041)	(.032)	(.045)	(.217)
Years of schooling	.077	.077	.074	.065	.062	.065
	(.001)	(.002)	(.003)	(.002)	(.003)	(.017)
Experience	.020	.045	.037	.018	.014	.004
	(.000)	(.002)	(.002)	(.002)	(.002)	(.013)
Experience squared (/100)	-.035	-.077	-.063	-.028	-.020	-.010
	(.001)	(.005)	(.005)	(.004)	(.005)	(.037)
Female	-.234	-.251	-.224	-.208	-.198	-.389
	(.002)	(.015)	(.012)	(.010)	(.013)	(.084)
R^2	.414	.457	.414	.410	.284	.273
σ_e	.241	.323	.286	.224	.272	.355
Sample size	43,532	2,496	2,213	2,246	1,795	117

[a]Wages have been inflated by 6 percent to adjust for bonuses in 1989.

[b]Easterners in the west includes 20 east Germans who migrated to western Germany and 97 east Germans who commute to work in western Germany.

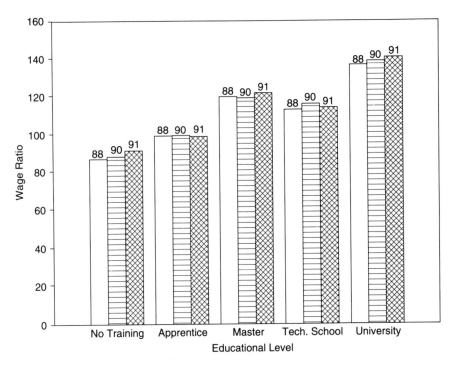

Fig. 12.7   Education wage differentials, 1988–91
Sources: 1988 Survey of Blue- and White-Collar Households and Labor Markets Monitor for the New German States (Bielinski and von Rosenbladt 1991).
Note: Apprenticeship = 100

from .077 to .062, suggesting that education attained under the Communist system is less valuable in the transition period. Official government statistics on earnings, which are summarized in figure 12.7, also show fairly stable education differentials.[20] According to these data, earnings increased by between 31 and 37 percent between 1988 and July 1991, depending on education level. Workers with no training experienced the most earnings growth, followed by university graduates.

Second, the already flat experience profiles in East Germany have become slightly flatter by 1991. We also find very low returns to seniority. Evidently, experience in the Communist labor market is now of less value. Third, the male-female wage gap has narrowed. The labor force participation rate for women in East Germany fell, moving in the direction of West German women, but the rate fell by almost as much for men. Fourth, the explanatory power of

20. The underlying data are from Bielinski and von Rosenbladt (1991) and our tabulations of the 1988 East German survey.

the regressions has dropped considerably, with the R^2 falling from 41 to 28 percent between 1990 and 1991. Finally, the residual variance increased by 47 percent (from .050 to .074) between 1990 and 1991. These findings suggest that there have been major changes in the valuation of individuals' characteristics since unification.

In other specifications, we have added a dummy variable indicating whether a worker is on short-time hours and a dummy indicating white-collar status. Workers on short-time hours earn about 23 percent less (t-ratio = -12) than full-time workers, other things being equal. This differential is about what one would expect since firms are required to supplement short-time workers' pay to 85–90 percent of their previous level. Including the short-time dummy reduces the return to education slightly and increases the male-female wage gap by about four points.

Interestingly, white-collar workers in the east now earn an 11 percent wage premium over blue-collar workers (t-ratio = 6.2). This may be contrasted with the 4 percent white-collar premium in East Germany in 1988 and the 19 percent premium in West Germany in 1988 that we document in table 12.6 above. As far as white-collar work is concerned, the wage structure in East Germany is approaching that in the west.

We have also examined the evolution of industry wage differentials in eastern Germany. Specifically, we added (broad) industry dummy variables to the wage regressions in table 12.2 and estimated industry wage differentials for East and West Germany. We then took deviations of each industry coefficient from the average, assigning a differential of zero to the omitted industry. To

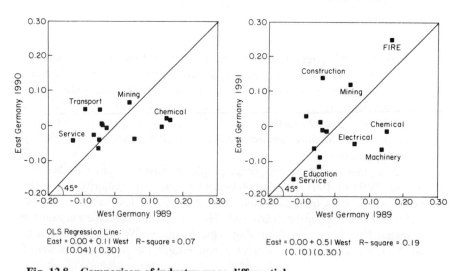

Fig. 12.8   Comparison of industry wage differentials
Sources: 1989 wave of the Socioeconomic Panel–West and 1990 and 1991 waves of the Socioeconomic Panel–East.

illustrate the evolution of industry wage differentials in eastern Germany relative to those in western Germany, figure 12.8 presents graphs of the east German differentials in 1990 or 1991 versus the West German differentials in 1989. The figures are striking. In 1990, east German industry wage differentials were extremely compressed, ranging less than 15 percent from highest to lowest paid industry; in West Germany the range was about 30 percent. Moreover, the correlation between industry wage differentials in the east and the west was statistically insignificant in 1990.

By 1991, the east German industry wage differentials were far more dispersed, with a range of 40 percent between the highest- and the lowest-paying industry. Finance, insurance, and real estate increased in position relative to the mean industry by 25 percentage points, while relative pay in the service industry fell by 10 points. Moreover, the pattern of industry differentials in eastern Germany now more closely resembles the west German pattern. The rapid change in the eastern interindustry wage structure is probably due, in large part, to the German unions' success in negotiating industry-level contracts that follow a similar pattern to western contracts.

12.6.3   Easterners Who Work in the West

A small number of eastern Germans surveyed in the SOEP-East migrated to the west since the initial wave of the survey was conducted.[21] For a sample of twenty migrants, we have complete wage and demographic information. An additional ninety-seven sampled individuals commute to work in the west but live in the east. These 117 easterners who work in the west have virtually the same level of education as easterners who work in the east but are about eight years younger, are much more likely to be men, are less likely to hold white-collar jobs (37 vs. 53 percent), and have much lower tenure (0.8 vs. 11 years). Bielinski and von Rosenbladt (1991) estimate that 28 percent of commuters received on-the-job training in a three-month period in 1991, as compared to 17 percent of those who do not commute.

The average easterner who works in the west earns DM 2,990 per month, which is 83 percent more per month than the average for easterners who work in the east but about 15 percent less than the average west German. The relatively small gap in earnings between easterners who commute or migrated to the west and native west Germans is noteworthy because the commuters/migrants have extremely low tenure and do not possess other observable characteristics that are particularly highly rewarded in the west German labor market.

Column 6 of table 12.12 presents the estimated log earnings equation for the small sample of eastern Germans who work in the west. Although the estimates are extremely imprecise, they reveal some interesting patterns.[22] First,

---

21. For a landmark study of migration between eastern and western Germany, see Akerlof et al. (1991).

22. We found qualitatively similar results for a larger sample of commuters using data from the 1991 Labor Markets Monitor Survey.

the return to education for workers who were educated in the east but work in the west is relatively large (.065). Although some caution is warranted because of sampling variance, this finding nonetheless suggests that the high level of education that East Germans received under the Communist system will receive a reasonable payoff as the east approaches a Western-style market economy. Second, the experience profile is virtually flat, again suggesting that work experience gained under the Communist system is of little value. Third, the male-female wage gap is greater for easterners who work in the west. Finally, the residual variance in earnings is quite close to the level for West Germany in 1988.

12.6.4 Unemployment

An important issue in addition to wage structure changes concerns the evolution of unemployment in eastern Germany. Unemployment in eastern Germany soared after unification, as it has in other former East-bloc countries. The probability of being unemployed in eastern Germany is inversely related to education level. We calculate that, in 1991, the unemployment rate was 6 percent for university graduates, 2 percent for master craftsmen, 10 percent for workers with apprenticeship training, and 33 percent for workers with no postsecondary training.[23] Similarly, workers with a low level of education were also much more likely to be placed on short-time hours. There was hardly any unemployment in 1988 in East Germany. The unemployment rates by education level in West Germany are much lower, especially at the low end of the education distribution. For example, Abraham and Houseman (chap. 11 in this volume) report that the unemployment rate in West Germany for workers with no postsecondary training in 1989 is 11.6 percent.

The high rate of unemployment for low-educated workers suggests that their wage rate is above the current equilibrium level. On the other hand, the more moderate rates of unemployment for highly skilled workers suggest that the wage structure is not far out of line for these workers. We note, however, that government policies to reduce unemployment (e.g., short-time work subsidies) may mask substantial imbalances in supply and demand.

We also note that, if the unemployed are very different from the employed in terms of unobserved characteristics, truncation bias may affect our regression estimates. On the other hand, this is not likely to be a serious problem because much of the unemployment is due to plant closings and mass layoffs, which affect a wide cross section of workers. Furthermore, we find that the results are qualitatively similar if we estimate the regressions for eastern Germany using just the subsample of individuals who were continuously employed between 1989 and 1991. This finding suggests that the differences in the wage structure that we document between 1989 and 1991 are not due to the changing composition of the samples.

---

23. We also find that the unemployment rate is almost twice as high for women as it is for men (13 vs. 7.6 percent) and that the probability of being unemployed increases with age.

12.7 Summary and Conclusion

We can summarize our main conclusions as follows.

1. In 1988, the wage structure was more compressed in East Germany than in West Germany, even though West Germany has low wage variability by U.S. standards.

2. In spite of the considerable wage compression in East Germany, education was relatively highly rewarded. The monetary payoff to a year of education was remarkably similar in East and West Germany. Furthermore, East Germans who migrated or commuted to western Germany after the collapse of East Germany appear to earn a comparable return to their education as native West Germans. Since East Germans are highly educated, this finding suggests that the unified Germany will have considerably more human capital.

3. Average earnings of eastern Germans grew rapidly following unification—by as much as 30–40 percent. Surprisingly, this great leap in wages occurred without unusually high variability in earnings growth across individuals. The cross-sectional variance in earnings growth in eastern Germany in 1990–91 was below the typical level for the United States but above the typical level for West Germany.

4. Wage regressions for 1990 and 1991 already show signs that the East German wage structure is quite different than it was in 1989. White-collar workers in eastern Germany now earn a substantial premium, although not as large a premium as white-collar workers earn in the west. Similarly, the industry wage structure in eastern Germany is approaching the West German structure. The remarkably low level of dispersion in earnings that we documented for East Germany in 1988 is gradually increasing, primarily because the right-hand tail of the distribution is stretching out. In addition, experience profiles have flattened out, suggesting that work experience gained under the Communist system is now of little value.

5. Eastern Germans who are observed working in western Germany earn almost as much as native West Germans, and, with the major exception of work experience, they appear to earn similar payoffs to their characteristics as West Germans.

6. The wage structure in eastern Germany, however, still has some distance to go until it mirrors the wage structure in western Germany. In particular, we expect that it will be a long time until the experience-earnings profile becomes as steep in eastern Germany as it is in the west. In addition, industry and occupation premiums are still compressed in the east relative to the west. Although wages served mainly a bookkeeping function in the former East Germany, they now serve as signals to firms and workers. The effect of the remaining differences in the wage structures on migration and capital flows between eastern and western Germany seems to us to be a worthy topic of future study.

We think that the facts documented in this paper are consistent with the view that German unions and government policies have maintained wages of low-skill workers above their current equilibrium level. Unions have imposed a wage structure that more closely mirrors the western wage structure. Government policy has protected low-skill workers. The Treuhandanstalt has pursued a policy of deliberately seeking new owners who would maintain employment, and the introduction of West German labor law has made it difficult to lay off workers or to deviate from union contracts. As a consequence, after unification high-income earners improved their position relative to middle-income earners, but low-income earners did not lose any ground relative to middle-income earners. The unemployment rate soared for low-skill workers, suggesting that employers' demand for low-skill workers is low at their current level of remuneration.

What will happen in the future? The German government and employers are providing a great deal of training to former East German workers, which should eventually improve the productivity and employment situation of less educated workers. Furthermore, more and better capital is flowing into eastern Germany, which would further raise productivity and sustain high wages for low-skill workers. Finally, our findings that commuters and migrants are doing quite well in the western German labor market and that the return to education has remained relatively high in eastern Germany suggest that worker skills are not the main problem in eastern Germany. Instead, outdated technology, insufficient capital, and inefficient management may be the main sources of low wages and productivity in the east. In any event, we conclude that the wage structure in eastern Germany has made substantial progress toward a new equilibrium that will eventually more closely resemble the West German wage structure.

Appendix

Description of Education Systems in the Germanies

Primary school in West Germany starts at the age of six and comprises the first four grades. After grade four, the secondary school system branches into three alternative routes. The most basic branch (*Hauptschule*) lasts up to grade 9 (or grade 10 in some states) and combines general education with certain preparatory courses for more technical or clerical vocations. It is supposed to lead to a subsequent apprenticeship or vocational training. The middle branch (*Realschule*) has a different vocational focus than the *Hauptschule* and offers a larger choice between liberal arts classes and courses with a more practical orientation. This branch ends after grade 10 and may lead to an apprenticeship, further education in vocational schools, or a switch into *Gymnasium,* which is the third branch of the secondary school system.

The *Gymnasium* is the most intellectually oriented track and is designed to provide a thorough education in the liberal arts that prepares students for further academic training. *Gymnasium* ends after grade 13 with a general exam (*Abitur*) that serves as a prerequisite for access to the university system. The last two years of *Gymnasium* are roughly comparable to the first years of college in the United States. Since the 1970s, some states have introduced integrated secondary schools (*Gesamtschulen*) combining all three branches and leading to the various secondary school degrees.

University training in West Germany is completely focused on the area of specialization and ends in a *Diploma.* The average time to completion was 6.9 years in 1987 (Scheuer 1990) and has increased even more since. In addition to academic universities, there is another kind of postsecondary institution known as *Fachhochschulen.* These institutions offer a more practically oriented training, usually in engineering or business disciplines; they are roughly comparable to professional colleges in the United States. Furthermore, the courses of study are generally shorter than in the universities (the average length was 4.4 years in 1987). *Fachhochschulen* can be entered after the twelfth grade in *Gymnasium* or after completion of a *Fachoberschule.* The latter comprises grades 11 and 12 and can be entered with a *Realschule* degree or the equivalent. It combines practical job-oriented training in workshops with more general education.

Vocational training in West Germany consists usually of an apprenticeship in a business firm combined with part-time schooling at a state run *Berufsschule.* Apprenticeships can last for two to four years, during which time apprentices earn a basic allowance from their employer. *Berufsschule* provides theoretical foundations for the profession in which an apprentice has trained as well as liberal arts education. A completed apprenticeship is a prerequisite to many skilled jobs in industry, administration, and the service sector. Two to three years after completion, trained workers can enroll in a two-year *Fachschule,* which enables them to become master craftsmen in their field.

East Germany

Owing to a series of reforms, the education system in East Germany is simpler. The main building block is the integrated *Polytechnische Oberschule* (POS), which is compulsory for everyone up to grade 10. Its quality and scope are generally regarded as comparable to the West German *Realschule.* Further secondary training is provided in the *Erweiterten Oberstufe* (EOS) for two more grades, leading to the East German *Abitur.* Access to the EOS is conditional on grades and political factors. In addition, social diversity in student representation is a consideration in admission to the EOS.

Unlike in West Germany, admission to a university is conditional on an additional entry exam. Admitted are EOS graduates, graduates of *Fachschulen* (see below), young workers who completed a three-year apprenticeship with *Abitur,* and graduates of the preparatory "Worker and Peasant Faculties" (for details, see Glaessner 1985). These indirect routes to university serve the purpose of creating a student body that reflects the social structure of the population and are quantitatively much more important than in the west. Since the 1970s, three-quarters of the students seeking admission to a university have had some work experience or completed their military training. This has led to the gradual introduction of a one-year practical training requirement for EOS graduates without professional training starting in 1976, basically lengthening their education by a year (Panorama DDR 1984).

Admissions to the various fields are regulated by state plan reflecting the prospective needs of a profession. This planning was apparently not always fully effective: many university graduates were overqualified for their jobs in the 1970s, which led to a reduction in the number of admissions (Scheuer 1990). This trend was reversed somewhat in the 1980s. Most university programs in East Germany are designed to be completed in four years; a one-year extension is granted only in exceptional cases. Only about three-quarters of university courses are devoted to the major field of study; the rest of the curriculum is taken up by courses in Marxism-Leninism, languages, and sports.

Fachschulen in East Germany are postsecondary institutions comparable to the West German *Fachhochschulen*. They mainly train engineers and technical experts and, since the 1970s, nurses. *Fachschulen* have three-year programs. They admit graduates of the EOS as well as young men and women who have completed practical training.

Like in the west, vocational training in the east consists of a dual education combining an apprenticeship with vocational school (*Berufsschule*). These schools are usually part of the enterprise offering the apprenticeship. Most apprenticeship programs last two years.

Derivation of Continuous Years of Schooling Variable

For the United States, years of school completed is collected directly in the Current Population Survey. For East Germany and West Germany, years of schooling is inferred from the worker's degree.

Education in our 1988 East German survey is measured in six discrete categories. The groups are less than tenth grade, completed tenth grade at a POS, apprenticeship training, master craftsmen, technical school (*Fachschule*), and university. Unfortunately, this is a rather coarse grouping; in particular, secondary school degrees and postsecondary qualifications are not coded separately. We report results with four education dummies as well as for a continuous schooling measure. The latter measure was constructed as follows. Nine years of schooling were assumed for workers who did not complete school, ten years if tenth grade was completed. The first group is rather unimportant and was lumped together with the second in the dummy variable regressions (this will be the base group). Two years of apprenticeship training was assumed, although a basic allowance is paid during this time by the employer. Four years of training was assumed for master craftsmen. Technical school lasts for three years and requires completion of the EOS or a two-year practical training, yielding a total of fifteen years of education. Finally, university courses last usually four years beyond EOS, yielding a total of sixteen. Since the mid-1970s, an additional one-year practical training requirement was introduced for EOS graduates. Thus, we assumed an additional year of schooling for everyone with university education who is under age thirty.

For the West German survey, we have more complete information on educational attainment. In particular, secondary school degrees and further training are coded separately. Education categories are formed as follows. Anyone who does not report any postsecondary training becomes part of the base group. The second group comprises everybody who completed an apprenticeship, *Berufsfachschule,* or schools for public-sector occupations. The third group comprises graduates of *Fachschulen* and anyone who reports holding a position as master craftsman. The next group includes graduates of *Fachhochschulen* and everyone who went to nursing school since this group has been trained at East German *Fachschulen* since the 1970s. University graduates form the last group.

The continuous schooling measure was constructed using the information on both secondary school degree and postsecondary training. For the group with no postsecondary education, the number of years to complete secondary school was used. Ten years of education were assumed for the category reporting other degrees (largely special schools) and nine years for anyone with no secondary degree. For completed apprenticeship, *Berufsfachschule,* public-sector training, and nursing schools, two years were added. For graduates of *Fachschulen,* 3.5 years were added since they must complete an apprenticeship, which can last for one or two years. We assumed *Fachhochschule* to last four years. It can be reached by a variety of different routes. For graduates with *Abitur* or *Fachhochschulreife,* thirteen and twelve years of secondary school were used. For graduates of *Hauptschule* and *Realschule,* three years of schooling beyond secondary school were assumed before *Fachhochschule* can be entered. Six years of university training were assumed, yielding a total of nineteen years for everyone with *Abitur.* We used twenty years for everyone who does not report *Abitur* since they probably reached university on a more roundabout route, for example, by attending *Fachhochschule* first.

Some of our assumptions may be debatable. For example, it is unclear whether for a certain degree only the minimum number of years necessary should be counted or a higher number if a more roundabout route was chosen. Helberger (1988) reviews the German literature and discusses these issues in detail without reaching a clear conclusion.

References

Abowd, John M., and David Card. 1989. On the covariance structure of earnings and hours changes. *Econometrica* 57:411–45.

Akerlof, George A., Andrew K. Rose, Janet L. Yellen, and Helga Hessenius. 1991. East Germany in from the cold: The economic aftermath of currency union. *Brookings Papers on Economic Activity,* no. 1:1–87.

Atkinson, Anthony B., and John Micklewright. 1992. *Economic transformation in Eastern Europe and the distribution of income.* Cambridge: Cambridge University Press.

Bellmann, Lutz, Saul Estrin, Hartmut Lehmann, and Jonathan Wadsworth. 1992. The eastern German labor market in transition: Gross flow estimates from panel data. Discussion Paper no. 102. London: London School of Economics, Centre for Economic Performance.

Bergson, Abraham. 1984. Income inequality under Soviet socialism. *Journal of Economic Literature* 22:1052–99.

Bielinski, Harald, and Bernhard von Rosenbladt. 1991. *Arbeitsmarktmonitor für die neuen Bundesländer: Umfrage 1990/1991 Tabellenband.* Beiträge zur Arbeitsmarkt und Berufsforschung 148.1–148.3. 3 vols. Nürnberg: Institut für Arbeitsmarkt- und Berufsforschung.

Bispinck, Reinhard, and WSI-Tarifarchiv. 1991. "Alle Dämme gebrochen"? Die Tarifpolitik in den neuen Bundesländern in 1. Halbjahr 1991. *WSI-Mitteilungen* 44:466–78.

Blanchflower, David G., and Richard B. Freeman. 1992. Unionism in the United States and other advanced OECD countries. In *Labor market institutions and the future role of unions,* ed. Mario F. Bognanno and Morris M. Kleiner. Oxford: Blackwell.

Boeri, Tito, and Mark Keese. 1992. Labour markets and the transition in Central and Eastern Europe. *OECD Economic Studies* 18:133–63.

Brown, Henry Phelps. 1977. *The inequality of pay.* Oxford: Oxford University Press.

Burda, Michael, and Jeffrey Sachs. 1988. Assessing high unemployment in West Germany. *World Economy* 11:543–63.

Führ, Christoph. 1989. *Schulen und Hochschulen in der Bundesrepublik Deutschland.* Studien und Dokumentationen zur Deutschen Bildungsgeschichte, vol. 39. Cologne: Bohlau.

Glaessner, Gert-Joachim. 1985. Universitäten und Hochschulen. In *DDR Handbuch,* vol. 2, ed. Bundesministerium für Innerdeutsche Beziehungen. Cologne: Verlag Wissenschaft und Politik.

Hauser, Richard. 1991. Die personelle Einkommensverteilung in den alten und neuen Bundesländern vor der Vereinigung—Probleme eines empirischen Vergleichs und der Abschätzung von Entwicklungstendenzen. University of Frankfurt. Typescript.

Helberger, Christof. 1988. Eine Überprüfung der Linearitätsannahme der Humankapitaltheorie. In *Bildung, Beruf, Arbeitsmarkt,* ed. Hans-Joachim Bodenhöfer. Berlin: Duncker & Humblot.

Krause, Peter, and Johannes Schwarze. 1990. Die Einkommensstichprobe in Arbeiterund Angestelltenhaushalten in der DDR vom August 1988—Erhebungskonzeption und Datenzugriff. Discussion Paper no. 11. Berlin: Deutsches Institut für Wirtschaftsforschung.

Mincer, Jacob. 1974. *Schooling, experience and earnings.* New York: National Bureau of Economic Research.

Panorama DDR. 1984. *Students and colleges: Higher education in the German Democratic Republic.* Dresden: Zeit im Bild.

Scheuer, Markus. 1990. Ausbildung und Qualifikation der Arbeitskräfte in der DDR. *RWI-Mitteilungen* 41:67–79.

Schmidt, Christoph M. 1991. Empirical analyses of the German labor market: Unions, unemployment, and wages. Ph.D. diss., Princeton University.

Schwarze, Johannes. 1991a. Ausbildung und Einkommen von Männern. Einkommensfunktionsschätzungen für die ehemalige DDR und die Bundesrepublik Deutschland. *Mitteilungen aus der Arbeitsmarkt- und Berufsforschung* 24:63–69.

————. 1991b. Einkommensverläufe in der DDR von 1989 bis 1990—Unbeobachtete Heterogenität und erste Auswirkungen der marktwirtschaftlichen Orientierung. In *Lebenslagen im Wandel—Zur Einkommensdynamik in Deutschland seit 1984,* ed. Ulrich Rendtel und Gert Wagner. Frankfurt and New York: Campus.

Siebert, Horst, and Holger Schmieding. 1992. Restructuring industry in the GDR. In *European industrial restructuring in the 1990s,* ed. Karen Cool, Damien Niven, and Ingo Walter. New York: New York University Press.

Statistisches Amt der DDR. 1990. Übersicht über die regelmäßigen repräsentativen Bevölkerungsbefragungen des Statistischen Amtes der DDR. Berlin. Typescript.

Stephan, Helga, and Eberhard Wiedemann. 1990. Lohnstruktur und Lohndifferenzierung in der DDR: Ergebnisse der Lohndatenerfassung vom September 1988. *Mitteilungen aus der Arbeitsmarkt- und Berufsforschung* 23:550–62.

Večerník, Jiří. 1991. Earnings distribution in Czechoslovakia: Intertemporal changes and international comparison. *European Sociological Review* 7:237–52.

Vortmann, Heinz. 1985. *Geldeinkommen in der DDR von 1955 bis zu Beginn der achziger Jahre.* Deutsches Institut für Wirtschaftsforschung, Beiträge zur Strukturforschung, vol. 85. Berlin: Duncker & Humblot.

Waterkamp, Dietmar. 1987. *Handbuch zum Bildungswesen der DDR.* Berlin: A. Spitz.

Contributors

John M. Abowd
School of Industrial and Labor Relations
    and Johnson School of Management
259 Ives Hall
Cornell University
Ithaca, NY 14853

Katharine G. Abraham
Department of Economics
University of Maryland
College Park, MD 20742

David G. Blanchflower
Department of Economics
Rockefeller Center
Dartmouth College
Hanover, NH 03755

Francine D. Blau
School of Industrial and Labor Relations
265 Ives Hall
Cornell University
Ithaca, NY 14853

Michael L. Bognanno
Temple University Japan
2–2 Minami Osawa
Hachioji-shi, Tokyo 192–03
Japan

Per-Anders Edin
Uppsala University
Department of Economics
Box 513
S-75120 Uppsala
Sweden

Christopher L. Erickson
Anderson Graduate School of
    Management
University of California, Los Angeles
405 Hilgard Avenue
Los Angeles, CA 90024

Richard B. Freeman
NBER
1050 Massachusetts Avenue
Cambridge, MA 02138

Robert S. Gibbons
Johnson Graduate School
507 Mallott Hall
Cornell University
Ithaca, NY 14853

Robert G. Gregory
Economics Program, RSSS
Australian National University
Canberra ACT 0200
Australia

Bertil Holmlund
Uppsala University
Department of Economics
Box 513
S-751 20 Uppsala
Sweden

Susan N. Houseman
W. E. Upjohn Institute
300 Westnedge Avenue
Kalamazoo, MI 49007

447

Andrea C. Ichino
IGIER-Bocconi University
Abazzia di Mirasole
20090 Opera Milan
Italy

Lawrence M. Kahn
School of Industrial and Labor Relations
264 Ives Hall
Cornell University
Ithaca, NY 14853

Lawrence F. Katz
Department of Economics
Harvard University
Cambridge, MA 02138

Dae-Il Kim
Department of Economics
6100 S. Main
Rice University
Houston, TX 77251

Alan B. Krueger
Industrial Relations Section
Firestone Library
Princeton University
Princeton, NJ 08544

Gary W. Loveman
Harvard University
Graduate School of Business Adminis-
    tration
Boston, MA 02163

Andrew J. Oswald
Centre for Economic Performance
London School of Economics
Houghton Street
London WC2A 2AE
United Kingdom

Jörn-Steffen Pischke
Department of Economics
Massachusetts Institute of Technology
77 Massachusetts Avenue
Cambridge, MA 02139

John Schmitt
Economic Policy Institute
1730 Rhode Island Avenue, NW
Room 200
Washington, DC 20036

Robert H. Topel
Graduate School of Business
University of Chicago
1101 East 58th Street
Chicago, IL 60637

Francis Vella
Department of Economics
P.O. Box 1892
Rice University
Houston, TX 77251

Author Index

449

Subject Index

Age
  comparison in U.S. and Italian labor force, 285–87
  Germany: trends in earnings by, 380, 382, 385; unemployment rates by, 399–400; working age population by, 395–96
  United States: wage differentials related to, 380, 390–91
Apprenticeship training, Germany, 396–97

Bargaining game, centralized, 353–61
Benefits
  country differences, 74; in analysis of executive compensation, 75–78
  per capita spending in OECD countries, 78–79

Centralization
  Swedish collective bargaining, 361–67
  of wage setting system, 347–51
Chief operating officer (CEO)
  comparison of total compensation levels, 81–83
  ratio of total compensation and replacement value to manufacturing total compensation, 85–86, 87f
  total compensation at PPP exchange rates (1984–92), 99f
Civil Rights Act (1964), U.S., 112
Collective bargaining
  country comparison, 115–18
  factors in decline of, 346
  model of centralized, 347–49

East Germany (GDR), post-unification, 409
France, 54–55, 346
Germany, 387–88
Italy: compensation structure, 275–83; roles of labor and employer, 268–75
Korea, 234
New Zealand, 346
Sweden, 309–13, 330–33, 346, 361–67
West Germany (FRG), 406–7
  See also Bargaining game, centralized; Wage setting
Comparable worth concept, 111, 112
Compensation
  differences in structure of CEO and HRD, 86, 88–89
  levels and standardization of different measures, 80–89
  private replacement value, 69, 74
  tax effects on stock-based, long-term, 92–95
  East Germany (GDR): components of, 407
  Italy: contractual compensation package, 275–82
Compensation, total
  of CEOs, HRDs, and manufacturing operatives, PPP exchange rates, 99–100f
  intercountry variance, 85–86
  tax effects on, 90–92
Compensation costs, total
  of firm, 70–71
  of firm for CEO, 71–72
Contractual minimum, Italy, 275–77